TOWARDS ELECTRONIC JOURNALS

REALITIES FOR SCIENTISTS, LIBRARIANS, AND PUBLISHERS

CAROL TENOPIR

AND

DONALD W. KING

SLAPUBLISHING

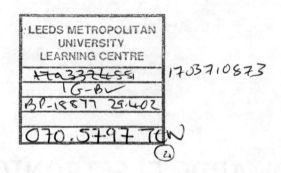

© 2000 by Special Libraries Association
1700 Eighteenth Street, NW
Washington, DC 20009-2514
1-202-234-4700
www.sla.org

Printed and bound in the United States of America.

ISBN 0-87111-507-7

Contents

LIST OF TABLES xi

PREFACE xvii

ACKNOWLEDGMENTS xxi

INTRODUCTION 1

PART I: BACKGROUND 15

CHAPTER 1—An Overview of Scientific Scholarly Journals 17
Background 17
The Evolution of Science and Scientific Communication 17
Growth in the Number of Scientists 18
Academic Science versus Science Done Elsewhere 19
Interdisciplinary versus Specialization 20
The Evolution of Scientific Scholarly Journals 21
Highlights 25
Are Scientific Scholarly Journals Worth Saving? 25
What Do Trends in the Scientific Scholarly Journal System Show? 27
What are the Consequences of Spiraling Scientific Journal Prices? 32
How Do Circulation, Cost, and Price Relationships
Contribute to Spiraling Prices? 34
What are the Financial Requirements for Scientific
Scholarly Journals? 36

Will Electronic Journals Make a Difference? 38
Implications for the Future of Scholarly Journal Publishing 44
Publishers 44
Large Publishers and Large Libraries 45
Large Publishers, Small Libraries, and Individuals 46
Small Publishers and Small Libraries 47
Academic and Research Libraries 48
Special Libraries 49
Scientists 51
Funders of Scientists and Libraries 52

CHAPTER 2—History of Traditional and Electronic Scientific
Journal Publishing 55
Introduction 55
History of Traditional Scientific Print Journals 56
Historical Perspectives on Electronic Journals 61
U.S. Scientific Communication Research Leading to
Electronic Journals in the 1960s 62
The Trail Blazed by the National Science Foundation (NSF)
and Others 62
Development of Scientific Communication Technologies 63
General Scientific Communication Studies 65
Perceived Problems with Scientific Scholarly Journals 66
Alternatives to Traditional Scholarly Journals 68
Experiments with Journals and Electronic Processes 68
U.S. Scientific Communication Research in the 1970s 70
Development of Scientific Publishing Technologies 70
Description and Assessment of Scientific Publishing 70
Systems Analysis of Alternatives to Traditional Scholarly Journals 71
Experiments with Electronic Journal Processes 73
Failed Attempts to Promote a U.S. National Periodicals Center 74
The European Trail Blazed by the British Library Research and
Development Department (BLRDD) and Others 75
Electronic Journal Research and Development in the 1980s
and Early 1990s 77
Development of Enabling Technologies in the 1980s 78
Experiments with Electronic Journals in the 1980s 80

CHAPTER 3—A Systems Framework for Assessing
Scholarly Journal Publishing 83
Introduction 83
Context for Scholarly Journal Publishing 84
Definition of Scientific Information 85

Scientific Journals in the Context of Research, Teaching,
    and Other Scientific Endeavors 86
Scientific Journals in the Context of the Life Cycle of
    Scientific Information 88
The Life Cycle of Scientific Information through
    Journal System Functions 90
Scholarly Journal Functions 92
    Scholarly Journal Functions and Processes 93
    Scholarly Journal System Roles 95
Scholarly Journal System Participants 95
    Scholarly Journal System Process Participants 96
Scholarly Journal System Attributes 98
    Generic Attributes of the Scholarly Journal System 99
Systemic and Economic Interdependencies in the
    Scholarly Journal System 101
Examples of Systemic Interdependencies 102
Examples of Economic Interdependencies 103

CHAPTER 4—Methods 105
    Introduction 105
    Framework for Examining Information Services and Products 106
    Statistical Surveys of Scientists and Institutions 111
    Cost Finding for Publishing and Information Services 117
    Journal Tracking Study 119
    Analysis of Electronic Publishing Directories 120

PART II: SCIENTISTS' PARTICIPATION 123

CHAPTER 5—Scientists as Authors, Readers, and Referees 125
    Introduction 125
    How Scientists Spend Their Time 126
    Scientific Authorship 130
    Scientific Readership 132
    Common Goals of Journal Authors and Readers 134
    Peer Review/Refereeing 136

CHAPTER 6— Authorship of Scientific Scholarly Articles 141
    Introduction 141
    Extent of Authorship 141
        Description of Journal Authors 142
        Trends in Authorship 144
    Cost of Authorship 145

Authors' Goals and Incentives 146
    Career Advancement 146
    Contributing to Knowledge 147
    Publishing for Posterity 149
    Protection of Intellectual Effort 150
    Other Factors 151
Factors that Affect Authors' Choice of Journals 152
Manuscript Exchange with Publishers 156

CHAPTER 7—Readership of Scientific Scholarly Journals 159
Introduction 159
Extent of Readership 159
    Early Misunderstanding Concerning Reading 161
    Trends in Readership 163
Cost of Reading 164
Readers' Goals 166
    Closer Relationships to Authors 167
The Usefulness and Value of Reading Scholarly Articles 168
    Usefulness of Journals to University Scientists 169
    Usefulness of Journals to Non-University Scientists 169
    Value of Scholarly Journals 170
Factors that Affect Readers' Decisions to Subscribe to a Journal 173

CHAPTER 8—Information-Seeking and Readership Patterns 177
Introduction 177
Identifying and Locating Scholarly Articles 177
Sources of Articles Read 178
Readership Patterns 183
    Frequency of Readership 183
    Frequency of Reading of Library-Provided Articles 186
    Reading Older Articles 188
Distribution and Use of Separate Copies of Scholarly Articles 191
    Interlibrary Borrowing and Document Delivery 191
    Distribution of Separate Copies of Articles 193
    Photocopying of Scholarly Articles 195
Serving Small Companies 196

PART III: LIBRARY PARTICIPATION 197

CHAPTER 9—Use and Economics of Libraries 199
Introduction 199
Use of Libraries by Scientists 200
A Framework for Examining Library Services 203
Unit Costs of Library Services 204

Indicators of Usefulness and Value of Libraries 205
Other Studies of the Usefulness and Value of Libraries 209

CHAPTER 10—Use and Economics of Library-Provided Scientific
        Scholarly Articles 213
Introduction 213
In-Library Use of Journals and Economic Aspects 215
    Use of Library Collections 215
    Cost of In-Library Use of Journals 216
    Usefulness and Value of Journal Collections 218
Use and Economics of Journal Routing 220
    Use of Routed Journals 220
    Cost of Journal Routing 221
    Value of Journal Routing 222
Purchase of Journals for Department or Personal Use 223
Use and Economics of Interlibrary Borrowing and
    Document Delivery Services 223
    Use of Interlibrary Borrowing and Document Delivery Services 223
    Trade-Off Analysis of Service Attributes 224
    Cost of Interlibrary Borrowing and Document Delivery 227
    Value of Interlibrary Borrowing 229
Comparison of Costs among Journal Services 229

PART IV: PUBLISHER PARTICIPATION 233

CHAPTER 11—Scientific Scholarly Journal Publishing 235
Introduction 235
A Recent Picture 236
    Number and Size of Scientific Scholarly Journals 236
    Scholarly Journal Costs 238
Scientific Scholarly Journal Prices, Size, and Circulation 239
Scientific Scholarly Journal Publishing Trends 242
    Trends in Number and Size 242
    Trends in Cost and Price 242
    Trends in Circulation 242
Unique Economic Properties and Characteristics 244
Cost, Price, and Demand Relationships 247

CHAPTER 12— Cost of Scientific Scholarly Journal Publishing 251
Introduction 251
Journal Publishing Activities 253
Sources of Publishing Cost Data 255
Article Processing Costs 256

Non-Article Processing Costs 259
Reproduction Costs 260
Distribution Costs 262
Publishing Support Costs 263
Total and Unit Publishing Costs 264
  Total Costs with 1995 Average Parameters 264
  Validation of the Cost Model 265
  Unit Costs with Varied Parameters 265
  A Cautionary Note in Comparing Costs 269
  Comparing Costs of the Four Types of Publishers 269

CHAPTER 13—Pricing of Scientific Scholarly Journals 273
Introduction 273
Scholarly Journal Prices and Demand 274
Trends in Scientific Scholarly Journal Prices 276
  Journal Tracking Prices 276
  Other Reported Price Information 278
  Reasons for Price Increases 281
Explaining Individual and Institutional Price
  and Demand Sensitivities 288
  Price and Demand of Individual Subscriptions 289
  Price and Demand of Institutional Subscriptions 294
Effects of Price Changes on Individual and Institutional Subscriptions . . 299

CHAPTER 14—Financing Scholarly Journals 301
Introduction 301
Investment Requirements for Scholarly Journal Publishing 302
  Start-Up Investment 302
  Operational Investment 304
Sources of Revenue and Their Interdependence 309
Profitability of Commercial Publishers 313
The Issue of a Publishing Monopoly 317

PART V: ELECTRONIC PUBLISHING 321

CHAPTER 15—Transformation to Electronic Publishing 323
Introduction 323
  New Models in Publishing 323
Changing Roles of Publishers 325
Electronic Journals 326
Electronic Format 328
  Character-based: ASCII 329
  Character-based: Encoded 330
  Image Only 330

Combination 331
Electronic Delivery 331
Commercial Online 331
Via Internet 331
Magnetic Tape 332
Diskettes 332
CD-ROM 332
DVD 333
Desk-Top Networks 333
Fax 333
Other 333
Degree of Interactivity 333
One-Way Communication 334
Interactive Journals 334
Collaborative Journals 334
Electronic Distributors 335
Authors 335
Libraries 335
Primary Publishers 335
Second-Party Distributors 335
Third-Party Distributors 336
Gateways 336
Subscription Agents 336
Information Brokers 337
Library Networks and Consortia 337
Granularity 337
Multiple Titles 337
Issue or Volume 338
Title 338
Article Only 338
Partial Document 338
Pricing Policy . . . .
No Direct Cost 339
Flat Fee 339
Potential Users (Site Licenses) 340
Simultaneous Users 340
By Usage 340
By Document 341
Electronic Journals Online and on CD-ROM 341
Number of Journals on the Internet 342
Other Aspects of Electronic Publishing 346
Economics 346
Contributing to Knowledge 347
Other Factors 348
Conclusion 349

CHAPTER 16—Economic Aspects of the Internet 351
 Introduction 351
  Economic Measures and Other Aspects 354
 Economic Aspects of the Communications Infrastructure 355
  Economic Costs of the Communications Infrastructure 355
  Internet Traffic/Outputs 357
  Internal Communications Infrastructure 358
  Communications Infrastructure Pricing 359
 Economic Aspects of the Internet Information Infrastructure 360
  Economic Costs of the Information Infrastructure 360
  "Free" Information on the Internet 361
  Other Economic Aspects 363
  Use of Information Provided by the Internet 366

CHAPTER 17—Cost of Electronic Scholarly Journal Publishing 369
 Introduction 369
 Cost of Electronic Journal Publishing 371
  Cost of Exclusively Electronic Journals 371
  Cost of Parallel Publishing 374
  Electronic Value-Added Features 376
 Cost to Readers of Using Electronic Scholarly Journals 376
 Cost to Libraries of Using Electronic Scholarly Journals 379
 Other Perspectives 381

CHAPTER 18—Electronic Scholarly Journal Pricing 385
 Introduction 385
 Electronic Journal Demand and Readership 386
  Demand for Electronic Journals 386
  Use of Electronic Journals 387
 The Context of Electronic Journal Pricing 390
 Alternative Pricing Strategies for Electronic Journals 392
  Three Types of Differential Pricing 394
  Pricing Government Information 396
  Billing and Payment Mechanisms for Transaction-Based Pricing 396
 Negotiated Site Licenses 398
 Risks in Parallel Journal Pricing 400
 Alternate Pricing Proposals 400

BIBLIOGRAPHY 403

AUTHOR INDEX 465

SUBJECT INDEX 477

Tables

Table 1 Components of Scientific Information Messages 85

Table 2 Functions and Processes Involving Information Content 94

Table 3 Functions and Processes Involving Information Media 94

Table 4 Perspectives for Examining Information Services and Products .. 106

Table 5 Estimates of the Proportion of Scientists' Time Spent
Communicating by Type of Communicator: 1958–1998 129

Table 6 Scientific Written Information Outputs Observed
in Two Studies: 1988–1993 132

Table 7 Annual Number of Readings Per Scientist by University
and Non-University Scientists: 1993–1998 133

Table 8 Proportion of Information Sources Used by Engineers
and Scientists: 1967 133

Table 9 Proportion of Information Sources Used for Technological
and Scientific Research Projects: 1980s 135

Table 10 Average Time Spent Writing and Reading an Article and
Annual Amout of Time Spent per Scientist by University
and Non-University Scientists: 1993–1998 135

Table 11 Time Required for Authorship of Life Science Articles: 1974 145

Table 12   Average Importance Ratings of Factors Used by
Authors for Selecting Journals, 1976, 1979 155

Table 13   Average Number of Scholarly Article Readings Per Year
by University and Non-University Scientists: 1977–1998 163

Table 14   Average Time Spent Reading Scholarly Scientific Journals
by University and Non-University Scientists: 1977–1998 164

Table 15   Time Spent Reading Journals by Scientists and Engineers
by Field of Science: 1960–1998 165

Table 16   Average Importance Ratings of Factors Used by Readers
to Select Journal Subscriptions: 1979 175

Table 17   Proportion of Readings of Scholarly Scientific Journals Identified
by Various Means by Univesity and Non-University Scientists
1977–1998 179

Table 18   Proportion of Readings of Scholarly Scientific Articles Obtained
from Various Sources by University and Non-University
Scientists: 1977–1998 180

Table 19   Average Number of Personal Subscriptions to Scholarly Journals
by University and Non-University Scientists: 1977–1998 181

Table 20   Average Journal Readings by Article Source: 1993–1998 182

Table 21   Proportion of Cumulative Proportion of Readers/Journals
at Various Levels of Reading: 1993–1998 183

Table 22   Proportion of Article Readings from Frequently and
Infrequently Read Journals by Source of Articles Read
by University and Non-University Scientists: 1993–1998 185

Table 23   Proportion of Article Readings from Frequently and
Infrequently Read Journals by Means of Identifying Articles
by University and Non-University Scientists: 1993–1998 186

Table 24   Proportion and Cumulated Proportion of Journals at Various
Levels of Reading Library Journals: 1993–1998 187

Table 25   Proportion of Readings by Age of Scholarly Article by
University and Non-University Scientists: 1993–1998 189

Table 26   Proportion of Readings by Source and by Age of Articles
Read by University and Non-University Scientists: 1993–1998 190

Table 27   Proportion of Readings by Means of Identification and
by Age of Articles Read by University and Non-University
Scientists: 1993–1998 191

Table 28   Estimates of Interlibrary Loans by Various Sources: 1987–1994 192

Table 29 Trends in Interlibrary Loans by the British Library: 1971–1993 192

Table 30 Trends in Interlibrary Lending and Borrowing 193

Table 31 Number of Separate Copies of Articles Received by
Scientists: 1977 194

Table 32 Average Number of Annual Uses of Libraries by University
and Non-University Scientists: 1982–1998 201

Table 33 Proportion of Scientists and Other Professions Who Do
Not Have a Library in Their Place of Work 202

Table 34 Unit Costs of Special Library Services by Cost to Library,
Scientists, and Their Funders: Adjusted to 1998 207

Table 35 Proportion Who Use and Average Annual Use per Scientist
of Two Types of Library Journal Collections by University
and Non-University Scientists: 1993–1998 215

Table 36 Cost per Reading of Journals Read in the Library at
Various Subscription Prices and Number of Readings 217

Table 37 Proportion of Readings by University Scientists Resulting
in Their Improved Performance by Source of Articles
Read: 1990–1993 219

Table 38 Proportion of Readings by Non-University Scientists Resulting
in Their Improved Performance by Source of Articles Read:
1994–1998 219

Table 39 Cost per Reading of Routed Journals at Various Subscription
Prices and Number of Readings per Title 222

Table 40 Attributes and Levels Used in Conjoint Analysis 225

Table 41 Normalized Utilities from Conjoint Analysis for Rush Orders
and Non-rush Orders (Special Libraries: R&D, Law
Business—1984) 226

Table 42 Normalized Utilities from Conjoint Analysis for Rush Orders
and Non-rush Orders (Academic Main Libraries—1984) 227

Table 43 Normalized Utilities from Conjoint Analysis for Rush Orders
and Non-rush Orders (ARL Libraries—1984) 228

Table 44 Break-even Point in Readings between Personally
Subscribing to Journals and Using the Library
at Various Journal Prices and Distance to the Library 231

Table 45 Break-even Point in Readings between Purchasing and
Using Document Delivery at Various Journal Prices and
Document Delivery Fees 231

Table 46 Break-even Point in Readings between Journal Routing
and Using Document Delivery at Various Journal
Prices and Document Delivery Fees 231

Table 47 Number of U.S. Scholarly Scientific Journals and Average
Number of Issues, Articles, and Pages per Title by Nine
Fields of Science: 1995 237

Table 48 Number of U.S. Scholarly Scientific Journals and Average
Number of Issues, Articles, and Pages per Title by Type of
Publisher: 1995 237

Table 49 Average Price, Number of Articles, and Circulation per
Journal by Field of Science: 1995 240

Table 50 Average Price, Number of Articles, and Circulation per
Journal by Type of Publisher: 1995 241

Table 51 Adjusted Estimates of Editing (C3) and Composition (C4)
Costs from Seven Sources 258

Table 52 Proportion of Direct and Publishing Support Costs
Reported by Six Sources 263

Table 53 Marks' Costs vs. Model Costs by Number of Subscribers 265

Table 54 Scholarly Journal Total Model Cost, Cost per Subscriber,
and Cost per Article by Number of Articles Published 267

Table 55 Scholarly Journal Publishing Parameters: 1975 and 1995 268

Table 56 Scholarly Journal Model Costs for Journals Published
in 1975 and 1995 268

Table 57 Cost per Subscriber by Quartiles of Numbers of Subscribers
Using the Cost Model Parameters 269

Table 58 Scholarly Journal Publishing Parameters by Type of Publisher:
1995 270

Table 59 Scholarly Journal Model Costs and Price by Type of Publisher 271

Table 60 Scholarly Journal Publishing Parameters by Type of Publisher:
1975 272

Table 61 Average Institutional Price and Average and Median
Circulation by Type of Publisher: 1965 275

Table 62 Average Price and Factor of Increase by Type of Publisher
1975 and 1995 277

Table 63 Trends in Average Prices of Scientific Scholarly Journals and
All Serials: 1960–1998 279

Table 64 Average Annual Rates of Price Increase in Constant Dollars for
Scientific Journals over Various Time Periods: 1960–1998 280

Table 65 Average Annual Rates of Price Increase in Constant Dollars for
All Journals over Various Time Periods: 1960–1998 280

Table 66 Break-Even Point in Readings between the Cost of Subscribing
at Various Individual Prices versus Using the Library: 1998 292

Table 67 Proportion of Readings from Library Collections by Distance
to the Library: 1990–1993 293

Table 68 Proportion and Cumulative Proportion of Readers/Journals
at Various Levels of Reading: 1993–1998 293

Table 69 Proportion of Journals to which Individuals Can Economically
Subscribe at Various Individual Subscription Prices: 1998 294

Table 70 Total Journal Costs by Academic and Special Libraries:
Projected to 1998 296

Table 71 Break-Even Point in Readings between Cost of Subscribing
and Obtaining Separate Copies of Articles: 1998 297

Table 72 Proportion and Cumulative Proportion of Journals at Various
Levels of Reading Library Journals: 1998 298

Table 73 Proportion of Journals to which Libraries Can Economically
Subscribe at Various Institutional Subscription Prices: 1998 298

Table 74 Effects of Price Changes on Number of Individual and
Institutional Subscribers (with 2,500 Subscription Base): 1998 299

Table 75 Timeframe for When Publishing Costs Are Incurred by Activity . . 306

Table 76 Cost Elements and Total Issue Cost by Time Prior to
Publication of an Issue 307

Table 77 Journal Publication Costs, Revenue, and Net Revenue over
Time before and after Publication 308

Table 78 Proportion of Revenue by Sources of Revenue Provided by
Several Sources of Data 310

Table 79 Rankings of Importance of Publishing Factors to Authors
and Subscribers: 1976, 1979 312

Table 80 Average Price, Number of Articles, and Circulation Per Journal
by Type of Publisher: 1995 314

Table 81 Number of Listservs by Type and by Subject: 1991–1995

Table 82 Number of Electronic Journals, Newsletters, and Conferences
by Type: 1991–1997 344

Table 83 Multiple-Journal Publishing on the World Wide Web: 1999 345

Table 84 Start-Up Ongoing Costs for an Electronic Journal 373

Table 85 Break-even Point in Readings between Individuals Purchasing
Electronic Journals and Electronic Access to Separate Copies of
Articles at Various Journal Prices and Article Access Fees: 1998 . . . 378

Table 86 Break-even Point in Readings between Libraries Purchasing
Electronic Journals and Electronic Access to Separate Copies of
Articles at Various Journal Prices and Article Access Fees: 1998 . . . 381

Table 87 Proportion of Scientists Who Use Various Sources to Obtain
Journal Articles at the University of Oklahoma: 1998 389

Preface

In 1994/95, F. W. Lancaster invited each of us to write an article for a special issue of *Library Trends* concerning electronic publishing.[1] In preparing these articles, it became apparent that much of the literature about electronic publishing was based on opinion and speculation with little data to support the many conjectures that were being made. Furthermore, a great deal of suspicion and antagonism was building among journal system participants based on this inadequate information and data. Moreover some of the studies we had performed over the years seemed to contradict some things that were being said about scholarly journals and electronic publishing.

Over the past twenty-five years, King Research, and more recently the University of Tennessee's School of Information Sciences, have performed more than 100 studies (many of them proprietary) that produced information and data that shed light on the roles played and the contributions made by scientists (as both authors and readers), publishers, and libraries to the scholarly journal system. These studies included statistical readership surveys of 13,591 scientists conducted from

---

[1]Also during this time one of the authors was serving on a National Research Council Committee ("Bits of Power: Issues in Global Access to Scientific Data") with co-member Paul Ginsparg. Ginsparg's discussions showed that electronic publishing was finally coming into its own, rekindling interest dating back to the 1970s and early 1980s when studies were being conducted by us for the National Science Foundation in this area.

1977 to 1998 for the National Science Foundation, journal publishers (e.g., *Science, Journal of the National Cancer Institute*), and thirty-two organizations such as the National Institutes of Health, AT&T Bell Laboratories, Oak Ridge National Laboratory, and the University of Tennessee. Another study tracked the characteristics of a sample of 715 scientific scholarly journals from 1960 to 1995 with adjustments for births, deaths, and twigging. Finally, a number of our studies involved in-depth cost finding in libraries and, to a lesser degree, in publishing operations.

We felt that the analysis of these data coupled with other research findings would help journal system participants (i.e., scientists, publishers, libraries, and their funders) to understand one another better. In particular, knowledge of the ways other participants process and use scholarly information, their contributions to the journal system, and their motives and goals can assist each participant in making more informed decisions concerning electronic journals in the future. To assist in this effort, we obtained a Steven I. Goldspiel Memorial Research Grant from the Special Libraries Association to write this book and to present the results in other ways.

In this book, we have assembled data and information that help clarify the following participant issues and questions:

Scientists. How do scientists spend their time communicating and in other activities? What are the trends in scholarly article authorship and readership? What motivates scientists to write and read? How much does it cost them to write and read? What factors are considered in choosing journals in which to publish and to which to subscribe? How do scientists identify the articles they read, and where do they obtain them? What are the consequences of reading scholarly articles? What are the trends in reading and information-seeking patterns?

Libraries. How extensively and for what purposes are libraries used by scientists? How do libraries contribute to the use, usefulness, and value of scholarly information? What library services provide access to scholarly articles; how much are they used; and how much do they cost? How much does it cost in scientists' time to use these services? What are the trends in library services, their use, and their cost?

Publishers. What are the trends in number of journals published, size of journals, price, and circulation? How much does it cost to publish scholarly journals, and what factors affect these costs? What factors affect individual (personal) and institutional (library) demand, and how much is demand affected by price changes? What are the financial considerations such as start-up costs, cash-flow requirements, capital expenditures, and risks? Are commercial publishers making an unreasonable profit?

Ultimately answers to these issues and questions also help address issues concerning electronic journals:

Electronic Scholarly Journals. What are the forms of electronic journals? What factors inhibit use or are of concern to each of the participants: publishers, libraries, and scientists? How much should electronic journals cost publishers, libraries, and scientists? How will electronic journals be priced? What are the overall implications of electronic journals to publishers, libraries, scientists, and their funders?

Abundant evidence is provided concerning these issues and other questions.

The book is based largely on data we collected plus the results of other studies that provide additional indications of trends or that support or refute our findings. For this reason, some otherwise useful publications are not mentioned or are mentioned only selectively. Indeed, some important aspects of scholarly journal publishing are not even addressed such as citation analysis, copyright, and the details of secondary publishing and other intermediary services. We felt that we could not add significant new data to these topics that have already been adequately covered in the literature.

Throughout the book we present several derived cost models (e.g., publishing costs, library service costs, and costs to readers of obtaining articles.) These models take a bottom-up approach to assessing costs as opposed to the economists' traditional top-down approach which employs various versions of multiple regression and correlation analysis. We believe both approaches contribute to understanding the dynamics of the scholarly journal system and its various interactions. In a conversation with King Research, Inc., in the 1970s, Yale Braunstein, then an economist at New York University, referred to our cost models as engineering models. Perhaps an even more appropriate characterization would be mechanic's models which require considerable hands-on analysis. The cost models were developed in all instances by sitting down with appropriate staff (or scientists) and asking them to describe the activities that are performed to publish a journal, provide a service, and read an article. They were then asked what resources are used to perform the activities (including staff time) and what factors affect or contribute to the application of these resources. The resulting analyses and models are in many ways simplistic, but hopefully they are useful in revealing the dynamics of publishing, service provision, and scientists' information-seeking patterns. In other words, these models should help to describe the extent to which various factors affect costs and to explain the economic rationale used by participants in their decision making.

We also provide a brief history of scientific scholarly journals and the evolution of electronic scholarly journals. The latter is somewhat colored by our own involvement in electronic publishing in the 1970s and beyond. Finally, even though we conducted surveys of over 8,000 other professionals, we decided to focus on science as the basis for our analysis both because so much of the effort involving electronic journals is in science and because our data were much more complete in this area.

Carol Tenopir
Donald W. King
June 1999

Acknowledgments

Research and preparation of this book required the time and effort of a large number of people. To begin with, over 13,500 scientists contributed by carefully responding to our questionnaires. A number of persons contributed, through interviews or formal discussion, by reviewing early drafts of the book or other related publications or by providing or exchanging information and data with us. Particularly important contributions were made by the following persons:

Janet D. Bailey	Robert Marks
Robert Campbell	Mark McCabe
Mary Case	Jack Meadows
Colin Day	Cathy Montalvo
José-Marie Griffiths	Sally Morris
Joyce Griffiths	Andrew Odlyzko
Karen Hunter	Robin Peek
Michael Mabe	

Others who also contributed in various ways include:

Juliette Arnheim	Joel Baron
Charles W. Bailey, Jr.	Susan Broughton

(continued)

Murray Browne
Michael Buckland
Paul Edwards
Francine Fialkoff
Stevan Harnad
Margaret Hedstrom
Michael Jensen
Richard T. Kaser
Paula Kaufman
Todd Kelly
Maurice Line
Clifford Lynch
Jeff MacKie-Mason
Al McCord

Sandra Meadow
Helen Miller
Norman Paskin
Sandra Paul
Stephen Robinson
William Robinson
Fytton Rowland
Judith Turner
Hal Varian
Susan Vianna
Thomas Walker
Sandy Won
Brendan Wyly

Students who spent a good deal of time as Graduate Assistants over the course of the research and writing include Lucy Park, Genevieve Innes, Eleanor Read, Barbara Sims, Jill Grogg, Elizabeth McSween, and Christopher Ryland. They all made substantial contributions to the research and the manuscript. We would like to acknowledge the particularly valiant effort on the part of Barbara Sims in editing multiple versions of the text and in helping to assemble the bibliography. She went well beyond our expectations in helping to improve our work.

We also thank the Special Libraries Association (Steven I. Goldspiel Memorial Grant) for their generous support. We also thank the many organizations that sponsored our research over the years, especially those who agreed to let us use their proprietary information and data.

To all of you: we thank you very much and hope that this book makes your support and contribution worthwhile.

CAROL TENOPIR
DONALD W. KING

This book is dedicated to

Jerry and Andy

and to

José, Rhiannon, Lisa, Kelly, Sara, Mary, Erin,

and the memory of Amy

Introduction

The past few decades have witnessed profound changes in science, scientific communication, and scientific scholarly journals. The dichotomy between greater specialization and big science has been increasing and is expected to continue to do so. Scientific research is also becoming more multidisciplinary, often involving many in-depth specialties coupled with more collaboration among universities, government and industry, and extending across national borders. Science education has also changed as more faculty teach and collaborate across disciplines, departments, and universities. Faculty and students alike are using new technologies extensively for teaching and learning, and research opportunities are increasingly incorporated into undergraduate curricula. Research results are often communicated rapidly to the public through traditional media and the Internet with both positive and negative consequences, the latter occurring when the results and/or conclusions are later found to be invalid. Some of these changes are a manifestation of new communication technologies; but such changes also create the need for new ways of communicating, which must be carefully explored.

Learning is fundamental to science, whether directly through research and discovery or through education and other forms of lifelong learning, and communication is at the heart of learning. We can learn by acquiring information and developing appropriate understandings. But learning can also result from the creativity associated with the thought processes needed to organize and explain our ideas through writing or personal discourse. Many have agreed with Garvey (1979) that communication is the "essence of science." Our studies have shown that information is one, if not the most important, resource used for performing research, teaching, and other scientific endeavors, and it is also the principal output of scientists' work that is communicated to others. Scientists spend a large proportion of their time communicating, and some evidence suggests that the proportion has increased from approximately 43 percent in the early 1960s to over 50 percent in recent years. Even though the total time spent communicating is consistently high among different types of scientists, the ways in which they communicate vary dramatically.

Scientists typically communicate by receiving information through such *modes* as observing, reading, and listening and by sending information through talking, writing, and creating images. This communication is accomplished through a number of communication *channels* including conferences and their proceedings, journal articles, and books. Each such channel can involve numerous *distribution means* (e.g., journal articles are communicated through personal subscriptions, local and remote library access, and preprints, reprints and photocopies provided by authors and colleagues) and several *media* (e.g., journals are found in paper, CD-ROM, online and microform). Together, the combination of channel distribution means and media form an extensive and complex pattern of information flow.

It is abundantly clear that individual scientists communicate using a variety of modes and channels, but the extent to which they are used varies among scientists, depending on their individual learning styles and abilities, the field of science, the type of work (e.g., basic or applied research, teaching), and other factors. Communication patterns are also a function of requirements for channel attributes such as information content accuracy, comprehensiveness and currentness , as well as, availability, accessibility, and costs. Because information needs and requirements differ, scientific communication has evolved into the multitude of modes, channels, distribution means, and media—each establishing an important niche in an array of communication processes that help scientists more effectively create, communicate, and use scientific information.

REDUNDANCY IN COMMUNICATION

One aspect of its complexity is that substantial redundancy has evolved in scientific communication. Specific research information (or modification of it) appears at different times in multiple channels. Also, since research builds on other research and, in turn, is used in further research, such research information has reasonable substitutes or approximations to it. Finally, specific information found in a particular channel, such as a journal article, is communicated through a variety of distribution means and media. Such redundancy reflects the varied needs of scientists and it has a significant bearing on information sources sought and used by them. This redundancy also serves as a context for examining scholarly journal communication and points to ways in which electronic publishing can help improve communication.

As mentioned, information describing a particular research result is communicated through a variety of channels, sometimes modified as it passes from channel to channel as a result of feedback from other scientists and further refinement. These redundant channels can include informal discussions and electronic messages with colleagues; laboratory notes and technical reports; formal presentations and lectures; conference presentations and published proceedings; scholarly articles; patent documents; state-of-the-art reviews; and textbooks, to name a few. Moreover, results from a research project can be reported in as many as eight scholarly articles, albeit with different emphases or addressed to different audiences. Clearly, the different channels serve various purposes and reach different audiences. However, communication researchers in the 1960s and 1970s felt that electronic publishing could compress time frames and eliminate some of the unnecessary redundancy. This probably holds true today (see, for example, Crawford, Hurd and Weller 1996).

Not only is specific information available from a number of sources, but other substitutes for the information are available as well. Odlyzko (1999) points out that any article is just one item in a "river of knowledge" and that this river is constantly growing. He contends that one can explain why the journal system works, even in light of its flaws, by thinking of it as a river of knowledge instead of a collection of unique and irreplaceable nuggets. Thus, not only are alternative sources of information available to scientists in their quest for information, but electronic publishing can improve information-seeking and use through hyperlinks to related sources of information.

Another type of redundancy involves multiple journal distribution means and media. Scientists and libraries can, and do, obtain specific articles through a variety of distribution means and media depending on the cost to them, extent of use, availability, and ease of access. Such redundancy options make the scholarly journal channel much more efficient. Our studies suggest that both scientists and libraries are well aware of the advantages of choosing from among sources and they generally select them in an economically rational manner. This bodes well for the future of electronic publishing and its value-added capabilities because scientists and libraries will ultimately recognize and utilize the beneficial aspects of electronic journals and text databases.

THE USEFULNESS AND VALUE OF SCHOLARLY JOURNALS

Studies over the past thirty to forty years have repeatedly shown the importance of reading (particularly of scholarly journals) and the benefits gained from this information such as increased productivity and higher-quality results. Furthermore, studies have shown that scientists spend a substantial amount of time reading journals and other materials, which shows how much they are willing to pay for this valuable information with the scarce resource of their time. Research over this period has also shown that scientists whose work has been recognized through achievement awards tend to read more than those whose work has not been formally recognized. Of course, some scientists rely more on personal communication and sources such as technical reports, but they still tend to also read scholarly articles extensively.

Not only are scholarly journals extremely useful and valuable, they involve an appreciable amount of resources. The entire scientific scholarly journal system in the U.S. currently expends about $45 billion in a year. The majority of these expenses cover scientists' time and other resources associated with authorship (9 percent of the total) and reading (78 percent). Publishers account for about 7 percent of the total and libraries and other intermediary services about 6 percent.[1] There are some important implications of this pattern of expenditure:

- The value of the system, as measured by what scientists are willing to pay in their time, far exceeds the communication costs of the system (i.e., publishing, distributing and providing access to the information). Even with some weaknesses this communication channel appears to be reasonably efficient.

- Scientists' time is a critical resource and any system innovations and service decisions should take into serious consideration the consequences on this time; for example, by minimizing the authors' time and readers' time required to identify, locate and acquire the information and the time spent reading and assimilating the information. Many of the value-added processes of publishing and library services do just that. For example, some

---

[1] These system costs do not include exchange of monies, such as payment for subscriptions.

aspects of editing are designed to assist readers by making text more concise and library services are shown to substantially reduce scientists' information-seeking time.

We believe that electronic journals and complementary text databases can be extremely helpful in further improving scientific communication and also in optimizing scientists' communication time, if applied in a cautious and enlightened manner.

The Internet and other advanced technologies have opened the floodgates to an enormous flow of data, images, and text (particularly informal messages). While new communication technologies create many opportunities, they can potentially place a burden on scientists. In the past fifteen to twenty years, it appears that scientists may have increased the amount of time spent on their work by as much as 150 hours per year. The increase is largely attributable to electronic messaging and increased time spent in informal meetings. Scientists seem to be reaching their capacity in terms of available work time and, as a result, will be forced to make difficult choices on how to spend their time, as increasing demands are made on it. The question arises as to how electronic publishing, particularly of scholarly journals, will affect the demands on individuals' time as well as improve overall communication processes.

THE EMERGENCE OF THE ELECTRONIC JOURNAL

Over the last three and one-half centuries, scientific scholarly journals have become the principal means of publishing scientific information. Our studies suggest that the amount of scholarly journal reading (and time spent reading) may have, if anything, increased slightly over the past few decades. Even though journals continue to be read and provide an extremely useful and valuable source of information to scientists in universities, government, and industry, over the past fifty years scientific scholarly journals have been subjected to intense scrutiny resulting from various perceived and imagined weaknesses. A number of alternatives have been proposed, experimented with and either failed or were not adopted. By the early 1970s, the alternative of choice for information scientists and communication researchers was the electronic journal. Since then, any number of prognosticators have predicted the imminent arrival of electronic journals with the subsequent demise of traditional print journals.

After nearly forty years of cut and try, scientists are just now beginning to benefit from comprehensive electronic publishing in which authors, readers, publishers, libraries, and the other intermediary services can all communicate easily and inexpensively online. Using the new technologies, electronic scholarly journal publishers and others are progressing through the phase of replicating tried and true ways of doing things, toward an innovative phase, in which limitless new opportunities are being explored.

Electronic scholarly journals have finally arrived, although not universally nor with the resounding success anticipated by many. A recent article in the *Chronicle of Higher Education* (Kiernan 1999) expresses the frustration felt by many, that some exclusively electronic journals have not met expectations. Speculation abounds as to the reasons for the failure of some electronic publications: authors are suspicious of their lack of prestige or continuity (which could affect tenure decisions), marketing is insufficient or non-existent, they are not covered by relevant bibliographic services, and libraries refuse to subscribe unless the journal is also available in print. It may be useful to examine these concerns in light of the current context and the history and evolution of traditional print scholarly journals.

To begin with, most of the exclusively electronic journals of concern are relatively new. The *Chronicle* quotes several publishers stating that not enough authors are contributing to these journals, and circulation is low (fewer than 200 subscribers are mentioned for some). Studies of factors that affect authors' choice of journals indicate that a journal's reputation and circulation are, among other factors, particularly important. These are characteristics not yet found in many exclusively electronic journals. In recent years, new print journals typically have experienced low circulation and have not grown as rapidly as in the past. Most new journals have been started by commercial publishers, with a typical journal requiring six years to reach 350 subscribers; whereas, twenty years ago, new journals commonly reached 600 subscribers in the same amount of time. It is often at least six years before new print journals accumulate sufficient profit to recover investment (Page, Campbell, and Meadows 1997). Thus, it may be that the exclusively electronic journals are merely following a recent industry-wide pattern in publishing.

The *Chronicle* article goes on to point out that systems such as Ginsparg's preprint and archival system (at the Los Alamos National Laboratory) appear to be highly successful. Ginsparg's system of electronic preprint distribution is said to log an average of 150 downloaded hits per article, considered by some to be surprisingly high. However, the fields of physics and some other sciences have long supported substantial preprint distribution and have had formal preprint exchanges from time to time. Such extensive distribution of separate copies of articles is not a new phenomenon. The King Research 1977 national survey for the National Science Foundation showed that scientists received 38 million separate copies of articles, or over 100 copies per article.[2] Currently we estimate that there are well over 100 million copies of articles distributed. For example, our surveys show that the number of interlibrary loans (and document delivery) of scholarly articles is over 40 million, up from 4 million in 1977.[3] In the late 1970s several studies strongly recommended the development of a one-stop shopping center (or centers) to more conveniently and less expensively satisfy the large demand for article separates.[4] It was anticipated that such a center would complement the extensive use of print journals and provide a small additional revenue to publishers. While Congress defeated a bill to create a federal center, it appears that the Los Alamos preprint (and archive) system and other systems are finally meeting this need for certain fields of science. Furthermore, such new systems may well exceed current distribution levels of over 100 million.[5]

These examples demonstrate that the enthusiasm for electronic journals has lacked an appropriate context and relevant historical perspective. When we started to write this book four years ago, it was evident that a great deal of opinion and speculation was, and continues to be, made in the absence of sound evidence. Coincidentally, over the past twenty years we had conducted readership surveys of scientists with over 13,500 responses, a scientific journal tracking study (1960-1995), and cost-finding studies of nearly 100 information services including libraries and publishers[6]. The purpose of this book is to present these data so that scientists (as both authors and readers), publishers, libraries, and others can better understand the economic and systemic nature of scholarly journals. Furthermore, they can begin to consider participant motives and incentives, why things are done as they are and what the lessons of the past can tell us about the future of electronic journals.

---

[2]These copies were in the form of preprints (2 million), reprints (27 million), and distributed photocopies including 4 million interlibrary loans and 5 million photocopies sent by authors and colleagues (King, McDonald, and Roderer 1981).

[3]The increase from 1.5 to 8 copies per scientist is due to libraries replacing high-priced, infrequently-read journals with individual copies of articles and the fact that ILL and document delivery services have improved.

[4]At that time many initial requests for interlibrary loans went unfilled because some requested libraries did not have the needed journal (there were few union lists of serials to locate them), needed articles were mutilated and issues were in binding, and some libraries refused to cooperate. Later some libraries received an unfair number of requests (e.g., libraries with names starting with the letter A).

[5]Communication patterns are like traffic patterns in the sense that the existence of a new highway creates far greater new, timely, and less expensive travel than would be expected based on strict origin-destination counts. Similarly, the Los Alamos system, and others like it, will undoubtedly create more new, timely, and less expensive article access.

[6]While some of the research was sponsored by the National Science Foundation and other agencies, much of this work was proprietary, but permissions have been granted to publish aggregate data.

WHAT ELECTRONIC JOURNALS WILL AND WILL NOT DO

Much of the hope for electronic journals has been in their potential to address some of the weaknesses of traditional print scholarly journals. The single greatest concern has been the spiraling prices of scientific scholarly journals, particularly those provided by commercial publishers. This concern is valid because the price increases, coupled with tightened library budgets in the 1970s and beyond, have resulted in diminished library availability of journals, books and other required materials. Furthermore, as a result of canceling personal subscriptions and using library copies instead, we show that scientists have lost some productivity because they are spending more of their time obtaining needed articles. Spiraling prices have also been detrimental to publishers in lower circulation and, perhaps, more importantly, in terms of lost prestige and appreciation for their contribution to science. Many factors contribute to the dramatic rise in prices, including inflation and larger journal sizes; although, these two only account for approximately 56 percent of the total price increase over the past two decades. Other causes include a 50 percent drop in personal subscriptions, requiring publishers to further increase prices to libraries to compensate for lost revenue. In turn, the accompanying relative decreases in library budgets accelerated subscription cancellations and, therefore, increased prices.[7] Will electronic journals alleviate this pricing problem? Probably not, unfortunately, because most publishing activities and corresponding costs are common to both traditional print and electronic media. In addition, the small savings from eliminating paper reproduction and most distribution costs are offset by increased investment in and costs associated with technology.[8] On the other hand, the flexibility afforded by electronic journals, along with carefully applied differential pricing, may help alleviate this critical problem.

A second problem with print scholarly journals is the delay from the date of initial manuscript submission to the actual distribution of its journal issue.

---

[7]Acceleration of price increases is exacerbated by the nature of unit costs of publishing journals and, thus, their prices. Because of high fixed costs, the unit cost per subscription increases in an almost geometric manner with reduced circulation under a critical mass of about 2,500 to 5,000 subscribers (about 60% of the journals have fewer than 2,500 subscribers). Thus, even small decreases in circulation under this amount result in spiraling increases in unit costs and prices.

[8]There is some evidence that small journals have lower per-article costs than large journals. It is not known, however, whether this is due to providing fewer bells and whistles, having lower overhead (and profit), or the donation or subsidization of some costs. Some new exclusively electronic journals are reported to cost less than their established print counterparts, perhaps for the same reasons. Price also appears to be related to the size of publishers (i.e., number of journals published).

Publishing delays generally declined during the 1970s, but the duration began increasing again in the early 1980s and appears to have leveled off and decreased since then. Electronic publishing may reduce the delay somewhat through electronic transmission and direct input to composition, although much of this delay is caused by the refereeing process which, despite the ability to communicate electronically, is not likely to change as much as desired. Electronic capabilities do, however, provide publishers greater freedom in assembling an issue for publication, which can reduce time delays.

Another concern has been anxiety over the "explosion" in amount of information available and the proliferation of scholarly journals. In fact, the number of articles (or pages) published has been highly correlated with the total number of scientists and, to a lesser degree, levels of research funding. The number of articles published per scientist appears to have increased somewhat from the 1960s to the 1970s, but recently decreased, but not close to the 1960s level. This concern with the growth of information was coupled with the perception by some that scholarly articles were neither useful nor read much.

A frequent criticism is that scholarly journals serve little useful purpose because most readers already know about the research. While some scientists do know about the reported research, most readers do not. It is a myth that authors merely communicate among themselves. In fact, particularly in the physical and life sciences, most of the reading is by non-authors located in industry and government. To be more specific, roughly 30 percent of all readings are by university scientists, with 70 percent by scientists working outside of academia. Even though this criticism is largely invalid, electronic journal capabilities will definitely enhance overall communication, both among authors and between authors and all readers.

Another related criticism has been that only a small proportion of the articles distributed in print are actually read by subscribers. In fact, over the years, an average of only 10 to 15 percent of the articles distributed by personal subscriptions are read by scientists. This does not mean that 85 to 90 percent of the articles are not read at all, despite the impression promoted by some. Clearly, different scientists read a varying number and different set of articles; although across all journals, readership of individual articles is highly skewed. In addition, estimated readership of journals from surveyed libraries is approximately ten times greater than from personal subscriptions, thus suggesting they are more thoroughly read. While this issue is important, it is typical of reading patterns of other print publications, such as magazines and newspapers. Electronic publishing should make article distribution significantly more efficient, since scientists and libraries will have the option of subscribing to electronic versions in addition to obtaining single-article copies to satisfy reading from infrequently read journals.

Another criticism has been that journals are not widely read. This is certainly true when compared to broadcast media with their enormous audiences, or media such as newspapers and magazines that are cast broadly. For a variety of reasons, however, past estimates of the amount of scholarly journal readership have been vastly understated in the literature (e.g., estimates of 5 to 20 readings per article are commonly cited in the literature). However, abundant evidence suggests that scientific scholarly articles are read an average of approximately 900 times and journals well over 100,000 times, although both of these estimates are derived from highly skewed distributions, in which some articles and journals are well read while many more are read relatively infrequently. Similarly, the distribution of journal circulation is highly skewed: with a median of 1,900 subscribers (averaging 5,800), one-fourth of the journals have fewer than 900 subscribers (averaging 520), while the highest one-fourth is over 5,700 subscribers (averaging 18,100). Journals read by individual scientists and those provided by libraries each tend to have highly skewed readership, in which some of the journals are read extensively, but most are not.

GLIMPSES INTO THE NEAR FUTURE

The print journal system has partially adapted to the distorted readership pattern through varied journal sizes (including the many small, specialized journals) and improved distribution of separate article copies. However, the pricing policies have hindered, rather than help adapt to the distribution patterns. The addition of electronic journal replicas and developing article text databases will make scholarly journals far more efficient, particularly if pricing is done properly. In the near future, several journal versions are likely to be needed, including traditional print complemented by electronic replica versions that can be obtained through subscription and by copies of articles on demand. Alternative versions will be required for journals that are well read and for those infrequently read (either by individuals or collectively in libraries) because the amount of reading is a critical economic variable in choosing among versions.[9] Furthermore, some scientists simply prefer one version over another.

---

[9]As an extreme example, it would cost a scientist approximately $266 to obtain only one article that is read from a $250 personal subscription, but $13.70 on average to go to a library to read the article. On the other hand, if a scientist reads 100 articles from a personal subscription, it costs $770 to subscribe and $1,370 to use the library. The distorted distributions of readings are actually even more relevant to electronic publishing, but these costs are not as well established. Break-even points in reading are given for comparing several alternative sources in Chapters 10, 13 and 17.

For the next five to ten years, scientific scholarly journals will probably remain similar to current journals in content, but will likely continue drifting to electronic versions as acceptance grows. Today's 100 million copies of articles distributed as preprints, reprints, interlibrary loan/document delivery and other photocopies will be replaced by electronic delivery as the articles become available electronically (e.g., most articles published before the mid-1990s are not yet available electronically). If done right, all of the characteristics that have made scholarly journals so useful and valuable to scientists can still be retained. Furthermore, the system can evolve in such a manner that all system participants can mutually benefit.

One aspect of pricing that might help is to "unbundle" the information content and the distribution/access aspects of scholarly journals; if not economically, at least philosophically. Information content and appropriate attributes (e.g., accuracy, conciseness, readability) are the principal "commodity" offered by publishers. The information content dominates publishing costs and prices, regardless of the distribution medium or whether the articles are grouped in a "journal" or a large text database. The print distribution and electronic access costs are relatively insignificant and cost per reading is indistinguishable when a journal is reasonably well read, since the difference in cost per reading between these two versions is below $1.00 per article reading (with more than 25 readings). Thus, with sufficient reading the choice of media depends not so much on price (and processing costs) but other factors such as how needed articles are identified, purpose of reading, and depth of reading, as well as trade-offs among required access attributes such as speed, ease of access, and so on. Looked upon in this way, it is clear that multiple versions make sense.

Innovative pricing strategies will be crucial to achieving all the benefits that can be derived from electronic journals and text databases. Some drastic forms of differential pricing may be needed. Among journals and articles, those with small audiences would continue to have higher prices than those with large audiences because of the large fixed costs. However, from the acquisition perspective (scientists or libraries) journals and articles that are infrequently read by users need to be charged less than those read extensively by them. Otherwise they will seek other sources for articles or equivalent information. The flexibility of subscribing to print or electronic versions and obtaining separate copies of articles facilitates such pricing policies. Also, large publishers and large libraries can negotiate relevant prices that differ from prices charged to small libraries and individuals. However, libraries need to pay only once for unrestricted use. Small libraries can also participate in consortia that can potentially achieve the benefits derived by large libraries. The point is that prices must reflect the distorted readership pattern in conjunction with available distribution means and media.

The second phase of development and implementation, in which the flexibility of digitized text and electronic dissemination can provide innovative services,[10] will probably evolve more slowly, both because flaws and complexities need to be resolved and because acceptance of innovation is often slow. It is the nature of users to indicate their enthusiasm for new services until it is time to actually obtain and use them, when excuses and reluctance to change begin to take over. This book attempts to provide the quantitative evidence to support these conclusions among many others.

ABOUT THIS BOOK

The background part of the book provides a context for examining the future of electronic scientific scholarly journals; particularly, the evolution of and prevailing trends in science, scientific communication and scholarly journals. We develop several themes throughout this book. The first theme addresses the interdependency between science and scientific communication. Each has grown more complex as has their interdependence, with science dependent on communication developments and communication becoming increasingly multi-channeled, in response to the changing science. A second theme deals with the complex nature of scientific communication that has evolved to encompass an array of modes and channels. To add to these complexities, the communication channels now involve combinations of multiple distribution means and media. A third theme relates how new channels evolve and why many old ones continue to exist.

When considering the future of scientific journals there is a tendency to think in black and white terms. That is, the journals must either be electronic or traditional print. In fact, scientific communication is likely to evolve into more channels and scholarly journals will undoubtedly splinter into additional combinations of distribution means and media. Major objectives of our research and this book are to describe the scientific communication system with emphasis on journals; identify and establish strengths and weaknesses of various distribution means and media; and determine what factors make each option viable.

---

[10]For example, to name a few innovative electronic services there are: multimedia; hyperlinks within and among documents; reducing redundancy among channels; providing options for different levels and types of information (e.g., multiple journals, single journals, articles, titles and abstracts, sections, paragraphs, citations, back-up data); providing a trail of modifications and updates; improving organization, control, identification, and retrieval; introducing multiple article reviewing and rating methods; establishing article usage data; and disseminating groups of articles selectively.

The remaining themes deal exclusively with a single channel—scientific scholarly journals. One theme pursues the sharp increase in the complexity of the journal system resulting from the introduction of new media and with drastically changing use across distribution means. Yet, even in light of such massive change, the overall journal system costs, use, usefulness and value have each remained relatively constant over the past few decades. Another theme addresses the recent turmoil within the journal system caused by spiraling subscription prices, the reasons for skyrocketing prices, the negative effects on the system, and how electronic capabilities might help. Finally, the evolution of electronic journals can be defined in terms of four distinct phases, spanning over fifty years. The first phase, starting in the 1940s and continuing today involves an examination of alternatives designed to overcome imperfections in the journal system. The second phase is characterized by the introduction of new technologies, mostly developed independently of scholarly publishing, that facilitate communication by authors, readers, libraries and other intermediaries, and publishers. This phase started in the 1960s. The third phase, largely covering the past decade, includes the realization of a comprehensive electronic journal, made possible by the economic and widespread use of some of these technologies. The final phase, into which we are just entering, will see the exploration, development and utilization of the full capabilities of the technologies, and the development of large article text databases.

The book is divided into five parts, the first of which provides an overview of scientific scholarly journals and background for the remaining parts including an historical discussion of scholarly print journals and the evolution of electronic journals (Chapter 2). Several timely questions regarding the sustainability of the scholarly journal system are highlighted in Chapter 1 and addressed in depth in subsequent chapters:

- Are scientific scholarly journals worth saving?
- What do trends in the scientific scholarly journal system show?
- What are the consequences of spiraling scientific journal prices?
- How do circulation, cost, and price relationships contribute to spiraling prices?
- What are the financial requirements for scientific scholarly journals?
- Will electronic journals make a difference?

The context for in-depth analysis and discussion is established through a systems analysis framework (Chapter 3) and description of the methods we used in readership surveys, journal tracking, and cost finding (Chapter 4). The next three parts focus on each of the three major participants in the scholarly journal system: scientists who are the journal authors and readers (Chapters 5, 6, 7, 8), libraries that increasingly provide access to the journals (Chapters 9 and 10), and publishers who add value to this channel by improving information and communication attributes (Chapters 11, 12, 13, 14). In each case, we discuss participant trends, incentives and motives, and their costs and other economic aspects of their involvement in the system. The final part specifically addresses electronic journals, including recent trends in their growth, modes of publishing, and economics, such as cost and pricing to the various system participants (Chapters 15, 16, 17, 18).

Part I

BACKGROUND

CHAPTER 1

An Overview of Scientific Scholarly Journals

BACKGROUND

In this chapter we provide a summary of the evolution of science, scientific communication, and scholarly journal publishing. Highlights of our research are also provided by answering some important questions such as: Are scholarly journals worth saving? What do the trends show? What are the economic aspects of pricing, costs, circulation, and financing? Will electronic journals make a difference? The research highlights section presents findings and conclusions on these issues. Finally, we speculate on the implications of the findings and conclusions for scientists, libraries, and publishers. The following chapters (2 through 18) provide much more in-depth analyses and over 600 citations to appropriate references.

THE EVOLUTION OF SCIENCE AND SCIENTIFIC COMMUNICATION

In the early stages of science, scientists (or natural philosophers as they were then called) tended to be either geographically dispersed individuals or gathered in a few small geographic clusters. Communication among these individuals and clusters was tedious and time consuming, largely accomplished through carefully constructed notes and letters, occasional monographs, and lengthy travel. Science was characterized by a high degree of cooperation among scientists, but there was fierce competition as well. Outside of the scientific community, the potential value of science was not widely appreciated except by benefactors and relatively few others. As science expanded in the seventeenth century, larger clusters of scientists with common interests developed, and they began to form scientific societies that eventually extended across national borders. Formal publications became a centerpiece of scientific communication, with scholarly journals initially emerging in the mid-seventeenth century in both France and England.

In the eighteenth century, scientific contributions to medicine and the military began to be recognized, and by the nineteenth century science contributed substantially to industrial change and growth. While these three applications continue to be extremely important, the twentieth century has demonstrated many additional scientific contributions to the understanding of space and our environment, the evolution of mankind and our planet, and to such diverse areas as agriculture, human behavior, and entertainment.

Growth in the Number of Scientists

The number of scientists has grown exponentially over the years. Price (1963) contended that the number of individuals with scientific and technical degrees doubles every ten years and increases ten-fold every fifty years at an annual rate somewhere between 6 and 7 percent. The numbers of scientists were estimated at 1,000 in 1800, 10,000 in 1850, 100,000 in 1900, and one million in 1950. Exact counts of the number of active scientists and engineers are difficult to determine for many reasons, however, including the fact that some persons with science degrees subsequently earn other degrees or migrate to non-scientific lines of work. Definitions of what constitutes a scientist also change over the years. For example, the National Science Foundation (NSF) for many years only counted psychologists as scientists if they had earned PhDs or the equivalent, but later relaxed that condition to include those with Masters and even Bachelor degrees.

As part of a series of studies performed for NSF in the 1970s,[1] we estimated the number of scientists in the U.S. engaged in research and development and teaching who were likely to be readers of scientific publications such as scholarly journals. This number grew from 1.87 million scientists in 1965 to 2.64 million in 1975, a growth rate of approximately 3.5 percent per year.[2] Our best estimate of the comparable number in 1995 based on recent NSF data is 5.74 million, which

---

[1]The name of the series was *Statistical Indicators of Scientific and Technical Information (STI) Communication.*
[2]In the 1970s the NSF classified scientists into eight fields: physical sciences, mathematics, computer sciences, environmental sciences, engineering, life sciences, psychology, and social sciences. In recent years, the fields have been reclassified. Throughout the book we collapse these fields and refer to them collectively as science.

represents a continued 3.5 percent annual increase with 6.8 million scientists by 2000.[3] Most scientists are located outside of universities and scientific activity and communication are somewhat different between university and other scientists.

Academic Science versus Science Done Elsewhere

University research differs in several ways from research done outside academia. Basic research is largely funded by the federal government and performed in universities, while applied research is largely funded and performed in industry. It appears that university scientists also tend to follow a single line (or related lines) of research throughout much of their careers, whereas in industry the focus of research changes more often depending on product requirements and managerial desires.[4]

These factors affect the communication patterns and practices of scientists. University scientists tend to develop long-term, collegial relationships with other university scientists in their specialties and to communicate through invisible colleges both informally and formally. For a variety of reasons they also publish more, and increasingly so, than other scientists. Scientists in industry rely heavily on these publications,[5] particularly in fields such as the physical and life sciences. Because they are required to change research directions, scientists in industry must rapidly bring themselves up to date in new specialties, which they largely accomplish through the published literature. In fact, even though they tend to read less (106 article readings per year per scientist vs. 188 readings by university scientists), there is far more reading of scholarly articles outside of universities than by the academic scientists who write most of the articles simply because many more scientists work outside of academia.

Boyer (1990) suggests that research universities in the United States have four basic roles: (1) to create knowledge by conducting basic research; (2) to transmit new knowledge through teaching, writing, publishing, meetings, and promotion; (3) to apply the knowledge through consulting and applied research; and (4) to preserve the knowledge through archives and libraries. To these four roles one might add a fifth, the increasing need in universities to protect the knowledge

---

[3]In 1980 we projected the rate to decrease to 3.0 percent by 1985. Many believe the rate must decrease eventually (Meadows 1998).

[4]These assertions are based on a number of personal and focus group interviews, but have never been validated through statistical surveys.

[5]Much more so than many university scientists appear to realize or appreciate, based on personal and focus group interviews.

created by them through patents, licensing, and copyright. Some national laboratories, government agencies, and companies also create knowledge, transmit it broadly, apply it in various ways, attempt to preserve it, and try to protect it, but with widely varying emphases depending on the mission of the organization.

Interdisciplinarity versus Specialization

The nature of science has evolved in several directions over time, a fact that has become increasingly evident in recent decades. On the one hand, traditional fields of science are becoming more specialized through fission and fusion of disciplines while, on the other hand, certain areas have expanded from big to even bigger science (e.g., the human genome project, the Hubble space telescope, space science, and high-energy physics). Multidisciplinary teaming is required in large, government, mission-oriented research projects and in industry where teams follow products from discovery through many processes to the marketplace. Collaboratories are flourishing with participation by scientists located throughout the world, and collaboration has increased dramatically among universities, industry, and government when they share common goals and objectives. One might even conclude that computer supported collaborative work (CSCW) is a manifestation of evolving communication patterns.

Large-scale multidisciplinary collaboration appears to be increasingly driven by complex social problems (e.g., environmental issues such as global warming) that require many disciplines applied on a very large scale. Another example of the need for collaboration is to help alleviate economic problems in specific areas of science. Budget decreases for particle physics led to international cooperation that took advantage of communication and information technologies. The World Wide Web originated at CERN in the late 1980s in order to share particle physics data and information among scientists in this community (Edwards 1999).

Science education is also becoming more multidisciplinary and collaborative in nature. Faculty are shared among departments and among universities, often for distance education programs and computer-supported collaboration. Highly qualified non-university scientists are utilized more as adjunct faculty. University students participate in research projects earlier in their education, increasingly in their undergraduate years, and science education in elementary and secondary schools is becoming more sophisticated in some schools, although valid concerns still exist about the level of science and mathematics education generally in the United States compared with other nations.

New approaches to communication have gained a degree of acceptance. For example, scientists in Europe have advocated witnessing techniques such as "virtual witnessing" in which experimental processes are presented in such a way that others can imagine being there and can potentially attempt to replicate the experiment. This innovative approach to communications was initially developed by Robert Boyle and the Royal Society. (See, for example, Shapin 1994; Shapin and Schaffer 1985.)

These diverse directions in science give rise to how science will affect and be affected by communication trends; how research can continue to contribute effectively to education and lifelong learning; and whether technological advancements in communication, electronic publishing, digital processing, and storage of large data sets will replace existing channels, transform communication patterns, or merely continue to evolve into a more discrete communication niche.

THE EVOLUTION OF SCIENTIFIC SCHOLARLY ELECTRONIC JOURNALS

The onslaught of documents produced by the Allies during World War II and the acquisition of Axis documents following the war triggered the need for new ways of organizing, storing, and accessing this enormous body of information. The solution at that time was believed to be microform, since digital storage was still on the horizon. Yet some of the innovative ideas being discussed today with electronic publishing were actually envisioned in the 1940s (see, for example, Bush 1945; and Rider 1944). While microform became a medium of choice for archival storage and preservation of government and other documents in the 1950s and 1960s, the creative ideas for processing information percolated until the late 1950s when science and scientific communication were rejuvenated in the United States as a result of Sputnik, the Cold War, and the post-war industrial growth.

In the 1960s, the National Science Foundation (NSF) began supporting a significant research effort on scientific (and technical) communication including surveys of scientists and their use of information and information services and products. The NSF and most other government agencies also supported research and development of electronic abstracting and indexing (A&I) databases and bibliographic information retrieval systems. By the end of the 1960s, over one hundred clearinghouses and information analysis centers were in service to process and analyze scientific and other types of information. Parallel developments were occurring in other advanced countries, most notably the United Kingdom, the Union of Soviet Socialist Republics, and Japan.

As a result of research in the 1960s, a number of real and imaginary problems with scientific scholarly journals were identified. These concerns included the crisis of the "information explosion," increasing publishing costs (and therefore prices), delays in publishing, replication of information in various publications, the invalid perception of low readership of articles, distribution inefficiencies, information in articles being already known by readers, and articles being written mostly to satisfy tenure requirements. Hundreds of studies and dozens of experiments were conducted in the 1960s addressing these perceived problems. Many of the innovations considered were quite imaginative, yet few of the proposed alternatives to traditional scholarly print journals survived beyond an experimental phase for a variety of reasons (see Chapter 2 for descriptions of some of these ideas). Perhaps the most compelling reason was that the traditional journal satisfied the common needs and requirements of all the participants involved (i.e., authors, publishers, libraries, secondary publishers, and readers). Change for the sake of change was simply not enough to alter this well-established and widely-accepted means of communication.

By the end of the 1960s it was generally recognized that any real advances in scholarly publishing and any realization of the early visions for scientific communication lay in the promise of electronic journals. Publishers became intrigued with successes observed with bibliographic databases and online searching. At the same time exciting technologies were emerging in the transmission of scientific data, computerized composition, mainframe and small computing, and magnetic tape and card typewriters. Thus, all the components of a comprehensive electronic journal system were developing, and all of the envisioned value-added features and services were seen as a distinct possibility in the future. Some even foresaw the imminent demise of traditional print-based journals as early as 1974. (See Samuel 1964, cited by Lesk 1998.)

In the 1970s, research in scientific communication focused on electronic publishing with a long-range goal of building one or more large, digital article databases from which a number of value-added processes and services could be derived. In addition to the bio-medical communication research at the National Library of Medicine, the National Science Foundation was the principal funder of scientific communication research at that time. NSF supported three avenues of electronic journal research. One line of research involved obtaining in-depth descriptions of scientific publishing, including obtaining accurate baseline estimates and trends of the number of publishers, journals, articles, costs, price, circulation, and use. Another approach addressed several detailed systems analyses of scientific journal publishing through both print and electronic media. A third avenue of research involved several experiments with electronic communication and publishing.

Few scientific publishers at that time were large enough to afford the relatively substantial capital investment required for computer composition and receipt of digital input from authors. To address this problem, NSF sponsored experiments with Editorial Processing Centers that could service small publishers and ultimately provide a database of digitized text. Some of the concepts and features were adapted in time by large publishers, but the concept of service centers never materialized. Several scientific societies (e.g., the American Chemical Society and the American Institute of Physics) began experiments to see if some of the technologies developed for A&I databases could be adopted for full-text, including special character sets such as mathematical equations and chemical compounds. These projects were the genesis of some of the current electronic journals. Another approach involved experiments which began with teleconferencing, but appeared to have the ultimate goal of compressing all the publications in which common research information is replicated (i.e., conference proceedings, articles, bibliographic databases, and books) into a manipulatable text database (see, for example, Turoff and Hiltz 1982). Because of extensive interlibrary lending and other distribution of copies of articles, another popular innovation was to develop a National Periodicals Center in the United States for distributing separate copies of articles on demand, ultimately electronically. This approach was defeated in Congress due, in large part, to the lobbying efforts of publishers and some large libraries.

By the late 1970s a great deal of hype surfaced concerning the imminent emergence of electronic scholarly journals or paperless journal systems. As with many technological innovations, hype and reality are sometimes far apart. A useful depiction of this phenomenon is presented in Figure 1 where the vertical dimension represents performance and the horizontal dimension, time. The hype shows

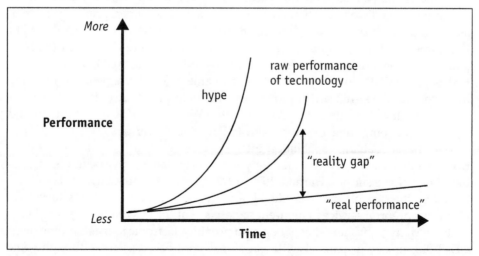

Figure 1. A familiar pattern: technology hype vs. reality.
(*Source: University of Michigan, School of Information*)

a sharp increase in anticipated performance over a brief period of time. In the 1970s, many communication researchers projected a widespread transformation to electronic journals within a few years.

These prognostications were unrealistic because standards were lacking for inputting digitized text from disparate sources; optical scanning was not economically or technically feasible; too few journal system participants (i.e., authors, editors, reviewers, publishers, libraries, readers) had adequate or compatible computing capabilities; and telecommunication was expensive and inadequate. The technology existed, but could not support a scalable comprehensive system. Finally, publishers remained lukewarm because they did not want to risk their steady revenue source, and scientists were generally unenthusiastic as well. The evolution of the Internet and related improved technologies unified the participants into a compatible system, and many of the earlier problems were overcome. Over the years, however, although hyperbole exceeds actual performance, progress is constantly being made toward the state the hyperbole describes.

A third condition in Figure 1 deals with the raw performance of technology which lies between hyperbole and real performance. In other words, the new technologies present possibilities for potential value-added processes which have not yet been achieved for a variety of reasons. Such possibilities include new ways of determining the quality of articles, providing author-reader interaction, compressing the channels in which research information appears, and developing the article databases from which these value-added processes can be derived.

In the 1980s, NSF support for research and development (R&D) on scientific communication dissolved. Thereafter new research was funded primarily by publishers and, in the United Kingdom, the British Library Research and Development Department (BLRDD). Input protocols and standards were developed (SGML), and several electronic journal experiments were launched: ADONIS, ARTEMIS, Red Sage, BLEND, ELVYN, and TULIP, to name a few. Perhaps more relevant, however, was the significant improvement and widespread use of facilitating technologies such as the Internet (followed by the Web in the 1990s), distributed and cost-effective computing, desktop workstations, and powerful software.

With these enabling capabilities, interest arose again in the potential of electronic scholarly journals led initially by some imaginative and vociferous proponents (see, for example, Harnad 1990, 1992; Stix 1994; and Odlyzko 1995) and fueled by the support of the digital libraries initiatives and Ginsparg's successful electronic preprint service in high-energy physics at the Los Alamos National Laboratory. Many publishers slowly began to provide electronic journals online or on CD-ROM, mostly in parallel with traditional print-based issues, although some exclusively electronic journals also emerged. Many of these electronic versions are merely replicas of the traditional print journals. The parallel publications are provided and priced in many ways. Still, few of the envisioned value-added processes and services are provided by publishers or vendors as of yet, with the exception of hyperlinks and limited multimedia.

HIGHLIGHTS
Are Scientific Scholarly Journals Worth Saving?
Findings of Journal Usefulness and Value

Scientific scholarly journals have long been one of the most important communication channels for scientists. Our recent studies show that university scientists average 188 readings of articles per year.[6] In universities, most of these readings are for research purposes (75 percent), with fewer for teaching (41 percent). A substantial amount of the reading also helps scientists keep current with their specialties. Over one-half of the readings for research are said to be essential to that activity, and most of the reading applied to teaching is considered essential to that purpose. Scientists in industry and government read less than their academic counterparts (approximately 106 readings versus 188 per year), but the information is extremely useful and valuable to them. In fact, when compared with five other resources used for research and several other activities, these scientists rated published information highest or second highest in importance for eleven of their activities.[7]

Another indicator of the usefulness of reading scholarly journals is the high correlation of achievement with amount of journal reading. In both environments, scientists whose work has been honored through achievement awards tend to read more than those whose work has not been formally recognized. The same is true for scientists who are given special assignments or are asked to serve on high-level committees or boards. In one company, it was found that twenty-five scientists who were considered particularly high achievers read 59 percent more than their colleagues and 52 percent more than their cohorts with similar specialties, equivalent degrees, and equivalent years of experience.

---

[6]Readings are defined as reading beyond the title and abstract to the body of an article. The average of 188 readings may not be the equivalent of reading 188 individual articles, however, because some articles may be read many times.

[7]These resources include laboratory instrumentation, computers, support staff, information staff, and advice from colleagues and consultants. The activities include primary research, secondary research, other R&D, professional development, management/executive, administration, technical support, legal/patent, consulting/advising others, writing, and presentations.

Abundant evidence demonstrates that scientists consider scholarly journals to be extremely valuable. From an economic perspective, value can be represented by the price one is willing to pay for the information as well as by the benefits derived from its use. Scientists pay for information in terms of the price paid for subscriptions and the time they expend in obtaining and reading the information, the latter typically being five to ten times the former when a dollar amount is assigned to time. University scientists each spend approximately 180 hours a year reading scholarly articles, while non-academic scientists spend nearly 100 hours obtaining (12 hours) and reading (88 hours) journal articles. Willingness to spend this amount of their scarce resource of time is a strong indicator of the value scientists place on the information obtained from scholarly journals.

Use value has been estimated in several ways. A high proportion of readings are said to improve the quality of research, teaching, or other purpose for which the information is read. Scientists also indicate that the information helps them perform better and faster, as well as saving them time or money (approximately $300 per reading).[8] We derived five indicators of scientists' productivity, and these measures were all correlated with the amount of reading in each of the six organizations in which observations were made.

The amount of scientific knowledge recorded in scholarly journals doubles approximately every fifteen to seventeen years. Consequently, when scientists graduate from college they have been exposed to only a fraction of the knowledge they will need during their careers, in fact, only approximately one-sixth of the knowledge that they ultimately must master during their careers. They must keep current or risk not achieving their full potential in research and teaching.

Conclusions as to What Must Be Continued

The evidence of the use, usefulness, and value of scholarly journals to scientists is overwhelming and, therefore, the system is well worth saving. For this reason, any changes in the journal system must take into account certain aspects of the system that have made it an enduring success. For example,

- Readers must have confidence that the information provided is trustworthy, replicable, and, to the degree possible, supported by other research.

---

[8]The average savings of $300 per reading does not imply a typical saving per reading because most of the savings come from a small proportion of readings (i.e., 1 or 2 percent of the readings, but some large outliers are excluded from the calculations).

- The information must be readily available to readers and accessible to an unlimited audience beyond the authors' primary or immediate community.

- The system must continue to provide an inexpensive means of communication (i.e., the communication costs are observed to be between a few pennies to approximately $30 per reading – which is the cost of an expensive interlibrary loan).

- The system should protect against plagiarism, copyright ownership violation, and unauthorized modification or altering.

- The scholarly journals should provide prestige and recognition for authors, their research, and their institutions.

- The system must continue to provide permanent, accessible archives for scientific information.

If electronic journals and subsequent alternatives can maintain these aspects of scholarly journals, they too may achieve a lasting success.

What Do Trends in the Scientific Scholarly Journal System Show?

Findings of Participant Trends

Our studies show evidence of the following participant trends:

Authorship. The estimated number of articles written per scientist has fluctuated over the three years for which rough estimates are available: 1965, 1975, and 1995. The averages are 0.093, 0.118, and 0.101 articles per scientist respectively or, conversely, the number of scientists per article published has decreased from 10.8 in 1965 to 8.5 in 1975, then increasing to 9.9 in 1995. Thus, authorship may be decreasing, but not appreciably so. The number of pages of scholarly articles published per scientist, however, increased significantly from 1975 to 1995 (1.0 pages per scientist to 1.7 pages). The increased length of articles may reflect the multidisciplinary nature of research and increase in number of co-authors. Historically most scholarly articles were written by university scientists, and that proportion appears to be increasing (62 percent in 1977 to 75 percent in 1995).[9] The cost of authoring scholarly articles was estimated in 1977 to be approximately $6,000 per

---

[9]The 62 and 75 percent estimates are based on our surveys. Henderson (1999) reports that "The academic sector produces about 70% of articles and citations in U.S. natural science and engineering journals—National Science Board 1996."

article (in current dollars), and evidence suggests that this has not changed appreciably in recent years. The average authorship cost per reading is estimated to be about $5 to $7 per reading.

Publishing. Several publishing trends are apparent over the recent twenty-year period:

- The number of titles published per publisher has increased dramatically because some professional societies turned their journals over to commercial and other publishers, a disproportionate number of new journals tend to be started by larger publishers, and the publishing industry experienced a rash of acquisitions and mergers of commercial publishers.

- The number of scientific scholarly journals is increasing at a rate well below that of the number of scientists (i.e., an increase in journals of 62 percent vs. 117 percent for scientists).

- The size of journals is increasing in terms of both the number of articles (85 to 123 articles per title) and the number of pages (820 to 1,723 pages per title including non-article pages).

- From 1975 to 1995 the price of scholarly journals has increased by a factor of 7.3 times or 2.6 times when adjusted for inflation. The increase is greatest for commercial publishers (8.9 times) and society publishers (8.2 times) and much less for educational and other publishers (5.4 and 3.0 times respectively).

- Circulation decreased from an average of 6,100 subscriptions per title in 1975 to 5,800 in 1995. The median number of subscriptions, however, has decreased from 2,900 to 1,900 which suggests that there is a higher proportion of both low- and high-circulation journals (i.e., "the rich are getting richer, and the poor are getting poorer" in terms of circulation).

- In 1977 it was estimated that scholarly articles are read an average of 638 times or 400 to 1,800 readings per article depending on the field of science. The readings per article have probably increased in the last two decades to an average of 900 readings per article based on the relationship among the growth in numbers of articles published, the number of scientists, and the average readings per scientist.

- Because there are more articles per journal and readership per article has increased, the average readership per journal has doubled over the past two decades from about 55,000 to 110,000 readings per journal.

- The cost per journal has increased (in current dollars) because the size has increased. The cost per page, however, has probably decreased somewhat, possibly reflecting the reduced costs for publishers that adopted computerized composition. The average cost per reading is estimated to be in the $4 to $6 per reading range, but varies widely among journals depending on circulation and size.

Library Services. While overall library use per scientist remains relatively constant, other drastic changes have occurred over the past two decades:

- Total library use per scientist appears, if anything, to have increased slightly over the sixteen-year period for which we have data (1982-1998) for both academic and special libraries.

- Libraries contribute appreciably to the usefulness and value of scholarly journal information by providing this information with greater accuracy and precision at less cost.

- Libraries are providing more journal-related services than in the past, including: management of department or branch libraries, journal routing, express delivery services, ordering personal subscriptions, improved photocopying services, and ordering by email.

- Library budgets, however, have generally declined on a per capita basis, particularly in the 1970s. Thus some services and acquisitions of journals and other materials have declined relative to the size of the user community.

- In order to provide access to cancelled subscriptions, the amount of interlibrary borrowing and document delivery of separate copies of articles has increased dramatically (approximately 1.5 copies per scientist in 1977 to over 8 during the 1994 to 1998 period).

- The library journal-related costs (i.e., acquisitions, maintenance, reshelving, photocopying, journal routing) totals approximately $5 to $7 per reading. From a total journal systems point of view (i.e., excluding price paid), however, it is closer to $2 to $4 per reading.[10]

---

[10]Other intermediaries account for about $1 per reading.

Scientists' Information-Seeking and Reading Patterns. While scientists' reading may have increased slightly, their information-seeking patterns have changed drastically.

- Amount of reading of articles increased from approximately 100 readings per scientist in 1977 to 122 in recent years, while time spent reading scholarly articles increased from approximately 80 hours to approximately 110 hours per scientist, or currently the monetary equivalent of approximately $5,200 per year. The average cost of time spent reading is about $43 per reading plus $9 for obtaining personal subscriptions (excluding price), going to the library, and receiving articles from other sources.

- Information-seeking patterns have also changed somewhat over the years, although browsing current journals remains the principal means of identifying articles to be read. Automated searches, however, now are used to identify a much higher proportion of articles that are read (from less than 1 percent in 1977 to over 12 percent in recent years).

- The source of articles read has migrated from predominately personal subscriptions to library-provided articles. For example, in 1977 60 percent of readings by university scientists were from personal subscriptions and 25 percent from libraries, but the 1990 to 1993 surveys showed a reversal to 36 percent from personal subscriptions and 54 percent from libraries.[11] For scientists in other organizations, readings from personal subscriptions declined from 72 percent in 1977 to 24 percent in the studies performed from 1994 to 1998; at the same time, library readings increased from 10 percent to 56 percent.

- Recent surveys observed that individual scientists read at least one article from an average of eighteen scholarly journals, up from thirteen journals observed earlier. Currently an average of 11.4 journals are provided by libraries, 2.7 journals from personal subscriptions, and the rest from other sources. Most of these journals are infrequently read by individuals (e.g., approximately 14 of the 18 are read 10 times or less), and articles from the infrequently-read journals are mostly provided by libraries.

Many articles are read well after the time they are published. Over one-third of the articles read are more than one year old. The newer articles tend to be found

---

[11]Other sources include obtaining copies from authors, colleagues, and elsewhere.

by browsing for the purpose of keeping current and the older ones are read for research and teaching purposes. The vast majority of older articles are obtained from libraries (e.g., approximately 70 percent of those older than one year and 94 percent of those older than five years). The readings of older articles tend to be more useful and have greater value than the readings of recently published articles, although the recent ones are sometimes read again later with specific research or teaching objectives in mind and thus take on greater usefulness and value.

Conclusions from Participant Trends

Scientific scholarly journals have thrived for three and one-half centuries through enormous changes in science and the expansion of scientific communication patterns. Over the past five decades, this communication channel has undergone intense scrutiny with many real and imaginary flaws identified. Numerous modifications and alternatives have been examined and many experiments conducted, but thus far no successful alternative has surfaced. In recent years publishing, library services, and information-seeking patterns have all undergone substantial changes. On the other hand, authorship and readership remain relatively stable, thus again demonstrating the strength of scientific scholarly journals.

Examination of the reading of older articles shows that they clearly need to be preserved because of their use, usefulness, and value. Publisher price increases have placed a particular burden on libraries because their budgets have not increased relative to the size of the communities served. While libraries are able to substitute interlibrary borrowing (or document delivery) for cancelled subscriptions, they still incur a large cost for these services. Clearly, something needs to be done to address this problem of spiraling prices.

Libraries will continue to be used extensively in the future, but will be providing greater access to external, rather than internal, sources of materials. Library search services and evaluation of retrieved items are likely to increase rather than diminish because scientists believe that search services can perform difficult searches better, faster and less expensively. Future searches may well become more difficult if articles are not linked to relevant bibliographic databases.

The trend of reading from more journals (but from fewer personal subscriptions) and the increased reliance on automated searches to identify important articles suggest that bibliographic databases and information retrieval systems are assuming a greater role and importance. Thus, the system participants need to ensure that reliable retrieval systems are utilized.

What are the Consequences of Spiraling Scientific Journal Prices?

Findings of How Spiraling Prices Affect Participants

The most visible and significant trend in the scholarly journal system has been the spiraling increases in journal prices. This one factor alone has triggered profound changes in the overall journal system that have neither been apparent nor well understood. Scholarly journal prices have been increasing at a rate well above inflation for at least forty years, but the full impact of the spiraling prices was not felt until the last twenty years when the following sequence of events occurred:

- Personal subscriptions dropped to less than one-half of that observed twenty years ago (i.e., the average number of subscriptions per scientist has decreased from 5.8 to 2.7).[12] In other words, considering the increase in the number of scientists in the United States there are currently 18 million fewer subscriptions than would have been expected had the average remained at 5.8 personal subscriptions. Thus publishers have lost billions of dollars in potential annual revenue even at 1975 prices inflated to current dollars.

To compensate for this lost revenue,

- Publishers generally increased their prices to libraries at a rate far greater than inflation and the increased journal sizes would warrant (i.e., these two factors account for only 56 percent of the increase).[13]

During this period library budget growth fell seriously behind R&D budgets and growth of science (Cummings, Witte, Bowen, Lazarus, and Ekman 1992, Brown 1996, Hawkins 1998, Henderson 1999). To stay within budgets,

- Libraries have generally cancelled duplicate subscriptions and infrequently-read journals and, as a consequence, dramatically increased the use of inter-library borrowing and document delivery services. They have also

---

[12]The price increases have resulted in reducing most personal subscriptions to those provided through society membership.

[13]Personal subscriptions are much more sensitive to price than library subscriptions because individual scientists read far less from journals than is collectively read from library journals. For example, a scientist can use a library or subscribe where the break-even point of a $250 journal is approximately 30 readings, and only 3 percent of journals read by them are above that amount (i.e., they would subscribe to 3% of journals priced at $250). The break-even point for library journals is 17 readings, and 78 percent of the journals are above that amount. Thus, a journal with 2,500 personal subscriptions at $250 would likely decrease to approximately 550 subscriptions at $500, but the journal with 2,500 library subscriptions at $250 would decrease to only 2,100 subscriptions at $500. The bases for these price sensitivities are described in detail in Chapter 13.

substantially reduced book and other collections to help pay for the higher priced serials and electronic resources.

In order to keep up with their reading,

- Scientists have replaced their reading of cancelled subscriptions largely through library-provided journals and articles. Scientists are paying for this change by sacrificing additional time to use the library collections.

Conclusions from Spiraling Prices

Everyone loses as a result of this sequence of events: scientists are paying more in their time to obtain needed articles, libraries are paying higher subscription fees while providing less information, and because of this, their funders are concerned and skeptical about increased costs. Publishers, on the other hand, are severely criticized, and they continue to lose subscribers, prestige, and the potential advertising revenue that accompanies higher circulation. In other words, the increased prices have resulted in a lose, lose, lose, lose situation for publishers, scientists, libraries, and their funders.

The frustrating aspect of this crisis is that the overall cost of the scholarly journal system has changed very little when considering the total amount of resources[14] applied to the system of authorship; primary publishing; library provision of articles, secondary publishing and other intermediary services; and obtaining and reading articles by scientists.[15] In current dollars, the cost per reading of the entire scientific scholarly journal system is about $60 to $70 per reading, up from $50 to $60 per reading in 1977. Authorship and readership costs dominate the totals (87 percent and 76 percent in 1998 and 1977 respectively). Both library and publishing costs per reading appear to be down slightly, but costs due to

---

[14]By resources, we mean input resources such as people's time, equipment, paper, space, furniture, and supplies. The total system cost here (adjusted for inflation and normalized over time by the number of scientists) does not include exchange of monies for purchasing journals. To include the purchase price paid would duplicate some of the overall system costs. The subscription price paid by libraries and scientists is a "cost" to them, but not an increase in system resources used. The cost of obtaining and processing journals is a valid system cost because of the resources such as labor and equipment are necessary to perform these activities.

[15]The cost per reading of the entire scientific scholarly journal system is estimated to be in the range of $60 to $70 per reading. Most of the system cost, however, comes from scientists' authorship (9%) and reading (78%). These costs include such items as support time, space, equipment, and photocopying. Publishing costs account for approximately 7% of the total, and library and other intermediaries another 6%. The library costs include all the resources (excluding the price of subscriptions) used in acquisition, collection maintenance, journal routing, automated searching, interlibrary borrowing, and all other journal-related activities performed in the library.

scientists' time and related expenses are up in current dollars. Thus, even though the system costs, use, usefulness, and value have remained relatively unchanged over the years, spiraling prices have had an appreciably negative effect on the journal system.

How Do Circulation, Cost, and Price Relationships Contribute to Spiraling Prices?

Findings of Why Some Journals Must Be Priced So High

The literature is full of conflicting or misleading statements concerning publishing costs. For example, publishing costs per article cited in the literature and at conferences have ranged from $200 to $8,000 per article. In partial recognition of the high, fixed costs of publishing, one sees such figures as 80 percent of publishing cost being attributable to the "first copy" or "pre-run" fixed costs and 20 percent to the variable costs of reproduction and distribution. None of these numbers has meaning without knowing more about the size of the journals, their circulation, and whether all costs are included. One must know the true cost of publishing and its dependence on circulation to adequately understand spiraling journal prices.

To address this issue, we developed a rough cost model of scholarly publishing, taking into account all the principal publishing activities and cost parameters such as the number of manuscripts received and articles published, the size of articles, and circulation. The generic activities include article processing (i.e., manuscript receipt and subsequent processing), non-article processing (e.g., preparation of covers, tables of contents, letters, reviews, advertising), reproduction (i.e., printing, collating, and binding), distribution (i.e., wrapping, labeling, mailing, storage, access, and subscription maintenance), and support (e.g., administration, marketing, legal work, financing). A model was developed for each of these five activities based on parameters observed from our journal tracking sample and unit costs observed in our studies and the literature over time.

The objectives of the model were to set forth a common basis for others to report cost data in the future, to determine which costs are likely to also be incurred by electronic journal publishing (for comparative purposes), and, since cost parameters have changed over time, to provide a basis to assess trends in total cost in light of the changes.[16]

---

[16]The model has been widely presented and published, and the resultant feedback has been incorporated into the versions presented in detail in Chapter 12.

The model, while rough, serves to show some of the dynamics of publishing costs and, therefore, pricing as follows:

- *Cost per subscription versus circulation.* Using estimated average journal parameters as constants,[17] the unit cost per subscription varies as follows:

No. of Subscribers	Cost per Subscription
500	$775
1,000	$404
2,500	$181
5,000	$107
10,000	$ 70

Unit costs approach an asymptote representing the reproduction and distribution costs which are in the $30 to $40 range, depending on the allocation of overhead or support costs. Thus, in order to cover costs, publishers must charge more for low-subscription journals than those having high circulation.

- *Fixed versus variable costs at levels of circulation.* The fixed, first-copy cost of a 500-subscriber journal is 89 percent of the total cost vs. 11 percent for reproduction and distribution, but only 13 percent and 87 percent respectively for a 50,000-subscriber journal.[18] Thus, the proportions are almost reversed. This is the reason that circulation data need to be presented in order for such proportions to be meaningful.

- *Cost per subscription versus number of articles published.* When the number of articles published in a journal increases, the cost per subscription also increases, but the cost per article does not increase. Assuming an average of 5,800 subscribers, 50 articles would cost approximately $58 per subscription, and 200 articles would increase the cost to $137 per subscription. The cost per article distributed, however, decreases. This may explain why publishers have tended in recent years to publish more articles rather than split journals (i.e., twig them) after they reach a certain size.

---

[17]Parameters include 205 manuscripts submitted, 123 articles per title, 11.7 pages per article, 289 non-article pages, 260 special graphics pages, 8.3 issues, and 200 over-run copies.

[18]Of course these values assume that the cost of activities and resources remains constant. In fact, large circulation journals tend to have more photographs (in color) and higher quality paper. Thus, other factors enter into these calculations.

- *Publishing cost versus price over time.* Publishers increased both the size of journals and the frequency of publishing over a twenty-year period. Taking inflation into account, the cost per subscriber has increased due to size and number of issues, although not nearly as much as have prices, and the cost per page has decreased slightly. Thus, other factors have clearly contributed to spiraling prices.

Publishing costs per subscription are very sensitive to the number of subscriptions below 2,500 subscribers due to the high fixed costs of journals. However, nearly 60 percent of scientific journals have fewer than 2,500 subscribers and, therefore, relatively higher prices, and the trend is for circulation decreasing to below the critical mass of 2,500 subscribers. Once subscriptions fall below the critical mass of 2,500 subscribers, the costs, and therefore prices, increase almost geometrically with lower circulation, thereby causing the spiraling price phenomenon. This partially explains why commercial publishers charge higher prices than the other publishers. The median circulation for commercial publishers is 1,400 subscriptions, but it is 5,600 for society publishers, with only 6 percent below 1,000.

Conclusions Concerning High Journal Prices

Some high journal prices are inevitable when circulation is low because publishers must recover the high cost of processing scholarly articles. However, this does not necessarily mean that all journal prices need to be as high as they currently are. Publishers need to be concerned about costs and librarians and readers should be vigilant about the reasonableness of journal prices.

What Are the Financial Requirements for Scientific Scholarly Journals?

Findings of What Investments Are Required

Some investment is required to publish scientific scholarly journals in order to (1) start a new journal, (2) provide operating support to cover costs that are incurred before revenue is received, and (3) recapitalize equipment and conduct research and development. These costs are detailed below.

- *Starting a new journal.* Many preliminary activities are required to start a journal including setting up editorial policies, soliciting authors, journal design, and marketing, to name a few. Even after the journal is launched, it can take as many as six years and up to a $50,000 investment before the journal recovers all costs, and many journals never do (Page, Campbell, and Meadows 1997).

- *Financing journal operations.* The cost model was used to demonstrate the cash flow of scholarly journal publishing (i.e., the difference of costs and revenue over time). It appears that costs start approximately fifteen months prior to publication of the first issue and build until revenue begins to flow, which is approximately three months before publication of the first issue. Soon after, revenues exceed the accumulated costs, and the journal begins a positive cash flow. This means that journal operations must be financed for a period of time. Even though the investment at one point is over $60,000 in our example, the return is approximately 40 percent of that amount in net profit. Thus, due to the cash flow, the return on investment of an ongoing journal can be very high.

- *Recapitalization investments.* Publishers also need to finance new equipment, facilities, and any requisite research and development. This is particularly relevant to excursions into electronic publishing which, in some ways, is almost like starting a new journal. The investment required depends a great deal on how much donated time is involved from editors and others and whether some costs are hidden in sponsoring organizations' overhead or in other ways.

Revenue is dominated by income from subscriptions, but advertising can also contribute revenue as well, particularly for journals with large circulation or that have audiences that lend themselves to directed advertising. For some publishers, revenue is also derived from page charges and sales of back issues and reprints.

Conclusions as to What Large Investment Means

Investment (in dollars or donated resources) is required for all scholarly journals, and the amount of investment can be substantial. This fact is probably the reason that most new journals in recent years have been started by commercial publishers, even though new journal success has not been as great lately. Societies and educational publishers do not have as many resources available to them to invest in new journals, although industrial and government publishers sometimes have other incentives which make this investment worthwhile. Commercial publishers obviously find this investment worthwhile or, otherwise, they would not continue to expand by adding new journals and through acquisition and merger.

Commercial publishers tend to charge significantly more than other types of publishers. Some of the higher prices can be explained by the fact that many of their journals are well below the circulation critical mass at which prices are relatively independent of the number of subscribers. Evidence suggests that high prices of some publishers may be due to large overhead and profit margins and that commercial publishers that provide a large number of journals tend to have higher prices than one would expect. The evidence is inconclusive, however, as to what proportion of commercial publishers charge unreasonably high prices.

Book publishers tend to use revenues from a few big winners to support the majority of marginal or losing publications. It seems that journal publishing has this characteristic as well. Within journals, a few articles tend to dominate reading and subscriber interests, and the same seems to be true among the array of journals provided by large publishers. This phenomenon is important to consider in the future in order to protect high-quality, useful journals and articles that serve small audiences.

Will Electronic Journals Make a Difference?

Findings as to How Electronic Journals Will Fit Into the Journal System

The power of technology affects all journal system participants, primarily in reducing costs, speeding transmission, and improving other attributes. While electronic journals were thought to be feasible in the early 1970s, one principal constraint was that the technologies were neither available to nor widely used by all the participants. Nevertheless, many of the scholarly publishers began to adopt computer composition technologies as early as the 1960s and therefore began to garner some limited benefits. Other advances in publishing standards, communication, and reduced computing costs benefited publishers and libraries. It is only in the past decade, however, that the other participants have widely used Internet and personal computers, thereby completing the requirements for a comprehensive electronic journal system. However, much of the cost savings and other advantages foreseen in the 1970s by electronic journal advocates have already been achieved, and, as we show below, lower costs and prices may not be the true advantage of electronic publishing.

In a time of uncertainty and evolution, the following trends in electronic publishing are beginning to emerge more clearly:

- Electronic processes now dominate all journal system functions from authorship to reading. Increased use of standards such as SGML, HTML, and XML and enhanced telecommunication infrastructures will continue to reduce costs and speed articles from authors to readers.

- We suspect that most journals and their articles will be distributed in a combination of electronic and traditional print media over at least the next five to ten years. New journals and journals with small circulation are more likely to be published exclusively in electronic media.

- Electronic processes will largely replace photocopy-based interlibrary borrowing and/or document delivery except for older articles. For this development to significantly impact library collection size, electronic access costs to the libraries must be somewhat below current external access costs. This will pressure the vendors to limit their cost and price increases. Publishers will be forced to charge larger royalties and fees in order to recover revenue lost to declining library subscriptions. Perhaps the move to central databases to process needed separate copies of articles will become more prominent in the near future.

- Regardless of how articles are distributed, publishers will continue to incur a large fixed (first-copy) cost which must be recouped through various sources of revenue. Traditionally the cost of high-quality, but infrequently read, articles has been recovered by bundling them in journals with frequently-read articles. To retain these important articles in an electronic environment, libraries and readers must be willing to pay a higher price just as they are currently doing for journals with low inherent demand.

- Site licenses and differential pricing may become a necessity in the long run. Both policies should reflect the extent of reading of journals with individual readers paying the lowest price, small organizations such as small high-tech firms paying more, and large organizations paying the highest price. Site licenses should charge enough to allow organizations to distribute copies of articles to their employees or students in any way they perceive necessary to optimize their use. Ultimately, pricing may be predominately based on extent of use, particularly in corporate environments.

Electronic scholarly journals are currently published in three ways. Two forms of electronic publishing are replicas of traditional print journals in CD-ROM or online; one being exclusively electronic and the other an electronic version published in parallel to the paper version. Publishers have adopted a variety of policies concerning subscriptions and access to separate copies of articles. Some offer

---

[19]Publishers sometimes turn over electronic versions to vendors (called aggregators by some) to provide access.

subscribers an option of the two media, while others insist that organizations subscribe to both versions. Some publishers provide access to separate online copies of articles, while others do not.[19] The third kind of electronic journal potentially involves one or more value-added features which distinguish it from traditional print versions. Such features include hypertext linking, multimedia, providing author and reader interaction and updates, batching articles and distributing them to readers or organizations based on profiles, rating the quality of articles in various ways, and providing pre-prints followed by refereed and edited copies. Each new approach has implications for costs and, therefore, pricing.

Scholarly journals that are exclusively electronic may achieve some cost savings associated with eliminating reproduction and distribution. These savings, however, are largely offset by the costs associated with implementing common standards, storage, and distribution of electronic subscriptions and articles. Even if the storage and online distribution functions are contracted to a vendor, the costs will still be reflected in prices to subscribers and users.

Scientists are likely to achieve some cost savings both by subscribing to electronic journals and by obtaining single copies of articles. Three components of potential cost savings to individuals emerge when using electronic subscriptions: the price paid; the cost of ordering, processing, and storing; and the cost of looking up articles and reading them. The subscription prices of exclusively electronic journals tend to be lower than the equivalent print journals, but may not remain so over the long term.[20] Electronic subscriptions should reduce ordering and maintenance costs by approximately $5 per subscription. On the other hand, look-up and reading costs are thought to be more for electronic journals, although not appreciably so. Thus, electronic subscriptions may save scientists some costs, but not a great deal. When scientists obtain single copies of articles from infrequently read journals, however, they may save as much as 40 percent of costs to them by using electronic access. Even print-outs of articles may save $1 to $2 over scientists having to photocopy articles.

Electronic subscriptions will also produce savings for libraries by potentially lowering prices, lowering processing and maintenance expenses, and eliminating photocopying and reshelving of used issues, but, again, these savings may not be significant, depending on amount of reading. Cost implications, however, are affected by how libraries handle electronic subscriptions: merely providing access

---

[20]The cost savings to publishers of not reproducing and distributing paper copies tend to be approximately $25 for a 500-subscriber journal, but falls slightly to $19 for a 50,000-subscriber journal.

from terminals located in the library, letting all users access online from their offices/rooms, or by using intranet or LAN capabilities. Elimination of issue processing and storage costs, however, is estimated to save approximately $70 per subscription, while the elimination of photocopying and reshelving costs should be approximately $1.48 per reading. Thus, if a journal is well read, the savings could be substantial. For example, an electronic journal that is read 200 times could yield savings as high as $366. Some of these savings, however, are offset by library technology costs. The cost of processing electronic articles on demand is likely to be $12 to $13 less than interlibrary borrowing or document delivery, with even higher savings on rush orders.

Site licenses are being implemented or explored by many academic, special, and large public libraries. This pricing approach has considerable potential for reversing the negative consequences of sky-rocketing prices. They can make all participants winners rather than losers, provided they incorporate the following principles: 1) guarantee publishers sufficient revenue to cover their article processing costs, 2) permit libraries to obtain as many subscriptions as necessary in either print or electronic media at near-distribution costs, and 3) allow the libraries and their users to obtain separate electronic copies of articles at near cost (more conditions are discussed in Chapter 18). With further stipulations, it is possible that such arrangements can satisfy all participants and reduce overall system costs. The problem is that these arrangements are likely to be relevant only to large publishers and large libraries. Ideally, small publishers could achieve similar benefits through participation in consortia or by using third parties. Small libraries that are not in a consortium and individuals would best be served through differential pricing that reflects actual use (e.g., counting hits) or potential use based on size of the organization.

Conclusions Concerning Adaptation of Electronic Journals

History is replete with examples of the introduction of technologies and devices into the communication process that have not replaced the fundamental channel, but simply facilitated it or enhanced information and/or media attributes. For example, written scientific communication has progressed from handwritten letters and notes to printed monographs, journals, and many forms of manual typesetting, computer typesetting, computerized composition, scanning, and electronic input from authors. Lectures have evolved from simple presentations to the use of microphones, slide projectors, overhead projectors, film and video, and computer displays. Photocopying has led to copies of articles being distributed among individuals, libraries distributing ILL photocopies of articles instead of issues or bound volumes, and individuals making copies from personal or library journals to read while traveling, to save, or to incorporate in laboratory notebooks.

The point is that these new technologies and devices have improved and broadened communication, but they have not fundamentally changed the traditional communication channels of lectures and documents. Authors, intermediaries, and readers have adapted to the changes. Electronic publishing may merely be an extension of these new devices in a well established means of communication. Many thoughtful scientists believe that traditional journals will fade away as a result of the enhancements made possible by the electronic technologies. We would do well to remember, however, that others predicted that movies were going to replace books (at least recreational books) and that television would supplant movies.[21] Yet all of these media have thrived, each finding a niche in the spectrum of communication channels. We believe that the transformation of print-base to electronic scholarly journals will follow this pattern, at least in the near future.

Journal participants will experience some cost savings, but not as appreciable as many hope. Publishers already achieved some savings as early as the 1970s. Thus large price decreases are not likely over the long run, but there will be cost savings to scientists and libraries that will make electronic subscriptions and access to single-article copies very attractive. In the near future, however, there is merit in large circulation journals (i.e., those over 2,500 subscribers) providing subscriptions in paper and electronic media, with back-up for electronic access to single copies of articles. Print versions should cost scientists less per reading for their personal subscriptions when they read them frequently and for browsing; some libraries or departmental branches may wish to continue current print periodicals as an option, and some scientists may simply prefer paper versions. It is important to have electronic access to single copies of articles to satisfy situations in which scientists and libraries do not have sufficient reading to justify a subscription. The latter capability will provide additional revenue to publishers, although not a significant amount.

Perhaps the single most important aspect of electronic publishing is to improve upon past pricing policies. There is no single magic bullet, however, that is likely to serve all publishers and all subscribers. Almost inevitably, for example, publishers that provide a large number of journals will have different pricing policies than small publishers. In both instances, the size of the subscriber base (in poten-

---

[21]Of course, there are examples where communication processes have died. For example, pony express survived only briefly due to the advent of the telegraph, railroads and other transportation.

tial total use) will have a bearing on pricing, whether through differential pricing or site licensing. Site and/or consortium licensing are likely to grow in popularity for all participants. Hopefully, innovative strategies can be tried such as charging per use or having libraries or funders provide scientists with discretionary funds to choose from alternative versions of journals (i.e., paper or electronic subscriptions and separate copies of articles).

Since the late 1960s, substantial research has examined electronic journals as a potential alternative to traditional print publishing. Early efforts failed to produce a viable comprehensive electronic journal system because of insufficient standards and the lack of widespread computer availability and capabilities. Some system functions utilize electronic technologies (e.g., digitized text input), and most of the system constraints have now been eliminated or at least minimized through new standards and vastly improved technologies. It is clear that the time is approaching for comprehensive electronic scholarly journal systems involving scientists, several intermediary services, libraries, and publishers. We feel, however, that all participants need to keep the following caveats in mind:

- Scientific scholarly journals continue to be perhaps the most useful and valuable formal communication channel for both authors and readers and therefore must be tampered with cautiously.

- While technologies show incredible promise, history has shown that both implementation and acceptance have lagged behind the technological capabilities available to scholarly journal publishers.

- Electronic capabilities are not likely to have a significant effect on overall system costs because all the system functions are labor-intensive and common to both media. Paper reproduction and distribution costs are largely replaced by the costs associated with the new technologies.

- For the near future, participants should not think in terms of exclusively electronic or exclusively paper, but rather combinations of each that best suit the individual reader's information needs and requirements. For some journals, exclusively electronic might well be the most appropriate, but for most, parallel publishing will prove most economic, with the emphasis initially on traditional print subscriptions backed by electronic distribution of article copies on demand.

- Many of the proposed major new changes in scholarly publishing must be carefully tested and gradually implemented. These changes will undoubtedly cost more and, therefore, must contribute corresponding value-added information content or service features.

- Perhaps the greatest challenge and best opportunity for electronic journals involves future pricing. It is clear that past strategies have not been successful and that new, truly innovative approaches will be required.

Future pricing and electronic journal systems must be examined in light of the consequences of change on all participants and of the ways in which all can mutually benefit.

IMPLICATIONS FOR THE FUTURE OF SCHOLARLY JOURNAL PUBLISHING

Electronic replica publishing will likely prevail for most scientific scholarly journals, although the manner in which electronic publishing is applied will depend on the size of the journal's audience, the age of the publication, and the number of journals provided by a publisher. The trend toward parallel media will continue, with exclusively electronic journals tending to be new journals and/or small-circulation journals. Some small publishers may adopt this approach much like publishing on a web site. It seems unlikely that the large publishers will convert all of their journals to the exclusively electronic medium, but rather will approach the medium on an experimental basis with a limited number of journals, perhaps even limiting their exposure to one journal. It is not likely that the total cost of publishing will decrease dramatically, if at all, unless editorial and other standards are revised. Pricing will be the most important issue that publishers, libraries, and scientists will face over the next decade.

In this section we describe some implications of electronic publishing to the journal system participants. We start with publishers in general and then discuss arrangements among the participants: large publishers and large libraries; large publishers, small libraries, and individuals; and small publishers and others. The remainder of the section is devoted to implications that are specific to academic and special libraries, scientists, and funders of scientists and libraries.

Publishers

Pricing will be a major issue for all types and sizes of publishers. Parallel journals will be accessed presumably through print subscriptions, electronic subscriptions, copies of individual articles, and combinations of these alternatives. The principal risk to publishers is that the price, and the resultant demand for one of the alternatives, does not overwhelm the total demand, which could yield insufficient revenue to cover costs. For example, if individual copies are priced too low, some subscribers will cancel their subscriptions and order articles on demand, perhaps with an overall reduction in revenue. Yet, if on-demand services are priced too high, publishers will lose potential revenue because libraries will obtain copies from other sources. Generally, electronic prices of single article copies should be set at a level that charges libraries less than the total cost of current on-demand services. This suggestion applies to both large and small publishers, regardless of whether they distribute their own copies or rely on a vendor for distribution.

Publishers will likely need to focus more intently on the requirements of all three sets of their customers (i.e., authors, readers, and libraries). Customer incentives are influenced by the perception of each customer of the motives of the publishers as well as the many other factors influencing their choices. For this reason, all publishers may benefit by reassuring their customers of the publisher's contributions to the journal communication system. It is time to emphasize, for example, the important contribution that publishers make to science through value-added processes and by making high quality, but low use, information available to scientists even when such articles do not make a profit. It is also critical that publishers make some arrangement to ensure that their electronic articles be available in perpetuity (e.g., in case either they or their journal cease to exist). They should also coordinate current electronic journals with the standards and other relevant aspects of the retrospective input of articles in the digital library initiatives so that past and future digital databases are seamless. Science publishers should continue to make their articles available to reputable abstracting and indexing services. Finally, publishers will undoubtedly need to actively pursue the additional value-added services made possible by new technologies and growing article databases.

Large Publishers and Large Libraries

Site licenses make a great deal of sense when both publishers and libraries are large, a situation where beneficial arrangements can be made in which publishers, libraries, and scientists all win. There are many ways this can be done. For example, this can be achieved by negotiating two types of charges: one charge for the availability of the information (i.e., reimbursement for the fixed, first-copy costs) and a second charge for unrestricted access to the information through a combination of print and electronic subscriptions (online or CD-ROM) and electronic access to separate copies of articles of journals to which the library does not subscribe. For example,

- The availability charge could be the sum of current subscription prices, less $25 to $35 per title now paid to cover reproduction and distribution costs. Thus, the publisher is ensured of continued revenue to recover relevant costs (including reasonable profits).

- The access charges could be the actual direct cost of reproduction and distribution for print and CD-ROM versions and online storage and access for electronic versions (plus a reasonable recovery of support costs).[22]

The latter charges permit libraries and their users to choose the options that are best suited to them. Libraries may choose only electronic online access in which case they could save approximately $70 per title in processing and maintenance costs and up to $1.48 per reading in avoiding photocopying and reshelving costs. Or they may chose to keep a current periodicals room (or departmental collections) in which case the savings would only involve storage and future per-reading costs of older materials. Either way, libraries achieve a savings. Scientists, too, can choose options that minimize effort and costs to them. Some can still choose print subscriptions that will cost them less with sufficient reading. Journals that are not subscribed to because it is less expensive to obtain copies of articles by interlibrary loan or document delivery, could probably be obtained electronically at a lower overall cost (See Chapter 18 for a detailed description of this example).

Thus, this or other schemes can be negotiated in ways in which everyone wins. It must be clear to all the participants, however, that each will lose some but gain more than they lose, all things considered. Furthermore, it seems clear that site licenses must be different for large academic and special libraries because their users are so different. Special libraries have the distinct advantage in such arrangements because their users are more homogeneous and the users are all paid by the parent organization. Thus, special library decisions can be based on minimizing the overall organization costs.

Large Publishers, Small Libraries, and Individuals

Many small, high-tech companies in the United States employ fewer than fifty scientists, and many scientists are independent consultants. In both instances, a strong argument exists for charging them less for subscriptions, but not necessarily less for access to separate copies of articles. This scenario is less appropriate for society journals than for commercial and some other types of publishers, because society pricing and membership benefits tend to be low enough that small libraries and individuals can afford needed journals. The high-priced journals, however, are even higher for small libraries when considered on a cost-per-reading basis.[23] Publishers currently lose revenue from these organizations because

---

[22]Additional details are provided in Chapters 12, 13, 17, and 18.

[23]Of course a large university can have small faculty in a specialized field for which the same conditions as a small firm hold. Large libraries, however, have the advantages of negotiating site licenses that average out frequently and infrequently-read journals.

reading is often done from journals provided by large public or academic libraries. In other words, scientists travel to these libraries to avoid paying the high subscription prices. In fact, the overall cost per reading for these scientists tends to be two to three times higher than for scientists located in large organizations. Thus, the high prices result in both publishers and scientists, not to mention their parent organizations, losing. Prices can be significantly lowered and still contribute substantially to recovering some of the cost of making the information available (i.e., the fixed publishing costs). As a rough rule of thumb, it costs these scientists $15 to $20 per reading to obtain articles from other sources. A charge of $1.50 per article published should result in a reasonable number of subscribers and sufficient contributions to recovered costs, (i.e., a 100 article journal would have a price of $150, most of which contributes to recovering fixed costs).

Small Publishers and Small Libraries

Small publishers face some problems that larger publishers do not have. For example, they cannot achieve the economies of scale afforded larger publishers in marketing, equipment purchases, and large article digital storage and retrieval capabilities. On the other hand, there has been a tendency toward lower costs (per article) for smaller publishers due to lower overhead, fewer extravagances, and the ability to attract donated time and other resources. There appears to be some merit in small publishers with low circulation journals moving toward providing exclusively electronic journals.

If this is done, however, marketing and acceptance by bibliographic services will be essential. One advantage with electronic access is that additional revenue will come from articles that are now made available through interlibrary loan and document delivery.[24] Pricing of subscriptions and on-demand articles will be very important. It may be necessary to provide electronic access through a vendor or consortium, in which case the revenue actually received by the publisher should be in the range of $5 to $10 per article disseminated in order to help pay for the article processing costs. A vendor (or consortium) may also be able to negotiate site licenses for a group of publishers in which some of the benefits of these arrangements can be achieved.

Small libraries and small organizations should consider joining a library consortium. The U.S. Department of Education has funded the development of multi-

---

[24]Our 1978 and 1984 copyright studies provided evidence that both small and large circulation journals can have appreciable numbers of interlibrary loans.

type library consortia in all states.[25] Most states have embarked on providing access to electronic publications, and others will follow. In this way, small libraries will able to obtain the advantages of site licenses.

Academic and Research Libraries

Site licenses with larger publishers provide a reasonable alternative because they offer the opportunity to negotiate terms in which all participants can benefit. For example, libraries might negotiate some concessions from publishers when electronic versions are offered in tandem with print versions.

- The library is purchasing information, so the purchase price will be no higher than previously paid, less $25 to $35 (for eliminated costs), and remain fixed (or with inflation increases) for a designated number of years.

- The library will be provided either paper or electronic versions of currently purchased titles, as desired, and on-demand electronic article copies of all the publisher's journals at a minimum negotiated price that covers distribution and, when appropriate, reproduction costs plus some overhead and profit.

- If the publisher maintains the electronic database, data on the amount of use (i.e., relevant hits) will be provided to the library on a periodic basis, perhaps quarterly.

- Since libraries are unlikely to maintain bound collections of these journals, the publishers need to provide some guarantee that there will be some future electronic access to them in case they cut back or go out of business.[26]

Libraries will experience savings from eliminating the costs of maintaining bound journals, reshelving and photocopying, and interlibrary borrowing (and eventually lending) or document delivery of the publisher's other journals (see Chapter 17 for details of cost savings).

---

[25]These consortia (or networks) are designed to provide economic services to libraries of all types and sizes. Most services are designed to take advantage of economies of scale that are not possible for small libraries.

[26]This is a useful service that a vendor or digital libraries could provide. However, publishers need to make that arrangement for their titles. Libraries can also work together to ensure a single last-paper copy of journal articles is also preserved.

For at least a decade, a movement has been growing to have authors, readers, libraries, and their funding sources essentially boycott commercial publishers (see description of SPARC in Chapter 15). This movement has three principal bases:

1. A number of studies established that the average prices of commercial journals are higher than those provided by other types of publishers, with a correspondingly higher rate of increase;

2. The stated reasons that their prices are so high are that commercial publishers are making an unreasonable profit and/or their growth in size through buy-outs and mergers have resulted in excessive overhead; and

3. Commercial publishers have created a monopoly which permits them to charge these high prices with impunity.

These accusations may well be correct, in which case the movement has considerable merit. However, we caution the library community not to take an all-or-nothing approach to this extremely important issue because it has not been adequately demonstrated that all commercial publishers are charging unreasonable prices. The high prices of some commercial publishers may be due to the size and circulation of their journals. Commercial journals tend to publish in highly specialized scientific areas in which the readership is small and, therefore, are likely to have small-circulation, high-unit costs, and correspondingly high prices. Some commercial publishers may indeed have unreasonable prices due to large overhead and profits, but that fact has not yet been sufficiently demonstrated.[27]

Furthermore, some organizations or other publishers must be willing to make enormous investments and assume the risks of publishing small-circulation journals. It is not at all clear that university presses and societies are either able or willing to do so. Finally, even if other publishers assume these risks, there is no reason to believe that libraries will eventually pay much less for this information unless the quality and other attributes are reduced.

Special Libraries

Over the years, special libraries (i.e., libraries in businesses, national laboratories, or government agencies) have shifted the role they play in providing access to scholarly journal articles. Sound economic rationale exists for acquiring and using

---

[27]See Chapter 14, Financing Scholarly Journals, for the pro and con arguments that have been made and why a different kind of analysis needs to be done to support these assertions.

journals through a variety of distribution means (e.g., personal and institutional subscriptions) and media (e.g., print and electronic subscriptions, electronic document delivery), depending on how often the journals are read and the comparative cost per reading from each source. From the parent organization's viewpoint, the overall cost of readers' time, payment for subscriptions, and library operations can be substantially reduced through careful allocation of these resources. In fact, special librarians have recently become more involved in such determination and resource allocation.

At one time, special librarians devoted most of their efforts to developing a centralized collection. Now many special librarians also order personal subscriptions and desk copies of books for individuals because they can do so less expensively than individuals. They help maintain unit or department collections and manage branch libraries in addition to their centralized collections. Special librarians also provide journal routing systems, current periodical rooms or space, and access through central CD-ROM collections that are sometimes distributed through local area networks. They are also much more active in providing access to external collections through document delivery services and multi-type library resource sharing. Special librarians need to broaden their perspective and responsibility, if indeed they have not already done so, to include all aspects of electronic publications as well.

To do this, special librarians must understand how publishing and access are changing. An essential issue which must be addressed is the economic implications of journal article access and use throughout their organization, including the price paid, the cost of processing and maintenance, and the cost to readers. These costs must be considered for all media and sources of articles. We have provided some examples of these costs to illustrate how this can be done. Armed with this information, special librarians can make rational decisions concerning any of the multitude of electronic alternatives they will confront in the future. Monitoring all of the options, selecting the best medium and distribution means for each title, negotiating site licenses, and optimizing information use throughout the organization are all essential roles for the special librarian.

Access to scholarly scientific and other journals remains vitally important to researchers and others in organizations. Providing the best and most cost-effective access to these resources is more complex than ever and requires someone who can weigh the advantages and disadvantages of all of the alternatives for every title and every potential user.

Thus librarians must ensure that the best information possible is provided to their user communities at a minimum cost to users and their organizations. That rarely means one single approach to dissemination because the wide variety of information-seeking and use patterns requires a range of dissemination means. Paper may be more appropriate for (1) individuals who read a journal extensively and are not near a shared collection, (2) library and unit collections of current periodicals available to those who are located nearby, and (3) centralized older collections that are not available electronically. Electronic access may be more appropriate for low-circulation journals, journals that are infrequently read by individuals, journals that are collectively infrequently read in an organization, and older articles from journals that are discarded because they are available electronically. Such an approach is based on minimizing the cost for each situation.

Ideally, site licenses for special libraries would be based on a fixed amount that makes all journals provided by a publisher available to the organization served by the library. The special library would then pay a nominal amount for paper distribution or electronic access, whichever minimizes costs to the library and its users. Paper distribution could be used for current periodical rooms, department collections, and individuals when there is a sufficient amount of reading to make it less expensive to use than electronic access. Note that the trade-off cost per reading involves only about $25 to $35 of reproduction and distribution costs for paper journals since recovery of the fixed costs is made by the agreed-upon fixed amount mentioned above. Electronic access would be made available for infrequently read materials and older articles, since binding and shelving should no longer be necessary (see Chapter 18 for details of such an approach).

Advantages of that approach include minimizing organization costs for each type of use by replacing journal ordering, interlibrary borrowing/document delivery, binding and storing future journals, and duplicate storage at various sites. It also has the advantage of reducing internal electronic-communication congestion and avoiding excessive reading from the computer screen. The disadvantages include the difficulty of establishing an equitable, fixed, availability fee and accepting some library budgeting uncertainty, although the commonly accepted means of document delivery already involves that element of uncertainty.

Scientists

Authors will undoubtedly continue to choose scholarly journals that meet their needs, but they need to also consider whether or not readership of these articles might be affected by journal prices, recognizing that prices must be high for journals serving small specialties. Authors who choose to publish largely on their own web sites need to recognize that readership, and therefore value, will be affected if their articles are not input to a reputable bibliographic database. Authors should also be aware that their greatest readership may be outside the academic community, especially if their articles are in the physical and life sciences. Peer review and editing are still important to readers and will undoubtedly continue to be sought by authors and readers. One important aspect of authorship is that the discipline necessary to put one's thoughts on paper, particularly with the knowledge that the manuscript will be critically reviewed, often actually enhances creativity.

Research demonstrates that scientific journals have tremendous use, usefulness, and value. This will undoubtedly continue to be the case regardless of whether articles are published in paper or electronic media as readers recognize that electronic publications provide an alternative, not necessarily a substitute, for traditional print journals. Readers need not be put off by screen displays because in-depth reading can be read from print-outs which are relatively inexpensive. Some of the most useful and valuable scientific information is found in older articles that typically are not yet available electronically and therefore require an alternative, more traditional means of acquisition.

For research and teaching purposes, it is important not to rely solely on Internet sources of information that do not provide some quality mechanisms, for either primary or secondary publications. Online searches are often best conducted on well-established databases because of their completeness and quality, preferably those sanctioned by a professional society (e.g., American Chemical Society) or that are well established such as the Science Citation Index. Librarians or information specialists will continue to be a valuable resource for identifying, locating, and assessing needed information. This service is likely to become even more relevant as information on the Internet becomes even more prolific. Users need to continually inform specialists about their information needs and requirements by utilizing specialists' strengths, including their intimate knowledge of both online and print collections and how to access them.

Funders of Scientists and Libraries

A large portion of an organization's resources are used for communication by professionals such as scientists who spend over half their time communicating. Some of this time is devoted to using information as a resource to do their work better and faster, and nearly half of this time involves conveying information to others. Overwhelming evidence shows that use of publications helps to achieve overall organizational goals, makes the staff more productive, and substantially increases the quality of work. For scientists, one of the most important resources in research and other scientific endeavors is the information provided by scholarly journals. Scientists are willing to pay for this information with hundreds of hours of their time to obtain and read scholarly journal articles. They choose to devote the scarce resource of their time to obtain this information because of its value to them in their work.

While thousands of scientific scholarly journals are published in the United States, on average scientists read more than 100 articles per year from approximately 18 of these journals. Some of the journals are heavily read, but most contain only a few articles that are read. With prices of journals increasing, it makes sense for scientists to personally purchase only the journals frequently read by them and to go to the library or other sources to read the rest. In fact, over the years, with spiraling journal prices, scientists and their libraries have achieved a nearly optimum balance of resources used to identify, locate, obtain, and use scholarly journals and other sources of needed information. A shift has occurred, however, from one resource—the purchase of an average of nearly six personal subscription to less than half that number—to the time required by scientists to go to the library to read their cancelled journals. Libraries have also cancelled subscriptions and replaced infrequently-read journals by ordering separate copies of their articles upon demand, a labor-intensive activity. Thus, fewer subscriptions are acquired, but at the cost of the valuable time of scientists and librarians, albeit still at a lower overall cost to the organization.

Scholarly journals are at the beginning of a major transition to electronic journals. Contrary to the belief and hopes of many administrators, electronic publishing is not a panacea to the costs of communication and libraries. In fact:

- Most scholarly journal prices will decrease little, if at all, because journal publishing is dominated by large fixed costs that may even rise a little with the new technology. Replaced reproduction and distribution costs will decrease, but they average only $25 to $35 per subscription.

- Space requirements for shelving will diminish over time, but some space will continue to be necessary because older scientific articles will continue to be needed and, as a practical matter, many older articles are not available electronically.

- Just as spiraling prices resulted in shifts among resources used for alternatives which minimized overall costs, electronic journals will also result in major shifts of resources. Evidence suggests, however, that some journals should continue to be acquired in traditional print form. Rather than thinking in either/or terms regarding journal media, it is important to ask which medium best suits scientists' needs at the minimum cost, and this can be expected to vary from journal to journal and among scientists. Librarians should continue to play an important role in ensuring that information is provided to scientists in the most economic manner possible.

- Large publishers and libraries are making arrangements to acquire journals through site licenses. This makes a great deal of sense, if the license permits the library to process articles in unrestricted ways that will optimize distribution to their users (i.e., print and electronic subscriptions and on-demand electronic article copies).

- There is a great deal of uncertainty among publishers, regarding pricing policies, thus leading to potential negotiation.

The flexibility of obtaining electronic subscriptions and access to separate copies of articles presents the opportunity for improved efficiencies, but the potential is also high for an economic downside because a new medium has been introduced into the journal system. Decisions necessary to allocate these resources optimally in an organization must at minimum take into account the scientists' time, purchase prices, equipment, space, and library costs. Here it is important to recognize that scientists' time dominates overall costs and, therefore, must be carefully considered when making information service decisions. Optimum results are contingent on allowing someone who is knowledgeable about communication costs and practices, such as librarians, to determine this allocation or at least be heavily involved in the decision-making process.

CHAPTER 2

History of Traditional and Electronic Scientific Journal Publishing

INTRODUCTION

The first traditional scientific print journals were conceived in Europe during the 1600s and began in the United States during the 1800s. From an historical perspective, scientific scholarly journals evolved rather unevenly over three and one-half centuries to their current special role in the complex array of scientific communication modes and channels. Today they are the primary publishing channel of scientists, and their usefulness and value have been abundantly demonstrated.

The history of electronic journals dates back to the 1960s, with a flurry of activity during the 1970s and early 1980s supported by extensive government funding. While technology development and acceptance were not as advanced as they are today, the early innovative concepts and their contribution to scientific communication are as relevant today as they were then. Because many of these creative ideas are still applicable today, we provide references to this largely untapped and currently ignored body of knowledge. This chapter examines their development as well as the later development of electronic journals up to the early 1990s. Recent growth and description are given in Chapter 15.

HISTORY OF TRADITIONAL SCIENTIFIC PRINT JOURNALS[1]

Two events, the development of newspapers and the formation of scientific societies, undoubtedly provided the impetus for the current scientific scholarly journal (Houghton 1975). While early versions of newspapers can be traced to China in the seventh century and the Roman Empire, the publication most resembling the modern newspaper was first published in 1594 in Germany, soon followed by other newspapers in England and other European countries.

At approximately the same time, the developing atmosphere of scientific discovery and collegiality required an improved means of communication. During the early 1600s, informal networks of scholars and philosophers, often referred to as "hidden colleges,"[2] communicated through personal contact and private written correspondence. These groups evolved into formalized academies and societies that clearly needed some means of communicating to groups of peers that were growing in size. One apparent solution seemed to be some form of newspaper-like means of communication. Efficient alternatives were non-existent: individual letters[3] and notes were inefficient, copyists used to reach multiple readers were very expensive, and book publishing was not timely. Thus, the scientific journal was a solution whose time had come.

The first scientific journal-like publication, *Le Journal des Scavans*, first appeared in January 1665. It was founded by M. de Sallo, a counselor of the French court of the Parliament, who "epitomized the new learning and who waged a constant battle against superstitions and prejudices rife at that time" (Houghton 1975). The first issue was twenty pages long and contained ten articles and some letters and notes. While censored by the crown for a short while, the journal still exists as a leading literary periodical. Later that same year, the Royal Society of London began a monthly journal of articles which recorded experiments of their members and other correspondence. This publication, *Philosophical Transactions*, contained sixteen pages consisting of nine articles, a dedication to the society, a listing of books, and other correspondence. It continues to this day, despite a seven-year hiatus.[4] Several other journals followed shortly thereafter, although the success of these early journals was far from guaranteed.

---

[1]Details of the history of scientific journals can be found in Kronick (1962), Meadows (1974), and Houghton (1975), among others. Meadows (1999) also contributed through personal comments.
[2]The "hidden colleges" are very much like the "invisible colleges" referred to by Derek Price (1963).
[3]The letters were typically one to many, a bit like Paul's letters in the New Testament.
[4]*Le Journal des Scavans* was intended to catalog and abstract books, provide obituaries, record legal decisions, describe developments in science and cover all topics of interest to men of letters. However, since the Royal Society was only concerned with "experimental learning", Meadows (1998) suggests that the *Philosophical Transactions* was the forerunner of the modern scientific journal.

The early journals were primarily written in the language of the country of origin, although some were written in Latin as a common language. Early articles often appeared in more than one journal and, for a long time, it was anticipated that they would eventually be published in a monograph. These practices do not seem much different from those of today.

By the end of the seventeenth century, somewhere between 30 and 90 scientific and medical journals were being published worldwide; in the next century this number rose to a total of 755 titles (Houghton 1975 and Garrison 1934). Until this time, most of the journals were fairly broad in their coverage, but specialization began to develop in both the societies and their journals. Kuhn (1962) argued that the formation of new scientific journals marked the consolidation of a new paradigm in science and demonstrated increasing specialization. Commercial publishers have recently started many of these new journals.

Price (1963) plotted the growth of a number of journals since their inception (Figure 2).[5] He points out that the number of journals doubles approximately every fifteen years, a rate of growth which has been relatively constant over the centuries. Price's forecasts have not been realized, perhaps due to his method of counting and since the number of journals per scientist has dampened (due in part to increased sizes). As the number of scientific journals began to proliferate worldwide, it became necessary to develop a means for identifying and locating articles. This requirement led to the development of journals of abstracts which were first published in the mid-1800s. At that time, there were approximately 300 scientific journals worldwide; since then, there has been approximately one new abstract journal for every 300 new scientific journals. A more recent estimate of the number of scholarly journals worldwide is 70,000 to 80,000 (Meadows and Singleton 1995).

The exact date of the founding of the first scientific journal in the United States is a matter of contention. A National Science Foundation (NSF) report (1964) indicates that the first such publication occurred in 1839. Houghton (1975) suggests that the *American Mechanics Magazine*[6] was first published in 1825, while *Scientific American* began in 1845. On the other hand, Meadows (in a personal review of this chapter) suggests that the earliest journal was one volume of *Transactions* produced by the Chemical Society in Philadelphia in 1813 (Brock 1992). He points out that the two titles above were magazines rather than journals, and that a problem

---

[5]Both Houghton and Meadows have recently described the character of this growth through its first two centuries. Earlier, Kronick provided an historical account of science journals. Price's data were questioned, not the least of which because he had little data on the death rate of journals.
[6]This journal later became the *Journal of the Franklin Institute*.

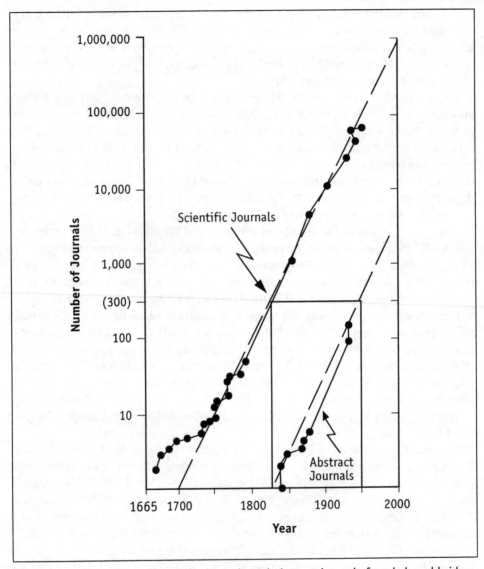

Figure 2. Total number of scientific journals and abstract journals founded worldwide, 1665–2000. (*Source: Price 1963*)

with identifying journal titles in both Europe and North America is that many of them, such as the *Transactions* were short-lived. He also indicates that reports from institutions such as the Chemical Society, geological survey, observatories, and so on, were probably as important as journals in early America.

The growth of journals published in the United States has also been very rapid, but in recent years it has lagged behind worldwide growth. In 1995 we estimate that there were 6,771 scientific scholarly journals published in the United States (Tenopir and King 1997). The number of journals in the United States, displayed in Figure 3, also doubled every fifteen years until recently when the rate in

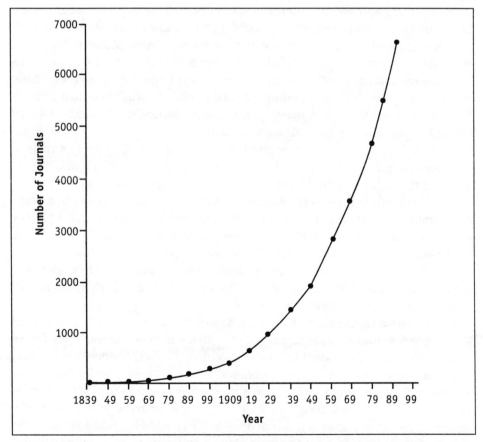

Figure 3. Total number of scientific and technical journals in the United States, 1839–2000. (*Source: King, McDonald, and Roderer 1981*)

number of titles decreased, although the number of pages has actually increased relative to the number of scientists. The growth exceeded worldwide growth until 1875; but then paralleled worldwide growth until the Great Depression in the 1930s. Since then, the rate appeared to be steady and linear on the logarithmic scale until recently.

Two other factors affect scientific and technical publishing in the United States. First, many scientific and technical periodicals that do not report primary research findings entered the field. These publications, which include trade journals, bulletins, and newsletters, are estimated to total 6,600 today, approximately equal to the number of scholarly scientific and technical journals. The second factor is related to the type of publishing entity. In the United States prior to 1945, nearly every scientific and technical journal was published by a professional society, unlike in Europe where many were published by commercial firms. After 1945, commercial publishers also became very active in the United States, to the extent that today they publish approximately 40 percent of all U.S. scientific scholarly journals (Tenopir and King 1997). Commercial publishers in the U.S. and Europe differ in several respects. For one, in Europe journal publishing was often their primary business, whereas in the U.S. many commercial publishers, until recently, focused on books with scholarly journals being a sideline. This, perhaps, led to the European publishers having to be more profit-oriented with regard to their journals.

Finally, communication research has demonstrated that scientific discovery is reported through a multitude of channels, some being interpersonal and others being in text. While there is substantial replication of specific information being communicated, each channel seems to fill a necessary niche. Lin and Garvey (1972), in reporting on seminal work in this area, concluded that all channels are important and "that to understand the differential use of information contained in various channels by scientists and technologists, it is important to understand the internal structure of and the interrelationship of the various channels as they provide a network of information sources . . .".

Various channels are used by different scientists depending on factors such as learning and communication capabilities and styles, field of science, type of work being performed, educational background, and years of experience.

Below we discuss some communication research in the 1960s that led to ambivalence concerning journals. Some research suggested that scientific scholarly journals were inefficient and unread. On the other hand, Kessler (1967) reporting on communication research done at MIT, concluded that scientific journals are "the most successful and ubiquitous carriers of scientific information in the entire history of science." Indeed, they have thrived for three and one-half centuries and continue to do so today. The abundant research reported in this book suggests that this situation is unlikely to change for some time to come.

HISTORICAL PERSPECTIVES ON ELECTRONIC JOURNALS

The past ten years have witnessed incredible interest and growth in electronic journals. Unfortunately, these recent developments do not seem to have fully benefited from extensive past research and experimentation in scientific communications in general and electronic journals in particular. Perhaps the most compelling reason for this oversight is that one of the funders of a substantial amount of the earlier research, the NSF, began to wind down this research from 1978 to 1982 and then essentially discontinued it until the recent digital libraries initiatives. While the efforts of the early years served as the genesis for recent developments, some of the findings have been effectively ignored, with the result that mistakes may be repeated as knowledge is rediscovered. Therefore, the results of some of the earlier research and experiments in electronic publishing are offered below.

There have certainly been a number of visionaries in the fields of knowledge and information, ranging from a global perspective (e.g., Wells 1938 and Otlet 1934, 1935) to its national importance (Machlup 1962), to general improvements in scientific communication (e.g., Bush 1945 and Rider 1944).[7] These and other visionaries provided the genesis for futuristic thinking that has led to electronic journals and, perhaps more importantly, what can be done with this information once it is recorded in flexible, digitized media. One of the works most cited as a precursor to the events of the 1960s and 1970s is Vannevar Bush's 1945 epic paper, "As We May Think." Bush envisioned a large office information system (memex) in which new technology could be used to store, organize, and retrieve the documented information found in books, journals, and other documents. He apparently foresaw both the flood of information that would arrive following the war and the need for new ways of dealing with this onslaught of documents. Lesk (1997) notes that, in addition to advocating large, local document banks, Bush had several prescient ideas. He suggested that individuals would plant links from one piece of knowledge to another, which he called 'trails' of information. These trails are the precursor of today's hypertext and the Web. Bush also emphasized the ease with which you could put your own information into the system. Many research efforts were made through the 1960s to help realize Bush's dreams. Some

---

[7]See, for example, brief summaries of Wells (Rayward 1999), Otlet (Buckland 1997), Machlup (Miller 1983), Bush (Buckland 1992) and Rider (Crawford, Hurd & Weller 1996).

of these began developing computerized extensions of knowledge work environments (e.g., Englebart 1970, Licklider 1968).

Two perspectives are critical to the achievement of recent developments in electronic journals and digital libraries. The first perspective derives from the enormous amount of research conducted from 1960 to 1980 in the United States,
largely under the auspices of the NSF. This research focused largely on three
areas: information retrieval systems; general scientific communication patterns
and innovations; and the potential of electronic journals. The greatest amount of
funding initially involved information retrieval, followed by funding for general
scientific communications and, finally, electronic journals. The second perspective
involves initiatives in Europe in the 1970s and 1980s. Some of that research was
funded through the British Library Research Development Department, in some
ways the NSF counterpart in the United Kingdom for information-related
research. The Royal Society, Office of Scientific and Technical Information (OSTI,
later Aslib), and scientific information providers (UKCIS, IEE, etc.) focused on
scientific communications in the U.K. Some of the research built upon projects
performed in the United States, and some involved European publishers. Finally,
other research studies and experiments were performed in the 1980s, primarily by
publishers in collaboration with university libraries.

U.S. SCIENTIFIC COMMUNICATION RESEARCH LEADING
TO ELECTRONIC JOURNALS IN THE 1960s

The Trail Blazed by the National Science Foundation (NSF) and Others

In the 1950s, the NSF, Office of Science Information Service began a series
of reports (Nonconventional Technical Information Systems in Current Use,
1957–1966) addressed to such issues as exploiting new technologies to the benefit
of scientific communications and how to take advantage of and the transfer of
scientific-related technologies from the military to universities and industry
(Henderson 1999).

The research performed in the 1960s followed four basic paths. First, there was
an enormous amount of research on technologies dealing with secondary
abstracting and indexing services that led to digital databases and automated
searches of these databases. NSF funded much of this research involving scientific
societies and their associated abstracting and indexing services. The National
Library of Medicine also supported a great deal of research, as did other government libraries and departments such as the National Aeronautics and Space
Administration (NASA), the Atomic Energy Commission (AEC), the Department
of Defense (DOD), and the U.S. Patent Office. Several companies, such as DuPont,

IBM and the Institute for Scientific Information (ISI), also conducted exemplary research in this area (see, for example, Kvalnes 1999, Gannett's description of Luhn's work 1973, and Wouters 1999). To a lesser degree at that time, NSF also supported research in the use of technologies in primary scientific publications.

The second line of research involved scientific communication through the use of a variety of channels such as primary and secondary publications, conferences, and informal word-of-mouth. Partially as a result of these studies, some problems appeared to emerge with the traditional scientific scholarly journals which were examined as part of a third research path. Finally, a series of studies and experiments were conducted to determine what might be done to solve the perceived weaknesses of the scholarly journal system.

Development of Scientific Communication Technologies

In the 1960s the NSF's Division of Science Information embarked on a series of projects designed to enhance scientific communication processes. In particular, substantial funding was directed toward improving information retrieval systems by directly funding, among others, the Chemical Abstracts Service, the American Institute of Physics, BIOSIS, the American Psychological Association, and the Engineering Index. This funding led to the creation of improved, comprehensive databases and test beds followed by research and experimentation with these systems. It seems clear that these development efforts paid off in valuable, widely used online retrieval systems in most fields of science. Some of the knowledge gained through that research, however, was ignored for many years. For example, research dealing with associative retrieval and other systems (e.g., Jones, Giuliano, and Curtice 1967a, b, c; Salton 1968) which showed such great promise in concept but lacked current technology capabilities at the time, has been lost and is being reinvented in digital library initiatives. Furthermore, the usefulness and value of traditional bibliographic databases are being ignored by many current electronic journal system advocates.[8]

Doebler (1970), a representative from the publishing industry, claims that publishers' full appreciation of technological innovation was stimulated by a 1964 special seminar in which leading information scientists, who had been engaged in the information retrieval research mentioned above, opened what proved to be a significant dialog with key publishers. They became intrigued by how far secondary

---

[8]Bourne and Bellardo Hahn (1999) provide an exhaustive history of this body of work.

publishing had progressed in the use of computer and communication technologies. It became clear to them that nearly all facets of primary publishing could benefit as well from these innovations.[9] This is not to say that serious investigations had not already begun in electronic publishing technology. For example, the American Chemical Society began investigating electronic innovations as early as 1958 when it acquired Photon photocomposition equipment (Kuney 1965, 1966).

Some of the early leaders in scientific applications of computer technology applied to primary publication text included a number of scientific societies (e.g., American Chemical Society and Chemical Abstracts Service, American Institute of Physics, American Geological Institute, American Mathematical Society, American Psychological Association, and IEEE) and several entrepreneurs (e.g., Lawrence F. Buckland, Ronald L. Henderson, J. N. Meade, and J. W. Seybold to name a few). For example, in 1966 the American Institute of Physics began research on computer composition of primary journals, and the American Mathematical Society began to examine the possibility of automating mathematical equations (Walker 1966).

By the end of 1967, North America boasted well over 400 computerized typesetting operations, and the American Chemical Society published three journals in which typesetting was computerized. Computerized photocomposition, however, was considered the most promising technology at that time (Kuney 1968). While computerized composition was thought to be an improvement over typesetting, it was clearly understood that obtaining digitized text opened up entirely new opportunities for scientific communication (see, for example, Licklider 1967). A seminal work was prepared by Barnett (1965) which illustrated how source data automation could be utilized from the author's original manuscript through publication and extending all the way through generation of indexes and abstracts.

The early years, while filled with promise, also held significant disappointments, most notably the inability to achieve anticipated economies (see the dialog among computer composition experts in Landau (ed.) 1971). Furthermore, Buckland (1966) clearly articulated the issue of a lack of standards for encoding the required symbols, both literal characters of text and function codes, for transformations of text to machine-readable format and for conversions between machines (or electronic input sources) which do not process the same symbol set.

Other technological breakthroughs that could ultimately affect electronic journals were also occurring in the 1960s. Digitized typewriting was just beginning with the use first of magnetic tapes and then magnetic cards; this opened the

---

[9]Lesk (1998) is particularly effective in showing the commonality between primary and secondary publishing technologies.

opportunity of directly entering author manuscripts. Both the Department of Defense (DOD) and NSF were developing advanced communication systems that could be used by segments of the scientific community. Collier (1998) points out that even the concept of the Internet is certainly not new. In the 1960s, Licklider and Taylor (1968) described an "intergalactic computer network" that would link scientists. Finally, some researchers were experimenting with the notion of searching full-text (i.e., natural language) of primary publications, article summaries, or abstracts (see a review of these studies by Tenopir and Ro 1990; Lesk 1998).

General Scientific Communication Studies

During the 1960s, the NSF and others also supported a large number of general scientific communication studies performed at institutions such as Case Institute of Technology (Ackoff and Martin), The Johns Hopkins University (Garvey and Griffith), the Massachusetts Institute of Technology (Licklider and Allen), Stanford University (Paisley and Parker), and the Harvard University (Rosenbloom and Wolek). These studies described scientific communication from several perspectives involving both oral and print media, including communication through scientific scholarly journals.

These studies represented four research approaches.

1. One approach examined new research findings and followed the resulting information through its life cycle through various communication channels, such as internal discussions and reporting in an organization, reporting at professional meetings, and through publication of meeting proceedings, journal articles, patents, books, and state-of-the-art reviews. The information is portrayed by a time line along which the information appears in the various channels (see, for example, Garvey and Griffith reports in the American Psychological Association's Project 1963, 1965, 1967, 1968).

2. A second approach to research involved observing scientists' communication patterns within organizations. Scientists were asked to indicate the specific information channels (i.e., sources) used by them to perform a recent or particularly important R&D task. This research helped determine the extent to which channels were used and their relative importance (see, for example, Allen 1970, Paisley 1965, Menzel 1962, Rosenbloom and Wolek 1970).

3. Allen (1966) was one of the first researchers who observed the extent to which specific individuals are used as an information source and the extent to which intra-unit, intra-organization, and external information channels are used. He found that certain scientists served as 'gatekeepers' of infor-

mation in their organizations. Allen and several others extended this kind of study with certain refinements into the 1970s and 1980s.

4. A fourth kind of research focused on scientists' reading and authorship. Garvey and Griffith (1971) observed readership of individuals and specific articles by having scientists indicate which articles were read from a journal's table of contents. Others simply asked how many journals or articles scientists read or how much time they spent reading journal articles during the last month.

Various aspects and results of these studies are discussed throughout this book.[10]

Perceived Problems with Scientific Scholarly Journals

Meadows (1999) recalls that some early events led some to believe that scholarly journal publishing could be improved. Two conferences in particular were addressed to these issues: The Royal Society Information Conference, Royal Society, London in 1948 and the International Conference on Scientific Information, NAS/NRC, Washington in 1959. The communication studies of the 1960s appeared to confirm concerns with scholarly journals and led to an examination of alternative forms of communication. In 1963, the Price research on the growth of scholarly journals and authorships triggered an enormous interest in journals. It also helped to encourage the perception that journals were at the heart of an emerging "information explosion" which needed to be addressed.[11] Some examples of statements at that time follow (Hammer 1967; Anderla 1985):

- "The body of recorded scientific and technical information now has a volume of about 10 trillion alphanumeric characters . . ." (Licklider 1966)

- ". . . the number of pages has been increasing at a rate of close to 10 percent per year in this post-World War II era. This rate of increase means that, in less than eight years, the number of technical pages will be doubled." (Willenbrock 1966)

---

[10]A review of communication studies performed in the 1950s and early 1960s is presented by Menzel (1966) and Herner and Herner (1967); other reviews and over 400 subsequent user studies performed from 1965 to 1994 are discussed by King (1994).

[11]The concerns with the information explosion are not new. Meadows (1998) cites a 1613 author imploring that "One of the diseases of this age is the multiplicity of books; they doth so overcharge the world that it is not able to digest the abundance of idle matter that is every day hatched and brought forth into the world," and Odlyzko (2000) points out that earlier Ecclesiastes 12:12 says that "of making many books there is no end; and much study is a weariness of the flesh."

- ". . . at the beginning of the nineteenth century, the number of scientific journals and periodicals was about 100; in 1850 it was 1,000; and by 1900 it had reached 10,000. Some estimates of the number at the present time [1966] go as high as 100,000.[12] If this rate of growth remains constant, it would give a figure in the neighborhood of one million at the end of this century [2000]." (Mountbatten 1966; Garvey and Compton 1967)

- "In every 24-hour period, approximately 2,000,000 words of technical information are being recorded. A reader capable of reading 1,000 words per minute would require 1.5 months, reading eight hours every day, to get through one day's technical output, and at the end of that period, he would have fallen 5.5 years behind in his reading!" (Murray 1966)

- "In the three centuries between 1660 and 1960, all indicators of the volume of science have increased by a factor of about one million." (Anderla 1985 citing Price 1963)

On the other hand, Anderla (1985) states that "In the case of scientific journals, the growth rate has been 3.5 percent, 3.7 percent, or 3.9 percent, depending on whether the number published at the present time [worldwide] is taken as 30,000, 50,000, or 100,000."[13] The 3.5 to 3.9 percent annual rates of growth convert to a doubling every eighteen to twenty years, a figure much closer to ours for the United States (King, McDonald, and Roderer 1981, Tenopir and King 1997) which reflects growth in the number of scientists in the United States. Regardless, in the 1960s the burgeoning information explosion was considered a significant problem that had to be addressed.

A related perceived problem was that journal articles were not read very much (e.g., a typical article is said to be read only an average of about 5 to 20 times) and that only about one-tenth of the articles distributed in journal issues were actually read. In fact, there was a serious misconception about the extent to which articles were read (see Chapter 7 for details), although the estimate which states that 10 to 15 percent of distributed articles are read was accurate and remains so to this day.[14]

---

[12]Note that these estimates are at odds with estimates mentioned above. In part this is a result of differing definitions of what comprises a journal.

[13]It is noted that in 1974 Anderla, in a report to NSF, predicted that the growth of the scientific and technical literature on a worldwide basis would increase four times, and possibly six or seven times, from 1970 to 1985. It is believed that he relied too heavily for his calculations on the published number of items abstracted and indexed which reflected growth in the literature, increased coverage, and increased duplication of coverage among services.

[14]Many publications such as newspapers and magazines, however, are not thoroughly read by most readers. Only about one-third of the outputs from automated information retrieval include items that are ultimately read.

These two factors led many to believe that scholarly journals were an inefficient communication medium (and a huge waste of paper). This problem was exacerbated by the finding that research reporting is replicated in many channels, several of which were informal or formal publications.[15] Furthermore, at that time there was a perception that most scientists already knew about the research being reported in scholarly journals, due in large part to the existence of "invisible colleges." One study (Garvey and Gottfreddson 1975) found that 73 percent of the workers active in a subject area of an article were likely to be acquainted with the research reported.[16] Finally, the time delay from initial manuscript submission to the time the journal issue was distributed was considered unacceptable by many. For example, Lin, Garvey, and Nelson (1970) reported that, on average, research started twenty-eight months prior to publication, was completed fifteen months before publication, and was written and submitted eight months prior to being published.

Alternatives to Traditional Scholarly Journals

As a result of these real and imagined problems with traditional scholarly journals a number of proposals were made to examine alternatives to them. While alternatives were attempted prior to the 1960s, that decade produced an intensive and organized effort to find solutions to these problems. Experiments were launched to improve the primary system through the use of preprints; the publication of briefs, synopses and smaller, more specialized journals; and pre-packaged groups of articles tailored to individual reader needs (see, for example, Brown, Pierce, and Traub 1967 and King ed. 1970). The time delay in publishing was addressed by publishing preliminary reports in the form of letters, advance abstracts, and preprints. Experiments with some of these alternatives continued into the 1970s.

Experiments with Journals and Electronic Processes

As mentioned above, several electronic components necessary for a comprehensive electronic journal system were emerging in the 1960s. The key appeared to be

---

[15]For example, Lin, Garvey and Nelson (1970) found that two-thirds of conference papers are eventually published in journals, although only one-fifth of journal articles were previously presented at national meetings. They also reported that a specific research finding could be reported in as many as eight separate journals, although mostly reporting different aspects of the work.

[16]Recent research does not seem to support this high proportion (see Chapter 8).

inputting digitized manuscripts into computerized composition,[17] but none of the experimental alternatives were particularly successful (Hagstrom 1970). The National Institutes of Health also experimented with the Information Exchange Group in 1960 (Aitchison 1974), but abandoned the idea after six years (Hills 1972). Cost and efficiency of journals were addressed by shortening papers and publishing synopses with full-archival backup (Terrant and Garson 1977; Staiger 1971).

A second approach was to distribute separate copies of articles independently of packaged journals (e.g., APA's *Journal of Applied Technology* and the Society of Automotive Engineers' *SAE Transactions*). This scheme permitted distribution of separates on demand or through pre-determined subjects. Sometimes the separates were, in effect, pre-prints, but some were later reviewed and published in journals. A third approach involved the ACS, Single Article Announcement Scheme, which emphasized fast announcement of contents pages from which separates of articles could be ordered.

One study (Paisley 1971) recommended multiple approaches to dissemination of articles including:

- dissemination of single articles on request

- automatic dissemination of single articles based on scientists' interest profile

- automatic dissemination of single articles according to group profiles, and

- packaging of several articles in "minijournals" according to composite profiles of groups

The American Chemical Society experimented with portions of these alternative approaches, but did not implement them on an ongoing basis. The American Psychological Association experimented with a plan to provide an array of information channels which addressed various author and reader needs (Van Cott 1970), but the system was never implemented in an ongoing way. Other multiple channels included a two-tier system of full text of some articles and abstracts of

---

[17]While local chapter president of ASIS, Donald King organized three conferences involving computerized text, two of which were held at the National Bureau of Standards (now NIST). The first conference, "Innovations in Communications," (King, ed. 1970) emphasized the electronic potential. The second, "Workshop on Computer Composition" (Landau, ed. 1971), dealt exclusively with this topic. The third conference, "Time-sharing Innovation for Operations Research and Decision-Making," (King and O'Neill, eds. 1969) attempted to demonstrate the usefulness of online text by inputting the text of talks prior to the meeting and having authors edit online at the meeting following comments. The proceedings were then published in book form shortly after the meeting.

others published with backups (Spillhaus and Holoviak 1971, 1972) and a system of paper, magnetic tape, and microform (Herschman 1970).

U.S. SCIENTIFIC COMMUNICATION RESEARCH IN THE 1970s
Development of Scientific Publishing Technologies

In 1973 Gannett reported that virtually all of the larger scientific and technical societies had totally converted to offset printing which hastened the implementation of computerized photocomposition. This innovation reduced costs by 15 to 25 percent with little sacrifice in appearance while allowing great flexibility in the use of mathematical notation and thus opened the way for other applications of computerized input. In the 1970s digital typewriters had become commonplace, CRTs were coming into their own, and the Advanced Research Projects Agency (ARPA) communications network was well established.

By this time many believed that electronic publishing held the greatest promise as an alternative to solve many of the problems with scholarly journals that had been identified in the 1960s. The ultimate goal seemed to be to develop one or more large databases of scholarly articles that could be searched and accessed in multiple ways. To achieve this, several related avenues of research began to emerge in the 1960s and carried out in the 1970s under Harold E. Bamford, Jr., Helen Brownson, and Eugene Pronko, and others at NSF. These avenues included three foci: 1) a more in-depth description and assessment of scientific publishing, 2) systems analysis of the scientific scholarly journal system, and 3) research and experimentation with electronic scholarly journals.

The first focus presented a deeper understanding of journal publishing and provided a benchmark for measuring effects of future changes. The second gave insights as to how electronic publishing could be achieved, and the third was designed to demonstrate how such a system could be implemented. Together they provided a well-conceived approach to the ultimate goals that were envisioned.

Description and Assessment of Scientific Publishing

Two large surveys of publishers and libraries were launched to establish the character of scientific publishing in the United States including cost, circulation, and pricing of books and journals (Fry and White 1976; Machlup and Leeson 1978).[18]

---

[18]Some results from these studies are reported in Chapters 12 and 13.

At that time, the NSF produced *Science Indicators* which relied largely on citation counts from the Institute for Scientific Information (ISI) database and patent awards as indicators of scientific communication. To gain a more complete picture of scientific communications and trends, the Division of Science Information awarded a contract, "Statistical Indicators of Scientific and Technical Information Communication" to King Research, Inc. While focusing on books and scholarly journals, the study also examined trends from 1960 to 1974 (with projections to 1980) in technical reports, patents, dissertations, libraries, secondary services, and numeric databases (King et al. 1976a, 1976b, 1977).[19] The trends focused on the growth in number of items (per capita), costs, price, and usage. Special analysis was performed on journal prices which showed increases from 1960 to 1974, even in constant dollars. When examined on a price-per-article and price-per-kiloword-page, however, the increases dampened to very small increases.

Systems Analysis of Alternatives to Traditional Scholarly Journals

Russell Ackoff, a renowned operations researcher, was awarded a grant by NSF to apply his innovative "idealized" approach to planning a national Scientific Communication and Technology Transfer (SCATT) System. This system was designed to "mobilize the large number of relatively autonomous subsystems of the current system into a collaborative effort directed at redesigning their system and implementing their design" (Ackoff, Cowan, Sachs, Meditz, Davis, Emery, and Elton 1976). Subsystems included audio (formal such as a prepared lecture or informal such as personal conversation), visual (formal such as reading a published article and informal such as exchange of personal messages), and three levels of messages: primary (messages that convey new information), secondary (messages about primary messages), and tertiary (messages about the content of other messages).

A University of Toronto systems study (Senders) focused primarily on a journal publishing system, adopting an industrial dynamics modeling process developed by Jay Forrester at the Massachusetts Institute of Technology (MIT). This model tracked the flow of materials through an industry and determined the interactive effects of changes among participants in the system. The study tracked past trends to determine their effects on the system and the effects of potential electronic

---

[19]Another study, "National Enquiry" (Booher and Bhagat) was performed later to describe communications in the humanities (Scholarly Communications 1979). This very large study was funded largely by the National Endowments for the Humanities and several foundations.

processes; it concluded that an electronic alternative to paper-based publishing was both inevitable and imminent (Senders, Anderson, and Hecht 1975).

Lancaster, Drasgow, and Marks (1980) conducted a Delphi study concerning the likely direction of communication technologies accompanied by a much discussed book, *Toward Paperless Information Systems* (Lancaster 1978), which foresaw the end of print-on-paper publishing. Among other systems analysis studies supported by NSF was a series of studies performed by Turoff, Hiltz, and colleagues on teleconferencing (Turoff 1975, Turoff and Hiltz 1982).

King Research, Inc. was awarded a contract to perform systems analysis on alternatives to paper-based systems. We were also optimistic about the promise of electronic journals, but more cautious in our prognostications (King and Roderer 1978; King, McDonald, and Roderer 1981). Electronic journals were clearly demonstrated to be both desirable and economically feasible. However, it was felt that acceptance and capabilities of all the necessary electronic processes (i.e., authorship, editing, composition, communication, library access and storage, and reading) would develop unevenly among participants and more slowly than predicted by some. Until all of the components were fully in place and universally used, the full potential of electronic publishing could not be realized.

For example, standards for text input were not yet in place, scanning text to complement digital input was not completely acceptable at that time, and problems still existed in handling mathematical equations, chemical compounds, and special graphics. From an economic standpoint it was felt that small-circulation journals (particularly new ones) were more likely to become exclusively electronic, but large-circulation journals would continue in paper, backed up with electronic distribution of separates for journals infrequently read in individual libraries and by individuals in small organizations. We predicted that it would be twenty years (1998) before comprehensive electronic journal systems would become commonplace.[20] By comprehensive we meant that all participants (i.e., authors, publishers, referees, secondary services, libraries, and readers) would have electronic communication capabilities, and all would apply them to processing manuscripts and articles and for their ultimate distribution and use.

---

[20]While this forecast was fairly accurate, others were not. For example, we were quite confident that a National Periodicals Center would be developed in the United States, although not necessarily as a government operation. We did predict the large increase in distribution of separates, but didn't come close on forecasts of journal prices. This demonstrates the truism that if one is to forecast, do it for a period beyond one's career.

Experiments with Electronic Journal Processes

Not many publishers were willing to invest in the technology needed to digitize input text, however. Publishers were constrained by the fact that only 2 percent of them published the minimum of ten journals believed necessary to justify purchasing the new technology.[21] It was felt that if authors could submit manuscripts in digitized form (magnetic tapes and cards), the publishers could save enough by eliminating costly, labor-intensive typesetting to justify the cost of the new equipment.

With this in mind, Bamford gathered a number of professionals from scientific societies and abstracting and indexing services to examine this idea and he was encouraged to pursue it. As a result, a competitive contract was awarded to Westat, Inc. (King) and their subcontractor, Aspen Systems, Inc. (Berul and Martin),[22] to explore the potential of forming Editorial Processing Centers (EPCs) that could serve small publishers by accepting digitized text for editorial processing, transmitting it to reviewers, and processing author revisions. The ultimate objective was to form the basis for large databases of article text that could be used for distribution of separates and other more imaginative ways of communicating. The study examined author and editorial-related costs; timing and extent of manuscripts transmitted; author ability to submit digitized text, formats for digital submissions; the potential for scanning text, and other aspects of an Editorial Processing Center (Berul, King, and Yates 1974). While the results demonstrated that input was more difficult than anticipated due to a lack of standards and other constraints, the potential cost savings led some of the larger publishers to test the concept, and many of the suggested features of an EPC were adopted.

Following the EPC experiments, Bamford envisioned the need to explore electronic journals further, and NSF funded Turoff at the New Jersey Institute of Technology for this purpose. The concept of computer conferencing was extended to include other forms of communication in an experimental system known as the Electronic Information Exchange System (EIES) (Turoff 1978). The components of the system included a personal notebook space, private communication space (like e-mail), a common conferencing space, and a directory of all the members

---

[21]Machlup and Leeson (1978), for example, showed that there were 1,634 publishers, and 86% of them published only one journal (57% of all journals) and 98% published fewer than 10 journals (81% of all journals).

[22]At that time Westat and Aspen Systems were sister companies in the Information Technology Group of American Can Co.

and groups. These components could then lead to an electronic journal since an author could compose a manuscript in the notebook space, send it to an editor and have it refereed in the conference space, and, if accepted, be published in a public conference space (Bamford and Savin 1978; Turoff and Hiltz 1982).

Failed Attempts to Promote a U.S. National Periodicals Center

Electronic publishing of journals meant more than replacing paper-based journals with electronic replicates available through traditional subscriptions. It was clear that an enormous number of copies of articles were being distributed through interlibrary loan and document delivery (King Research 1977). With the potential for an electronic database of scholarly articles, several studies were performed to establish the feasibility and plans for a U.S. National Periodical Center (NPC) similar to the British Library Lending Division in the United Kingdom, but fully automated (see, for example, Palmour, Bellassai, and Gray 1974; U.S. National Commission on Libraries and Information Science (NCLIS) 1977; Council on Library Resources (CLR) 1978; and King, McDonald, and Roderer 1981). These studies all pointed out the enormous economic and systemic advantages of one-stop shopping and a comprehensive database, not to mention the ability to provide multiple services from the database.

Unfortunately, when proposed to Congress, publishers and some large libraries successfully lobbied against it. Publishers erroneously feared that they would lose control of their revenue source, although in actuality the Center would have resulted in additional royalty revenue which was being lost through the interlibrary loan process. Later, in the 1980s, several article document delivery centers developed that distributed articles initially in photocopies hand delivered or sent by mail, then facsimile for rush orders, and finally in electronic format.

In the late 1970s, the American Institute of Physics, under NSF funding, complemented an information retrieval database (SPIN) with the ability to obtain copies of identified articles. A number of libraries including the National Library of Medicine, Linda Hall Library, and the Center for Research Libraries joined other organizations in providing such services: for example, the UMI Article Clearinghouse (now ProQuest), Online Computer Library Center (OCLC), ISI/OATS (Original Article Tear Sheets), CARL, and DIALOG among others. Contrary to the belief of many in the 1970s, the demand for article separates grew dramatically in the 1980s (see Chapter 10).

THE EUROPEAN TRAIL BLAZED BY THE BRITISH LIBRARY RESEARCH AND DEVELOPMENT DEPARTMENT (BLRDD) AND OTHERS[23]

The British Library Research and Development Department (BLRDD) supported a range of communication studies and experiments similar to those funded by the National Science Foundation in the United States; they differed from the U.S. effort in that the overall level of effort was somewhat less and did not focus on science, although science was considered important. Some of the research and experimentation involving bibliographic retrieval systems actually led the U.S. effort (see, for example, Cleverdon, Mills, and Keen 1966; Sparck Jones and Kay 1973; Robertson 1997). They also performed a number of general user studies, including some in the physical sciences and the social sciences which were particularly revealing (see, for example, Institute of Physics 1976; Hall, Clague, and Aitchison 1972). Results of some of these studies are presented in Chapters 6, 7 and 8.

Lambert (1985) provides an historical discussion of electronic journals, particularly from a European perspective. She indicates that the genesis of electronic journals in Europe involved adaptation of the Editorial Processing Centers (EPCs) led by the Aslib Research and Development Department which investigated their potential (Woodward 1976a, 1976b). It was recognized that EPCs were merely a means to the end (i.e., electronic journals) since the EPCs were intended to use technologies to achieve economies in journal production, but the digitized input would lead to a complete electronic alternative to paper-based publishing.

Meadows and Singleton (1995) provide a schema depicting electronic publishing experiments supported by the BLRDD from 1976 to the mid-1990s. The initial study was performed by Aslib in 1976 involving an assessment of the electronic journal based partially on secondary sources of information. This study led to two series of studies: one performed from 1977 to 1986 by the Primary Communications Research Centre was entitled "New Technology and Developments in the Communication of Research in 1980s: New Methods and Techniques," and the other was done by BNRBF in 1983, "Impact of New Technology". BLRDD was joined by the NSF which examined an "Experimental Multi-Disciplinary Teleconference and Electronic Journal". Simultaneously the University College London performed "Studies of the Electronic Document" (1980-85) while the Royal Society performed a "Study of the Scientific Information System in the UK" (1980–81).

---

[23]Much of the discussion below is based on Lambert (1985), Meadows (1994), and Rowland, McKnight, and Meadows, eds. (1995).

These studies all tied into the Birmingham Loughborough Electronic Network Development (BLEND) project led by the HUSAT Research Group, Loughborough, from 1980 to 1985. The project is discussed in some detail below. Out of this project came alternative forms of communication through an electronic journal (*Computer Human Factors Journal*) and support infrastructure called the Loughborough Information Network Community (The LINC). From BLEND and a joint project with IEPRC publishers, ADONIS, and the British Library, came Project Quartet involving four British universities and running from 1986 to 1989. These efforts spawned experiments involving automated document delivery, electronic publishing, document interchange, transmission of images, and enabling software and hardware. Later studies were conducted by the Royal Society "Scientific, Technical, and Medical Information System in the UK" (1993), Institute of Physics "Electronic Journals on SuperJANET" (1993), ELVYN Scholarly Journal Publishing and SCONUL (1992-94) which examined the feasibility of electronic delivery of a scholarly journal from the publisher to libraries.

One EIES experiment, The Mental Workload Group, established an experimental electronic journal from 1978 to 1980.[24] Scientists in the United Kingdom were included in the experimental group under BLRDD funding, although the British telecommunication authorities constrained the computer-based text messaging. BLEND strongly resembled the EIES communication and electronic journal initiative (Schackel 1983). In addition to a refereed journal, the system was designed to facilitate short papers and letters, annotated abstracts, news and bulletins, cooperative writing of papers, poster papers, and an inquiry and answer system. Approximately sixty scientists participated in the initial experiment, and an electronic journal, *Computer Human Factors Journal*, was formed in 1982 (although it ultimately failed). The BLEND System researchers, at that time, experienced problems with handling special graphics, archiving, lack of user acceptance, and diversity of hardware and limited standardization (much the same as observed in the King and Roderer study performed in 1978.)

As in the United States, the first aspect of electronic publishing that was widely recognized was its ability to deliver separate copies of articles in lieu of current interlibrary lending and document delivery. Thus, a traditional print-on-paper journal could become minimally electronic by providing separates electronically. In the 1960s and 1970s, electronic ordering of separate photocopies of articles became commonplace and was extensively implemented through the British Library Lending Division (BLLD).

---

[24]This project may well have built upon the electronic laboratory notebook developed and used by scientists at the National Physical Laboratory in the early 1970s.

An online information retrieval system was developed in the 1970s by the British Library Information Service (BLAISE). They introduced an electronic system for ordering separate copies of articles, largely from the BLLD. This system, called the Automated Document Request Service (ADRS), was not particularly successful in 1978. It was found that fast response of full-text was needed, and several approaches to achieve this end were attempted unsuccessfully during the late 1970s and early 1980s.

As a result, several studies were commissioned to investigate the best means for achieving electronic article delivery. The initial study, funded by PIRA, concluded that cost might be a constraint, although the technology was technically feasible (Gates 1983). Another study, funded by the Commission of the European Communities (CEC) and conducted by Arthur D. Little, Inc. (ADL), examined alternative approaches to electronic delivery of articles and concluded that a system they envisioned[25] was economically and technically feasible (ADL 1981). The system generated a great deal of interest, but was never implemented due to lack of funding. Another approach was investigated using satellite capabilities (Gurnsey 1982). This initiative, called APOLLO (Article Procurement with Online Local Ordering), was also funded by CEC with support from the European Space Agency (ESA). Another similar project, Project HERMES, tested the use of teletex in 1981 (Amy 1983).

In 1984, the BLRDD apparently decided that digital input of text was not feasible in the short term and opted for facsimile transmission as the optimum system at that time to electronically transmit separate copies of articles. To facilitate this option they initiated an experiment by installing machines in libraries to receive and send copies of articles normally distributed through interlibrary lending. This practice became widespread during the 1980s.

ELECTRONIC JOURNAL RESEARCH AND DEVELOPMENT IN THE 1980s AND EARLY 1990s

Much of the enthusiasm for electronic journals that existed in the U.S. in the late 1970s subsided,[26] although not completely. In addition to some continued experimentation, particularly in Europe and by publishers, the facilitating technology advances that have made electronic journals a reality came piecemeal in several unrelated areas, including enabling word processing and publishing software,

---

[25]ARTEMIS (Automatic Retrieval of Text from Europe's Multinational Information Service).

[26]Rowland (1995) mentions that Senders (1977), an early advocate (see above) who felt that electronic journals were on the brink, "commented afterwards that he had seen the future, and it didn't work."

introduction and availability of the Internet and local area networks (LANs), and the appearance of PCs and workstations on the desks of scientists that were initially used for bibliographic online searching and electronic mail, but later for manuscript input and article retrieval. These technologies are discussed briefly below; followed by a description of some of the electronic journal experimentation of the 1980s and early 1990s.

Development of Enabling Technologies in the 1980s[27]

By 1990 the U.S. information industry had grown to approximately $500 billion, and 7.6 million computers were shipped domestically in 1991. In the 1980s, the growth in sales was far greater for microcomputers than other types: approximately $1 billion to $18 billion from 1980 to 1990 for microcomputers; $7 billion to $9.5 billion for minicomputers; and $9.5 billion to $12 billion for mainframes. By 1990, 40 million PCs had been sold in the United States compared with 1.2 million in use in business in 1981. In the late 1980s, over 85 percent of scientists in the United States used computers at their work (King, et al. survey 1984; U.S. Census Bureau 1989). Clearly by 1990 computing was rapidly becoming commonplace with improvements in the spectrum of both large-scale mainframes and individual desktop computers.

Telecommunication technologies were also making tremendous advances through satellites, ground linkages using fiber optics, and general networking capabilities. This facilitated the increase in the installed base of supercomputers which were shared by many researchers, developers, and educators through the communication networks. It also enabled individual scientists to communicate more freely with one another. By 1990 there were well over 100 computer networks dedicated to research, but the level of implementation of and access to these networks was uneven among, as well as within, institutions.

In 1989, legislation was first proposed to create a high-capacity electronic national research and education network (NREN) to link supercomputer centers, educational institutions, and other R&D facilities in the United States. NSF coordinated the final effort by upgrading its backbone network; by assisting regional networks to upgrade facilities, capacity, and bandwidth; and by interconnecting the backbone networks of other agencies. DARPA was involved with coordinating R&D efforts on very high-speed switches, protocols, and computer interfaces

---

[27]Much of this discussion was extracted from a report prepared for NSF by J-M. Griffiths (Griffiths, Carroll, King, Williams, and Sheetz 1991). For details concerning relevant technologies, see Lesk 1998.

aimed at developing gigabyte-per-second capability. NSFNET and other backbones (NSINET, DRINET, DDN/MILNET, and ESNET) connected approximately 2,000 computer networks to the international Internet which existed in 1990. In early 1990 NSFNET was passing well over 3 billion packets per month. The traffic at that time on the NSFNET backbone (i.e., the heart of the Internet) was divided among interactive applications (18 percent), electronic mail (27 percent), file transfers (28 percent), domain name lookups (10 percent), and other protocols and services (17 percent) according to Brownrigg (1990). At this time the federal government was funding intercampus networking facilities at a level of approximately $50 million per year.

The ultimate success of the Internet depended on developing the communication capabilities of individual organizations. By 1988, companies had spent $5.7 billion on internal networks (up to $17.9 billion in 1993). At that time, however, improvements were still needed in LAN integration, hardware and link capabilities, and remote LAN capabilities. Still in question was which of several alternatives—fiber optics, microwave radio, infrared light, or cellular radio—would dominate. The truly global expansion of the Internet occurred after breakthrough developments like the NCSA's Mosaic leading to CERNS's World Wide Web.

Visualization (i.e., image understanding and image synthesis) was also emerging as a technology that eventually could have a major impact on electronic publishing. This tool interprets image data fed into a computer and generates images from complex multidimensional data sets. Also, the wide availability of microprocessors combined with the rapidly growing use of CD-ROM players created the potential for multimedia databases with graphics, pictures, animation, and sound with which to enhance the printed word. Finally, hypertext emerged to take advantage of the random access capabilities of computers to overcome the strictly sequential medium of print on paper. Thus, elements could be linked within a single document or among multiple documents.

Increasingly widespread use of automated bibliographic searching has hastened the acceptance of electronic journals. The number of automated searches performed by scientists increased from 8.1 million in 1984 to 14.4 million five years later (King et al. surveys 1984-1990). According to Williams (1989), library and information center searching doubled from 1982 to 1989, and by the late 1980s over 80 percent of academic institutions were using CD-ROM databases. The databases themselves were also growing rapidly. Database records numbered approximately 200,000 in 1980, but had grown to 3.7 billion by 1990 (Williams 1991). Contrary to many predictions, automated searches performed by intermediaries for scientists actually increased in the 1980s, largely because of the time required of scientists and the complexity of searches.

Experiments with Electronic Journals in the 1980s

Some important research and development in the 1980s addressed the problem of the standardization of digital input. For example, in the early 1980s, the Association of American Publishers (AAP) let a contract to Aspen System Corporation (the company that did the technical work on the Editorial Processing Centers in the early 1970s) to assess the feasibility of digitizing text and, in particular, of standardizing digitized text received in various formats. Actual tagging standards were developed by the AAP (i.e., Electronic Manuscript Standards) and others. This work ultimately led to the Standard Generalized Markup Language, (SGML). SGML provides a flexible syntax and philosophy for tagging input of text.

A number of experiments with electronic journals were conducted in the 1980s and beyond with mixed outcomes (see, for example, Brown 1996, Lesk 1998, and Rowland 1995). A consortium of commercial publishers established one of the most heralded efforts in Europe and the United States.[28] The ADONIS project, mentioned earlier, was born out of the concern that interlibrary lending (i.e., photocopies) resulted in cancelled subscriptions, but yielded no revenue in return for distribution of separate copies of articles. The system underwent several technological designs (e.g., one depended heavily on satellite transmission) before one was selected (see, for example, Stern 1982). The system was abandoned after three of the members withdrew, although the system was considered technologically sound.[29] More recently, in the system several hundred journals were scanned and images stored on CD-ROM. These databases were maintained at several libraries and used as a general document delivery service with the CD-ROMs being the source for the copies of articles (Stern 1992).

Red Sage[30] was an experiment undertaken by Springer-Verlag, AT&T Bell Labs, and the University of California at San Francisco library from 1993 to 1995 (Badger and Wallace 1993). This project involved approximately forty Springer journals in molecular biology and radiology. The journals were also scanned and processed with OCR software to allow searchable text (not available in ADONIS).

MUSE is a joint project involving The Johns Hopkins University library and University Press in which the Press' journals are digitally input and made available on the World Wide Web with hypertext links and other special features. The

---

[28]Elsevier Science Publishers, Blackwell-Science, Springer-Verlag, Pergamon, John Wiley, and Academic Press.

[29]Griffiths and King (1982) examined the fundamental system and suggested alternative approaches that they considered to be more feasible.

[30]Named after the restaurant in Washington, D.C. at which the idea was conceived.

University Licensing Program (TULIP) was an Elsevier project involving nine academic libraries (TULIP Final Report 1996). It was an experiment to test systems for networked delivery to, and use of journals at, the user's desktop. A database of forty-two journals in the field of material science were delivered through Engineering Information after being customized for individual requirements. The file was developed with OCR scanning of bit-mapped page images, plus a digital file that was searchable but not displayed.

All of these projects, while promising, are not by any means considered unqualified successes. For example, the TULIP report indicates that "A common view which all TULIP participants share is that the transition to a digital library will go slower than they expected before starting the project." Many digital library initiatives seem to have also come to similar conclusions.[31] Today many services provide access to journal articles, including the American Chemical Society, Bell & Howell ProQuest Direct, CARL UnCover (Lenzini and Shaw 1992), OCLC, ISI, and several online vendors and subscription agents. A unique system is the Los Alamos National Laboratory's (LANL) electronic preprint system developed by Ginsparg (1994).[32] While there has been concern that this system will eliminate or replace refereed journals (as has been the concern for such systems in the past), it has been said that 80 percent of its preprints are eventually published in a traditional journal.

Throughout the 1990s, a number of professional societies (e.g., the American Chemical Society, the American Institute of Physics, and IEEE, to name a few) have started or experimented with electronic journals. In addition, there are also several exclusively electronic science journals in full operation or being experimentally tried. Probably the most publicized of these journals in the mid-1990s were *Psycoloquy* (published by the American Psychological Association) and the *Online Journal of Current Clinical Trials* (published by AAAS and OCLC). Harnad, (1990, 1992, 1996) editor of *Psycoloquy*, has been particularly outspoken about electronic journals and predicted that by 2010, approximately 80 percent of the world journals will have stopped paper publication. Others such as Stix (1995), Odlyzko (1995), and Walker (1998) have also been thoughtful advocates of electronic journals. Among other early exclusively electronic journals are the *Chicago Journal of Theoretical Computer Science* (Fisher 1994) and the *Journal of Electronic Publishing*

---

[31]Drabenstott (1994) provides an early description of the digital library initiatives.

[32]Interestingly enough, however, the concept for such a system in high energy physics was first proposed in 1965 by Moravesik (1965, 1966) for a system called the Physics Information Exchange; also it has been pointed out that physicists used preprints more than any other field in the late 1970s (King and Roderer 1982).

(University of Michigan Press). In 1995 it was estimated that there were approximately 100 refereed electronic journals; not necessarily exclusively electronic or scientific journals (Woodward 1995). In Chapter 15, we update events and discuss electronic scholarly journals and their recent growth in greater depth.

CHAPTER 3

A Systems Framework for Assessing Scholarly Journal Publishing

INTRODUCTION[1]

In order to assess scholarly publishing, it is useful to identify and describe the many facets of publishing that affect the economics, information seeking patterns, and use of scientific information. These facets comprise the following dimensions of the systems-like framework we used to assemble information and data concerning scientific scholarly publishing.

The dimensions of this framework are itemized below.

- the context of journal publishing

- the principal functions performed

- the participants in the system who perform these functions

- the attributes of information and communication processes, and

- the systemic and economic relationships among these functions and participants.

---

[1]An early version of this chapter may be found in Tenopir and King (1996).

The context defines scientific information, describes the various means by which it is communicated, and portrays the purposes for which it is used. Scientific scholarly journals clearly constitute one of the most important sources of information for scientists, but to be effective in that role a number of functions must be performed on both the information content and the media used to communicate the information. Over the years, a number of system participants[2] have evolved to perform these functions in ways that add value to the information. Usually value is added by improving the attributes of information content or communication processes in ways that make the information more accessible, relevant, and usable. Abundant evidence demonstrates that any changes in the way in which these functions are performed will affect other functions and participants. For example, author submission of manuscripts in standardized electronic formats affects publisher processes and economic costs, thereby leading to potential reductions in journal prices. These facets are presented in this chapter, and detailed information and data are provided in subsequent chapters for many of these dimensions of the publishing system.

CONTEXT FOR SCHOLARLY JOURNAL PUBLISHING

The decision to use science as the focus for our examination of scholarly journal publishing is based on the fact that our knowledge is not only greater in the scientific fields, but electronic publishing is likely to have a greater impact in the near future in these disciplines than elsewhere. Components of the context described herein include:

- defining scientific information
- establishing the critical role of information as a principal input resource for and output of scientific research, teaching, and other scientific endeavors
- describing the life cycle of information through several communication channels, including scholarly journals, and
- detailing the life cycle of information among functions performed in the scholarly journal system.

---

[2]We chose to use the term, participant, rather than the more common term, stakeholder, because the latter tends to imply an adversarial involvement.

Definition of Scientific Information

Definitions of scientific information are not lacking, but we have adapted one appropriate for this framework from a National Science Foundation study (Griffiths, Carroll, King, Sheetz, and Williams 1991). In a broad context, scientific information is simply messages about basic and applied research resulting from the efforts and knowledge of scientists and engineers. These messages basically present new theory and information obtained from experimentation, observations, instrumentation, or computation in the form of text, numeric data, or images. Once information is created, it may be further transformed, described, evaluated, and synthesized. Finally, its usefulness and value to a wide spectrum of users may be increased by recording and distributing it through a variety of media such as paper, microform, electronic transmission, or magnetic devices.

The messages conveyed by scientific information can be viewed as having the three major components illustrated in Table 1. Integrating electronic technologies into these processes significantly affects the attributes associated with these three information components. For example, in the scholarly journal system, peer review and editing is incorporated to assure that the information content is not only meaningful, accurate, and precise, but is presented in a comprehensible and usable form to convey a message to other specialists. Since this message has value

Table 1	Components of Scientific Information Messages
Information Component	**Purpose**
Content	Conveys the meaning of the message
Form	Format or type of information, e.g., text, mathematical model, numeric data, coded data, imagery, graphics
	Structure or expression of content, e.g., language; syntactic or semantic structures of text; type of mathematical model; pie charts, bar charts or other types of graphics; structure of numeric tables
Medium	Package in which content is recorded and distributed, e.g., print-on-paper, electronic Web pages or CD-ROM

over time, the information medium must first provide storage until the information is needed and then provide logical and physical access on a timely and economical basis. Any changes in an information medium affect input costs and output attributes of journal system processes and thereby will affect the use, usefulness, and value of the information (see Chapter 4 for details concerning this framework).

Scientific Journals in the Context of Research, Teaching, and Other Scientific Endeavors

To determine value, one must consider what scientists do and how the availability of scientific information affects, and is affected by, what they do. One simple model of this relationship is displayed in Figure 4. At the heart of this model are the activities that scientists perform such as research, teaching, and management. Many resources are used to perform these scientific activities including the scientists' time, workstations, instrumentation, office and classroom facilities, and support staff.

Scientific information has been shown to be one of the most important input resources for most scientific activities and has a bearing on how well scientists perform (see Chapter 7). Such information is received through several channels (e.g., journal articles) and from a variety of distribution means (e.g., personal subscriptions and libraries). Similarly, this information is also one of the most important outputs from scientific endeavors. The fourth component of this simple model involves the systems used to communicate these outputs to the rest of the scientific community, including those found in a scientist's own organization as well as elsewhere. From an economic point of view, the scholarly journals that provide this service are not only an essential input resource for scientific activities, but also serve as an output from these activities. Throughout the book we have described the input costs and quantities of output for each of the four components (i.e., scientific activities, input and output from these activities, and communication processes).

This model provides an important context because scientists spend over 50 percent of their time communicating through activities such as listening, reading, presenting, and writing (See Chapter 5). Furthermore, studies have shown that scientists who read more tend to be more productive and high achievers (See Chapter 7). Thus any changes in the way in which journals communicate scientific information must take into account their effects on scientific endeavors such as research and teaching, which in turn create scientific information. Several

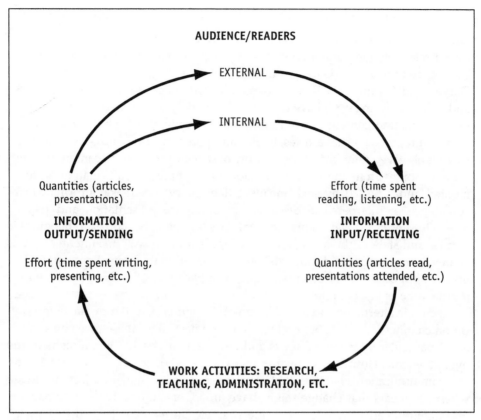

Figure 4. Scientists' communication cycle.
(Source: Adapted from Griffiths and King 1993)

information researchers (Krockel 1991 and Little 1989) have considered the integral role of scientific information in research. Changes in scientific endeavors can have a bearing on the amount and attributes of information produced. Furthermore, early studies have shown that the number of articles written is correlated, with a lag of three to five years, to research funding (King, McDonald, and Roderer 1981). Other evidence provided by Brown (1996) and Anderla (1985) shows a positive correlation between papers written and countries' GNP and other indicators.

Scientific Journals in the Context of the Life Cycle of Scientific Information

Once scientific information is created, it may be communicated in many ways over a relatively long time period. Garvey and colleagues at The Johns Hopkins University and others [Garvey, Lin and Nelson (1970), Lin and Nelson (1970), Garvey and Griffith (1972)], and Yokote and Utterback (1974), Lancaster (1978)] and Subramanyam (1981) have described the variety of channels by which scientific information content is communicated: informal and formal presentations, technical reports, journal articles, books, and patent documents. Garvey and colleagues observed time frames for the flow of specific information content through these channels from the time of creation to the time the information is documented and reported by such means as laboratory notebooks, informal correspondence or interpersonal discussions, conference presentation and papers, research reports, dissertations, journal articles, patents, books, bibliographic entries, and state-of-the-art reviews (See Figure 5). Less well documented in this context is the timeframe during which the information is obtained and applied by users as opposed to its first appearance in publications. This is documented for journal articles in Chapter 8.

Electronic alternatives to journals can affect and be affected by the communication channels and distribution means. In the past, all of these mechanisms satisfied particular information needs and requirements, each filling a niche in the overall scheme. However, there appears to be a kind of ecological balance among the communication channels that must be monitored and interjections made when it appears that change might have an adverse effect. For example, some infrequently-read articles have considerable relevance and value to their readers, and many older articles are discovered and read many years after they are published. The current system protects the infrequently-read articles by bundling them with frequently read articles and the older articles by archiving them in library collections.

Some have suggested that electronic articles need never have a final version. Rather the research can be documented in a dynamic form in which changes are continuously made, but not necessarily finalized. In a sense, the life cycle of information found in multiple channels achieves a similar dynamic form in which each channel is a stage in its life. Thus, one should consider electronic processes as particularly applicable for all the appropriate channels.

Crawford, Hurd, and Weller (1996) discuss the Johns Hopkins (i.e., Garvey and Griffith) scientific communication model that tracks research results through the various channels of communication. They see this model as a means of addressing big science communication of the future by examining all the channels (and

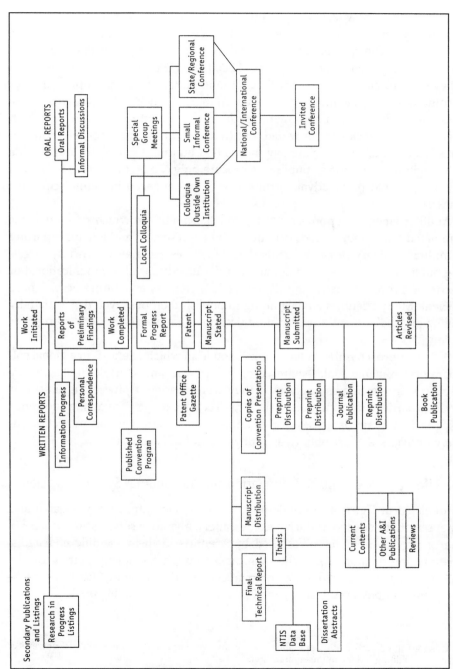

Figure 5. The dissemination of scientific and technical research results. *(Source: Adapted from Garvey, Lin and Nelson 1970, Lin, Garvey and Nelson 1970, and Garvey and Griffith 1972)*

processes) to see how technology is involved and how innovative approaches can improve communication. They suggest that electronic mail and listservs have already significantly changed information communication and the support of invisible colleges with their estimated 12,000 to 15,000 discussion groups. They believe that electronic journals will result in important new and improved ways of communicating traditional peer-reviewed journal articles.

Other models that might emerge include the "no-journal model" in which peer-reviewed articles are provided, but hypertext links and other selection features made possible by technology means that bundling articles by journal title may begin to disappear as publishers procure only the best articles. This model obviously would prove advantageous to scientists engaged in multidisciplinary research.

Another emerging approach is an "unvetted model" in which peer review is eliminated. This model speeds communication of research[3] and it helps reporting of multidisciplinary research results that sometimes experience difficulty in getting published. Of course, traditional preprints already speed communication, but electronic processes makes the dissemination, storage, and future access more efficient. Many scientists are beginning to publish their own web pages, thereby relying on feedback and updated modification as a means of circumventing peer review.

A final approach is the "collaboratory model" in which scientists in a global collaboratory exchange data, share computer power, and consult digital library resources, interacting as easily as if they were sharing a physical facility. This model is particularly applicable to the largest science projects involving enormous dispersed numeric databases, for example, the human genome project, high-energy physics, and astronomy, astrophysics, and space physics.

The Life Cycle of Scientific Information through Journal System Functions

As depicted in Figure 4, scientific information is one output from research and other scientific endeavors which becomes, after a myriad of services and processes, one of several input resources used by scientists in their scientific endeavors. Scientific information that is communicated through a scholarly journal can be characterized by a spiral of the traditional generic processing functions of generation, composition, reproduction, and distribution as shown in Figure 6.

---

[3]This is said to be particularly applicable when it involves large numbers of scientists where peer review and editing is done in the organization.

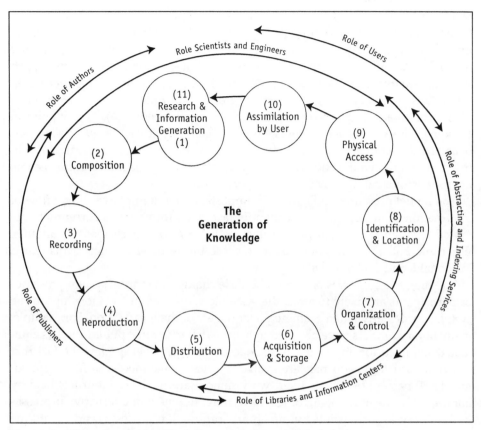

Figure 6. Life cycle of scientific information through scholarly journal system functions. *(Source: King, McDonald and Roderer 1981)*

The spiral begins with information generation or creation from research (1). This information, at some time, is composed (2) for article publication (i.e., written, reviewed, and edited). When ready for formal publication the information is recorded (3) in a physical form that can be reproduced (4) and distributed (5). Currently, the time to complete this process of journal publishing from composition to initial publication and distribution can range from a few months to years (King, Lancaster, McDonald, Roderer, and Wood 1976b). Of course the information is distributed more quickly to peers and reviewers through preprints.

The life of the information in journal articles, considered to be from initial publication to use, tends to follow a highly skewed distribution of use over time, not unlike a nuclear decay curve. Thus, the information must be acquired and stored (6) for future physical access. Since a substantial proportion of use involves journals that are infrequently read by some scientists or are needed long after publication, it is necessary to organize and control the information (7) and to facilitate identification and location (i.e., logical access) when needed (8). At any point in the journal life cycle, scientists must be able to gain physical access (9) to all or part of an article in order to assimilate (10) and use the information for research, teaching, and other scientific endeavors. Only in this way can the information become a resource for creating new scientific information.

The model presented in Figure 6 is simplistic in that it implies a simple flow of information from function to function. In fact, the information is currently transmitted through more than fifty distinct paths from one participant to another. Electronic publishing might actually increase the number of such paths (King, McDonald, and Roderer 1981).

The life cycle context is important because changes in journal system processes or participants are likely to affect the systemic and economic relationships in the system, particularly when examined over the life of the information. For example, many library funders have been led to believe that electronic publishing has eliminated the need for library in-house collections. This belief ignores the fact that few older articles or journals are available in electronic media; in fact, approximately 80 percent of articles over two years old are read from journals held by libraries.[4] On the other hand, others have suggested new or alternative processes in the life cycle such as integrating library information processes earlier into the cycle (see, for example, Lucier 1993). Thus, it is useful to understand how such earlier integration is likely to affect subsequent processes.

SCHOLARLY JOURNAL SYSTEM FUNCTIONS

Descriptions and analyses of the functions of scholarly journals have long appeared in the literature. In fact, a study and report of an Association of American Universities (AAU) Research Libraries project (1994) presented an updated list of functions. Examination of their list demonstrates two types of

---

[4]The JSTOR project (discussed in Chapter 15) is the most ambitious project to date to digitize old print journals. Some commercial vendors, notably Chadwyck-Healy in the humanities, are actively digitizing older journals.

functions. The first describes the generic processes of the scholarly journal system, while the second more accurately describes what the scholarly journal system should accomplish. In order to clarify this distinction, we will refer to the latter type of function as scholarly journal system roles.

Scholarly Journal Functions and Processes

A number of researchers[5] have identified and described the functions and processes of publishing scholarly journals. While some of these researchers focused on generic scientific communication functions, the principles are never-the-less appropriate to the scholarly journal system. The functions and processes which relate to the life cycle of information range from creation and composition through assimilation and use.

Creation of information involves scientific processes such as development of new theory and hypotheses, performing experimentation, sampling, observations, correlating or linking information from several sources, and evaluation and analyses. Some refer to this as generation of information or knowledge. Composition consists of documenting or writing about newly created information, including authorship of article text, derivation of models, preparation of tables, and graphics.

Assimilation of information involves processes for receiving and absorbing information through reading article text and looking at charts and graphs. Use of information involves the ways information is used or the purposes to which the information is put such as research, teaching, keeping current, or professional development.

Two other sets of functions involve processes that address information content and deal with information media. The functions and processes which focus on information content are delineated in Table 2.

Some functions and processes focus on the way in which information is packaged. Examples of media-related process functions are detailed in Table 3.

Each function or process can be expressed in terms of input and output. Input is both the amount of input resources (staff, equipment, and space) applied to perform the process (or the total cost of these resources) and the attributes of these resources (e.g., staff competence or modem access speeds). Output is both the amount of output (e.g., number of articles published) and the attributes of output (e.g., quality of articles published). Change in any process will affect its input

---

[5]See Griffiths, Carroll, King, Sheetz, and Williams (1991).

Table 2	Functions and Processes Involving Information Content

Information-Related Functions	Examples of Processes
Transformation	Translating from one language to another, subject or text editing
Description and Synthesis	Validating information through peer review, facilitating logical access through preparation of abstracts, indexes, catalogs, and metadata, preparation of reviews, especially state-of-the-art reviews
Logical Access	Identifying and locating sources through reference searching, referral, linking
Evaluation/Analysis	Assessment on behalf of users, annotated search output, data evaluation by Information Analysis Centers

Table 3	Functions and Processes Involving Information Media

Media-Related Functions	Examples of Processes
Communications	Information transfer, e.g., author to publisher, scientist to scientist, publishers to scientists, libraries to libraries
Recording	Inputting to physical media, e.g., page masters, computer storage, CD-ROM disks
Reproduction	Multiple copying, e.g., issues of journals, CD-ROM disks
Physical Transformation	Conversion, e.g., paper to microform, electronic to paper
Storage	Providing access over time, e.g., libraries, computer files
Preservation	Ensuring that information on the media or the media themselves do not deteriorate over time and reproduction or restoration of information on deteriorating media
Physical Access	Delivery, e.g., personal subscriptions, library subscriptions, photocopies through interlibrary loan (ILL), terminal displays, computer printouts

and/or output as well as potentially affecting other processes. Therefore when developing alternatives to the present journal system, one must consider the effects on every process with its concomitant inputs and outputs.

Scholarly Journal System Roles

The scholarly journal system plays several important roles for science.

- Its primary role is to serve as a means of communicating new, edited, and peer-reviewed scientific information to an unlimited audience beyond an author's primary or immediate community.
- The information content can be addressed to specific audiences with particular interests; in fact, it can be said that journals bundle like articles addressed to the same audience. In a sense, journals serve as a selective dissemination device, yet one can also gain access to a single article whenever necessary.
- The discipline of authoring manuscripts, particularly ones that will be refereed, serves as an integral part of creativity in that new ideas are often created or ideas are modified during the writing process.
- Journal publishing provides an inexpensive means of communicating, considering the cost per reading of articles.
- The journal process protects against plagiarism and establishes copyright ownership.
- It provides assurance that the record of ideas, discovery, and hypotheses tested are not altered (Spilhaus 1998, Borgman 2000)
- Publishing in scholarly journals serves to convey prestige and recognition to authors, their research, and their institutions.
- Journals serve as a permanent archive for scientific information.

If science is to continue to play its creative role in our education, business and society, it seems that the evolving electronic publishing and distribution system must either continue to fulfill these roles or otherwise justify the discontinuance of any one of them.

SCHOLARLY JOURNAL SYSTEM PARTICIPANTS

Each of these generic functions and specific processes involve one or more participants who can be characterized as belonging to groups of individuals (e.g., authors, readers), institutions (e.g., publishers, vendors, libraries) or organizations or communities to which the groups or institutions belong (e.g., library and reader parent organizations, professional societies). Some of the participants perform the processes (e.g., publishers, libraries, scientists) and others exert external influence (e.g., funders of research, copyright authorities). This section briefly describes all of these participants because all are driven by their own motivation, incentives, and information needs and requirements. Some understanding and appreciation of the interplay of these factors is important when considering alternatives to the current scholarly journal system.

Scholarly Journal System Process Participants

The principal participants in the processes of the scholarly journal system include: creators and authors (and their support participants such as graphics designers, word processors, and technical writers), reviewers/referees, primary publishers (and their staff, subject editors, translators, printers), secondary information publishers (abstracting and indexing services, catalog vendors, printers), second party distributors (contracted to distribute the primary publishers' work), third party distributors (contracted to distribute copies of record party articles), gateway organizations, libraries, subscription agents, information brokers, resource sharing services or library networks, computer centers, and readers. These participants are described briefly below.

Creators are the scientists, engineers, and other professionals whose experiments, observations, and ideas create new information. They initiate the life cycle as the knowledge they create is then communicated to others and ultimately assimilated into a body of personal knowledge which is, in turn, applied, taught, and reviewed. These creators have many motivations ranging from the desire to discover and learn to job- assigned research areas (see Chapters 5 and 6).

Authors, who are more often than not the creators, document research results in a number of ways, including scholarly journal articles. Various motivations to write include the enjoyment of writing and documenting one's work to the necessity to "publish or perish" (Tenopir 1995). Reviewers and referees provide authentication of the accuracy and validity of information in an article. They are usually unpaid, but do the reviews to keep up with their peers' work, as a contribution to their profession, and sometimes to reciprocate for review of their own manuscripts.

Primary publishers of scholarly journals perform a number of important value-added processes including, among others, starting a journal, acquiring solicited and unsolicited manuscripts, arranging for copyright ownership, subject editing, arranging peer review, managing interaction (among authors, editors and referees), redaction, developing master images, reproduction, and distribution. Some of these processes, such as printing, are often sub-contracted. Publishers basically fall into four groups: commercial publishers who must make a profit to recover the financial investment in the journal; professional societies who provide journals as a service to their membership (as both authors and readers) and others; educational institutions who provide an outlet for their authors, prestige for the university, and an educational tool for students; and others such as non-profit organizations, government agencies, and advocates for a research field.

Secondary publishers such as abstracting and indexing services provide description and synthesis of journal article information to enable scientists to achieve logical access to the information. They perform many of the same publication processes as primary publishers, but currently rely heavily on electronic media and access. They tend to cluster in particular scientific fields and specialties, and many of them are non-profit organizations who were at one time partially subsidized by the National Science Foundation and/or professional societies.

Second party distributors are typically for-profit organizations who obtain permission from a variety of publishers to distribute articles electronically through CD-ROM, online databases, and magnetic tape. A royalty, typically based on use or units sold, is paid to the primary publishers. Some librarians serve this function, with and without permission, by downloading articles available through the Internet and then distributing them to their users. Document delivery services also fall into this category. Third-party distributors contract with a second party to provide further distribution of electronic publications for which the second party has obtained permission. They are often for-profit vendors. The vendors may serve as a third party for some electronic publications, as well as a secondary party with others if they contract directly with the primary publisher. Gateway organizations provide access to third party online services. In this role they typically provide only hardware, software, and telecommunication links.

Libraries serve as intermediaries in that they acquire scholarly journals to be shared among their users and to serve as an archive, a facility to distribute and/or reproduce copies for subsequent use, and a means of identifying, locating, and obtaining copies of articles as needed. Some libraries are given the responsibility of managing all acquisitions and distribution of journals in their parent organizations. All traditional types of libraries, (i.e., academic {higher education}, special, public, and school {K through 12}) process some scholarly scientific journals, although academic and special libraries generally do so to a much greater degree.

Subscription agents are for-profit organizations that have developed a niche to maintain the tedious process of negotiating, claiming, and renewing subscriptions with primary publishers for libraries. Some are beginning to also distribute electronic subscriptions and copies of articles.

Information brokers are for-profit organizations or individual consultants that provide reference search services, services to obtain copies of articles, and other related services to libraries and small companies that do not have libraries. Library networks or consortia represent unique organizations throughout the country that were developed to serve groups of libraries by providing combined services such as acquisitions and cataloging in which economies of scale can be achieved and by facilitating interlibrary lending. Most states fund these organizations with substantial Federal support, although universities sometimes form cooperative groups, particularly for interlibrary lending. Such cooperatives are now licensing and distributing electronic journals.

Computer centers and intranet facilities in large academic, industry, and government agencies serve to download, store, and provide access to electronic full-text and bibliographic databases.

Readers are scientists and others who use scientific articles to perform their work. Evidence has documented that those who spend more time reading these materials tend to perform their work better and more productively (see Chapter 7).

Some participants who do not directly process information or media nevertheless significantly affect the system. For example, government and others who fund research and development partially determine the extent of research and, therefore, indirectly the number of articles written. Unfortunately, however, they often do not provide sufficient funding to ensure that the results of the research are adequately communicated. Another type of funding source includes parent organizations which support authors, readers, libraries, computer centers, and other information-related participants. Copyright granting and royalty collection agencies are important participants in the system since they protect against plagiarism and provide some economic protection for publishers. Finally, professional societies contribute substantially by facilitating scientific publications and other communication channels. Each of these participants affect and are affected by changes in scholarly journal processes.

SCHOLARLY JOURNAL SYSTEM ATTRIBUTES

The scholarly journal system includes two disparate sets of attributes: the generic attributes required by the overall system and the specific attributes of the input resources and of the output of each process in the system. In a sense, the roles of the system can be stated in terms of achieving satisfactory levels of such attributes.

Generic Attributes of the Scholarly Journal System

Three versions of the generic attributes of the scholarly journal system have been reported in the literature over the last 40 years. Association of American Universities Research Project 1994, Goodwin 1959, and King 1981 provide some examples of these attributes, which are combined below:

- accuracy: factually described, with the correct meaning conveyed to both authors and readers

- reliability

- precision: conveyed in the appropriate dosage required by readers

- brevity

- prioritized information with auxiliary information

- practicality: meaningful, comprehensible, and usable

- availability: in the required information format, structure, and medium

- accessibility: where needed

- promptness: information provided to users in a reasonable time frame following creation

- timeliness: information provided when the need for the information arises, and

- economic: in terms of price and ease of use.

Additional generic attributes were prescribed by the Association of American Universities Research Project (1994) and Goodwin (1959) as indicated below:

- authority of information source

- reliability, especially of negative results

- Predictability. How reliable and consistent is the system in maintaining levels of quality and availability?

- Adaptability. How flexible is the system in providing new approaches to information or providing access for unanticipated users?

- Eligibility. Who has access to information in the system?

- Recovery. How well is the system able to avert or recover from errors of mismanagement and lack of resources to make the system work?

- Innovation. How well does the system perform research and development to provide system innovation?

- Extensibility. How well does the system integrate between media? Between disciplines? What is the system's ability to build and extend itself without a total restructuring?

Taylor (1986) provides an exhaustive set of specific attributes, which he calls values, which he associates with various specific communication service processes.

Price (or user charge) is also an attribute of a service or product. Pricing in scholarly journals is becoming very complex, particularly in electronic publishing. Strategies range from:

- no charge where publishers provide journals free (usually a company using the journal for promotional purposes)

- no charge with an understanding of reciprocal services such as interlibrary loans

- bundled price that includes membership in a society that provides one or more journals, conference registration, and other discounts

- discriminatory pricing with different prices for personal, institutional, and foreign subscriptions

- flat fee subscriptions which offer the purchaser unlimited usage rights within the constraints of the Copyright Act

- fee based on the number of potential users such as staff size or number of people in an organization

- fee based on number of simultaneous users by counting the number of online ports allocated, the number of active online passwords, or the number of workstations connected to a CD-ROM or locally loaded system

- fee based on usage, and

- fee based on documents selected by users either to be viewed or to be delivered in full.

Chapters 13 and 18 address the issue of scholarly journal pricing in greater detail.

SYSTEMIC AND ECONOMIC INTERDEPENDENCIES
IN THE SCHOLARLY JOURNAL SYSTEM

Thus far we have discussed the functions, participants, and attributes of the scholarly journal as well as the context in which it operates. The context which we have described is essentially static. However, the reality in which scholarly journals operate is anything but static. In order to better understand the scholarly journal system and the probable effect of the emerging new technologies on it, we must recognize the dynamic nature of the system. The best way to examine this dynamic nature is to observe trends over time and to analyze the systemic and economic interdependencies among functions and participants.

A number of principles dominate the systemic and economic interdependencies of most systems of scientific information services and products and particularly of scholarly journal publishing. For example, communities of information users tend to follow a skewed distribution somewhat like a lognormal distribution. In other words, while some information enjoys a very large audience, most is useful to only a small group of scientists. This fact partially accounts for the highly skewed distribution of journal circulation where the median circulation is approximately 1,900 subscriptions, although the circulation for several journals numbers in the hundreds of thousands.

Most information services and products have high front-end fixed costs and relatively small variable costs for reproduction and distribution. Thus, the subscription price required to recover costs tends to be much higher for journals with a small circulation than for journals with a large circulation because, in the latter case, the prices approach an asymptote near the reproduction and distribution costs. In fact, electronic processes may exacerbate the discrepancy between fixed and variable costs since fixed costs may increase, while variable costs decrease.

Many high-quality articles are infrequently read because the number of potential readers is small. In the current system, these articles become economically viable by being bundled with other articles in one issue of a journal. Electronic publishing would do well to encourage continued access to such articles.

The distribution of the amount of individual and library use of journals tends to also be highly skewed. For example, the average scientist reads at least one article from approximately eighteen different journals, but reads or rereads fewer than five articles in more than half of the eighteen journals, while reading or rereading over twenty-five articles in at least one of the journals.

Purchase of journals, whether for personal or institutional use, tends to involve a high fixed cost associated with the purchase price and processing relative to the variable cost of accessing the articles read. In other words, excluding the costs of the time spent reading, the cost per reading of journals in which only a few articles are read is much higher than for frequently-read journals. In fact, the cost per reading of alternative sources, to both personal and institutional subscribers, is usually far less than the cost of a subscription to infrequently-read journals; on the other hand, it is much higher for the frequently-read journals. In other words, there is an economic break-even point in the amount of reading below which it is less expensive to use an alternative to subscribing. For example, a personal subscriber would read a library copy or an institutional subscriber would substitute an interlibrary loan or document delivery. Evidence suggests that most individuals and libraries do, in fact, make exactly such choices. In an electronic environment, article copies provided electronically will significantly affect the break-even points.

Users tend to factor in their time and ease of use in choosing among alternative sources of information. Other information and service attributes such as quality, accuracy, timeliness, accessibility, and availability are additional important factors that affect not only decisions to use, but also the determination of the price one is willing to pay.

Each use of information is based on a unique combination of purpose of use and desired attributes such as the when, where, and cost of use. Thus, in order to satisfy the array of necessary combinations of uses and attributes, in the future there is likely to be a variety of services and products, electronic and otherwise, which fulfill the needs of smaller and smaller specific niche markets. For example, researchers under tight deadlines might happily pay a premium to receive the methods section of a 5-year-old article in their office within one day of their request regardless of the cost.

In the current market, the cost to individuals of using information, including their time, tends to be orders of magnitude higher than the actual price charged by providers. This principle is most obvious in the case of non-charging providers such as libraries and, more recently, the majority of the Internet services, but it is also true for most commercial publishers and especially for scholarly journals.

Some examples of systemic and economic interdependencies are detailed below.

Examples of Systemic Interdependencies

Systemic interdependency, by definition, means that any changes in the system, such as adaptation of new technologies to perform system functions, will affect not only the functions and participants directly, but will also cause a ripple effect on other functions and participants in the system. Such changes can affect the amount and timeliness of the flow patterns of information through its life cycle. Recent technological developments enable most authors of scholarly articles to input their manuscript into standardized electronic media which can be sent electronically to publishers, and from publishers to reviewers and editors and eventually to page masters for reproduction, storage, and distribution. Use of electronic media has not been exploited nearly as extensively as is technically possible because of the wide variety of non-compatible formats. Electronic processes should speed the flow of manuscripts and improve quality at a lower cost. Journal authors can also save time by salvaging and editing previous text (e.g., internal reports and conference proceedings), references, and graphics already in electronic form.

One aspect of systemic interdependency is that the participants are required to be separate and distinct for the system to function effectively. For example, authors can not effectively referee their own manuscripts and can probably benefit substantially from independent editorial review. Most readers, in fact, do not also write articles. The prediction that electronic processes will eventually make all traditional interdependencies irrelevant is highly unlikely in our view.

Some academic presses and libraries are beginning to pressure faculty and researchers to publish primarily through their university. By agreement, universities would provide logical and physical access to articles in electronic form, perhaps with no charge to requesting universities, much as is being done now with interlibrary lending. Such a new process could adversely affect non-university scientists who collectively read more articles than university scientists (simply because there are more of them), and they rely heavily on scholarly articles. Thus, other participants should be considered if and when such transformation takes place; otherwise the potential value of scientific information will not be fully achieved.

Examples of Economic Interdependencies[6]

Information users generally choose from several alternative sources to obtain the information they desire. As mentioned earlier, these choices depend on price, ease of use, availability, timeliness, and a host of other attributes. A change in any one attribute such as price can affect not only buyers and sellers, but other participants as well. For example, over the past twenty years increases in the price of personal subscriptions have resulted in fewer subscribers, and thus reduced revenue for publishers. Since institutional subscriptions are less sensitive to price changes,

---

[6]Economic interdependencies among journal prices, page charges, circulation, article separates, etc. and their attributes are discussed in Chapter 14.

many publishers apparently have increased the prices of institutional subscriptions at an even higher rate to compensate for the reduced revenue resulting from lost personal subscriptions. Subsequent increased library use, increased prices, and increased reliance on interlibrary loans and document delivery have led to increased library costs, thus affecting their other services. The allocation of time by users has changed as they use libraries more frequently for journal reading. Despite the fact that the spiraling effects of journal price increases have dramatically changed usage patterns, we have found that the extent of use and the cost per use (considering cost to all participants and inflationary increases) has not changed appreciably over the past twenty years.

Substantial evidence exists that improved library services such as higher quality and more timely automated bibliographic search services have resulted in a greater use of the services (Griffiths and King 1993). Continued improvement in services, in turn, will require more input resources due to the increased demand as users realize that they can save time and improve their performance in terms of productivity and quality of work when they use these services more extensively.

Systems such as the scientific scholarly journal system resemble a link chain in that a break in any link can diminish or eliminate the effectiveness of the entire system. Furthermore, changes in any of the system processes can have a ripple effect throughout the entire system. Throughout the book we have tried to identify some of these interdependencies as they have occurred over the past twenty or thirty years.

CHAPTER 4

Methods

INTRODUCTION

This chapter discusses the methods used to observe and analyze the data produced by King Research, Inc. over the past 23 years and with more recent contributions by the University of Tennessee, School of Information Sciences' Center for Information Studies and Hodges Library. These studies include the following six types:

- statistical surveys of scientists to determine both journal and other readership and use of information services

- statistical surveys of libraries, small businesses, and other institutions to estimate service provision, cost, and use (e.g., amount of interlibrary loan)

- a sample of scientific scholarly journals[1] from which data were tracked from 1960 to 1995

- cost finding and modeling of scientists' activities, library services, publishing, and other processes in the journal system

- assessment of the growth of electronic journals, and

- a review of secondary sources of information.

---

[1]Throughout this book, scholarly journals are defined as periodicals that report scientific research and often include a peer review or refereeing process to aid in screening manuscripts for editorial quality control.

Over the course of the years, a framework of measures evolved for the purpose of describing and assessing information services and products. This framework is described in detail in the next section. Later sections describe methods for surveying scientists, observing costs, and tracking scholarly journals for those who wish to interpret the data in greater detail.

FRAMEWORK FOR EXAMINING INFORMATION SERVICES AND PRODUCTS

This section describes our evolving research framework and provides examples related to scholarly journals, access to library journals and library services, and online access to electronic journals in lieu of interlibrary borrowing. One aspect of this framework is to consider the different perspectives of those who are affected by scholarly journals as shown in Table 4.

The first perspective addresses the producers of the service itself and all the activities and resources necessary to provide a service or produce a product. It also includes the factors and conditions that affect the amount and quality of services or products.

The second perspective focuses on the actual and potential user communities and their information needs and requirements. It not only includes factors that affect the use of a service or product, but the available alternatives and features which make them preferable to the alternatives.

Table 4	Perspectives for Examining Information Services and Products		
	SERVICE/PRODUCT		
PERSPECTIVE	Scholarly Journal	Access to Library Journal Collection	Access to Electronic Journal Database
Service/Product	Journal	Access to Collection	Access to Database
User (Actual/Potential)	Scientists/Others	Scientists/Others	Scientists/Others
User Organization	University Company Govt. Agency Natl. Lab	University Company Govt. Agency Natl. Lab	University Company Govt. Agency Natl. Lab
Scientific Community			
Society			

The third perspective focuses on the user parent (or funding) organization. It is essential to gain an understanding of the goals of the parent organization and how the service or product contributes to achieving these goals. Funders of libraries are concerned with resource allocation among many units including the library, but they often fail to recognize that one major role of libraries is to reduce the cost of scientists' time and other organization resources outside of the library.

Finally, there are the beneficiaries of those affected by the scholarly journal system. One purpose for reading scholarly journals is to create new knowledge and communicate that knowledge to the scientific community so that it may be applied to serve not only that community but ultimately all of society. Throughout the book we have tried to make observations and develop measures to represent each of these perspectives.

Throughout this research framework, we used five generic types of measures: service or product inputs, outputs, usage, outcomes, and domain. Figure 7 depicts the perspectives above (column 1), the five generic measures and specific measures within each type (column 2), and the derived measures developed from the generic and specific measures (column 3).

Input measures include the amount of resources applied to provide a service or produce a product (e.g., staff hours, equipment, and supplies or dollars as a common unit among resources) and attributes of the resources (e.g., competence of staff and capacity and speed of equipment). Resources used in publishing include items such as manuscripts, staff, equipment, facilities, and supplies (which are discussed in depth in Chapter 12). Access to library journals involves not only the journal collection, but also the other input resources such as shelving, space, and service staff. These costs are discussed in greater detail in Chapters 9 and 10. Access to electronic journals requires equipment, internal storage, service staff, and supplies. Examples of attributes of resources include the quality and length of manuscripts; whether back issues are bound, the location of the journal collection (i.e., current periodicals or stacks); and the age and comprehensiveness of the electronic journal database. Each of these resource attributes affects input costs.

Output measures include amount of services provided or products produced and their attributes. Journal publishing outputs are measured in number of issues, articles, or pages, with the attributes being subscription price, quality of the information content, age of the information, and appearance. The output measure for access to a library's journal collection is the size of the journal collection, and its attributes include comprehensiveness, availability (e.g., hours clients may access the collection) and accessibility measured by distance to users and ease of use (open or closed stacks). The output measure for service access to electronic jour-

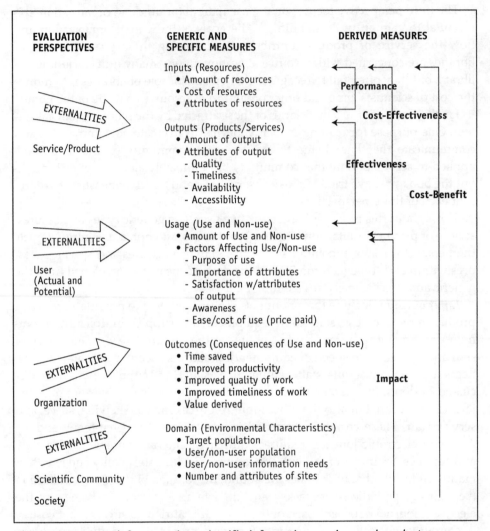

Figure 7. Framework for assessing scientific information services and products.

nals is normally the number of requests, and its service attributes are measured by ease of access and speed of response to the requests.

Usage measures count the number of times a service or product is used or might potentially be used. Use can be measured either by the number of journal issues examined or by the number of article readings. The use of an issue, bound volume, or electronic document can involve multiple readings of articles (as explained in Chapters 7, 8, and 10). Usage is also measured by factors that affect use, such as purposes of use (e.g., research, teaching, or current awareness), perceptions of the importance of and satisfaction with the journal or electronic services, and their attributes. Ease of use or time required by users to obtain the journal or access the services can also affect use. Another usage factor is the user's awareness of the existence of the journal or services.

Outcome measures describe the consequences of using information found in the journals. Such outcomes include improved research or teaching, saving time or money, increasing productivity, and helping achieve organizational, scientific, or societal goals. Some of these outcomes are measured by having scientists report the outcomes of their last reading of a scholarly journal article. (See Chapters 7 and 8.)

Domain measures include descriptions of the environment or characteristics of the target population of actual and potential journal readers and service users. Characteristics might include the number of scientists in a discipline, the number of scientists in a company or university and their primary role (e.g., teaching or research), or the amount of available discretionary information-related funds and access to equipment and local area networks.

These generic measures convey little meaning by themselves. For example, journal costs are relatively meaningless without knowing the number of articles published and the number of subscribers. For this reason, we derived measures from two or more of the five generic measures shown in Figure 7. One such set of relationships involves input and output. For journals this can be the unit cost of a subscripion or the journal, issues, articles, or pages. The unit cost of a scholarly journal subscription, of course, must correspond to the price charged. For a journal collection, the cost is often computed as the library cost per journal title divided by the number of years held. For a service providing access to an electronic journal database, the relationship could be the unit cost per article retrieved or productivity of the service, such as articles provided per staff hour or dollars expended. Such relationships are defined here as *performance measures*. Both input and output attributes affect performance. For example, editor competence can affect input cost (i.e., salary) as well as the quantity and quality of a journal's output.

Output attributes also affect usage. For example, journal price clearly partially determines demand (i.e., number of subscribers). Comprehensiveness, availability, and accessibility of a library journal collection all affect the extent to which a collection is used. Delivery speed of electronically retrieved articles affects the continued use of the service. These relationships are defined here as *effectiveness measures*.

Input cost and usage are also related as *cost-effectiveness measures*. For example, by applying higher quality but more costly resources, a journal may attract more readers and subscribers. Likewise, a library service can utilize better, more expensive equipment for electronic retrieval, thereby increasing usage which in turn affects the performance of scientists and ultimately saves organization resources. *Impact* can be the relation of use and outcomes. It can also be measured by the extent to which outcomes are affected by population size, the cost per capita of services or products, or a shifting of readers from alternative sources to the service of interest.

The final type of derived measure involves *cost-benefit* relationships. These relationships are somewhat more complex than those described above. At one time, we thought of benefits as the favorable higher-order effects of services or outcomes (King and Bryant 1971). This approach proved to be oversimplified, however. One problem was that both favorable and unfavorable results of modifying a service involve costs. For example, one can use a more expensive automated system to provide a service, in which case the additional cost is unfavorable. Yet such a system may result in saving users considerable time, in which case the reduced cost of users' time is favorable. To overcome that problem, we adapted an approach presented by Bickner (1983) in which cost and benefit analysis involves comparisons between alternatives such as providing a service or not providing a service or providing a service at specified levels of quality.

Alternatives can be compared at each level of measure: input (costs), output (quantities and attributes), usage, and outcomes. These comparisons are categorized as to whether they are unfavorable ("costs") or favorable ("benefits"). Note that these "costs" are not defined in the same way as input costs or usage costs. A "benefit" can be expressed in terms of reduced input or usage costs, since a decreased cost is favorable; conversely, increased input or usage costs are unfavorable and would be termed "costs." A better term for "costs" might be "detriments," but common usage requires that we continue using "costs" and "benefits."

We present measures of "costs" and "benefits" in several places in this book. For example, we often ask scientists what they would do to obtain information if there were no service or library and what it would cost them to obtain their information using alternative sources. Thus, the alternative examined is having or not having a service, such as a library-provided journal. "Costs" of having the service (or "benefits" of not having it) include the total output costs of the service (since the library would have no costs as an alternative) and usage costs of users (i.e., their time required to use the service). "Benefits" of having the service (or "costs" of not having it) are measured by the additional usage costs required to obtain information using alternative sources. For example, when a reader has the option of subscribing to a journal or using a library copy, we show the cost of both alternatives at different levels of use. The same analysis is applied to a library's decision to purchase a journal or obtain it through an interlibrary loan or document delivery.

Some examples of derived cost and benefit relationships include the ratio of the cost difference of using alternatives (i.e., "benefits" expressed in dollars) to current costs (i.e., "costs" expressed in dollars). At a higher level of comparison, we have estimated what it would cost users not to have library collections in terms of savings from lost information since users would have less time to read since they would be required to spend more time acquiring information. Again, these "benefits" are compared with "costs" in the form of a ratio. In a sense, the last two ratios are like a return on investment or what might better be called a return on information (ROI).

Changes in service performance or output attributes should affect usage by altering the factors that affect use. Suppose the publisher decides to replace a departing editor with one who has a stronger educational background with a relevant subject degree and considerably more experience. Clearly such a change will cost the publisher more in salary. However, such a change also may result in better quality and faster turnarounds, which in turn might result in more readership and subscriptions. Unless the new editor is sufficiently more productive than the old one, additional input resources will be required. One should consider not only the increase in input costs (from increased salary and additional service requirements) but also the potential increased revenue. Increased subscriptions may reduce the cost per subscription and increase net revenue. For example, with an increased number of subscribers, the average unit cost may actually decrease, thereby further increasing net "benefit." These relationships demonstrate the interactions or feedback in the evaluation model.

Externalities are extraneous factors that affect measurements at all levels or perspectives. Externalities affecting publisher or library inputs and outputs include such factors as the organization's economic standing, general attitude of investors or funders, the physical location of the library in the organization, the price and quality of external sources of service (e.g., printers, vendors and brokers), the quality and salaries of the local community's sources of labor, the existing staff and their competencies, and the remoteness of the organization from the labor market. In comparing publisher or library inputs, outputs, and performance to the results presented in this book, it is important to consider such externalities.

STATISTICAL SURVEYS OF SCIENTISTS AND INSTITUTIONS

The data reported here emerged from three national surveys of scientists performed in 1977 and 1984 under contract to the National Science Foundation (NSF) and in 1984 for University Microfilms International (now Bell & Howell). These surveys focused primarily on readership of scholarly journals, but they also gathered information on the use of libraries and other information services.

In the late 1970s, two readership surveys were conducted for *Science* and for John Bailar, editor of the *Journal of the National Cancer Institute*. From 1981 through 1998, a series of statistical surveys of scientists were performed under contract for different companies, government agencies, and national laboratories.[2] Every one of these studies by King Research, Inc. included a battery of surveys which focused on user activities such as readership, general communication patterns, library use, or use of other information services. Two surveys were performed in the early 1990s for The Johns Hopkins University (Eisenhower Library) and by the University of Tennessee (Hodges Library).[3]

In all instances, respondents from these surveys who indicated, sometimes indirectly, that they were scientists according to the former nine NSF fields of science were included in the data for this book. A total of 13,591 scientists responded to these surveys, as did over 8,000 professionals from other disciplines who are not included in these analyses.

The institutional statistical surveys were conducted for several different purposes. A national survey conducted in 1985 determined how small, high-tech firms obtain information. Two national surveys in 1978 and 1982 were completed for the U.S. Copyright Office concerning the 1976 revision to the copyright law. These surveys provide detailed data concerning photocopying and interlibrary loan/document delivery. Statewide studies[4] also obtained detailed information concerning library use, cost of services, and extent of interlibrary loan/document delivery.

All of the surveys were based on statistical sampling (Griffiths and King 1991) with only two of the surveys yielding less than 50 percent response rates.

---

[2]Air Products and Chemicals, Inc. (2 studies), Alabama Power Company, AT&T Bell Laboratories, Baxter Healthcare, Bristol-Myers Squibb, Colgate-Palmolive Company, Eastman Chemicals Company, Eastman Kodak Company, FBI Academy, E. I. DuPont De Nemours and Company (2 studies), Johnson & Johnson Orthopedics, Johnson & Johnson Vistakon, National Institutes of Health (2 studies), National Oceanic and Atmospheric Administration, National Rural Electrical Cooperatives Association, Oak Ridge National Laboratories, Proctor & Gamble (2 studies), Public Service Electric and Gas Company, U.S. Department of Justice, U.S. Department of Labor, U.S. Department of Transportation, Rocky Flats Nuclear Center, Rockwell International, Volpe National Transportation Systems Center, and one other that requested that we not reveal its name when granting use of the data. One study was performed by the University of Illinois, Graduate School of Library and Information Science, Library Research Center for the International Atomic Energy Agency (Lancaster and King 1998).

[3]When results of these surveys (1977-1998) are reported, the source is cited as King et al. surveys (relevant year or years in which the surveys were conducted).

[4]Arizona, Massachusetts, New York, Pennsylvania, and Wisconsin.

Sampling frames for the national surveys of scientists involved lists compiled by a vendor from memberships in professional societies and other sources. Since scientists often belong to multiple societies, an overlapping strata statistical method was used to weight survey results. Sometimes non-respondents were mailed postcards with brief questions or called to establish any bias that might involve readership or service use. There did not appear to be any major source or amount of bias due to non-response.

The sampling frames within organizations consisted of lists provided by personnel units in which professionals, their specialties, and exempt staff were designated and used to employ a statistical sample design. Sometimes samples from strata such as scientists or professionals from R&D units were picked with higher probability of selection. All observations were properly weighted, sometimes using known population totals. Institutional sampling frames were developed from existing lists of companies, government agencies, and universities, including lists of libraries when relevant. Sometimes the samples were chosen with probability proportional to size, while other times ratio estimation was used, especially when the appropriate covariates were known.

All the surveys were preceded with five to twenty in-depth personal interviews and from one to twelve focus group interviews. Each survey itself constituted a self-administered questionnaire. Sometimes telephone calls were made to non-respondents to increase response rates to over 50 percent. The responses invariably relied on recall and memories of events. To minimize bias, we varied the recall time periods to specific services depending on their likely frequency of use. For example, questions concerning the amount of reading asked respondents to recall their activities for the last week or month, whereas questions concerning online bibliographic searches required respondents to remember over longer periods of time up to one year. Whenever possible, we also tried to obtain other sources of information to validate results. For example, the amount of reading is corroborated with questions on other surveys by King Research and with other studies concerning the amount of time spent reading; estimates of the use of library services were also compared with known statistics.

Nearly all surveys of scientists in organizations involved multiple questionnaires. Some questions such as the amount of reading, the number of personal subscriptions, library use and distance to the library, and general demographic information are common to all the questionnaires. Each questionnaire also addressed specific issues such as readership (of scholarly journals or other publications), use of specific services, and communication patterns. A survey of one company used twelve separate questionnaires, although four to five instruments was more common.

To the degree possible, the exact wording of questions remained the same among surveys in order to permit comparisons over time and among organizations. Some changes were made when it was clear that respondents did not interpret the question properly or when circumstances changed as, for example, when electronic journals were introduced. Most questions involved pre-coded answers, although open-ended responses were available as an option, and a section was always included for comments.

All the surveys of readership and specific services involved estimates of total reading and use as well as critical-incident questions concerning the last article read or service used. With scholarly articles, the critical-incident questions started with identification of the article title or topic of the article in order to help respondents focus on a specific reading. The follow-up questions established the date of publication, previous knowledge of the article or information, the amount of time spent reading the article, the method of identifying the article, the source of the copy obtained (e.g., personal subscription or copy obtained from the library or a colleague), and whether the article was photocopied. A series of questions were asked concerning the time spent identifying, locating, obtaining, and photocopying the article and the purposes and consequences of reading the article.

Typical purposes of reading included such activities as research, teaching, and administration. Sometimes the level of specificity included tasks that correspond to outputs used in the general communication survey such as consulting or advising others, making formal presentations, and writing articles, proposals, and internal reports. Consequences of the last reading were related to specific purposes such as the extent to which the reading affected performance of the activity in terms of quality or in savings of labor time or other resources. In the latter instance, respondents were asked to specify:

- the type of savings (e.g., avoiding having to do some work) and the amount of savings achieved both in resources (e.g., equipment) and labor (e.g., time of oneself and co-workers)[5]

- other beneficial outcomes such as initiated ideas, reinforced hypothesis, or improved confidence in work.

We also determined the respondent's anticipated action when the normal source of the article (e.g., personal subscription, library copy) was not available. Would they obtain the article or equally useful information, and, if so, where

---

[5]To avoid duplicating the costs of scientists, we divided by the number of co-workers involved.

would they obtain it, and how much additional time and/or money would be required to use the source? Our results showed that for approximately 30 to 40 percent of the readings, the scientist would not seek another source, in which case the costs would be zero and added as such when calculating average costs.

In the demographics section, we asked whether the scientists had received any organization or other awards or special recognition during the past two years and, if so, to designate the awards to enable us to eliminate those of lesser importance. These responses were used to correlate and assess the amount of reading with achievement.

In some organizations, such as AT&T Bell Laboratories and the National Institutes of Health, we established the amount of work-related time spent on various activities including time spent inputting information to scientists' work (e.g., attending meetings and reading), and time spent outputting information from work (e.g., consulting or advising others, making presentations, and writing). The total time for each scientist included respondent estimates of the number of hours per year devoted to work or professional development above a normal eight-hour workday, but did not include vacation, holidays, and sick leave.

We estimated communication inputs in terms of the number of discussions, meetings attended, and articles, book, internal reports, and e-mail messages read; as well as time required to receive these inputs. We also estimated communication outputs such as number of presentations made, the number of articles, books, internal reports, proposals, and e-mail messages written, and the time to provide these outputs. Every output was adjusted by the number of co-authors or co-presentors.

A general communication survey served several purposes, including demonstrating the amount of time spent communicating in organizations and the importance of information services in optimizing the utilization of this time and other resources. Estimates of the amount of time spent reading served to validate estimates of time from the readership surveys (i.e., average amount of time spent reading times number of readings of articles and books,). Since the communication outputs such as number of articles written also serve as indicators of the output of scientists, these outputs can serve as indicators of performance in terms of productivity (i.e., the numerator). This, in fact, was done with five indicators of productivity which were correlated with such factors as amount of reading and library use.

For each of the various activities performed by scientists, we asked them to note the importance of six resources potentially available to them. The resources included computing equipment/terminals, other equipment/instrumentation, information found in documents (e.g., articles, books, patents, and research or technical reports), library staff, and advice from consultants or colleagues. The activities corresponded to scientists' activities reported in the general communication survey and the purposes of reading reported in the readership survey. Some resources were not applicable to an activity; the rest were rated in importance from one (not at all important) to five (absolutely essential).

Critical-incident questions were used for both the library and information services questionnaires. These surveys also focused on factors that affect use such as awareness of services, distance to the service, or availability of electronic requests, as well as the importance of and satisfaction with the services and service attributes such as existence of a fee and quality and speed of delivery of the service. For every service, respondents were given four choices: not aware of the service, yet need it, or do not need it and aware of the service, but have never used it, or have used it.

The first and second responses show the potential use of the service with better publicity or initial indoctrination. If respondents had used the service, they were asked the number of uses during the past month and their rating of the service in importance and satisfaction on a scale from one to five. For some services, respondents were asked to rate the importance of and their satisfaction with service attributes such as completeness of the journal collection or interlibrary loan/document delivery response time. Amount of use of services is usually correlated with ratings of importance and/or satisfaction. Some surveys incorporated conjoint measurement (Griffiths and King 1991, 1993) which establishes the relative utility of service attributes such as price, speed of delivery, and quality of presentation. (See Chapter 10 for examples.)

One question provided analysis of the amount of reading in the journals read by the respondent. For a critical incident of the last reading of a scholarly article, the scientists were asked how many articles they had read from the journal in the past twelve months. That information provided a basis for assessing individual journal readership by the source of the journal read. Since frequently-read journals are more likely to be observed than infrequently-read ones, the data needed to be adjusted to account for the probability of entering the sample. In other words, a journal read 100 times by a scientist is more likely to be reported on a critical incident of a journal reading than a journal read only once. Thus, the two results were not treated equally in estimating proportions and averages. Similarly, one must not directly attribute observations of readings to samples of individuals without adjustments for an individual's total amount of reading. Details of these adjustments are described in Griffiths and King (1991).

Most of the specific and derived measures can be made for journal article readership and service use questionnaires as demonstrated in the Framework section of this chapter. Journal and service input, output, and performance measures, however, were estimated from the cost finding studies described in the following section.

COST FINDING FOR PUBLISHING AND INFORMATION SERVICES

Earlier in this chapter we described a framework for assessing information services and products. One aspect of this framework addresses input and output of services and the relationship between these two measures, otherwise defined as service performance. Over the years we developed methods for measuring input, output, and performance in terms of transaction unit costs and productivity. Input costs were measured by the dollar cost of all resources directly applied to provide a service (e.g., interlibrary borrowing/document delivery) or produce a product (e.g., a scholarly journal). In these methods, all operational and administrative activity costs were allocated to the services and/or products. Therefore, the unit costs of services accounted for all costs incurred by a publisher or a library. This costing method was used in a National Science Foundation study in the late 1970s for three publishers and their presses. It has also been applied to fifty-seven special libraries, seven academic libraries, and over fifty public libraries. The general approach to measuring input cost, output, and unit cost is described briefly below.

We emphasize that the following approach to costing would not withstand the scrutiny of a formal audit because it lacks the necessary rigor. On the other hand, the approach does provide a way of establishing rough orders of magnitude for unit costs, recognizing that if the unit cost of one service or product is low (e.g., journal routing or editing a journal), another must be high (e.g., access to current periodicals or composition) because all resources and costs have been considered. It also provides a means of establishing the relationships among the various cost parameters (e.g., number of subscribers and number of pages) for publishing journals. The steps used in this costing approach are outlined below:

- identify all services or products and the principal activities performed by the organization
- identify the resources (e.g., staff, equipment, facilities, and supplies) required to perform the activities
- allocate the total amount of resources and their cost to the relevant activities
- determine which activities are directly related to a service such as journal routing and which are related to a product such as subject editing

- allocate administrative (support) costs to service costs and operational activities such as collection development in libraries

- allocate operational activities to services in a rational manner, i.e., collection development to services such as current periodicals, journal routing, and interlibrary lending

- determine relevant output quantities for all services, and

- derive unit costs and/or cost elements for cost models.

Examples of this cost finding approach are given in Griffiths and King (1993). Allocation of resources can sometimes be done reasonably accurately, although usually they involve a degree of subjectivity. Therefore, each unit cost is tested for reasonableness against a multitude of other data. Careless allocations are usually caught and corrected by this process. In fact, most unit costs fall within a reasonable range of the overall average among libraries.

We must emphasize that service unit costs, particularly the publishing cost model presented in Chapter 12, does vary from organization to organization because circumstances can vary dramatically. The publishing cost model is based on an in-depth study of three publishers in the late 1970s and validated by other data collected under the NSF studies (King, McDonald and Roderer 1981, King and Roderer 1978). To our knowledge, a replication of this kind of study has not been conducted since that time. Therefore, we have extrapolated these data using rates of inflation, known changes in cost parameters, and comparisons of cost elements with reported data in the literature which, in turn, has been adjusted as appropriate to compensate for inflation.[6]

One reason for producing a cost model which can not be completely validated is to demonstrate how cost parameters such as number of articles, pages, and subscribers can substantially affect costs. One can substitute any values of cost elements that reflect a particular organization. Another reason to apply a version of this model is to demonstrate that the cost of an average size journal can be misleading. For example, the word, average, is often used in the literature to denote both mean circulation size, which is 5,800 subscribers for scholarly journals, as well as the median size, which is only 1,900. This model demonstrates that the

---

[6]Validation of the rough cost model was achieved by asking several commercial, society, and university publishers to review the model parameters and cost elements, a result of which was to make some modifications. We also asked readers of a publication (King and Tenopir 1999) to report any invalid data.

unit cost per subscriber is considerably different for the two since the number of subscribers has a significant effect on unit cost per subscriber.

We also estimate cost of author, reader, and user time for several analyses. This was done by determining average compensation of scientists (i.e., salary, FICA, Medicare, insurance, pension, etc.) and adding an organization's overhead costs (about 50% of compensation). This amount is divided by the reported number of hours worked in a year (excluding vacation, sick leave, holidays) to determine an hourly rate. In 1998 this rate comes to $48.30 per hour or $0.805 per minute.

JOURNAL TRACKING STUDY

During the 1970s, King Research, Inc. completed a series of contracts with the National Science Foundation under the title, Statistical Indicators of Scientific and Technical Information (STI) Communication. One aspect of this body of work was to establish trends in scientific scholarly journal indicators such as price, size, circulation, and cost. To gather these data we established a unique list of scholarly scientific journals compiled from an Institute for Scientific Information (ISI) list, *Ulrich's International Periodicals Directory* (New York: Bowker), and a smaller list developed by Fry and White at Indiana University. This combined list contained 4,447 titles published by U.S. publishers. We used *Ulrich's* designation of country of origin where some titles are designated U.S. and others as U.S. and non-U.S. (which include those with offices and/or operations both within and outside the U.S.). In 1975, 7.4 percent of the journals were published by the latter category (U.S. and non-U.S. publishers), while in 1995 this proportion is estimated to have grown to 18.1 percent. Most of these are commercial publishers (93 percent).

A sample of 432 titles was chosen from this combined 1977 list of 4,447 titles, and information was obtained about each journal from *Ulrich's* and other sources (e.g., prices, circulation, name of publisher, issues per year, and year when first published). A sub-sample of twenty-five titles was drawn from each of the eight fields of science as defined at that time by NSF, plus a category for multi-field titles. All 225 sub-sampled journals were examined in libraries, and in-depth data were collected for every other year back to 1960 or to the year a journal was first published. A sample was also brought forward to establish deaths (i.e., cessation of journals). These data were collected from samples of issues and samples of articles within issues found in libraries. They included reported prices, number of articles, pages/article, words per page, graphics, authors, author affiliations, citations, number of non-article pages, amount of advertising, and page charges or fees. All of these data were statistically weighted, taking into account births, deaths, and twigging (i.e., a journal splitting into two or more journals) and the varied sizes of fields of science. These data are published in King, McDonald, and Roderer (1981).

Under NSF contract to the University of Tennessee, School of Information Sciences, in 1991, we updated the list of journals with a new sample of 150 journal titles from *Ulrich's* to incorporate births and deaths and *Ulrich's* most recent data on prices. In 1995 we took another sample of 133 titles to establish births and deaths, price, and circulation. Finally, in 1995 an in-depth review was performed on the original 225 journals, located in the university library, to obtain equivalent updated information on these journals. Even though no attempt was made to assess journal quality, we made some cursory assessment to ensure that the scholarly scientific journals reported scientific research and/or employed a peer review or refereeing process to aid in screening manuscripts for editorial quality control. While the focus of these journals is on reporting research findings, methods, concepts, or other scholarly information, these journals also often publish other forms of professional communication such as letters, book reviews, editorials, news, and advertising. The *National Science & Engineering Indicators 1996* published by NSF reports that the Institute for Scientific Information, *Science Citation Index* journal database has 4,681 natural science and engineering refereed journals published worldwide. These do not include social sciences and behavioral sciences. Thus, the direct comparison is 4,681 ISI journals versus 4,289 for our estimates. The ISI database provides a valid and useful core of scientific journals (Tenopir and King 1997).

ANALYSIS OF ELECTRONIC PUBLISHING DIRECTORIES

Ulrich's was used to trace the growth of print journals over time, but more recent specialized directories were used to track the recent growth of the electronic publishing discussed in Chapter 15. Three directories are especially important in tracing electronic publishing: the Association of Research Libraries' (ARL) annual *Directory of Electronic Journals, Newsletters, and Academic Discussion Lists*, the twice yearly *Fulltext Sources Online*, and the twice yearly *Gale Directory of Databases*.

The *Directory of Electronic Journals, Newsletters, and Academic Discussion Lists* was originally published as a printed directory to keep track of a fast growing world of electronic-only intellectual works. Since 1996 it is available only in electronic form (from ARL) like the journals it covers. It is the most complete source for electronic-only publications, including those created by individuals, academic institutions, government agencies, other not-for-profit organizations, and commercial publishers. Watching it grow from a few funded titles in 1991 (mostly lists and discussion groups) to many thousands by the late 1990s (mostly web sites) is the best evidence for the growth of electronic publishing in the 1990s. Chapter 15 provides some analysis of this change in content and describes in-depth analyses reported by Hitchcock, Carr, and Hall (1996) and McEldowney (1995).

Fulltext Sources Online was published twice a year by Bibliodata until 1998 when it was purchased by Information Today, Inc. It is an alphabetical listing by journal title of all journals, magazines, and newspapers available on the major commercial online services such as DIALOG or LEXIS-NEXIS. Almost all of its titles are electronic versions of print publications, so it has little overlap with the journals covered in the ARL directory.

The third important directory for electronic publications is the *Gale Directory of Databases*. Gale purchased the two earliest database directories dating from the late 1970s that were originally published by Carlos Cuadra and Martha E. Williams. (Martha Williams still writes the introduction to the *Gale Directory*.)

Unlike the other directories, Gale's directory includes listings for all electronic databases from commercial or government sources, including bibliographic, directory, statistical, and other types of databases in addition to full-text journals.

No one source alone gives a complete picture of electronic publishing. In fact, even these three sources together can not keep up with the constantly changing electronic publishing picture. The over ten million World Wide Web sites alone makes the idea of counting problematic.

Part II

SCIENTISTS' PARTICIPATION

CHAPTER 5

Scientists as Authors, Readers, and Referees

INTRODUCTION

In Chapter 3 we described several conceptual models of communication and identified the role of scholarly journals within each model. One simple model involves scientists' principal activities such as research, teaching, and administration. In order to perform these activities, scientists apply several kinds of resources, including their time, equipment, instrumentation, support staff, facilities, and information. Aside from their time, information is certainly one, if not the most important, resource for performing most scientific work. The application of resources to perform work results in output such as completed assignments, new ideas, internal thoughts, and information that is communicated to others. Thus, information is not only an important input to scientific endeavors, but its principal output as well.

Both information input and output consist primarily of documents or recorded information (e.g., journals, books, reports, and video) and verbal or interpersonal modes (e.g., conversations, conference presentations, classroom lectures, and informal meetings). Information input and output can involve communication that is internal to the organization where the scientist works or external to it; that is, sending information to and from scientists working in other organizations.[1]

---

[1]The simple model depicting such communication is presented in Figure 4 (Chapter 3).

Receiving and sending information are two distinct scientific activities, each of which requires input resources such as time spent reading or writing and each of which measures output quantities by number of articles read or articles written. In this chapter we provide quantitative evidence of the extent to which journal articles, other documents, and verbal information are used as information input to scientific activities such as research and teaching and the extent to which articles, other documents, and verbal information are produced. We also examine the effort involved in receiving and sending this information.

Finally, we describe the common goals of authors and readers of scientific journal articles. We also discuss the importance of peer review and refereeing scholarly articles and provide estimates of the amount of time spent in these activities. The simple model presented in this chapter does not show all the processes involved in communicating information. These processes are discussed in greater detail in the earlier models and in subsequent chapters. For example, in Chapters 6 and 7, we provide substantial detail concerning authorship and use of scientific journal articles and trends from 1977 to 1998.

HOW SCIENTISTS SPEND THEIR TIME

In order to establish the use, usefulness, and value of scientific information in general and scholarly articles in particular, surveys of scientists were conducted from 1984 to 1998 in companies, government agencies, and national laboratories to establish how scientists spend their time and the contribution that information makes to their work. The results of these studies provide a context for discussing both authorship and use of scientific journal articles (Griffiths and King 1993).

We found that scientists average slightly less than 2,400 hours working for their organizations excluding vacation, holidays, and sick leave; this amounts to nearly 600 hours a year over and above a normal 8 hour workday. About 78 percent of this time is spent on primary research (e.g., experimentation and data collection), engineering, systems development, and background information research. Three percent of their time is spent on professional development, and the rest (19 percent) is spent on managing, budgeting, manufacturing, or operations-related activities. Thus, for the most part, these surveyed scientists (n=904) spend most of their time in scientific endeavors.

Examined from another perspective, over one-half of their time (1,386 hours) is spent in communications-related activities. Thus, less than one-half of their time is spent thinking, conducting experiments, and other non-communication tasks. Over half of the communication time (687 hours) is spent on information input such as identifying and accessing documents (34 hours), reading (370 hours), attending internal meetings (127 hours), attending external meetings (36 hours), and reading electronic messages (120 hours). Information output involves approximately 524 hours. Output accounting for the remaining time includes preparing documents such as writing internal reports, computer programs, and proposals (181 hours), preparing electronic messages (40 hours), and creating external documents (only 19 hours). Most of this output time involves consulting or advising others (175 hours) and making internal (77 hours) or external (32 hours) presentations and workshops. Informal discussions (175 hours) are common to both input and outputs. Thus, reading documents and electronic messages consumes over 71 percent of the input time, while writing involves approximately 46 percent of the output time (excluding informal discussion).

Some evidence suggests that communication time has increased approximately 150 hours over the past 15 years, due in large part to electronic messaging and an increase in the number of informal meetings. Unfortunately, we do not have estimates of how university scientists allocate their time, although communication activities undoubtedly dominate their time. It must be remembered that a minority of scientists work in universities, although they dominate the production of scientific scholarly articles.

A study in 1958 (Halbert and Ackoff 1958) revealed that chemists spent about 44 percent of their time communicating (33.4 in scientific communication and 10.4 percent in business communication). In 1960, Menzel, Lieberman and Dulchin found that university chemists spent approximately one-fourth of their time in scientific communication, while industrial scientists spent approximately one-third of their time in this way. A careful[2] and revealing study conducted for NSF in 1960 by the Operations Research Group, Case Institute of Technology, (Martin and Ackoff 1963) found that physical scientists spent 42 percent of their time engaged in scientific communication, 27 percent working on equipment, 8 percent on data treatment, 6 percent in thinking and planning, and 17 percent on business administration. They spent about 16.5 hours per week in scientific communication. This finding was considered significant because scientists spent considerably more time in scientific communication than in any other scientific activity including work with scientific equipment. The Case study involved 701 physicists and chemists located in 55 industries, 13 universities, and 3 government agencies.

---

[2]Time spent in various activities was observed through random alarm devices. More specifically, each time the alarm sounded, scientists were asked to record what they were doing.

One focus of the Case study addressed the amount of time spent reading scientific journals. They found that the surveyed scientists spent an average of 142 hours per year reading scientific journals. Some comparable data exists for recent years. In two national sample surveys of scientists and engineers (King et al. NSF surveys 1977 and 1984), it was estimated that physical scientists spent 110 hours reading articles from scholarly journals in 1977 and 122 hours in 1984.

Ample additional recent evidence exists to document the substantial amount of time spent by scientists in communicating, both as input to their work by reading and listening and as output resulting from their work as written documents and presentations as shown in Table 5. Other more recent studies report that between 40 and 67 percent of scientists' time is spent communicating.

Although scientists spend a substantial amount of their time communicating, they choose to do so because their performance depends on communication. Research reported over the years indicates that those who spend more time reading perform better or are high achievers (e.g., King and Griffiths 1993; Katz and Tushman 1979; Lufkin and Miller 1966). Research also suggests that projects have a better outcome when the project staff communicates more (Allen 1966). In recent years there has been an interest in designating as learning organizations those companies that take advantage of opportunities to learn from outside sources of information.

Another aspect of scientific communication is the many modes and channels used for communication, ranging from the published literature and formal presentations to interpersonal conversations. The literature reports a wide difference in findings of the relative importance of various channels of communication. The relative importance of the literature versus interpersonal sources of information, however, may reflect the scientist's information content needs and attribute requirements. Clearly, most communication researchers have found that ease of use or time required by the users dictates the information sources used by scientists. However, the purpose of use (and/or stage of a project) also affects the sources used. For example, Gerstenfeld and Berger (1980) show that written sources are more commonly used for basic research, while interpersonal sources are more often used for applied research. Allen and Gerstberger (1964) indicate that experience and the scientist's personality are related to literature use; in other words, gatekeepers read more than other scientists.

Obviously, one purpose of the effort expended in formally recording or orally communicating the output of one's work is to provide evidence of accomplishment. Other consequences, however, undoubtedly far outweigh that purpose. One immediate consequence is to gain feedback from others, and this is particularly well achieved through communications by means of interpersonal

Table 5	Estimates of the Proportion of Scientists' Time Spent Communicating by Type of Communicator: 1958–1998

Year	Communicator	Proportion of Time (in percent)

1958	Chemists	Total: 44%
		   Scientific: 33.4%
		   Business: 10.4%

1960	University chemists Industry chemists	Scientific: 25% Scientific: 33%
1960	Physical scientists	Total: 42%

1964	Chemists	Total: 61%
		   Writing: 16%
		   Reading: 10%
		   Oral: 35%

1975	Scientists	Writing: 25% Input: 30%
1975	Scientists	Total: 67%

1979	R&D	Total: 40%
		   Reading: 9.8%
		   Interpersonal: 23.3%
		   Other: 7.0%

1988	R&D	Total: 48%

1989	Engineers	Total: 66%
		   Input: 31%
		   Output: 35%

1994–1998	R&D (non-academic)	Total: 58.4%
		   Reading: 20.6%
		   Other input: 8.3%
		   Writing: 10.1%
		   Other output: 12.0%
		   Discussions: 7.4%

Sources: Halbert and Ackoff 1958; Menzel, Lieberman and Dulchin 1960; Operations Research Group 1960; Hinrichs 1964; Davis 1975; Turoff and Scher 1975; Mick, Lindsey, Callahan and Spielberg 1979, Allen 1988, Pinelli, Glassman, Oliu and Barclay 1989; King, et al. surveys 1994–1998.

information. A longer range beneficial consequence is the consumption and use of the information by others. Thus, scientists communicate the results of their work for various purposes in various ways (internal, external, formal, and informal).

SCIENTIFIC AUTHORSHIP

Scientists and engineers are prolific writers, although those from academia and government tend to write more for external consumption, while those from industry write more for the internal use in their company. Documenting research findings is an essential part of research because the discipline of writing is, in itself, part of the creative process and often leads to new creation. Pinelli, Glassman, Oliu, and Barclay (1989) have summarized some aspects of the importance of writing. Portions of these results are quoted below:

> Davis (1975) published the results of a survey to determine, among other things, the importance of technical communications to successful engineers. In response to the question of how important writing is and if the ability to write effectively is needed, approximately 96 percent (134 respondents) indicated that the writing they did was either very important (51 percent) or was critically important (45 percent) in their position. None of the respondents indicated that their writing was unimportant. In response to the question of whether the ability to write can effectively delay or prevent advancement for an individual who is otherwise qualified, 89 percent of the respondents stated that, other considerations aside, the ability to write is usually an important or a critical consideration when a subordinate is considered for advancement.

> Spretnak (1982) conducted a survey in 1980 which was mailed to 1,000 engineering alumni of the University of California, Berkeley. In response to the question, "Do you have any general comments about the importance or relative unimportance of writing and speaking skills in engineering careers?" none of the respondents indicated that writing and speaking skills were unimportant. Excerpts from the responses to Spretnak's (1982) open-ended question appear below.

> 1. Technical communications is the key to success for every engineer.

> 2. No doubt writing is the most important skill an engineer can possess.

> 3. Writing and speaking should receive the same attention as technical writing.

> Seventy-three percent reported that writing skills had aided their advancement. Ninety-five percent said they would consider writing ability in deciding

whether to hire or promote an engineer, while 42 percent of the total respondents said that they would weigh writing and presentation skills "greatly."

The importance of writing to engineering students as well as science students is echoed by David (1982) who states:

> The single, greatest complaint our students make when polled about their undergraduate preparation consists of questions of the form: "Why don't you teach us how to write?" They have found, much to their amazement, that one of their main jobs in the real world is writing and that they are woefully unprepared to fulfill that part of their duties.

Davis (1975) reported that respondents to his study spent approximately 25 percent of their time writing technical communications and approximately 30 percent of their time working with technical communications prepared by others. Approximately 63 percent of the respondents reported that as their responsibilities increased, so did the time they spent writing, and 94 percent of the respondents indicated that they spent more time working with written material as their responsibilities increased. According to Davis (1975), "As their responsibilities increased, respondents spent less of their time developing the actual details of specific jobs and more time considering the work of others, making decisions from it, and inaugurating and carrying out appropriate action."

Average information outputs for aeronautical engineers in the past 6 months projected to 12 months are shown in comparison with the average information outputs found in King et al. surveys 1988–1993 in Table 6. These results are certainly of the same order of magnitude. The NASA study also mentioned 44 letters, 0.6 technical manuals, 0.6 press releases, and 13.2 audiovisual materials per year. Our survey also included 2.2 laboratory notebooks, 3.5 items of technical correspondence, 0.03 patent awards, 0.02 books, and 6.1 other documents.

A survey conducted at the University of Tennessee (n=404) in 1993 shows that scientists indicate that they authored or co-authored[3] only 0.5 internal reports compared with an average of 2.2 scholarly journal articles per scientist, 0.9 trade journal contributions, 0.2 scholarly books, and 1.2 other documents intended for external use such as technical reports or substantive electronic documents. Thus, the assertion that university scientists tend to write significantly more for external consumption than do other scientists appears to be valid.

---

[3]These averages are authorships per scientist, not the number of articles written per scientist because the sample could include two or more scientists who co-authored the same document.

Table 6	Scientific Written Information Outputs Observed in Two Studies: 1988-1993 (in Number of Items Authored)	
Common Output	Engineers 1989	Scientists & Engineers 1988-1993
Technical Reports	7.0	5.1
Proposals	3.6	2.2
Specifications	6.4	5.2
Computer Program Documentation	2.6	2.8
Journal Articles and Trade Literature	1.4	0.1
Conference/Meeting Papers	2.2	0.5
Speeches	4.4	2.5
Memos	57.6	19.0

Sources: Pinelli, Glassman, Oliu, and Barclay 1989; King et al. surveys 1988–1993

SCIENTIFIC READERSHIP

In terms of reading, university scientists tend to read more than other scientists, although not dramatically so, as shown in Table 7. While university scientists average reading far more scholarly articles per scientist than other scientists (188 vs. 106 readings per year), most readings of scientific scholarly articles are read by non-academic scientists simply because non-academic scientists greatly outnumber academic scientists. Journals appear to have been read more than other documents in the 1950s. For example, Shaw (1956) found that 70 percent of all reading by scientists and engineers was from journals. This is still true of university scientists when trade journals are included. Rosenbloom and Wolek (1967) surveyed more than 3,000 engineers and scientists in large corporations, including a sample of members of the Institute of Electrical and Electronic Engineers. One principal focus of the data collection was to determine the information sources used by engineers and scientists to perform their work. Respondents were asked to report the most recent instance in which an item of information proved to be useful in their work, excluding information from someone in their immediate circle of colleagues. Sources reported are summarized in Table 8.

Clearly, the engineers in the 1960s relied much more on sources found in their own organization than on external sources (63 percent versus 37 percent), and they relied more on interpersonal sources than on written materials (62 percent

| Table 7 | Annual Number of Readings* Per Scientist by University and Non-University Scientists: 1993-1998 |

Type of Document	University	Non-University
Scholarly journal articles	188	106
Trade journals	74	51
Professional books	48	53
External reports	20	12
Internal reports	26	53
Other materials	14	22
Total	370	297

*By reading we mean going beyond the contents page, title and abstract to the text of the document. A reading means a single incident of reading, recognizing that a particular document may be read on several occasions.

Source: King et al. surveys 1993–1998

| Table 8 | Proportion of Information Sources Used by Engineers and Scientists: 1967 (in Percent) |

Information Sources	Proportion of Instances	
	Engineers	Scientists
Sources within own company		
Interpersonal		
Local source (within establishment)	25	18
Other corporate	26	9
Written media (documents)	12	6
Sources outside company		
Interpersonal (anyone outside company)	11	16
Written media		
Professional (books, articles, conference papers)	15	42
Trade (trade magazines, catalogs, technical reports)	11	9
Total	100	100

Source: Rosenbloom and Wolek 1967

versus 38 percent). Scientists relied more on outside sources (67 percent), and their most important source was the published literature (51 percent of instances).

Allen (1988) reports comparisons observed in the early 1980s between information sources used in performing technological projects and scientific research projects. Sources used in these projects are summarized in Table 9.

These results suggest that engineers more recently are more dependent on colleagues and that scientists use the literature much more than engineers. Allen points out that engineers also need different kinds of journals since they use the literature for entirely different purposes. Engineers spend only 7.9 percent of their time using the literature versus 18.2 percent by scientists.

COMMON GOALS OF JOURNAL AUTHORS AND READERS

Scientists' time is obviously a critical resource for research, teaching, and other scientific endeavors. How they choose to spend this time is an extremely important decision. As mentioned earlier, both authors and readers devote a substantial amount of time to writing and reading. The time spent writing and reading scholarly journal articles, estimated from our surveys, is outlined in Table 10. Clearly, scientific authors and writers choose to devote many hours to writing and reading scholarly journal articles. However, while the average time spent writing an article and reading an article are roughly the same for university and non-university scientists, the total amount of time spent per scientist reflects their overall journal authorship and readership displayed in Tables 6 and 7.

Ultimately the key to success for any electronic publication lies with the two predominant participants that appear first and last in every model. Authors must be willing to write, and readers must feel compelled to read. Kaplan (1993) depicts the relationship between author and reader as a constant that "has not changed since the first writings were rendered as cave markings."

Downplaying or eliminating the role of the publisher revolves around the widely held belief that authors and readers share common goals and that these common goals conflict with the goals of commercial publishers. Authors and readers are depicted as integrated units as electronic journals "shift the emphasis of scholarship . . . from the single author to the corporate author [which is made up of] writers and their readers" (Amiran, Orr, and Unsworth 1991).

Certainly authors and readers share some goals, but in reality, are they now, or can they ever be a single unified entity? Is this unification necessary for the success of electronic publishing? An examination of their respective motivations and goals with scholarly publications may help to answer these questions (see Chapters 6 and 7).

Table 9	Proportion of Information Sources Used for Technological and Scientific Research Projects: 1980s (in Percent)

Information Sources	Proportion of Instances	
	17 Technological Projects	2 Scientific Research Projects
Literature	8	51
Vendors	14	0
Customer	19	0
Other external sources	9	14
Lab technical staff	6	3
Company research programs	5	3
Analysis and experimentation	31	9
Previous personal experience	8	20
Total	100	100

Source: Allen 1988

Table 10	Average Time Spent Writing and Reading an Article and Annual Amount of Time Spent per Scientist by University and Non-University Scientists: 1993-1998 (in Hours)

Scientific Scholarly Articles	University		Non-University	
	Average/ Article*	Annual Total	Average/ Article*	Annual Total
Writing	85	187	100	10
Reading	0.97	182	0.83	88

*Averages are only for scientists who recently wrote or read scholarly articles (i.e., authors and readers).
Source: King et al. surveys 1993–1998

PEER REVIEW/REFEREEING

The author's goal of academic achievement may be met by inculcating the accepted practice of peer review/refereeing into scholarly electronic journals and ensuring that this is understood and accepted by academic decision makers. The editors of the successful electronic (and peer reviewed) journal *Postmodern Culture* report having trouble getting contributions from junior faculty because tenure committees fail to recognize the legitimacy of electronic publications (Amiran, Orr, and Unsworth 1991). They believe it must be conveyed to these decision makers that "Institutional legitimization is a matter of the peer-review process and not a question of the medium in which peer-reviewed work is distributed." They hope to convey the belief that "an electronic journal that uses methods as careful and reviewers as qualified as those used by responsible print journals ought to be considered a valid form of professional publication."

A 1981 study by Seiler and Raben (1981) provides an early view of the challenge of fostering such acceptance. They surveyed attitudes toward refereed electronic journals by 677 assistant, associate, and full professors in U.S. academic institutions that have graduate programs. Respondents were asked to envision publications that were available only through computer networks, but were national in scope, were in their subject specialty, and were refereed. Given this scenario (futuristic in 1981), 52 percent of the respondents "considered electronic publication equivalent to print publication." Many either believed it inferior (37 percent) or would totally disregard it (6 percent), and Seiler and Raben found "virtually no support (1 percent) for the idea that electronic publication is superior to print publication as a basis for promotion."

Not surprisingly, in schools oriented toward teaching, a higher proportion of the respondents believed the electronic medium for journals would be equal to or superior to print for promotion to full professor than did those in schools oriented toward research (62 percent to 42 percent) (Seiler and Raben 1981).

Nowhere is the peer review issue more important and more discussed than in the medical and biomedical fields. Health-service professors publish more refereed articles in their careers than any other scientists (Griffiths, Carroll, King, Williams, and Sheetz 1991) and the amount and prestige of these publications is essential for competitive external funding, as well as academic success. Much of the discussion has centered around the problems of a peer review system for grant proposals and journal articles that use potential competitors as reviewers in a highly competitive scientific environment. Recently, discussions have focused on the role of peer review in electronic journals as well.

In the early 1990s, the International Committee of Medical Journal Editors added a statement about electronic publication to their "Uniform Requirements for Manuscripts Submitted to Biomedical Journals" (Flanagin, Glass, and Lundberg 1992). They wanted to convey to authors, editors, academicians, and institutions their belief that:

> Scientific reports disseminated through an electronic journal—especially one that publishes original, peer-reviewed, and copyright-protected articles —should be considered 'published' material and thus held to the same standards that apply to information published in conventional print journals.

When it works as it should, peer review is an essential ingredient of ensuring that only the best quality papers get published. It provides decision makers at universities with a criteria for quality that they can accept without question. It thus serves the academic author's primary motivation.

But merely bringing the old processes of print into an electronic world may not serve the interests of all authors or all readers. Judson (1994) surveyed the troubled history of peer review in medicine—a process that is dominated by an old boy network and conflicting interests and competition, where the best work does not always get into print. Merely moving this old system into a new delivery medium would not solve the fundamental problems, but there is the possibility of a better peer review system in the future with the more open environment that electronic publishing will bring. He sees hope in the future because:

> A new generation of journal editors will arise who have grown up with electronic editing and publishing. In ten years' time, although procedures will be followed that some journals will still label "refereeing" or "journal peer review," these procedures will be startlingly different from those put into place in the years after the second world war, which, despite their brief history, seem so monolithic and unchangeable today [T]he transformation will open up the processes by which scientists judge each other's work, making them less anonymous, capricious, rigid, and subject to abuse, and more thorough, responsible, and accountable.

In many, less competitive disciplines, it may be a long time before this new vision serves the advancement goals of authors. It does, however, clearly serve the next major goal of authors—that of contributing to the knowledge base of their field.

Peer review serves the needs of readers by providing a quality filter. When functioning correctly, peer review guarantees that published papers have merit, although there are many complaints that too many articles are published and that the filtering mechanism should be tighter.

Readers, especially those who are not experienced researchers and authors, need to have confidence that what they read is accurate and authoritative. Amiran,

Unsworth, and Chaski (1992) quote a proposal to establish *The Chicago Journal of Computer Theoretical Science* by Mike J. O'Donnell and Abraham Bookstein on the needs of readers of scholarly publications. They maintained that readers need to have:

> a high confidence that they are all reading precisely the same article created by the author and accepted by the editor, and that this acceptance is an accurate certificate of the value of the article. The basic protocol of publication in a scholarly journal—the author freely chooses to submit an article, the editor takes the advice of several independent and anonymous referees, insists on revisions if appropriate, then accepts or rejects the article—is independent of the medium. There is no reason to change that highly successful protocol in converting from print to electronic network publication.

As discussed earlier, rigorous peer review is facilitated by electronic communication since more reviewers can evaluate a manuscript in less time. Reviewers' comments can be attached to electronic preprints of a manuscript before a more final version is completed. There is no reason why peer review has to be less rigorous, and, indeed, it could be more rigorous. Stevan Harnad, editor of *Behavioral and Brain Sciences* and the electronic *Psycoloquy* is an articulate proponent of rigorous peer reviewing for both print and electronic journals.

In 1978 Roistacher proposed a unique way for electronic journals to serve both goals of readers—the goal to see more articles published and the goal to have a quality filter. He proposed imposing no limits on the amount of material published, but attaching numerical scores assigned by referees to each article. Readers could follow a threshold score when they wanted to read only the best articles. Subsequent readers could attach their own scores to articles, extending the refereeing process forward in time and to a larger audience.

Rogers and Hurt (1990) provide detailed suggestions on how an electronic Scholarly Communication System could meet a variety of authors' and readers' goals for quantity and quality of publications. Scholars would submit papers electronically where they would be filed by subject category and would be available for readers' comments. After six months on the system each article would be flagged for review and authors would be notified. Authors could use the comments from readers to prepare a final draft of their article.

If an author submits a final, revised copy it would be sent for formal review, otherwise the article would be purged from the system. Review boards would place each article in one of seven categories, including:

- original contribution to literature in a field

- logical extension of research in a field

- application of a theoretical perspective or method developed in one content area to another content area

- restatement or interpretation of existing research

- review of the status of research on a particular topic

- seriously flawed in research design, experimental technique, or conclusion, and

- no scholarly contribution.

Time spent by scientists in reviewing article manuscripts is not insignificant. In 1977, reviewers averaged 6 hours per manuscript for rejected manuscripts and 6.25 hours for accepted articles (King, McDonald, and Roderer 1981). Campanario (1998 a, b) cites three recent studies that give ranges from 3.0 to 5.4 hours per manuscript for peer review. The extrapolated 1977 cost of reviewing articles, while largely donated, is approximately $480 per article, based on average costs of scientists' time. This includes both review and critical annotation. While a relatively costly activity, on balance, review appears to be important to both authors and readers, particularly non-university readers who are not members of the invisible college.

CHAPTER 6

Authorship of Scientific Scholarly Articles

INTRODUCTION

This chapter presents the extent of authorship in terms of the proportion of scientists who write scholarly articles, the number of articles written by those who do write, and trends in authorship. We show evidence as to the cost of preparing scholarly articles in scientists' time and application of other resources. There are many reasons why scientists are willing to devote their time to authoring, including to achieve academic advancement and tenure, to contribute to the body of knowledge in one's field, to establish one's posterity, and to protect one's intellectual effort and discovery. Finally, we discuss reasons why authors choose one journal in which to publish over another and the extent of manuscript exchange with publishers.

EXTENT OF AUTHORSHIP

Our national survey in 1984 estimated that 6 percent of scientists write and publish at least one scholarly article every year, and those who write regularly average 2.0 articles per year. Mooney (1991) reported that approximately 70 percent of the professors from research universities wrote an article in 1986 or 1987, and the average number of articles ranged from 2.1 articles for social sciences to 4.3 for health sciences. A series of in-depth surveys of scientists revealed an average of 2.2 articles per annum published by university scientists and 0.1 articles per scientist in companies and government agencies (King et al. surveys 1993–1998). A study by Pinelli, Glassman, Oliu, and Barclay (1989) of aeronautical engineers and scientists from academia, industry, and government indicated that they averaged 1.4 journal articles and contributions to the trade literature per year.

Description of Journal Authors

The scientific community represents the universe of potential authors of scientific and technical journal articles, but not all scientists publish regularly or even one time. The characteristics of the author community are therefore somewhat different from the characteristics of the scientific community as a whole. For example, in 1977, 72 percent had a doctorate (vs. 17 percent of the population), 62 percent were in a university (vs. 13 percent), 81 percent were engaged in research or teaching (vs. 38 percent), 64 percent were under 40 years of age (vs. 43 percent), and 90 percent were male (vs. 95 percent) (King, McDonald, and Roderer 1981).

Price and Gursey, in their *Studies in Scientometrics (1974)*, have distinguished authors among seven groups in the scientific community, and have estimated their sizes. These groups are:

a. Transients, who publish only during a single year

b. Recruits, who begin publishing during the year considered and will continue publishing

c. Terminators, who have published previously, but end their publishing during the year

d. Core continuants, who publish in the year in question and every year over a long period

e. Noncore publishing continuants, who publish this year and are likely to publish frequently, but not annually, over a long period of time

f. Nonpublishing continuants, who are noncore continuants who do not happen to publish in the particular year in question

g. Nonauthors, who do not publish during the year, but are not nonpublishing continuants. This group includes past and future transients who have published or will publish in another year and authors who have terminated previously.

According to Price and Gursey, groups a. through e., respectively, comprise 22, 11, 4, 20, and 47 percent of the scientists publishing in any given year. (Terminators appear to overlap with continuants in this percentage breakdown.) In total, then, 67 percent of the authors in a particular year are continuants, either core or noncore. Nonpublishing continuants are equal in number to approximately one-third of the publishing authors. It is more difficult to determine the size of the nonauthor group in a given year, although this can be derived by inference from authorship data from several sources.

From 2 to 17 percent of scientists, depending on the field of science, will author at least one article in a particular year. Approximately 80 percent of these (2 to 14 percent) will be continuants in some sense; in other words, they have authored or will author articles in other years. (Included in the 80 percent are Price and Gursey's groups a. to e.) Core continuants, or authors who publish every year, account for approximately 20 percent of the authors in a given year, or 0.5 to 3 percent of all scientists.

In an additional refinement, Price and Gursey subdivided authors according to the number of articles published. In a small sample, they found that transients produced 1.1 authorships per year and that the production of continuants increased in relation to the length of continuance (for example, two-year continuants produced an average 1.5 articles per year, five-year continuants 3.7 articles per year, and nine-year continuants 4.3 articles). These results correspond well to Price's law, which states that the number of authors with at least n authorships is proportional to $1/(n(k + n))$. Here k is a parameter of approximately fifteen authorships per author per lifetime. This marks a boundary between very high and normal production.

Lotka's Law provides a similar picture (see, for example, Schauder 1994), which says that the number of people producing n papers is proportional to $1/n^2$. In other words, for every 1,000 academics who produce three professional articles in their lifetimes, there are 100 who produce ten, and there is only one who produces 100.[1] Schauder then cites evidence that this may apply to "little science," but not to "big science." He was told by Stephan Schwartz that in experimental High Energy Physics, scientists work in large teams, ranging up to 700 individuals. These teams normally publish with all members as authors, so if fifty papers are produced, there will be so many hundreds of authors having fifty papers each.[2]

---

[1]Lancaster (1978) summarizes several other similar models.
[2]This partially explains why the number of authorships (i.e., number of authors per article) is increasing. It also confirms personal discussions with Paul Ginsparg in which he feels that some reported research, such as that done in National Labs, is less in need of external review since there is so much internal collaboration and review.

Trends in Authorship

U.S. scientists wrote nearly as many articles per scientist in 1995 as in 1975. Journal tracking data (Tenopir and King 1997) show that the total number of articles published in U.S. journals has more than doubled from 353,700 articles in 1975 to 831,300 in 1995 due to the increase in the total number of scientists. Of these, 273,100 and 504,900 articles respectively are estimated from author affiliations to be authored by U.S. scientists. U.S. scientists also publish in non-U.S. journals. We estimated that they wrote approximately 39,100 such articles in 1975. We do not have equivalent 1995 data, but if the proportion of articles published in non-U.S. journals compared with U.S. journals remains the same, 72,200 articles would have been published in non-U.S. journals by U.S. scientists in 1995. Thus, in 1975, 2.64 million U.S. scientists are estimated to have published 312,200 articles in U.S. and non-U.S. journals or approximately 0.118 articles per scientist[3] (or 8.5 scientists per article written). In 1995, an estimated 577,100 articles were prepared by 5.74 million scientists for an average 0.101 articles per scientist (or 9.9 scientists per article written).

Another way to estimate the average number of articles written per scientist is to ask the scientists themselves to report such information in surveys. Surveys in 1977, 1984, 1993 reveal that university scientists appear to be writing increasingly more articles; that is, respectively 1.0, 1.4, and 2.2 articles per scientist in the last year, while other scientists are writing approximately the same number (about 0.10 articles per scientist).

Other studies show results that are similar to our 1990s averages. As mentioned above, a study in the late 1980s (Mooney 1991) showed 2.1 to 4.3 articles per professional in research universities depending on the discipline, and a recent study (Von Seggern and Jourdain 1996) in three government defense laboratories shows 0.8 journal articles per year per laboratory scientist and engineer.[4]

Examination of articles in libraries (journal tracking) shows that the authorship seems to be shifting further to university scientists (from 62 percent of all articles in 1975 to 75 percent in 1995). This supports the data reported above that was collected from surveys of university scientists. The biggest change is the drop in the proportion of articles that are written by company scientists from 19 percent in 1975 to 10 percent in 1995.

---

[3]In 1965, the number of articles per scientist was estimated to be 0.093 articles (or 10.8 scientists per article written).

[4]Studies of authorship can be biased when comparing over time because the number of authors per article is increasing over time. Averaging reported number of articles written by a number of respondents overestimates the number of articles written per scientist, since more than one co-author could be sampled.

COST OF AUTHORSHIP

The amount of time spent authoring was estimated to be 82 hours per article in 1977 and 80 hours in 1984. We have no comparable data from recent years other than from companies, government laboratories, and agencies where reported time is approximately 100 hours per article. The extrapolated 1977 cost of writing, reworking articles, and resubmission (including salaries of authors and support staff, facilities and postage) is approximately $6,000 per article in 1998.

Authorship encompasses the initial set of activities in the communication cycle, those grouped in our generic functions under composition (see Figure 6). In the development of a scientific journal article under the current system, authorship encompasses literature search, bibliography preparation, manuscript writing, manuscript transcription, graphics, peer edit and review, revision, proofreading, transcribing revisions, manuscript photocopying, dispatching manuscript, reprint orders, and page charge payments, alterations, and reprints.

These activities were used as the basis for estimating the cost of authorship in a study conducted for the National Science Foundation (Green and Hill 1974). In that study, life scientists identified as authors were asked how much time they, their co-authors, and their support staffs spent in preparing a particular journal article. A summary of their responses is shown in Table 11, with a breakdown for the various activities for the initial manuscript and each revision cycle.

Table 11	Time Required for Authorship of Life Science Articles: 1974 (in Hours)					
Activity	Initial Manuscript	First Revision	Second Revision	Third Revision	Fourth Revision	Fifth Revision
Literature search	30.6	4.8	3.5	3.0	2.7	2.5
Preparing bibliography	7.1	1.8	1.7	1.7	1.7	1.7
Writing manuscript	53.5	9.6	5.8	3.6	2.8	2.0
Typing manuscript	7.9	4.8	4.0	3.6	3.5	3.4
Informal internal edit	6.6	3.1	1.9	1.5	1.2	1.0
Formal internal edit	6.9	2.1	2.2	2.2	2.2	2.2
Proofreading typeset manuscript	2.5	1.8	1.7	1.7	1.7	1.7
Subtotal						
Author time	79.1	15.4	10.1	7.5	6.4	5.4
Support time	36.0	12.6	10.7	9.9	9.5	9.2
Proofreading/alteration of galleys (author)	2.5	2.0	2.4	2.4	2.4	2.4

Source: Green and Hill 1974

These data, combined with knowledge of the numbers of articles and of revision cycles, permit estimation of the total author and support time spent on published articles. In addition, one must also account for rejected articles, including time spent reworking articles to be resubmitted to another journal but excluding time spent on articles rejected and not resubmitted. It is estimated that 15 hours of a scientist's time are required, on average, to rework an article after initial rejection.

AUTHORS' GOALS AND INCENTIVES

The motivation to publish in scholarly journals has been examined often, long before electronic journals were a reality or even a possibility. The two primary motivating factors of scholarly authors are 1) recognition for career advancement, including tenure, promotion, and salary increases popularly known as publish-or-perish, and 2) the desire to contribute to the body of knowledge in a field or to the archive of the scholarly knowledge in a field and to be recognized for their contribution by their peers. Several studies in the last 15 years have shown that these are still the primary motivating factors for authors.

Career Advancement

Academicians publish to external audiences far more than scientists from industry and government (see Table 6 in Chapter 5). This partially coincides with Price's observations thirty years earlier that scientists (mainly in academe) "want to write but not read" and the technologists (mainly in industry and government) "want to read but not write" (Price 1975). Since far more academicians publish, the motivation of academic recognition and advancement through tenure and promotion must surely be a major goal in scholarly publishing.

This goal is not new—the phrase, publish-or-perish, was probably first used by Wilson in 1942 (cited in Tenopir 1995), and academic institutions still weigh research output very heavily when making tenure and promotion decisions. A 1986 survey by the American Council of Learned Societies (cited by Lubans 1987) found that 29 percent of academic scholars felt that the pressure to publish was "extremely strong," while an additional 31 percent felt that it was "strong."

In his review of the literature describing motivations and problems with academic pressure to produce, Schauder (1994) concludes that:

> the need by academics to publish in recognized refereed journals is a very important factor supporting the continuation and growth of formal academic publishing. It might be even more important than the need to read

such journals. An academic with a poor publishing record is deemed to be underperforming.

Schauder's (1994) survey of 743 senior academics in Australia, the United States, and the United Kingdom reinforced the perception that career advancement is a major motivator for academic authors. He found that 82 percent felt that the publishing of professional articles was "important" to advancement in their careers, while an additional 14 percent felt such publishing was of "some importance" to their careers.

The goal of publication as a career advancement mechanism may not yet be served by electronic journals since universities have been slow to recognize their scholarly potential. One of the earliest attempts at developing a refereed scholarly electronic journal was the *Mental Workload* journal of the Electronic Information Exchange System (EIES) (Turoff & Hiltz 1982). A major reason for its failure was the unwillingness of authors to contribute to a journal that promised no recognition in tenure or promotion decisions, no royalties, and no role in advancing their reputations or careers.

A small study by Shamp (1992) reinforced the reluctance of universities to recognize electronic journals. He surveyed eighty-five academic users of Comserve, a communications electronic discussion group on Bitnet, to discover factors influencing their willingness to contribute articles to scholarly electronic journals. Seventy-seven percent of the respondents who were Assistant, Associate, or Full Professors "did not believe their institutions would accept electronic publication as evidence of scholarly productivity."

Without a doubt, the success of electronic journals rests on the number and quality of the articles submitted and published. The early adopters of technology surveyed by Shamp (1992) are the most likely candidates to submit electronic articles, and yet:

> sixty percent of the respondents' decisions to submit were in line with their perceptions of their universities' policy on electronic publication—22.1% said their university would accept and that they would submit while 37.1% thought their university would not accept and they would not submit. No respondents indicated they would not submit when they believed their university would accept the publication.

Contributing to Knowledge

While motivation for career advancement may be a pragmatic view of authoring, a more idealistic view is that an author's prime goal is to contribute to the knowledge of his or her discipline. Ideally this is not a one-way process or a one-step process, but an iterative communication process with established peers and at least some of the wider body of readers of scholarly works. Anderson (1993) quotes Harnad's (1992) expression of this loftier communication contribution goal:

> Surely the motive of the true scholar/scientist is to advance human inquiry. And, just as surely, such an enterprise is, and always has been, a collective, cumulative and collaborative one: Scholars publish in order to inform their peers of their findings, and, equally important, to be informed by them in turn, to interact with them, in the cycles of reciprocal influence that constitute an evolving body of scholarly research. In a word, the purpose of scholarly publication is communication with peers and for posterity.

Feedback in an electronic environment can be instantaneous and from a wider group of readers than the established peer group. Implied in this communication function is the frequently mentioned advantage of becoming closer to readers and of fostering more collaboration, which even now in its incipient form is already beginning to change the fundamental nature of research.

Authors will be able to enter into a dialog, or dialectic, with readers as research and writing evolve through continuous interaction (Lederberg 1993). A collaboratory or electronic community, as expounded by Wulf (1993), is composed of scientists who both cooperate and compete and who do their own reviewing in an open manner "that concatenates publication and responses" (Judson 1994).

In the ideal view, electronic publications will include all evolving versions of an article, from preliminary drafts through a number of revisions to an accepted final version, replacing the old preprint function. In a more revolutionary mode, it could also include comments from referees; criticism and suggestions from readers; rebuttals, corrections and retractions; and perhaps even raw data (Judson 1994).

Electronic publishing facilitates this cooperation among peers as it incorporates the long-term functions of the scholarly invisible college. Writing evolves from an idea to a research or conference report, to a preprint, and finally to a formally published article, honed and supported at every stage by peer involvement and cooperation. Invisible colleges by definition are exclusive groups, as graphically described by Price in *Science Since Babylon* (1975):[5]

> [Scientists] get by in what are now called 'invisible colleges' of little groups of peers. They are small societies of everybody who is anybody in each little particular specialty. These groups are very efficient for their purpose and, somewhere along the line, people eventually write up their work so that

---

[5]These views show the lack of appreciation that non-authors extensively read scholarly articles.

graduate students can read it and get to the research front. By the time it gets published, however, it is so old that all the good research juice has been squeezed out of it, so it is not worth reading if you are really in the business at the research front.

Publishing for Posterity

Communicating with contemporary readers is not the only motive in formal scholarly publishing. An author's goal may be to ensure a place for himself for posterity by making a journal contribution that becomes part of a discipline's future knowledge base or that ensures personal fame and recognition in his field. This process may be independent of contemporary readers as an author looks ahead to his or her place in history. For this purpose, the process of writing and publishing are essential to the work of a scientific scholar, but a wide readership of contemporaries is not (Schauder 1994).

Taken to an extreme, authors and readers might be completely separated. According to Garcia (1994):

> The view that texts are meant for audiences and thus that an audience, either actual or imagined, is a necessary condition of texts is one of those assumptions that, even if seldom explicitly stated, is generally implicitly accepted in the pertinent literature. Recently this view has come under fire, however, from some authors who claim that their business is not with an audience at all. Practitioners of the *nouveau roman*, such as Alain Robbe-Grillet, believe that for a writer the aim is to write, and whether what the writer writes is read or not is actually unimportant. From this point of view, an audience is neither necessary nor important for the author, and if that is so, then its consideration could neither be necessary nor important for the existence or understanding of a text.[6]

He argues that there is always at least one audience for every publication – the author as his own audience. Perhaps this extreme view is limited to fiction or philosophy and is not true in scientific publishing, but authors may not have an audience clearly in mind when they write. The needs of readers may be inconsequential when compared to the author's need to publish or the urge to record for posterity.

---

[6]This is precisely the reason given by Fritz Machlup when asked why he was engaged in writing a 12-volume series on information while approaching his 80th birthday.

Protection of Intellectual Effort

Although it is not an explicit motivating factor for publishing, protection of ideas from theft or misuse is implied if the primary goals of authors are to be achieved. It is a goal that is shared by publishers, although publishers and authors may be in conflict over who owns the published intellectual property. Protection against unauthorized copying, plagiarism, being quoted out of context, or theft of ideas concerns authors in all disciplines. Justified or not, the fear seems to be greater with electronic publications.

Staking a claim to a research idea before it can be formally published or claimed by someone else is more easily done electronically. In competitive fields, the desire to get credit for an idea, or process, or discovery has a long tradition. It is tied to the motivation of recognition by peers and by posterity. Although only the expression of ideas and not the ideas themselves can be copyrighted, scholarly research has a long tradition of granting credit to the first person to publish an idea. Electronic communication has changed the traditional channels of going public and may even allow some ideas to go public before they should. (The cold fusion issue is a good example.) More cautious researchers may be penalized.

On the other hand, some readers may not consider casual mention in an electronic forum as staking a claim. To protect a researcher's interest, all readers must be made aware that using someone's ideas that have been articulated in a casual manner on a listserv without ascription or taking credit for another's work is "intellectual theft" (Hauptman and Motin 1994.)

If authors' prime motivators of career advancement and securing a place for themselves in their discipline are to be met in an electronic environment, the work of an author must be clearly differentiated from the interactive comments or extensions by readers. Even in co-authored publications, the work by the authors of the institute or organization must be easily identifiable.

Copyright laws originated to protect the investment by both authors and publishers of time, creativity, and capital. In the United States, copyright is guaranteed in the Constitution by giving Congress the power "to promote the progress of science and useful arts . . . by securing for limited times to authors and inventors the exclusive rights to their respective writings and discoveries." According to Rawlins (1993), in book publishing that protection is eroding rapidly because "there is no long-term copy protection scheme suitable for marketable electronic books; the user can always scan the book and copy it perfectly. It will merely take longer to make the first copy".

With electronic distribution of journals the process is even easier since entire articles can be quickly downloaded and imported into a reader's word processor. The potential for misuse is vast.

Some of the copyright abuse in scholarly electronic communication is surely unintentional. In an interactive environment of give and take with informal-looking communications, the author of an original idea may be obscured. As lines blur between readers, authors, and publishers, a reader may appropriate an idea or, mistakenly, an entire interactive document. In this situation, the author's motivation of self-protection is not best served by informal or highly interactive electronic publications.

Outright plagiarism is a topic that is gaining renewed concern, although some maintain that the fear is unfounded (Amiran, Unsworth, and Chaski 1992). Still, downloading full articles is easy to do and ". . . from there, it is easy to change a sentence here and there and incorporate the downloaded information into one's own research paper and claim it as one's own work. How to catch plagiarism is a major problem" (Reichel 1989). Reichel calls for librarians to teach ethics of information use to students along with techniques for accessing electronic information.

Plagiarism may be less of a problem with formal electronic journals that appear at regular intervals and have copyright notices clearly displayed than with e-mail communications (Bailey 1991 cited in Amiran, Orr, and Unsworth 1991).

The fear of having their intellectual output read out of context or quoted out of context is one that is not often articulated by authors, but may be present none-the-less. Some authors fear in particular the capabilities offered in electronic versions of texts that make viewing small segments of texts so easy. The ability to read only chunks or paragraphs from multiple articles on a topic is seen as an advantage by readers of electronic texts, but as a disadvantage by some authors (Tenopir 1988).

Involvement of a formal editorial and formal publishing function may help authors to protect themselves from copyright infringement, theft of ideas, or plagiarism. Commercial publishers and authors share a common goal in this situation. Amiran and Unsworth (1991) quote Bailey (1991) who points out that

> perhaps the situation is worst [sic] for electronic communications that bear the least resemblance to traditional print journals. . . . Some print publishers are already moving into electronic text, and if they become a major force in this medium (or if software companies do), then some of these questions might eventually become moot or meaningless. (Amiran, Orr, and Unsworth 1991)

Other Factors

Thus, the two primary motivating factors of career advancement and contribution to the discipline are independent of the publication medium. In addition, authors see advantages in electronic publishing that are not present in traditional print publishing. Many of these advantages, which are outlined below, result in a publication more closely aligned with the needs of readers.

- timeliness (articles are published more quickly)
- less pressure to condense the length of articles in order to conform to arbitrary page restrictions
- lower cost—no need to pay for publication or reprints
- increased opportunities for non-traditional writers or topics
- errata can be connected to the original text and authors who change their names can update previous publications, and
- financial reward does not seem to be an important motivating factor for authors of scholarly articles. (Amiran, Orr, and Unsworth 1991; DeLoughry 1989; Judson 1994; Seiler and Raben 1981)

The last point may be based on the pragmatic realization that financial reward for scholarly publishing is unlikely. Only 4 percent of Schauder's (1994) respondents felt personal financial return was "important," while an additional 17 percent felt it had "some importance." Seventy-six percent had never been paid for an article in a journal, while another 19 percent had been charged a fee to publish in a journal at least once.

FACTORS THAT AFFECT AUTHOR'S CHOICE OF JOURNALS

Numerous factors are involved in the process that scientists use to select journals to which to submit articles. Uppermost is the selection of a journal with the appropriate subject scope. Kochen and Tagliacozzo (1974), in a discussion of these factors, stated that authors selected the most prestigious journals with the largest circulation and the shortest publication lag. They also reported research that suggested that, in pre-paradigm fields, authors' selection of an appropriate journal for publishing was more difficult than in fields with more highly-developed identities.

In the same article, Kochen and Taliacozzo described a hypothetical service, primarily for novice authors or authors new to a field. This service would aid in the selection of a journal to which to submit an article. It would use a mathematical model to calculate a score for the desirability or relative preference of a given journal as a publishing outlet for a given article. The model incorporated the following variables:

- relevance based on readers sharing authors' interests
- high acceptance rate

- wide, appropriate, circulation (the total number of copies perhaps being of secondary importance to the type of readership)

- prestige, perhaps measured by journal age, and

- short publication lag.

With regard to publication lag (or *publication speed*—a term preferred by some journal publishers), Garvey, Lin, and Tomita (1972) reported that journal article authors who had previously disseminated their research findings via conference and other channels were less interested in speed of article publication than those who had not done so.

A common thread throughout these and other studies is the stated importance of concepts such as *prestige, quality, and value.* These difficult-to-define concepts were among those treated in a study by McDonald (1979) investigating the factors, or attributes, that were related to scientists' selection of particular journals in which to publish their research findings. This study looked at three different types of variables potentially related to authors' decisions:

- directly measurable journal characteristics such as price, frequency of publication, and publication speed

- variables describing authors' past experience with the journal such as number of articles submitted and number of articles read, and

- subjectively scored journal attributes representing both quantitative and qualitative concepts such as emphasis on methodology, benefit to career, perceptions of price, and publication delay.

Through surveys conducted with authors of *Cancer Research* and *Astrophysical Journal*, it was found that the third group of journal attributes was more effective in discriminating between journals considered for publishing and those not considered for publishing. Based on their perceived importance and on their ability to discriminate among groups of similar journals, the following seven journal attributes were selected for analysis:

- the proportion of people I wanted to read my paper who were regular readers of this journal

- the benefit to my career, professional prestige, job status, or salary of publishing in this journal

- the quality of the printed appearance of papers published by this journal

- the competence and fairness of this journal's refereeing of submitted papers' scientific content

- the speed with which this journal publishes a paper once its author is notified of the paper's acceptance

- the probability of my paper's acceptance by this journal, and

- this journal's emphasis on theory.

Author-supplied data regarding the importance of these attributes[7] was combined with authors' scores[8] on the same attributes for journals similar to *Cancer Research* and *Astrophysical Journal*. To test the hypothesis that authors' relative preferences for journals can be simulated using basic utility theory concepts, McDonald used a functional formula to calculate utility scores. He found that the utility scores calculated using the model were significantly higher for *Cancer Research* and *Astrophysical Journal* than for journals identified by these journals' authors as being similar to them. Additional analysis suggested that the utility scores for other journals considered for publishing were higher than the utility scores for journals not considered for publishing.

Respondents to two comparable surveys in the 1970s were asked to note the importance of various factors in their selection of a journal in which to publish. In both instances, the scientists were physicists—the first study surveyed physicists worldwide, while the second focused on authors published in the *Astrophysical Journal*. For comparison importance was rated "not important" as 1, "very low and somewhat low" as 2; "marginally important" and "neither high nor low" as 3; and "very important" as 4, and "somewhat high and very high" as 5. Average ratings of importance are given in Table 12.

Interestingly, factors dealing with readership rated highest in both surveys. Speed of publishing and refereeing were rated highly in both surveys, namely second and fourth, and fourth and third respectively. Quality was also rated nearly equally in each survey, namely fifth and sixth. In the worldwide survey, the publisher's reputation was found to be far more important than whether the journal was published by a member society (i.e., 4.12, and 1.76 average ratings of importance). Similar results were observed by Garvey, Lin, and Nelson (1970) where authors in their surveys indicated that they selected a particular journal largely because the audience was appropriate, the journal publishing speed was good, and the editorial policy was desirable.

---

[7]Attribute importance was ranked on a zero-to-six scale.
[8]Supplied by authors on a five-point "very high" to "very low" scale.

Table 12	Average Importance Ratings of Factors Used by Authors for Selecting Journals: 1976, 1979

Factors	Worldwide Physics Authors	Factors	Astrophysical Journal Authors
Circulation	4.60	Audience might	4.95
Speed of Publication	4.40	Problems of acceptance	4.27
Publisher's reputation	4.12	Refereeing good	3.35
Refereeing arrangements	3.93	Speed of publishing	3.24
Quality of production	3.70	Benefit career	3.16
Available within own institution	3.58	Quality of appearance	3.15
Frequency of publication	3.42	Not asked to shorten	2.55
Page charges	3.30	Little effort for changes	2.15
Charges for off-prints	2.20	Speed of notification	2.15
Price of journal	2.16	Emphasis on theory	2.05
Tradition within dept.	1.86	Emphasis on methods	2.03
Published by member society	1.76	Emphasis on data	1.69
Instructed to do so	1.52	Low or no page charges	1.55

Sources: Institute of Physics 1976; McDonald 1979

In the Institute of Physics survey, all of the economic issues were rated at the bottom in importance. At that time, the price of the journal did not seem to be a particularly important consideration, rating an average 2.16 in importance. In the survey of astrophysicists, issues of the interaction with the publisher such as "would not be asked to shorten," "little effort required for changes," and "speed of notification, " were all rated low in importance. Having low or no page charges was rated very low in importance (1.55 average rating). In another survey, (Green and Hill 1974) life sciences authors indicated they would be willing to pay $45[9] more in page charges in return for a 50 percent reduction in publication time from an 8.7 month average, thus providing an indication of the value placed on publishing time.

---

[9]In 1998 dollars.

MANUSCRIPT EXCHANGE WITH PUBLISHERS

We have already demonstrated that authors spent an average of 80 to 100 hours in writing and other author-related activities to which support staff, prior to electronic advances, added approximately 40 additional hours. In the late 1970s an author survey (King, McDonald and Roderer 1981) showed that publishers rejected approximately 44 percent of the manuscripts submitted to them.[10] Of those rejected, nearly two-thirds were re-submitted to other journals, while the rest were simply dropped. Some manuscripts are accepted without revision, but most require at least one revision, with a very few being revised from two to five times. For those in which a revision is required, the average number of revisions is 1.2 revisions per accepted manuscript. At that time, the average elapsed time from the first submission to the date of publication was 10.3 months.[11] Subsequent studies showed that publishing times seemed to decrease until the early 1980s, at which time the trend reversed.

A detailed stochastic model of the interchange between authors and publishers was developed in which probabilities were established for various events in the flow of (or responsibility for) manuscripts in terms of acceptance, rejection, or modification (King, McDonald and Roderer 1981). Stations in the model represent the author, managing editor, technical reviewer, rejection, publication in the original journal, and submission to another journal. Examples of transition probabilities are displayed in Figure 8. The model permits the simulation of a range of input, process, and output conditions including considerations of timing and of querying by participants of one another. The results show that electronic transmission of manuscripts can only reduce the publication time marginally because most of the delays occur while the manuscript awaits action by editors and authors.

---

[10]The rejection rates were highest in psychology and lowest in the environmental sciences.
[11]The longest average time was in the field of mathematics, and the shortest was "other" sciences.

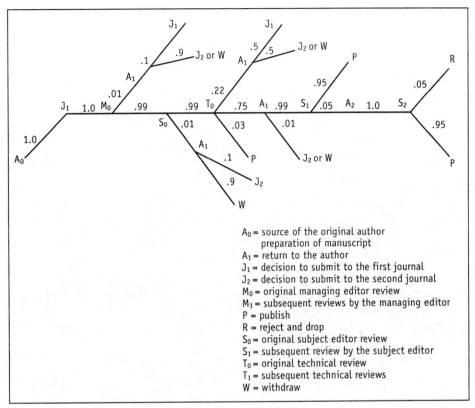

Figure 8. Tree diagram of transition probabilities—Markov chain.

CHAPTER 7

Readership of Scientific Scholarly Journals

INTRODUCTION

This chapter discusses the amount of readership of scholarly journal articles. Most of the evidence is extracted from our surveys conducted from 1977 to 1998. In every survey we conducted, scientists were observed to read many more scholarly articles than any other type of document. Journals are read more than other types of publication because they cover a range of topics, editors attempt to maintain content quality, the information is relatively current, and the articles serve a variety of purposes such as research, teaching, and administration. Also presented are estimates of the extent of readership in recent years and trends in readership; readers' goals and incentives for reading; the usefulness and value of reading scholarly articles; and reasons that scientists choose the journals to which they subscribe.

EXTENT OF READERSHIP

A readership study done for the University of Tennessee, Hodges Library (1993) and four studies done for companies (1994–1998) show that readership of scientific scholarly journals is appreciable (i.e., 188 average readings per year per university scientist[1] and 106 readings for scientists elsewhere). Not only do these scientists extensively read scholarly articles, they spend a substantial amount of time reading these articles (i.e., an average of 182 and 88 hours per scientist per year respectively).

Other studies report similar results. For example, Meadows (1974) found that medical researchers read approximately 7.4 papers per week (approximately 380 per year), and engineers read approximately 1.5 papers per week (approximately 75 per year). Pinelli, Glassman, Barclay, and Oliu (1989) observed that engineers read an average of 6.7 readings of articles per month (approximately 80 readings annually). The engineering averages of 75 and 80 readings compare to 80 readings in our recent surveys. A number of studies validate the amount of time spend reading and, therefore, the amount of reading. These study results range from 2.2 hours per month per scientist (engineers—approximately 26 hours per year) to 24 hours per month for cancer researchers or approximately 288 hours per year. The median of the 17 averages is 11.7 hours per month or 140 hours per year. Since readings tend to average less than one hour per reading, the amount of time spent reading appears to validate the assertion that journals are well read.

We found abundant evidence that scholarly journals are not only widely read, but are extremely useful and important to scientists' work, whether that work be teaching, research, administration, or other activities. Furthermore, the value of the information was clearly established, whether measured by what users were willing to pay for it (purchase value) or by the benefits derived from its use (use value). In addition, information attributes (e.g., relevance, quality, accuracy) and communication attributes (e.g., availability, accessibility, ease of use, or cost to use) were documented as contributing to the use, usefulness, and value of the information. These results are discussed in detail below.

The amount of reading by scientists suggests that articles and journals are well read in the aggregate. In fact, among nine fields of science—physical sciences, mathematics and statistics, computer sciences, environmental sciences, engineering, life sciences, psychology, social sciences, and other fields—the average number of readings per article is estimated to range between 500 and 1,500. On average, there are about 900 readings per article and scientific journal experiences over 100,000 article readings, but the distribution for both article readings and journal readings is highly skewed. In other words, many scientific specialties have few scientists, and journals in such specialties therefore have relatively few read-

---

[1]We define "reading" as going beyond the table of contents, the title and the abstract to the body of the article. We count each time an article is read as a single reading (King et al. surveys 1977–1998).

ings. A small number of journals—*Science* is one—have large circulations with readings numbering in the millions.

Early Misunderstanding Concerning Reading

During the 1960s there was a great deal of confusion concerning how much scholarly journals are read and their usefulness and value. The misunderstanding was largely based on three ways in which the amount of reading of articles was presented. The first way assumed that citations, and thus citation counts, were actually measures of total reading of articles and journals. Several studies reported statistics on the amount of reading based on samples of scientists, but did not extrapolate estimates to the entire population from which samples were chosen. Finally, some researchers reported the proportion of readings of all article copies distributed as being an indicator of the usefulness of journals.

Schauder (1994) and Lancaster (1978) summarize some of the studies that suggested low readership. Reports of surveys conducted by the American Psychological Association (APA)[2] showed that the average article in the APA's journals was read by only 17 people, while Williams (1975) stated that chemical journals had an average readership of only 10 persons per article. Lancaster, in reviewing the APA studies, reported that, within two months of publication, about one-half of journal articles were read or scanned by 1 percent or less of the random sample of psychologists, and, at the highest end, that no research report is likely to be read by more than 7 percent of the sample of psychologists.

The problem with these conclusions is that reported results of both the average readings per article and the proportion of copies read are estimates from sample observations only and include only current reading of the articles (i.e., within 2 months of publication).[3] After discussing these limitations with William Garvey, a co-investigator for the APA studies, it was concluded that the total reading (from the entire population from which the samples were drawn and also projected over the life of the articles) is about 25 to 50 times that observed in the sample and

---

[2]Actually in one report (Garvey and Griffith 1963) it was reported that the APA journal articles were read an average of 520 times by psychologists. The psychologists averaged reading 58 articles from the APA journals which averaged 480 articles per title. Thus, they read approximately 12 percent of the total articles received (King and Bryant 1971).

[3]The surveys involved statistical samples of psychologists (and later other scientists). Respondents were provided Tables of Contents and asked to indicate the articles that they had read. It is noted that these estimates are of "articles read," whereas, our estimates are usually of number of "article readings," which can involve repeated readings of a particular article by a scientist.

much more when reading from reprints and other sources are included. We estimated in 1977 that approximately 865 readings per article were obtained from all sources for psychology; that is, 642 readings from personal subscriptions, 216 from library copies, and 7 from authors (King, McDonald, and Roderer 1981).

In 1977, King Research was asked by John Bailar (editor) to evaluate the *Journal of the National Cancer Institute (JNCI)* (King, McDonald, and Olsen 1978). This provided us with an opportunity to replicate the Garvey and Griffith (1963) method of surveying readership from Tables of Contents and comparing those results with other estimates. As it turns out, the *JNCI* was a highly-read journal as were other journals reporting cancer research. A total of 521 responses were analyzed from a mailing of 953 questionnaires, of which 121 were not qualified or not locatable (i.e., 63 percent response rate). At that time, the *JNCI* annually published approximately 420 articles in 12 issues. The Table of Contents of 37 articles for one issue, published three months prior to the survey, was included as part of the questionnaire. Respondents were asked to "circle the page numbers of all the items which you read in this issue of *JNCI*."

The average number of readings per article by the 521 respondents was 52 (46 was the median). All of the articles were read at least 11 times, and one was read 151 times. Approximately one-fourth of the respondents did not read any of the articles, most of these being non-subscribers (80 percent). Projected over the entire population sampled and over time, the average number of readings per article is estimated at approximately 1,800 readings per article, with an average time per reading of 50 minutes. The 1,800 readings per article is much higher than the average 638 readings per article for science journals in general in 1977, but time spent per article is approximately the same: 54 minutes vs. 50 minutes.

Schauder and Lancaster also mention other studies that suggest low reading of articles. For example, subscribers to the *Journal of Organic Chemistry* glanced at or began to read approximately 17 percent of the papers in a typical issue (Moore 1972), while a pre-1960s study indicated that a single article in a specialized periodical is of interest to only 10 percent of the workers in the subject area covered by the journal (Astle 1989). Baruch and Bhagat (1975) also found that the average journal subscriber reads fewer than one percent of the articles received. Studies such as these led many to believe that scientific scholarly journals were no longer viable and needed to be replaced by some alternative (see Chapter 2).

Yet the low proportion of articles distributed that are not read is not inconsistent with our results. For example, our 1977 survey results suggested that the average readings per article copy distributed was only 0.12 readings, yet the average readings per article was 638. Our recent data show that the average reading in a personal subscription is 13.4 readings per journal per scientist.[4] With an average of 123 articles per journal, this means that one of nine article copies distributed is read. For library journals on the other hand, the average is much higher (e.g., 1.1 times per article distributed in academic libraries).

Trends in Readership

Recent surveys show that scientists continue to read scientific scholarly journals extensively (see Table 13). Scientists at the University of Tennessee average 188 readings of scholarly articles per year (1993), while scientists in companies in our studies average 106 scholarly articles readings annually (1994-98). While these results reflect statistical surveys from organizations that chose to ask us to conduct a survey, they are similar to results from national surveys of scientists performed for the National Science Foundation in 1977 and 1984.

Survey results for years other than 1977 and 1984 represent samples of scientists selected for studies in universities, companies, government agencies, and national laboratories as well as for studies of journal readership conducted for *Science* and the *Journal of the National Cancer Institute*. Thus readership in those years reflects the composition of scientists in organizations that requested studies (e.g.,

Table 13	Average Number of Scholarly Article Readings Per Year by University and Non-University Scientists: 1977-1998 (Readings per Scientist per Year)					
	YEARS OF OBSERVATION					
	1977	**1978–1983**	**1984**	**1985–1989**	**1990–1993**	**1994–1998**
University	150	—	172	—	188	—
Non-University	90	91	99	75	80	106

Sources: King, McDonald, and Roderer 1981; Tenopir and King 1997; Griffiths and King 1993; King et al. surveys 1977–1998

[4]Assuming that the average journal publishes 123 articles per year that are sent to 5,800 subscribers, it would distribute 713,400 individual copies of articles. If the average number of readings per article is still 900 readings, the total would be 110,700 readings for the 123 articles, which means that the average number of readings per article copy distributed is 0.155 readings or about one of 6½ articles distributed.

a dominance of chemists in selected companies, medical researchers at the National Institutes of Health, and physicists in national labs) and potential journal readers (e.g., cancer researchers). Therefore, the differences in reading over the twenty-two years may be an accurate predictor of the situation in other sciences, or they may reflect differences in composition of the study participants rather than actual trends. The amount of article reading by scientists outside of universities, however, appears to be relatively constant and may even be increasing with university scientists. While university scientists tend to read more on average than other scientists, the total number of articles read is undoubtedly far greater in industry and government than in universities because of the greater number of scientists employed there.

COST OF READING

The average amount of time spent reading scholarly articles has remained relatively constant over the years as shown in Table 14. The times are estimated by multiplying the average time per reading by the estimated annual number of readings. The time spent reading is validated from other methods of observing reading time (King, McDonald, and Roderer 1981; Griffiths and King 1993). We have no explanation for the higher 1984 survey estimates of average time per reading since the questions were worded the same in every survey. Other studies over the years have shown similar results as depicted in Table 15.

Table 14	Average Time Spent Reading Scholarly Scientific Journals by University and Non-University Scientists: 1977-1998 (Hours per Scientist per Year)					
	YEARS OF OBSERVATION					
	1977	1978–1983	1984	1985–1989	1990–1993	1994–1998
University	120	—	259	—	182	—
Non-University	70	86	101	70	68	88

Sources: King, McDonald, and Roderer 1981; Tenopir and King 1997; Griffiths and King 1993; King et al. surveys 1977–1998

Table 15	Time Spent Reading Journals by Scientists and Engineers by Field of Science: 1960-1998

Field of Science	Hours per Month Reading Journals	Hours per Month Reading All Literature
Physical Sciences	9.0	
	25.1	36.8
	11.7	24.3
	4.8–11.7	
	24.0	
Engineers	<4.0	
	5.0	
	19.1	45.1
	2.2–3.5	8.6–13.8
Life Sciences	8.1	
	24.1	
Psychology	4.8	
	13.9[a]	27.7
All Fields	6.8	
	7.8–10.4	15.6–20.8
	11.7[a]	23.4
	9.2	

[a]Computed as one-half of the total literature.

Sources: Operations Research Group, Case Institute of Technology 1960; Weil 1977; Allen 1966; King, McDonald, and Olsen 1978; American Psychological Association 1963; King, McDonald, and Roderer 1978; Hall, Clague, and Aitchison 1972; Pinelli et al. 1989; Brown 1999; King et al. surveys 1993-1998.

The average time spent reading an article ranges from 30 minutes across several fields to nearly 4 hours in mathematics (King, McDonald, and Roderer 1981). Related data on the level and purpose of reading do not provide any direct justification for the amount of reading time spent by mathematicians; in fact, they indicate that a higher proportion of articles in mathematics are read simply for the idea and for a variety of purposes. One explanation might be the length of mathematics articles which, at 10.2 pages, are considerably longer than the overall average length of 7.5 pages (1975). Reading time is also high in both the social sciences and other sciences. In the social sciences, we again find a relatively low level of intensity of reading, many purposes of use, and even lengthier articles (13.3 pages). In other sciences, the uses mentioned are the more general, time-consuming ones.

READERS' GOALS

Clearly, not all of the goals or concerns of authors are shared by readers. Some are in direct conflict; while others may be shared in an electronic environment whereas they were not in a traditional print world; still others are important to both groups. Finally, readers have additional unique goals.

Olsen examines journal-reading habits for professors of chemistry, sociology, and humanities as well as their requirements for electronic journals. Olsen found that academic readers unanimously find journal literature to be "indispensable" to their work. They read journals for many reasons, including gathering background knowledge on a topic, current awareness, and looking for specific facts or items. Chemists use literature the most frequently—62 percent read journals daily (Olsen 1993).

When preparing to do research in a new area such as preparing a grant proposal or writing a manuscript, readers use retrospective literature as well as current articles. They scan or browse through vast amounts of material, using articles to trigger new ideas.

Olsen found that the parts of an article that are ultimately read or used to determine pertinence vary with the subject discipline of the reader. Chemists most often look first at the abstracts and the figures including captions; sociologists, however, look at the abstract, introduction, conclusion, and figures; while humanists either scan the entire article or look at the first few paragraphs and footnotes.

When an article is deemed useful, chemists typically do not read the entire article; in fact, they often read the interesting parts out of sequential order. Humanists are the most likely to read the entire article in sequence, probably because articles in their fields do not have the regular structure that articles in chemistry or social sciences usually exhibit.

Olsen's findings suggest that the concerns of authors that electronic publishing will lead to sections of their works being read out of context are not only valid, but are happening already in the print environment. Chemists and many social scientists do not always read an entire print article, but extract the information they need from the sections they deem useful.

These same scholars, however, indicated to Olsen that skimming articles in print does not result in losing context. Instead, they skim to get a feeling of the whole article and place the parts in which they are interested into the context of the whole. They expressed concern that scrolling on a computer screen does not retain the same level of context; neither does it facilitate the browsing that is so important to them. In this instance, the concerns of academic readers mesh with those of the authors.

Olsen's findings also suggest that scholars will embrace electronic versions, but only if they serve real fundamental needs. She concludes that:

> while scholars may express their purposes as 'finding the comprehensive background knowledge on a topic,' or 'browsing to keep up to date' or 'finding articles in my research areas,' their actual purposes in interacting with the literature are learning, creative thinking, and analytical thinking. This is a crucial distinction because functions such as selecting articles or browsing the latest literature appear to be tasks which a computer can be programmed to perform well, but in practice the computer performs them quickly, but not well. Assuming technological barriers (hardware and access to networks) are overcome, electronic publishing serves many interests of readers. Clearly good software design that facilitates searching, scanning, and browsing are crucial elements in electronic publications from the reader's point of view.

Low costs and pricing mechanisms that facilitate this natural behavior are also important factors. Griffiths and King (1993) found that the number of personal journal subscriptions held by scientists has declined as prices have risen, the price of the journal being the most important reason for not purchasing a personal subscription. Surely this applies to electronic journals as well.

Closer Relationships to Authors

As discussed earlier under authors, the advantage of closer relationships between authors and readers is seen as a major advantage of electronic publishing for readers. At the simplest level, a reader's natural impulse to interact with an author can be easily met in electronic publishing. Comments to and from the author can be stored and viewed by others if desired (Seiler and Raben 1981).

At its fullest extension, a new form of cooperative, collaborative writing would "entwine ideas and response to them (more ideas) in a totally new vision of the cumulative scholar's journal" (Okerson 1992). Harnad (1990) calls this "scholarly skywriting;" Lederberg (1993) calls it "a dialectic;" and Judson (1994) sees it as a revolution that moves scholarly work from a hierarchical model to an egalitarian one.

But readers' goals of learning and keeping up in their field are not always best met by collaboration and interaction. As articulated by Price (1975) and demonstrated in the Griffiths, Carroll, King, Williams, and Sheetz study (1991), not all readers want to write or even to be known to the authors they read. Anonymous reading of the experts' polished work is still a valuable goal of many readers. They often want to annotate, underline, and make notes about an article, but not for public consumption (Olsen, 1993). Traditional publishing models support this behavior by creating a buffer between readers and authors.

THE USEFULNESS AND VALUE OF READING SCHOLARLY ARTICLES

In this section we discuss evidence of the purposes for which scientific scholarly journals are read and the importance of information in achieving these purposes. We also provide several indicators of the consequences of reading these articles on scientists' research, teaching, and other activities. The consequences are measured in terms of how the information affects the quality, speed, and cost of these activities. With information outputs serving as a measure of work output, five indicators of productivity are compared with the amount of reading to see if the amount of reading is positively correlated with productivity. Finally, we examine whether achievers in organizations tend to read more than non-achievers. Throughout this section we distinguish between university and non-university scientists because both their work and their reading habits are somewhat different.

Scholarly articles are read for a variety of purposes ranging from self-education or keeping up with a discipline to applying the information to ongoing research or teaching. This means that one might read an article when it is first published out of general interest, but re-read it one or more times later to apply the information when a need arises. In fact, only around 60 percent of total readings represent articles being read for the first time. Thus, 188 readings per year by university scientists might involve only 110 articles.[5]

We find from questions dealing with the most recent reading of journal articles that the time spent reading an article ranges from a few minutes to hours. Most

---

[5]The question leading to estimates of amount of reading was: "In the past month, approximately how many of each of the following types of documents have you read in connection with your work? Reading is defined as going beyond the title, contents page, and abstract of the document. A reading should be counted every time you pick up the document to read; you may have many readings of any given document, and you do not need to read the entire document to count it as a reading." Two designated responses are "professional or scholarly journal articles" and "trade journals." Only the former is counted.

readings of articles (about 60 percent) take place within six months of publication. Nevertheless, many of those articles are re-read later for scientific research or teaching purposes. For example, 37 percent of the scientists who read articles more than two years old were not reading them for the first time. The amount of readings of articles diminishes slowly over time much like a nuclear decay curve. Most quick reading involves recently published articles, while most in-depth reading is of older articles. In other words, a substantial amount of readings are for the purpose of current awareness or professional development.

Usefulness of Journals to University Scientists

University scientists were asked several questions concerning the last article they read. One critical incident question concerned the purposes for which they used or planned to use the information.[6] Over one-half of the readings were for current awareness or professional development. When applied to work, the information is frequently used to support research (75 percent) and teaching (41 percent). Administration accounted for 13 percent of the total. Brown (1999) also found that scientists at the University of Oklahoma relied on journals more for research than for teaching. These scientists also used the information to prepare formal publications and formal talks or presentations (32 percent of readings).

Readers were asked to rate the importance of the information read in achieving teaching or research objectives, with a rating scale of 1 (not at all important) to 7 (absolutely essential), with 4 being somewhat important. Scientists reading for input to teaching rated the importance of the information to achieving teaching objectives at 4.8. The information appears to be slightly more important for research (5.0). Both ratings are above the rating of 'somewhat important,' but well below 'absolutely essential.' Over the period of a year, the scientists indicated that an average of thirteen readings per scientist were absolutely essential to their teaching, while twenty-three readings were absolutely essential to research.

Usefulness of Journals to Non-University Scientists

While non-university scientists read scholarly journals less frequently and spend less time reading them, the journal literature is, nevertheless, extremely important to their work. Comparable surveys in companies (e.g., Bell Laboratories), government agencies (e.g., National Institutes of Health), and national laboratories (e.g.,

---

[6]Totals do not add to 100 percent because respondents were permitted multiple responses.

Oak Ridge National Labs) provide evidence of the use, usefulness, and value of scholarly journal information in these environments (Griffiths and King 1993). Scholarly journals are read an average of 106 times per year by these scientists. They spend an average of twelve hours acquiring the articles and eighty-eight hours reading them. Approximately 30 percent of the readings are primarily for current awareness and professional development. Most of the readings were for background information research (26 percent), conducting primary research (17 percent), conducting other R&D activities (11 percent), and management and other (3 percent). Readings for communications-related activities include consulting or giving advice (4 percent), writing (7 percent), and making presentations (3 percent).

These scientists were asked to rate the importance of several resources used in performing various work activities. These resources include computing equipment/workstations, other equipment/instrumentation, information found in documents (including articles), support staff (e.g., technicians), information staff, and advice from consultants or colleagues. The importance ratings were 1 to 5 (1—not at all important, 3—neutral, 5—absolutely essential). Information in documents is found to be very important for the scientists' work. For primary research, information in documents had an average importance rating of 4.03, second among resources only to computing at 4.11. The importance of this information to other R&D activities is rated highest among the resources, with a 3.87 average rating. For communication-related activities this information had the highest or second highest average ratings: writing (3.76—highest), consulting/advising (3.60—second), and presentations (3.31—third). It appears that this information is also very important to professional development (4.05—highest among the resources).

Our recent surveys merely reflect the findings of earlier studies. For example, an American Psychological Association survey found that journals were rated highest in importance in furnishing the required scientific information among sixteen types of publications, scientific meetings, and personal communication (APA 1964). Menzel (1970) found that chemists used different sources depending on the purpose of seeking information. For deliberate searching, articles are mentioned most frequently as the main source for information sought. Articles also rank first for serendipitous acquisition of useful information and second for "brushing up."

Value of Scholarly Journals

Two different types of value result from the information provided in scholarly articles: the purchase value and the use value (Machlup 1979). Purchase value is what scientists are willing to pay for the information in terms of money exchanged and the time expended in obtaining and reading the information. Use value is the consequences of using the information.[7] With scholarly journals, the purchase value equals an average of nearly $6,000 per scientist per year,[8] and the use value is estimated at over $25,000 per scientist. Both estimates represent the lower boundaries of value. The purchase dollar value is actually higher because it does not include expenditures for purchasing subscriptions, document delivery, or photocopying. The use value is much higher because it does not include all the other favorable outcomes or consequences of reading mentioned above.

The use value is examined through several indicators, including perceived effects on scientists' activities and their productivity. Nearly all university readers (95 percent) indicated some favorable outcomes from some of their readings. They said two-thirds of the readings improved the quality of teaching, research, or other activity for which they read the article. They also indicated that reading helped them perform the activity better (33 percent of readings), faster (14 percent), or saved them time or money (19 percent).

In our most recent surveys (1993–1998) we found that the average university scientist purchased 3.9 journal subscriptions a year, and the average scientist outside the university purchased 2.4 subscriptions a year. The average university scientist spent 182 hours a year reading articles, while the average scientist outside the university spent 88 hours reading articles, plus another 12 hours obtaining those articles. Even assuming that the average journal subscription is $300 a year and the average scientist's compensation is $48 an hour actually spent working, the value of the time spent obtaining and reading journals is much greater than the cost of the journals. Since a scientist's time is a scarce and valuable resource, his or her willingness to expend it on information found in articles in scholarly publications is an indicator of the value of the information to the scientist (i.e., the purchase value).

Article information appears to affect the research and other work of scientists in several ways. One way is by improving the quality of scientists' activities. To determine this, non-university scientists were asked to indicate the principal activity for which they last read a journal article and to indicate whether the information resulted in better quality of the activity. Approximately two-thirds of the readings are said to have improved the quality. In those instances, they were

---

[7]These two values can vary dramatically from product to product. Gems have a high purchase, but low use value. Air has a low purchase, but high use value.

[8]Estimates are based on compensation (salary, FICA, pension, insurance) plus support costs divided by hours actually worked in a year.

asked to rate the quality before and after the information was read. The ratings are on a scale of 1 to 7 (1—low quality, 4—medium, 7—high). Before the readings, quality of the activity was rated at an average of 4.04 and after at 5.82, a rather remarkable increase in this indicator of the effect of reading on quality. Other indicators of favorable outcomes from reading journal articles follow:

- 32 percent of readings resulted in faster performance or completion of the activity (for activities in which timeliness is applicable—60 percent)

- 42 percent helped reinforce an hypothesis or increased confidence in one's work

- 26 percent resulted in initiating ideas for research

- 23 percent broadened options concerning research, and

- 6 percent narrowed options.

One of the most important outcomes involves productivity of scientists' work. This was examined in two ways. Productivity was observed by the outputs of an activity divided by the time spent on it. Five outputs were measured: number of formal records of research (e.g., lab notes), number of consultations, number of presentations, number of written proposals or plans, and number of formal publications (e.g., articles). All five indicators of productivity were found to be somewhat correlated with the amount of scholarly journal reading (Griffiths and King 1993).

Organizational productivity is affected by cost savings of research and other activities. Savings were found to be achieved from 26 percent of the readings. The average amount of savings based on all readings averaged $300 per reading.[9] The savings were achieved by avoiding the necessity of conducting some primary research; abandoning an unproductive line of research; and modifying research, analysis, or engineering design.

Orr (1970) showed that in the 1950s and 1960s evidence existed for the relationship between the amount of reading and the output and productivity of scientists (Maizell 1958; Operations Research Group, Case Institute of Technology 1960; Shilling and Bernard 1964; Allen and Andrien 1965). Parker, Lingwood, and Paisley (1968) found, using a series of multiple regression analyses, that the amount of information scientists input is the strongest predictor of how much

---

[9]These averages should not be thought of as typical because a very low proportion of readings (1 or 2%) contribute to nearly all the savings observed.

they produce. The relative importance of the various information sources, however, depends on the disciplines involved (Allen 1988 and Allen and Gerstberger 1968).

Improved performance and higher productivity of scientists suggest that their research be recognized through achievement awards, technical awards, and patent recognition. The surveys showed that such award winners read 53 percent more journal articles than non-awardees. Another indicator of competence or achievement is whether scientists are asked to serve on high-level projects or problem-solving teams or special committees. Such persons read about 21 percent more articles than others. In one company, the personnel office agreed to provide the names of twenty-five persons who were considered to be particularly high achievers. These persons read 59 percent more articles than their colleagues. The same finding holds true when compared with cohorts who have similar fields of specialty, equivalent degrees, and years of experience.

No matter where they are employed, scientists who read more articles tend to receive achievement awards and other special honors. In universities, those whose teaching has been honored read approximately 26 percent more articles, while those honored for research read approximately 33 percent more articles. Lufkin and Miller (1966) also found that achievers tend to read more than non-achievers. That does not necessarily suggest a cause and effect relationship between reading and achievement, but it does suggest that this important resource should not be denied those who require it to succeed.

We have tried to illustrate the usefulness and value of scholarly journal articles from a range of viewpoints and perspectives. They all serve to demonstrate that this information is extremely important to scientists in both the university setting and elsewhere. One factor helps explain why scientists must continue to read. Throughout history the amount of recorded knowledge in science doubles approximately every 15 to 17 years. Thus, in 1998, all the knowledge recorded throughout the history of humankind up to 1983 has now doubled, and will likely double again at least by the year 2015. By the time a scientist graduates from college there is a body of knowledge that represents only a fraction of the new knowledge that will be created during one's career. In fact, that base knowledge represents only about one-sixth of the knowledge that scientists must master during their careers. It is no wonder scientists read so much and that those who read more appear to perform better.

FACTORS THAT AFFECT READERS' DECISIONS TO SUBSCRIBE TO A JOURNAL

Chapter 8 provides evidence that traditionally scientists tend to subscribe to journals that they frequently read, while they use their libraries to gain access to journals infrequently read by them. Furthermore, the journal price and distance to the library also have an important bearing in that higher prices require more reading to justify subscribing; thus scientists are more likely to subscribe when further away (in time) from the library.

A study by the Charles River Associates for the National Science Foundation (1978) clearly supports the importance of frequency of reading, journal price, and distance to the library in the decision by physicists to subscribe to their most important journal. The study developed a stochastic model to establish factors that explain the probability of physicists subscribing to their more important journal. The top four factors which explain the probability of subscribing are, in rank order, (1) availability of the journal in a library frequently used by them, (2) convenience of location to their library, (3) the subscription price, and (4) the proportion of articles read. Other factors included whether it was an association journal and the physicist's out-of-pocket expenditures on information services. It is noted that physicists indicated that they read their most important journal an average of seventy times per year, with a range of reported readings from 4 to 1,000 readings annually. It was observed, in 1979, that 61 percent of the readings of physics articles were from the physicist's personal copy, 31 percent from a library copy, 4 percent from an author, and 4 percent from a colleague's copy.

Astrophysicists were asked by McDonald (1979) to rate the importance of the attributes of the *Astrophysical Journal* to their work or research. Average ratings of importance—ranging from 1 (very low) to 5 (very high)—are presented in Table 16 in order of their average importance ratings.

Attributes of information content dominated importance ratings of subscribers to this journal. Price, at this time, was rated low (3.24). A survey of worldwide physicists reported low importance ratings for features of journals such as layout, typestyle, and size, while price was rated at the 2.32 level of importance, echoing the other survey results (Institute of Physics 1976).

Table 16	Average Importance Ratings of Factors Used by Readers to Select Journal Subscriptions: 1979

Factors	Importance Rating
Papers are interesting	4.80
Publication relevant to work	4.70
Papers by people whose work is relevant	4.66
Refereeing is competent and fair	4.44
Publishes unfamiliar work	4.24
Work not obsolete	3.74
Quality of printed appearance	3.48
Price is low	3.24
Presentation of data	3.08
Emphasis on theory	2.94
Emphasis on methods	2.64
Length of papers	2.62
High acceptance rate	2.28

Source: McDonald 1979

CHAPTER 8

Information-Seeking and Readership Patterns

INTRODUCTION

In Chapter 5 we discussed the general communication patterns of scientists: how they spend their time and the extent of their reading and writing. Chapter 6 described authorship trends and costs and discussed scientists' incentives to write journal articles and the factors that affect their selection of journals in which to publish their research results. The next chapter provided in-depth results of readership surveys including the number of articles read by scientists, trends and costs of reading, and the consequences of reading. This chapter addresses the information seeking and readership patterns of scientists based on our surveys.

We found that information-seeking and readership patterns vary dramatically among user groups, distribution means, journals, and even articles within the same journal. Yet the usefulness and value of the information remained high for all of those patterns. Therefore publishers of electronic journals need to recognize, replicate, and even enhance the important attributes of paper journals if they are to serve their readers.

IDENTIFYING AND LOCATING SCHOLARLY ARTICLES

Scholarly articles are identified for reading in five basic ways: browsing, automated searches, citations from the literature, recommendations by other people, and current-awareness tools. Browsing can take place in personal subscriptions, library copies (including journals routed primarily in non-university organizations), and shared office or unit copies. Our surveys show that university scientists identify about 60 percent of their readings by browsing, with a comparable number, 64 percent, for scientists elsewhere. Williams (1993) reports that U.K. chemists also found papers most often by browsing (about 56 percent).

Other methods of identification are used in a similar way by scientists in both types of organizations: automated searches conducted online or from CD-ROM (15 percent of total readings in universities, 11 percent elsewhere); citations found in other articles and books (7 percent in each); colleagues, authors, or other persons (10 percent universities and 12 percent elsewhere); and, finally, current-awareness tools such as *Current Contents* and printed indexes (10 percent universities and 7 percent elsewhere).

Williams' results from the U.K. reveal a similar pattern: about 11 percent found by online search; told by a colleague—8 percent; hardcopy abstract—9 percent; and other means—16 percent. The principal difference observed between universities and other organizations is that many special libraries route journals; in fact, approximately 16 percent of their total readings are identified in that manner. This relatively slow and expensive practice is already being replaced by online viewing of journal articles.

Trends in how scientists identify and locate articles are show in Table 17. Results over the last twenty years show that scientists still rely heavily on browsing to identify scholarly articles to read, but are using online searches more. In fact, the proportion of readings identified through online searches appears to be increasing, while use of the remaining means—except for browsing—has been decreasing. Thus, to the degree possible, electronic publishing should facilitate browsing and automated searching because those are the preferred means of gathering information by growing numbers of scientists.

SOURCES OF ARTICLES READ

Scientists obtain their articles primarily through personal subscriptions, nearby libraries, and other sources such as shared office collections, colleagues, and authors. Our most recent surveys indicate that university scientists rely on personal subscriptions for approximately 36 percent of readings, but personal subscriptions are used less frequently (24 percent of readings) by scientists outside universities. Scientists in universities obtain 54 percent of their readings from libraries, including reading in the university library or department library, having someone obtain photocopies of articles from the library, and ordering from inter-

Table 17	Proportion of Readings of Scholarly Scientific Journals Identified by Various Means by University and Non-University Scientists: 1977-1998 (in Percent)				
			YEARS OF OBSERVATION		
Means of Identifying Articles	1977	1984	1985–1989	1990–1993	1994–1998
University					
Browsing	58.5	54.1	—	59.7	—
Automated Searches	0.7	1.1	—	14.6	—
Citations	6.7	13.1	—	6.5	—
Other Persons	17.7	15.3	—	9.7	—
Other	16.4	16.4	—	9.5	—
Total	100.0	100.0	—	100.0	—
Non-Universities					
Browsing	49.6	67.4	72.8	57.1	63.6
Automated Searches	0.2	2.7	2.1	7.0	11.1
Citations	11.3	6.3	6.4	5.4	6.6
Other Persons	18.1	11.3	12.0	16.9	12.1
Other	20.8	12.4	6.6	13.6	6.7
Total	100.0	100.0	99.9	100.0	100.1

Sources: King, McDonald, and Roderer 1981; Tenopir and King 1997; Griffiths and King 1993; King et al. surveys 1977-1998

library loan or a document delivery service. Approximately 11 percent of university readings come from other sources such as colleagues and authors.

Outside the university, scientists rely even more on libraries: 19 percent of readings come from organization library collections, 23 percent from routed journals, 11 percent from interlibrary loans and document-delivery services, and 3 percent from academic, public, and government libraries. The more recent (1998) surveys of scientists working in industry and government show that nearly 10 percent of their readings are from electronic sources. Approximately the same

Table 18	Proportion of Readings of Scholarly Scientific Articles Obtained from Various Sources by University and Non-University Scientists: 1977-1998 (in Percent)				

			YEARS OF OBSERVATION		
Means of Identifying Articles	1977	1984	1985–1989	1990–1993	1994–1998
University					
Personal Subscription	60.0	53.0	—	35.5	—
Library	24.8	30.1	—	53.8	—
Other	15.2	16.9	—	10.7	—
Total	100.0	100.0		100.0	
Non-University					
Personal Subscription	72.0	66.3	53.8	49.0	24.0
Library	10.4	20.5	32.1	37.3	55.5
Online	—	—	—	0.1	9.8
Other	17.6	13.2	14.1	13.6	10.7
Total	100.0	100.0	100.0	100.0	100.0

Sources: King, McDonald, and Roderer 1981, Tenopir and King 1997, Griffiths and King 1993, King et al. surveys 1977-1998

amount of readings came from sources such as shared department or unit collections, colleagues, and authors.

The sources of scholarly articles read by scientists have changed dramatically over the last two decades (see Table 18). Scientist in all locales have steadily increased the amount of reading they do from library-provided articles. From 1977 to 1993, the proportion of those readings rose from 24.8 percent to 53.8 percent in universities and from 10.4 percent in 1977 to 55.5 percent in industry and government during the 1994 to 1998 period.[1] This increase in library provision was largely at the expense of reading from personal subscriptions and, to a lesser degree, reading from other sources. Table 19 documents the decline in personal

---

[1]Actually, this number is still higher when online access is done through the library.

Table 19	Average Number of Personal Subscriptions to Scholarly Journals by University and Non-University Scientists: 1977-1998 (Number of Personal Subscriptions per Scientist)					
	YEARS OF OBSERVATION					
Location of Scientists	1977	1978– 1983	1984	1985– 1989	1990– 1993	1994– 1998
University	4.21	—	3.96	—	3.86	—
Non-University	6.20	4.60	4.26	3.70	2.98	2.44

Sources: King, McDonald, and Roderer 1981; Tenopir and King 1997; Griffiths and King 1993; King et al. surveys 1977-1998

subscriptions to journals. In particular, scientists working in industry, government agencies, and national laboratories have been subscribing to fewer scholarly journals in recent years (2.44 subscriptions per scientist) than in 1977 (6.20 subscriptions). The rationale behind this decline in subscriptions is discussed in-depth in Chapter 13. Scientists average reading at least one article from approximately 18 journals, up from 13 in earlier observations[2] (Griffiths and King 1993). Most (11.4) of those journals are provided by libraries, including interlibrary borrowing and document delivery. Personal subscriptions account for 2.7 of the journals read. The scientists read from one or two electronic journals (either online or CD-ROM), and approximately the same number of journals provided by colleagues, authors, and other sources. These are allocated to personal subscriptions and libraries in Table 20.

Each scientist reads an average of 13.4 articles per personal-subscription journal each year (counting articles that are read more than once). Library-provided journals are read an average of 6.4 times per scientist, but collectively each journal is read an average of 136 times per year when readings by students and others are included. Each electronic journal is read about seven times per scientist per

---

[2]In the 1960s, it appeared that pure scientists scanned approximately ten journals on a regular basis and additional titles spasmodically. Martin (1962) found that ten journals accounted for half the reading done by a physicist or a chemist, but Menzel, Lieberman and Dulchin (1960) found that 60 percent of reading by chemists came from these journals. This is closer to the Kingma (1995) findings presented in Chapter 13. White's (1970) results were in the middle: applied scientists and engineers looked at five or six journals on a regular basis.

Table 20	Average Journal Readings by Article Source: 1993-1998			
Source of Articles	Avg. No. of Readings per Scientist	Avg. No. of Journals Read per Scientist	Avg. Readings per Journal per Scientist	Avg. Total Readings per Journal
Personal Subscriptions	36.2	2.7	13.4	13.4
Libraries	73.1	11.4	6.4	136
Other	13.1	3.7	3.5	—
All Sources	122.4	17.8	6.9	—

Source: King et al. surveys 1977–1998

year. Other sources of journals include shared department or unit collections and copies obtained from others, such as authors and colleagues.

The average readership per journal in academic libraries may be somewhat higher. Wilder (1998) quoted the results of a University of Illinois study in which 120 titles are said to have a total of 29,368 uses, which comes to an average of 584 uses per title.[3] In this study, the uses per title vary with type of publisher: U.S. association (1,440 uses per title), U.S. commercial publishers (175 uses), non-U.S. associations (94 uses), and non-U.S. commercial (391 uses).

The number of library-provided journals read per scientist has increased since earlier observations. We think that the increase reflects both an increase in readings identified by automated searches, which potentially broadens the range of journals read, and a reduction in personal subscriptions. Perhaps scientists use online searches of bibliographic databases to identify articles in journals that are otherwise scarcely read, requesting them through interlibrary loan or document delivery.

Such trends have appreciable implications concerning electronic journals. Several aspects of traditional scholarly publishing and use must be considered in electronic publication. First, universities clearly differ from the rest of the world in terms of the extent to which journals are read by scientists and the purposes for which they are read, despite the similarity in the methods for identifying and, to

---

[3]Of course, the total uses reflect use over all ages of journals, but not future uses. Thus, the averages calculated in this way should be reasonably close to the uses for one year's publication. This is largely true for older journals that have not changed much in content or size. Also, a 'use' may not reflect a 'reading' depending on how the data are collected.

a lesser degree, obtaining articles. University libraries also differ in that they serve students and external users such as researchers from small high-tech companies. For these reasons, we have separated trends for universities and other sites.

In addition, electronic publications may serve niche audiences differently than paper publications, especially for journals with small readerships. The electronic versions may also serve libraries differently than paper versions. Similarly, journals that are infrequently and frequently read in libraries may be served differently with electronic journals. Another issue involves the very large, and rapidly increasing, number of articles obtained through photocopying, interlibrary loan, document delivery, preprints, and reprints. Still another issue is that scholarly journals are read over a long period of time following publication.

READERSHIP PATTERNS

Frequency of Readership

Examination of readership in recent years shows that most scientists do not read every article in every issue of a journal, even if they do read some articles. Scientists were asked how many articles they read in the last year from the journal most recently read. The results are summarized below. These results show that in approximately 53 percent of the journals read by a scientist, he or she reads five or fewer articles per year, and in 80 percent of the journals, he or she reads ten or fewer articles. Only in approximately 1 percent of the journals does a scientist read fifty or more articles per year.

Table 21	Proportion and Cumulative Proportion of Readers/Journals at Various Levels of Reading: 1993-1998 (in Percent)	
An Individual's Number of Readings per Journal	Proportion of Readers/Journals	Cumulative Proportion of Readers/Journals
1-5	53.0	53.0
6-10	27.5	80.5
11-15	7.0	87.5
16-20	5.1	92.6
21-25	2.7	95.3
26-50	3.8	99.1
51-100	0.7	99.8
>100	0.2	100.0

Source: King et al. surveys 1993-1998

Of course, scientists read some articles more than once, and they are more likely to do repeat reading in frequently-read journals: 65.5 percent of articles in frequently-read journals are read more than once versus 43.3 percent of articles in infrequently-read journals. University scientists report, however, that the usefulness of articles in infrequently-read journals is greater. Average importance ratings (1 = not at all important to 7 = absolutely essential) of readings used for teaching are 5.11 for infrequently-read journals and 4.64 for frequently-read ones. Those read for research have ratings of 5.23 and 4.88 respectively. Thus, articles in infrequently-read journals tend to be more important. However, the two sets have approximately equal "purchase" value to university scientists since they spend approximately the same amount of time reading an article from an infrequently-read journal as from a frequently-read journal. This finding was observed in studies both inside and outside the university setting.

Frequency of readings of journals by individuals is a critical measure because the amount of reading and the price of the journals have contributed to the decision to subscribe to journals. With high subscription prices, the cost per reading of articles in infrequently-read journals becomes prohibitive, yet some of the relatively inexpensive journals (less than $500) are read more than 50 times. For those journals, the subscription cost per reading (at most $10) is less than the cost of most alternative sources of articles, since the typical cost of reading library-provided articles averages approximately $13.70 per reading (Tenopir and King 1997). If a scientist reads from eighteen journals on average, and 1 percent of all subscriptions have more than fifty readings by a scientist, then nearly one million journals read at least once by a scientist would have at least that level of reading by a scientist.[4] When the price and cost per reading climb too high, scientists most often turn to library-provided articles as an alternative to personal journal subscriptions. Thus, as demonstrated in Table 22, most readings of infrequently-read journals are from those provided by libraries (71 percent of those in universities, and 66 percent of the others).

Nevertheless, some personal subscriptions are infrequently read, and some of the journals frequently read by individuals are provided by libraries. For example, approximately 16 percent of non-university readings are in journals in which the scientist reads many articles, but to which he or she does not have a subscription. That is partially because a cost break-even point is dependent on the price of jour-

[4]Assuming that most of these journals are personal subscriptions, about 6 percent of all personal subscriptions would have at least this level of readership.

Table 22	Proportion of Article Readings from Frequently and Infrequently Read Journals by Source of Articles Read by University and Non-University Scientists: 1993-1998 (in Percent)			

	READINGS			
Sources of Articles Read*	By University Scientists		By Non-University Scientists	
	≤10	>10	≤10	>10
Personal Subscription	16.1	54.1	15.4	28.9
Library	71.0	40.5	66.0	51.3
Online	—	—	6.4	11.8
Other	12.9	5.4	12.3	8.0
Total	100.1	100.0	100.0	100.0

*Note that proportions differ from Table 18 because some scientists did not respond to the question of how many times a journal was read.

Source: King et al. surveys 1993–1998

nals, distance to the library, and the availability of journal routing. For example, at an average distance to the library (i.e., just over 5 minutes) and a price of $100, the break-even point is thirteen readings. In other words, for fewer than thirteen readings it is less expensive to go to the library, while above that number it is less expensive to subscribe. The cost to scientists of subscribing includes both ordering and maintaining journals as well as the time to look up citations or to browse. The cost of using a library is based on reading approximately three articles per visit and includes the time to locate, obtain, and photocopy the article. At a journal price of $250, the break-even point is 30 readings; at $500 it is 59 readings; and at $1,000 it is 118 readings. (See Chapter 13 for details.)

Browsing is by far the most prevalent means of identifying articles, but Table 23 shows that university scientists identify only 34 percent of the articles in infrequently-read journals by browsing, compared with 54 percent identified by other scientists. This suggests that electronic journals should provide a strong browsing capability, regardless of the frequency with which journals are read. Automated searching of indexes and abstracts is also important for identifying articles located in infrequently-read journals.

Table 23	Proportion of Article Readings from Frequently and Infrequently Read Journals by Means of Identifying Articles by University and Non-University Scientists: 1993-1998 (in Percent)			

	READINGS			
Means of Identifying Articles*	By University Scientists		By Non-University Scientists	
	≤10	>10	≤10	>10
Browsing	34.4	80.0	54.0	68.7
Automated Searches	18.8	3.3	12.7	9.8
Citations	12.5	3.3	11.1	4.9
Other Persons	12.5	6.7	15.8	9.8
Other	21.9	6.7	6.4	6.8
Total	100.1	100.0	100.0	100.0

*Note that proportions differ slightly from Table 17 because some scientists did not respond to questions of how many times a journal was read.

Source: King et al. surveys 1993-1998

Frequency of Reading of Library-Provided Articles

The distribution of reading library-provided journals tends to be skewed because many journals are infrequently read while some are extensively read. For example, Kingma (1995) collected data on the use of 787 journals in university libraries. We show his results in Table 24 (with uses adjusted to readings). Approximately 30 percent of the journals had fewer than 25 article reading during the year, but in 6.6 percent of the journals, there were more than 500 article readings.

Like individuals, if the cost per reading of a journal subscription is too high, libraries have the choice of obtaining article copies from alternative sources, in this case usually interlibrary borrowing or document delivery services. In fact, in comparing the costs of subscribing and obtaining copies of articles elsewhere, the break-even point is approximately nine readings when a journal is priced at $100. The break-even point for a $250 journal is seventeen readings, thirty readings for a $500 journal, and fifty-seven readings for a $1,000 journal. The cost per reading of heavily read journals—those with more than 500 article readings per year —is very low. The costs of interlibrary borrowing and document delivery range from $6 to $27 (Tenopir and King 1997; Kingma 1995; Jackson 1997) with costs partially

Table 24	Proportion and Cumulated Proportion of Journals at Various Levels of Reading Library Journals: 1993-1998 (in Percent)		
Total Readings per Journal		Proportion of Journals	Cumulative Proportion
1-10		12.9	12.9
11-25		17.1	30.0
26-50		17.6	47.6
51-100		18.3	65.9
101-250		19.1	85.0
251-500		8.4	93.4
>500		6.6	100.0

Source: Tenopir and King 1997

dependent on the number of transactions due to economies of scale. If copies of electronic journal articles can be made available at a much lower cost, the dynamics of journal purchasing for both individuals and libraries will change dramatically.

The use of journal collections in libraries is fairly extensive. A full 97 percent of scientists at the University of Tennessee and The Johns Hopkins University indicate that they have used their university journal collection at some time, averaging sixty-five uses per scientist per year.[5] That use (which is not necessarily the same as the number of readings) is in line with the estimated number of readings from library-provided articles (101 per scientist per year including external libraries). A smaller proportion of scientists outside universities indicate that they used the journal collection in their organization's library (56 percent during 1990-93 and 78 percent during 1994-1998). The average number of uses is substantially less: eighteen and thirty-eight uses per year for the same range of years. While the overall use per scientist nearly doubled, the number of uses per scientist increased from less than thirty-two to fifty-three uses.

We asked journal readers to consider how much it would cost them to find the information they obtained from library-provided articles if there were no library

---

[5]These estimates include uses of both trade and scholarly journals.

(Griffiths and King 1993; and King et al. surveys 1977-1998). We asked if they knew about the information prior to reading the article. Could that information—or equally useful information—have been obtained elsewhere? If so, where would they obtain the information? Then, considering the least-expensive alternative source, how much would it cost to obtain the information, including the time to identify, locate, and obtain the source, as well as costs due to telephone calls, travel, and photocopying.

Approximately 50 percent of the readings involved articles with information that was new to the reader. Of the readings in which the information was not new, the information could be obtained most frequently from a colleague. Other sources included another library (35 percent of readings) and a consultant (7 percent of readings). The estimated cost of alternatives was approximately three times the library's cost to purchase and maintain the journals plus the user's time required to obtain and use them. Thus, shared library collections achieve a substantial savings for both users and their employers.

Reading Older Articles

Scientific scholarly journals are read for a long time after publication; the pattern is very much that of a nuclear-decay curve. As shown in Table 25, both inside and outside the university setting, a majority of readings take place in the year following publication, with only 5 percent of the readings involving articles more than fifteen years old. In fact, the oldest critical incident of reading observed in these samples was an article published in 1935. Interestingly enough, a 1960 readership study of physical scientists (Operations Research Group, Case Institute of Technology 1960) showed a remarkably similar pattern: 1st year 61.5%; 2—13.3%; 3—2.6%; 4,5—8.4%; 6 to 10—10.2%; 11–15—1.7%; over 15—2.3%.

The pattern of the age of articles read has implications for electronic journals because most of the older articles are not available in electronic media. When journals become available electronically, they are rarely made available retrospectively, although some digital library initiatives are addressing that concern. The danger in the future is that older articles will be ignored because they are not available electronically. The question then becomes whether the older, less frequently-read articles are important enough to worry about since only 15 percent of the articles read by university scientists and 11 percent of the articles read by other scientists are more than five years old.

When university scientists said they needed an article for research or teaching purposes, they were asked: "How important is this article to achieving your research or teaching objectives?" They rated importance from 1 (not at all impor-

Table 25	Proportion of Readings by Age of Scholarly Article by University and Non-University Scientists: 1993-1998 (in Percent)	

Age of Articles Read (Years Since Publication)	University Scientists	Non-University Scientists
1	58.5	66.9
2	12.3	15.1
3	6.2	1.7
4-5	7.7	5.2
6-10	9.3	2.9
11-15	1.5	2.9
>15	4.6	5.2
Total	100.1	99.9

Sources: King et al. surveys 1993-1998

tant) to 7 (absolutely essential). The average importance rating for research articles less than a year old is 4.78; for those articles over a year old the rating is 5.26. For teaching, the averages are 4.76 and 5.00 respectively. The average time spent reading articles less than one year old is forty-three minutes per article; it is sixty-one minutes for articles more than one year old and slightly more for those over five years of age. Outside the universities, the average reading times are thirty-five minutes for articles equal to or less than one year old, forty-nine minutes for those older than one year, and fifty-three minutes for those over five years old.

Older articles are often read for research purposes; newer articles may be read for casual interest. In universities, age is clearly a factor in the purposes for which the articles are read. For example, about one-half of the articles less than a year old are read for teaching purposes, but that proportion declines as the articles become older (30 percent for articles over a year old and 20 percent for articles more than five years old). The opposite is true for articles read for research purposes.[6] Under one year, 66 percent of the articles are read for research purposes, compared with 74 percent of articles older than one year and 80 percent of those older than five years.

---

[6]Note that some articles are read for both teaching and research purposes.

These findings are consistent with the fact that a higher proportion of older articles are consulted to prepare a formal publication such as an article or book. In other words, approximately 26 percent of new articles are reported to be read for that purpose compared with 42 percent of older articles. It seems clear that, although there are fewer readings of older materials, they are useful and valuable to readers and should continue to be made available in the electronic world.

As shown in Table 26, libraries are the primary source of older articles as the proportion of readings from personal subscriptions decreases dramatically with age. Nearly 95 percent of readings of articles over five years old are obtained in or by libraries both inside and outside the university setting. Some of the readings of older articles obtained from libraries involve articles originally read through personal subscriptions that were later discarded. For example, about one-third of older articles have been read at least once before. Some of the earlier articles were initially read to keep abreast of the literature or, perhaps, for teaching purposes, but later a research need for the information arose.

Table 26	Proportion of Readings by Source and by Age of Articles Read by University and Non-University Scientists: 1993-1998 (in Percent)					
	AGE OF ARTICLES READ (Years Since Publication)					
Source of Articles Read	**University Scientists**			**Non-University Scientists**		
	≤1	**>1**	**>5**	**≤1**	**>1**	**>5**
Personal Subscription	55.3	7.4	6.7	29.6	9.2	—
Library	42.1	70.4	93.3	53.0	72.3	94.7
Online	—	—	—	3.5	5.6	—
Other	2.6	22.2	—	13.9	13.0	5.3
Total	100.0	100.0	100.0	100.0	100.1	100.0

Source: King et al. surveys 1993–1998.

The proportion of articles identified by browsing declines substantially over time as might be expected, as shown in Table 27. Other means, such as automated searches and citations in other articles, become more prevalent as articles age. Thus, it is also important that traditional bibliographic databases and other comparable sources continue to be updated and made available to scientists and librarians in order to help identify older articles in the electronic era.

Table 27	Proportion of Readings by Means of Identification and by Age of Articles Read by University and Non-University Scientists: 1993-1998 (in Percent)

	AGE OF ARTICLES READ (Years Since Publication)					
Means of Identifying Articles	University Scientists			Non-University Scientists		
	≤1	>1	>5	≤1	>1	>5
Browsing	76.3	18.5	6.7	74.3	39.6	15.8
Automated Searches	5.3	14.8	20.0	6.2	17.0	15.8
Citations	5.3	11.1	13.3	1.8	18.9	42.1
Other Persons	5.3	18.5	21.1	8.8	17.0	15.8
Other	7.9	37.0	38.9	8.8	7.5	10.5
Total	100.1	99.9	100.0	99.9	100.1	100.0

Source: King et al. surveys 1993-1998

DISTRIBUTION AND USE OF SEPARATE COPIES OF SCHOLARLY ARTICLES

We indicated earlier that scientists and their libraries rely heavily on interlibrary borrowing and document delivery to obtain copies of articles not available in their collections. Scientists also obtain preprints and reprints of articles directly from authors and publishers. Finally, scientists extensively photocopy articles, particularly those obtained from libraries. Estimates and trends for these methods of obtaining articles are discussed below.

Interlibrary Borrowing and Document Delivery

The use of interlibrary borrowing and document-delivery services has grown dramatically over the years. Two studies for the U.S. Copyright Office (King Research 1978; McDonald and Bush 1982) showed that approximately 4 million interlibrary loans of science articles (including document delivery) were executed in 1977, climbing to 7.5 million in 1982. It is expected that the number could currently surpass 40 million for scholarly scientific articles.

A recent survey of 119 libraries by the Association of Research Libraries (Jackson 1997) reported an average of 12,200 items per library obtained from interlibrary borrowing and document delivery. Our 1993 surveys of university scientists showed that nearly 90 percent had used library interlibrary loan services and the scientists averaged 7.5 uses of the service per year. Non-university scientists averaged using these services 14.3 times per year per scientist (1994–1998). Surveys from 1990 to 1993 showed that approximately 30 percent of scientists outside the universities used interlibrary loan and/or document delivery services; they averaged 6.1 uses per scientist per year. Studies from 1994 to 1998 showed a substantial increase to 64 percent who were users, with 14.3 uses per scientist per year.

Some other indicators of size and growth of separate copies are provided by Kaser (ed. 1995). In that report, Finnigan reports the following estimates of interlibrary loans.[7]

Table 28	Estimates of Interlibrary Loans by Various Sources: 1987-1994		
All U.S. Academic Libraries	6,600,000	J. Williams	1994
CISTI	>470,000	NRC	1993
British Library	> 3,630,000	Carrigan	1993
OCLC	> 7,000,000	Dean	1994
ARL	> 2,800,000	ARL	1987
ACRL	> 800,000	ACRL	1989
Docline	> 2,800,000	Fishel	1994
Information Brokers	> 2,000,000	Rugge	1994

Source: Finnigan 1995

The British Library amount grew as follows (Carrigan 1993):

Table 29	Trends in Interlibrary Loans by the British Library: 1971-1993

Year	ILL
1962-63	229,000
1971-72	1,529,000
1978-79	2,861,000
1993	3,630,000

Source: Carrigan 1993

---

[7]The values represent both books and photocopies of articles (e.g., articles represent 54% of ARL loans and 41% of ACRL loans in 1983-84), and there is some overlapped reporting.

Associates of Research Libraries (ARL) had the following growth:

Table 30	**Trends in Interlibrary Lending and Borrowing** Reported by Association of Research Libraries Members: 1983-1993	
	Loaned	**Borrowed**
1983-84	2,781,662	859,551
1986-87	3,232,349	1,044,417
1992-93	4,266,134	1,531,149
Source: Association of Research Libraries 1993		

Growth of document delivery services is another indication of a rapid increase in the use of separate copies of articles (Coffman and Wiedensohler 1993). They show that the number of document delivery services grew from 35 in 1986 to 445 in 1993.

Abundant evidence exists for the size and growth of the distribution and use of separate copies of articles. If scientists in the United States averaged eight items per year (see above), there would be well over 40 million separate copies of articles obtained in one year or nearly 6,000 copies per scholarly journal. That represents only approximately five percent of total readings. However, the availability of copies of articles from electronic journals might increase that amount appreciably, particularly if the electronic-access cost is less than the cost of current interlibrary borrowing and document delivery charges.

Distribution of Separate Copies of Articles

In 1977, over 38 million articles were distributed as separates (i.e., separate copies of articles such as preprints, reprints, and photocopies) and 32.5 million photocopies were made by scientists themselves or by library staff for them, as shown in Table 31.

In 1985 it was estimated from a series of national surveys (King 1985) that approximately 90 million copies of articles were made by or provided to scientists, including photocopies made by libraries from their collections or by scientists themselves (10.1 million and 32.8 million respectively). Copies also originated from ILL (5.4 million), document delivery services (8.6 million), authors and

Table 31	Number of Separate Copies of Articles Received by Scientists: 1977

Document Type	Number Distributed (in millions)
Preprints	
From authors	2.0
From colleagues	0.1
Reprints	
From authors	26.0
From publishers	0.6
From colleagues	0.3
From libraries	0.3
Photocopies given to users	
By ILL	4.0
By colleagues	3.5
By author	1.5
Photocopies made by/for users	
By scientists themselves	25.0
By library staff	7.5
TOTAL	70.8

Source: King, McDonald, and Roderer 1981

colleagues (9.7 million), publishers (13.1 million), and other sources such as information analysis centers and clearinghouses (10.3 million). While in recent years we have less definitive survey results concerning the sources of reading for separate copies of articles, there is some indication that those sources continue to grow at a rate exceeding the growth in the number of scientists and their reading. Thus, the number of separate copies distributed by preprints, reprints, ILL and document delivery, and photocopies given to users by colleagues and authors was estimated to be 38 million in 1977/78 and 47 million in 1984/85. this amount is thought to be well over 100 million currently. Electronic distribution of individual copies of articles could probably replace most of that activity at a reduced cost.

After 1985 we discontinued collecting data on readings from preprints and reprints. One particularly interesting aspect of the distribution of preprints involves Paul Ginsparg's highly successful system for distributing preprints electronically. Initially, the system—developed at Los Alamos National Laboratory—involved high-energy physics manuscripts, but it has expanded to other physics specialties and other fields of science. Preprints are commonly distributed in physics (Tenopir and King 1997; King and Roderer 1981, 1982): in 1981 scientists read 20,000 separate copies of articles from the American Institute of Physics journals; 2,000 were reprints, 4,500 were preprints, and 13,500 were distributed photocopies. At that time physical sciences authors, including chemists, distributed an average of 51 reprints per article and approximately 110 preprints per article. Other fields of science generally distributed fewer preprints, but averaged 69 reprints, with mathematics having the fewest (21) and life sciences the most (110).

Photocopying of Scholarly Articles

Articles in journals held by libraries are photocopied extensively. In The Johns Hopkins University and the University of Tennessee libraries (1993), over three-fourths of the scientists say they have used library photocopy machines to copy journal articles, with the amount of use averaging seventeen uses per scientist per year. About 56 percent say they have asked library staff to photocopy an average of six times per year. Outside the university setting, approximately 62 percent of scientists say they have used the library for photocopying forty-four times per year (thirty times personally and fourteen times by library staff). In companies, at least 27 percent of all photocopies are made of articles in the scientist's own copy of the journal. Colleagues provide approximately 15 percent of all photocopies. About 14 percent of photocopying involves interlibrary borrowing or document delivery copies. The remainder—44 percent—is from journals to which the library subscribes.

Photocopying is done in order to read articles more conveniently (e.g., while traveling), to permit annotation or highlighting, for retention in personal files for future reference, or to file with laboratory notes or other documentation. Only about one-fourth of those photocopies are loaned or given to others (Griffiths and King 1993).

Photocopying library journals costs the library approximately $1.84 per article copied in supplies, equipment, and reshelving.[8] The cost climbs to $6.67 when the user's time is included (Griffiths and King 1993). When the library staff does the photocopying, the cost to the library is $2.53 per article copied as compared to $5.27 when the scientist's time is included. Thus photocopying is not an inexpensive alternative. In fact, ultimately it may be less expensive to obtain copies from electronic sources, particularly if the time the scientists spend locating and reproducing the article is reduced (see Chapter 17).

SERVING SMALL COMPANIES

An appreciable number of scientists work in small high-technology research and development firms. A King Research study for the Small Business Administration in the mid-1980s identified nearly 14,000 such firms with a median of 8 employees and an average of approximately 100 employees (Liston, King, Kutner, and Havelock 1985). Because of their size, only 13 percent of those firms have information-support staff or librarians, and, because of economies of scale, they spend more than twice the amount per scientist for information that larger companies spend. Higher costs per reading arise from having fewer scientists share in the cost of library collections and from the cost in additional time necessary to obtain information services from academic libraries and other sources.

In order to avoid the high out-of-pocket costs of scholarly journals, many scientists in small firms travel to academic, public, and other libraries periodically to read the literature. That, of course, is very expensive in terms of labor costs even though the scientists batch their reading by designating long periods of time in the library to do their reading or to photocopy for later reading. It would seem that electronic journals could be particularly helpful to that community of perhaps 250,000 to 500,000 scientists. In this area, journal price differentiation could be particularly effective (see Chapters 13 and 18).

---

[8]Note that the $1.84 per article copied is distinguished from $1.48 per reading mentioned elsewhere.

Part III

LIBRARY PARTICIPATION

CHAPTER 9

Use and Economics of Libraries

INTRODUCTION

This chapter addresses the general use of libraries by scientists. Chapter 10 provides details concerning scholarly journal-related services such as access to internal collections (i.e., current and shelved journals, journal routing and interlibrary lending), access to external collections (i.e., interlibrary borrowing and document delivery services), ordering for unit collections or personal use, and photocopying.

Scientists use libraries an average of two to three times a week, including visits, calls, or e-mail requests to the library. Use also includes visits or requests made by someone on behalf of a scientist. Most use involves the organization's main or central library, but also includes use for work-related purposes of other organization libraries as well as external libraries. Based on observation of library use over the past two decades, we provide extensive evidence of the usefulness and value of academic and special libraries. Finally, we provide estimates of the unit cost of twenty-six library services. The unit costs are those incurred by the library including all direct costs and allocated operational and support costs. Estimates are also made for the cost to users (mostly in terms of their time) and finally the total cost to funders (i.e., the cost to both libraries and users).

USE OF LIBRARIES BY SCIENTISTS

Over 100,000 libraries in the United States serve universities, companies, government agencies, schools, and the general public. Scientists use their organization libraries extensively, but also use other external libraries as well (see Table 32). Scientists in universities (1990-1993) indicate that they use the main university library an average of 119 times per year.[1] This amount of use is greater than that observed in a national survey conducted in 1984 when the estimated average for university scientists was 77 uses per year.[2]

At the University of Tennessee (Hodges Library), scientists who are primarily engaged in research tend to use the library more (128 times annually per scientist) than those primarily involved in teaching (101 times), administration (79 times), or other activities (94 times). The university scientists also use other libraries at their university approximately eight times per year and departmental collections approximately once a month. They also use libraries outside the university for work-related purposes approximately once per month on average. During the last month, nearly all of the scientists used the main library, while fewer used other available libraries: other local university (14 percent), department (27 percent), academic (13 percent), government (6 percent), and public (14 percent).

Non-university scientists also use their main site library extensively, and it appears that this amount of use may be increasing over time. The greatest amount of use observed over time was during the 1994-1998 period at 100 times per scientist. This growth in use reflects the increase in reading from library-provided scholarly journals discussed in Chapter 8. Scientists use the libraries of other organizations and shared unit collections approximately nine times per year each and external libraries about five times for work-related purposes. Nearly all of the scientists have used their main library, and approximately 81 percent have used the library in the last month.

Other older studies show ample use of libraries. For example, Orr (1970) reported that staff in five medical schools used their library an average of 18 to 70 times per year. Engineers tend to use libraries less than scientists in other fields. For example, Pinelli, Glassman, Oliu and Barclay (1989) report that engineers use libraries an average of 3.2 times per month or approximately 38 times per year.

---

[1]Uses include visits and additional uses (e.g., e-mail, telephone) by scientists themselves or by others for them.
[2]In this particular survey (1984), the question(s) concerning amount of use differed from all the other surveys conducted by King Research and the University of Tennessee in that uses by others on behalf of scientists are not included.

Table 32	Average Number of Annual Uses of Libraries by University and Non-University Scientists: 1982–1998				

	YEARS OF OBSERVATION				
	1982–1983	1984	1985–1989	1990–1993	1994–1998
Universities					
Main library	—	77.2	—	119.3	—
Other local university libraries	—	NR*	—	8.4	—
Department collections	—	NR	—	13.2	—
Other academic libraries			—	3.9	—
Government libraries	—	NR	—	5.1	—
Public libraries	—	NR	—	4.5	—
Total	—	—	—	154.4	—
Non-Universities					
Main site library	33.0	87.9	51.0	79.5	99.8
Other organizational libraries	8.0	NR	12.0	4.4	9.2
Shared unit collections	10.0	NR	15.0	5.5	9.3
Academic libraries	NR	NR	2.0	3.4	1.6
Government libraries	NR	NR	0	0.2	0.6
Public libraries	NR	NR	10.0	4.5	3.0
Total	—	—	90.0	97.5	123.5

*NR means that the researchers did not ask about these libraries.

Sources: King et al. surveys 1977–1998

Siess (1982) reports an average of between 28 and 64 times per year for engineers depending on the type of research being done, and King et al. surveys reveal visits 54 times per year by engineers based on the 1984 national survey. Roderer (1998) reported that Yale University Medical Center staff used their library nearly 100 times per year.

Unfortunately, some scientists outside of universities do not have libraries in their organizations, although scientists in general tend to have access to organization libraries more frequently than other professions as demonstrated in Table 33. One reason that some organizations do not have libraries is their small size. A national survey sampled from 13,950 small businesses engaged in research and

Table 33	Proportion of Scientists and Other Professions Who Do Not Have a Library in Their Place of Work (in Percent)

Field	Proportion of Professionals
Science	18
Engineering	20
Education	12
Medical Practice	26
Business	55
Law	54

Source: King et al. national survey 1984 (n=749)

development shows that only approximately 10 percent of firms with fewer than 50 employees (and even fewer scientists) have a librarian or other information support staff, while 24 percent of R&D businesses with 50 to 500 employees have such library support (Liston, King, Kutner, and Havelock 1985). The problem is that such small businesses do not have a sufficient volume of library use to justify a librarian since they do not enjoy the economies of scale (discussed in a later section) from which larger companies benefit. These smaller firms tend to meet their needs by relying on academic, government, and public libraries as well as multi-type library cooperatives and private or government information services.

Many public and school libraries provide access to scientific information. For example, a statewide survey of libraries in Massachusetts (King and Griffiths 1991) showed that nearly all public libraries at that time are used for scientific purposes. About 55 percent of school libraries have scientific materials and 60 percent have mathematical collections, although the adequacy of these collections is rated lower than the other types of collections.

Libraries in the United States have been ingenious in sharing resources. Approximately 1,000 formal library cooperatives or networks provide: 1) access to collections through interlibrary loan and reciprocal borrowing agreements, 2) reference and referral services, and 3) other operational functions and services—including scientific materials or related services (King and Griffiths 1987). Some states have supported large libraries and resource sharing to specifically serve the research community (e.g., New York and Boston Public Libraries and the Reference and Research Library Resources Systems in New York).

A FRAMEWORK FOR EXAMINING LIBRARY SERVICES

Over the years we have developed a framework for examining information products and services, including library services (Griffiths and King 1989, 1993). This framework, depicted in Figure 7 in Chapter 4 is based on five types of measures including service inputs, outputs, usage, outcomes, and domain.

For every service, *inputs* comprise the amount of resources applied to provide the service (primarily measured in dollars[3]) and attributes of the resources (e.g., competence of staff, reliability of equipment). *Outputs* are described in terms of amount of services provided (e.g., number of journals available locally, number of articles obtained from document delivery services, number of searches) and service attributes (e.g., accessibility of a journal collection, speed of response, quality of searches).

Usage is measured from the user's perspective in terms of amount of use,[4] which is sometimes the same as the amount of service output. Since requests for services may not result in use of the service output, however, they should be observed independently. In other words, just because an article copy is provided does not necessarily mean it is used, on the one hand, or then again the copy may be read many times by several scientists. Usage measures also include factors that affect use such as awareness of the services, ease of use, or cost to use the services, as well as the importance of and satisfaction with service attributes.

Outcomes of information use include how it affects scientists' research and teaching in terms of saving time and improving the quality, timeliness, and productivity of these activities. Information use can also have even higher order effects on organizations and society. *Domain* measures include the environmental characteristics of the user population such as the number of users (and non-users), their scientific specialty, and type of work.

From these five measures one can derive other, perhaps, more relevant measures. Relating service input and output provides measures of unit costs and productivity which are indicators of service *performance*. Of course these measures are also dependent on input attributes such as staff competence and attributes of outputs produced such as quality.

Effectiveness of the services is demonstrated by the relationship of service output and use of information provided. Service attributes such as speed of delivery, quality, and accessibility all affect the extent to which services are used. If libraries

---

[3]Amount of resources can be observed by amount of staff time, equipment time, space, and supplies. However, a common unit of measure for all the resources is dollars.

[4]Generally use in this context refers to the use of information provided by the service.

charge for services, the amount of the fee will affect the demand for services in measurable ways. Relating input cost and use (i.e., *cost-effectiveness*) provides a useful indicator of how effectively resources are applied. Ultimately, however, relating service cost, output attributes, and usage to outcomes or consequences of information serve as meaningful indicators of the impact of library services. Furthermore, relating cost and use, for example, to domain measures is illuminating. Service cost per capita or use per capita are commonly used as measures of this effect.

Cost and benefit measures provide comparison of services and their alternatives using the measures discussed above. In this case, favorable comparisons are considered benefits, and unfavorable ones are costs (better called detriments). For example, if the service costs less and offers better quality than an alternative, these would be considered benefits, whereas the reverse would be costs (or detriments). Examples of this phenomenon are given in this and the following chapter for library services involving access to scholarly journals.

The remaining sections in this chapter provide a further discussion of the economic aspects of library services including measures of the usefulness and value of such services. The next chapter addresses specific library services that involve access to scientific scholarly journals. Such services include reference services, in-library access, purchase for individuals, journal routing, interlibrary borrowing, and document delivery in both paper and electronic form. Each section provides such estimates of input costs (including cost to users) as usage and costs per reading.

UNIT COSTS OF LIBRARY SERVICES

In the previous section we briefly described one measure, input cost, that, while important by itself, also serves as a component of derived measures such as unit cost (i.e., cost per item produced) and cost-effectiveness (i.e., cost per use of a service or per reading in the case of journals or other documents). In this section we present estimates of input cost[5] for each of the services discussed.

Another kind of cost which must be considered, however, involves the cost to the user of requesting a service or obtaining journals.[6] The reason that user costs are included is to provide the library funder's perspective on costs, although one can argue that this should be the same perspective as that of the librarian. This perspective seems to be particularly important when considering acquisition of alter-

---

[5]Library service costs are defined as the direct costs of all resources (e.g., labor, equipment, collection, facilities) applied to provide the service, plus an allocation of operational costs (e.g., collection development, ordering) and support and overhead costs (e.g., personnel, finance, utilities).
[6]User costs include the user's compensation (e.g.., salary and wages, retirement benefits, insurance) and support and overhead costs (e.g., payroll, space, furniture, equipment).

native journal media (i.e., traditional paper and electronic subscriptions as well as separate copies in both media). It will be shown that, at certain levels of use, results or decisions vary depending on whether or not user costs are considered.

Unit costs of services are discussed here because they provide a common and revealing way to examine services. This enables a meaningful comparison of costs among services and among alternative ways of providing information (e.g., purchasing journals versus using interlibrary borrowing or electronic access). Another important aspect of unit cost analysis is that unit costs can vary dramatically depending on the number of units involved. For example, with online searching the cost per search can be relatively high for a small number of searches and, on the other hand, low for a large number of searches. Such economies of scale exist because there is a high fixed cost of such line items as equipment, staff training, and the purchase of reference materials. In other words, these costs are incurred irrespective of the number of searches.

Another source of economies of scale involves processing costs in which the cost per item processed is greater for a small number of items processed than for a large number. This is typically true with such services as interlibrary lending and borrowing (Griffiths and King 1989, 1993) because a staff member who performs regularly can do it more skillfully and productively than one who does the same task only intermittently.

Cost per use (or reading in the case of journal-related services) has many of the same aspects and relevance as unit cost. For example, the high fixed costs associated with purchasing, processing, and storing journals means that a journal read infrequently will have a much higher cost per reading than journals read more often. This is important when comparing purchasing versus obtaining separate copies of articles regardless of media. Here again, user cost per reading can be an important aspect when comparing alternative services. For example, library cost per reading for current periodical rooms tends to be somewhat less than for journal routing. When the cost of scientists' time travelling to the current periodicals room is factored in, however, their cost can be substantially higher, than for journal routing.

Table 34 gives examples of unit costs for a variety of library services (Griffiths and King 1993). The unit costs are given by total library costs, user costs, and cost to the library and user funder (i.e., the total of the two costs).

INDICATORS OF USEFULNESS AND VALUE OF LIBRARIES

Griffiths and King (1993) summarize the results of a number of studies that examine the usefulness and value of special libraries serving scientists among others.

While these results address the entire library, the results summarized actually present usefulness and value indicators for twenty-six individual services, some of which are presented in the next chapter. In every one of these studies, organizational goals were established and attempts were made to demonstrate how the libraries helped to achieve these goals. For example, the libraries have contributed to the following organizational goals:

1. **Improved quality of work**
   - Scientists and others indicate that the library is absolutely essential to their work for approximately 40 percent of the uses of the library.
   - Quality of work is improved in nearly 60 percent of the uses of the library.
   - Quality of work improves in 57 percent of readings from library-provided documents compared with 49 percent from other sources.
   - Scientists and others whose work has been recognized through awards use libraries more than non-award winners.
   - In one organization, it was found that twenty-five fast trackers used libraries substantially more than cohorts with similar backgrounds.

2. **Increased productivity**
   - More than one-third of scientists and others who use the library save time and often other expenditures as well.
   - Such savings are achieved in 45 percent of readings of library-provided documents, compared with 32 percent from other sources.
   - Five indicators of user productivity are positively correlated with the amount of library use.
   - Looked at in another way, Van House (1990) reported from research at twenty-seven large research and academic libraries that there were positive correlations between library resources (e.g., collections acquired and held) and indicators of productivity at the organizations served by them.
   - Five industry-wide studies show a positive correlation between information-related expenditures and profit and/or productivity (Hayes and Erickson 1982, Braunstein 1985, Koenig and Gans 1975, Jonscher 1983, Terleckyj 1984)

3. **Shorter product lead time from discovery to the marketplace**
   - We identified twenty-one organizational activities that affect product lead time and found that approximately 38 percent of library uses help scientists and others to perform these activities faster.

Table 34	Unit Costs of Special Library Services by Cost to Library, Scientists, and Their Funders: Adjusted to 1998 (in Dollars)			

| Library Function/Service | Unit Cost | | | Type of Unit/Per: |
	Library	Scientist	Funder	
Access to Library Collections				
Circulation	11.23	5.39	16.62	Reading
Materials read in library	6.96	12.22	19.18	Reading
Current periodicals room	1.61	6.08	7.69	Reading
Journal routing	6.34	5.10	11.94	Reading
Audiovisual use	7.22	15.86	23.08	Use
Interlibrary lending	24.10	n/a	24.10	Item
Access to External Collections				
Interlibrary borrowing	21.50	11.34	32.84	Item
Document delivery	22.75	11.34	34.09	Item
Purchase of materials for department/personal use	8.26	3.18	11.44	Document
Photocopying				
By library staff	2.53	2.74	5.27	Document
Self-service	1.84	4.83	6.67	Document
Reference and Research Services				
Directional/assistance	1.40	4.20	5.60	Incident
Brief reference	3.15	6.82	9.97	Request
In-depth reference	21.69	16.10	37.79	Search
Online catalog—library	2.80	20.62	23.32	Search
—office	4.95	12.94	17.89	Search
Database search	160.04	10.71	170.75	Search
Current Awareness Services (SDI/bulletins)	11.83	15.47	27.30	Issue
Translation Services	130.66	11.90	142.56	Item
User Instruction				
Exhibits	812.70	—	812.70	Exhibit
Tours/briefings	29.24	—	29.24	Incident
Training sessions/demos	123.52	34.27	157.79	Session
Access to Facilities				
Reading room/study space	0.51	23.80	24.31	Use
Individual carrels or rooms	3.06	35.70	38.76	Use
PCs/CD-ROM workstations	2.64	7.38	10.02	Use
Microform reader/printers	0.66	7.94	8.60	Use

Source: King et al. surveys 1985–1998 ($ adjusted to 1998)

- Approximately 31 percent of readings of library-provided documents lead to completing work faster, compared with 17 percent from other sources.

Libraries also contribute to organizational productivity by providing information less expensively than other alternative sources and by saving scientists and others considerable time that they can more appropriately apply to research, thinking, and other tasks. Special libraries typically cost organizations about $725 per professional per year. Users spend approximately $1,300 per year per professional (including non-users) acquiring library-provided information. Thus the annual cost of libraries to an organization is in the range of $2,025 per year per professional.

One can place a value on libraries in two ways: 1) purchase value or the amount users are willing to pay for library-provided information, and 2) use value which is derived from library services and the use of its information.

1. **Purchase value.** Scientists and others do not pay directly for library-provided information, but they are willing to pay to acquire and use information provided by their libraries with their most valuable resource—their time. In fact, they spend an average of $6,180 per professional per year in this manner (including reading time). This value is approximately 8.5 times the actual cost of the library or $725 per professional per year.

2. **Use value.** As previously discussed, indicators of use value are defined as the ways in which libraries help to achieve organizational goals. Benefits of libraries can also be measured, however, in terms of how much less it costs scientists and others to obtain needed information from libraries compared to the cost of acquiring the information if there were no library.

Were there no library, it would cost an average of $5,960 per professional to obtain the library-provided information absolutely required by scientists and others to do their jobs, or approximately 2.9 times the current library cost of $2,025.

Furthermore, when factoring in the benefits that would be lost by not having the necessary information, it actually would cost approximately 7.2 times more not to have a library than it does to have one.

From another perspective, larger organizations typically have approximately one library staff member per 120 scientists and other professionals served. With a library, scientists and others spend approximately 27 hours acquiring library-provided information; without the library, they would have to spend approximately 121 hours acquiring the same information. Thus, having a library saves them approximately 94 hours per year that can be used for research, thinking, and the other endeavors for which they were hired. When these savings are applied to all 120 professionals (per library staff) the time savings mount to approximately 11,300 hours or the equivalent of nearly five scientists' time for every library staff member.[7]

We approached the question of usefulness, value, and impact of information and libraries from a variety of perspectives, and found confirming evidence of positive results from every angle. Some data are more robust than others, however. For example, estimates of the amount of reading, time spent reading, and extent of library use are all from large sample sizes and are validated in a number of ways. Other estimates, such as the impact of reading and library use, depend on a degree of recall and judgment on the part of respondents. Nevertheless, we have been struck by the strength of conviction with which readers and users have related their favorable experiences in hundreds of in-depth interviews conducted by us personally, thereby reinforcing the statistical survey responses.

Furthermore, we are encouraged by the fact that our results appear to be consistent in a wide range of environments and in our national surveys of professionals. In new studies, we often use different methods to confirm or deny earlier findings, and in no instance have we found evidence contrary to previous results. Finally, we wish to point out that results showing the correlation between reading or library use and such indicators as productivity and achievement also indicate that some successful professionals do not read or use their libraries extensively. Conversely, extensive reading and library use do not ensure success. Regardless, most professionals do consider information and libraries to be essential to their work.

OTHER STUDIES OF THE USEFULNESS AND VALUE OF LIBRARIES

We first studied organizational libraries in conjunction with a study of the value of information services (King, Griffiths, Sweet, and Wiederkehr 1984). This study included one of the first literature reviews on research into the value of information and information products and services (Griffiths 1982). In that review, the literature was divided into two categories: 1) descriptions of the concept of value and approaches to measuring value, and 2) descriptions of the application of the measures of value to information products and services. The former category contained considerably more literature than the latter, a situation that persists even to this day.

---

[7]Of course, this analysis ignores the library expenditure on other resources such as the collection, equipment, and facilities.

Several others also conducted reviews of the literature concerning the value of information and libraries for the *Annual Review of Information Science and Technology*, including Griffiths (1982), Repo (1986), and Koenig (1990). Recent reviews also include Broadbent and Lofgren (1991), Keyes (1995), Saracevic and Kantor (1997), and Nelke (1998). In 1987, the Special Libraries Association (SLA) published the report of the President's Task Force on the Value of the Information Professional. The task force addressed three basic approaches to measuring value: measuring time, and its monetary equivalent saved by information services and products; determining real savings, financial gains, or liability avoidance; and assessing the worth of qualitative, anecdotal evidence. Using several approaches to value measurement, the task force demonstrated that the value of the information professional can be determined quantitatively (in terms of real cost savings) and qualitatively (in terms of time savings and increased productivity). The task force recommended further research into how the corporate world values its libraries and information centers.

In 1990, SLA published *Valuing Corporate Libraries* (SLA 1990), the results of a study by Matarazzo and Prusak. The authors surveyed corporate officials from a sample of 164 companies about the value they placed on the information professional and on the corporate library or information center. The survey also aimed at identifying emerging trends for special libraries. The study gathered mostly qualitative statements of value of the corporate library and corporate librarian to the firm. Key conclusions of this study included:

- *a lack of managerial consensus* on how the library adds specific value to the firm's performance or how value should be measured

- *a lack of input by librarians* to the firm's information policies and mission (Few respondents could state the exact function of the library within the firm's information structure.)

- *a lack of planning by librarians* and their managers on the future role of libraries within the firm as end-user database systems and other information technologies have major impact on business and other operations, and

- *a strong reservoir of good will and affection for the library* and librarians—often based on an intuitive feeling that the service is valuable and worthy of continued support.

This study provided an indication of the prevailing corporate climate and attitudes toward the library and its personnel on the part of the corporate executives responsible for the library or information center.

Prusak and Matarazzo (1992) studied the information environment in Japanese firms. They set out to identify the characteristics of the Japanese approach to acquiring, managing, and disseminating the kinds of information they consider to be critical to business success. Brief case studies were developed through interpersonal interviews with executives and managers of several Japanese firms. The findings included:

- Japanese firms place a tremendous value on information and do not feel the need to justify information management expenditures.

- The mission of the information function is already aligned with the strategic thrust of the organization.

- Information technology is seen as an enabler for information management, not the primary component.

- Management of the information function is rotated among all company managers.

- Japanese management reads a great deal.

Again, this study did not aim to actually measure the value of information in Japanese firms, but rather to provide a description of the environment within which Japanese corporate libraries and information centers operate.

Koenig (1991, 1992) reviewed the literature on the effects of information services on user and organizational productivity, and, in 1992, he reviewed several studies that attempted to calculate the value of information services. He compares various ratios of value (variously defined) to the marginal cost of providing the services derived from several of the studies and finds remarkably similar results. He states, "the magnitude of the effects [value derived to cost] reported in these studies is quite striking, as is the high degree of their consistency, both across different techniques and across different cases. This creates a high degree of confidence that the findings are not mere artifacts, but that they reflect a genuine phenomenon."

In 1991, Marshall was funded by an SLA Steven I. Goldspiel grant to measure the impact on corporate decision making of information provided by special libraries. The results showed that, when libraries are used in decision-making situations, the information provided is frequently perceived by managers and executives as having a significant impact on their actions. Marshall (1993) measured impact in terms of:

- behavioral change as a result of the information received from special libraries

- increase in the managers' or executives' level of confidence in making decisions

- information enabling the managers or executives to take courses of action, and

- allowing the users to avoid potentially negative consequences for the organization.

Marshall based her methodology on that of David King (1987). Assessments of the value of information provided by the libraries were grouped into three areas: quality of information, cognitive value, and value for decision making. Respondents to the survey were asked to agree or disagree with various statements about the information received. This study did not attempt to quantify the value of the information or the services provided. It did gather information about the value of financial transactions (if involved) associated with the decision making and found over 40 percent to involve amounts over $1 million.

It is abundantly clear that libraries remain extremely useful and valuable and are likely to remain so in the future even in light of electronic publishing and the availability of the Internet (see, for example, Griffiths 1998 and Henderson 1999).

CHAPTER 10

Use and Economics of Library-Provided Scientific Scholarly Articles

INTRODUCTION

In Chapter 8, we showed that scientists obtain the articles they actually read from four basic sources: personal subscriptions, libraries (e.g., subscriptions and document delivery), departmental collections, and other sources such as author reprints and colleagues. Generally, scientists appear to make rational choices among alternative sources based on economic considerations such as the price of journals, how frequently they read the journals, and the cost of using alternative sources. Other factors are also considered such as the age of the articles when the information is needed and the service attributes of alternative sources. In this chapter we focus on the library service provision of scientific scholarly journals and its economic aspects.

Libraries provide access to scientific journals from internal as well as external collections. Internal collections include recent journals in current periodical rooms, older bound copies of journals in stacks, and, particularly in special libraries, journal routing of current issues. External access involves interlibrary borrowing (especially by university libraries) and use of document delivery services (mostly by special libraries). Substantial photocopying takes place in all types of libraries. There is internal and external electronic access.

In this chapter, we reiterate that a higher proportion of readings comes from library-provided articles than in the past and a high proportion of scientists use their library to obtain articles. The extent to which these articles are read, however, depends somewhat on user perceptions of the importance of and satisfaction with the comprehensiveness of the library's journal collections. Use of library journals also depends on the distance of users from the library and the availability and accessibility of other sources of articles. Journal routing is used in many organizations served by special libraries, but the success of the service depends on the timeliness of delivery which is a function of the length of the routing lists and the extent to which the routed journals are read.

Over the past twenty years, the journal subscription prices charged to libraries have increased far faster than inflation. Because of these increased prices, libraries have been faced with increasingly difficult decisions concerning whether to purchase journals or to rely on external sources such as interlibrary borrowing, document delivery services, and, more recently, electronic access to journals and articles.

Choices among these alternatives are examined below from the standpoint of their costs. Clearly, journals that are infrequently read should not be purchased by libraries, but rather have use satisfied by separate copies of articles (interlibrary borrowing or document delivery—photocopy or electronic). On the other hand, those journals that are very frequently read probably should continue to be purchased by libraries based on cost per reading. Somewhere between the two extremes are break-even points that depend largely on the cost of journal purchases (including both subscription price and processing), the cost of obtaining separate copies of articles, and the amount of reading of the journals. Tables in this chapter illustrate break-even points derived over a range of journal subscription prices and alternative costs of separate copies of articles. We also present estimates of the use, usefulness, and value of all the various services for providing articles to scientists.

These extremely large increases in subscription prices have resulted in some significant trends concerning the use of library-provided journals. In effect, the large increase in journal prices has resulted in an appreciable decrease in the number of personal subscriptions because demand for personal subscriptions is particularly sensitive to price changes (discussed in depth in Chapter 13). The amount of reading per scientist, however, has remained relatively constant over the past twenty years and perhaps is even increasing somewhat with academic scientists. Thus, scientists have sought, and found, alternative sources for journals including colleagues and, particularly, libraries.

IN-LIBRARY USE OF JOURNALS AND ECONOMIC ASPECTS

Use of Library Collections

Both university and special libraries have large scholarly journal collections in current periodical rooms, with the older collections housed in the stacks. These collections are extensively used by scientists and are highly rated by them in importance. Average use of these collections is presented in Table 35.

Table 35	Proportion Who Use and Average Annual Use per Scientist of Two Types of Library Journal Collections by University and Non-University Scientists: 1993–1998			
	Type of Collection			
	Current		**Stacks**	
Location of Scientists	**Proportion Who Use %**	**Avg.Use/ Scientist**	**Proportion Who Use %**	**Avg. Use/ Scientist**
University	96.5	34.8	96.4	31.2
Non-University	69.7	28.3	67.8	24.5

Source: King et al. surveys 1993-1998

It is clear that a high proportion of scientists not only use their library's journal collections, but use them extensively. Looked at in a different way, approximately forty-six readings per scientist per year of university library-provided scholarly journals are from journals published less than one year prior to reading.[1] Similarly outside of the universities approximately thirty-eight such readings are from current scholarly journals, although only twenty-four of the readings are from in-library reading, the rest being from routed journals.

Very few studies observe the amount of reading of individual library journals. A most recent estimate of journal use was conducted for universities in New York by Kingma (1995). Other estimates were made at the University of Pittsburgh

---

[1]Use of journal collections reported in Table 35 include both scholarly and trade journals since that is the way the question was posed in the survey instruments.

(Kent, Montgomery, Cohen, Williams, Bulick, Flynn, Sabar, and Kern 1978) and at MIT (Chen 1972). These studies provide averages of use per title as well as distributions of journal use among journals (see the section below on comparison among alternatives). The average use per journal title for the Kingma study is 37 uses per title; in the earlier Pittsburgh study the average uses per title were 33.2 for physics, 28.4 for chemistry and 21.2 for life sciences.[2]

Estimates of use, however, are not estimates of reading because readers often read more than one article when an issue or bound volume is picked up to be used. The distinction between use and readings is important when comparing among alternatives. For example, if one compares purchasing journals versus interlibrary borrowing, an article borrowed should be compared with the amount of reading of library journals. Our estimate of the amount of reading per use is 3.7 readings per use, based on an exit survey done at the National Institutes of Health. This estimate is used to extrapolate Kingma's average use (and distribution of use) to average readings of 136 readings per title in universities.[3] In special libraries the total number of readings of scholarly journals is estimated to be approximately 102 readings per title. Of these readings, approximately 46 readings per title are actually read in the library.

Cost of In-Library Use of Journals

The unit cost[4] of processing and maintaining purchased journals has been estimated at $71 per title for university libraries (Kingma 1995) and $81 for special libraries (Griffiths and King 1993). To these values one should add the subscription price of the journals. In addition to the fixed costs of purchasing and processing journals, readers and libraries incur additional costs for each reading of the journal. For the library these costs involve reshelving and photocopying. In university libraries, Kingma (1995) estimates these costs at $1.05 (adjusted to 1998 dollars) per reading. In special libraries the library cost is $1.48, including $0.04 per item reshelved and $1.44 for photocopying.[5]

---

[2]The average uses per title included both active and inactive titles (i.e., those no longer subscribed).
[3]On the other hand, Wilder (1998) reports that 120 journals in a University of Illinois library had a total of 70,072 library uses (or 584 uses per title).
[4]Estimated costs are adjusted to account for inflation from the time estimates were made to 1998.
[5]Since reshelving involves a use of an issue or bound volume, the cost per reading is $0.04 since there are 3.7 readings per use (i.e., $0.157 divided by 3.7). The cost per article photocopied is $2.53, but only 57 percent of the readings involve photocopying, thus yielding a cost of $1.44 per reading.

We asked scientists how much time they spent going to their library to identify, locate, obtain, and photocopy the articles they will read. This cost is estimated at $8.93 per reading. Sometimes, scientists ask others to go to the library for them to obtain copies. This cost is estimated at $3.29 per reading, yielding a total cost of $12.22 per reading of an article obtained in the library.[6] The cost per reading of current journals is $3.80 per reading for browsing the collection, $1.30 for photocopying 27 percent of readings, plus the cost per reading of traveling to and from the library ($2.18 per reading). The cost of other readings is much higher due to searching and so on. Table 36 presents the average costs per reading at different journal prices and amount of reading at $13.70 per reading (i.e., $1.48 library cost and $12.22 user cost).

Table 36	Cost per Reading of Journals Read in the Library at Various Subscription Prices and Number of Readings (in Dollars)		
		Price	
Number of Readings	$250	$500	$1,000
10	46.80	71.80	121.80
25	26.90	37.00	57.00
50	20.30	25.30	35.30
75	18.10	21.50	28.10
100	17.00	19.50	24.50
250	15.00	16.00	18.00
500	14.40	14.90	15.90
1,000	14.00	14.30	14.80

The total costs include the journal price, library processing costs (at $81 per title), reshelving, photocopying, and all user costs. It is clear that cost per reading varies dramatically by journal price at low levels of reading but very little as the number of readings climb above 250. This shows that the cost per reading of frequently-read journals is insensitive to the price of the journal. It also shows that

---

[6]These costs include instances in which scientists obtain the article themselves and those in which they ask others to do so; that is, the denominator for each average is the total number of readings.

the cost per reading of infrequently-read journals is high for $250 and $1,000 journals compared with interlibrary borrowing costs. These aspects of costs are explored in detail in Chapter 13.

Usefulness and Value of Journal Collections

Journal collections are considered very important to scientists with average importance ratings (where 1 = not at all important and 5 = very important) ranging from 4.27 to 4.72 for current and permanent collections in academic and special libraries. Satisfaction ratings tend to be lower than importance ratings, however, ranging from 3.59 to 3.73. Lack of comprehensiveness generally accounts for the low satisfaction ratings.

Library-provided scholarly journals tend to be more useful and valuable than journals and articles obtained from other sources. Scientists at the University of Tennessee indicate that a lower proportion of library-provided articles (versus those obtained from other sources) are read for teaching purposes (29.7 percent versus 53.1 percent), but the importance of the information contained in the article to the teaching objective is rated higher for library articles (5.27 versus 4.53 on a scale of 1 = not at all important to 7 = absolutely essential).[7] The proportion of readings for research purposes are about the same (75.7 percent for library-provided articles versus 75.0 percent), but again ratings of importance is much higher (5.41 versus 4.50 on a scale of 1 to 7). Reading for current awareness/keeping up and continuing education for oneself is done much less often from library-provided articles (45.9 percent versus 71.9 percent), but roughly the same for preparing a formal publication (37.8 percent versus 25.0 percent) and for preparing a formal talk or presentation (18.9 percent versus 25.0 percent).

In terms of outcomes or consequences resulting from reading, there is little difference in proportion of readings achieving the outcomes from the two sources as shown in Table 37. University scientists spend more time reading library-provided articles, however, indicating their willingness to pay more in their time for the information, i.e., seventy minutes per reading versus forty-four minutes.

In Chapter 9 we demonstrated the usefulness and value of special libraries to scientists and their organizations. Below we demonstrate that library-provided journals tend to be more useful and valuable than other sources of journals and articles. For example, Table 38 shows that a higher proportion of readings from

---

[7]Based on questions posed about their last reading of a scholarly journal article (King et al. survey 1993).

Table 37	Proportion of Readings by University Scientists Resulting in Their Improved Performance by Source of Articles Read: 1990–1993 (in Percent)		

		Source of Article Read	
Performance Indicator		**Library**	**Other**
Saved time or money		16.7	17.2
Improved quality of activity		63.3	62.1
Helped perform activity better		33.3	37.9
Helped complete activity faster		16.7	13.8

Source: King et al. surveys 1990–1993

Table 38	Proportion of Readings by Non-University Scientists Resulting in Their Improved Performance by Source of Articles Read: 1994-1998 (in Percent)		

		Source of Article Read	
Performance Indicator		**Library**	**Other**
Saved time or money		32	23
Improved quality of activity		52	41
Work done faster		25	18

Source: King et al. surveys 1994-1998

special library-provided journals result in savings, in improved quality, and in performing work faster.

Approximately 32 percent of readings from library-provided journals result in savings to readers versus 23 percent of readings from other sources, and the average amount of savings from library-provided readings is nearly 50 percent higher. The amount of time spent reading library-provided articles is fifty-five minutes per reading versus forty-six minutes for other sources. Thus the value these scientists are willing to pay for the information is somewhat higher for library-provided journals.

We examined the value of the library-provided journals by asking scientists what it might cost them to obtain the last article they read if no library existed. A sequence of questions was developed to establish this information. It was observed that approximately one-half of the library-provided readings involved new information. Of the readings in which the information was new, approximately 40 percent said the information could be obtained from a colleague or consultant, another library (35 percent), or by purchasing the journal (25 percent). The total cost to the reader of obtaining the information from another source is estimated by the readers to be $69.10 per reading.[8] Assuming 137 readings from a $500 journal, the current cost is $17.97 per reading including $4.27 per reading attributable to purchasing and processing journals, $1.48 per reading for reshelving and photocopying, and $12.22 per reading for readers going to the library and acquiring the articles. Thus it would cost nearly four times as much to use alternative sources as it now costs to provide a $500 journal in the library.

USE AND ECONOMICS OF JOURNAL ROUTING

Use of Routed Journals

Journal routing is most prevalent in organizations served by special libraries, and our data below reflect surveys and cost-finding studies performed in companies and government agencies from 1994 to 1998. A high proportion of scientists in the surveyed organizations use routing services (59 percent), and they average receiving 2.4 journals in this manner. Altogether the number of readings from these journals is 22.9 readings per scientist or 9.6 readings per journal title received compared with 13.4 readings per personal subscription.

Approximately 30 percent of the items read from routed journals are photocopied. Routing serves a dual role in providing current awareness and access to the articles. Depending on the number of scientists on the routing lists, however, there can be a considerable delay in receiving routed issues. Furthermore, while being routed the issues are not available to users if a need arises unless another copy is available in the library or elsewhere.

The number of names on a routing list is typically six to fifteen, with an average receipt time of thirty-six days from the initial distribution date. Because of this delay, average ratings of satisfaction with receipt time is low (3.07 on a scale of 1

---

[8]This estimated average cost per reading includes those readings in which there would be no attempt to obtain the information because it was already known (i.e., the cost of such instances is $0).

to 5—with 1 being very dissatisfied and 5 being very satisfied). Of course time of receipt and satisfaction varies by placement on the routing list. The average wait for those who are first through sixth on the list is eighteen days, and their satisfaction rating is 3.73. For those above sixth position on the list, the average wait is 51 days with a satisfaction rating of 2.65. Position on the list seems to have a minimal effect on the amount of reading (i.e., those on the top half read about 12 percent more articles than those on the bottom half). It is desirable, if possible, to keep the number of recipients to less than eight.

Cost of Journal Routing

In this section we examine the unit cost, cost per reading, impact, and cost-benefit of journal routing. Journal costs can be subdivided into the fixed cost of purchase (price) and the processes necessary to make the journals available for access.[9] The unit cost of processing these journals is found to be approximately $81 per title.

A more useful measure in comparing alternative journal distribution and access, however, is to allocate the total fixed cost by amount of reading (i.e., cost per reading). This amounts to approximately $1.05 per reading with eight persons reading 9.6 articles apiece and excluding the purchase price. In addition to the fixed costs of purchasing and processing journals, there are costs associated with journal routing including routing list maintenance (approximately $6.80 per user per title), actual journal routing ($1.10 per issue routed), and collection maintenance and shelving (approximately $0.60 per issue routed). Together, these costs typically total approximately $0.89 per reading.[10] Thus, the total library processing cost is approximately $1.94 per reading, excluding the journal price. This comes to a total of $149 per title. For each scientist who receives a routed journal, the total library processing cost is estimated at $18.69 per recipient based on an average of eight scientists receiving the journal.

To this cost, one can add the purchase price allocated by readings which runs approximately $3.26 per reading for a $250 journal (assuming 9.6 readings per title received and eight persons on the list), $6.51 for a $500 journal, and $13.02 for a $1,000 journal. The cost to readers is estimated at $5.10 per reading attributable to browsing through issues and making photocopies as needed. They average nineteen minutes reading the articles, amounting to $15.30 per reading.

---

[9]Processing costs involve such activities as serials acquisition, check-in and processing, collection development (allocated), mail sorting (allocated), and collection maintenance.

[10]Assuming an average of 8.3 issues per journal (see Chapter 11).

Thus with 76.8 average readings of a $250 journal, it costs the organization approximately $10.30 per reading, not including reading time. With changes in parameters, the average varies as shown in Table 39. One can see that the cost per reading is not significantly affected at high levels of reading: over 50 readings at a journal price of $250; over 75 readings at $500; and over 150 readings at $1,000.

Table 39	Cost per Reading of Routed Journals at Various Subscription Prices and Number of Readings per Title (in Dollars)		
		Price	
Number of Readings	$250	$500	$1,000
10	32.05	57.05	107.05
25	17.05	27.05	47.05
50	12.05	17.05	27.05
75	10.40	13.70	20.40
100	9.55	12.05	17.05
150	8.70	10.40	13.70
200	8.30	9.55	12.05

Value of Journal Routing

Readers were asked about the articles read from journal routing and what they would do to get the information elsewhere if necessary. About 60 percent of the readings involved information of which readers were unaware prior to reading the journal article. If they did not have journal routing, the readers speculated that it would cost them approximately $67 per reading to use another source considering such costs as their time (or the time of another staff member), journal subscriptions, and photocopying. Thus, for a $500 journal the cost to the parent organization is:

- $8.45 per reading for library purchase and processing
- $5.10 per reading for a reader to obtain the information, and
- $15.30 per reading of user time spent reading.

Under these assumptions, library costs are approximately 40 percent of the cost in user time to obtain and read articles. The total cost to the organization to provide the information (prior to reading) is $13.55 per reading which is about one-fifth of what it would cost the organization if the service were not provided (i.e., $67 per reading).

PURCHASE OF JOURNALS FOR DEPARTMENT OR PERSONAL USE

Some libraries, special libraries in particular, assume the responsibility for ordering journals and other information materials for departmental or personal use. Approximately 43 percent of scientists in organizations offering such a service say that they use it on average over two times a year. The service is not rated high in importance (3.70 average rating) nor high in satisfaction (3.91). Scientists say they use the service for approximately 70 percent of their orders because the service saves their time or that of another staff member. About two-thirds of them believe that library staff can place orders faster.

The cost to the library is approximately $8.26 and the cost to users runs approximately $3.18. If the library did not provide the service, scientists say they would handle the order themselves 61 percent of the time, delegate the order to someone else on staff 32 percent of the time, and go elsewhere to place the order 7 percent of the time. Scientists indicate that it would cost them approximately thirty-two more minutes of their time, or seventeen minutes of someone else's time, and $3.27 in ancillary costs such as telephone calls and fees. These resources would cost approximately $36.00 or 3.1 times the current cost to the library of $8.26 and to users of $3.18.

USE AND ECONOMICS OF INTERLIBRARY BORROWING AND DOCUMENT DELIVERY SERVICES

Use of Interlibrary Borrowing and Document Delivery Services

In Chapter 8 we showed that not only do scientists rely heavily on interlibrary borrowing and document delivery services, but that such use is growing. The 1993 surveys of university scientists showed that nearly 90 percent of them had used library interlibrary loan services, and they averaged 7.5 uses of the service per year (including non-users). Studies of non-university scientists surveyed from 1994 to 1998 showed 64 percent of scientists being users of these services, with 14.3 uses per scientist per year.

Interlibrary loan includes both interlibrary borrowing and interlibrary lending, and many of the larger libraries lend more articles than they borrow (i.e., they are net lenders).[11] Interlibrary borrowing is considered very important by university and other scientists: average importance of 4.74 and 4.27 respectively (where 1 = very little importance and 5 = very important). However, satisfaction ratings tend to be lower (4.05 and 3.88 respectively), mostly due to delay in response times (where satisfaction with response times are 3.60 and 3.72 respectively) and the fact that not all requests are filled. The average response time is about 14 days for research libraries (Jackson 1997) and 10 days for college libraries (Oberlin Group) with fill rates of 85 percent and 91 percent respectively. Our survey at the University of Tennessee showed an average turnaround time of 13 days, but this is reduced to 6 days when document delivery services are used. To these times, one day is added for internal processing.

Our surveys showed that about one-third of the requests for interlibrary borrowing and document delivery required fast delivery,[12] with methods such as courier services and fax being used to satisfy these rush requests. In one study (King and Griffiths 1984), a conjoint measurement analysis was done to show the relative utility of three service attributes: price, speed of delivery, and quality of reproduction.

Trade-Off Analysis of Service Attributes

Conjoint analysis is a method that can aid in estimating the relative importance of a combination of several product attributes.[13] This technique requires that potential consumers make overall judgments about a set of complex alternatives involving different combinations of the product attributes. These rankings are then used to arrive at a set of utility scales for the product attributes that are compatible with the original overall rankings.

In our particular situation, three attributes or factors are expected to influence consumer preference: price, speed of delivery, and quality of reproduction. Under

---

[11]At one time, lending of journal articles involved mailing issues or bound volumes, much like lending books. Now this practice is rare, however, since articles are routinely photocopied and sent. Yet it is still called interlibrary lending.

[12]In special libraries, scientists need articles in less than one day 30 percent of the time and in 2 to 5 days 16 percent of the time.

[13]The general researcher will find a good introduction to conjoint measurement in: Richard M. Johnson, "Trade-Off Analysis of Consumer Values," *Journal of Marketing Research* 11 (May 1974) 121-127 and Paul E. Green and Yoram Wind, "New Way to Measure Consumers' Judgments," *Harvard Business Review*, July-August 1975, pp. 107-118.

consideration are four alternative prices: $4.00, $10.00, $20.00, and $30.00 (in current dollars) and four different speeds of delivery: within an hour, within a day, overnight, and within a week. Also under consideration are two different qualities of reproduction: high and low. These levels are summarized in Table 40.

Although it is possible to have potential users rank alternatives in which all three attributes (price, speed, and quality of reproduction) vary at the same time, keeping track of multiple attributes is confusing to most potential users. Therefore we requested that the responding libraries rank only pairwise combinations of these attributes.

The conjoint measurement analysis enables the rankings to be converted to a relative utility (or value) for the different levels of each attribute. The utility is an indicator of the importance of the attribute to the respondents. For example, computed utilities for rush orders and non-rush orders are given in Table 41.

One can see, under rush orders for example, that a $4.00 price has a much higher utility (36) than a $20.00 price (11). Responding within an hour has a higher utility (29) than within a week (0). Compared across attributes, the $4.00 price (36) is more important than delivering within an hour (29). One can also compare the utilities of the attributes of rush orders versus non-rush orders.

Table 40	Attributes and Levels Used in Conjoint Analysis
Attribute	**Level**
Price	$ 4.00
	$10.00
	$20.00
	$30.00
Speed of Delivery	Within an hour
	Within a day
	Overnight
	Within a week
Quality of Reproduction	High
	Low

| Table 41 | Normalized Utilities from Conjoint Analysis for Rush Orders and Non-rush Orders (Special Libraries: R&D, Law, Business—1984) | | | |

Attribute	Level	Rush	Non-Rush
Price	$ 4.00	36	37
	$10.00	22	21
	$20.00	11	11
	$30.00	0	0
Speed of Delivery	Within an hour	29	26
	Within a day	21	17
	Overnight	14	11
	Within a week	0	0
Quality of Reproduction	High	18	19
	Low	0	0

Source: King et al. survey 1984

Since the importance of speed of delivery is generally greater for rush orders than non-rush orders, the relative magnitudes of the utility measures seem to make sense, or are as one would expect them to be.

The total utility of a service can be calculated by adding the appropriate utility associated with the level of the attribute provided by that service. For example, suppose a document delivery service had a price (rush orders) of $20.00 (11), speed of delivery of overnight (14), and high quality of reproduction (18), but special graphics were not available (0)—the total quality for that service would be 43. If they lowered their price to $4.00 their total utility would increase to 68.

The data were collected for the conjoint measurement analysis by having library respondents indicate their preferences for the last article copy order made by them (i.e., a critical incident). It was felt that they could focus better on the importance of such attributes as speed of delivery and price if a specific incident were used. Also, every order for an individual article copy is different. They were asked whether the last order was a rush order as well. Utilities were then calculated for rush or non-rush orders and for several types of libraries (i.e., public, academic department, academic main, ARL, federal government, state government, and special: medical, R&D, law, and business). Results of some of these computations are presented in Tables 42 and 43. The utilities do not seem to vary significantly across the various types of libraries, although the level of price seems to be less important for libraries that serve private organizations such as R&D, law, and business libraries.

Cost of Interlibrary Borrowing and Document Delivery

The cost to libraries of interlibrary borrowing includes request processing, bibliographic look-up, follow-up, occasional re-submittal to another library,[14] and receipt processing. Kingma (1995) estimates the cost by a university library to obtain an external copy of an article to be in the range of $15.60 to $20.90 (adjusted for inflation). The ARL study (Jackson 1997) estimates a unit cost of $18.35 for

Table 42	Normalized Utilities from Conjoint Analysis for Rush Orders and Non-rush Orders (Academic Main Libraries—1984)		
Attribute	**Level**	**Rush**	**Non-Rush**
Price	$4.00	39	42
	$10.00	25	24
	$20.00	15	12
	$30.00	0	0
Speed of Delivery	Within an hour	25	23
	Within a day	17	15
	Overnight	13	12
	Within a week	0	0
Quality of Reproduction	High	16	17
	Low	3	1
Source: King et al. survey 1984			

---

[14]At one time fill rates were quite low, but development of union serials lists and other mechanisms have reduced this problem in recent years.

Table 43	**Normalized Utilities from Conjoint Analysis for Rush Orders and Non-rush Orders** (ARL Libraries—1984)

Attribute	Level	Non-Rush
Price	$ 4.00	39
	$10.00	22
	$20.00	11
	$30.00	0
Speed of Delivery	Within an hour	24
	Within a day	15
	Overnight	11
	Within a week	0
Quality of Reproduction	High	19
	Low	0

Source: King et al. survey 1984

research libraries ($9.76 low, $27.84 high) and $12.08 for college libraries ($6.39 low, $18.50 high). To this is added an estimated user cost of $2.90 per reading (Kingma 1995). Estimates of cost from the special library studies are $21.50 for interlibrary borrowing and $22.75 for document delivery services (including fees of approximately $10.00). The cost to users for identifying, requesting, and receiving borrowed articles is approximately $11.34 or $32.84 total.

It is noted that the provision of interlibrary services implies that a library accepts the cost of interlibrary loan requests made by the library in addition to interlibrary borrowing costs. These costs are estimated at $9.48 in research libraries, $7.25 in college libraries (Jackson 1997), and $24.10 in special libraries (Griffiths and King 1993, adjusted). Kingma (1995) estimated this cost at $3.60 to $12.30. Studies (Griffiths and King 1989, King and Griffiths 1990) have shown that economies of scale exist in interlibrary lending and borrowing processing. The critical mass at which unit costs level out is approximately 1,000 items per year.

Value of Interlibrary Borrowing

If the library does not have an interlibrary loan service, 15 percent of scientists say that they would not bother pursuing the information, but most of those who would search further for the information say that they would go to another library (68 percent), the publisher (6 percent), another document (6 percent), or another service (11 percent). The scientists estimate that this would cost them $175 or approximately 5.3 times the current costs of $21.50 to the library and $11.34 to the user.

COMPARISON OF COSTS AMONG JOURNAL SERVICES

In previous sections we provided estimates of costs for several library services involving scholarly journals: in-library use of journals (including current periodicals), journal routing, purchase of journals for departments or personal use, and access to external collections through interlibrary borrowing or document delivery services. Electronic publishing provides additional access to journal subscriptions and copies of individual articles. Librarians are faced increasingly with deciding among many electronic alternatives for individual articles, issues, titles, or groups of scholarly journals.

In this section we provide some guidance for choosing among alternatives based on the likely cost per reading including the cost to the library and the cost to users. Each service has certain parameters that affect cost, such as price for purchasing subscriptions, distance to a library for in-library reading, fee for obtaining separate copies of articles, and amount of reading for all services. It is emphasized that cost estimates may or may not apply to a specific library, but they do represent relative orders of magnitude and reflect differences in cost due to the variations of these parameters.

As prices increase, scientists are faced with a choice of subscribing to journals or going to the library to read the journal in the library. The subscription cost is the price of the journal plus the cost to the reader of ordering, receiving, and storing the journal ($11.00 per title). There is also a cost associated with browsing through the journal and making photocopies when needed, which averages $5.10 per reading. Both the library and reader incur costs when the library is used. It costs the library an average of $1.48 per reading to reshelve and photocopy, and it costs the user approximately $10.04 to locate and identify the articles that they read plus the time necessary to go to the library, which depends on the distance to the library. Also, this latter cost is spread over an average of 3.7 readings per visit. One can establish the amount of reading necessary to justify subscribing versus going to the library while recognizing that costs vary by journal prices and distance to the library. Such break-even points are displayed in Table 44. The break-even points determine whether to subscribe; in other words, one should subscribe above the break-even amount of reading.

For example, above twenty-seven readings of a $250 journal at a distance from the library of five to ten minutes, one should subscribe to the journal. If one is close to the library (under five minutes), it is less expensive for readers to go to the library if there are fewer than thirty-five readings. However, as the distance increases, it costs less per reading to subscribe when the amount of reading is sufficient. For example, if a scientist is over ten minutes away and has over twenty readings in a $250 journal, it is less expensive to subscribe to the journal.

Similarly, one can establish break-even points for whether a library should subscribe or rely on a document delivery service to obtain separate copies, including electronic copies. The cost of document delivery is $12.75 plus a fee and $11.34 for user costs. These break-even points are presented in Table 45.

Above these break-even points a library should subscribe to a journal, and below them the library should rely on separate copies of articles. For example, if a journal is priced at $500 and the document delivery fee is $10, the break-even point is twenty-nine readings. Thus if there are more than this number of readings, the library should subscribe; otherwise using the document delivery service proves more cost-effective. One can also add a penalty cost for time delays to the fees. For example, if the penalty is $5, one adds the $5 to the fee and looks up the corresponding break-even value. Since the break-even point is very insensitive to the fee, there is not much gained in adding the penalty. Clearly, journal prices dominate the break-even points.

One could also compare the costs using journal routing at various prices versus document delivery at various service fees. The break-even for these alternatives is presented in Table 46. The break-even readings are similar to purchasing and document delivery, but tend to be lower for the journal routing comparison except at the $100 price and $20 and $30 fees and the $250 price and $30 fee.

The comparisons given above provide a rough guide for deciding among alternative sources. One can develop such break-even points by knowing costs and being able to observe the amount of reading of specific journal titles. Hopefully, electronic journal access by subscription or on demand will simplify this process by tallying use (see Chapters 17 and 18).

Table 44	Break-even Point in Readings between Personally Subscribing to Journals and Using the Library at Various Journal Prices and Distances to the Library

	Distance to Library (Minutes)		
Journal Prices	<5	5 to 10	>10
$ 100	14.8	11.5	8.6
$ 250	34.8	26.9	20.2
$ 500	68.0	52.7	39.5
$1,000	134.6	104.3	78.1

Table 45	Break-even Point in Readings between Purchasing and Using Document Delivery at Various Journal Prices and Document Delivery Fees

	Document Delivery Fees				
Journal Prices	$0	$5	$10	$20	$30
$ 100	17.4	11.8	8.9	6.0	4.5
$ 250	31.9	21.5	16.2	10.9	8.2
$ 500	55.9	37.8	28.5	19.1	14.4
$ 1,000	104.0	70.2	53.0	35.6	26.8

Table 46	Break-even Point in Readings between Journal Routing and Using Document Delivery at Various Journal Prices and Document Delivery Fees

	Document Delivery Fees				
Journal Prices	$0	$5	$10	$20	$30
$ 100	13.1	10.4	8.6	6.4	5.1
$ 250	21.0	16.7	13.8	10.2	8.2
$ 500	34.2	27.1	22.4	16.7	13.3
$ 1,000	60.5	47.9	39.7	29.5	23.5

PUBLISHER PARTICIPATION

CHAPTER 11

Scientific Scholarly Journal Publishing

INTRODUCTION

In this chapter we provide an overview of scientific scholarly publishing including a recent description of the number, size, price, and circulation of scientific scholarly journals published in the United States. These aspects of scholarly journals are shown to have changed dramatically over the past two decades; for example, growth in the number of journal titles published has diminished from the numbers historically observed. These aspects are also shown to vary among fields of science and by types of publishers (i.e., commercial, society, educational, and "other").

We also briefly describe current journal publishing costs and prices and their trends over two decades. The costs are shown to vary by journal size and circulation, which accounts for over one-half of the increase in prices from 1975 to 1995. We also show that there is a dynamic relationship among journal cost (and size), price, and demand that is not one-sided. In other words, increased prices result in reduced demand, but equally valid is the possibility that low demand (sometimes determined by the size of a discipline) requires high prices.

We also discuss some unique economic properties and characteristics of scientific scholarly publishing. While one can demonstrate quantitatively relationships among cost, price, and demand, there are many qualitative aspects of publishing that help explain why scholarly journals differ from the typical consumer products and services. Chapters 12, 13, and 14 delve much more deeply into scientific, scholarly journal publishing costs, pricing, and financing.

A RECENT PICTURE[1]

Number and Size of Scientific Scholarly Journals

In 1995, U.S. publishers produced an estimated 6,771 scholarly scientific journals (see Chapter 4 for the definitions and methods used to collect the data). We characterize these journals by four types of publishers (commercial, society, educational, and other) and by nine scientific fields. We adopted the nine fields of science designated by the National Science Foundation (NSF) in the 1970s as shown in Table 47[2]. We reported these nine fields in order to compare trends from 1975 to 1995. Other fields and multi-fields include other fields of science such as the information sciences and multi-field publications such as *Science*. Table 47 shows the number and size of current scientific scholarly journals by field of science.

The number of journals is dominated by engineering (828), life sciences (2,104), and social sciences (2,140), which together represent 75 percent of all scientific scholarly journals. The journals in psychology and the social sciences tend to be smaller in size in both numbers of articles and pages, and they also publish less frequently (number of issues) than the other seven fields. In the other fields, the number of issues ranges from 8.8 to 14.2 per year, and the number of pages published ranges from 1,600 to 4,500.

Table 48 shows comparable information by type of publisher. Commercial publishers account for approximately 40 percent (2,679) of the titles published in 1995, with one-half of these involving life sciences journals such as clinical medicine and biology. Professional society journals account for nearly one-fourth of the journals (1,557), and all scientific fields are well represented by society publications with the exception of the social sciences (including economics), where only 7 percent of the titles in this field are society publications. Nearly one-half of physical sciences journals such as physics and chemistry are society publications.

---

[1]Most of this section is taken from Tenopir and King (1997) with permission.
[2]Recently NSF has formed four general categories by combining computer sciences, mathematics, and portions of other sciences (information science), as well as psychology and social sciences. The two current final groups are engineering and the remaining fields which collectively are called the natural sciences.

Table 47	**Number of U.S. Scholarly Scientific Journals and Average Number of Issues, Articles, and Pages per Title by Nine Fields of Science: 1995**

| | | Average Number per Title | | | |
| | Number of | | | Article | All |
Field of Science	Journals	Issues	Articles	Pages	Pages
Physical sciences	432	14.2	306	2604	3342
Mathematics, statistics	206	9.1	127	2069	2276
Computer sciences	126	8.8	165	1947	2370
Environmental sciences	322	9.8	117	1641	1807
Engineering	828	9.0	163	1830	2039
Life sciences	2104	11.0	130	1396	1596
Psychology	342	4.5	49	757	842
Social sciences	2140	3.9	38	918	1099
Other fields/multi-fields	271	12.1	396	2742	4535
All fields	6771	8.3	123	1434	1723

Source: Tenopir and King 1997

Table 48	**Number of U.S. Scholarly Scientific Journals and Average Number of Issues, Articles, and Pages per Title by Type of Publisher: 1995**

| | | Average Number per Title | | | |
| | Number of | | | Article | All |
Type of Publisher	Journals	Issues	Articles	Pages	Pages
Commercial	2679	9.9	118	1533	1811
Society	1557	9.3	202	1813	2296
Educational	1106	4.3	70	1500	1742
Other	1429	7.3	84	786	919
All publishers	6771	8.3	123	1434	1723

Source: Tenopir and King 1997

University presses and other educational publishers account for 16 percent of scholarly titles, with 70 percent of these titles being social science titles. "Other" publishers include government, government laboratories, non-profit organizations, and businesses such as AT&T Bell Laboratories. About one-fifth of the titles are published by these organizations; in fact, 63 percent of their publications are social sciences journals.

Educational and "other" publishers tend to both publish less frequently than commercial and society publishers and to publish fewer articles per title. While publications in the educational sector publish fewer articles, their articles tend to be longer and, therefore, they publish nearly as many pages annually as the commercial and society publishers. Society publishers tend to publish more non-article pages than other types of publishers, often in order to present member-related information.

Scholarly Journal Costs

Publishing costs and a cost model are discussed in detail in Chapter 12. The cost model consists of five types of activities: article processing, non-article processing, reproduction, distribution, and publishing support. Based on the average parameters of journals estimated in 1995 discussed in this chapter,[3] the direct cost to provide the first copy of an article is about $1,545.[4] Non-article processing involves preparation of items such as issue covers, Tables of Contents, book reviews, letters, brief communications, and advertisements. Journals average about 289 non-article pages which cost about $19,415 annually or $65 per page compared with $130 per article page. With a total of 1,723 pages and an average of 5,800 subscribers, the direct cost of reproduction and distribution totals less than $31 per subscriber. Publishing support activities[5] are those not directly attributable to article or non-article processing, reproduction, and distribution. For the parameters and costs discussed above, the indirect costs are estimated to be $168,541.

---

[3]Publishing parameters that affect cost include, among others, number of issues, articles, pages, and subscriptions.

[4]The article processing begins with receipt of an article manuscript and ends with first-copy composition, typesetting, and engraving. Specific activities include receipt processing, disposition decision-making, identifying reviewers, review processing, subject editing, indexing and coding, redaction, and preparation of master images.

[5]Support activities include administration (e.g., accounting, management, equipment management, and facilities), marketing, rights and copyright management, financial activities (e.g., research and development, capitalization of equipment, and profit), and other indirect sources/costs such as insurance, taxes, and utilities. They also include staff costs such as vacation, sick leave, holidays, pension, and insurance.

For the purposes of our cost analysis, support costs are allocated in the following manner: article and non-article costs are increased by 35 percent; reproduction and distribution costs are increased by 15 percent; and the support cost of approximately $68,000 is treated as "fixed" because some costs such as marketing and rights management are incurred regardless of the size and circulation of the journal. Thus, with support costs allocated, the article processing costs amount to $2,085 per article, and reproduction and distribution costs amount to approximately $36 per subscription.

With the parameters given the total cost is estimated to be $559,535. Of course, journal costs vary dramatically among journals depending on the level of effort applied to the various activities, quality of paper, and number of issues. The number of pages published affects first-copy costs, as well as reproduction and distribution costs. At the parameters and costs listed above, we have shown that a journal will have a dramatically lower unit cost per subscription as the number of subscriptions increases; for example the unit cost is $775 per subscription with 500 subscribers, $181 with 2,500 subscribers, $107 with 5,000, and $70 with 10,000. Thus, in order to recover costs, journals with low circulation must charge a higher price. This fact is highly significant in understanding why some journals and publishers have high prices.

SCIENTIFIC SCHOLARLY JOURNAL PRICES, SIZE, AND CIRCULATION

Publishers sometimes use differential pricing by charging individual subscribers a lower price than institutional subscribers such as libraries. Nearly every publisher has a different price for foreign subscribers. Society publishers provide subscriptions bundled as part of a membership package and sometimes charge other individuals a non-member price which is yet a different price from that charged to institutions. Across all journals, the estimated average institutional price is $284, and the average individual price is $255.[6,7] Most journals (76 percent) charge a single price for individual and institutional subscriptions. Subscription prices vary dramatically by type of publisher and field of science reflecting their journal sizes and circulation.

---

[6]In Chapter 13, we show that others have observed average prices that are higher than here. These prices and trends are discussed in detail in that chapter.

[7]It is noted that the average price per subscriber is only approximately 40 percent of the average price per journal because some journals have a very large circulation, and their low prices tend to dominate calculations of the average price per subscriber.

The individual price, institutional price, average annual number of articles published per journal, and average number of subscriptions per journal are listed in Table 49 for each of the nine fields of science. The average prices (individual, institutional) per journal range from a low in the social sciences ($80, $89) to a high in the physical sciences ($553, $616). The average prices reflect, to some degree, the number of articles published and the number of subscriptions, although there is always a danger in interpreting the meaning of averages when skewed distributions are involved. For example, based on averages, one would expect mathematics journals to have lower costs and prices than physical science journals because they tend to have fewer articles and similar circulations. The apparent lower article-related cost of physical science journals may be partially offset in mathematics, however, by the high cost of typesetting or composing mathemati-

Table 49	Average Price, Number of Articles, and Circulation per Journal by Field of Science: 1995			
Field of Science/ No. of Titles	Average Individual Price per Journals	Average Institutional Price per Journal	Average No. of Articles per Journal	Average Circulation per Journal
Physical sciences/432	$553	$616	306	4,700
Mathematics, statistics/206	$527	$570	127	6,200
Computer sciences/126	$328	$331	165	13,700
Environmental sciences/322	$441	$458	117	4,900
Engineering/828	$268	$357	163	10,000
Life sciences/2,104	$344	$366	130	4,000
Psychology/342	$130	$166	49	3,000
Social sciences/2,140	$ 80	$ 89	38	3,200
Other fields/multi-fields/271	$134	$137	396	29,400
All fields/6,771	$255	$284	123	5,800

Source: Tenopir and King 1997.

cal equations (Odlyzko 1995). The price of environmental science journals is approximately the same as mathematics, but the apparent high price cannot also be explained by unusual composition or typesetting costs. Prices for computer science and engineering journals appear to be lower because of the low number of articles published and the high number of subscriptions. The very low number of articles published in psychology and social science journals seems to partially account for their very low costs and prices.

The average individual price, institutional price, proportion of journals having a single price, average number of articles, and average number of subscribers are listed by type of publisher in Table 50. As shown in Table 50, the estimated average reported circulation for scholarly journals is 5,800 subscriptions per journal, with society publishers averaging 13,300 subscriptions, comercial publishers averaging 3,700 subscriptions, and educational publishers averaging 1,700 subscriptions. The circulation numbers for specific titles in our sample of 715 scholarly journals range from 150 subscriptions to over 600,000, demonstrating a highly skewed distribution. In fact, the median number of subscriptions is very near 1,900, with one-fourth of the titles having fewer than 900 subscriptions and one-fourth surpassing 5,700. The median number of subscriptions for commercial publishers is 1,400, with 41 percent

Table 50	Average Price, Number of Articles, and Circulation per Journal by Type of Publisher: 1995				
Type of Publisher/ No. of Titles	Individual Price per Journal ($)	Institution Price per Journal ($)	Avg. No. of Articles per Journal	Proportion of Journals with Single Price	Average Circulation per Journal
Commercial/2,679	$463	$487	118	85%	3,700
Society/1,557	$178	$229	202	69%	13,300
Educational/1,106	$47	$81	70	60%	1,700
Other/1,429	$112	$119	84	80%	4,600
All publishers/6,771	$255	$284	123	76%	5,800

Source: Tenopir and King 1997

of the journals having fewer than 1,000 subscribers. The median for society publishers is 5,600, with only 6 percent having fewer than 1,000. The median for educational publishers is about as high as the average (1,500 versus 1,700), and 24 percent are below 1,000. The median for other publishers is 3,500, with very few journals having less than 1,000 subscribers. Circulation and pricing are discussed in depth in Chapter 13.

It appears that the community served and pricing strategies vary dramatically among the four types of publishers. A somewhat different picture emerges when we consider the price per article published or the price per page published. For example, average institutional journal price, price per article, and price per page are as follows:

- *Commercial publishers:* $487, $4.10 per article, $0.27 per page
- *Society publishers:* $229, $1.10 per article, $0.10 per page
- *Educational publishers:* $ 81, $1.20 per article, $0.05 per page
- *Other publishers:* $119, $1.40 per article, $0.13 per page.

Overall, publishers' prices are $284 per journal, $2.30 per article, and $0.16 per page.

SCIENTIFIC SCHOLARLY JOURNAL PUBLISHING TRENDS

Trends in Number and Size

In 1975, there were 4,175 print scientific scholarly journals published in the United States (as defined by *Ulrich's*), increasing to 6,771 in 1995. Since the number of scientists more than doubled during this time period, it is clear that the number of journals published per scientist has dropped appreciably. Since journals now tend to provide more articles (123 articles per journal in 1995 versus 85 in 1975), however, the number of articles per scientist has not changed significantly. Not only are publishers providing more articles per journal, but the number of issues, article pages, and total pages have increased as well. The average number of issues has increased from 6.5 to 8.3 per year; article pages per title have increased from 630 to 1,434, and total pages from 820 to 1,723. In fact, the number of pages published per scientist has even increased approximately 50 percent.

Compared with 1975, the proportion of journals published by societies has apparently diminished from 39 percent to 23 percent, while education publishers remained about the same (18 percent and 16 percent). Both commercial and other publishers have gained share (from 35 percent to 40 percent and from 8 percent to 21 percent respectively).

Trends in Cost and Price

As clearly demonstrated in the literature, scholarly journal prices have increased at a phenomenal rate over the past two decades (see Chapter 13). Prices of the journals in our tracking sample increased from an average of $39 in 1975 to $284 in 1995 for institutional subscriptions. This 7.3 fold increase can not be nearly explained by inflation or increases in the size of the journals. In fact, of the $245 absolute amount of increase, only 56 percent can be explained by these two factors.

A number of other plausible explanations exist (see Chapter 13), but one that is particularly compelling is the sharp decline over this period in personal subscriptions from approximately 5.8 subscriptions per scientist to 2.7. This drop, reflecting the extreme sensitivity of personal subscription demand to price changes, has resulted in an annual loss of billions of dollars in revenue that has been recovered through exceptionally high prices which libraries pay due to their relatively less sensitivity to price increases. As a result, scientists rely much more on library-provided articles at a cost to them in time; libraries, in order to stay within budgets, now provide less information at a much higher cost per unit of information;[8] and funders are disillusioned concerning these services.

Trends in Circulation

Some, but not all, of the circulation data reported in this section were obtained from *Ulrich's*, although those data may be somewhat unreliable (see Chapter 4). Nevertheless, we are presenting them here as a general indicator of trends. Based on the journal tracking data, the average circulation per journal was 5,800 subscriptions in 1995, with a median around 1,900. The average in 1975 was estimated at around 6,100, and the median was near 2,900. Of the 6,100 subscriptions in 1975, approximately 3,700 were individual subscriptions. We do not have a comparable breakdown for 1995, although we estimate that an average of approximately 2,300 of the 5,800 subscriptions were U.S. individual subscriptions. From surveys of scientists, we estimate the current average number of personal subscriptions to be 2.7 subscriptions per scientist per year, an obvious decrease from 5.8 in 1975 (4.2 to 3.9 subscriptions per for university scientist and 6.2 to 2.4 for non-university scientists).

---

[8]Less information is provided because they subscribe to fewer journals and tightened budgets mean that many fewer books and other materials are purchased.

In 1975, the total number of subscriptions was estimated at 25.5 million, of which approximately 22.2 million were U.S. subscribers. By 1995, subscriptions had climbed to an estimated 39.3 million.

UNIQUE ECONOMIC PROPERTIES AND CHARACTERISTICS

Scholarly journal publications are unique economic entities by virtue of the following properties and characteristics:

- The product of scholarly journal publishing is the information content in the articles and its special attributes such as accuracy, understandability (readability), comprehensiveness, timeliness, accessibility, availability and provision in the appropriate dosage required (see Chapter 3 for a more complete list of attributes).

- Information is a non-depletive commodity in the sense that use by one person neither depletes the supply nor denies its use by others. Packages of information in issues or bound volumes, however, are depletive. Otherwise, interlibrary loan might still involve lending issues or bound volumes instead of the current process of distributing photocopies and electronic versions of articles.

- Economists have long tried to characterize published information, resulting in strong disagreements as to whether it should be considered as private goods, public goods, or merit goods. Some argue that information is like a commodity, while others suggest it is more like a service. No single traditional economic concept seems to apply, and we do not pretend to settle such issues here.

Some important journal system characteristics follow:

- The scholarly journal system encompasses a number of participants including authors, publishers, secondary services, libraries, and readers, each of whom contribute toward improving and enhancing information attributes.

- Examination of all the resources (e.g., labor, equipment, facilities, and supplies) applied by the participants demonstrates that labor costs dominate, particularly the time devoted by authors and readers.

- Total resources expended by all participants (excluding the monetary exchange of purchasing subscriptions) have not changed much when calculated on a per scientist, per article, or per reading basis and factoring in inflation. Yet subscription prices have increased well beyond inflation rates, and the patterns of sources used to obtain articles have changed—most notably from personal subscriptions to library-provided journals and photocopies.

The important characteristics of scholarly journals follow:

- Infrequently-read articles are often bundled with frequently-read ones in journal issues, and journal subscriptions, in turn, are sometimes bundled with other professional society member benefits which are supported by membership fees.

- Since frequency of reading cannot be known ahead of time, bundling of articles reduces risks, or more accurately, spreads costs and prices over a larger number of articles. This has the benefit of providing high-quality, but low-use, articles at a reasonable price.

- Functionally, journals are packages of articles. Whether purchased by individuals or by libraries, scholarly journals have a highly skewed distribution of use that dictates which journals should be purchased and by whom. A few articles and journals are widely read, but most articles and journals are relatively infrequently read.

- The price paid to obtain and use article information is dominated by the cost of scientists' time compared with dollars exchanged between subscribers and publishers for subscriptions or for purchases of alternative sources (e.g. document delivery).

- Alternative sources are always available for obtaining the information found in scholarly journal articles such as the author, a professional society presentation (and published proceedings), personal subscriptions, library subscriptions, external copies, a colleague's knowledge from reading, and a colleague's copy of the article.

- Scientists consistently make economically rational choices in deciding among the alternative sources available to them.

The characteristics of journal use and demand that one should keep in mind follow:

- Demand for information found in scholarly journal articles varies dramatically from article to article depending on the specialty covered, the purpose for which the article is read, the time at which the need for information arises following publication, and the varied or relative importance of the various information attributes.

- The reading of an article by a scientist can involve multiple readings at different times for different purposes and can result in a multitude of different values derived from the use of that information. For example, the first reading right after publication could be for keeping current, and then much later new research or a different phase of research could require re-reading an article.

- Individuals and libraries purchase journals sight unseen. In other words, they purchase them based on past experience and expectations of the usefulness and value of the information for them in the future.

- Scientists often purchase journals using funds provided by their organizations, and therefore demand is partially determined by organization policies.

- Journal subscription payments are made before some costs are incurred, making the publication of journals financially attractive to investors because of this favorable cash flow (see Chapter 14).

- National surveys and a number of studies have shown that the information in scholarly articles is extensively read and contributes substantially to the scientists' research, teaching, and other work of its readers.

- Article information is one of many resources used by scholars and researchers to support their work, but it is consistently rated in surveys as one of their most important resources. Scientists whose work has been formally recognized tend to read more than their colleagues.

- The value of journal information includes both purchase value and use value. Purchase value represents the price buyers are willing to pay for the information. Typically scientists pay far more in their time to acquire and use the information than the price of a subscription. Use value, on the other hand, represents the outcomes of reading the information; in the case of scholarly journals, use results in both increased productivity and improved research and teaching.

In order to place these unique characteristics in perspective, it is useful to understand the economic issues faced by publishers. To this end, we have compiled data from our studies and the literature on publishing costs, pricing, and financing in Chapters 12, 13, and 14. The next section discusses the interrelationship of these three aspects.

COST, PRICE, AND DEMAND RELATIONSHIPS

User demand for journals is clearly a function of price, among other factors. An increase in the subscription price of a journal will most certainly result in at least some cancellations.[9] Perhaps at least as important in the price and demand relationship, however, is the fact that the size of the potential readership dictates the price that must be charged in order to recover the large fixed, first-copy costs. Journals with small potential readerships require very high subscription prices, whereas journals with very large potential readerships can offer subscriptions at a price near the reproduction and distribution costs. Scholarly communities and their interests tend to consist of some large fields of knowledge and many narrow specialties.

To demonstrate how publishing prices are affected by potential demand, we can show how important the large first-copy costs are in determining the minimum price required to recover costs. Publishing costs can be divided into two components: fixed costs that are incurred regardless of the number of subscribers and variable costs that are associated with each subscription. *Fixed costs* involve three types of activities: article processing (e.g., receipt, review, editing, coding for SGML or HTML, and composition), non-article text processing (e.g., preparation of covers, letters to the editor, book reviews, and advertising), and publishing support activities (e.g., marketing, administration, and financing). Activities contributing to *variable costs* include reproduction costs such as printing and binding as well as distribution costs such as wrapping, mailing, and subscription maintenance. The *incremental costs* are those attributable to each subscription (i.e., reproduction and distribution of one subscription).

Total journal publishing costs are large even when there are no subscribers, and they increase incrementally with each subscriber, that is nearly linear as a function of the number of subscriptions as shown in Figure 9.

Subscription prices are partially determined by the unit cost per subscription. This "average" cost should be equal to or less than the price of the journal in the absence of other sources of revenue. The average cost is the total cost divided by the number of subscriptions. This cost tends to be high in journals with a small number of subscriptions, but decreases as the number of subscriptions increases as depicted in Figure 10.

---

[9]This does not necessarily mean a reduction in readership because readers can use alternative sources to obtain the information. For example, a canceled personal subscription is often replaced by library reading, a canceled library subscription might be one of multiple subscriptions or could be replaced by obtaining copies of articles from interlibrary loan or document delivery services.

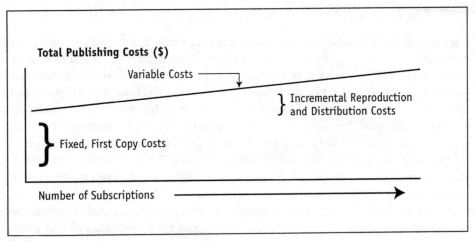

Figure 9. Total costs of journal publishing.

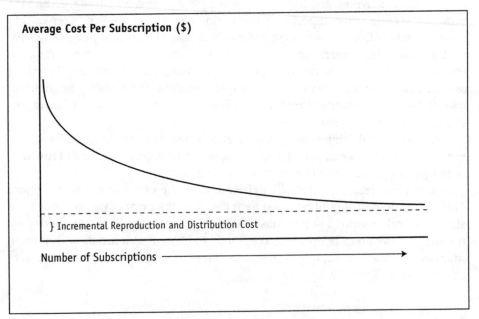

Figure 10. Average cost per subscriber of journal publishing.

Here the average cost per subscriber with only one subscriber is the fixed cost plus the incremental cost of the one subscription. With two subscribers, the average cost is the fixed cost plus the incremental cost of two subscriptions divided by two. Thus, the average cost decreases rapidly over the first few hundred subscriptions and then decreases at a slow pace toward an asymptote which it never reaches (where the asymptote is the incremental reproduction and distribution cost). Thus, at each subscription level, publishers must price subscriptions at least at the average cost in order to recover enough revenue to cover the costs of all five types of activities, i.e., article processing, non-article processing, reproduction, distribution, and publishing support.

The problem is that most scholarly journals publish information that has a potential readership well below the number of subscribers at which the average cost per subscription approaches anywhere near the incremental costs. In fact, journal subscriptions of less than 1,000 can require prices that are orders of magnitude above incremental costs. On the other hand, journals with circulation over 100,000 subscribers have average costs very near the incremental cost of reproduction and distribution.[10]

In order to fully appreciate the relationship of publishing cost and subscription demand, it is useful to know the relative costs of fixed and variable publishing activities. The literature contains few details of such costs or even circulation statistics, perhaps because publishers do not wish to reveal their costs and circulation to their competitors. Regardless, because of the importance of understanding these costs we have tried to derive estimates of these costs in the following chapter.

---

[10]Very few scientific scholarly journals, perhaps a handful, have over 100,000 subscribers.

CHAPTER 12

Cost of Scientific Scholarly Journal Publishing

INTRODUCTION

Scholarly journal publishing involves a large number of typical publishing activities performed by all publishers, most of which also need to be performed to produce electronic journals. However, specifics as to procedures, input cost and attributes of resources, and output quantities such as number of articles, issues, pages, and copies circulated vary among journals and publishers. It is useful to understand how such publishing parameters affect journal costs, and thus prices, since these parameters vary so significantly among journals and among types of publishers. Unfortunately, there has been a paucity of detailed information and data on publishing parameters and their relationship to costs.

In this chapter we assemble publishing cost information dating back to the 1970s, a time when the National Science Foundation was sponsoring a number of detailed cost studies. We analyze these and more recent data (adjusted for inflation) and derive a set of cost models that consider the effects of some of the parameters mentioned above. Clearly, for example, journal costs depend on such cost parameters as number of manuscripts submitted, number of articles published, number of issues published, number of article and non-article pages, and number of special graphics. These models attempt to consider the effects of such parameters. From these analyses and models we hope to:

- Encourage researchers to report common publishing cost data. Too often publishing costs are reported as proportions of first copy and subscription costs which are meaningless without clarification, e.g., number of subscriptions. Some costs are reported without indicating which cost components have been included and which resources, if any, have been donated.

- Establish which publishing activities (and their costs) are common to both paper and electronic journals and which are unique to each medium. With this basis for comparing the two media, publishers may hopefully make more reasoned decisions when converting to electronic publishing.

- Provide a model for assessing trends and comparing publications with different cost parameters particularly regarding size and circulation, among the four types of publishers: commercial, society, educational, and "other."

- Establish a basis for understanding how circulation affects journal prices and to carefully examine electronic journal pricing.

- Obtain feedback concerning estimated cost elements and overall publishing costs.

Detailed costs are presented in this chapter to achieve these objectives. It should be kept in mind, however, that the models are merely indicative of publishing costs. They are designed to show the dynamics of publishing costs in light of the parameters mentioned above.

In order to assess publishing costs, it is helpful to first describe all the activities that are necessary to publish scholarly journals. We have divided these activities into five categories: 1) article processing or all article-related activities required to produce the first copy of a journal issue; 2) non-article processing of covers, Tables of Contents, letters, editorials, and book reviews; 3) journal reproduction or printing and binding the final product; 4) distribution including subscription maintenance, wrapping and mailing; and 5) publishing support activities such as marketing and sales, administration, finance, other indirect cost activities, and non-allocated resources.

The cost of these activities is discussed below, along with an approximate cost model consisting of cost parameters (number of pages published, number of subscribers) and specific cost elements related to these parameters. The cost parameters are taken from estimates of 1995 scientific scholarly journal averages (Tenopir and King 1997), while the cost elements are derived from one or more sources of data found in the literature, or failing that, educated guesses. Derived estimates of total cost for each of the five sets of activities are combined, leading to an estimate of the total cost of a 'typical' scientific scholarly journal. Thus, we can project a probable journal price to enable publishers to recover publishing costs at various levels of circulation. Comparable costs of traditional print publications and electronic journals are discussed in Chapter 17.

JOURNAL PUBLISHING ACTIVITIES

The activities presented here are those that publishers and their representatives perform as part of traditional print journal publishing. The total cost of the first type of publishing activity, article processing, is largely a function of the number and size of the articles in a scholarly journal. The cost of non-article processing, on the other hand, is examined in isolation because it is a significant cost which is often ignored when discussing costs of scholarly journals. Total article and non-article processing costs are fixed costs identified with a particular journal which are not affected, or are affected very little, by the number of subscriptions. These are often called pre-run or first-copy costs because they include all the costs required to prepare the first copy. A different kind of fixed cost involves the indirect support costs of marketing and administration such as accounting, personnel, rights management, copyright protection, and finance. Finally, variable costs are those involving journal reproduction and distribution activities. These costs are largely a function of the number of subscribers, the frequency of publication, and the size of the journals. It is these activities which are critical to this analysis because they are the ones most affected by the transformation of publishing from print to the electronic arena.

A partial list of scholarly journal publishing activities is grouped below by five categories (article processing, non-article processing, reproduction, distribution, and support).[1] Article processing involves a number of activities that begin with receipt of an article manuscript and end with first-copy composition, typesetting, and engraving. These activities include receipt processing, initial disposition decision-making, identifying reviewers or referees, review processing, subject editing, special graphic and other preparation, formatting, copy editing, processing author approval, indexing, coding, redaction, and preparation of master images. Most of these activities are designed to enhance favorable attributes of article

---

[1]These activities are extracted from several sources including Page, Campbell, and Meadows (1987, 1997), Robert Ubell Associates' report to the Coalition on Networked Information (CNI) reported in 1996, Marks (1995), Scoville (1995), and King and Roderer (1978).

information and its presentation such as making the context concise, accurate, and readable.

Non-article processing involves essentially the same activities as article processing although authors are often internal staff members, and peer review is not required. Subject editing may involve less effort, and special graphics may be minimal. Master images may be provided by advertisers. One special kind of non-article activity involves preparation of issue covers, while another requires preparation of the Table of Contents and indexes. Reproduction activities include printing, collating, and binding. Publishers often print more copies of issues than required for circulation in order to have back issues available for sale, promotion and claims; for orders that come in later in the year and need to be back started; and for gracing old subscribers who renew late. They also will print individual copies of articles for authors or for sales of reprints. Distribution includes costs of wrapping, labeling, sorting by zip code, and mailing. The important activity of subscription maintenance includes keeping an updated list of subscribers, their addresses, and their payment status. This activity is common to electronic journals as well.

Support activities (variously called conducting business, general and administration, overhead, and indirect costs) include:

- Marketing and promotion such as preparation and arrangement for direct mail and other advertising, catalogs, exhibits, and telemarketing. It also includes arrangements with abstracting and indexing services. Resources include sales staff and support, staff-related resources (e.g., space, furniture, equipment, and supplies), use of outside vendors, and travel and entertainment.

- Rights management and copyright protection activities include copyright registration, administering permissions, licensing, and legal counsel.

- Administration includes maintaining personnel records and payroll, accounting, managing, equipment maintenance and administration, space allocation, legal and insurance administration, royalty and author payment administration.

- Finance activities and costs include new product research and development, inventory management, interest payment, capitalization of equipment and other resources, profit or return-on-investment, and payment of taxes on profit.

- Other indirect sources of cost include organization insurance and taxes (federal, state, and local), utilities, janitorial services, and unallocated resources such as space, parking, and travel.

Sometimes staff benefits are not included in the direct staff costs that are reported in the literature. These costs can include slack time, vacation, sick leave and holidays, as well as health and life insurance and payroll-related taxes.

These support activities and costs represent an appreciable portion of total publishing costs. Costs of marketing and rights management are fixed in the sense that they are incurred independently of the size of a journal. The other support costs will vary somewhat by the amount of labor involved.

SOURCES OF PUBLISHING COST DATA

Background research produced several sources of traditional print scholarly publishing cost data. Our analysis started with three studies sponsored by the National Science Foundation (NSF) in the 1970s because they appear to be the most recent comprehensive studies performed on scholarly publishing costs. Two of the studies, Machlup and Leeson (1978) and Fry and White (1976), surveyed scholarly publishers in 1975 and 1973 respectively. These surveys obtained information on journal (and book) publishing costs, circulation, price, and financial aspects. While providing very useful data and insights, the two studies suffered from low response rates. Presentation of results were also limiting for a comparative study because the amount of costs attributed to publishing activities such as editing, composition, printing, and mailing were presented as proportions of total direct costs.

The problem here is that total direct costs involve large fixed, first-copy costs and small variable printing and distribution costs per subscription. The proportions attributable to fixed or variable costs depend a great deal on the number of subscriptions. In fact, the proportion of all fixed cost activities (e.g., editing, composition, and support) for a low-subscription journal could typically equal 90 percent, but for a large subscription journal it could be as low as 10 percent. Thus, presentation of proportions does not help one to interpret relative costs unless more information is provided such as total costs, circulation amount, and size of the journals. Fortunately, Machlup and Leeson do provide some of these data to complement the proportions.

The third NSF-sponsored study of journal publishing costs involved a series of studies summarized by King, McDonald, and Roderer (1981). The approach taken in these studies was to visit three publishers and their presses to establish how cost resources such as staff and equipment were allocated to 15 specific publishing activities. This approach led to detailed cost models which were used to estimate publishing costs over time based on trends in resource costs (e.g., labor and paper) and cost parameters (e.g., number of articles/pages, issues, subscriptions).

Extension and modification of these models are given in the following sections for the five categories of journal publishing costs.

While we are unaware of more recent comprehensive publishing studies, some articles and book chapters have presented typical publishing costs for some activities. These include 1996 average costs per page of various activities (Holmes 1997), 1996 average costs per page of various activities for an unidentified journal (Ludwig 1997), 1995 ranges of cost data for various American Chemical Society publishing activities (Marks 1995), and 1983 total cost budgets for several American Institute of Physics journals (Lerner 1984) along with total pages and subscriptions for these journals. Marshall (1988) provides an example of a commercial journal cost for the years 1988 and 1979, and Page, Campbell, and Meadows (1997) provide similar data for later years. Some scientific activity cost data are reported by Day (1973) for editing, Bowen (1979) for internal and external review, Fisher (1995) for editing, Lago (1993) for composition, and Brogan (1979) for copy editing. Finally, we obtained some 1995 vendor cost quotes of printing, binding, and mailing along with postal rates from the U.S. Postal Service. Cost data presented in past years are all adjusted for inflation (CPI) to 1995 to provide a common basis for comparison.

ARTICLE PROCESSING COSTS

Article processing involves all publishing activities required to produce the first copy from which, in traditional print journals, copies are reproduced for distribution. These pre-run activities listed above must be performed regardless of whether articles are distributed electronically or on paper. The principal parameters for article processing costs are the number and length of manuscripts and articles, the number of special graphics, the number of pages produced, and the number of issues involved (because each issue requires some effort to 'put to bed').

A rough cost model for article processing follows:

$$C_A = C_1 I + C_2 P_A M + (C_3 + C_4) A P_A + C_5 G$$

where:

C_A is total annual article processing costs

C_1 is the fixed direct cost per issue

C_2 is the cost per page of receiving, processing, and reviewing a manuscript

C_3 is the cost per page associated with editing and proofing articles

C_4 is the cost per page of composition/typesetting

C_5 is the cost per unit of processing special graphics and other non-text materials

Parameters of the model include:

I – number of issues

M- number of manuscripts submitted

A – number of articles

P_A – average number of pages per article, and

G – number of special graphics and other materials.

Average values of the parameters for scientific scholarly journals in 1995 (Tenopir and King 1997) include: 8.3 issues per year (I), 123 articles published per year (A), 205 original manuscripts submitted,[2] 11.7 pages per article (P_A) and an unknown number of special graphics pages (G), but assumed to be about 260 pages based on 18 percent of all pages in 1977 (King, McDonald, and Roderer 1981).

Cost elements are found to vary in the literature or are not available. For example, we do not have sound evidence of how much staff time and other costs are directly attributable to processing journal issues, but we assume that C_1 is about $500 per issue. This cost includes final checking of the entire issue and dealing with printers. There is also a fixed cost (C_2) in staff and other resources associated with receiving, reading for initial disposition, managing and processing the manuscript, and processing the manuscript for review. Marks (1995) indicates that the cost of editorial management of American Chemical Society journals ranges from $15 to $50 per published page. Editorial management cost includes manuscript receipt processing, the selection of at least two referees, and review processing. Taking the mid-point from above, adjusted to the number of manuscripts, the cost (C_2) per manuscript page would be approximately $20 per manuscript page received.[3]

Seven sources over the years have provided editing and composition, and typesetting costs. Adjusting for inflation and other factors, estimates of these costs are given in Table 51. Since the Marks' estimate may be the only one that does not include the editorial management activities (C_2), we will use his estimate for this activity and subtract $20 per page from the other values, resulting in an estimate

---

[2]We assume a manuscript rejection rate of approximately 40 percent based on Marks (1995) mention of 20 to 56 percent rejection for American Chemical Society journals. Thus the total number of manuscripts processed (M) would be 205 (i.e., 123 ÷ 0.6).

[3]However, some publishers actually pay staff or external reviewers. For example, Bowen (1979) indicates that review cost of internal professional, technically trained staff ranges from $110 to $250 per manuscript and $280 to $560 per manuscript for part-time reviewers. Some review journals are said to cost as much as $1,980 per article to review. All figures are adjusted to 1995 dollars.

Table 51	Adjusted Estimates of Editing (C3) and Composition (C4) Costs from Seven Sources (in $/page)		
Author		**C3***	**C4***
Machlup & Leeson (1978)		70	120
King et al. (1981)		90	100
Lerner (1984)		50	70
Marks (1995) mid-points		40	60
Holmes (1997)		60	25
Anonymous 1 (1996)		100	33
Anonymous 2 (1997)		—	22

*Costs adjusted for inflation and other factors.

of $50 per page for C_3. For composition/typesetting costs (C_4), we use $35 which represents an average of the most recent data[4] (i.e., 1995 and later).

The cost of special graphics such as mathematical equations can vary dramatically. For example, medical illustrations are said to cost as much as $1,000 each. Adjusted cost estimates for C_5 vary widely among four of the sources of data specified in Table 51: Machlup and Leeson (1978) quote $32 per special graphics page with King, McDonald, and Roderer (1981) at $123 per page, Marks (1995) at $71 per page, and Lerner (1984) at $15 per page. Without further evidence, by averaging the most recent data we estimate C5 to be approximately $60 per special graphics page.

From these model parameters and costs, we arrive at a total publishing cost of article processing by applying the following formula:

$$C_A = \$500(8.3) + \$20\,(11.7)\,(205) + (\$50 + \$35)\,(123)\,(11.7) + \$60\,(260)$$
$$= \$190{,}045$$

----

[4]One publisher told us that the electronic processes have helped to reduce typesetting costs by over 60%. Thus the earlier data would reflect these differences in the processes available at that time.

which amounts to approximately \$1,545 per article published or approximately \$130 per article page published.[5] We emphasize that model parameters and costs vary from journal to journal and publisher to publisher.

The article processing costs reported in the literature vary substantially, particularly by those attempting to make the case for electronic publishing. Some of these authors report costs that are a fraction of the costs listed above. We suspect that some of these costs are low because they do not include some of the hidden costs such as space and fringe benefits for staff. Odlyzko (1997) provides another plausible explanation however. He believes that publishers of small journals tend to avoid the extra attributes or bells and whistles found in the more established publications, especially those issued by the larger commercial and society publishers. He cites one publisher as saying that "a \$250 paper gets you 90% of the quality that a \$1,000 paper gets you."[6]

Some older evidence to support this notion was provided to King Research by Machlup and Leeson in the late 1970s while the two groups were cooperating closely under NSF sponsorship. They provided special data on editorial costs by size of journals as defined by circulation and number of pages published. It turns out that the editorial costs of small journals tend to be less than for large journals. For example, the average editorial costs per page for journals with more than 3,000 circulation was over three times the amount of those with a circulation of 3,000 or less. Those with more than 1,000 pages average 25 percent higher costs than those with 1,000 or fewer pages. At the time, we ignored these data because the established principle of economies of scale in larger operations suggested opposite results. Perhaps Odlyzko's conjecture might have been valid, however, even in the 1970s. A publisher of approximately twenty-five journals indicated anonymously that he had experienced a rise in costs up to a certain size at which point unit costs then decline.

NON-ARTICLE PROCESSING COSTS

Scientific scholarly journals are estimated to publish an average of 289 non-article pages annually. The corresponding cost is not believed to be as high as for article processing. A rough cost model for non-article pages as follows:

$$C_N = (C_6 + C_7) I + (C_8 + C_9) P_N$$

---

[5]Numbers are rounded to nearest five or ten throughout the chapter.
[6]Eric Hellman, editor of the *MARS Internet Journal of Nitride Semi-Conductor Research* (electronic).

where:

C_N is the total annual cost of processing non-article pages

C_6 is the fixed cost of handling the non-article materials each issue

C_7 is the cost of preparing covers for each issue

C_8 is the cost of editing and proofing these pages

C_9 is the cost of composition/typesetting

There may also be special graphics costs, but these are ignored here. I is 8.3 issues per year, and P_N is 289 non-article pages published annually. In the absence of evidence, we assume C_6 and C_7 to be $50 and $200 per issue, C_8 to be ½ of article costs (i.e., $25 per page), and C_9 to be the same as article pages (i.e., $35 per page). Thus, total non-article processing costs with these assumptions comprise:

$$C_N = (\$50 + \$200)\,(8.3) + (\$25 + \$35)\,(289) = \$19{,}415$$

or approximately $65 per non-article page as compared to $130 per article page.

REPRODUCTION COSTS

Once a master image is produced, a traditional print journal can be reproduced and distributed. Of course the reproduction and distribution activities of traditional print journals are not incurred by journals that are exclusively electronic publications. In fact, the most relevant comparison of electronic journals with print journals may lie in a comparison of these traditional print costs with the costs of electronic storage, distribution, and receipt, especially if it can be shown that the first-copy costs are essentially the same for both types of journals.

As with costs of other journal publishing activities, some relatively good cost data are provided through National Science Foundation contracts in the 1970s (King, McDonald, and Roderer 1981; Machlup and Leeson 1978), with further evidence provided by Holmes (1997), Marshall (1988), Page, Campbell, and Meadows (1987, 1997), and Lerner (1984). In addition, we obtained several vendor printing and distribution quotes for four journals ranging in size from 16 to 100 pages per issue. All of these costs were projected to 1995 using CPI inflation rates and are incorporated in our reproduction and distribution models.[7]

---

[7]Dates here represent the year the data were observed published, however years in which data were observed are, respectively: 1977, 1975, 1996, 1988 and 1979, 1987 and 1997, and 1983.

Reproduction involves printing from a composed image and binding. These two activities involve labor, equipment, paper, and other supporting resources such as space. The reproduction cost model follows:

$$C_R = I\,[C_{10} + (C_{11} \times P_I) + (C_{12} + C_{13})\,(S + O) + (C_{14} + C_{15})\,P_I \times (S + O)]$$

where:
   C_R is the annual print and binding cost
   C_{10} is the setup cost associated with one issue
   C_{11} is the plate making and/or collating cost per page
   C_{12} is the binding cost per copy
   C_{13} is the cost per copy of special covers
   C_{14} is the labor and equipment cost per impression (one copy of one page)
   C_{15} is the paper cost per impression (i.e., twice one piece)

and model parameters are:
   I is the number of annual issues
   P_I is the number of pages in an issue
   $(S + O)$ is the number of copies made for an issue (i.e., number of subscriptions
        plus some overrun).

Instead of multiplying by I, one could more accurately sum the equation without I for each issue over a year.

A typical 1995 scientific scholarly journal (Tenopir and King 1997) has 8.3 issues, 5,800 subscribers (plus 200 copies for overrun), and 1,723 pages (or 208 pages per issue). Thus, one issue has an average of 1,248,000 impressions. We estimate C_{10} (one issue set-up cost) to range from $550 to $1,360 per issue or an average of approximately $950 per issue for four observations. The first set-up costs account for from 3 to 9 percent of the total direct reproduction costs. Platemaking (C_{11}) is roughly estimated to be $4 per page (one issue) or approximately 4 to 11 percent of the total.

The binding cost per copy (C_{12}) depends on the type of binding (typically saddle stitch or perfect binding), but is observed to be in the range of $0.05 to $0.20 per copy or an average of approximately $0.125 per copy. Special covers appear to cost about $0.15 per copy ($C_{13}$), but can be much higher. Thus, binding and special cover costs tend to account for a relatively small portion of total costs for scholarly journals (10 to 16 percent). Total cost per impression ($C_{14} + C_{15}$) amounts to roughly $0.007 or less than one cent per printed page, assuming no color or photograph requirements. These print costs account for about 75 percent of the total direct reproduction costs depending on the size of journal (i.e., number of pages), number of copies (i.e., number of subscriptions), and other factors such as quality of paper. A typical journal as defined by the above parameters ($I = 8.3$, $P_1 = 208$, and $S + O = 5,800 + 200$) would have direct costs for reproduction of $100,995 or approximately $17.00 per subscription mailed.

The data above were largely based on 1995 vendor quotes. The seven other sources mentioned above provided estimates for the reproduction costs per annual subscription. These estimates ranged from $12 per subscription (Anonymous 1997) to $27 (Machlup and Leeson 1978) compared with the model estimate of $17 per subscription.[8] Thus, the model appears to hold reasonably well considering this rough validation approach.

DISTRIBUTION COSTS

The distribution total cost includes the same three parameters as reproduction costs (i.e., number of issues, number of subscriptions, and number of pages per issue). The cost model follows:

$$C_D = C_{16}I + (C_{17} + C_{18})SI + C_{19}S + C_{20}SIP_1$$

where:

C_D is the total direct distribution cost

C_{16} is the fixed cost associated with each issue mail processing

C_{17} is the mail processing cost per item or copy including such costs as inserting, sorting, sealing, and labeling

C_{18} is the postal rate per copy, which depends on the proportion of advertising pages

C_{19} is the subscription maintenance cost per subscription

C_{20} is the postage cost per page per copy mailed (also based on proportion of weight due to advertising)

Using the current typical scholarly scientific journal parameters of 8.3 issues, 5,800 subscriptions, and 208 pages per issue, we arrived at the following distribution costs:

C_{16} = $50 per issue mailing

C_{17} = $0.35 per copy mailed

C_{18} is $0.263 (assuming 5 percent advertising pages)

C_{19} is approximately $7.00 per subscription

C_{20} is approximately $0.001 per page per copy mailed (again assuming 5 percent advertising pages)

---

[8]Adjusted for inflation, currency differences, and reproduction parameters upon which the estimates were made.

Thus, the total distribution cost of a current scholarly journal with the parameters and costs discussed above is $80,540 or approximately $14 per subscription. A number of factors can affect these costs such as whether the journal copies are wrapped, how heavy the pages are (including special covers), and whether a mailer has the non-profit designation to obtain preferred postal rates.

The proportion of distribution costs due to processing and to postal rates are 71.7 percent and 28.3 percent respectively. Machlup and Leeson (1978) give these proportions as 77.0 and 23.0 percent respectively, so that these costs, perhaps, have not changed significantly over the years.

PUBLISHING SUPPORT COSTS

Publishing support involves non-direct cost elements such as general and administration (G&A) costs, space and utilities, and taxes. It also includes marketing, cost of research, investment, and other items mentioned previously in this chapter. Not a great deal has been said in the literature about such costs, although Holmes (1997), Ludwig (1997), Scoville (1995), Marks (1998), Marshall (1988), and Page, Campbell, and Meadows (1987) give examples of proportions of total costs attributable to support activities. Proportion of costs are given in Table 52.

We assume that support costs, excluding finance, are approximately 39 percent of total costs. Of these costs, about $68,000 are fixed (e.g., marketing, rights management, facilities). The article and non-article processing support costs are estimated to be approximately 35 percent of direct costs since these costs are labor intensive. They are estimated to be 15 percent of reproduction and distribution costs since they are often contracted out and, therefore labor-related activities are

Table 52	Proportion of Direct and Publishing Support Costs Reported by Six Sources (in Percent)					
	Marks 1998	Holmes 1997	Ludwig 1997	Scovill 1995	Marshall 1988	Page et al. 1987
Direct Cost	80	51	63	56	70	52
Publishing Support	20	49	37	44	30	48
(Marketing)	—	—	(6)	(12)		(15)
(Administrative, rent)	—	—	(20)	(18)		(22)
(Reinvestment, finance)	—	—	(1)	(14)		(11)

not involved. Thus total publishing support costs, would be represented by the following equation:

$$C_S = 0.35 (C_A + C_N) + 0.15 (C_R + C_D) + C_M$$

where:

C_S represents the costs attributable to support activities
C_A represents the total article processing costs
C_N represents the total non-article processing costs
C_R represents the total reproduction costs
C_D represents the total distribution costs
C_M represents fixed costs such as marketing (including overhead)

As an example,

C_S = 0.35 ($190,045 + $19,415) + 0.15 ($100,995 + $80,540) + $68,000 = $168,540.

Thus, publishing support costs represent an appreciable proportion of all direct costs. These costs can vary dramatically, particularly by size and by type of publisher.

TOTAL AND UNIT PUBLISHING COSTS

Total Costs with 1995 Average Parameters

Based on the approximate costs of the five functions or group or publishing activities, the total costs of publishing a typical scientific scholarly journal is represented by the following equation:

$$C_P = C_A + C_N + C_R + C_D + C_S$$
$$= \$190,045 + \$19,415 + \$100,995 + \$80,540 + \$168,540$$
$$= \$559,535$$

This cost comes to an average of $4,550 per article or $325 per page published. This compares to Holmes (1997) total publication cost per page of $331.49. If we eliminate non-article pages and allocate support costs, the first-copy cost totals $256,560 or $2,085 per article. Without allocating support costs, the article processing costs are 49 percent of the entire direct cost.[9]

---

[9]The issue of the large fixed cost and its effect on price is not new; for example, Kuney (1962) showed that the break-even price for publishing high-circulation journals (at 1,000 pages) is $10–$15 (i.e., $60 to $90 in current dollars) and is $25 to $35 for smaller circulation journals (i.e., $150 to $200).

Validation of the Cost Model

It is emphasized that the costs cited above and the model parameters are merely indicative of what a journal might cost. For example, Marks (1995) indicates that article first-copy costs range from $60 to $185 per page at the American Chemical Society. Reproduction and distribution costs range from $32 to $41 per subscription. Leaving non-article processing costs at $91 per page (with support allocation), these total publishing costs (using current parameters and model support costs) would be, at a minimum, $424,300 and, at most, $727,160. This compares with the model figures of $559,535. At the minimum and maximum costs, the price required to recover costs is given in Table 53. Of course, the Marks' minimum and maximum are extreme because the journal with the minimum first copy cost might not be the one with the minimum reproduction and distribution cost and the same with maximum costs. However, Marks' data demonstrate that our model costs may not represent any one publisher, since their costs vary so much.

Scott (1998) presented some detailed costs for a hypothetical journal, along with cost parameters. Presumably these costs were some typical costs observed at American Institute of Physics where he worked until his recent retirement. Applying his parameters to our cost model, we find that the model total cost is 11 percent below his total hypothetical cost, thus validating the model to some degree.

Table 53	Marks' Costs vs. Model Costs by Number of Subscribers (in Dollars)		
Number of Subscribers	Marks' Costs/Subscription		Model Costs/ Subscription
	Minimum	*Maximum*	
500	459	955	775
1,000	248	501	404
2,500	121	229	181
5,000	79	138	107
10,000	58	93	70

Source: Marks 1995

Unit Costs with Varied Parameters

First we examine the effect of circulation on the average cost per subscription. The minimum price necessary to recover publishing costs for various circulation levels

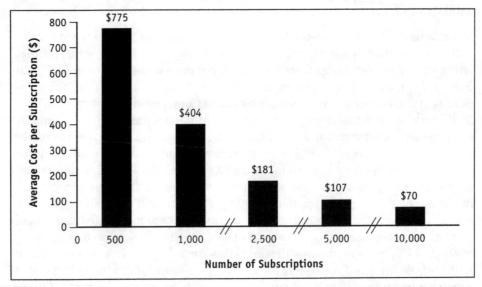

Figure 11. The minimum price necessary to recover costs at various levels of circulation.

would be as follows for a journal with other parameters remaining as described above. [10]

The price necessary to recover costs at 500 subscribers is at least $775 per subscription, but decreases to $107 per subscription when subscriptions total 5,000. At 50,000 subscriptions, the required price drops to approximately $40 per subscription which approaches the incremental reproduction and distribution cost of $31 per subscription. [11] At 500,000 subscribers, the price falls to approximately $2 above the incremental cost. Other various levels are displayed in Figure 11.

In the tables below we vary some of the other cost parameters to test sensitivity of total unit costs to them. The cost parameters are primarily number of subscriptions, number of issues, number of article and non-article pages, and number of special graphics pages. Scientific scholarly journals were estimated in 1995 to have the following average parameter values: 5,800 subscribers, 8.3 issues per year, 11.7 pages per article, 289 non-article pages, and 260 special pages. In the

---

[10]Support costs are allocated at 35 percent of first-copy costs ($C_A + C_N$) and 15 percent of reproduction and distribution costs ($C_R + C_D$), plus $68,000.

[11]For those who like to quote proportions of first-copy versus reproduction and distribution direct costs, the proportions are 89% and 11%; 57% and 43%; 13% and 87%; and 1% and 99% for 500; 5,000; 50,000; and 500,000 subscribers respectively based on the cost model.

previous analysis, we varied the number of subscribers. Now we will vary the number of articles, with the number of manuscripts, non-article pages, and special pages remaining proportionately the same. Pages per article and the other parameters remain the same.

Thus, as shown in Table 54, increasing the number of articles (and other related parameters) by increments of 50 articles results in an increase in cost per subscription (with 5,800 subscribers) of approximately $26 per subscription, or $0.52 per article distributed. However, the cost per article decreases. This may help explain why publishers have tended to publish more articles per title rather than publish more titles, i.e., twig. Further evidence of this is provided by comparing costs with the 1975 and 1995 parameters.

Over the 20-year period from 1975 to 1995, the number of scientific scholarly journals published in the United States has increased at a rate far less than the growth of the number of scientists (Tenopir and King 1997), but the number of articles published per scientist in the United States has remained relatively constant. This can be attributed to a substantial increase in the average size and frequency of publication. From 1975 to 1995, the number of scientists in the United States also increased from approximately 2.6 million to 5.7 million, an increase of approximately 119 percent. The number of scientific scholarly journals is estimated to have increased from 4,170 to 6,771, an increase of 62 percent. Referring to cost model parameters, the changes in size and frequency of publishing are depicted in Table 55.[12] Applying 1995 cost estimates in the cost models to the 1975 parameters produces a total cost of $266,785 per journal compared with $433,140 using 1995 parameters.

Table 54	Scholarly Journal Total Model Cost, Cost per Subscriber, and Cost per Article by Number of Articles Published (in 1995 Dollars)		
No. of Articles	**Total Cost**	**Cost per Subscriber**	**Cost per Article**
50	$335,564	$ 58	$6,711
100	$488,977	$ 84	$4,889
150	$642,393	$111	$4,283
200	$795,678	$137	$3,978

---

[12]Median number of subscribers is used because results better reflect average cost per subscription.

Table 55	**Scholarly Journal Publishing Parameters: 1975 and 1995**		
Cost Model Parameter		**Year**	
		1975	1995
No. of Issues		6.5	8.3
No. of Articles/Title		85	123
No. of Manuscripts Submitted		90	205
No. of Article Pages		630	1,439
No. of Special Graphics Pages		114	260
No. of Total Pages		820	1,728
No. of Subscriptions (Median)		2,900	1,900

Sources: King, McDonald and Roderer 1981, Tenopir and King 1997.

In Table 56 below we compare 1975 and 1995 size journals in terms of total cost and unit cost. Thus, it may be that increasing the size of journals as opposed to increasing the number of journals has kept costs down—at least on a cost-per-page basis. Unfortunately, looked at from the buyer's perspective, prices have increased far more than one might expect considering the increased size of the journals (i.e., information provided) and inflation. Prices are discussed in more detail in the next chapter.

Table 56	**Scholarly Journal Model Costs for Journals Published in 1975 and 1995 (in 1995 Dollars)**		
Total and Unit Costs		1975 ($)	1995 ($)
Total Cost/Title		266,785	433,140
Cost per Issue		41,045	52,185
Cost per Article		3,140	3,520
Cost per Page		325	250
Cost per Subscriber		90	230

Values rounded to nearest $5.

A Cautionary Note in Comparing Costs

Comparing average cost per subscriber per journal using parameter averages for the cost model above can be misleading, particularly when important parameters such as circulation are highly skewed. That is, the unit cost of an average journal is *not* the average cost of journals. For example, the average circulation per title is 5,800 subscribers, but the median circulation is 1,900 subscribers; in other words, 50 percent of the journals have fewer than 1,900 subscribers. Using the cost model with 5,800 subscribers, the model cost is approximately $96 per subscription. However, if we take the number of subscribers for each journal and compute the costs for that journal, the average cost rises to $350 per subscription per title.

This phenomenon can be demonstrated by subdividing journals into quartiles based on subscribers as shown in Table 57. Thus, one-fourth of the titles have between 150 and 900 subscribers, and they average 520 subscribers, which, other parameters holding, brings their cost for a journal to $747 per subscriber. Averaging costs of the four ranges would be $315 per subscriber per title, which is considerably higher than the $96 cost model estimate at the 5,800 subscriber average. Even averaging within the quartiles underestimates the true average by about 10 percent.

Table 57	Cost per Subscriber by Quartiles of Numbers of Subscribers Using the Cost Model Parameters (in 1995 Dollars)		
Quartile	Circulation Range	Average Circulation within Range	Cost per Subscriber
0–25%	150–900	520	$747
26–50%	901–1900	1,310	$316
51–75%	1,901–5,700	3,290	$145
76–100%	5,701+	18,100	$ 53

Comparing Costs of the Four Types of Publishers

The four different types of publishers tend to publish different sizes of scientific scholarly journals and with varied frequency. Furthermore, in addition to the differences in publishing parameters, there is some evidence that cost elements also vary among types of publishers. First, we examine the publishing parameters for the four types of publishers, namely commercial, society, educational, and "other." As shown in Table 58, commercial and society publishers tend to publish more articles and more frequently than educational and "other" publishers, although educational publishers publish nearly as many pages. For this analysis, we use the median circulation for publishers since this provides an estimate which is closer to the average cost per subscriber per title, although perhaps still two-thirds of the actual average.

Applying 1995 cost estimates in the models to the parameters above, produces the total and unit costs depicted in Table 59. A major discrepancy clearly exists between the estimated model cost and price of educational publishers and the other three types of publishers. Here the model cost is substantially higher than the average price per subscriber, whereas the model cost and price are comparable to the other three types of publishers. There are several possible explanations

Table 58	Scholarly Journal Publishing Parameters by Type of Publisher: 1995			

Cost Model Parameter	Type of Publisher			
	Commercial	Society	Educational	Other
No. of Issues	9.9	9.3	4.3	7.3
No. of Articles/Title	118	202	70	84
No. of Manuscripts Submitted*	197	337	117	140
No. of Article Pages	1,533	1,813	1,500	786
No. of Special Graphics Pages	276	326	270	141
No. of all Pages**	1,811	2,296	1,742	919
No. of Subscriptions				
Median	1,400	5,600	1,500	3,500
Average	3,700	13,300	1,700	4,600

*Based on 40% rejection rate for all types of publishers.
**Based on 18% of article pages for all types of publishers.

Source: Tenopir & King 1997

Table 59	Scholarly Journal Model Costs and Price by Type of Publisher (in 1995 Dollars)			
Unit Costs and Average Price	Type of Publisher			
	Commercial	Society	Educational	Other
Cost per Subscriber	441	174	337	80
Average Price*	487	229	81	119

*(institutional price)

Source: Tenopir & King, 1997

for this discrepancy. Some educational publishing costs may be subsidized by their institutions or through volunteer labor, thereby allowing them to charge less. As mentioned previously, it may be that these publishers of small scholarly journals reduce costs by avoiding publishing extras as suggested by Odlyzko (1997) or that they, by necessity, are extremely cost efficient. Whatever the explanation, something appears to be different about the educational publishers.

Machlup and Leeson (1978) provide evidence that this difference may not have changed over the years. They show that in 1975 the average publishing cost of journals published by university presses is far less than commercial or society journals: $41,300 versus $152,500 and $259,700 respectively (excluding general and administrative costs). Furthermore, the gross margin (i.e., revenue less manufacturer's costs) is far less for university journals in 1975: $14,300 for university presses, $133,800 for commercial publishers, and $193,000 for learned society publishers. Furthermore, some university presses show a negative gross margin of as much as $26,000 in 1975 dollars. The publishing parameters provided by Machlup and Leeson for the observed journals are listed in Table 60. Note that these data include journals from all disciplines, whereas the publishing parameters above include only science.

Table 60	Scholarly Journal Publishing Parameters by Type of Publisher: 1975		
	Type of Publisher		
Publishing Parameters	**Commercial**	**Society**	**University Press**
Circulation (median)	1,040	5,270	2,780
Average No. of Pages	1,200	1,510	520

Source: Machlup and Leeson 1978

CHAPTER 13

Pricing of Scientific Scholarly Journals

INTRODUCTION

In this chapter we reinforce the notion that the price of scientific scholarly journals has increased at a rate far greater than would be expected based on inflation. Observations from the journal tracking sample show that the average journal price has experienced more than a seven-fold increase from 1975 to 1995; this translates into an increase factor of 2.6 even when adjusted for inflation. Other sources of data indicate an even greater increase in prices, particularly in recent years. Evidence from our journal tracking study shows that the size of scientific scholarly journals is increasing while their circulation is decreasing. Furthermore, our cost models (Chapter 12) show that these changes in size and circulation have substantially increased costs per subscription and, therefore, have further affected price increases. Other explanations for the spiraling prices are also posited.

A number of studies have related price and demand of scholarly journals using variations of regression analysis. We have found it useful, however, to take a different, bottom-up approach to explain price and demand relationships. This approach is based on the premise that purchasers choose among alternative sources of journals based on cost and convenience to them. Both libraries and individuals have alternatives to purchasing journals. Individuals can go to a library to read journals, and libraries can use interlibrary borrowing or document-delivery services to obtain separate copies of articles for their users. In both instances, the frequency of reading of a journal dictates whether or not it is more cost-effective to purchase a journal subscription than to rely on the alternative source.

Since personal subscriptions are read relatively infrequently (approximately 13 times per scientist), their demand is extremely sensitive to price. Thus price increases have led to a sharp decline in personal subscriptions over a twenty-year period. In fact, this decline has resulted in publishers losing an estimated annual revenue in excess of one billion dollars. Publishers have only been able to compensate for this loss by drastically increasing library subscription prices which they have been able to do because they are read frequently enough that their demand has been relatively insensitive to price changes. Some rough cost data illustrate the dynamics of these two pricing relationships on demand.

SCHOLARLY JOURNAL PRICES AND DEMAND

In Chapter 11 we indicated that, based on the journal tracking study, scientific scholarly journals in 1995 averaged $255 for personal subscriptions and $284 for institutional subscriptions.[1,2] Approximately three-fourths of the journals had a single price for these two types of subscribers. The estimated average prices varied a great deal among the fields of science and the four types of publishers. We also showed that, while the average circulation per title is 5,800 subscriptions, the average varies substantially among fields of science and types of publishers and the median circulation is generally much lower than average circulation. Table 61 displays estimated average prices and average and median circulation by of publisher.

Generally, with commercial and society publishers, there appears to be an inverse relationship between price and demand. That is, commercial publishers have a low demand and high price, while the opposite is true for society publishers. Educational and "other" publisher journals defy this economic reality for reasons discussed in Chapters 11 and 12.

Much has been said in the literature about the inverse relationship between journal price and demand. Clearly price increases typically result in reduced cir-

---

[1]We interchange the terms "institutional" and "library" as well as "individual" and "personal" subscription prices.
[2]It is noted that the average price per **subscriber** is only around 40 percent of the average price per **journal** because some journals with a very large circulation and low prices tend to skew the calculation of the average price per subscriber.

Table 61	Average Institutional Price and Average and Median Circulation by Type of Publisher: 1995			
Type of Publisher	Number of Titles	Average Price ($)	Average Circulation (Subscriptions)	Median Circulation (Subscriptions)
Commercial	2,679	487	3,700	1,400
Society	1,557	229	13,300	5,600
Educational	1,106	81	1,700	1,500
Other	1,429	119	4,600	3,500
All Publishers	6,771	284	5,800	1,900

Source: Tenopir and King 1997

culation. However, there is a chicken and egg aspect to price and demand of journals. That is, a small scientific discipline would suggest low circulation for journals in that discipline, therefore, requiring high prices of the journals. Thus one must be careful in interpreting price and circulation relationships across all journals as, for example, Noll and Steinmueller (1992) and others have done. They have shown that such relationships, when plotted across all journals, present a shotgun-like appearance, although illustrating a rough negative price and demand correlation. Our journal tracking data show a similar scattered pattern, with the average institutional price of low-circulation journals (i.e., the low 50 percent) being approximately $370 compared with $170 for the high-circulation journals in the top half.

The inverse price and demand phenomenon is more likely to be attributable to the size of audience served.[3] Each journal has unique information that is not found in any other journal, although it may be available to potential readers from other sources such as directly from the author, formal conference proceedings, and technical reports. When a scientific specialty represents a relatively small community of scientists, the circulation will normally be even smaller because some journals are shared and some articles are obtained from other sources. Low

---

[3]The audience or market comprises the scientists who have an interest in the information conveyed by specific journals.

circulation, as demonstrated in Chapter 12, results in a high unit cost and, therefore, a corresponding high price per subscription. Thus, since individuals cannot afford high-priced journals, most of these journals are purchased by libraries in order to share the cost among clusters of scientists. Science seems to be characterized by a highly skewed distribution of specialties representing very small scientific communities and a few large communities. Thus, one would expect most journals to be high priced and a much smaller number to be low priced.

Another way to assess the price and demand relationship is to compare circulation and price changes over time for specific titles or titles having similar circulation sizes. The former was done in the early 1980s, and results yielded a fair degree of predictability of demand as a result of price changes that were actually made (King and Roderer 1981).

In order to compare journal costs and prices, we estimated unit costs per subscription for a small sample of journals based on the cost models outlined in Chapter 12, applying observed articles per issue, number of issues, reported circulation, and other parameters. These expected prices were compared with reported prices. Across all journals for which we compiled such data, the expected prices (i.e., costs) run approximately 10 percent lower than reported prices. This suggests that the costs mentioned above are roughly correct. Some variation by audience exists: commercial publisher's expected prices tend to be slightly lower than reported prices with some notable exceptions, while society and educational publishers are much more likely to charge lower prices than expected based on anticipated costs. The latter might be explained by the absorption of some of the overhead publishing costs by their institutions and membership fees. Furthermore, some society publishers require authors to pay page charges, which cover some of the fixed article costs. Finally, it may be that the social and behavioral science journals favored by educational publishers have publishing attributes or processes that tend to have lower costs.

TRENDS IN SCIENTIFIC SCHOLARLY JOURNAL PRICES

Journal Tracking Prices

Based on our journal tracking data the average institutional prices of current journals have increased from approximately $39 in 1975 to $284 in 1995, 7.3 times higher (see Chapter 11). Thus, journals today are priced an average of $245 more than in 1975. Obviously, part of the price increase is attributable to inflation and part to the increased size of journals. With inflation alone, one would expect the 1975 journals currently to cost approximately $110 compared with $39 in 1975.

Thus, inflation accounts for nearly 30 percent of the increase (i.e., $71 of the $245). With the size increase alone, we would expect the $39 journal to cost approximately $136 more in 1995 when adjusted for inflation. Thus, size and inflation together would explain approximately 56 percent of the increase or $136 of the $245 difference between 1975 and 1995. Cost components such as paper, labor, and capitalization of equipment account for some of the remaining increase since the cost of these resources is believed to be increasing at a rate greater than inflation, although less than sometimes implied in the literature.

We believe that the majority of the remaining increase in price is attributable to the pricing policies of commercial publishers and, to a lesser degree, the society publishers. To examine this hypothesis, it is useful to know where the largest price increases occur. Examination by type of publisher depicts the increases in Table 62.

In summary, the average price of journals in 1975 was $39 per journal. The average price in 1995 ($284) was 7.3 times as high. When adjusted for inflation, the price was 2.6 times as high. Commercial and society journal price increases far exceed those of educational and "other" publishers. Some of this discrepancy is correlated with the fields that these types of publishers address. For example, the price of physical sciences journals increased from $62 to $616 (a factor of 9.9), and 86 percent of these journals are published by commercial or society publishers. Social science journal prices increased from $28 to $89 (a factor of only 3.2 or

Table 62	Average Price and Factor of Increase by Type of Publisher: 1975 and 1995 (in Current and Constant Dollars)			
TYPE OF PUBLISHER	**AVERAGE PRICE**		**INCREASE FACTOR IN:**	
	1975	**1995**	**Current Dollars**	**Constant Dollars**
Commercial	$55	$487	8.9	3.1
Society	$28	$229	8.2	2.9
Educational	$15	$ 81	5.4	1.9
Other	$40	$119	3.0	1.1
All Types	$39	$284	7.3	2.6

Source: Tenopir and King 1997

12 percent above inflation), and only 22 percent of these journals are published by commercial and society publishers. Commercial and society publishers' price increases for social science journals only increased by a factor of 3.7 and 3.9 respectively.

The average number of individual subscriptions per scientist has decreased substantially over twenty years from 5.8 in 1975 to 2.7 in 1995. Prices began to increase dramatically in the late 1970s which caused the individual subscription base to erode rapidly for most commercial publishers and some society publishers. It appears that an attempt was made by some publishers to address the sudden drop in individual subscription revenue by increasing institutional prices at a rate far greater than inflationary and size increases could explain. This effort was partially successful because of the relative insensitivity of demand to price increases of institutional subscriptions. Attempts have also been made, with some success, to reduce the cost of journal publishing. Some publishers may have tried to maintain or recapture lost subscribers by providing more articles (and pages), but the accompanying large increase in fixed and variable costs required even higher prices.

Other Reported Price Information

In comparing journals in the tracking sample that survived[4] from 1975 to 1995, the scientific scholarly journal prices increased by a factor of 9.26. Even adjusted for inflation, the prices still increased by a factor of 3.24 or approximately 6.0 percent per year. These price increases are not a recent phenomenon. Using the same sample of journals from 1960 to 1975, we estimated an increase from $8.51 to $30.66[5] for an average increase of 4.7 percent per year. Thus, the rate of increase appears to be rising over time. Other studies show similar increases as depicted in Table 63.

The scientific scholarly journal prices estimated from the journal-tracking sample (source 1 in the table) appear to be lower than prices observed in other studies. It is believed that this may be due to the completeness of the database

---

[4]The tracking sample changed some over the years in order to take into account journal births, deaths, and twigging of one journal into two or more journals. This meant that the average price was $30.66 vs. $39 reported when all sampled journals in 1975 are included.

[5]Prices in 1975 varied by type of subscriber and by field of science. For example, the society member price averaged $13.54, while the non-member price was $23.80; individual subscriptions averaged $30.87; institutional subscriptions, $38.57; and non-U.S. subscriptions, $33.37. Among fields of science, the physical sciences charged the highest average price ($82.66) and social sciences the lowest ($16.58). The differences in price among the fields were much less in 1960.

Table 63	**Trends in Average Prices of Scientific Scholarly Journals and All Serials: 1960-1998** (in Dollars)	

Year	Scientific Scholarly Journals	All Serials
1960	8.51 (1)	5.32 (5)
1962	9.33 (1)	
	14.11 (2)	
1967	27.93 (3)	
1972		13.23 (4)
1975	30.66 (1)	19.94 (5)
	37.01 (5)	21.00 (4)
1986/87	279.64 (3)	88.81 (4)
1988		77.93 (4)
1991	179.00 (6a)	254.00 (6c)
	290.00 (6b)	
1994		191.13 (4)
1995	284.00 (1)	369.00 (6c)
	278.00 (6a)	
	424.00 (6b)	
1998	356 (7d)	501 (7f)
	598 (7e)	

Sources:
(1) King, McDonald and Roderer 1981, Tenopir and King 1997 (n = 775)
(2) Campbell and Edmisten 1964 (n = 209)
(3) Marks, Nielsen, Petersen and Wagner 1991 (n = 370)
(4) Association of Research Libraries (ARL) statistics: Okerson 1989, Stubbs 1995
(5) Wootton 1977 based on *Library Journal* data (n = 954)
(6) Ketcham and Born 1995, based on ISI Citation Index database
(7) Ketcham-VanOrsdel and Born 1998, based on ISI Citation Index and EBSCO databases.

Notes:
(a) U.S. Science journals only (n=2,072); (b) All science journals (n = 5,020); (c) All journals (n = 6,027)
(d) U.S. Science journals only (n=2,855; (e) All science journals (n = 5,630); (f) All journals (n = 7,201).

from which the sample was drawn, particularly since there were more social science journals involved in the sample compared with journals observed by others. The rates of increase in constant dollars are summarized in Table 64 for the scientific journal prices obtained from several sources. The rates of increase go from 4.7 percent (1960–1975) steadily upward to 8.8 percent (1995–1998). Thus, the rate of price increase also appears to be rising. A similar conclusion might be drawn from the prices of all journals or serials as depicted in Table 65. The prices for the

| Table 64 | **Average Annual Rates of Price Increase in Constant Dollars for Scientific Journals over Various Time Periods: 1960-1998** (in Percent) |

Time Period	Average Annual Increase (%)
1960-1975	4.7 (1)
1967-1986	4.8 (3)
1972-1988	5.3 (4)
1975-1995	6.0 (1)
1991-1995	8.6 (4a)
1995-1998	8.8 (5b)

Note that rates of price increase from 1995 to 1998 are based on a different sample for 1995 with a different price than that shown in the table.

Sources:
(1) King, McDonald and Roderer 1981, Tenopir and King 1997 (n = 775)
(2) Marks, Nielsen, Petersen and Wagner 1991 (n = 370)
(3) Association of Research Libraries (ARL) statistics: Okerson 1989, Stubbs 1995
(4) Ketcham and Born 1995, based on ISI Citation Index database
(5) Ketcham-VanOrsdel and Born 1998, based on ISI Citation Index and EBSCO databases 1995-1998
    (n = 2,855)

Notes:
(a) U.S. Science journals only (n=2,072); (b) U.S. Science journals only 1995-1998 (n = 2,855)

| Table 65 | **Average Annual Rates of Price Increase in Constant Dollars for All Journals over Various Time Periods: 1960-1998** (in Percent) |

Time Period	Average Annual Increase (%)
1960-1975	4.7 (1)
1960-1975	5.0 (1)
1972-1988	4.7 (2)
1975-1986	6.9 (2)
1986-1994	5.3 (2)
1991-1995	6.9 (3)
1995-1998	9.4 (4)

Note that rates of price increase from 1995 to 1998 are based on a different sample for 1995 with a different price than that shown in the table.

Sources:
(1) Wootton 1977 based on *Library Journal* data (n = 954)
(2) Association of Research Libraries (ARL) statistics: Okerson 1989, Stubbs 1995
(3) Ketcham and Born 1995, based on ISI Citation Index database 1991-1995 (n = 6,027)
(4) Ketcham-VanOrsdel and Born 1998, based on ISI Citation Index and EBSCO databases 1995-1998
    (n = 7,201)

broader set of periodicals are increasing in constant dollars, but not necessarily accelerating as fast as with scientific journals.

Annual price data are also reported elsewhere such as in *American Libraries* and EBSCO (At Your Service).

Reasons for Price Increases

There is a well-established theory and sound empirical evidence concerning the inverse relationship between the price of and demand for journals. Thus, when publishers increase prices, circulation nearly always decreases. Conversely when circulation drops even at a constant price, the price of a journal must be increased in order to recover costs.[6] Since the 1970s, prices have increased astronomically and average circulation has decreased substantially. For example, the average price of scientific scholarly journals has increased over seven-fold over a twenty year period and the rate of increase continues to grow while, as mentioned above, personal subscriptions have decreased from 5.8 subscriptions per scientist to 2.7 over the same period.[7] The question is what triggered this unhealthy trend? Was it started by large increases in price or by a decline in circulation? While there is no definitive answer, it appears that a little of each was occurring simultaneously during the 1970s.

It is clear that some, but not nearly all, of the price increases result from inflation and increased size of the journals (i.e., over 20 years about 56 percent of the increase can be attributed to these factors).[8] However, other factors must have contributed to the remaining 44 percent increase. For example, the publishing costs and, thus, prices were hurt in the 1970s by severe inflation rates (at times well over 10 percent), inflationary cost of labor (publishing is highly labor-

---

[6]There are, of course, exceptions to these circumstances. For example, circulation could increase, even in light of a higher price, if attributes such as quality are improved. When circulation goes down, publishers could also take cost cutting action or develop other sources of revenue in order to maintain a price.

[7]Over the twenty year period the average circulation per journal has decreased from 6,100 subscriptions to 5,800, but with the increase in number of scientists and relative decrease in number of journals, one would expect the average circulation to be 9,800 subscribers. The median circulation decreased from 2,900 to 1,900 subscriptions which suggests that the larger circulation journals are getting larger, but small ones are decreasing.

[8]It is interesting to note that Faxon recently (1997) reported that they expected subscription prices to increase by 10.3 percent: 2.8 percent resulting from general inflation, 3.0 percent attributable to increasing number of pages (with these two factor contributing 56 percent of the total increase—the same as our findings). The remaining 4.5 percent is said to be caused by decreasing number of subscriptions (cited in Odlyzko 1996)

intensive, King, McDonald and Roderer 1981), and fluctuating international exchange rates (see, for example, Sandler 1988). In addition, a trend in publisher size may have contributed to price increases, because there is evidence that higher prices are related to the size of publisher portfolios (i.e., number of journals published) (see McCabe 1998, Chapter 14). At the same time subscriptions dropped because library budgets did not grow as fast in the 1970s and 1980s as observed with the steady growth in R&D funding[9] and number of scientists (Henderson 1999), scientists (particularly in companies and government agencies) had less discretionary funds for purchasing journals, and libraries were developing improved alternative journal-related services such as interlibrary borrowing and journal routing. The combination of these factors appears to have triggered a spiraling effect of increased prices, declining circulation, even higher prices, and so on which has accelerated over the years.

One reason for this spiraling effect is that publishing costs increase at an accelerated rate as circulation decreases below the 2,500 level (see Chapter 12). For example, if circulation decreases by 100 subscribers from a 2,500 level, the additional cost at 2,400 subscribers would be $6 more per subscriber; but at 500, a drop of 100 subscribers would cost $186 more per subscriber (assuming all other publishing parameters such as number of pages remain the same). Decreases of 100 subscribers would result in the following increases in cost: at 2,500—$6; at 2,000—$8; at 1,500—$18; at 1,000—$41; and at 500—$186. Thus, at low circulation small decreases in circulation can initially require a small increase in price resulting in lower circulation leading to larger increases in price and larger drops in circulation. The more publishers attempt to maintain sufficient revenue at these levels, the deeper the hole they dig. Unfortunately, an increasing number of journals have backed into this dangerous territory (e.g., in 1975 about 900 journals are estimated to have had under 1,000 subscribers, but in 1995 nearly 1,900 journals had fewer that 1,000 subscribers).

Since personal subscriptions are much more sensitive to price changes than library subscriptions, the spiraling effect was initially observed in the area of personal subscriptions (see the next section for an explanation of this phenomenon). Over the twenty year period there are now about 18 million fewer personal sub-

---

[9]From 1970 to 1985 world science expenditures doubled (in constant $) and academic R&D increased by 50 percent. Meanwhile, U.S. libraries' expenditures increased about 20 percent, but remained "absolutely flat between 1970 to 1980" (Henderson 1999). Brown (1996) points out that supply (research) doubled from 1976 to 1990, but demand (libraries) rose only by one-half. Thus, he contends that it is impossible for libraries to handle the over-supply of research. Henderson (1999) has another perspective in that the capacity of libraries (as suppliers) cannot meet the demand for the requirements of research.

scriptions than would be expected had personal subscription levels remained the same. This fact has undoubtedly cost publishers billions in lost revenue which was recovered through higher prices to the relatively price-insensitive library market.

There are further subtle effects of spiraling prices on library budgets. One consequence of cancelled personal subscriptions is increased demand on library-provided journals since reading of these journals has shifted to those provided by libraries. This extensive shift in reading has resulted in an additional annual cost of about $75 per title for reshelving and photocopying. This additional cost further reduces funds available to purchase journals and other materials. Interlibrary borrowing and document delivery services are often used to provide articles from cancelled subscriptions. However, contrary to the belief of many, a cancelled subscription often saves far less than the cost of the subscription and the cost of processing the journal (typically about $81). The reason for this is that an additional cost is incurred for obtaining copies of articles needed by users (e.g., the cost of interlibrary borrowing is about $21.50 per item). As an example, assume that a $400 journal is cancelled and 10 items are later borrowed. The library would save about $481 in price and processing, but would also incur an additional cost of $215, so that the saving is not $481 but rather less at $266. Thus, there are economic effects within the journal market that are not entirely apparent.

There are many other thoughts concerning reasons for such dramatic price increases. For example, the 1967 to 1986/7 study (Marks, Nielsen, Petersen and Wagner 1991) considers both inflation and number of pages by comparing the average price per page over that time period in constant dollars, and the increase appears to surpass 50 percent (based on a graph). These data, based on institutional prices, total approximately 2.2 percent per year. Using institutional prices for the journal-tracking sample, we find that the equivalent price per page increase from 1975 to 1995 is approximately 1.8 percent per year. Under contract to the ARL in 1989, the Economic Consulting Services, Inc. (ECS) also provides price per page comparisons from 1973 to 1987 for 165 commercially published journals in five fields of science. Reading from charts, index values (starting at 100 in 1973) increase to about 525 for physical science, 450 for technology (with a large increase from around 300 in 1986), 475 for medical (with an increase from around 340 in 1986), 400 for earth science, and 590 for biology.[9] The average increases are 12.6, 11.4, 11.8, 12.1, and 13.5 percent respectively.

---

[9]An index approach is used by ECS to avoid the problem of comparing increases among journals having substantial differences in price. It appears that inflation was not taken into account.

Librarians in particular have lamented the large increases in journal prices, but this is not a new phenomenon. For example, Okerson (1989) cites the following from the 1927 Association of American Universities: "Librarians are suffering because of the increasing volume of publications and rapidly rising prices." In 1977, DeGennaro wrote a strongly worded article, "Escalating Journal Prices: Time to Fight Back." Much of the blame has been directed toward commercial publishers because their prices and rates of increase tend to be higher. As a result, academic libraries have begun to advocate that researchers (and universities) eschew commercial publishers. Okerson (1989), while not the first, made the following recommendation to ARL:[10]

> ARL should strongly advocate the transfer of publication research results from serials produced by commercial publishers to existing noncommercial journals. ARL should specifically encourage the creation of innovative, non-profit alternatives to traditional commercial publishers.

Both Economic Consulting Services, Inc. (ECS) (1989) and Okerson (1989) present reasons for the dramatic price increases. ECS presents these five possible explanations:

- Size of journal: as journal articles proliferate, the journals increase in volume.

- Subject matter: certain fields have become more technical, and the added technical language, mathematical equations, and graphics included in these articles cause publishing costs to increase.

- Exchange rate trends: as the value of the dollar decreases relative to foreign currencies, it becomes more difficult for foreign publishers to cover their costs if they receive constant dollar prices.

- Exchange rate fluctuations: the increasing volatility of exchange rates has made it difficult for foreign firms to set U.S. prices and still guarantee themselves a profit.

- Circulation: the highly specialized nature of serials implies a limited circulation level. A limited circulation level implies higher unit costs.

Conspicuously absent from this rationale are the inflation rates.

Okerson (1989) categorizes the causes of the high prices into three groups: a consumer problem, a systemic problem, and a classic economic problem. The

---

[10]A qualifying argument concerning this solution is presented in Chapter 14.

consumer problem relates to the lack of knowledge of libraries to pricing issues such as:

- dual pricing (i.e., price differentiation) in which institutions, especially U.S. libraries, are charged more than both individuals in the United States and libraries in other countries,

- foreign exchange fluctuations over the years has made budgeting difficult and has benefited non-U.S. publishers,

- government privatization policies in which publications which were published by government below cost are transferred to commercial publishers,

- concentration of key, expensive journals within certain publishing companies which have become monopolistic, and

- publisher increases far in excess of general inflation and the Consumer Price Index.

Part of the latter increases are said to be attributable to a growth in the size of journals: a greater degree in specialization; photocopying, electronic transmission, library resource sharing, and budget cutbacks; elimination of page charges by some journals—requiring higher prices to compensate for lost revenue; and the higher prices charged by commercial publishers compared to society publishers.

The systemic argument places the blame for high prices on the system due to:

- Sheer size—The number of scientists and journal literature has increased dramatically.

- Competition for grant and research funds has led to a necessity to publish.

- The academic tenure system spurs publication and multiple authorship.

- The information system is open-ended and library budgets are based on factors other than use.

- Research libraries have historical expectations regarding the completeness of their collections.

- Faculty have expectations that they will get articles exactly when needed in their roles as editors and society members.

- Publishers play a role in satisfying the demand for additional author outlets and commercial publishers' need to place profit before any notion of a larger community benefit.

The classical economic argument explaining the trend to high prices includes the following precepts:

- Publishing requires high fixed costs and low marginal costs of reproduction and distribution.

- The market (demand) for scholarly journals is limited.

- Library acquisition (demand) has low elasticity.

- The intersection of supply and demand curves occurs at a very <u>low</u> quantity and a very *high* price for serials sold at a single price.

- In the absence of a mechanism for the common good, publishers have pursued a policy of multiple-tier pricing to regain some of their otherwise lost economic benefit.

- In a marketplace in which a publisher holds a natural monopoly, wasteful behavior by the publisher, such as economically unproductive growth in the size of the serial, can occur without correction, particularly with the unwitting cooperation of editors and scholars.

While we agree that most of these factors lead to high prices and incorporate some of them into the following section on price sensitivities, we have come to some different conclusions (see Chapters 1 and 14).

Literally hundreds of articles discuss journal pricing and price/demand relationships. Most of the quantitative studies take a top-down approach using some form of multiple regression analysis to explain the large variation in price among journals. In the next section of this chapter, we provide a different, bottom-up approach which examines why individuals and librarians decide to purchase journals in light of alternative sources for the information (i.e., libraries as an alternative to purchase for individuals and separate copies of articles for librarians). The top-down approach generally involves observations of the price and demand relationship over a large number of journals in a given year or of the changes in price in constant dollars over time which are then related to number of subscribers. Some problems with these approaches are outlined below:

- Journals with small demand (<2,500 subscribers) have unit costs per subscriber that vary sharply because of high fixed costs.

- The perceived value and number of potential readers vary substantially among journals.

- Information from journals can be obtained in several ways (e.g., personal subscriptions, library copies, document delivery/ILL, reprints, copies from colleagues, etc.) so that, if a price is too high, reasonable alternatives are available (i.e., a classic example of substitution of equivalent goods).

- Journals, and most especially society journals, bundle other services or information, making it difficult to assess the actual cost of publishing a journal as opposed to its price which is a cost to libraries (Ordover and Baumol 1975; Chuang and Sirbu 1997).

- Awareness of the existence of journals is not always high.

- The shape of the price-demand curve is unknown.

One should review top-down results with these caveats in mind.

Berg (1973) provides a top-down analysis for both individual and library subscriptions and demonstrates the difference in price elasticities of the two. Petersen (1989) uses a multiple regression analysis to establish variables that affect variations in prices and concludes that "more pages, additional issues, and photos, figures, and art in the journal are associated with higher prices. Advertising reduces prices." These conclusions are consistent with the cost model presented in Chapter 12. Petersen also found that journals involving commercial publishers, non-U.S. publishers, and physical sciences are more expensive even when cost factors are held constant. Noll and Steinmueller (1992) provide charts of Faxon subscription prices and paid circulation (1988) for a sample of 1,400 journals. The chart shows that prices range up to $950 with circulation under 10,000 and all journals with circulation over that amount are priced under $150.

Chressanthis and Chressanthis (1994) studied the top 99 journals in economics. They concluded:

> Contrary to the malevolent intentions charged by libraries against publishers for the levels and changes in library prices, the empirical results suggest that systematic variations in library prices across economics journals exist for explainable reasons. The results show that library prices vary according to the degree of third-degree price discrimination practiced by publishers; variations in the production and distribution cost structure as measured by the existence of illustrations, geography of publication, journal age, journal quality, total pages printed, and journal circulation; and finally by the nonprofit versus for-profit status of publishers.

An entirely different conclusion is drawn by Stoller, Christopherson and Miranda (1996). They summarized many of the pricing studies and concluded:

> An economic analysis of the journal industry indicates that high and discriminatory prices result from the existence of monopoly power among publishers. University and library administrators can alleviate

this problem in several ways: (1) by providing journal users with an incentive for keeping prices lower; (2) by encouraging library organizations and university consortia to exploit their potential monopsony (i.e., a buying monopoly) power into a bilateral monopoly situation; and (3) by attempting to create and demonstrate high elasticity of demand for journals in any way possible. Even if some degree of price discrimination is justified by consumer equity considerations, the current pricing situation is far from equitable and can be improved if publishers can be coerced to change their pricing practices.

They point out that high prices tend to be attributable to "a few commercial publishing firms, primarily located in Western Europe and to be limited to a few disciplines." In light of the fact that "recent data show that the problem is not simply going to disappear," they feel that "the pricing practices and profitability of these firms need to be explored further to determine whether there is any cost-based justification for their high prices and to develop a more complete understanding of the journal price problem."

In Chapter 14 we discuss the issue of profitability of commercial publishers in substantial detail. First, it is useful to understand price sensitivities from the buyers' perspective as discussed below.

EXPLAINING INDIVIDUAL AND INSTITUTIONAL PRICE AND DEMAND SENSITIVITIES

As described in Chapter 8, scientists and engineers use a variety of sources for scholarly journals including individual subscriptions, journals provided by their organizational libraries, journals found in shared office collections, and articles provided by other sources such as colleagues, authors, and non-organization libraries. The choice of source for a particular journal depends on its price, the frequency with which the journal is read, the age of an article when needed, and the ease of gaining access to an article when needed. Scientists average about 122 readings of scholarly articles per year.

Some of the 122 readings are from personal subscriptions (36 readings per scientist), parent organization libraries (73 readings per scientist), and 13 of the readings are from journals found in shared office collections and articles obtained from other sources such as colleagues and authors.[11]

---

[11]Some of the 122 readings (9.8) come from electronic journals, but are included in the sources mentioned.

Although some scientists do not read scholarly articles, a typical scientist reads at least one article from an average of 17.8 scholarly journals. Scientists in the particular surveys from which the data are obtained averaged about 2.7 personal (individual) subscriptions from which they averaged reading about 13.4 articles per annual subscription. The largest share of the 17.8 journals that are read are provided by an organizational library (an average of 11.4 journals). Each of these journals is read an average of 6.4 times per year per scientist. Other sources account for approximately 3.5 of the journals read.[12]

The mixture of journal sources used by scientists may appear to be rather chaotic. When assessed from an economic perspective, however, the utilization of a variety of sources makes perfect sense in terms of economic costs to scientists and libraries, ease of use, and availability. Each source serves a relevant niche, and scientists typically make economically rational choices among these alternative sources.

Price and Demand of Individual Subscriptions

Generally scientists choose to subscribe to relatively inexpensive journals which they read frequently and/or are available through society memberships. They use their shared office collections and organizational libraries for expensive journals, those that they read relatively infrequently, and older articles. In other words, they are willing to trade their time to travel to the library to avoid the cost of subscribing to expensive and/or infrequently read journals. From cost studies we can demonstrate the hypothetical cost trade-off of subscribing to a journal versus periodically travelling to a library to read journals.

We provide economic costs based on surveys of scientists and other professionals and cost finding studies of special libraries (Griffiths and King 1993). The overall cost to readers for using individual subscriptions consists of the one-time subscription price, as well as the time and effort to order, receive, and retain copies of the journal and the time per reading to browse through a new issue and to look up older articles. For the purpose of our example, we assume an average individual subscription price of $303 in 1998 dollars. Reader surveys have shown that it costs approximately $11.00 to process new personal journal subscriptions and retain them. This total cost ($314) is shown in Figure 12 as the fixed cost incurred prior to reading the journal.

---

[12]Approximately 1.4 of the 17.8 journals are electronic, and these are read about 7.0 times per year per scientist.

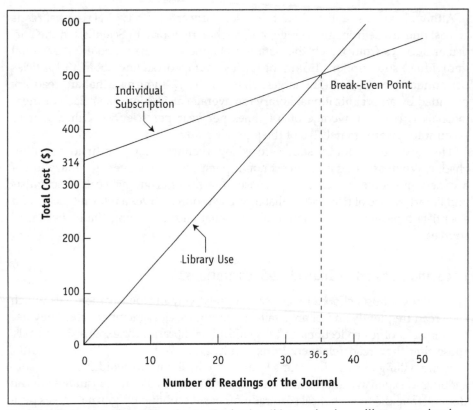

Figure 12. Comparative costs of scientists' subscribing and using a library over levels of reading a journal: 1998

The average cost in a scientist's time of one reading including browsing or looking up articles and making some photocopies is estimated to be $5.10 per reading. With the average of thirteen readings from personal subscriptions, this cost of browsing and look-up amounts to approximately $66.30. This cost does not include the average of fifty minutes spent reading the article. As shown in Figure 12, total cost increases with number of readings at an incremental rate of $5.10.

Looked at in another way, the cost per reading with only one reading is approximately $319.10. With thirteen readings (i.e., the average per individual subscription) the total cost is $380.30 or $29.25 per reading. With fifty readings, the average cost is approximately $11.38 per reading. If a journal contains 123 articles (the average number of articles per journal), and every article is read once, the average cost per reading is approximately $7.65.

Readers can avoid the high cost per reading of journals they read infrequently by going to their library or a shared office collection instead. This option does incur costs to them (or to a delegated person) such as travelling to and from the library, browsing issues, looking up articles, and photocopying some of the articles. Typically, scientists read or make photocopies of several articles during each library visit.

Our surveys show that the total cost per reading from library-owned journals is approximately $13.70.[13] The cost of reading library copies is shown on the figure as a line going through the origin (zero cost) with no reading and rising incrementally at $13.70 per reading. This line crosses the individual subscription cost line at 36.5 readings. In other words, at a subscription price of $303, it costs less to go to the library if one reads the journal fewer than thirty-seven times, and it costs less to subscribe if there are more than thirty-seven readings. Since only approximately two percent of scientific journals read by individuals are read more than thirty-seven times, it is clear why few journals are purchased by individuals at that price. If one does not include the incremental cost to the library for reshelving and photocopying ($1.48 per reading from library copies), the break-even point increases to forty-four readings.

The break-even points in Table 66 show the effects of pricing at various levels. It seems clear that one needs to read journals very frequently to justify ordering individual subscriptions, particularly with prices at their current high levels. In addition to price, the break-even point is also affected by distance of the reader to the library, extent of reading of all journals that are read in the library, and availability of other sources of the journal such as journal routing and shared office collections. The following evidence from our surveys suggests that distance to the library has a bearing on the source of journals selected by scientists (Griffiths and King 1993):

- Scientists close to libraries purchase fewer individual subscriptions than those farther away (1.8 subscriptions for those less than ten minutes away versus 2.6 for those ten or more minutes away).

---

[13]This amount includes time for travel, browsing or look-up, and photocopying (both by oneself and by library staff). It also includes instances in which the scientist sends someone to the library to obtain an article copy.

Table 66	Break-Even Point in Readings between the Cost of Subscribing at Various Individual Prices versus Using the Library: 1998 (in Readings)

Individual Price ($)	Break-Even Point (Readings)
$100	12.9
$150	18.7
$250	30.3
$500	59.4
$1,000	117.6

- Scientists close to libraries and shared department collections read more from these sources than from individual subscriptions as depicted in Table 67.

While the economic model above does not fully explain choices as to sources of journals used, it is a good indicator of some contributing factors.

Individual subscriptions are particularly sensitive to price because individuals tend to read extensively from a few journals and little from most others. We mentioned earlier that a typical scientist reads at least one article per year from approximately 17.8 journals. We also indicated that scientists need to read a $303 journal about thirty-seven times to cost justify a personal subscription.[14] Across all scientists and journals, our readership survey shows that fewer than 2 percent of the journals are read more than thirty-seven times by individual scientists. The observed distribution of scientific journal readings is presented in Table 68.

This distribution demonstrates that 53 percent of scientists who read a journal at least once read only five or fewer articles from the journal; 80.5 percent of the readers read ten or fewer articles, with readership steadily declining thereafter. In other words, of 5,000 scientists who might read at least one article from a journal during a year, approximately 4,025 scientists will read fewer than eleven articles from that journal or, conversely, fewer than 975 scientists will read more than ten articles.

---

[14]The break-even point of 37 readings involves the trade-off in which library costs are included.

Table 67	Proportion of Readings from Library Collections by Distance to the Library: 1990–1993 (in Percent)

Number of Minutes	Proportion of Readings from Library and Shared Department Collections
Less than 5	91
5 to 10	65
More than 10	43

Source: King, et al. surveys 1990–1993

Table 68	Proportion and Cumulative Proportion of Readers/Journals at Various Levels of Reading: 1993-1998 (in Percent)

An Individual's Number of Readings per Journal (Readings)	Proportion of Readers/Journals	Cumulative Proportion of Readers/Journals
1-5	53.0	53.0
6-10	27.5	80.5
11-15	7.0	87.5
16-20	5.1	92.6
21-25	2.7	95.3
26-50	3.8	99.1
51-100	0.7	99.8
>100	0.2	100.0

Source: King et al. surveys 1993-1998

Earlier we presented break-even points for five personal subscription prices ranging from $100 to $1,000. At these prices and break-even points, the proportion of
journals to which scientists could economically subscribe is presented in Table 69.
Thus, if a scientist reads at least one article from eighteen journals, less than three
of them would be subscribed to at $100 (0.15 × 18), 1.6 of them at $150, and less
than one at $250. Clearly, individual or personal subscription demand is extremely
sensitive to changes in price, with the typical costs and distribution of journal
reading given in our example.

Table 69	Proportion of Journals to which Individuals Can Economically Subscribe at Various Individual Subscription Prices: 1998 (in Percent)
Individual Price	**Proportion of Journals to which Scientists Can Economically Subscribe**
$ 100	15.0
$ 150	8.7
$ 250	3.2
$ 500	0.7
$1,000	<0.1

Source: King, et al. surveys 1993–1998

Price and Demand of Institutional Subscriptions

A cost trade-off very much like the one discussed above for individuals also
applies to institutional or library subscriptions. Libraries can subscribe to journals
or provide their users with copies of articles obtained by interlibrary borrowing or
from a document delivery service. Journals which are collectively read frequently
by users generally should be purchased, and infrequently-read journals are better
obtained as copies of articles from elsewhere.

In fact, this economic reality is the basis for the guidelines agreed to by publishers and libraries after the 1976 revision to the U.S. Copyright Law in which five
and under items borrowed from a journal during one year by a library are not
subject to royalty payment. At the time the Law was passed, the level of journal

prices[15] made it cost effective to subscribe to journals when there were six or more readings of the journal. Thus, royalty payments for interlibrary loans were not necessary for most journals. However, as we will show below, escalating journal prices have increased the break-even point well above the five and under agreement for most journals.

A series of special library cost studies have documented detailed costs of interlibrary borrowing and document delivery requests (Griffiths and King 1993). A more recent study by Kingma (1995) has provided academic libraries with both careful cost estimates and decision criteria for purchase versus external access; in fact, a 1995/96 ARL study (Jackson 1997) has validated the cost of interlibrary borrowing and lending (see Chapter 10).

When libraries purchase journals, they incur the cost represented by the price of the journal plus processing costs associated with collection development, acquisitions, input processing, shelving, and storage, binding, and weeding. When a library journal is read, the library incurs further costs of reshelving and sometimes photocopying of articles. In addition, users incur costs to travel to the library, browse, and look up articles for subsequent reading. These costs are summarized in Table 70 for both academic and special libraries, assuming an average institutional subscription price of $338 established from the journal tracking study and adjusted to current dollars.

Prior to any reading, the cost to purchase and own a typical science journal is $419 in special libraries (i.e., $338 plus $81 processing costs). Each reading costs special libraries an average of $1.48 per reading for reshelving and photocopying. (Patrons of academic libraries are more likely to pay the photocopying costs). Users invest an average of $12.22 per reading in their time or that of someone they delegate. Thus, if a typical $338 journal has 136 readings in a library as documented in Chapter 8, the total cost to the library averages approximately $620 or $4.56 per reading. Users add a cost of $12.22 per reading, so the total cost to a company, government agency, or an institution averages $16.78 per reading. The total cost of owning the $338 journal is depicted in Figure 13 by amount of reading.

The cost incurred by an academic library to obtain an external copy of an article by interlibrary loan is $13.90 to $18.60; the cost incurred by the user is $2.55. The cost for a special library to obtain the same copy is $21.50, while the cost to its user is estimated to be $11.34. Kingma (1995) also presents costs to lending libraries ($3.21–$10.93) depending on the service vendor, and special library costs of lending are estimated to be about $24 per item loaned.

---

[15]An average journal institutional price in 1976 was approximately $40.

Table 70	Total Journal Costs by Academic and Special Libraries: Projected to 1998 (in Dollars)	
Cost to Libraries and Users	**Academic Libraries**	**Special Libraries**
Subscription price	338.00	338.00
One-time processing costs	75.00	81.00
Shelving and photocopying costs per reading	1.12	1.48
Costs to users per reading	1.04	12.22

Sources: Kingma 1995; Griffiths and King 1993; costs adjusted to 1998

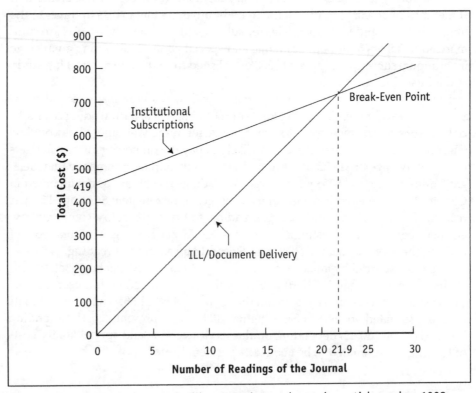

Figure 13. Comparative costs of a library owning vs. borrowing article copies: 1998

In special libraries, the break-even point between owning versus external access of a $338 journal is 20.9 readings when user costs are not considered and 21.9 readings when user costs are included.[16] Again, journal prices have a significant bearing on the break-even points as shown in Table 71.

Kingma (1995) has computed the costs for 787 journals and determined, under various assumptions, whether or not each is less expensive to own or to rely on external copies. Unfortunately, there have been few studies that have observed the distribution of readership of library journals. Kingma graciously made a special computer run for us to analyze the extent of reading of journals for which he had data. Others who have performed such studies include Chen (1972) and Kent, Montgomery, Cohen, Williams, Bulick, Flynn, Sabar, and Kern (1978). The average number of uses for Kingma's journals is 37.2 uses per journal.

To apply the academic library example, we expanded the lognormal distribution of Kingma's data by a factor of 3.6 (i.e., 136 ÷ 37.2). The resultant distributions are presented in Table 72.

Thus, 12.9 percent of the journals have less than eleven readings; and 30 percent have less than twenty-six readings, with a continued diminution in the number of readings.

Translating the break-even points for the five prices ($100 to $1,000) into the proportion of journals to which libraries can economically subscribe, one arrives at the values presented in Table 73. Thus, the proportions decrease with increases

Table 71	Break-Even Point in Readings between Cost of Subscribing and Obtaining Separate Copies of Articles: 1998 (in Readings)

Institutional Price	Break-Even Point in Number of Readings
$ 100	9.5
$ 150	12.1
$ 250	17.3
$ 500	30.4
$1,000	56.5

[16]User costs involve $12.22 when an article is read in the library and $11.34 when an article is ordered by document delivery or interlibrary loan. Thus, the net difference is $0.88 in favor of obtaining separate copies. Neither cost includes actual time spent reading.

Table 72	Proportion and Cumulative Proportion of Journals at Various Levels of Reading Library Journals: 1998 (in Percent)	
Total Readings per Journal	**Proportion of Journals**	**Cumulative Proportion of Journals**
1-10	12.9	12.9
11-25	17.1	30.0
26-50	17.6	47.6
51-100	18.3	65.9
101-250	19.1	85.0
251-500	8.4	93.4
>500	6.6	100.0

Source: Adapted from Kingma 1995

Table 73	Proportion of Journals to which Libraries Can Economically Subscribe at Various Institutional Subscription Prices: 1998 (in Percent)
Institutional Price	**Proportion of Journals to which Libraries Can Economically Subscribe**
$ 100	88.9
$ 150	84.6
$ 250	78.2
$ 500	65.5
$1,000	49.0

in price, but not nearly as sharply as with individual subscriptions. Even journals priced as high as $1,000 should be purchased about one-half the time under these assumptions. These sensitivities are illustrated below.

Effects of Price Changes on Individual and Institutional Subscriptions

Library journals are much less sensitive to price changes because they tend to be read much more than individual subscriptions. For example, if a $100 journal has 1,000 individual and institutional subscriptions each, a price change to $250 would reduce individual subscriptions from 1,000 to 213 for a loss of 887 subscriptions,[17] but the number of institutional subscriptions would only drop from 1,000 to 880 for a loss of only 120 subscriptions.

To expand on examples of the price sensitivities of individual and institutional subscriptions, we assume that 2,500 journals might be read from individual subscriptions and 2,500 might be read from institutional subscriptions prior to a price change. Under the hypothetical conditions discussed above, we would expect the following changes in demand as a function of the price changes presented in Table 74.

Under these conditions, increasing an individual price from $100 to $150 would result in a loss of about 1,050 subscriptions. A comparable institutional price

Table 74	Effects of Price Changes on Number of Individual and Institutional Subscribers (with 2,500 Subscription Base): 1998						
Price Changes		**Individual Subscriptions**			**Institutional Subscriptions**		
From	*To*	*From*	*To*	*Loss*	*From*	*To*	*Loss*
$100	$ 150	2,500	1,450	1,050	2,500	2,379	121
$150	$ 250	2,500	920	1,580	2,500	2,311	189
$250	$ 500	2,500	547	1,953	2,500	2,094	406
$500	$1,000	2,500	111	2,389	2,500	1,870	630

---

[17]There would be a total of 6,667 readers of the journal, of which 1,000 readers would subscribe at $100 (i.e., at 15.0%). At $250, only 3.2% would subscribe or the equivalent of 213 readers.

change would result in a loss of only 121 subscriptions. Clearly, individual subscriptions are much more sensitive to price changes than are institutional subscriptions.

Somewhat similar results were observed in a 1981 study (King and Roderer) in which it was observed that a 50 percent increase in individual subscription prices would reduce personal subscriptions by approximately 40 percent, but such an increase would affect institutional subscriptions by only 6 to 8 percent.[18] This result is not too different from that presented in Table 74 for increasing prices from $100 to $150 (i.e., 42 percent for individual subscriptions and 4.8 percent for library subscriptions). The $100 to $150 prices are similar to prices in constant dollars during the 1981 study. Further confirmation that institutional demand is less sensitive to price was cited by McCarthy (1994). He stated that the number of library subscriptions dropped 5 percent from 1986 to 1994, but that libraries are spending 100 percent more for the reduced number of subscriptions.

Individual price increases affect the number of both individual and institutional subscriptions. When individuals stop subscribing to a journal, they will normally go to a library to read the journal. Thus, when individuals stop subscribing, the number of readings of a library copy increases, meaning that fewer library journals should be canceled in lieu of interlibrary borrowing or document delivery.

---

[18]These data were observed from actual price increases and changes in demand over time for physics journals.

CHAPTER 14

Financing Scholarly Journals

INTRODUCTION

The previous two chapters discussed the possible contributions of costs and pricing of scholarly journals to some severe problems in the scholarly journal system. The financial aspect of publishing is overlooked by many when considering the publishing environment. Every publisher requires funds to start new journals and to keep operations afloat. Furthermore, publishers also require capital to purchase new equipment and facilities and to perform research and development, particularly in order to achieve a successful transformation into electronic publishing. Source of investment, in particular, delineates the four types of publishers. The incentive to invest in scholarly journals is entirely different for commercial stockholders, professional societies, universities and government agencies, and others who support journal publication.

This chapter examines the basic investment required to publish, sources of revenue and their interdependence, and then addresses more specifically commercial publishers and scrutinizes the issue of commercial publisher profitability. We also discuss the fact that some frequently-read articles, in effect, subsidize the infrequently-read ones, whether or not they are of higher quality. This is accomplished by bundling all articles from a specialty, regardless of potential readership, into one journal. Furthermore, marginal journals are sometimes financially subsidized by the publisher's other more profitable journals. We believe this to be far less true with journal publishing, however, than with book publishing where a few popular books tend to compensate for a relatively large number of unprofitable books. In Chapter 15 on electronic journals, we focus on the importance of investment in making these journals successful.

INVESTMENT REQUIREMENTS FOR SCHOLARLY JOURNAL PUBLISHING

Start-Up Investment

In order to start and maintain a scholarly journal, a substantial up-front investment is required by the publisher, its parent organization, or sponsors (Page, Campbell, and Meadows 1997). The principal up-front costs include the staff time and the materials to complete the start-up such as those given below:

- investigate the need for a new journal
- line up an editor
- set up an editorial office
- establish a list of potential authors and referees
- establish an editorial board
- create a five-year plan and budget
- establish editorial policies and criteria for acceptance and rejection
- determine non-article materials to include
- prepare instructions to authors
- identify potential subscribers
- establish and implement a marketing and sales strategy including promotion (mainly advertising leaflets and free copies)
- solicit authors
- design covers and other formats
- assemble the initial issue
- send copies to subscribers and potential subscribers, and
- distribute copies at relevant conferences

Even after the first issue is completed, it can still be several years before the annual revenue equals the annual publishing costs, thus requiring an additional investment to cover losses during that period. In some cases revenue never exceeds costs, and the journal must either be terminated or the costs must be absorbed by profits from other journals. In fact, this is the major risk for investors in journal publishing. Commercial publishers pay for new journals from stockholder investment or from undistributed profits. In either case, scholarly journal publishing must show a reasonable return-on-investment or the stockholders simply will not continue investing in the enterprise.

When a new journal is launched, circulation growth typically continues for five to seven years before beginning to taper off; furthermore, the level at which growth peaks seems to be decreasing over time (Page, Campbell, and Meadows 1997). Unfortunately, the costs of publishing journals in their early stages appear to far exceed revenue, and journals do not usually break even until approximately the sixth year. This picture of losses for a small journal is depicted in Figure 14 adapted from Page, Campbell, and Meadows (1997). It converts pounds into dollars and adjusts for inflation.

Figure 14 shows that a typical new scholarly journal does not recover accumulated costs through accumulated revenue for approximately six years. In fact, some publishers indicate that an even longer period of time is more realistic.[1] The

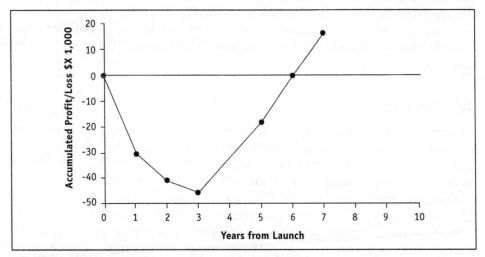

Figure 14. Accumulated profit and loss by number of years from launch of a scholarly journal. (*Source:* Adapted from Page, Campbell and Meadows 1997 and adjusted to 1998 U.S. $s)

---

[1]For example, Meadows (1974) reports that it was thirty years before even *Nature*, a popular general scientific publication, made a profit.

figures show that annual revenue first exceeds costs in approximately the third year of publication. During these three years, losses can amount to approximately $45,000 for a small journal, thus requiring a fairly substantial investment by the publisher without a positive return-on-investment for approximately six years. In fact, present value analysis shows that the actual return probably takes even longer if one considers the alternative uses of the invested funds (e.g., a savings account).

The question becomes one of the capability of publishers to provide sufficient money or capital to make such an investment. Professional societies can obtain capital from excess dues or by borrowing. In recent years, in the field of science at least, societies appear to be more likely to increase the size of existing journals than to launch new ones. The number of scientific scholarly journals published by societies has increased little, if at all, over the past twenty years. Educational and other scholarly journal publishers are undoubtedly subsidized by their parent organizations because of other incentives, which may be the reason that educational and other publishers have initiated more new journals than society publishers. On the other hand, from 1975 to 1995 the number of commercial journals has increased significantly more than the other types.[2] Thus, commercial publishers must find the risk of starting new journals rewarding; otherwise they could not justify the investment required for ongoing publication costs from the standpoint of return-on-investment. Investors would simply place their funds in other ventures.

Operational Investment

Operational investment is required for those periods of time when costs exceed revenue. Revenue from subscriptions is not received all at once; in fact, most of it appears to arrive after some operational costs have been incurred, but before all costs have been expended. We illustrate below how this takes place.

Page, Campbell, and Meadows (1997) give an example of journal revenue and costs for a small journal. In their example, they show that approximately 37 percent of revenue is received prior to publication of the first issue, 34 percent in the first two months of a new year, 12 percent in the second two months, 9 percent in

---

[2]There has also been a trend toward small societies arranging to have commercial publishers process their journals. In our tracking survey we continued to classify these as society publications when clearly identified as such, e.g., *Journal of the American Society for Information Science.* This issue is addressed in greater detail in Chapter 11.

the third two months, and 3.7 percent, 3.4 percent, and 1.8 percent over the remaining two-month periods. Costs incurred to prepare and provide the journals, however, vary by the timing of the different types of publishing activities. In Chapter 12, Cost of Scientific Scholarly Journal Publishing, we presented examples of five kinds of publishing activities and their costs, including the cost of article processing, non-article processing, reproduction, distribution, and publishing support. An example of costs is presented here based on the following cost parameters: 6 issues per year, 120 articles, 10 pages per article, 180 initial manuscripts, 240 special graphics pages, 1,800 subscriptions (180 overrun), and 300 non-article pages. The appropriate unit costs are those presented in Chapter 12, but they are distributed over time with publishing support costs allocated as shown in Table 75.

We assume that support costs represent 35 percent of all article and non-article processing costs, 15 percent of reproduction and distribution costs, and a fixed cost of approximately $68,000. Total costs equal $376,211 including support costs. The costs are conceptually distributed over time as depicted in Table 76.

We also spread the one-year costs of a publication (i.e., issues) over a period of twenty-seven months beginning fifteen months prior to the first of six issues until the sixth issue is published. The costs of subscription maintenance ($17,687) is not listed above but is assumed to occur approximately one month after subscriptions are made. Of course, the costs cover only one year's publication (i.e., 6 issues). Since the costs are distributed over twenty-seven months, other year's subscriptions would overlap, but here we are interested only in comparing costs and revenue over time to demonstrate the favorable cash flow for journal publishing. We assume subscription revenue to be approximately 15 percent above costs; thus subscription revenue would total $432,647 beginning four months prior to publication of the first issue. Costs and revenue are displayed in Table 77 where months are presented in pairs.

The cost distribution over time shows that the costs of each issue begin approximately fifteen months prior to publication of the issue and end with subscription maintenance costs of $17,687 running from five months before the first issue is mailed through the tenth month after publication. The cost of each issue totals $59,754. The total cost up to the time the first issue is published (including six issues) is $158,714, and the accumulated costs prior to any revenue being received is $53,929.

The net revenue is positive for a total of 12 of 27 months, albeit highly profitable for only one of those months. Immediately following the beginning of the publishing year, the journal operates in the black. In fact, actual cash flow might be more favorable than shown in the table because actual expenditure may come as much as one month later than the date the costs are incurred. For example,

	Table 75	Timeframe for When Publishing Costs Are Incurred by Activity (in 1998 Dollars)		
	Activity	**Cost**	**Unit of Measure**	**Timeframe**
C_1	Set-up	$500	issue	Spread over the 2-month preparation period
C_2	Processing manuscripts	$20	manuscript page	12 to 15 months prior to publication
C_3	Editorial	$50	article page	approximately 6 months prior to publication
C_4	Article composition/ typesetting	$35	article page	2 to 4 months prior to publication
C_5	Special graphics	$60	special graphics page	2 to 4 months prior to publication
C_6	Set-up non article materials	$50	issue	2 to 4 months prior to publication
C_7	Covers	$200	per issue	2 to 4 months prior to publication
C_8	Editing non-article materials	$25	page	2 to 4 months prior to publication
C_9	Non-article composition	$35	page	2 to 4 months prior to publication
C_{10}	Printing set-up	$950	issue	2 months prior to publication
C_{11}	Plate making and/or collating	$4	page	2 months prior to publication
C_{12}	Binding	$0.125	copy	2 months prior to publication
C_{13}	Special cover	$0.15	copy	2 months prior to publication
C_{14} and C_{15}	Printing	$0.007	impression	2 months prior to publication
C_{16}	Set-up for mail processing	$50	issue	1 month prior to publication
C_{17}	Mail processing	$0.35	copy mailed	1 month prior to publication
C_{18}	Postage (rate based on advertising)	$0.263	copy	1 month prior to publication
C_{19}	Subscription maintenance	$7	subscription	when an order is placed (assumed to be 1 month prior to the receipt of revenue)
C_{20}	Postage (rate based on weight)	$0.001	page per copy	1 month prior to publication

Table 76	Cost Elements and Total Issue Cost by Time Prior to Publication of an Issue (in 1998 Dollars)	
Months Prior to Publication of an Issue	**Cost Elements**	**Total Cost of One Issue**
6-15	C_2, $1/6C_3$	$12,633
5	$1/6C_3$	$ 2,746
4	$1/6C_3$, $1/3$ [C_4, C_5, C_6, C_7, C_8, C_9]	$ 9,695
3	$1/6C_3$, $1/3$ [C_4, C_5, C_6, C_7, C_8, C_9]	$ 9,695
2	$1/2C_1$, $1/6$ C_3, $1/3[C_4$, C_5, C_6, C_7, C_8, C_9] C_{10}, C_{11}, C_{12}, C_{13}, C_{14}, C_{15}	$19,475
0-1	$1/2C_1$, $1/6C_3$, C_{16}, C_{17}, C_{18}, $C_{19}C_{20}$	$ 5,510

outside printers might wait thirty days for payment, and staff is normally paid at the end of the month. The general picture is drawn to demonstrate the typical distribution of expenses in journal publishing and the need for some subsidy or investment, at least initially, to support ongoing operations.[3]

To operate under the hypothetical conditions set forth above, the accumulated deficit of $63,187 must be financed. Societies typically partially overcome these early deficits by surplus membership fees and page charges. Obviously publishers can borrow during the fifteen months prior to publication when revenue is insufficient to cover costs, in which case the publisher must pay interest under the assumption that the interest paid will be balanced by collecting interest when there is a surplus. The problem is that, while the deficit and surplus end up being nearly equal, the deficit is spread over a longer period, and therefore requires a greater interest outlay than received. Furthermore, banks usually charge more for interest on loans than they pay for interest on surplus balances. If a commercial publisher receives 15 percent gross profit (approximately one-half of which goes to taxes), the return-on-investment ranks as a good investment. Before publishing the first issue, $63,187 is tied up for a time, but that investment yields approxi-

---

[3]McCabe (1999) points out that the cost model applied here involves cost incurred at various points in time. Thus, true "economic" costs should include the time value of funds which was not done here (although done in some other models).

Table 77 Journal Publication Costs, Revenue, and Net Revenue over Time before and after Publication (in 1998 Dollars)

Months Before/After Start	Subscription Maintenance Costs	Costs* by Issue						Total Cost	Revenue		
		Issues							Total Revenue	Net Revenue	Accumulative Revenue
		1	2	3	4	5	6				
-14, 15		2,527						2,527		(2,527)	(2,527)
-12, 13		2,526	2,527					5,053		(5,053)	(7,580)
-10, 11		2,527	2,526	2,527				7,580		(7,580)	(15,160)
-8, 9		2,526	2,527	2,526	2,527			10,106		(10,106)	(25,266)
-6, 7		2,527	2,526	2,527	2,526	2,527		12,633		(12,633)	(37,899)
-5	651	2,746	2,527	2,526	2,527	2,526	2,527	16,030		(16,030)	(53,929)
-4	1,302	9,695	2,746	2,527	2,526	2,527	2,526	23,849	15,921	(7,928)	(61,857)
-3	1,953	9,695	9,695	2,746	2,527	2,526	2,527	31,669	31,843	174	(61,683)
-2	2,603	19,475	9,695	9,695	2,746	2,527	2,526	49,267	47,763	(1,504)	(63,187)
0, -1	6,021	5,510	19,475	9,695	9,695	2,746	2,527	55,669	63,685	8,016	(55,171)
1, 2	2,115		5,510	19,475	9,695	9,695	2,746	49,236	147,272	98,036	42,865
3, 4	1,627			5,510	19,475	9,695	9,695	46,002	51,744	5,742	48,607
5, 6	651				5,510	19,475	9,695	35,331	39,803	4,472	53,079
7, 8	439					5,510	19,475	25,424	15,921	(9,503)	43,576
9, 10	325						5,510	5,835	10,730	4,895	48,471
11,12								--	7,961	7,961	56,432
Total	17,687	59,754	59,754	59,754	59,754	59,754	59,754	376,211	432,643	56,432	56,432

* Some numbers are slightly off due to rounding.

mately $28,000 in net profit. Thus, the return-on-investment is very high. This profit also must cover both start-up investment and start-up risks for a new journal and potential losses for an existing journal. (The latter risk is discussed later).

These data apply roughly to all journals having the same parameters (i.e., number of issues, articles, and pages) regardless of the number of subscribers, and hence, the subscription price. However, changes in these parameters do affect cash flow. For example, the number of articles published appreciably affects early deficits. In other words, journals with more articles have higher early deficits. This may be one reason that commercial publishers tend to publish fewer articles than society publishers. Fewer issues also affect cash flow favorably. These two factors may explain why educational and other publishers have fewer articles and issues than society and commercial publishers since they typically have less recourse to capital and borrowing sources.

SOURCES OF REVENUE AND THEIR INTERDEPENDENCE

Thus far we have restricted our discussion concerning revenue to that produced exclusively from subscriptions. Publishers do obtain revenue from other sources as well, however, including page charges, advertising, reprints, back issues, licenses, and royalty fees. Page charges aside, other sources of revenue help dampen the effects of risk, although there are also costs associated with these services. To illustrate the extent to which these sources produce revenue, we present examples cited in the literature dating back to the 1970s (see Table 78). Evidence shows that revenue sources do not change appreciably over time. Subscriptions tend to dominate revenue, with advertising and page charges being the next most prevalent sources of revenue. Advertising revenue depends on the degree to which the journal specialty fits the market niche of the service or product being advertised and/or the circulation of the journal. Thus, the large-circulation journals are more likely to have the high advertising revenues, while it is the small-circulation journals that most need advertising revenue to lower prices.

Page charges represent another source of revenue. Across all types of publishers, it appears that this revenue source represents approximately 2 to 8 percent of revenue. Societies, such as those represented by the American Institute of Physics (AIP), can earn nearly one-third of their revenue from this source.[4] Machlup and

---

[4]Societies are reducing the number of journals in which page charges are required, however. Commercial publishers very rarely charge for pages. In fact, even the AAP estimate of 2.4% is said to have decreased since 1991.

Table 78   Proportion of Revenue by Sources of Revenue Provided by Several Sources of Data (in Percent)

Source of Revenue	Fry/ White 1973	Machlup/ Leeson 1975	King et al. 1977	Lerner 1984**	Page et al. 1977*	Page et al. 1987*	Page et al. 1996*	Marshall 1988*	AAP (In CLR/AAP-1995)*** 1991	Soc. 1991	AAUP 1991
Subscriptions	74.9	64.5	81.1	61.9	86.7	88.6	74	96.4	72.0	59.0	73.9
Page Charges	5.1	8.3	6.6	32.8	--	--	12	--	2.4	1.8	7.0
Advertising	3.2	13.7	4.5	0.9	9.6	3.2	2	--	17.7	29.7	3.0
Back Issues	1.5	2.2	2.5	0.5	--	7.3	2	1.3	--	--	--
Reprints	3.3	4.8	5.3	2.3	2.4	0.1	8	2.4	--	--	--
Subsidies	5.4	--	--	--	--	--	--	--	--	--	--
Other	6.6	6.5	--	1.6	1.2	0.7	2	--	7.9	9.5	16.1

*Commercial publisher only. These are very small journals.
**American Institute of Physics (AIP)
***American Association of Publishers (AAP), Association of American University Presses (AAUP). Commercial publishers rarely require page charges. Recent results suggest less than 2%.

Leeson (1978) show that page charges in learned societies in the 1970s earned, on average, approximately 20 percent of revenue. Using AIP as an example (Lerner 1984), a 33 percent reduction in costs means that the subscription price can be reduced by approximately 25 percent.

A further interdependency exists between page charges and subscription demand because the existence and amount of page charges could possibly affect the number, size, and quality of submissions to a journal. Number and size of articles submitted affect cost, but quality can affect readership and demand for a journal. The interrelationship of subscription price and demand with article page charges and submissions is depicted on the schema in Figure 15 based on King and Roderer (1981). As shown in Chapter 13, price for journals affect their demand (link a) whether for personal subscriptions (link b) or institutional subscriptions (link c). There is also an interdependence of price and demand

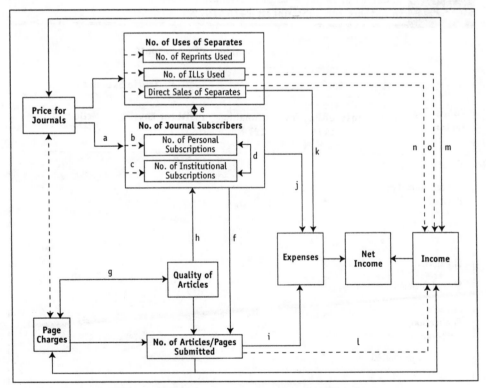

Figure 15. Costs, price, and demand relationships for AIP journals.
(*Source:* The AIP Journal System, King and Roderer 1981.)

between personal and institutional subscriptions (d) because personal subscription demand is much more sensitive to price and, when personal subscriptions are canceled, they are often replaced by reading library copies. When library copies are canceled, much of the reading is achieved through use of separate copies of articles (e).

Many factors enter into the author's selection of journals in which to publish (Tenopir 1995). One important factor is the journal's circulation (f), which is ranked the highest of thirteen factors in two studies (see Table 79). Thus, an increase in price will likely result in some cancellations which can, in the long run, diminish the attractiveness for authors to publish in the journal. Another important factor is the author's perception of the journal's quality. As measured by

Table 79	Rankings of Importance of Publishing Factors to Authors and Subscribers: 1976, 1979			
	Rankings of Importance			
	Journal Demand		**Article Submission**	
Publishing Factors	**Inst. of Physics 1976**	**McDonald 1979**	**Instit. of Physics 1976**	**McDonald 1979**
Price	2	8	10	*
Content Quality-Related	*	1, 2, 3, 4	3, 4	3, 8, 9
Format Quality-Related	1, 3, 4	7, 9	5	4
Circulation	1	1	1	1
Size of Articles	5	11	*	10
Speed of Publication/ Acceptance Rate	*	*	2	2, 6
Page Charge-related	*	*	7	13

*Indicates that factor was not considered. Some factors are given that are not in table.
Source: King and Roderer 1981

reputation (ranked third—Table 79) and refereeing (ranked third and fourth), it appears that quality of content is also very important. Yet both the number and quality of manuscripts can be affected by page charges (g) as well as circulation size. Thus, increased page charges can reduce the number and quality of manuscripts submitted which, in turn, also can reduce demand for the journal (h).

In summary, publishing costs are affected by the number of articles and pages submitted (i), the number of subscribers (j), and the number of reprints sold (k). Revenue, on the other hand, is a function of the level of page charges and the number and size of articles on which they are paid (1), subscription prices and subsequent demand (m), and sales of reprints (n). The number of interlibrary loans and document delivery can reduce subscription revenue, that is, have a negative effect (o). Net revenue, then, is the total revenue less cost, which varies over time as shown in the last section.

The point of this discussion is to demonstrate the interdependencies of price and page charges that extend well beyond the fact that revenue from page charges has a direct bearing on subscription price. A change in either can have an unintended ripple effect that significantly affects cost and revenue. In addition to price and page charges, other publishing attributes also affect both journal demand and article submission.

Along with refereeing, both content and format quality seem to be important to both readers and authors. Page charges do not appear to be relatively important to the physics authors surveyed in either study (Institute of Physics 1976 and McDonald 1979). This assertion is confirmed by an attempt to correlate changes in page charges in constant dollars over time with changes in the number of article pages submitted (King and Roderer 1981). The amount of page charges levied dropped appreciably in constant dollars over the years studied, but the trend in number of pages published increased for half the journals and decreased for the other half. It is possible that the reason that the size of page charges was relatively unimportant at the time of the study is that only 18 percent of those who paid these charges did so out of their personal finances. Over half of the charges were paid by the government, and approximately one-fourth were paid by other sources (King, McDonald, and Roderer 1981). In 1977, one-third of all scientific articles required page charges or other fees, with the average amount being $208 (approximately $570 in 1998 dollars).

PROFITABILITY OF COMMERCIAL PUBLISHERS

Page, Campbell, and Meadows (1997) have found that not only does it take new journals many years to reach their potential circulation, but the ultimate circulation is declining substantially for scientific, technical, and medical research journals which are launched independently of any society. For example, journals which started from 1968 to 1974 reached their potential of approximately 600 subscribers in six years, while from 1988 to 1993, circulation reached only approximately 350 in six years. Clearly, the price of these recent journals must be relatively higher to cover costs. Furthermore, the start-up risks must be increasing because an increasing number of new journals may not survive or may need to be subsidized by profitable journals.

A great deal has been said in the literature about the particularly large increases in prices charged by commercial publishers, with emphasis on the fact that their journal prices are much higher than those of other types of publishers (see Chapters 12 and 13). In Table 80 (repeated from Table 50), we provide supporting evidence of this assertion from our tracking sample of journals.

Average commercial journal prices per title are more than double that of society journals and over four times those of educational and other journals. Nevertheless, we are aware of little evidence to suggest that U. S. commercial publishers in general are making an excessive profit on journals, although some very well may be. Some suggest that most commercial publishers are not making an unreasonable profit, although studies indicate that some European publishers may be making a large profit (as described later). Rowland (1982) shows that society journals (including some processed by commercial publishers) have also achieved a "surplus," at least in the 1970s.

Table 80	Average Price, Number of Articles, and Circulation Per Journal by Type of Publisher: 1995				
Type of Publisher/ No of titles	Individual Price per Journal ($)	Institution Price per Journal ($)	Avg. No. of Articles per Journal	Proportion of Journals with Single Price	Average Circulation per Journal
Commercial/2,679	$463	$487	118	85%	3,700
Society/1,557	$178	$229	202	69%	13,300
Educational/1,106	$47	$81	70	60%	1,700
Other/1,429	$112	$119	84	80%	4,600
All Publishers/6,771	$255	$284	123	76%	5,800

Source: Tenopir and King 1997

To confirm our economic cost model, we compared prices and estimated costs per subscriber based on the cost model (Chapter 12) for a small sample of journals in which the relevant parameters are known (i.e., circulation, number of issues, observed articles per issue, and pages). Thus, we compared reported journal prices with "expected" prices based on the model. Across journals provided by the four types of publishers for which cost parameters and prices were available, we found that the average expected prices (i.e., costs) of journals tend to be below actual prices, but few of them appreciably so. On the other hand, the expected prices of some journals are observed to be higher than reported prices. Thus, publishing costs, in some instances, are higher than might be expected, or perhaps other sources of revenue offset the lower reported prices. In other words, page charges and membership dues may offset lower reported subscription prices of society journals, while educational institutions may absorb some overhead costs for educational journals. The expected prices of commercial journals observed tend to be approximately 10 to 20 percent lower than reported prices on average, which suggests a profit of approximately that amount, although some journals in the sample had a larger spread. We must emphasize, however, that we have complete data (i.e., both circulation and price) for only around 40 percent of commercial journals, so some non-reporting bias may exist, especially with the circulation data found in *Ulrich's*.[5] Therefore, these results are merely indicative, not statistically validated. they are presented here partially to demonstrate that such analysis is possible and should be done with a valid sample.

When profit data are reported in the literature, some have reported amounts that are not particularly high. In an early study, Fry and White (1976) report a before-tax profit of 11 percent in 1969 and 14.1 percent in 1973 for U.S. commercial publishers. They are quoted as saying, "this income percentage can by no stretch of the imagination be considered exorbitant or even substantial, when it is recognized that approximately half of all net income before taxes does in fact go to federal taxes." In the United Kingdom, studies showed increases in the surplus of society publishers from 1973 to 1978, but with a fallback in 1979 (Royal Society 1981). The financial examples given by Page, Campbell, and Meadows (1987 and 1997) place the profit of a small journal at approximately 10 or 11 percent of sales.

---

[5]Some of *Ulrich's* data on circulation are suspect because circulation data are often the same from year to year, leaving one to believe that they are not always updated. Also, circulation data are missing for many journals, particularly commercial journals. Therefore, we obtained some circulation data from commercial publishers with a promise of anonymity. Some data were merely distributions of circulation so we could not use both price and circulation for these journals in the expected cost calculations.

Scoville (1995) indicates that shareholders of large publishing corporations antici-pate a return of 10 to 14 percent on their stock investment.

Wyly (1998) has done a thorough updated analysis of the revenue, net margin (profit to stockholders), and return on equity (i.e., return on ordinary owner investment) of four large commercial publishers.[6] The net margin ranges from 4.7 percent for J. Wiley & Sons to 24.4 percent for Plenum Publishing. Some of these amounts represent very high profit margins compared with the Standard and Poor (S&P) 500 companies and with periodical publishers in general (5.0 percent median). When considering the profit ratio to the investment necessary to oper-ate, the values are even more impressive, ranging from 41.7 percent (Wolters Kluwer) to 20.2 percent (Plenum Publishing). This compares with an 18.8 percent median for periodical publishers; 28.2 percent for consumer S&P 500 companies; and 15.8 percent for bank S&P 500 companies.

Wyly did a special analysis (with some necessary assumptions) to isolate the scholarly science and medical publications from other aspects of the businesses. Results show that scholarly publishing is probably the most profitable segment of these companies. He then shows that there could be considerable differences in the total value of sales and revenue for these publications if their net margins were kept at the level of periodical publishing net margin and/or return-on-equity medians. He concludes that the suppliers (authors) and buyers (libraries/readers) should take into account the financial aspects of publishers when considering their decisions to do business with them.

Wyly goes so far as to suggest that profit making is not necessarily bad since

> a financially sound company can be more safely relied upon if the intention is to build a long-term relationship. The profitability of a vendor may also indi-cate the superiority of its products and services or a better understanding of the market served. If a competitive market is operating, the very definition of a free market means that successful companies succeed for these reasons. . . However, if a competitive market is not operating, the finances of vendors can show the absence of competition.

Wyly quantifies some of the "economic consequences" of what he concludes is the task of a competitive market for customers of commercial scholarly publishers. "When these consequences are clear, customers may come to understand that they must seek to change the situation . . ." Nonetheless, Wyly also notes that "many for-profit publishers are adopting business philosophies and practices that may ultimately contribute to a more competitive and viable marketplace for schol-arly communication."

---

[6]Wolters Kluwer, Reed Elsevier, J. Wiley & Sons, and Plenum Publishing.

One of the most stinging condemnations of commercial publishers was made by Carrigan (1996). He cited the financial experience of Reed Elsevier (a joint venture between Reed International, a British firm, and Elsevier, a Dutch firm).

> Reed Elsevier has business interests in addition to publishing academic journals. According to the author of the *Forbes* article (Hayes 1995), the firm in 1995 had total revenues estimated at $5.5 billion, up from $5.1 billion in 1994. What is especially noteworthy was that, for 1994, the pretax margin on the $600 million segment of the business concerned with academic journals was estimated to be nearly 40 percent, whereas it was 20 percent on the remaining $4.5 billion.

This margin seems high on sales of $600 million, in fact far higher than estimated by others. Also, it may reflect sales of trade journals which have a higher circulation and, therefore, also higher advertising revenue.

Carrigan also discusses the birth and growth of Robert Maxwell's Pergamon Press. He cites Maxwell (Wade 1963) as saying, "I set up a perpetual financing machine through advance subscriptions as well as the profits on the sales themselves. It is a cash generator twice over." This financial aspect of scholarly journal publishing was discussed earlier in the cash flow analysis. Maxwell was alluding to the potential favorable aspects of the cash flow of journal publishing which, when added to profits even at 5 to 10 percent of revenue, can be attractive to investors from a return-on-investment standpoint. This is depicted in both our cash flow analysis and the Wyly analysis discussed above.

THE ISSUE OF A PUBLISHING MONOPOLY

Many feel that the reason for high prices is that the growth of commercial publishers has created a monopolistic-like market. To examine this issue, McCabe (1998) and colleague David Reitman developed economic models and performed an economic analysis to determine if "portfolio size" (i.e., number of titles published) is related to price and, further, if mergers are related to even higher prices. They recognized that the cost per use (in libraries) and quality as measured by an ISI-citation level are both important considerations. Prices were regressed on several variables: portfolio size, journal quality, an assessment of whether journals are specialized or generalized, and other relevant factors.[7] The results showed that prices are positively related to portfolio size, and it was concluded that a

---

[7]In a sense, the journal quality (i.e., ISI-citation level) and specialization vs. generalization are redundant variables in that they are both indicators of the potential readership and/or circulation potential which, as we have shown in Chapter 13, affect price at certain levels of circulation.

merger between Wolters Kluwer and Waverly would increase the average price of their medical journals 20 to 30 percent (presumably projecting the price in the regression model by increasing the portfolio size variable an appropriate amount). Of course, if all journals in the portfolio were low-circulation journals, the prices would be higher. Commercial publishers tend to start more new journals rather than publish a few journals that become much larger in size.

Based on rules of thumb concerning share of market and monopolistic effects on price, the potential merger of Wolters Kluwer and Waverly might not affect price as much as predicted. Two possible explanations are given:

- libraries purchase journals from "as many sellers as possible," thus delivering more market power to small publishers, which affects strategies for maximizing profits, and

- a complementary contribution exists which can be explained by the theory that the entrance of new journals forces prices up as well.[8]

Another possibility is that overhead costs increase relative to direct costs. That is, the ratio of overhead to direct costs in labor-intensive organizations tend to be higher for large firms than small ones.[9] A final possible explanation is that large publishers have a higher profit margin as suggested by Wyly, although this was not the case for the U.S. publisher, J. Wiley & Sons.

The question of whether a monopoly exists in the scholarly publishing industry is a very complex one. The product that is supplied, bought, and sold is unique pieces of information for which there continues to be a free market in the sense that purchasers always have several alternative sources for the information available to them. As shown in Chapter 13, the market appears to freely use these alternatives when prices become too high. Libraries can and do use document delivery and interlibrary borrowing services for infrequently-read journals, although perhaps not as much as they should (see Kingma 1995). One problem for libraries is that the document delivery alternative to journal purchase is valid only for low readership, and most journals purchased have readership well above the break-even point, even with high prices (see Chapter 13). This means that library demand is relatively insensitive to price, which some commercial publishers have

---

[8]These rules of thumb are primarily legal criteria which bear no necessary relation to market power and anticompetition effects in a particular market (McCabe 1999).

[9]This phenomenon is discussed briefly in Chapter 12. Odlyzko (1999) is adamant about this factor and cites the experience of the *Encyclopaedia Britannica* in which failure is attributed to bloated sales and administrative costs.

recognized. McCabe (1999) also indicates that libraries often buy "portfolios" of journals which also contributes to the insensitivity to price. Thus, the high prices may not be due to a monopolistic industry, but rather to the reality of the marketplace. On the other hand, McCabe suggests that although monopoly may not exist in this market, market power almost definitely does, and larger publishers probably have more power than their smaller counterparts.

It does make sense for both authors and readers to be aware of the pricing dilemma and to take it into account, along with other factors, in their journal-selection decisions. The scientific and library communities, however, should not overreact to this problem by condemning all commercial publishers for the following reasons.

- Journal costs and prices are generally a function of the size and the circulation of the journal. While some studies have considered one parameter (that of size or number of pages), no studies of which we are aware have considered both the parameters of circulation and size.[10] Because of high fixed costs, any journal with fewer than 2,500 circulation is going to have 'abnormally' high unit costs and, therefore, prices. Well over half of the commercial journals have fewer than this number of subscribers. This suggests that each journal (and publisher) should be examined as to the 'reasonableness' of their prices in light of their size, circulation, and other relevant cost parameters.[11]

- Tests of reasonableness using our cost model suggest that most, but not all, of the observed U.S. commercial journals are priced reasonably. It may be that differences in reasonableness of cost vs. price among journals published exists for particular publishers. That is, they may have a few winners that support marginal and losing journals. This is generally true of book publishing, and it is the nature of individual articles published (i.e., bundled) in a journal. The willingness of publishers to do this is important to scientific communication because it makes high-quality articles in small specialties available to the scientific community. It also may be that some commercial publishers' scholarly journals are supported by trade journals and other

---

[10]McCabe (1999) reports that his recent research incorporates circulation and size data for almost two thousand journals held by 200 medical libraries.

[11]It is noted that this comparison only tests whether prices are reasonable in light of expected costs. Price and demand relationships over a range of prices could reveal a much better result (with higher or lower prices) in terms of readership and overall costs and yet yield comparable reasonable profits to the publisher.

kinds of profitable information services, although Wyly's analysis seems to dispute this possibility for at least some publishers.

- Many commercial publishers may, in fact, charge reasonable prices, at least in the aggregate. If so, libraries will continue paying nearly as much for the articles purchased by them, even if the articles are published by societies or university presses, assuming, of course, that the quality remains the same. This is because the article processing costs should be about the same (particularly when "donated" costs are included).

- It is not clear that the funders of university presses are willing to support a large increase in the volume of journals that they might 'inherit' from commercial publishers. Similarly, society membership may resist publishing journals in specialties that are not germane to their members. Furthermore, both university presses and society publishers may not be willing to assume the high risk of starting a large number of new journals, nor do many of them have the investment capital to do so. This concern is partially addressed by the SPARC initiative (see Chapter 15).

We have tried to present arguments, both pro and con, concerning issues of journal monopolistic markets and commercial profitability. These complex issues are being examined by competent economists and some experiments may prove enlightening. However, as of yet, the jury is still out concerning these issues and journal system participants should proceed in a cautious and enlightened manner. Electronic journals may prove to be one solution to the problem as may less expensive electronic access to separate copies of articles for infrequently-read journals (see Chapters 17 and 18). New pricing policies, however, will be critical to a brighter future.

Part V

ELECTRONIC PUBLISHING

CHAPTER 15

Transformation to Electronic Publishing

INTRODUCTION

New Models in Publishing

Over the years, an elaborate structure has developed around traditional print publishing that includes publishers, printers, indexers, database vendors, subscription agents, libraries, microfilmers, back issue dealers, cataloging utilities, and interlibrary loan networks, in addition to the authors and readers who form the raison d'être for the system. Other value-added parts of the structure include reviewers and editors.

These many "intervening agents" between authors and readers have proliferated over the years. Potter (1986) points out that, historically, journals grew out of personal correspondence between scientists, but today "with the sheer number of journals, the complexities of serials, and the sociological baggage involved in publishing, an elaborate structure has been built to provide the channel that connects the author and reader." In Chapter 2 we described historical aspects of scientific scholarly journals and electronic publishing up to the early 1990s. In this chapter we will bring this discussion up to 1999.

Electronic publishing allows many new models by providing flexibility in the ways these various agents interact with each other. Williams (1990) describes seven links in the information generation-database use chain that focuses on the participants responsible for each link: 1) author/originator; 2) primary publisher; 3) secondary publisher/database producer; 4) tertiary publisher/online vendor; 5) gateway; 6) searcher/analyst; and 7) end user/requestor. Anderson (1993) identifies four crucial links in the electronic information delivery chain: 1) authors, 2) publishers, 3) libraries, and 4) readers. Distribution is assumed to move from publishers via the Internet to readers or from publishers through libraries to readers.[1] Schauder (1994) describes these links as "dependency patterns." In print publishing he identifies three patterns: 1) author to publisher to vendor to librarian to reader; 2) author to publisher to reader; and 3) author to publisher to vendor to reader. These might be characterized as communication paths.[2] In every case, the author and reader are dependent on the publisher as the key link in conveying information, although additional links may also be present.

In electronic publishing, Schauder expands the possible patterns to fifteen variations incorporating in various permutations the links of author, publisher, vendor, librarian, consortium (of publisher/vendor, publisher/vendor/librarian, publisher/librarian, or vendor/librarian), and reader. Unlike print publishing, the publisher is not involved in every pattern. The pattern may proceed directly from author to reader, or it may go from author to vendor to reader, or from author to library/vendor consortium to reader. Four of the fifteen dependency patterns exclude publishers, and when a publisher is involved it may be only as part of a consortium.

All of these descriptions of the links or structure recognize the separate, but interrelated, participants in the electronic transfer of information. In all cases the participants begin with the intellectual creator (the author) and end with the reader or user. This is, of course, the essence of any type of oral, written, or electronic knowledge dissemination—the linking of creators, or creators' ideas, with readers. As Potter (1986) succinctly puts it, "the situation today, as volatile as it may seem to us, is still essentially a reader looking for an author and an author looking for a reader."

---

[1]This echoes earlier work by King, McDonald, and Roderer (1981) involving ten links (i.e., functions performed) and the separate, but interrelated, roles of authors, publishers, A&I services, libraries, and readers in scientific communication through scientific print journals. (See Figure 3, Chapter 3).

[2]In 1977 we identified fourteen such paths and estimated that there were 1.9 billion journal-related items sent on these paths that year. Such items included requests for articles and responses; manuscripts and related correspondence; journal issues; searches, requests, and responses; and preprints, reprints, and photocopies, to name a few (King, McDonald, and Roderer 1981).

CHANGING ROLES OF PUBLISHERS

One unique aspect of electronic publishing of scientific journals is the wide variety of ways the participants can be connected to achieve the communication purposes. New ways of linking authors more directly to readers have developed as the direct communication via the Internet replaces the formal role of vendors, distributors, or publishers. Such use of the Internet usually plays a more passive and less formal communications role than traditional vendors or publishers in linking authors to readers.

Much of the early dissemination of scholarly journals on the Internet did not involve formal publishers. After an extensive survey of scholarly electronic publishing efforts, Schauder (1994) concluded that as of mid-1993 most of the publishing on networks such as the Internet were non-commercial enterprises which depended on volunteer effort and institutional or personal subsidies of money, labor, or facilities. However, widespread commercial electronic publishing ventures over the Internet by not-for-profit and for-profit organizations were introduced as early as 1994. The early involvement of OCLC in conjunction with the American Association for the Advancement of Science (AAAS) and pilot projects by commercial scholarly publishers such as Elsevier's TULIP project foreshadowed future developments.

Many proponents of electronic publishing call for a downplaying of publishers' roles (or even the elimination of publishers as we now know them) as a way to bring authors and readers closer. Certainly the lines between publishers, authors, and readers are blurring in electronic publishing or, as Anderson (1993) points out, "the boundaries between the players—authors, publishers, libraries, readers— have become very fluid and permeable."

Okerson (1992b) sees the solution to a range of long-term problems by eliminating traditional commercial publishers in the scholarly publishing that emanates from academe. She attributes problems such as high prices and loss of information ownership to scholarly publishing through the commercial sector. Because of this perception by many, the Association of Research Libraries (ARL) is directly challenging the high prices of commercial scholarly journals with their SPARC initiative. SPARC (Scholarly Publishing and Academic Resources Coalition) offers financial and/or marketing support for society or other not-for-profit organizations or individuals who are willing to start journals that will directly compete with commercial titles. SPARC-supported journals may be exclusively electronic publications, print publications, or both, but they must be priced substantially lower than their commercial competition. SPARC is targeting scientific and technical titles. (See Chapter 14 for a discussion of commercial publisher prices and profits.)

Other advantages to the elimination of middlemen, be they commercial or other publishers, are cited by proponents of a new model for electronic scholarly publishing. These include faster transmission from author to reader (Arms 1992), circumventing the exorbitant prices of serials (Bailey 1992), providing equal access for all scholars (Okerson 1992a), and breaking out of a biased and closed review system (Judson 1994). Odlyzko (1999) has also been a strong proponent of direct communication between authors and readers.

Few believe that publishers should be completely eliminated from electronic publishing. The advantages and commitment that formal publishing bring are historical and far-reaching. They touch all parts of the publishing process including the soliciting and evaluation of quality manuscripts, supervising the refereeing function, editing and advising authors of needed changes, copyediting final drafts, disseminating issues on a regular schedule, and protecting copyright. The formality and regularity of the process bring legitimacy and constancy to scholarly journals.

Even publishers agree that the role of the publisher is very likely to change, however, including the stable, long-term relationships between publishers and writers and those between publishers and readers (Kaplan 1993). Scholarly publishing is especially ripe for change, and an increased role may be assumed by universities or other participants outside the mainstream of traditional print publishing.

With emerging electronic alternatives to scholarly journals, more emphasis is likely to be placed on the marketing and promotion role of non-traditional publishers. With the likely continued proliferation of published materials in an electronic environment, even scholarly publishers can bring an increased effort to identifying markets, linking author's ideas to appropriate readers, and serving as clearinghouses (Kaplan 1993; Horowitz and Curtis 1982; Varian 1999).

Other possible expanded roles for publishers and librarians have been suggested as enforcers of an author's individual copyright, as developers of better access and display software, as providers of better links between related research, and as maintainers of quality over time by including errata or updated information in conjunction with older articles.

ELECTRONIC JOURNALS

The number and availability of scholarly electronic journals is increasing dramatically and will continue to do so in the future. This expansion is attributable in part to the many advantages of electronic publishing for publishers, librarians, and readers. A wide variation in types of electronic journals makes an exact count difficult, but the amount of unique scholarly scientific material available electronically is still probably well below that available in print. Some electronic journals are merely electronic equivalents of their print counterparts and are used mainly for the purpose of document delivery. Others are unique entities that are beginning to more fully exploit the expanded capabilities offered by digital and electronic media.

One explanation for the variation in types of electronic journals is a natural, "evolutionary" process of electronic journals (Lancaster 1985). According to Lancaster, journals evolve in six stages in the progression towards a truly digital age. In the first stage, computers are used merely to produce better print publications, while in the second stage the same journal is distributed in both print and electronic media. New publications are first developed solely for electronic distribution in the third evolutionary stage, but with their design still rooted in the world of print. The fourth, fifth, and sixth stages provide a more accelerated exploitation of digital and electronic capabilities. In the fourth stage, some electronic journals incorporate interaction and collaboration between authors and readers. Participation includes direct connection between readers and authors, creating publications that continuously evolve and grow as readers interact with the content. In the fifth stage, multimedia texts go beyond print capabilities. Finally, in the sixth and final stage, electronic journals combine both participatory and multimedia capabilities. This does not necessarily mean that all scholarly journals will evolve to the sixth stage, but that some may be found in each of the six stages, depending on the field of science, purpose of the article, and other factors. Thus, there will be a niche for all these types of publications.

Lancaster's first stage has, of course, been standard operating procedure in the publishing world for many years. Hawkins (1992) makes a distinction between Lancaster's first stage and true electronic publishing. He defines electronic-aided publishing (equivalent to Lancaster's first stage) as using computers and electronic processes solely for production, while delivery is accomplished by conventional (print) methods. True electronic publishing, on the other hand, must involve not only production, but also delivery of information in electronic form.[3]

---

[3]We have gone two steps further in that manuscripts are prepared and sent electronically and distribution to bibliographic services and other vendors are sent electronically in a "comprehensive electronic journal" (King, McDonald, and Roderer 1981).

It can be argued that in the late 1990s, scholarly journals are being created as both electronic-aided and true electronic publications; thus we are simultaneously functioning at all six of Lancaster's evolutionary stages. We are truly in the throes of evolution, a position that is slightly chaotic and confusing to a majority of the participants. Even within each of these stages, further variety emerges in such procedures as distribution means, pricing, and format. Publishers and purchasers alike are faced with an array of design and policy choices.

To better understand the design and policy options for electronic journals today, it is useful to describe these options in a matrix of decision elements. The principal decision elements, and thus distinctions, among electronic journals are depicted in Figure 16. They include: 1) format, 2) medium of distribution or delivery, 3) degree of interactivity, 4) distributors, 5) granularity, and 6) pricing policy. Although presented in Figure 16 as separate, these decision elements are interwoven in a complex mixture of options that require decisions that affect every publisher, author, reader, library, and distributor.

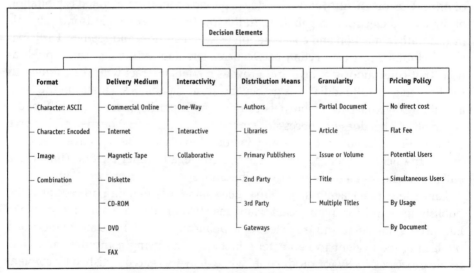

Figure 16. Decision elements for journal system participant consideration.

ELECTRONIC FORMAT

Just as electronic journals currently coexist in all six of Lancaster's evolutionary stages, the current state of electronic scholarly journals shows great variety in form and format. This is mainly due to the rapid pace of development—electronic formats, hardware, and software develop and change so quickly that all participants in the journal system (including authors, readers, libraries, and publishers) do not convert to new forms immediately. This variety leads to a fairly complex matrix of possibilities for electronic publishing as shown in Figure 16. Each of the variables is briefly described below.[4]

Character-based: ASCII

Full-text journal databases have been accessible from commercial online systems since the early 1980s and on CD-ROM since the late 1980s. The first databases were almost entirely character-based text of ASCII (American Standard Code for Information Interchange) files. Surprisingly, text-only files remain a common option, but more attractive formats are also available.

Character-based text hearkens back to an age when computers were mainly used to more easily generate print publications; at that time electronic journals were perceived merely as a byproduct of word processing. Character-based electronic journal articles still exist because, as a textual common denominator, ASCII text is an inexpensive, yet necessary, step in most document creation processes; furthermore, it conserves computer storage space and can be quickly and easily transmitted over voice-grade, analog telephone lines. With proper software, every word of these character-based texts can be searched, displayed, manipulated, and downloaded, thus providing sophisticated search and retrieval capabilities.

Journals of pure ASCII text have many limitations, however. Character-based texts cannot represent graphics, fonts, columnar formats, illustrations, figures, mathematical formulae, or most tabular data. Without this type of information, the look and feel of print journals must be sacrificed. Character-based texts must be formatted by software by both the provider and the user, so the publisher has little control over the appearance of the final product.

Character-based electronic publications by definition exclude images since they are created and distributed in a digital, text-only format. This text format may or may not add typesetting and other special characters to the basic ASCII text. Customers often prefer to receive ASCII texts because they can be downloaded, manipulated, and re-used in digital form even when the customer does not have the same text-creation software as the distributor.

---

[4]For a more in-depth examination of the electronic publishing technologies and their evolution, see Lesk (1997).

Character-based: Encoded

Although ASCII distribution has been the most common format, character-based publications may also be distributed in a word processing format such as Word or WordPerfect, in a typesetting language such as TeX, or, increasingly, in the Standard Generalized Mark-up Language (SGML) or its subset, Hypertext Mark-up Language (HTML). SGML encoding is used by a growing number of publishers as a print-formatting language. When used for electronic distribution, SGML offers the advantage of standard formatting for users with compatible software.

Although much of SGML's promise is not yet being exploited, retrieval can be improved when SGML is coupled with search and retrieval software that recognizes the embedded SGML tags. For example, software can assign a greater weight to words found in certain parts of a document (as defined by the SGML tags) such as titles, main headings, chapter headings, or summaries.

As the mark-up language for the World Wide Web, HTML is currently the most prolific type of electronic text. Although HTML is based on the SGML international standard, various vendors are using their own proprietary variations of HTML so that its standardization has been compromised. Texts marked up with word processing software may also be output into a PDF (personal document format) file that can be output and read by proprietary software such as Adobe's Acrobat. PDF files retain the look defined by the creator of the word processing file, so all readers will see the same formatting (e.g., fonts and indentation). Acrobat readers may be downloaded without charge, making PDF document distribution a low-cost option.

Image Only

Image files can be created by a variety of technologies and stored in a variety of standard encoding schemes such as GIF and JPEG. In these imaging schemes, characters are not individually recognized, but are stored as digital representations of light and dark much like a photocopier image. With current technology, most imaging files are not directly searchable; they require the establishment of an accompanying ASCII database in order to provide a search capability.

Image-only electronic journals provide access to scanned page-images from existing print journals. They retain the look and feel of the print publication, including type fonts, format, and the inclusion of graphics. In a sense, an image-only journal article is like a digital photograph of a printed work. It is more easily distributed and preserved than its print counterpart, but it must rely on a linked bibliographic or ASCII full-text file to provide search and retrieval capabilities. Image-only journals were pioneered by UMI Inc. (now Bell and Howell Information and Learning Company) to distribute their massive print and microfilm journal archives in large CD-ROM collections and are used today primarily for preservation and archiving purposes.

Combination

Combination ASCII-image or encoded databases offer the best of both worlds. They provide the searchability of ASCII with the standardized appearance of encoded files or images. In reality, a combination database is two databases linked together. An ASCII file is used for searching and relevance ranking, while the other file is used for reading and printing. Either may be used for downloading, depending on the user's needs. Such combination files are available in both online and CD-ROM environments and are extensively used for World Wide Web publications.

ELECTRONIC DELIVERY

The mechanism for delivery of electronic journals is dependent on rapidly changing technology. New viable alternatives emerge regularly, such as commercial online in the early 1970s, CD-ROM in the mid 1980s, and the World Wide Web in the early 1990s. Rarely do new options completely supplant the old; typically they are added to the existing store of viable alternatives from which to choose.

Commercial Online

With a history of nearly three decades, remote online delivery of electronic publications was the first viable electronic delivery option. Systems such as DIALOG, LEXIS-NEXIS (Reed International), and Orbit (Questel) have stayed the course, although with different owners. This option also includes government-sponsored online systems: for example, the National Library of Medicine was a pioneer with their MEDLARS/MEDLINE system.

The online systems described above are designed to serve information professionals or researchers. A second group of online systems are more consumer oriented; the more well-known of these include CompuServe, and America Online. Scholarly journals are generally restricted to the online systems serving the research community.

Via Internet

Commercial online systems can be accessed by using the Internet as a telecommunications channel to access the Telnet function (in addition to a variety of packet-switching networks such as BT Tymnet and SprintNet) or more directly on the World Wide Web. Users may access electronic journals via the Internet through a library, university, or directly from a government agency or commercial publisher. There may or may not be a charge for access, although many people assume that if something is available exclusively via the Internet it should be free, particularly if the distributor has a .edu or .gov address.

By far the most popular Internet application in the late 1990s is the World Wide Web, with web sites estimated in the tens of millions. Listservs, Newsgroups, FTP (file transfer protocol), and gopher sites are other Internet options for the distribution of publications.

Magnetic Tape

Electronic publications may be supplied on magnetic tape to an organization for subsequent loading on its local computers. Magnetic tape is only a distribution medium: the digital information is transferred to another storage medium, such as magnetic disks, for daily use. In library publications, this option is often referred to as locally loaded databases. Individual access to the locally loaded publication is determined by pricing policy.

Diskettes

Diskettes, previously called floppy disks, are another medium used exclusively for distribution. Once customers receive a publication on diskette, normally they load it on another storage medium such as a fixed disk for daily use. Since the capacity of a diskette is limited, this option is usually reserved for small subject-specific subsets of a larger database. Some believe diskettes will become obsolete as better, higher capacity, distribution systems take over.

CD-ROM

CD-ROM is popular as a combination distribution and storage medium. CD-ROM products first became commercially available in 1985, with widespread use in libraries by the late 1980s, and finally expanded to common use by individuals in the 1990s. The wide appeal of CD-ROMs extends beyond their technological advantages of high-density storage and robustness to their attractive pricing policies. Typically they are priced by flat fee or, in a networked environment, by number of simultaneous users.

DVD

High-density compact disks became available in 1997. DVDs (digital video disks or digital versatile disks) have a capacity four to fifteen times that of CD-ROM's 650 megabyte capacity. The first DVD applications were entertainment since, unlike a CD-ROM, a DVD can hold an entire feature-length movie. In addition, DVD holds promise for distribution of image and multimedia electronic journals.

Desk-Top Networks

Many vendors make electronic versions of journals available for use by defined user groups on local area networks. A user group will subscribe to a journal or set of journals electronically and can then view or print these journals from their locally networked computer. Often only those journals or articles that match an individual's pre-set topical profile are delivered to individual's desktop. These versions are variously called desktop networked publications, desktop filtering, or intelligent agents. These networks are often connected to a corporate intranet for distribution throughout the organization.

Fax

The facsimile machine is most typically used as a fast way to transmit a photocopy since it is in essence a photocopier with an attached telephone line. In most cases it is strictly for document delivery purposes, and no electronic copy is stored. Facsimile transmissions using a fax board on a computer, however, do generate a digital copy although, like the image-only option, this copy cannot be searched without first constructing a companion ASCII database. Fax is still commonly used for document delivery of article separates.

Other

New technological alternatives for delivery of electronic publications are developed every few years, and there is every reason to believe that this trend will continue. New alternatives will undoubtedly initially coexist with existing alternatives, but may eventually replace one or more of them for the communication of scholarly works.

DEGREE OF INTERACTIVITY

Scientific communication involves several levels of participation by both senders and receivers. For example, a scientist can communicate with another individual (in person, e-mail), small groups (lectures, e-mail), large groups (publications, Internet), or masses (radio, television). Senders can also be groups of individuals such as speakers or co-authors, and they also can be a group communicating to a few or one (an audience response) or many to a few or one (e.g., survey respondents). Both traditional print and exclusively electronic journals fit the individual or small group models of senders, with the potential receivers located at all levels. Digital text and electronic technologies, however, are capable of reaching the entire range of levels of communication by both senders and receivers.

One-Way Communication

Like their print counterparts, electronic journals are currently primarily one-way communications where an author communicates to readers, but formal communication from a reader to an author is restricted to letters to the editor. Electronic journals which reproduce a print product by definition fall into this category. In fact, they may have less interactivity than their print counterparts since letters to the editor are often omitted from electronic article collections. One-way interactivity can also characterize journals distributed online or via the Internet, but it is particularly typical of CD-ROM, diskette, and magnetic tape distribution, all of which experience a significant time lag between publication and distribution.

Interactive Journals

More interactivity is facilitated when the Internet is used as a distribution option and when the electronic version takes advantage of the electronic environment to offer capabilities not possible in print versions. For example, letters to the editor may be more immediate and may be tied directly to an article, or comments from authors and other readers may be presented in the context of the article. This model is more interactive, but still retains the formal relationship between author and reader.

Collaborative Journals

Interactivity has its logical conclusion in truly collaborative publications. In collaborative journals, the lines between authors, readers, and editors become blurred as articles develop and are revised over time and space. Articles are refined as comments or sections are added through an interactive process. The Internet is the logical forum for this process of creating truly collaborative journals.

ELECTRONIC DISTRIBUTORS

Distributors may be organizations or individuals involved in electronic document creation and distribution. They are the sellers or distributors as opposed to the buyers.

Authors

Authors may choose to distribute their own works, exclusively or in addition to other distribution agents. This option has become more popular since the Internet has become available as a viable delivery mechanism. There are, of course, costs in terms of the author's time, equipment, and connectivity expenses, but often there is no direct charge to the recipient. Many authors today routinely place their works on their personal web pages. Search and retrieval of these works become problematic, thereby reducing their value to the scientific community.

Libraries

Libraries sometimes serve as authors, publishers, and distributors of electronic publications. According to American Library Association guidelines, only libraries may participate in interlibrary loans. If both parties are not libraries, the same action becomes document delivery rather than interlibrary loan, and copyright fees must be paid, regardless of the number of copies made from any one journal title.[5]

Primary Publishers

Primary publishers are those commercial organizations, societies, universities, or other entities who are directly responsible for the solicitation, editing, packaging, and distribution of intellectual property. At the present time, buyers face an unsettled marketplace when trying to identify distributors. Primary publishers of print materials, for example, were slow to enter the electronic publishing realm, but favor the World Wide Web when they do so.

Second-Party Distributors

A primary publisher may choose to allow a second party to distribute its intellectual work. Second-party distributors such as Bell and Howell or The Gale Group

---

[5]Of course under interlibrary loan guidelines libraries borrowing more than five photocopied items from a single journal must also pay royalty fees.

are usually profit-making organizations who gain permission from a variety of publishers to distribute articles electronically through CD-ROM, online, and the Web. A royalty, typically based on use or units sold, is paid by the second party to the primary publishers. Some librarians serve this function, with or without permission, by downloading databases available through the Internet and distributing them to their users. Document delivery services also fall into this category.

Third-Party Distributors

A third party may contract with a second party to distribute the electronic publications for which the second party has obtained distribution permission from the primary publishers. Such third parties are often referred to as vendors or aggregators. Major third-party companies such as DIALOG, LEXIS-NEXIS, and Silver Platter may contract with second parties to distribute their contracted electronic publications via online, CD-ROM, the Web, or other delivery medium.

It should be noted that aggregators may serve as a third party for some electronic publications, but as a second party with others for which they contract directly with the primary publisher. DIALOG, for example, serves as a third party to distribute the publications contracted by Bell and Howell and The Gale Group, but at the same time serves as a second party to distribute the *Harvard Business Review* and the newspapers of its former parent company, Knight-Ridder.

Gateways

Gateways are organizations that provide access to third-party online services. In this role they provide hardware, software, and telecommunications links only. Telebase's EasyNet gateway linked to over a dozen third-party online services, and America Online serves as a gateway to other online services. Westlaw serves as a gateway to DIALOG in addition to its other capacities as an online and CD-ROM vendor and secondary publisher. Engineering Information Village is a web-based gateway (or "portal") to a variety of web and online engineering content.

Subscription Agents

Subscription agents are profit-making organizations that have developed a niche for brokering subscription negotiation, claiming, and renewal between libraries and primary publishers. Companies such as EBSCO and Blackwell's are now often also serving as second- or third-party distributors in addition to their subscription agent role. Subscription agents save money for their customers by offering volume discounts and reduced paperwork.

Information Brokers

Information brokers are profit-making organizations or individual consultants that provide reference search services, services to obtain copies of articles, and other related services to libraries and small companies.

Library Networks and Consortia

Library consortia are unique organizations throughout the country that developed to provide groups of libraries with economies of scale by sharing technical services such as acquisitions and cataloging, by cooperative purchases of electronic resources, and by facilitating interlibrary lending. Most states fund these organizations, with substantial Federal support, although universities sometimes form cooperative groups, particularly for interlibrary lending. Consortia may include multiple types of libraries (public, school, special, and academic) or a single type.

GRANULARITY

Granularity is a term that defines the amount of an electronic publication to be made available to or requested by a buyer.[6] For example, a buyer may wish to subscribe to multiple journals or to purchase multiple issues of journals, a single issue or volume, a single article, or even a single paragraph or other part of an article. The same buyer is likely to make different granularity decisions for different titles or for the same title under different circumstances. Publishers may decide to provide a single option or a combination of options for all buyers or for certain classes of buyers.

Multiple Titles

Sometimes a publisher bundles together several related titles as a package or allows a buyer to select several titles of interest to create an individualized

---

[6]This publishing attribute is also sometimes called information dosage (see Chapter 3).

package. They are usually related titles, such as titles by the same publisher, on the same topic, or for the same audience.

Multiple-title bundling is especially prevalent when a second party contracts with a primary publisher for distribution rights to a number of his titles or contracts with several publishers for electronic rights. Bundling may also be used for direct distribution by a primary publisher who publishes more than one title. For example, at one time Ziff/Davis published and distributed the multi-title CD-ROM publication, Computer Select, which included many of their titles. Bell and Howell and The Gale Group both package multiple titles in single offerings, such as the Business Periodicals Collection, the Magazine Database, and the Trade and Industry Database.

Issue or Volume

Distribution may be for a single issue or volume of a title rather than, or in addition to, a standing order for an entire run of a title. A single issue may be purchased because it covers a special topic that is marketed more widely than the journal as a whole.

Title

Distribution by title implies that the buyer selects an entire work, for example a journal, and purchases an entire set or run of this title or an entire run within a set subscription period. This is the standard method with print subscriptions and is also popular with some CD-ROM and Web publications of particular newspapers.

Article Only

Article-only delivery may be the most popular option of the future. Already it is the most popular item in interlibrary loan and document delivery services and is now available from many commercial online services. To be successful, it requires a good search tool to enable buyers to identify individual articles for purchase. An added benefit is its ease for tracking copyrights. Libraries and scientists usually obtain copies of articles from infrequently-read journals as discussed in Chapters 10, 13, and 17.

Partial Document

In an electronic environment, a user may request delivery of a single part of a document that meets his or her search criteria. For example, after retrieving a set of documents that meet a subject search in an online or CD-ROM publication, many search systems allow the user to display selected paragraphs (e.g., lead paragraph) or selected pages (e.g., first page), or selected portions (e.g., KWIC {Keyword in Context}) of documents. In a Web site a reader may want only a picture or a sound file from a large document.

PRICING POLICY

Pricing policy refers to the policies the supplier sets for the purchaser, be it a library or an individual. These policies are set forth in terms and conditions based on the Copyright Act of 1976 and are often supplemented by a contract. Policies may differ by class of purchaser. For example, one price or one set of terms and conditions may be set for libraries, with another for individuals, or one price or terms and conditions may be set for publicly supported libraries, with another for libraries in private organizations. (See Chapters 13 and 18 for further discussion of pricing.)

No Direct Cost

In this scenario, the purchaser does not pay the supplier for the publication, although the purchaser will always incur indirect costs associated with requesting and processing publication orders. This is typical for many interlibrary loans, where the supplying library may not charge the requesting library to provide a copy of an article. The original publisher of the item often does not receive a copyright royalty payment for these transactions, either through the Copyright Clearance Center or another channel. It is also the case in some periodicals on the Web that are subsidized by advertising or grant support.

Flat Fee

Without contractual constraints, flat fee subscriptions offer the purchaser unlimited usage rights within the constraints of the Copyright Act. By far the most common pricing policy for print periodicals, it is also common with consumer online services such as America Online which offers access to core materials or a set amount of usage for a fixed monthly fee. Flat fee subscriptions often provide additional usage or premium materials under a separate pricing policy.

Some electronic publications also charge a flat fee that does not include a subscription. More common with books, one-time flat fees provide unlimited use within copyright restrictions, but do not include updates.

Potential Users (Site Licenses)

Pricing is set by a contract, usually negotiated annually, between the purchaser and seller, with a price based on potential users. Potential users may be the total number of people within the purchaser's organization or constituency. For example, in a university with 25,000 students and 1,000 faculty members, the total number of potential users would be 26,000. The purchase price for *Encyclopaedia Britannica* at this imaginary university, for example, may be $1.00 per potential user for an annual access fee of $26,000.

Public and university libraries with large constituencies may regard this pricing scenario as unfair. A public library system serving a total population of 2 million people may be charged for each of those 2 million (or minimally for the 500,000 with library cards), but the likelihood of many of those 2 million (or even 500,000) ever using even one publication is small.

A common variation in site licenses involves charging by the number of people in an organization who are likely to use a specific journal. Organizations initially estimate the number of persons in their operation who would benefit from a publication, after which usage may be tracked intermittently to verify the continuing accuracy of the original estimate. Another example of charging by number of potential users is that of the Copyright Clearance Center where negotiated royalty payments in a company are established by type of company and number of employees.

Another variation on site licenses involves setting the price on a sliding scale based on the size of an organization's budget. For years the H.W. Wilson Company used this pricing strategy for its print indexes and abstract publications. (A suggestion for site licensing is presented in Chapter 18).

Simultaneous Users

The number of simultaneous users can be easily limited by contract and enforced by technical means: the number of online ports allocated to a purchaser, the number of simultaneously active online passwords, or the number of workstations connected to a CD-ROM or locally loaded system. This option is popular in public and academic libraries because they can adjust their costs based on the popularity of a title; corporations, however, may not view this as a viable option because access is denied to users whenever the simultaneous capacity is reached.

By Usage

Payment by usage can be inexpensive for individuals or organizations that are infrequent users of electronic publications, but it proves exceedingly expensive for heavily used items. Nevertheless, it was the standard strategy for accessing commercial online resources from the early 1970s until the early 1990s, and it is still somewhat common in the commercial online world.

Payment by usage can be computed by connect time; computer resources used; number, size, or type of databases selected; documents or parts of documents viewed; or by any combination of these.

By Document

Although document viewing may be a part of payment-by-usage fees, some systems charge for every document selected by a user to be viewed, while others only charge for those delivered in full. This is common in some interlibrary loan situations and is also typical of document delivery services that use fax or other methods of document transmission. Many online services based on the Web are moving in this direction because readers find it understandable and equitable.

ELECTRONIC JOURNALS ONLINE AND ON CD-ROM

In 1996 the print guide, *Fulltext Sources Online*, listed 2,107 scientific, technical, or medical full-text sources in character-based text format available from nineteen commercial online vendors. Based on an examination of their titles, approximately 220 of these were scholarly journals, which represents approximately 3 percent of all U.S. scientific scholarly journals. Almost all of these text-only portions of articles appear in more complete form in print journals. Major commercial online vendors currently distributing scholarly journals include LEXIS-NEXIS, DIALOG, OVID, STN International, Westlaw, and ProQuest Direct. As of spring 1999, *Fulltext Sources Online* included nearly 9,000 entries, many of which are journals. This is an increase from approximately 7,600 in 1997. Many are scholarly journals.

CD-ROM is used less for scholarly publications than for news media and trade journals, but it is used to publish both image files of journals as well as text-only versions. In the *Gale Directory of Databases*, CD-ROM entries grew from only 433 databases in 1989 to 4,168 in 1998. CD-ROM represented only 7 percent of the total database listings in the directory in 1989, as opposed to 34 percent in the 1998 directory. The CD-ROM databases in the directory include character-based databases, image-only databases, and combination character-image databases.

The main motivation for primary publishers to make electronic full-text versions of their print publications available through commercial online or CD-ROM vendors is to provide controlled electronic access to article copies that heretofore were distributed as preprints, reprints, and facsimiles or photocopies obtained through interlibrary loan or document delivery (see Chapter 10). There are several sources for online full-text copies of articles. In addition to the commercial systems mentioned above, a large database of the full text of physics, nuclear, and other related preprints is available online on request from the Los Alamos National Laboratory, and replication of this process is being started by biological scientists and medical researchers.

Odlyzko (1999) reports that the entire American Mathematical Society e-math system has approximately 1.2 million hits per month while JSTOR (1998) has approximately 0.45 million hits per month. The Los Alamos system experiences 2 million hits per month, and the netlib system of Dongarra and Grosse receives about 2.5 million hits per month. These, of course, do not represent full-article downloads (e.g., Los Alamos observes 7 million of these per year), but they do demonstrate the enormous potential of single-article distribution online.

Most full-text publications are stored on commercial online systems as articles. Rarely is an entire journal issue or volume retrieved online or from a CD-ROM. Thus, many so-called electronic journals, that are based on a print journal, are really not journals at all. Instead they are repositories of selected articles from specific journal titles. If an author retains copyright or an article is shorter than the norm, these articles may be excluded in electronic versions.

As mentioned earlier, in many cases, the electronic versions of journals are made available by a party (or parties) other than the publishers themselves. Full-text electronic versions of these journals differ from the print version in several ways. The most notable difference is that the cover-to-cover information in these journals is not always made available electronically. Secondary material such as book reviews, letters to the editors, short news items, and announcements are often not included in the electronic version.

NUMBER OF JOURNALS ON THE INTERNET

Many scientific scholarly journals are available on the Internet in various formats. Most of these journals are electronic versions of a print equivalent, although a growing number are published exclusively online. Some exclusively electronic journals do not yet fully exploit the potential features of the electronic media, namely multimedia and interactivity.

Some older Internet journals are ASCII based and therefore do not include graphics, formulae, audio, or video. These are typically available via listservs, file transfer protocol (FTP), or gopher applications. This category of electronic publications grew rapidly with the initial expansion of the Internet in the late 1980s and early 1990s. According to the *Directory of Electronic Journals, Newsletters and Academic Discussion Lists*, published annually since 1991, the number of scholarly electronic listservs in the sciences grew impressively during this timeframe as shown by McEldowney (1995) and depicted in Table 81.

During the same time frame, the number of scholarly electronic journals on the Internet experienced similar growth. Although the Directory does not divide this category by subject, McEldowney (1995) provides the indicators of growth depicted in the last line of Table 81.

Since 1995, the number of electronic journals, including many multimedia journals available on the Web, has grown quickly. The Foreword to the 1997 edition of the *Directory of Electronic Journals, Newsletters and Academic Discussion Lists* separates the publication by types and characteristics. Table 82 breaks down the growth of journals from other types of publications and further documents how many journals were reviewed by peers.

Many electronic journals have clearly evolved beyond the mere simulation of print publications in an electronic format. They typically exist in both print and electronic versions, although they originated as print publications. The print versions of the publication continue to be a strong source of revenue for the

Table 81	Number of Listservs by Type and by Subject: 1991–1995				
Type of Journals	**July 1991**	**March 1992**	**April 1993**	**May 1994**	**May 1995**
Journals by Subject					
Computers	—	—	126	311	359
Biological Science	104	125	124	155	222
Physics	71	102	151	245	272
Total	175	227	401	711	853
Academic Electronic Journals	27	36	45	181	306

Source: *Directory of Electronic Journals* 1995 and McEldowney 1995

Table 82	Number of Electronic Journals, Newsletters, and Conferences by Type: 1991–1997						
Type	1991	1992	1993	1994	1995	1996	1997
Electronic Journals and 'Zines	27	36	45	181	306	1,093	2,459
Peer Reviewed	7	15	29	73	139	417	1,049
Electronic Newsletters & Other	83	97	175	262	369	596	955
Electronic Conferences	517	769	1,152	1,785	2,480	3,118	3,807

Source: Directory of Electronic Journals 1997

publisher, but the electronic versions are not simply a sideline. They are important entities unto themselves, exploiting the capabilities of electronic media in ways that add value to the content of the publication, making the electronic version superior in some ways to the print version.

Many electronic scholarly publications originally were individual journal titles mounted electronically, usually by the same entity that published the print version or by a third-party distributor. A study by Hitchcock, Carr, and Hall (1996) surveyed such journals. Some publishers and distributors of scholarly journals who pioneered electronic publishing projects of groups of journals on the Web include OCLC with their electronic journals online project, BioMedNet, Elsevier's TULIP, and The Johns Hopkins University's Project MUSE.

In 1999, an estimated 4,000 journal titles were available electronically, either directly from the primary publishers or through second or third-party aggregators (Getz 1999). The major suppliers of these titles are listed in Table 83.

A further evolution involves journals that represent a true shift of focus from print media to electronic media. They have their genesis in the electronic arena, and they take full advantage of the electronic capabilities of multimedia and interactivity. These journals are currently available on the World Wide Web, although it must be assumed that their capabilities will continue to expand as new technologies develop.

Table 83	Multiple-Journal Publishing on the World Wide Web: 1999

Publishers Distributing E-Journals Directly	Number of Titles
Elsevier Science Direct	1,100
Springer Link	300
American Chemical Society	33
Institute of Physics	33
University of Chicago Press	9
(a partial list)	

Aggregates Supporting Electronic Distribution of E-Journals (selected list)	Number of Titles
HighWire	90
OCLC (29 publishers)	1,200
Academic Press	175
JSTOR	68
Muse	40
Kluwer	120
Blackwell	150
MIT Press	9
Taylor and Francis	50

Source: Getz 1999

These journals typically reside online as complete entities, rather than as mere collections of articles. They include extensive editorial and subscription information, instructions to authors and readers, and copyright and use restriction information. The articles in these journals include multimedia, complete graphical and tabular information, and links to related or cited material. They also typically include an online forum for discussion, whether it be directly between readers and authors or in the form of letters to the editors.

Of the sample of eighty-three journals studied by Hitchcock, Carr, and Hall (1996), thirty-five were published exclusively in electronic form. It is interesting to note that some of these journals (five of the thirty-five) were planning or considering producing both print and CD-ROM editions or cumulations of the journals. For these journals, print had become the sideline or afterthought medium. Ten of the thirty-five journals were published by commercial publishers, four by society publishers, and twenty-one by other sources. Journals in the latter group were sponsored by a mix of commercial and society or association publishers, by government or educational research grants, or by author fees. Many of the thirty-five were free of charge, while others required a subscription. Personal subscriptions to most of these journals were priced under $100.

Most of the journals were available for viewing or downloading in multiple file formats, allowing the user to choose a preferred viewing option. Use restrictions varied from journal to journal, with some offering unlimited use by placing their documents in the public domain and others restricting use for commercial purposes.

In the mid-1990s, Web interactive journals were the smallest group of scholarly electronic journal because they were the newest. With more scientists (authors and readers), publishers, and libraries gaining access to the World Wide Web, however, and with continued dissatisfaction of the current state of the scholarly publishing system, this category has grown rapidly. Examples of some early interactive journals include: *Complexity International, Electronic Journal of Differential Equations,* and *Electronic Research Announcements of the American Mathematical Society.*

OTHER ASPECTS OF ELECTRONIC PUBLISHING

Economics

The evolution toward electronic publishing will undoubtedly change the dynamics of journal economics and price. These issues are discussed more fully in Chapters 1, 17, and 18. There is insufficient hard data to make any long-term predictions, but carefully considered design decisions and policies can lead to a situation from which publishers, libraries, individual authors, readers, and funders can all benefit. It is useful, however, to take a bottom-up approach using models which illustrate the dynamics of the many factors described in detail in Chapters 12, 13, 17, and 18.

Contributing to Knowledge

Electronic journals will definitely impact both authors and readers. For example, electronic communication facilitates more timely access to the small peer group of invisible college members, which is clearly an advantage to authors within the college. The ability to easily expand the invisible college to include other peers who were previously excluded, particularly those in companies and other countries who may not be able to attend professional conferences, should assist researchers as well.

Electronic communication has the potential of opening up the invisible college to a much wider world of readers beyond research peers. This includes students, researchers in other disciplines, readers outside of academia, and any interested laypersons. Surely this is an advantage to readers or new authors who can be included in a process that once excluded them, but is it an advantage to authors who are already members of the more exclusive peer group?

This is perhaps an unanswerable question as cogent arguments can be made on both sides. From the purely selfish perspective of an individual author, too much feedback, especially from those with little depth of knowledge in a subject specialty, may not be of as much service as the ideal view proposes. Widespread distribution of referees' comments, or disagreements from anyone who wishes to post them, may discourage some authors from publishing.

Even Stevan Harnad, an early creator and proponent of electronic journals, is described by *Scientific American* (Stix 1994) as:

> no populist. Unlike Internet evangelists who view the network as the ultimate equalizer for dismantling hierarchy, Harnad is an unabashed academic snob. The best thinkers in a field, he believes, should have access to one another, undisturbed by the noise of crowds milling outside the ivory tower.

Perhaps it is wise to keep communication and publishing separate at some level. King (1992) advises viewing the process and products separately: "just because researchers use e-mail frequently for informal communications does not mean that e-mail will become the publishing medium of preference for formal publication." Invisible colleges are one type of informal communication means; less selective lists and bulletin boards are others.

Other Factors

Readers will need to be convinced that electronic publishing is superior to traditional print publishing if they are to happily make the switch (July 1992). Nevertheless, many indicators suggest that the transformation is already taking place in many subject disciplines and is picking up speed.

The extensive transformation from print journals in the research areas of physics and mathematics has been well reported (Stix 1994). Many examples of successful refereed electronic journals now exist, including *Postmodern Culture, Psycoloquy*, and the *Electronic Journal of Combinatorics*.

As technology improves, convincing readers to make the switch becomes easier to do. In addition to the speed and convenience of delivery now present, multimedia electronic journals are beginning to provide types of information not available in print. Stix (1994) describes the future look of electronic journals for the extensive audience of *Scientific American*.

Additional factors that are important advantages to readers of electronic publishing include:

- opportunity to experiment with electronic media (Amiran, Orr, and Unsworth 1991)

- timeliness of publication (Anderson 1993; Stix 1994)

- location independence (Anderson 1993)

- instant updates and revisions (Rawlins 1993)

- improved searchability (Olsen 1993)

- ability to create own personal electronic file of articles (Olsen 1993)

- space savings (Olsen 1993), and

- not reliant on library collection (Stix 1994)

Clearly some of the goals of authors and readers are in harmony. Most authors and readers, for example, want a process that allows articles to be disseminated in a timely manner. It is in both of their interests to keep the costs of creating and distributing journal articles low and to support a system of publishing that allows widespread dissemination.

Although the primary motivation may vary, the ultimate goals of both groups are served by some sort of peer review/refereeing process that serves as a quality filter and is acknowledged as such by academic institutions and decision makers. Many authors and readers benefit from increased feedback and connection, although this benefit is less clear for some groups. Non-academic researchers are often readers, but rarely become authors. They may have neither the job incentives nor the desire to do so. Electronic communication may allow them to connect with authors or other readers on a less formal basis, however.

Other goals may never coincide. Authors value their historical place in a discipline over time, the academic and professional stature that comes with formal publishing, and protection of their individual ideas.

Readers value the ability to access relevant information in a timely manner and use it for their own needs. They may want to comment on electronic texts or author's ideas even in areas where they are on the periphery. They may want to download, alter, or retain personal files of electronic journal articles at a low cost.

Still, uniting all of the goals of authors and readers may not be necessary for electronic publishing to ultimately replace print, if a variety of electronic communication and publication models are able to coexist. The goals of communication can be met with informal e-mail, more formal listservs and bulletin boards, and still more restrictive invisible colleges. The goals of collaboration and interactive publication can be met with all of these options, supported by an electronic preprint function that distributes drafts for peer review and comment. Finally, the goals of recognizing quality work and ensuring importance over time can be met with rigorous formal refereed electronic journals.

The traditional links of editors, reviewers, referees, and publishers enable this last model and allow disparate goals to coexist. Publishing has worked in a print mode without complete commonality of goals between readers and writers, and it can continue to do so in the electronic world as long as all of its critical needs are met.

CONCLUSION

The technology which makes electronic versions more than afterthought publications is the World Wide Web. Debate continues over whether the Web is actually a revolutionary new communication paradigm or merely a new, albeit interesting, distribution medium. We contend that in the context of scientific scholarly publishing, the Web is much more than a distribution medium because it incorporates two key electronic elements which have the potential to revolutionize the scholarly communication system: (1) the use of multimedia applications, and (2) interactivity between authors and readers. Other means of electronic publication provide either multimedia applications (e.g., CD-ROM) or interactivity (e.g., listservs and discussion groups), but the Web is the first medium in which these capabilities can be easily combined.

CHAPTER 16

Economic Aspects of the Internet[1]

INTRODUCTION

Most Internet studies have focused on the costs and pricing structures of linked networks. To establish a context for the spectrum of economic aspects of the Internet, this chapter takes a broader, more systems-like view of the Internet which includes all the various processes, services, and participants necessary to communicate information.[2] Thus Figure 17 depicts four generic groups of processes: (1) **creation** of Internet information, (2) **end-use** of that information, (3) all the information processes, services, and participants which we call the **Internet information infrastructure**, and (4) all the processes, services and participants involved in actually transmitting information which we call **the Internet communications infrastructure**. Together they form an Internet system. All four types of processes are considered because any changes in process costs, prices, or attributes can have a significant ripple effect across all four types of processes. This in turn can affect the amount of use, usefulness, and value of Internet information (see Chapters 3 and 4).

---

[1]Much of this chapter is taken with permission from King (1998).
[2]Some prefer the term, 'content.' However, by definition (see Chapter 3), we use the broader term, 'information.'

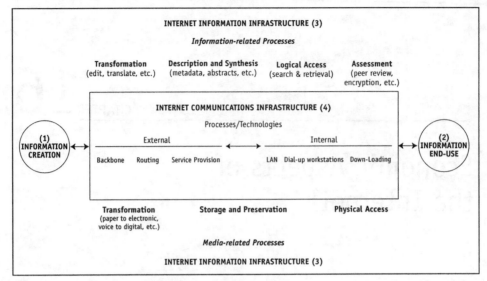

Figure 17. Four types of Internet processes.

The Internet involves a great deal of commercial and personal information. Our focus is on the economic aspects that affect scientists and their communication and the effect of changes in that communication on journal publishing. Research information on the Internet ranges from individuals formulating ideas or opinions through informal and formal research to the big science projects sponsored by government (e.g., the Hubble Space Telescope, the human genome research, and LANDSAT.). Regardless of the type of information created, there is a cost of creation ranging from a single individual's time and use of other resources that help to formulate ideas all the way to the billions of dollars spent by the government on the big science projects which create information. Incentives are required to expend the resources necessary to create this information, but sometimes the mere existence of the Internet justifies or encourages such creation, although information is usually created to share ideas, to promote oneself or an organization, or to earn money.

The largest single use of the Internet is electronic mail, followed by data transfers from one computer to another, and lastly logging into a computer that is running elsewhere (MacKie-Mason and Varian 1997). Internet users are often discussed in terms of end-users, yet Internet users also include information creators and the information infrastructure participants who depend on the Internet to provide their services. With electronic journals, for example, many types of communication take place: authors communicate with peers and publishers, editors with referees, publishers with secondary database producers, libraries with libraries, and database vendors with intermediary searchers, to name a few. The cost to users of Internet charges is usually far less than the cost of acquiring Internet information in terms of their time and other resources. In fact, the cost of using the information is often higher than the cost of acquiring the information.

The Internet communications infrastructure provides a means for individuals to create information and communicate it to others. Sometimes, as with e-mail and journal articles, the Internet merely provides a means for sending messages that can be stored and read when a need arises. It also provides a convenient mechanism for sending research data, software, and a host of other kinds of information from creators to users. The economic role of the communications infrastructure is to facilitate communication and to add value to the information communicated by providing rapid transmission, enhanced accessibility, greater availability, ease of access, low cost, and other such favorable attributes.

The Internet communications infrastructure consists of communication technologies such as the network of backbone channels or connected pipes through which packets of information are transmitted and the computer traffic cops that route the packets through the appropriate network of channels by means of complex protocols (e.g., TCP/IP—transmission control protocol/Internet Protocol and user-defined protocols—UDP). This infrastructure also includes participants that provide the backbone of the communications infrastructure (e.g., MCI, UUNet, and Sprint) and Internet service providers (e.g., America Online, PSI, and Netcom) who connect users to the Internet backbone. (See Lynch 1998 for a more detailed description.)

The communications infrastructure includes a second component consisting of organizations with internal communications infrastructures connected to the main Internet infrastructure described above. The internal infrastructures include internal extensions of the Internet, local area networks (LAN), independent dial-up workstations, or combinations of these. These internal infrastructures have considerable economic implications because of their high cost and because their technologies can either enhance or critically impede the flow of Internet information and services, thus affecting their usefulness and value.

The Internet information infrastructure involves processing information and media. Participants include, among others, libraries, secondary and primary publishers, and vendors. Their economic role is to provide value-added processes that make the information more usable, accessible, and relevant. They improve information content through editing, translation, and organized access. Some processes are designed to describe and synthesize information to enhance its identification, location, and retrieval. Information is also assessed to help assure its accuracy and quality and screened to filter out non-requisite information, ensure privacy, provide security, or protect children from inappropriate information.

Information is transported on networks in various formats such as text, voice, image (still and moving), and data. All formats are frequently transformed into digital formats which can be carried by a range of delivery mechanisms. Thus, not only is information transformed from one medium to another, but from various formats to a digital (electronic) format. These digitization processes can be expensive to develop, but will provide further efficiencies as communications technologies become more commonly used. Other processes store, preserve, and provide access when needed.

Economic Measures and Other Aspects

Figure 7 from the economic framework presented in Chapter Four, depicts four basic economic measures of Internet processes. The first involves inputs to processes; that is, the amount of resources applied, usually measured in dollars, and the attributes of these resources. The other three economic measures include outputs of processes and their attributes (e.g., quality, timeliness, accessibility), the amount of use of the information and factors that affect use (e.g., price, awareness, satisfaction with attributes), and the outcomes of information use in terms of the effects of information on personal well-being, life-long learning, and work performance.

Economic analyses address the relationships among these economic measures such as between service costs and outputs (e.g., productivity, unit costs, and economies of scale), price and demand, cost and use, and cost and benefit comparisons of alternatives across all measures. Early Internet economic analysis studied communication infrastructure costs and pricing, but a more recent focus has added information-related services. Thus far there has been much less analysis of the other measures, however, partially because they are not easily defined or obtained.

Two equally important aspects of the economic costs of Internet processes answer the questions: how much does it cost and who pays for these costs—the service provider (and its investor), the government, service consumers, or advertisers? Generally, the costs of Internet processes include very large fixed, one-time (or periodic) costs and relatively small incremental costs associated with service delivery. This is an important economic aspect because the large fixed costs involve an investment prior to revenue that must somehow be recovered from one or more of these participants.

Even though the literature has focused on communications infrastructure costs, it is useful to consider costs of all four types of processes because the communications infrastructure probably represents the smallest proportion of the total cost. A reasonable ranking of total cost would probably place use as having the highest cost, with creation the second highest, while the information and communication infrastructures would take a distant third and fourth place, depending on the types of information involved. For example, the information infrastructure costs of electronic journals are much higher than the communication infrastructure costs of transmitting articles. Finally, the total cost to organizations of the internal infrastructure is normally much higher than is the payment for use of the main external infrastructure.

Many of the information-related costs have been donated or subsidized, thus creating the illusion to at least some end-users that the Internet is essentially free. As the novelty of Internet involvement by services dwindles and economic realities set in, many service providers may no longer provide their services without a charge. The issue of who pays may increasingly involve end-users or their organizations, and a re-examination of pricing policies may be warranted.

ECONOMIC ASPECTS OF THE COMMUNICATIONS INFRASTRUCTURE

Economic Costs of the Communications Infrastructure

An indicator of the Internet system cost (excluding use) is the amount of sales of network services; hardware including routers, modems and computers; software; enabling services; information content providers; and Internet-related expertise ranging from system integrators to business consultants. A study in 1995 by Hambrecht and Quist estimated the market to be about $1 billion, and it is expected to grow to $23 billion by 2000 (Hambrecht and Quist (1995) cited by Werbach 1997). In 1996 the *Boardwatch Directory of Internet Service Providers* (Fall 1996) listed approximately 3,000 ISPs.

One major cost of the communications infrastructure involves R&D. Certainly the government has been a major contributor to the development of the Internet communication infrastructure. This federal support has contributed to the major impact of the Internet on our economy, but, in recent years, the spur to growth has been the significant commercial involvement, particularly by telephone companies. McKnight and Bailey (1997) claim that government involvement is no longer significant. They state that the National Science Foundation (NSF) paid less than 10 percent of the Internet costs and even less when all costs are considered. Varian (1996a) indicates that NSF spent only $12 million on the initial backbone supplemented by $8 million per year in subsidies. Even though the contributions may be relatively small, Hallgren and McAdams (1997) argue that some benefits yielded by federal support will not be achieved through private initiatives, if left to themselves, because of the inherent economic properties of the Internet. Regardless, the type and extent of future participation by the federal government is an on-going issue.

The government involvement does appear to be changing. For example, in 1995 NSF implemented a privatization plan which stopped support of the NSFNET backbone and support of regionals (i.e., mid-level networks connected to one or more backbones) over a five-year period, but they continued to fund creation of network access points and development of a very high speed network. Three initiatives were announced by Federal agencies and others in 1998: (1) the Next Generation Internet (NGI) involving federal R&D agencies and laboratories, (2) the Internet 2 to create a test bed for advanced technology involving over 100 major universities (sponsored by the University Corporation for Advanced Internet Development); and (3) an initiative involving the Universal Service Fund, as required by the Telecommunications Act of 1995, to help connect schools and public libraries to the Internet by the year 2000. A fourth related involvement is a second round of digital library funding by NSF and other agencies.

A great deal of discussion centers on the dramatic reduction in costs of communication technologies. Moore's Law suggests that the maximum power of a microchip, at a given price, doubles roughly every eighteen months. This helps to speed traffic through networks and to eliminate hot spots. A major cost beyond the purchase price of improved hardware and software, however, lies in installation and maintenance. In other words, the cost reduction of microchips does not necessarily mean that they all will be replaced every year or two. Thus, there may be a lag in realizing the economic advantages of new technologies, although competition among providers tends to minimize the lag period. Another source of delay is that some suppliers of microchips cannot keep up with the demand.

Operational costing of Internet communications is extremely complex. Much of the communications infrastructure cost involves one-time fixed costs of laying wire (e.g., optical fiber), installing computers, and developing software. Actual recurring costs of operations like maintenance and support, however, are not only less understood, but are not even widely discussed in the literature. The ongoing flow of information through the Internet costs relatively little. Most of the discussions of costs really involve how the initial investment or expenditures can be recouped through allocation of the use of backbone and service providers.

Internet Traffic/Outputs

Few doubt that Internet traffic is increasing dramatically, particularly since the introduction of the World Wide Web, to the point that rush-hour traffic jams or congestion have already begun (Varian 1996a and others). Traffic through the network of networks means that any given message can traverse a dozen networks, many of which are independently owned. The varied capabilities (e.g., different bandwidths, faster or slower routers, larger or smaller buffers) means that some participants provide and receive poorer service than others. Providers must pay to maintain routing tables which direct traffic and keep track of the paths followed through the network. Thus, the weakest link in the chain of networks dictates the overall quality and speed of transmission. Yet, since these costly mechanisms vary among network providers, there are attempts to direct traffic to the best ones, thereby placing a burden on them. Varian also points out that bit-intensive transmissions involving display images, graphics, and real-time audio or video require broader bandwidths and higher level equity among participating networks.

The service attributes of the Internet make it more valuable to an end-user. The increasingly larger number of sources of information and individuals with whom one can communicate by e-mail makes the Internet increasingly attractive. Other attributes such as being available 24 hours a day (at convenient times to users) and providing particularly interesting information (e.g., the landing on Mars) lead to more use and congestion at peak times.

Congestion also occurs for transmissions overseas (e.g., between the United States and Europe where the normal eight business hours coincide only for two or three hours per day). Congestion can occur at several points: on the network backbones, at the public switched telephone network (when used to access the Internet), at the ISP connection (e.g., America Online) and, for organizations, at their interface and through local networks. Regardless of the location, congestion can create delays for Internet use, which in turn diminishes the amount of use and, consequently, the favorable outcomes of the information use. One way to address congestion is to build a larger backbone and improved networks. One extreme estimate of the cost to provide high bandwidth fiber to every home in the United States is $100 billion or $1,000 per household. The question arises as to who might pay for this enormous investment. Similarly, a universal packet-switching network that optimizes digital transmissions instead of analog voice is unlikely to be developed by the telephone companies because of the current uncertainty of revenue levels, but might be attractive to cable TV.

One issue with the communications infrastructure is how to measure input costs (e.g., allocation of all the resources involved in development, implementation, and operations of individual networks.), output quantities (e.g., defining chunks of information), relating outputs (network flow of information), and revenue (network flow of money). Little information exists concerning the attributes of output other than price and speed (or the lack thereof due to congestion). Usage is roughly measured in terms of total use (although not uniformly defined), but there is little information about how factors concerning use such as purpose and ease of use actually affect use. MacKie-Mason, Murphy and Murphy (1997) have suggested incorporating user satisfaction as a measure, not so much for economic assessment but as an operational tool to help control the effectiveness of the Internet.

Internal Communications Infrastructure

Perhaps the weakest link in the communication chain involves the internal communications infrastructure.[3] The development and operational costs of a communications infrastructure for a university, company, or government agency are usually far greater than the cost to them of using the external Internet. The cost of external Internet access for a large university is typically in the low hundreds of thousands of dollars per year or somewhat less than $10 per student. On the other hand, installing lines, developing and operating computer support, maintenance, and other internal communication infrastructure resources can cost in the tens of millions of dollars. Because of the high cost, many organizations operating under tight budgets are reluctant to expend the resources necessary to ensure an adequate communications infrastructure. Even library funders are beginning to question whether the usefulness and value of Internet services justify the large expenditures, particularly since these expenditures are made at the expense of other information resources and services. Public libraries, for example, can spend hundreds of thousands of dollars on Internet access and internal wiring, equipment, software, staff, and space (McClure, Brett, and Beachboard 1995). Some valid measures of output, use, and outcomes would help to resolve this issue (see Chapter 4).

---

[3]Local networks are commonly called intranets to which one can add extranets which involve linkages among private business or cooperating organizations located outside a corporate firewall. Examples include private newsgroups, groupware, and training programs (Collier 1998).

Communications Infrastructure Pricing

The Internet communications infrastructure usually charges a user fee to recover costs. The fee can range from monthly charges for individuals (e.g., $20 to $40 per month) to connection charges for organizations based on the number of ports or workstations and access to the Internet (i.e., through Internet, other internal networks, or direct individual terminal access). Arrangements are usually negotiated for the first two options and sometimes the last one. Once negotiated, the rates are fixed or flat for monthly or annual fees. Anania and Soloman (1997) argue that flat rate pricing is preferable because of the tradition with telephone rates, difficulty in counting usage, and convenience to customers.

Nevertheless, MacKie-Mason and Varian (1995) suggest that usage-based pricing is inevitable for the Internet, and they present some benefits of this pricing strategy such as dealing with congestion, accommodating price discrimination based on usage, and improving the desirable aspects of service financing (e.g., guiding investment decisions and expansion of capacity). They also mention some drawbacks such as the cost of accounting for usage-based pricing.

They point out that customer usage-based charges of a phone call consist of three components: an allocation of fixed costs, the incremental cost of a call, and the incremental cost associated with billing (i.e., an itemized cost per call, a cost per invoice, and an overall maintenance cost per month). The itemized billing costs are more than one-half the total incremental costs of a call; however, these costs (0.7 to 1.2 cents per call) are generally much smaller than the other costs (with a relatively small number of calls). They emphasize that usage-based pricing on the Internet is much more complex than telephone calls because the definition or measurement of usage is less clear. Furthermore, backbone providers have not yet established the identity of the end-users since servers, not end-users, initiate a transaction.

Another possibility is that the pricing reflect what users are most willing to pay for: namely, speed of service. This strategy would use a bidding scheme in which packets of information are prioritized by speed instead of first in, first out. Shenker, Clark, Estrin, and Herzog (1996) argue that flat pricing and usage-based pricing are but two ends of a pricing continuum and that hybrids of the two are likely to prevail in the end.

Part of the problem is that the "flow" of reimbursement money often does not match the actual flow of information. This is partially attributable to the lack of an accurate means of measuring traffic. At any rate, there is substantial disagreement as to adequate pricing and payment mechanisms. Some networks take a simplistic equity approach to payment (e.g., disregarding distance and carrier charges as well as inequities in provider capacities and capabilities). There are even some processes for which no way has yet been established to compensate providers for their costs. For example, NSF-funded networks provided good routing tables, but the new private providers are reluctant to utilize them because they are not adequately compensated for using them (Clark and Varian presentations, reported by Oram 1997).

ECONOMIC ASPECTS OF THE INTERNET INFORMATION INFRASTRUCTURE

Economic Costs of the Information Infrastructure

The cost of preparing information for the Internet can range widely. For example, the cost to maintain large company Web sites can be substantial. A survey of 104 large companies by Buck Consultants indicates that they typically spend $200,000 to $300,000 on staff compensation alone. Only 15 of the companies said they ran the sites to generate revenue. Most indicated they maintained a Web presence to showcase products or to provide financial information to investors. (*USA Today* 1997).

Another important economic aspect of information involves big science. Funders of such research tend to direct their funding allocations first to the creation or generation of information, then to research on or analysis of the information, and only then, if at all, to its dissemination and application. In Europe and the United States controversy about the economic properties of such information has been rampant. For example, is information a public, private, or other type of economic good? Should value-added information transfer processes be made available through the government or privatized? A recent report (National Research Council 1997) tackled this issue for many large data-gathering science projects. Rather than polarizing into an either/or approach, they addressed the problem by identifying conditions that lent themselves to one economic solution or another, for example, whether the information should be privatized and what pricing strategies should be employed. Suggested questions (i.e., conditions) concerning privatization include:

- Can the distribution of data be separated easily from their generation?

- Is the scientific data set used by others beyond the research community?

- Is the potential market enough to support several data distributors?

- Is it easy to discriminate prices or differentiate products between scientific users and other users?

- Is it costly to separate the distribution of data to scientists from their distribution to other users, such as commercial users?

Answers of yes to these questions suggest that privatization should be an option for distribution of the information whether by Internet or some other means, although the report focuses on Internet access. The report strongly recommends federal funding of distribution technologies such as those utilized in the Internet communications infrastructure and processes involving the Internet information infrastructure.

The relationship between service input (cost) and output (quantities) is an important economic aspect of services. The cost per unit of output is important because cost per unit must be equal to or less than the price paid or costs will not be recovered through sales. Since the costs of Internet services tend to be dominated by fixed costs, the cost per unit will be extremely high with low usage, but will approach the very low incremental distribution costs at extremely high levels of use. For example, an electronic journal with a fixed cost of $400,000 requires a minimum subscription price of slightly more than $800 at 500 subscribers in order to recover costs, while at 10,000 subscribers, the price could drop to $40 (both depending on transmission costs). Unfortunately, few scholarly journals address disciplines which have a readership anywhere near the number where price is close to the incremental costs of distribution on the Internet (see Chapters 12, 13, and 14).

"Free" Information on the Internet

Value-added processes are designed to improve information or access to it, but the economic cost associated with them must be borne by individuals, private organizations, or government. To date, the resources involving many information-related activities have been donated by individuals or are supported by academic institutions, companies, or government. It is likely, however, that the incentives to provide such "free" services will diminish, and user charges more frequently will be required.

Consider for example, the case where some electronic journals are provided free on the Internet. The incentive for participants to donate or absorb costs range from altruistic to obtaining recognition for the participants in a discipline to obtaining publicity for an organization. Whether such incentives will continue to warrant free journals over the long run is difficult to predict. Current print publishers are struggling with the decision of whether to provide Internet access for their entire journals or separate copies of articles and, if so, how much to charge for such services. The problem is that their information infrastructure costs are very high, and these costs must be recovered regardless of whether the articles are distributed in paper or electronic media (see Chapter 13). Since both paper and electronic media have relatively small incremental costs,[4] electronic publishing of equivalent information can reduce the journal prices somewhat, but not dramatically so. Other Internet benefits such as speeding up publication, enhancing peer participation and review, automated assessment of, and rapid access to individual copies of articles may be more important to the reader than price.

Going from free to charging does not necessarily mean that the service or product will fail. For example, Collier (1998) gives an example of a large publishing company that placed 21 magazines online free for one year. After the year, it charged $160, but essentially maintained its circulation of 6,000 subscribers.

According to an Ernst and Young report (1997), many magazines are not financially viable on the Internet. Their survey of magazine publishers showed that only 20 percent who have online magazines say they will earn a profit. At the same time, the publishers project revenue to triple during the next two years, at which time a minimal profit will be earned. In 1997, approximately 25 percent of revenue is earned from subscription or transaction fees. Advertising dominates revenue.

Another example (described by Crawford, Hurd and Weller 1996, Stix 1994, and others) involves the availability of high-energy physics and other scholarly article preprints through the Los Alamos National Laboratory (LANL). This highly acclaimed and heavily used service developed by Paul Ginsparg is touted as being free, although Ginsparg developed the system as an employee of LANL. Furthermore the system is stored and made available through the LANL, and the NSF has funded the project for more than $1 million. This is not to detract from the considerable merits of the service, but merely to point out that some day the LANL may decide to charge for costs incurred or to turn the system over to an information service organization that must charge for it.[5]

---

[4]See Chapters 12 and 17 for details on such costs.

[5]Referring to the National Research Council report, public vs. privatization questions were asked concerning information produced by big science projects to determine desirability or privatization. It well may be that high-energy physics information does not meet the criterion for privatization (i.e., the information is created and used by essentially the same community). This condition is not true for many scientific disciplines in which there is far more reading of scientific articles outside the academic community (which creates the information) than within. Chemistry and many life sciences are examples of such disciplines.

Other Economic Aspects

The Internet has been described as the best vehicle ever developed to disseminate opinion. This creates an economic concern that information found on the Internet may not be accurate. Clearly, anyone can claim to be an expert and present his information as being factual. One only has to do homework at a grade school level to find different answers on the Internet to questions for which there should be no ambiguity. Some now argue that peer review or refereeing of scholarly articles is not only too costly, but is no longer necessary because, on the one hand, the Internet allows iterative interaction among peers, and, on the other, the Internet will permit readers to rate articles concerning various attributes which can serve as indicators of their validity, usefulness, and value on a topic. Regardless of the merits of these arguments, any changes in current practices for electronic journals on the Internet will affect information attributes and make the information more or less useful and valuable.

With so much new information being made available on the Internet and with a substantial amount of it being sent to individuals at the discretion of its creators, end-users are beginning to feel swamped with unwanted and unneeded information. Furthermore, searches for very specific information often result in hundreds of identified hits when perhaps only a few are needed. Such lack of precision in the dissemination and retrieval of information can cost users substantially in time that they are less and less willing to spend. The information science community will need to exhibit greater involvement and entrepreneurship in attacking these issues.

The Internet features two kinds of information retrieval: one that identifies and locates information resident on Internet hosts that can be accessed through the Internet and another that identifies and locates information from sources external to the Internet as represented by library catalogs and bibliographic databases. The accuracy and precision of the former generally are inferior to the latter because of the nature of the information described, the ad hoc development of some, and the lack of attention to standardization of terminology. Williams (1994) points out that the traditional bibliographic database vendors (e.g., DIALOG, National Library of Medicine, LEXIS-NEXIS, and West) encourage access through the Internet. This has the advantage of saving telecommunication expenditures, which amount to approximately 3 percent of the out-of-pocket costs of searching online, depending on factors such as transmission speeds.

The growth of both electronic publishing and digital library initiatives mean that traditional abstracting and indexing services and databases may not be sufficient for searching large text databases. Improvements to current Internet search engines and new search engines are certainly necessary and, perhaps, a revisit to the full-text associative retrieval systems of the 1960s is warranted provided they prove scalable in today's environment. Even the traditional bibliographic database services often do not include exclusively electronic publications or research articles where authors choose to publish exclusively on their own Web pages. Finally, some electronic journals bypass bibliographic database producers and traditional online vendors, which makes their materials less accessible and creates a false sense of comprehensiveness on the part of the bibliographic databases.

Some in the library and information science community have lamented their future in light of the Internet. Yet the initial chaotic nature of searching the Internet means that end users must rely on information professionals to assist in navigating through the maze of sources of information and to build a knowledge of the strengths and weaknesses of information and information sources (i.e., what sources can you trust?). Just as end-users tended to rely on intermediaries to perform traditional searches in companies, they may find it even more necessary to do so because of the competence necessary and the increasing time (and cost) required to search for information. As Griffiths (1998) points out, the Web is not a library and should not be considered as such.

Archiving and preservation of information on the Internet is becoming a problem. One issue involves information that is frequently modified or changed. For example, some researchers are constantly updating and modifying the formal documentation of their research and, as a result, sometimes no permanent record of the process is maintained. A second issue is that no one assumes responsibility for archiving some important types of information. For example, traditional print journal articles can be obtained from the publishers and large libraries, but there may be no such source for some electronic journals. Another aspect of preservation is that information stored in a digital format has a much shorter life span than the traditional print on paper. Finally, some information is lost because it has been input and stored using outdated technologies that limit retrieval with current technologies (see Schwartz 1998).

Some of the major preservation and digital library initiatives are focusing on these issues, but the solutions can be very expensive. For example, digitizing through scanning is expensive since human intervention is still required. Because of the enormous costs, retrospective input of text should not be duplicated by competing initiatives or among countries, and the digital structure of retrospective text should be coordinated and made compatible with newly created digital text.

The Internet changes the basic concept of the way information is stored because information on the Internet is stored on 16 million host computers (Network Wizards Internet Domain Survey, 1997 cited in Werbach 1997). These computers are found almost anywhere in the world, and access is extremely simple, fast (with the exception of potential congestion delays), and available 24 hours a day. While some information is stored on supercomputers, there is less need for central storage since an information creator can locally store information to be used at the discretion of end-users. This distributed storage capability made possible by the Internet has certainly resulted in new sources of information, but, on the other hand, has made identification and access more chaotic.

The extensive number of computer hosts and end-use access provided by the Internet has created a need to filter access in some instances. Privacy of personal information such as medical records, personal finances and tax information, and personnel records are all now potentially subject to access on the Internet resulting from this information being stored on computers that are also used for other network access. Companies are also concerned about pirated access to proprietary research and financial and marketing information that can be harmful in the hands of competitors. Finally, governments have classified information that should not be accessible on the Internet. In order to provide Internet exchange of appropriate information, but deny access to inappropriate information, several technologies and software are designed to build firewalls to limit inappropriate access. All of these means are expensive to implement and maintain.

Limited access can be achieved through encryption which was developed for the intelligence community. Encryption uses a key or key process to transform information into a code so that only the recipient(s) of the information who have the key can read the information. The basic encryption algorithms are short and simple and can be used by relatively technically unsophisticated users. According to Varian (1996a) this has led to an attempt to regulate or ban the export of algorithms to deny their use to criminals and terrorists who could then communicate without detection and future prosecution. Varian and others feel that this attempt is useless and that the U.S. government will abandon the idea.

One very controversial issue involves pornographic and other materials on the Internet that are deemed inappropriate for children. One attempt to address this problem was made in the now-defunct US Communications Decency Act of 1995. This Act would have made it unlawful for an interactive computer service to display such information to a person under 18 years of age. Another approach is a system called Platform for Internet Content Selection (PICS) which permits users to designate agencies which rate the information found at different Internet sites. The system selection protocol provides ratings which allow users to configure browsers to display only information that is appropriately rated. Varian (1996a) points out that this system can also be used by groups such as Consumers Union or local libraries to filter information by rating information sources. Using Group

Lens, for example, readers can also rate materials by various attributes so that subsequent users can screen their reading by others' opinions of the material. Furthermore, one can further weight a person's rating by how much one has agreed with the person in the past.

Use of Information Provided by the Internet

Liebscher, Abels, and Denman (1997) reported that the number of Internet users nearly doubled from November 1993 to November 1994, while the amount of traffic in bytes doubled. The following year, the number of Internet hosts more than doubled. The enormous growth of Internet use is well documented by Werbach (1997) as follows:

- 47 million subscribers in the United States. (Intellquest Survey, 1997)

- 50.6 million adults in the United States and Canada accessed the Internet at least once during December 1996 (Nielsen Media Research) compared with 18.7 million in the spring of 1996

- approximately 100,000 business accounts in 1995, projected to approximately 2.5 million in 2000 (Yankee Group 1996)

- approximately 9 million consumer households in 1995, projected to more than 40 million in 2000 (Yankee Group 1996), and

- the number of users in 2000 is estimated at 500 million (Taylor 1996).

For those who cannot or do not wish to use their own terminals or modified TV, nearly all public, school, and other libraries are expected to provide access services to their users by the year 2000. It is emphasized that growth in users and use has accelerated much more rapidly since the implementation of the World Wide Web. Thus, growth patterns before that time may not be indicative of future reality.

Of course, much of this use is recreational or at least non-work related. There is, however, little question that the Internet is heavily used in the workplace as well. Bishop (1994) found widespread use by engineers for professional and administrative tasks with little social or recreational use. Recent studies in the industry (King et al. surveys 1994-1998) showed that professionals spent an average of 120 hours per year receiving online messages from internal and Internet sources and 40 hours inputting information online. In the 1994-1995 time period, fewer than five readings per year per professional were found to involve substantive electronic documents (e.g., e-journals and listservs). More recent survey results (1998) show approximately ten readings per scientist of electronic scholarly journals (see Chapter 7).

A similar 1993/1994 study performed at the University of Tennessee showed that 84 percent of faculty and staff used networks for electronic mail (more than once per day—56.3%, 1 to 5 times per week—34.3%, less than once per week—9.4%). They averaged two hours per week (or 100 hours per year) preparing, sending, receiving, and reading electronic mail messages and an additional 45 minutes per week spent by someone performing these activities on their behalf. In addition, 72 percent of the faculty use the network for accessing databases and purposes other than e-mail (more than once a day—26.8 percent, 1 to 5 times per week—45.0 percent, and less than once a week - 28.2 percent). The amount of time spent by them and others for them averages one hour and five minutes per week respectively. Thus, they spend a total of approximately 200 hours per year both sending and receiving information in these ways.

Similar university results have been reported by others. For example, Lazinger, Bar-Ilan and Peritz (1997) report that 80.3 percent of the faculty at Hebrew University of Jerusalem were Internet users in 1995, ranging from 59.3 percent for those in Law, Social Work, and Library Science to 90.7 percent for the Science, Dental, and Medical faculty. Estimated hours per week for e-mail use were: 0–1 hour (44 percent), >1 to <5 hours (41 percent), >5 hours (15 percent). These numbers could roughly be converted to 100 to 150 hours per year per faculty member. Liebscher, Abels, and Denman (1997) report that 89 percent of science and engineering faculty at six small universities in the US. sent or received electronic discussion group messages in a typical work week, and 97.1 percent sent or received e-mail messages. Chu (1994) indicated that 42 percent of the faculty at two U.S. universities used e-mail in scientific communication. Wei He and Jacobson (1996) indicate that 53 percent of library users at the University of Albany were Internet users.

The university studies indicate that a very high proportion of the population of university faculty use the Internet, suggesting that a number of users and, perhaps, uses are becoming saturated. Studies over time (King et al. surveys 1984-1998) indicate that the amount of time professionals in industry and government spend on their work is increasing, perhaps by as much as 150 hours per person over the last fifteen years. Most of this additional time appears to involve using the Internet and informal meetings. It seems that the total amount of time spent working is becoming saturated. Thus, any substantial increases in time spent for Internet communication must come at the expense of other work-related activities. This is not necessarily bad, but it does point out that there is a limit on the growth of the Internet system for work-related purposes as the proportion of the work force who use the Internet and the number of users and their available time reach a saturation point.

The price paid by end-users includes both server fees and the application of user resources (e.g., their time, equipment, and facilities). Server subscription fees are typically $20 per month (with local phone charges added as appropriate) or $40 to $50 per month for cable or high-speed access (e.g., ISDN, ADSL). The terminal costs include the proportion of terminal expense (e.g., $1,000) or TV linkage device (e.g., $300) involved in Internet use. A person's time may or may not have an appropriate dollar value, but in organizations the average user time spent receiving information (120 hours per year) averages $5,800 per professional per year. Allocated equipment, furniture, space, and supplies might cost $500 per person per year. If an organization's Internet access cost was $240 per year per workstation or less, it is obvious that this cost is small compared with the resources expended to use the networks. This is probably true even when internal network implementation, operations, and maintenance costs per user are considered.

Internet-provided information is used for a wide variety of purposes including personal recreation, problem solving, shopping, life-long learning from preschool through formal education during one's occupation and into retirement; and for work regardless of one's occupation. There are certainly many anecdotes describing ways in which information has improved quality of life. With information found in electronic journals, abundant evidence has shown that readership is highly correlated with reader productivity and other indicators of performance (See Chapter 7). Unfortunately, information can be detrimental as well. For example, some information is inappropriate for children. Just as television viewing by children can detract from reading, over-use of the Internet for recreational purposes could have a detrimental affect as well. Misleading or inaccurate information found on the Internet can lead to unfortunate decisions or invalid application. Unanticipated transmission delays due to congestion can be extremely detrimental for work-related uses, research, or resolution of personal problems. Finally, the Internet opens the door to potential violation and use of private information.

CHAPTER 17

Cost of Electronic Scholarly Journal Publishing

INTRODUCTION

Electronic journals today comprise a rapidly growing proportion of scholarly journal publications as demonstrated by the self-proclaimed, authoritative source of scholarly electronic journals being developed by CIC, a consortium of university libraries for the Big Ten and the University of Chicago. Of the several different types of electronic journals, two are replicates of paper journals. Some publishers duplicate the journals in parallel, offering both electronic and paper copies, while other electronic journals which offer no paper counterpart nevertheless replicate the features of print journals. A third type of electronic journal includes enhanced features which add value to traditional journals. A variety of secondary sources are available to assist the user in identifying these journals including the University of Houston index supplemented by Charles W. Bailey's Scholarly Electronic Bibliography. The University of California at San Diego also hosts NewJour, a broader list of electronic journals. Three other directories are: (1) *Directory of Electronic Journals, Newsletters, and Academic Discussion Lists*, (2) *Fulltext Sources Online*, and (3) *Gale Directory of Databases*.

In this chapter we discuss the cost of electronic scholarly journals from the perspective of publishers, individuals, and libraries. The electronic cost to publishers varies depending on whether the journal is exclusively electronic or published in parallel paper and electronic versions. The exclusively electronic journal appears

to cost less than the paper version because the savings from reduced paper reproduction and distribution costs can be greater than the additional costs required for
equipment, software, and staff with the appropriate expertise, particularly for
large-circulation journals. In fact, the proportion of savings of electronic journals
to total costs increases as the circulation of the journal increases because additional costs are relatively fixed, but savings due to eliminating reproduction and
distribution costs increase with amount of circulation. Total costs increase with
parallel publishing because less savings occur with reproduction and distribution
costs even though new technology costs are incurred for the electronic version.
Additional costs tend to be in the 20 percent range, although some savings are
incurred when publishers offer the journal in either paper or electronic medium
(but not both) because electronic subscriptions avoid the bulk of the reproduction
and distribution costs.

Individuals incur two kinds of costs to read an article; the first being acquisition
and retention including the purchase price of electronic subscriptions or electronic access to journals and the second being the time required to identify, display, and print selected articles. The price of exclusively electronic journals can be
less because the cost of publishing and distributing the journals is less. Sometimes
paper versions cost readers less and sometimes more, depending on how much a
journal is read. It may cost a reader less to rely on separate copies as will be
demonstrated through simulated examples of these reader costs and break-even
points in amount of reading. In other words, if a scientist typically reads every
article in a journal, it is generally less expensive to acquire the paper version. Electronic versions are less expensive for journals infrequently-read by purchasers.

Another aspect of cost is the ease of use. There continues to be a cost penalty
and reluctance to read articles on a screen. However, with fast printers and better
quality screen display this problem will soon disappear. Another realistic choice in
the future will be to subscribe to electronic journals or to rely on obtaining separate electronic copies of articles. Rough cost estimates show that the break-even
point in readings depends on the journal price, article copy fees, and extent of
reading.

Libraries are currently faced with a choice of subscribing to journals or relying
on obtaining separate copies of articles through interlibrary borrowing or document delivery. The difficulties with these choices are exacerbated by the availability of electronic subscriptions, online or CD-ROM, and by access to electronic separates. We present simulated cost estimates of these alternatives along with break-
even points based on the amount of reading. One important aspect of the cost to
libraries is whether a year's electronic subscription permits access to those articles
beyond the year subscribed (even after subscriptions are stopped in later years). If

it does, libraries no longer need to bind, store, and weed issues, resulting in substantial savings in maintenance. Another related cost issue is whether or not electronic journals can be downloaded and printed out or whether they are only made available to read online. Finally, we present some other perspectives and potential value-added processes and services.

COST OF ELECTRONIC SCHOLARLY JOURNAL PUBLISHING

Cost of Exclusively Electronic Journals

The literature offers numerous examples of the low cost of article processing for electronic journals, including the aforementioned CIC in its annual report. Nevertheless, it is not clear that all costs have been included in these figures such as the costs of preparing intellectual content, computer and telecommunications infrastructure costs, and storage costs. Furthermore, most of these quoted low costs are for small journals which may have relatively lower support costs. We have re-examined both the 1970s and 1990s data and found that the unit cost of small journals is less than that of larger journals, contrary to the notion of economies of scale (see Chapter 12). Evidence suggests that the fixed costs per article tend to be relatively low for small journals, to rise significantly for medium-sized journals, and to fall again for the largest journals. However, it appears to increase by size of the publisher.

It may be that the low costs quoted for exclusively electronic journals is a mute issue; the point being that one could publish these journals in paper at the same cost plus an additional $25 to $35 for reproduction and distribution. Clearly, some purchasers might prefer to pay that amount in order to receive a version that is preferred by them (for whatever reason). In fact, Odlyzko (1998) mentions that a commercial publisher is selling a paper version of the *Electronic Journal of Combinatorics*, the most successful of the free electronic publications in mathematics.

Exclusively electronic journals typically save reproduction and distribution as well as some other costs associated with paper issues such as non-article processing of issue covers and other information. However, these savings are partially offset by electronic storage, software, and typically higher labor costs.

Thus, it appears that the costs of exclusively electronic publishing are less than paper, although not appreciably so (Holmes 1997). The reason for this similarity in total cost is that many publishing activities are common to both electronic and traditional paper publishing. For example, article and most non-article processing is common to both media, although electronic copy editing tends to cost more, while first-copy composition costs less. The major difference between the two media lies in production costs where the cost of paper reproduction is replaced by the cost of electronic storage for online access and disk production for CD-ROM. Paper distribution is also replaced by online or CD-ROM distribution, although subscription maintenance exists for both, and the actual billing activity tends to cost approximately $5 to $15 per subscription depending on allocation of support costs. Thus, electronic production and distribution costs are much lower than paper costs. However, these costs represent a relatively small percentage of the total costs for the low-circulation journals serving low-population disciplines.

Boyce (1996) indicates that publishing costs do not decrease appreciably with electronic journals. Odlyzko (1995) reports that the American Mathematics Society (AMS) found electronic costs to be 90 percent of paper costs. The *Canadian Journal of Communications* is said to have reduced costs by 25 percent after going electronic, with savings in reproduction and distribution offset by the cost of the expertise and technology required for electronic publishing (Brandao 1996). On the other hand, Harnad (1992) claims that electronic publishing can achieve savings of 75 percent over paper.

One large publisher anonymously shared cost data with us. They indicated that savings in reproduction, distribution, and composition costs are partially offset by new electronic processing costs, but that, when compared to the reproduction, distribution, and composition costs, amounted to only two to three percent of total publishing costs per 100 copies produced. It is noted that these savings increase as circulation increases, but the cost of electronic processes are relatively fixed so that net savings depend on circulation. To demonstrate this point we return to the cost model in Chapter 12 and substitute cost elements observed for electronic publishing. At 500 subscribers, we estimated savings to be approximately 4 percent, but at 5,000 subscribers the savings amounted to nearly 25 percent, and at 50,000 they climbed to over 50 percent. These data assume that all publishing parameters, but circulation, and other costs remain the same, but in practice computer-related costs are likely to proportionately increase for larger circulation journals.

Another set of cost data was presented at a 1998 conference in Oxford, England by VandenBos (1998). These data represent potential and real costs observed in modifying an existing American Psychological Association journal from paper to an exclusively electronic journal. The implied start-up and on-going costs are displayed in Table 84.

Some factors result in a range of costs: editors have a range of equipment needs, clerical support, and whether or not an honorarium is involved; marketing might be low, if the journal is free, to somewhat high (i.e., $25,000 start-up and

| Table 84 | Start-Up Ongoing Costs for an Electronic Journal (in Dollars) |

	Start-Up	Ongoing
STEP ONE		
System/Site design	9,000	500
Or		
Annual licensing fee	1,000	500
Adaptation/modification costs	0	500
Basic system costs	168,000	49,000
Maintenance costs/licenses	12,000	72,500
STEP TWO		
Editor start-up	0–7,500	0
Editor office support	1–3,000	1–10,000
Editor honorarium	0–10,000	1–10,000
Copy editing	0	600–1,000
Coding for display	0	700–1,000
STEP THREE		
Marketing/advertising	0–25,000	0–10,000
Subscription accounting	0–25,000	10,000
STEP FOUR		
Accessing/authorizing subscribers	0–5,000	1,250
Customer Service	0–15,000	20,000
Ongoing content maintenance (e.g., back-up, archiving)	0–5,000	1,250

Source: VandenBos 1998

$10,000 ongoing); subscription costs being low, if the journal is free, to high, if the ordering process involves phone calls and other follow-up.

VandenBos indicates that savings achieved by electronic journals are offset by other costs (e.g., equipment, highly skilled staff) and offers the following new law of conservation: "for every innovation that results in lower costs in one area of publishing, there is an expense that will equal the savings."

He does say that electronic publishing reduces processing time from six months to two weeks,[1] and the technologies provide value-added features such as links to full data sets or additional material, online commentary, online or links to audio visuals, and inexpensive color. He does not indicate whether such features contribute more to costs, and, if so, the extent of the additional outlay.

One reason that exclusively electronic publishing is said to be less expensive is that computer storage costs are decreasing rapidly as is online access to storage. Odlyzko (1995) indicates that 7 gigabytes of storage cost about $200 then (but far less now), and 50,000 articles (about 80 scholarly journals stored over 5 years) require only 2.5 gigabytes of storage. Of course, this cost only represents storage costs.[2]

Other costs are required for access to such a database including expertise, software, and billing. Billing is estimated at approximately $5 to $15 per subscription, and $0.20 to $0.30 per transaction for accessing separate electronic copies of articles when using a credit card (Sirbu 1995). Another cost to publishers is the use of a second or third party to distribute electronic versions of subscriptions and to provide access to separate copies of articles. For this service subscription agents require a discount from the publisher.[3] The discount is usually a fixed proportion of the journal price, but publishers are pushing for a fixed amount since costs incurred by vendors are independent of the journal's price to subscribers.

Cost of Parallel Publishing

Publishers continue to publish in parallel because they are concerned about losing revenue from subscribers who can not or will not receive journals electronically. The distribution of parallel publications include those that require both paper distribution and electronic access to subscribers; paper or electronic access to

---

[1]O'Shea and Hansen (1998) claim that the peer review process for their physics journal (at Lindsay Ross) dropped from six to seven weeks to three to four weeks due to email transmission. They also claim that "real cost savings due to electronic publishing continue to be elusive."

[2]Lambert (1985) estimates storage costs for electronic journals in 1978. In today's dollars, the costs would be nearly 5,000 times as high as Odlyzko's estimates (1995, 1996), demonstrating the drop in costs. She also estimated that electronic input costs would be approximately $19 per page in today's dollars.

[3]Others receive their revenue through a service charge to librarians.

subscribers; the latter two options with or without electronic access to separate copies of articles; and electronic subscriptions versus available online which can also be downloaded. Regardless of the distribution policy, the article and non-article processing costs for parallel paper and electronic publications are typically higher than for paper alone because systems-related costs are added to the traditional paper costs, and paper reproduction and distribution costs continue to be involved.

Holmes (1997) suggests, however, that such costs are not appreciably higher. She claims for her journals that editing, pre-marking, and coding or tagging costs are lower (94.9 percent of paper costs), but that layout/typesetting costs are higher (74.3 percent higher). Overall, article (and presumably non-article) processing costs are 18 percent higher than for paper alone when editorial costs are included.[4] Holmes (1997) indicates that the average increase in the cost of her journals is Canadian $20.61 per page, which is not too different from the APS reported increase of U.S. $10 per page. Others who maintain both paper and electronic versions, such as the American Chemical Society—ACS (Okerson and O'Donnell 1995) and the American Physical Society—APS (Lustig 1996), report similar results.

Some publishers provide both versions to all their subscribers. This can be achieved with little additional cost due to access and record keeping, but electronic costs are added, and paper reproduction and distribution costs remain. Assuming that electronic versions remain available in the future, this permits the relevant library and individual subscribers to avoid processing paper issues, thus avoiding maintenance, storage, and weeding costs of as high as $70 per journal. Instead, they can rely on future identification and access to older articles through electronic separates. If libraries download the subscriptions, there must be some provision for future preservation.

Other parallel publishers offer subscribers a choice of paper or electronic versions. There is a savings, of course, of approximately $25 to $35 per subscription in reproduction and distribution costs for the electronic version. However, not all costs are eliminated (e.g., subscription maintenance costs continue), and the cost per subscription of paper decreases as subscriptions to the paper format increase. In fact, the cost models in Chapter 12 demonstrate that some reproduction and

---

[4]These costs are said to not include overhead involving management and facilities including equipment, hardware, software, connectivity, and network support which may or may not be incurred with paper alone. Thus, the parallel difference could be even higher if the technology costs are added to provide electronic journals.

distribution costs are independent of the number of subscriptions, namely reproduction set-up cost per issue (C_6 = $950 per issue), plate making and/or collating cost per page (C_7 = $4 per page per issue), and distribution set-up costs per issue (C_{12} = $50 per issue). Thus, with 8.3 issues and 208 pages per issue, these costs would equal approximately $15,200, which translates to $30 per subscription for 500 subscribers or $3 per subscription for 5,000 subscribers.

Electronic Value-Added Features

While the wide range of potential value-added processes available with exclusively electronic journals will improve communication, they probably will also raise the cost significantly. For example, publishers will be able to provide a database of their current and archival journals, single journals, individual articles, or selected sections of articles. Various levels of information can be offered for reader examination, including titles, abstracts, reviews of the article, accompanying data, and appendices. Sets of articles on specific topics can be sent automatically to users based on a profile of reader interests. Quality of older articles can be assessed by citation counts of authors (before or after publication), ratings offered by readers, or ratings garnered from a panel of invited referees. With multimedia (e.g., sound, motion, and extended graphics), interactivity is possible among users (e.g., between readers and data, among readers, and between readers and authors); complete data can be provided (e.g., spectral, chromatographic, gene sequencing); computer programs can be included to help users manipulate data and other literature; and scientific databases can be hyperlinked (Heller 1997 cited by Collier 1998). These are only some examples of features which can be added to electronic journals. Pricing strategies will need to be established for each feature since these changes will affect costs, information and service attributes, and use.

COST TO READERS OF USING ELECTRONIC SCHOLARLY JOURNALS

One cost to readers of using electronic scholarly journals is the purchase price, and generally the price for journals published exclusively electronically could be somewhat less. We pointed out earlier that the proportion of savings to publishers increases as the size of the journal increases. If these savings are passed on in the price to subscribers, however, the absolute amount of savings to users does not vary substantially over the range of circulation size. For example, the subscription price would be about $25 less for a journal with 500 subscribers, $22 less with a 5,000 subscription journal, and $19 less with a 50,000-subscription journal. Thus, to a publisher, the difference in savings for a 50,000-subscription journal would be nearly $1 million, but only in the range of $12,500 for a 500-circulation journal. Thus, the savings tend to be much more important to some publishers than to specific subscribers.

Another aspect of purchasing paper journals is the cost of ordering and storing copies, usually for less than 2 years for individual subscribers. Ordering costs are common to both paper and electronic versions, but perhaps less so for the latter. The ordering, receiving, and retention costs of a personal subscription to scholarly journals is estimated to be about $11 per subscription (i.e., $6.30 for ordering and $4.70 for storing). Thus, subscriptions to electronic journals might cost $6.30 versus $11 for paper subscriptions. If individuals maintain an article in either electronic or print-out form, there will be a small storage cost.

The second element of cost involves the time of readers. The estimated time spent browsing and looking up articles from personal paper subscriptions is estimated to be about $3.90 per reading or about five minutes per reading plus nearly $1.30 for photocopying. It is believed that this time is greater for online browsing and look-up, even up to seven or eight minutes per reading. Furthermore, research has shown that it takes longer to read on screen than from paper (see, for example, Lee 1996), although we ignore this time and cost for reasons discussed later in this section. We estimate scientists' time at $0.805 per minute and other such expenses as equipment and facilities at $0.06 per minute.[5] Printing is estimated to cost $0.53 per article ($0.045 X 11.7 pages).[6] Thus, the reader cost per reading for obtaining an electronic article online from a subscription is approximately $7.00 per reading versus $5.10 for reading paper versions. At most, with the rough assumptions above, the additional cost of obtaining articles online from a subscription is $1.90, but electronic subscriptions are likely to cost about $20 less (including the lower cost for storing plus any reduced publisher costs passed on to the subscribers). Therefore, it costs less for the electronic version up to 10.5 readings (or more), while it costs more electronically above that amount, although the difference is not enough to be of great concern. Of more importance is whether an individual should subscribe or rely on obtaining separate electronic

---

[5]Scientists' compensation rate is based on their spending 2,400 hours annually on work-related activities. Their average total compensation (e.g., salary, fringe benefits, social security) plus 50% for direct overhead is divided by 2,400 to establish an hourly rate. Supporting equipment costs are divided by the estimated proportions of time used by scientists on the average (25% in 1994).

[6]Lambert (1978) presents data which provide some evidence that costs have dropped considerably. Printing costs have gone from $0.33 per page (in 1998 dollars) to $0.045. Equipment costs have decreased from $0.21 per minute to $0.06.

copies of articles, which is estimated to take about 15 minutes per article or $13.50 per reading including printing.

Using the estimated costs above, one can establish the break-even point for the amount of reading below which one should use electronic access to separate copies and above which should subscribe to an electronic journal. Examples of these break-even points are presented in Table 85 for various subscription prices and fees charged to readers.

With these cost conditions, one would conclude that the amount of journal prices and fees charged for electronic separate copies significantly affects the break-even points. At low subscription prices and high document delivery fees, journal subscriptions will most often be cost effective because the reading break-even points are so low, but the opposite is true with high-priced journal and low document delivery fees.

Many researchers of online journals have found that readers simply do not want to read articles on a screen. For example, Schauder (1994) found that 75 percent of respondents to his survey would prefer to read articles received in electronic form as print-outs (assuming laser-quality printing rather than on screen). At the University of Tennessee, we asked scientists questions about the last scholarly journal article they read, including their attitude about obtaining the article electronically. First we asked, "Would it affect the information's usefulness to you if the document had been transmitted to you electronically to be read on a screen or printed out?" Most of the scientists said no (57 percent), but several mentioned

| Table 85 | Break-even Point in Readings between Individuals Purchasing Electronic Journals and Electronic Access to Separate Copies of Articles at Various Journal Prices and Article Access Fees: 1998 |

	Document Delivery Fees (in dollars)				
Journal Prices	$0	$5	$10	$20	$30
$100	16.4	9.2	6.4	4.0	2.9
$250	39.4	22.3	15.3	9.7	7.0
$500	77.9	44.0	30.7	19.1	13.9
$1,000	154.8	87.5	61.0	38.0	27.6

positive as well as negative ways they believed that usefulness might be affected. We also asked scientists to rate their preference for reading in electronic or traditional paper by rating from "1—Much prefer electronic format" to "7—Much prefer traditional paper format," with 4 being neutral. Results show that about one-half prefer the traditional paper (15 percent much prefer), 29 percent are neutral, and 22 percent prefer electronic (7 percent much prefer).

The objection to reading on screen may not be valid in practice, because most articles identified or accessed electronically will be printed before being read. This does not differ considerably from paper since many articles read from a library or personal subscription are also photocopied (i.e., 57% of read articles). In fact, the cost of printout on a laser printer is estimated to be $0.045 per page or $0.53 for an average sized article of 11.7 pages. The $0.53 cost per article for printout from electronic sources compares with $2.53 per article for library photocopies, and $1.84 per article for personal photocopies. Thus electronic access and printout may actually save $1 to $2 per article copied.

COST TO LIBRARIES OF USING ELECTRONIC SCHOLARLY JOURNALS

Once an electronic journal becomes established and accepted by readers, there will be economic advantages to libraries to subscribe to them. First, there should be some cost savings to publishers for publishing electronic journals as discussed above, at least some of which may be passed on to libraries in the form of lower prices. The greater savings, however, are likely to be the elimination of costs to maintain, store, and weed paper journals, which is estimated to be in the range of $70 per title.

Another saving to the library is the reduction in reshelving and photocopying costs for journal articles; this saving is estimated to be $1.48 per reading. We have estimated that scholarly journals average 136 readings per title, making this source of savings approximately $201 per title and bringing the total savings from subscribing to electronic journals to at least $271 per title (and more if publisher savings are passed through).[7] It will cost less to use electronic subscriptions up to

---

[7]Wilder (1998) reports that the University of Illinois estimates 70,072 uses of 120 journals in their library (i.e., 584 uses per title) so savings for these titles could be about $864 per title for reshelving and photocopying alone. Note that Wilder's data were reported as uses, which might actually mean that the number of readings are higher. Thus, the savings per title would even be higher than $864 because the $1.48 figure is based on readings, not uses.

a breakeven point of 37 readings and less to use paper copies above that number of readings since it costs users less to browse paper versions.[8]

There are two downsides: the cost to users will be higher (see above), but only if they continue to go to the library to read. Since many of these readings of electronic journals can be done in the office, avoiding time to visit the library, user costs will decline as well. The other additional cost is to the library in equipment, software, communications, and staff with the appropriate expertise to provide access to electronic journals online. Some of these costs can be fixed purchases, which are amortized over time, while others are annual recurring costs. Justification of these technology costs requires the availability and demand for a reasonable number of electronic journals. As a rule of thumb, one can divide technology costs by 138 to determine the break-even number of titles required. For example, if annual technology costs are $50,000, there would have to be approximately 360 electronic journals to justify this annual expense. Note, however, that the frequency of reading and the amount of savings due to the elimination of reshelving and photocopying have a significant bearing on the number used to determine the break-even point. Also, the rapid growth in the number of electronic journals may make this calculation irrelevant for most libraries as the majority of required journals become electronic.

One other very important aspect of electronic publishing is the opportunity to gain online access to separate copies of articles. This service should be less expensive (i.e., $3.45 vs $12.75 per transaction) than the cost of current interlibrary borrowing and document delivery. With a less expensive process, the break-even point of readings between purchasing a subscription and document delivery will increase, regardless of whether subscriptions are to paper or electronic versions.[9] The most important question is the price publishers and vendors will charge for the separate copy. Table 86 is presented below to guide librarians in their decision-making. The break-even points show that access fees should be kept low if publishers wish to promote separate copy distribution. It is hoped that the figures in Table 86 provide some insight to the effect of electronic alternatives on purchasing decisions.

Chapter 18 addresses in greater detail the ways in which such results affect publisher revenue.

---

[8]The costs assume that scientists go to the library to read (i.e., browse) electronic subscriptions at a cost per reading of $9.18 (i.e., $2.18 for travel and $7.00 for browsing, equipment, and printout) and paper browsing of $7.28 (i.e., $2.18 for travel, $3.30 for browsing, and $1.30 for photocopying).

[9]The costs assume that the electronic subscription cost is the price plus $11 for acquisition processing and $9.18 for browsing. Article access costs are the document delivery fee plus a library cost of $3.45 and user cost of $11.34.

Table 86	Break-even Point in Readings between Libraries Purchasing Electronic Journals and Electronic Access to Separate Copies of Articles at Various Journal Prices and Article Access Fees: 1998				
Subscription	Article Access Fees				
Price ($)	$0	$5	$10	$20	$30
$100	19.6	10.4	7.1	4.3	3.1
$250	46.0	24.4	16.7	10.2	7.3
$500	90.1	47.8	32.6	19.9	14.3
$1,000	178.3	94.8	64.5	39.4	28.3

OTHER PERSPECTIVES

Givler (1999) provides a synopsis of understanding concerning electronic publishing over the past decade:

What is the future of scholarly communication in a world of electronic information? Until recently, our answers were shaped by the liberating awareness that publishing need no longer be constrained by the mortal clay of real books and journals. In cyberspace, knowledge could be weightless and disembodied, and data could be transmitted at the speed of thought. Information just wanted to be free.

That fantasy of weightlessness, and its imagined consequences, permeated early ideas about electronic publishing. Because a writer's words didn't have to be embodied in ink on paper, it was assumed that the costs of publishing would abruptly drop. Because use of the Internet was virtually free, distribution costs—warehouses, shipping, retail stores—would vanish. Because copyright was fatally dependent on an outdated, earth-bound manufacturing technology, it would become irrelevant. Anyone with a P.C. and access to the Net could be a publisher, and anyone who doubted would be road kill on the infobahn.

That was only 10 years ago. Since then, we've discovered that, even in deepest cyberspace, gravity works. Scientific papers and poems may be liberated from their centuries-old marriage to the printed page, but they still have to be incarnate in something. The new costs of engineering that ill-defined something (research and development, software, hardware, training) are significant, and the traditional costs of making scholarship socially useful (insuring that it is accurate, consistent readable, searchable, findable) are still there. Thus, publishing costs have gone up, not down.

This reality, however, does not detract from the approaching potential uses of technology in scholarly publishing as envisioned by Odlyzko (1995, 1999), and others.

Odlyzko (1998) summarizes much of his recent thinking concerning the evolution of electronic scholarly journals by emphasizing weaknesses in current system costs and by recommending steps necessary to reach a completely digitized journal system. He qualifies his essay by limiting it to low-circulation journals, say, those under 1,000 subscribers because these are the "source of the research library crisis" and, presumably, because they are amenable to exclusively electronic publications.[10] He contends that the journal system is full of unnecessary costs for both publishers and libraries. He implies, through example, that much of the high costs of journal publishing are due to sales and administration, as well as, publishing activities that can be eliminated through digitization. He believes that "unnecessary library costs are far greater than those of publishers," in fact probably about double the amount.[11] He believes that Ginsparg's Los Alamos National Laboratory system demonstrates that articles can be digitized and disseminated without intervention of publishers and, particularly, libraries.

---

[10]We have long held that new and low-circulation journals are best suited to be exclusively electronic journals (King and Roderer 1979; King, McDonald, and Roderer 1981).

[11]In making his arguments, Odlyzko (1998) presents some cost data from ARL statistics. However, these data are somewhat different from data we observed from special libraries, suggesting a difference by type and size of library. He maintains that the journal system costs libraries about $4,000 per article in compensation to publishers and an additional $8,000 in library costs including staff, space, shelving, equipment, and so on. He bases these figures on examples of total academic library budgets. The data seem to ignore all the non-journal services and activities performed in libraries. Our library cost studies did not deal with large academic libraries (Griffiths and King 1986; 1993), but we did in-depth cost studies of 13 medium size special libraries (e.g., National Institutes of Health, Bristol Myers Squibb). A typical library had a budget of $2.1 million of which 24% is attributable to journals (i.e., current periodicals room, older materials, journal routing, interlibrary loan/document delivery, and photocopying). About 25 percent was attributable to reference and research services (including database search services), 1 percent to user instruction and access to study space and workstations, and about one-half to other materials (primarily internal documents) and other services. He suggests that "institutions are paying at least $60 for each article read." Our reading costs, which include price, all library resources applied, and indirect costs (see Chapter 4) come to $1.61 per reading of current periodicals, $6.96 for older journals, $6.34 for journal routing, and $21.50 for interlibrary borrowing (see Chapter 9). Thus, in the special library environment, doing away with journals would not have nearly the impact suggested by Odlyzko's data. However, this does not detract from his conclusions, many of which coincide with ours.

There are three steps necessary to arrive at a completely digitized environment. The first step, well on its way, involves digitizing current journals, albeit mostly in parallel with print versions. The second step is to eliminate print editions entirely and the third is to retrospectively convert old issues to a digitized medium (e.g., JSTOR, Guthrie 1999). This means that libraries will no longer have a role in journal distribution and archiving. However, he feels that libraries will adjust easily to a paperless journal environment because monographs will again become more prevalent, reference librarians are likely to thrive, and there will be a greater requirement to collect, classify, and navigate the database (see also Griffiths 1998). They will also play a larger role in negotiating and enforcing site licenses and cooperative arrangements.

He cites the example of the Florida Entomological Society project (Walker 1998) in which a high quality digital version is achieved at $0.60 per page. He estimates that back issues can be converted at costs between $0.20 and $2.00 per page. Thus, citing mathematics as an example, the entire mathematical literature collected throughout history could be digitized at a cost of less than 10 percent of the current annual cost of mathematical journals. He also addresses some issues of interlibrary loan, browsing, and pricing (see Chapter 18).

In the past, both publishers and some libraries have resisted electronic distribution of interlibrary loans. Prohibition by publishers meant that libraries had to continue relying on expensive and slow acquisition of photocopies. Now electronic versions are used to satisfy many interlibrary loan requests, but some involve printing out and then sending copies to borrowing libraries. In the future such inhibiting practices should not be necessary and can be made part of site licensing and consortium arrangements. Others should be able to obtain copies online from publishers (see, for example, Walker 1998), vendors, or aggregators. He believes that browsing will be done online with better results made possible through hyperlinks. Ultimately, publishers will begin to add intellectual value through more review publications which will catch on faster than online versions of primary research journals. Again, linking capabilities will enhance this innovation.

In addition to Odlyzko, Varian (1996, 1999) and others have envisioned a number of value-added processes and services that can be achieved with digitized journal capabilities. One possibility is to address the redundancy of information in multiple channels such as technical reports, conference proceedings, articles, reviews, and books. Word processing provides inputs that are common to channels, albeit modified to some degree. While not in the redundancy context of channels, several authors have suggested electronic journal articles can yield a trail of updates and modification, sometimes resulting from author-reader interactions. In a sense, such processes could lead to a compression of redundant channels. Varian suggests that author-reader interactions can complement traditional reviewing processes as can use of citations for this purpose. Articles can be rated by readers concerning various aspects of information content. Citation counts of previous publications by authors can be used as an indicator of their capability and contribution to a discipline and subsequent citation counts to an article can be a guide to later readers of an article. Here hyperlinks and citation methods begin to blur.

Varian also envisions a variety of forms of publications. Multimedia can be injected when one form can convey messages more appropriately than others. Information can be replicated in multiple forms to accommodate different learning styles and capabilities. Electronic processes also facilitate access to various levels and types of information and writing can be done (and edited) to accommodate readers in seeking levels that will satisfy their information needs. Levels can include hyperlinked databases of journals, single journals, or individual articles. Within articles levels can relatively easily include titles and abstracts for screening purposes; text revealing various aspects of research such as findings, analysis, and methods; details of tables, models, and raw data; and linkages among these parts. Digitized text and data permit much more detailed document identification, location, and retrieval tools. Such tools can be used to develop automated dissemination of information based on reader/user profiles (much like the ballyhooed Selective Dissemination of Information—SDI—services of the early 1960s).

It is clear that new technologies open the door to imaginings that will undoubtedly lead to better scientific communication. The real promise is that "electronic publishing could offer new ways to communicate the results of scholarship, and may even, one day, give us new methods of doing scholarship itself" (Givler 1999).

Electronic Scholarly Journal Pricing

INTRODUCTION

In Chapter 13, Pricing of Scientific Scholarly Journals, we described the incredible rate of growth of journal prices, examined some reasons for the phenomenon, and discussed its consequences for scientists, libraries, and publishers. Electronic versions of scholarly journals are thought by some to be the salvation for this state of affairs because they can now be provided free (Walker 1998) or, at a minimum, reduce publishers' costs and, therefore, subscription prices.[1]

In Chapter 17, Cost of Electronic Scholarly Journals, we did, indeed, suggest potential cost savings for publishers, libraries, and readers. However, significantly more savings to libraries may be achieved from eliminating storage, maintenance, re-shelving, and photocopying costs than from reducing journal prices. Thus, unless some innovative approaches to pricing are established, publishing may continue on its current path, to the detriment of all participants. In this chapter we first discuss electronic journal demand and use. We then examine the effects of

---

[1]The reported low publishing costs and prices of many exclusively electronic journals are irrelevant in that these journals could be distributed in print for only about $25 to $35 per subscription more than the current price. Some scientists and libraries would prefer the print version.

alternative pricing strategies on decisions to purchase journals by both individuals and libraries versus using other alternatives. The options of differential pricing and site licensing are discussed in detail.

ELECTRONIC JOURNAL DEMAND AND READERSHIP

Demand for Electronic Journals

When relatively primitive technologies were in place in the late 1960s, it was clear that the journal system was not ready for a comprehensive electronic journal in which authors, readers, publisher, libraries, and intermediary services could all extensively use computer and communication technologies. By the late 1970s such a comprehensive system still seemed unobtainable for about twenty years (King, McDonald, and Roderer 1981). Even in the mid-1980s scientists as authors and readers had inadequate tools to participate in a comprehensive electronic journal system (Case 1985). However, by the early 1990s the Internet (and Web), extensive use of personal computers, facilitating software, and publishing standards finally ushered in the capabilities necessary for publishing electronic journals in a comprehensive system.

In 1999 a substantial number of journals are now available in electronic media and several preprint and article databases have been developed to help electronically fulfill the enormous amount of separate copy distribution. Most electronic journals are currently published in parallel to traditional print issues, but some journals are published exclusively in electronic media (see Chapter 15). The problem seems to be that most exclusively electronic journals have a small circulation in the hundreds, although a few have circulation in the thousands (Kiernan 1999). Walker (1998) provides an example of circulation trends for the small electronic *Florida Entomologist* which was provided free on the Web in 1994. From 1994 to 1998 the number of institutional subscriptions declined 3 percent, but actually increased 5 percent from 1997 to 1998. On the other hand, Rous (1999) discusses an ACM initiative that gained 30,000 paying subscribers in a little over one year of online service.

In the early 1990s, the ACM developed a Digital Library that consisted of a "body of well-indexed literature, with a variety of views into it, supporting the scholar's need to browse, search, bookmark, retrieve, and store articles of interest, from his own desktop, at any time." The service grew rapidly in the first few years, but at a decrease of over 25 percent in printed subscriptions. However, the overall revenue had increased. Rous believes that many subscribers still see an advantage to receiving their specialty journals in print, but use the Digital Library to search and retrieve additional articles from journals they cannot afford (see Chapters 13 and 17 for further cost implications). During this time, ACM membership continued to increase, particularly with student members. However, the number of individual members of the Digital Library access grew faster than institutional members. The ACM also provides a discount price to consortium and this market has helped open up new markets in the U.S. and elsewhere.

The Association of Research Libraries (ARL) began reporting the electronic serials expenditures of their members in the fiscal year 1994–95. In that year the libraries responding to this item in a survey (76 members) reported total expenditures of $11.8 million or an average of $188,057 per library. In the second year (1995–996), the number of libraries reporting this item went up to 87, but the average expenditures decreased to $174,379 indicating that the additional reporting libraries probably had lower electronic serial expenditures. However, the proportion of library materials expenditures attributable to electronic serials increased from 2.4 percent to 2.7 percent over the two years. Thus, the demand for electronic serials appears to be low in 1996, but increasing slightly.

Use of Electronic Journals

There are two distinct distribution means for uses of electronic journals, the first involving traditional subscriptions to the journals and the second is gaining online access to separate copies of articles. We have shown that there is a break-even point in amount of reading below which it costs less (per reading) to obtain separate copies of articles and above which one should subscribe (Chapters 13 and 17). The discussion above concerning ACM's Digital Library seems to confirm that such a choice is being made. There are estimated to be over 100 million separate copies of articles distributed through interlibrary loan and document delivery, preprints, reprints, and photocopies of articles sent (or given) to scientists by authors, colleagues, and other scientists. Most of this distribution can be done less expensively and faster electronically. However, one constraint in achieving electronic distribution is willingness of publishers to distribute these copies or grant others license to do so. This barrier seems to be coming down after 20 or more years of resistance. Clearly some revenue can come to publishers from this source, but not a significant amount over the next five years or so.[2] Another problem has to do with identifying, locating, and gaining access to electronic copies of articles. This

---

[2]For example, if publishers could clear a $5 per separate copy surplus on 100 million separate copies the revenue would increase only about 10 to 15 percent, but the $5 surplus might be on the high side and electronic distribution of the entire 100 million copies is unrealistic.

problem is addressed through reliable bibliographic databases that, at minimum, direct users to electronic sources and, at most, actually provide access to full text of articles. It also helps to have large databases of articles that are readily identified with scientific disciplines such as the ACM Digital Library (22,000 articles in computer science); Ginsparg's Los Alamos National Library database of preprints in theoretical high-energy physics, other areas of physics, computer science, and mathematics (24,000 submissions in 1998); American Mathematical Society e-math system; the American Chemical Society system; the netlib system of Dongarra and Grosse; several aggregators; and some large publishers. There are clear advantages to having "one-stop shopping" for article separates and that seems to be the direction that some are going. Usage from these systems is hard to measure and counts of "hits" that can be related to readings are not available as yet.[3] Some data are reported by users. For example, the University of Vermont (MacLennan 1999) tracked electronic journal usage from Sage with statistical software that logs the number of times each link is accessed or "hit" by users. For the fall quarter, there were the following hits: Project Muse Journal list—134 hits, SIAM Journals Online list—34 hits, Springer-Verlag Online Journals list—74 hits, and HighWire Press list—61 hits. This is equivalent to about 1,200 hits per year, but does not include hits on individual titles accessed from Sage.

Our surveys of readership show that about 10 percent of readings by scientists surveyed are from electronic journal publications[4] (see Chapter 7 and 8). Prior to 1994 there was just a trace of readings from electronic journals. Several studies in recent years give some indication of growing use of electronic journals by scientists and others. In 1995, Budd and Connaway (1997) surveyed faculty of several universities of whom 63 percent were scientists. About 14 percent of respondents indicated that they subscribed to an electronic journal (omitting listservs, bulletin boards, Usenet), although 23 percent of those who do not subscribe, do occasionally read the content of electronic journals (most often on the computer screen—83 percent). Three percent of the respondents have ever submitted a paper to an electronic journal. At the Yale University Medical Center, about one-half of the faculty and staff had used their computer to access electronic journals (Grajek 1997).

In 1998 and 1999 surveys were conducted of faculty from one-third of academic ARL institutions (Lenares 1999). Respondents indicated that 61 percent of faculty

---

[3]However, Odlyzko appears to be collecting data along this line and may have published these data by the time this book is released.

[4]This is true of surveys in the U.S. (King et al. surveys 1994–1998) as well as in Europe (Lancaster and King 1999), but all the surveys were heavily represented by physical scientists.

use electronic journals in 1999, up from 48 percent in 1998. There was an increase in all fields (physical, biological, and social sciences) with the largest increase in physical sciences (from about 60 to 90 percent). Nearly one-fourth of the users say they use electronic journals frequently. The use of print journals decreased over this year from 74 percent of all respondents to 65 percent.

At the University of Oklahoma, science faculty were surveyed about their information seeking patterns (Brown 1999). In particular the scientists were asked whether or not they used various electronic media to obtain journal articles including: personal subscriptions to electronic journals, a library's electronic version, a free electronic version, and document delivery (some of which are electronic). Results of services used to obtain journal articles are summarized in Table 87. Even though data are presented as proportion of scientists who use various distribution means, the results confirm our 1993 university survey results (involving total and average readings), except that a higher proportion of scien-

Table 87	Proportion of Scientists Who Use Various Sources to Obtain Journal Articles at the University of Oklahoma: 1998 (in Percent)		
	Scientific Discipline		
Source of Articles	**Chemistry Biochemistry**	**Mathematics**	**Physics Astronomy**
Personal subscription	55	23	38
Library copy	75	62	75
Photocopy library's copy	90	100	81
Personal subscription to electronic version	5	8	6
Library electronic version	5	8	19
Free electronic version	20	31	44
ILL	60	46	44
Document delivery	45[1]	15	25[2]

[1] 89 percent indicated *Carl UnCover*
[2] 75 percent *Carl UnCover*, Los Alamos National Laboratory Preprint Archive, or Stanford Public Information Retrieval System (SPIES)

Source: Brown 1999

tists now use electronic sources (see Chapter 8). Electronic sources are being used by an appreciable proportion of scientists, particularly those in physics and astronomy. At OU, campus wide access is available to 5 American Physical Society and 23 Institute of Physics journals. While there is clearly a trend to greater use of electronic journals in the U.S., Harter (1998) found that there are few citations as of yet emanating from electronic journals.

In the Netherlands, a nationwide survey of university students, faculty, and researchers (63 percent scientists) showed similar use of electronic journals (Voorbij 1999). Over one-half of the respondents indicated that they use electronic journals, with 8.5 percent using once a week or more. Of those who use the Internet for electronic journals, an average of 1.2 journals are consulted regularly. About one-fourth indicate that the service is important or very important. About one-third use the Internet for document delivery, with 2.9 percent using it once a week or more for this service and 22 percent consider it important or very important. Lower use was observed in the U.S. for business school faculty (Speier, Palmer, Wren and Hahn 1999). Only 16 percent or respondents had read articles in electronic journals and 7 percent had submitted a manuscript to an electronic journal. Part of the problem with business faculty is that awareness of electronic journals is somewhat low[5] and they also did not consider electronic journals to be as high quality as paper versions. This mirrors earlier scientist use, awareness, and attitude toward electronic journals.

Kling and McKim (1999) provide an interesting analysis of 16 journal media and distribution means in terms of three communication attributes: publicity, access, and trust. The distribution means and media range from simple electronic postings to personal and institutional Web postings to traditional print. They imply that the Internet has made communication much more complex and that scholars and publishers need to develop guidelines to help "maximize effective communication through multiple media and through a deep understanding of these multiple media." They also point out the problems with multiple appearances of information content and what constitutes a publication. Many journal publishers are becoming wary of this practice.

THE CONTEXT OF ELECTRONIC JOURNAL PRICING

Libraries are experiencing an untenable situation because spiraling prices are causing them to spend more for fewer journals. While that fact dominates discus-

---

[5]Lenares (1999) also reported that 54 percent of academics in her survey in 1999 "did not know of respected e-journals in my field." This proportion is down from 61 percent in 1998.

sions among publishers, librarians, and scientists, it is useful to examine how much resources (e.g., labor, equipment, space, supplies) are expended in the overall journal system involving authors, publishers, secondary services, libraries, and readers. The systems approach ignores money exchanges and focuses instead on the total resources expended in the journal system, normalized by the number of scientists and taking inflation into account. That approach represents the true cost of the journal system to the scientific community or society.

The amount of resources used to write articles is increasing, although not appreciably. Total publishing resources may have risen moderately due in part to the overhead of larger publishers and the fact that the number of pages published per scientist has increased—offsetting cost advantages of new publishing technologies. At the same time, the amount of library journal-processing resources have fallen because processing systems are better, and fewer journals are acquired. Resources used to obtain separate copies of articles have risen due to an increase in this activity, so that the overall cost of resources, again ignoring exchange of money, has fallen slightly. The amount of resources applied to secondary services is thought to have risen slightly, but that has not been confirmed, and the readers' time expended has increased appreciably, partially because of the additional time that must be spent traveling to libraries to obtain articles.

Thus, the overall system resources expended per scientist and per use has increased, although apparently very little. In current dollars the journal system cost per reading is about $60 to $70 per reading, up from $50 to $60 in 1977 (with most of the cost due to authorship and reading—87 percent in 1998). The biggest change is that the resource expenditures are shifting among the participants. Another systems view takes into account money exchanged among participants and the effects of price-and-demand relationships. Pricing policies have led to publishers losing subscribers, higher subscription budgets for fewer journals in libraries, readers paying more in their time per reading, and library and reader funding sources becoming dissatisfied because they are receiving less for their expenditures.

It is clear that traditional scholarly publishing has serious economic problems, despite a greater number of both articles and readers. With the emergence of electronic publishing, we are concerned that the economic difficulties of the past not be repeated. Yet pricing policies are currently chaotic, with little information or sound principles on which to develop valid replacement policies.

Journal pricing is becoming extremely complex and will become more so with electronic delivery. Some examples of current pricing policies include (see Chapter 15):

- no charge, i.e., some publishers provide journals free—sometimes a company will use the journal for promotional purposes or publications are wholly supported by advertising

- no charge with understanding of reciprocal services, e.g., interlibrary loan
- bundled price that includes membership in a society that provides one or more journals, conference registration, and other discounts
- differential pricing, i.e., different prices for personal, institutional, and non-U.S. subscriptions
- flat fee subscriptions which offer the purchaser unlimited usage rights within the constraints of the Copyright Act
- fee based on number of potential users, i.e., staff size or number of people in an organization
- fee based on number of simultaneous users, i.e., number of online ports allocated, number of active online passwords, or agreement that stipulates the number of workstations connected to a CD-ROM or locally loaded system
- fee based on usage, and
- fee based on documents selected by users to be viewed or delivered in full.

Many electronic publishing distributors do not yet have an established pricing policy, but rather choose to negotiate with each library, consortium, or company individually. Thus, the prices or licenses can cover a wide range of options depending on the knowledge and negotiating skill of the buyers.

ALTERNATIVE PRICING STRATEGIES FOR ELECTRONIC JOURNALS

The pricing structure and strategies of electronic services and products are in a state of flux. One common form of pricing, the flat subscription rate, will undoubtedly continue to be used for many information services. The potential flexibility provided by electronic publishing, however, means that a flat subscription price does not necessarily make sense.[6]

Electronic access introduces three aspects of flexibility that influence pricing strategies. The first involves defining an information product by the amount of information provided. For example, electronic information can be sold as a database of journals, as individual articles, or as individual pages, paragraphs, or even bits.

Secondly, the possibility of customization is introduced with electronic journals. For example, one could obtain early preprints of articles and later edited

---

[6]Some news organizations, however, continue to charge for annual subscriptions to Web sites; for example, the *Wall Street Journal* charges $49 ($26 if one purchases the print version) to 70,000 Web subscribers, and *The Economist* charges $48, but access is free for print subscribers (Collier 1998).

versions. The quality of articles could be rated by citation counts of authors, by past readers, by referees, or by any combination of the preceding participants. Selective Dissemination of Information could be upgraded to the announcement, or even distribution, of sets of articles to readers based on their profile or specific search and retrieval terms. Customization could be expanded to include sequential levels of information such as titles, abstracts, reviews, entire articles, accompanying data, or appendices (see, for example, Varian 1996b and Brown 1996).

The third aspect makes a practical possibility of charging on the basis of how much the information is used, whether by an individual, group of individuals in an organization, or across all users; the depth of use; and the purposes for which the information is used (e.g., research or teaching). The usefulness and value of these readings can vary dramatically, thereby warranting alternative prices and pricing strategies.

It is clear that the notion of bundling vs. unbundling journal titles, groups of individual titles, and articles is becoming an important issue for electronic journals. For example, examination of journal bundling leads MacKie-Mason and Jankovich (1997) to the conclusion that future pricing may depend on the value of attributes to user groups, the size of the reader audience, and how often readers use a journal or journals. Chuang and Sirbu (1997) suggest that neither pure bundling nor pure unbundling is best, but suggest mixed bundling as the best strategy (at least under the conditions set forth by them). Kiernan (1997) points out that acceptance of bundled electronic journals is receiving varied responses by academic librarians, partially because there is currently inconsistency in the way in which licenses or deals are negotiated. An emerging drawback of licensing is that it is becoming harder to establish organization use through traditional user IDs or passwords, thus requiring a formal means of authentication.

The flexibility of the electronic medium implies that a range of economic costs, pricing strategies, and corresponding payment mechanisms will emerge to serve all participants far better than in the past. The range of prices should reflect different units of output (i.e., amount of information exchanged and customized versions of the information) and the needs of the various groups of users. Niche markets will undoubtedly emerge for combinations of amount and customization that will determine the type and amount of use.

Since pricing may depart from flat rates in order to reflect, in various ways, the amount of use by end-users, some form of price differentiation will predominate in which prices vary with different units of access and/or with different classes of buyers. Different units of access may be defined by different amounts of output (e.g., an article, a page, bits), different delivery media (e.g., printed journals or online), different service attributes (e.g., rush document delivery through priority processing and rapid transmission such as online, fax, or courier versus regular processing), and different levels of customization (e.g., preprints without editing and refereeing vs. edited and refereed copies). Classes of buyers can be differentiated by ability or willingness to pay (e.g., faculty versus students), by membership in a society, by amount of use of a service or product (e.g., individual or library subscriptions), or by processing cost necessitated by buyer location (e.g., U.S. versus non-U.S. subscribers).

Three Types of Differential Pricing

Varian (1996a) gives examples for three types of price differentiation,[7] all of which seem applicable to journal publishing, whether print or electronic, as follows:

- First-degree price discrimination: the producer sells different units of output for different prices that differ from buyer to buyer. Different units of output can refer to the amount of information purchased and/or the degree of customization of journals. For example, a multiple-journal publisher negotiates with each organization or library on how many of their journals will be purchased and at what price (e.g., a negotiated site license agreement). This kind of arrangement could apply to either print copies or electronic access (online or CD-ROM). A further desirable refinement of this strategy is to also provide infrequently-read journals by document delivery (i.e., separate copies of articles on demand). Librarians can minimize how much they pay, however, by knowing the likely use and unit cost per use for each journal as well as the cost of alternative sources.

- Second-degree price discrimination: the producer sells different units of output for different prices, but everyone who buys the same amount pays the same price. In this scenario typically used by subscription agents, publishers set volume discounts for all buyers (e.g., for purchasing more titles and/or more copies of titles). Obviously, library consortia, and other cooperatives such as networks, use this pricing strategy to their advantage to achieve economies of scale. In a sense, this form of pricing is contrary to usage-based pricing since large libraries pay less per reading for highly used journals, and small libraries pay more per reading for the same journals because they are relatively infrequently used. Thus, with volume discounts, the cost

---

[7]Varian (1996a) refers to Pigou (1920) who uses the term price discrimination vis-à-vis price differentiation, thus suggesting that the two terms are interchangeable.

per use will be much less for large libraries than for smaller libraries and individuals.

- Third-degree price discrimination: the producer sells the same units of output to different classes of people at different prices. One example is the fairly standard price differentiation for domestic and foreign subscribers.

The latter type of price discrimination was applied by some print publishers in the past to both individual and institutional prices. Varian argues that small, niche markets—which accurately describe most scholarly publishing—are generally not well served if the producer is required to charge a uniform, single price, and he presents some simple examples to prove his point (Varian 1996c). This strategy may well be a contributory factor to the spiraling prices of scholarly publications (see Chapter 13). Individuals will not pay as much as a library for the same journal because, when looked at from a cost per reading standpoint, it is less expensive for them to use alternative sources (e.g., a library) than to pay a high price for an infrequently-read journal. The same principle applies to small organizations and libraries where the alternative to purchasing an expensive or infrequently-read journal is to either borrow copies or use a document delivery service.

Thus, the amount of reading serves as a useful means for identifying classes of subscribers (e.g., large libraries, small libraries, and individuals). There is certainly evidence that such price discrimination would have avoided much of the dramatic price increases of journals in the past, thus benefiting purchasers and readers as well as publishers.

Electronic publishing provides a perfect vehicle for extending this third form of price discrimination to an optimum level in which prices are charged on the basis of usage (i.e., amount of reading) and where most reading is accessed online by readers. The marginal costs to publishers of electronic distribution approaches zero, but the unit price (per reading) must be sufficient to recover all the high fixed costs of publishing mentioned earlier (Chapter 12). Publishers seem to be reluctant to provide journals by electronic media because they are afraid they will lose revenue from traditional subscriptions; they do not seem to realize that most reading is done from journals for which individual readers are not paying anyway. Libraries seem reluctant because they perceive that they will lose some of their services; they do not seem to realize that electronic publishing will also create new services and better utilization of information resources for their clientele. This pricing strategy has the strong potential of win-win-win-win for the publishers, libraries, readers, and funders of libraries and readers. Of course, if usage categories are used to discriminate, it will be necessary to be able to accurately and honestly distinguish readership categories among some subscribers. This is why, ultimately, electronic access may lead to a price per access at some level such as article, page, or paragraph.

A counter argument is that current journal practice bundles frequently-read articles with infrequently-read ones. This has the distinct advantage of providing a mechanism for distribution and access to high-quality articles in a discipline that inherently has a small audience or readership. If electronic journal articles are completely unbundled, as may ultimately happen, it may be necessary to over-charge for frequently-read articles by charging the same unit price for all articles, even though some will be profitable due to a large inherent readership, and others, while unprofitable, will at least, be available. Another negative aspect of usage pricing is that it is much riskier than journal subscriptions because the potential use of new articles is inherently unknown.

Pricing Government Information

When government provides information on the Internet, a real question arises of how much of the costs should be covered by government and how much by buyers. The possible levels of cost recovery include only the cost of reproduction (which is obviously not applicable to the electronic journals) and distribution (or incremental use), plus the total service cost, plus the cost of creation or generation. Generally, the policy is to charge for the cost to make the information available to users, but not the cost of obtaining and maintaining the information that is collected initially for government use. Since government information—such as scientific data—is monopolistic, there is merit in using a Ramsey pricing strategy (National Research Council 1997). This strategy suggests that, when total costs are not likely to be recovered, differential prices should be employed where high prices should be charged to buyers whose demand is relatively inelastic (e.g., library subscribers). In a sense, and to a lesser degree, electronic publishing can facilitate such a strategy for government-produced information.

Billing and Payment Mechanisms for Transaction-Based Pricing

As more and more information and services require payment and the variety of pricing schemes increase, complementary payment mechanisms must be developed. Sirbu (1995) suggests several features of payment mechanisms that contribute to their success, and he also describes types of payment mechanisms. He presents the following necessary features of payment mechanisms:

- They should be widely accepted.

- The processing costs of each transaction must be low; otherwise information providers will require larger chunks of information (i.e., if the cost of recording and billing for a single article in a journal is as high as the cost of obtaining the article, publishers would require purchase of the entire bundle of articles).

- Information delivery must be limited to paying customers only, thus requiring some form of security such as encryption for payment and information delivery.

- There should be one-for-one adherence of the charge for the information and the delivery of the information (i.e., no under- or over-charges).

An additional feature not mentioned by Sirbu is the speed of billing and payment which encourages information providers to place their information for sale on the Internet. One reason that journal publishers have been reluctant to depart from traditional subscription pricing is that the print revenue precedes much of the costs, thus ensuring a more favorable cash flow than, for example, book sales where nearly all costs precede the sales revenue (see Chapter 14).

Sirbu (1995) describes three kinds of payment models that he calls the department store model, the boutique model, and the transaction-based model. In the department store model, the provider (server) acquires information from a number of sources (e.g., several publishers, secondary services, document delivery services) and then charges users for services obtained during a specified period (e.g., monthly, quarterly). This permits one-stop shopping for users and avoids multiple billings and payments. On the other hand, this mechanism delays payment to the providers, much the same way credit cards do. In fact, credit cards are being implemented for this type of payment mechanism to make payment possible from one or more of them.

The boutique model involves a small information provider whose customers to do not have much repeat use. To avoid relatively costly invoicing for small accounts, the provider can rely on bank card companies, recognizing that credit card transactions cost providers about 20 to 30 cents per transaction. Thus, the sales transaction must be relatively high compared with the credit card cost.

The third model involves a transaction-based system in which a server and protocols permit identification of an information transaction and, at the same time, debit the buyers account and credit the providers account (both in a banking institution). This mechanism would be flexible in the amount or type of information transferred (e.g., page, article, database search output, or software program), the price identified with the information unit, and the buyer to allow an array of differential pricing as described above. Charges could involve such strategies as individual transactions and subscriptions allowing unlimited access.

Ultimately, the Internet may provide micro charges for very small chunks of information. It is clear that a comparable payment mechanism is necessary for transaction pricing to succeed.

NEGOTIATED SITE LICENSES

Site licensing has long been advocated as a reasonable, even highly desirable, method of buying and selling between large libraries and multi-journal publishers. King (1987) suggested, however, that site licenses be negotiated so that an organization licensee could use the journals in any way necessary to reduce costs within their organizations without further penalty of royalty payments as long as use was limited to employees and students of the organization.[8] Electronic publishing lends itself to multiple ways in which libraries can provide access to journals which can increase revenue to publishers, reduce costs to libraries and readers, and serve organizations in an optimum manner. Unrestricted library distribution means that libraries, as an organization negotiation party, must have a number of options available to them depending on the resultant cost to the organization. They can subscribe to electronic journals, obtain paper versions, or obtain electronic separate copies for one or all classes of subscribers: the library, department collections, or individuals.

Site licenses can be constructed in a variety of ways. They need to be written, however, so that all participants can gain. For example, one site-license option (among many) is to negotiate two basic charges: one large charge for unlimited access to the publisher's electronic journal database (i.e., an *availability charge*) and one smaller charge to cover *distribution* of the contents of the database by paper or electronic means. The availability charge would be used by the publishers to recover article and non-article processing costs and allocated support costs (see Chapter 12).[9] The distribution charge would recover both print and electronic distribution costs plus allocated support costs. One possible scheme to achieve this type of site license is detailed below:

- The license would cover all journals currently provided to the organization by the publisher, regardless of whether the library, organization, department, or any employee subscribes to the journal.

---

[8]It was suggested that the Copyright Clearance Center (CCC) should serve as an arbiter and facilitator in such negotiations, somewhat in the manner employed recently by Okerson (1999).
[9]Support costs would include a profit when appropriate.

- The library and publisher would establish the current subscription cost of all subscriptions to the publisher's journals in the organization.

- The first annual availability charge would be this current subscription amount less current distribution costs (i.e., the total number of subscriptions times a distribution amount, say, $25 to $35).

- Access to paper issues from any of the journals would be the reproduction, distribution, and allocated support costs (e.g., $25 times 1.15 or approximately $29 per annum). Any electronic access to currently purchased journals would be at cost. Electronic access to any other journals available from the publisher would be at a calculated cost per reading (plus allocated support costs, e.g., 35 percent).

- During the first year, each access to the articles would be counted electronically and used by the library to make decisions concerning future subscription vs. separate article access. It can also be used for future charges on a cost per reading basis.

- The publisher must agree to ensure future access to all the journals covered by the term of the agreement, thus permitting the library to discard all relevant paper issues.

This type of site license provides advantages to every participant. While libraries and their constituents pay nearly the same amount to publishers, they achieve considerable savings in storage and maintenance (e.g., approximately $70 per subscription) . They also save an estimated $1.48 per reading by avoiding current reshelving and photocopying costs (which for a frequently read journal can be as much as the subscription price). Libraries also save on interlibrary borrowing or document delivery costs from journals in the publisher's database that they did not purchase. Finally, the library has the option to retain certain current periodicals or department collections in paper. These savings far exceed any advantages they might have achieved from reduced electronic journal prices.

Publishers have the advantage of maintaining cash flow and retaining any cost savings they obtain from electronic publishing, plus they receive additional revenue from distribution of electronic article separates that were previously obtained outside of their control.

Readers benefit by having the choice of obtaining articles in paper or electronic versions, both at substantial savings in their time and to their parent organizations. In other words, by this kind of negotiation, publishers win, libraries win, readers win, and funding sources win. Such as an agreement, of course, may have downsides, but it is given to demonstrate the need to arrive at arrangements that can be beneficial to all participants in order to end the adverse effects of current pricing strategies.

RISKS IN PARALLEL JOURNAL PRICING

New pricing policies are fraught with risks and can be potentially damaging to the overall journal system. For example, in the last 30 years there have been several instances of pricing mistakes made when information services provided multiple services from a single database or common type of publication. Two prime examples involved pricing printed and online versions of abstracts and indexes, and pricing of paper and microform versions of National Technical Information Service (NTIS) documents (King 1977, 1982).

One medium can be priced high (e.g., paper documents) to force the market into using the other medium (i.e., microfiche), but at a sacrifice to the revenue stream from the one medium (paper) which has a legitimate niche. That is, both media are needed and should contribute to revenue. At NTIS in the early 1970s, unfortunately, they not only more than doubled the price of paper copies, but also reduced the price of on-demand microfiche below the cost to process requests. The strategy worked in shifting demand to microfiche, but at a considerable loss to NTIS.

A similar phenomenon existed with printed and online versions of abstracting and indexing (A&I) databases. In fact, from an economic cost and ease of use standpoint, each version served a useful purpose. Print versions were best for quick look-up, bibliographic verifications, and online for in-depth research into new areas. Yet, pricing strategies by some A&I services forced subscribers into online only, probably at a loss of revenue in the long run.

Parallel publishing of scientific journals run the same risk. However, maximum revenue and market satisfaction can be achieved, but only by seeking appropriate prices to both print and electronic subscriptions and separate article copies. It appears that "appropriate" prices would be to charge about $40 more for print subscriptions than electronic subscriptions and to strive for less than $5 surplus per article (and $10 to $15 total) for separate copies. This does not mean that price differentiation cannot take place, but rather that the appropriate prices hold for specific purchasers or within site license agreements.

ALTERNATE PRICING PROPOSALS

In the Introduction we suggested that a clear distinction needs to be made between publishers making information content available with appropriate attributes and the media used to gain access to the information (i.e., online, CD-ROM, and paper). Making the information available dominates publisher costs and usually a major portion of the price.[10] Improving information attributes such as quality normally increases cost by the same amount to both print and electronic versions. The distribution costs become insignificant between the two versions with a sufficient amount of reading (e.g., less than $1 per reading of a subscription read more than 25 times). This means that access attributes such as speed of delivery, ease of access, and browsibility become the motivating force in choosing between the two versions. Both versions have advantages to different scientists.

The distinction between availability and access is made because the availability costs and prices are what must be ultimately be addressed. Somehow publishers must receive enough revenue, at least in the aggregate, to recover these high costs. One way this has been done in the past is through page charges, mostly by scientific societies. Even though this practice is declining, some have suggested revisiting this method of compensating publishers for making information available (see, for example, *Florida Entomologist*—Thomas Walker, Ed. cited in *Nature*). The argument for this policy is that it avoids most of the "shifting of funds" that have led to spiralling prices. As mentioned earlier, the scientific journal system currently involves about $45 billion per annum. A substantial portion of the scientist's time (authoring and reading) and library budgets come from common sources. There is merit in taking the portion of library budgets devoted to paying for scientific journal subscriptions and directly funding the "availability" aspect of journal publication (and page charges is one way of doing this). Choices of journals in which to publish can be made on the basis of quality, speed of publishing, and so on. Libraries and individual scientists can then make more rational choices among print or electronic subscriptions or separate copies of articles. From a system economic standpoint, a great deal would be gained. One disadvantage, however, is that basic research funders would bear a larger burden because so much reading is done by scientists in industry with little revenue derived from this use. Yet, society would benefit because more use and, therefore, value would be derived from the basic research findings.

On another vein, Getz (1999) has suggested that readers be given personal debit accounts with their library to access separate copies of articles. This would permit scientists to order separate copies from services depending on attributes of

---

[10]The exception to this statement is when circulation of a print version is very high and reproduction and distribution costs dominate (see Chapter 12).

speed, image, quality, and accessibility that are provided at appropriate prices. This interesting notion, of course, can be extended to subscriptions in print or electronic media and other related services as well. Getz feels that such an account would end up serving users more effectively and relieve libraries from some clerical-like activities. The examples given involve academic libraries, but are even more feasible in a special library environment.

Bibliography

Abels, Eileen G. 1994. A new challenge for intermediary-client communication: The electronic network. *The Reference Librarian* 41/42: 185-96.

Abels, Eileen G., and Lois F. Lunin. eds. 1996. Perspectives on costs and pricing of library and information services in transition. *Journal of the American Society for Information Science* 47(3).

Abels, Eileen G., Paul B. Kantor, and Tefko Saracevic. 1996. Studying the cost and value of library and information services applying functional cost analysis to the library in transition. *Journal of the American Society for Information Science* 47(3): 217-27.

Ackoff, Russell L., T. A. Cowan, W. M. Sachs, M. L. Meditz, P. Davis, J. C. Emery, and M. C. J. Elton. 1976. *The SCATT Report: Designing a National Scientific and Technological Communication System.* Philadelphia: University of Pennsylvania Press.

Ackoff, Russell. 1967. *Choice, Communication, and Conflict.* Philadelphia: Management Service Center, University of Pennsylvania.

Aitchison, J. 1974. *Alternatives to the Scientific Periodical: A Review of Methods Reported in the Literature.* London: Office for Scientific and Technical Information.

Albritton, Everett C. 1965. *The Information Exchange Groups—An Experiment in Communication.* Presentation to the Institute on Advances in Biomedical Communication. 9 March American University and George Washington University, Washington, D.C.

Alexander, Adrian, and Julie S. Alexander. 1990. Intellectual property rights and the 'sacred engine': Scholarly publishing in the electronic age. In *Advances in Library Resource Sharing*, eds. Jennifer Cargill and Diane Graves, 176-92. Westport, Conn.: Mecklermedia. Out of print.

Alexander, Adrian, and Marilu Goodyear. 2000. BioOne: Changing the role of research libraries in scholarly communication. *Journal of Electronic Publishing* 5(3). Available from <http://www.press.umich.edu/jep/05-03/alexander.html>.

Allen, Bryce. 1995. Academic information services: A library management perspective. *Library Trends* 43(4): 645-62.

—. 1996. Information and measurement (book review). *Library Quarterly* 66(4): 482-83. Chicago: University of Chicago Press.

Allen, Thomas J. 1964. *The Utilization of Information Sources During R&D Proposal Preparation* Report No. 97-64. Cambridge: Sloan School of Management, Massachusetts Institute of Technology.

—. 1965. *Sources of Ideas and Their Effectiveness in Parallel R&D Projects.* Report No. 130-65. Research Program on the Management of Science and Technology. Cambridge: Massachusetts Institute of Technology.

—. 1966a. *Managing the Flow of Scientific and Technical Information.* Ph.D. diss., Massachusetts Institute of Technology, Cambridge.

—. 1966b. Studies of the problem solving process in engineering design. IEEE *Transactions on Engineering Management* 13(2): 72-83.

—. 1968. Organizational aspects of information flow in technology. ASLIB Proceedings, 20. Reprinted in *Key Papers in Information Science,* ed. Belver C. Griffith, 74-95. White Plains, N.Y.: Knowledge Industry Publications, 1980.

—. 1969. Information needs and uses. In *Annual Review of Information Science and Technology*, ed. Carlos A. Cuadra, vol. 4, 3-29. Chicago: Encyclopedia Brittanica.

—. 1970a. Roles in technical communication networks. In *Communication Among Scientists and Engineers*, 191-208. Lexington, Mass.: Heath Lexington Books.

—. 1970b. Communication networks in R&D laboratories. R&D Management, 1. Reprinted in *Key Papers in Information Science,* ed. Belver C. Griffith, 66-73. White Plains, N.Y.: Knowledge Industry Publications, 1980.

—. 1988. Distinguishing engineers from scientist. In *Managing Professionals in Innovative Organizations: A Collection of Readings*, 3-18. Cambridge, Mass.: Ballinger Publishing Co.

Allen, Thomas J., and Maurice P. Andrien, Jr. 1965. *Time Allocation Among Three Technical Information Channels by R&D engineers*. Cambridge: Massachusetts Institute of Technology.

Allen, Thomas J., and Stephen I. Cohen. 1969. Information flow in research and development laboratories. *Administrative Science Quarterly* 4: 12-19.

Allen, Thomas J. and Peter G. Gerstberger. 1964. *Criteria for Selection of an Information Source*. Cambridge: Massachusetts Institute of Technology.

Allen, Thomas J., A. Gerstenfeld, and Peter G. Gerstberger. 1968. *The Problem of Internal Consulting in R & D Organizations*. Working Paper, 319-68. Cambridge: Sloan School of Management, Massachusetts Institute of Technology.

Almquist, E. 1991. *An Examination of Work-Related Information Acquisitions and Usage Among Scientific, Technical and Medical Fields*. Faxon Institute 1991 Annual Conference: Creating Pathways to Electronic Information: Electronic Conferencing System; 28-30 April; Reston, VA. Westwood, Mass.: Faxon Institute for Advanced Studies in Scholarly and Scientific Communication.

Altbach, Philip G. 1989. Examining the conflicts. *The Journal of Academic Librarianship* 15(2): 71-72.

American Chemical Society. *Will Science Publishing Perish? The Paradox of Contemporary Science Journals*. Washington, D.C.: ACS Publications.

American Mathematical Society. 1992 *Survey of American Research Journals 1988-1992*.

American Psychological Association. 1965-1968. *Reports of the American Psychological Association's Project on Scientific Information Exchange in Psychology*. Vol. 1 Overview Report and Reports 1-9, 1965; Vol. 2 Reports 10-15, 1966; Vol. 3 Reports 16-19, 1968. Washington, D.C.: American Psychological Association.

Amiran, Eyal, Elaine Orr, and John Unsworth. 1991. Refereed electronic journals and the future of scholarly publishing. *Advances in Library Automation and Networking* 4: 25-53.

Amiran, Eyal, John Unsworth, and C. Chaski. 1992. Networked academic publishing and the rhetorics of its reception. *The Centennial Review* 36(1): 43-58.

Amy, S. 1983. *Proposals for Project HERMES*. London: SCICON.

Anania, L., and R. J. Soloman. 1997. Flat — The minimalist price. In *Internet Economics*, eds. L. W. McKnight and J. P. Bailey, 91-118. Cambridge: The MIT Press.

Anderla, J. Georges, ed. 1974. *The Growth of Scientific and Technical Information: A Challenge*. Meeting held in Washington, D.C. by the National Science Foundation, Office of Science Information Service.

—. 1985. *Information in 1985: A Forecasting Study of Information Needs and Resources*. Paris: Organization for Economic Cooperation and Development.

Anderson, G. 1993. Virtual qualities for electronic publishing. In *The Virtual Library*, ed. Laverna Saunders, 87-109. Westport, Conn.: Mecklermedia.

Anthony, L. J., H. East, and M. J. Slater. 1969. The Growth of literature in physics. *Reports of Progress in Physics* 32: 709-67.

Ardito, Stephanie C. 1996. Electronic copyright under siege. *Online* 20(5): 83-88.

Arms, William Y. 1992. Scholarly publishing on the national networks. *Scholarly Publishing* 23(3): 158-69.

Armstrong, C. J. 1995. The eye of the beholder. In *Electronic Information Delivery: Ensuring Quality and Value*, ed. Reva Basch, 221-44. Brookfield, Vt.: Gower Publishing.

Arnold, Kenneth. 1995. Virtual transformations: The evolution of publication media. *Library Trends* 43(4): 609-26.

Arnold, Stephen E. 1995. Information manufacturing: A historical view of quality engineering. In *Electronic Information Delivery: Ensuring Quality and Value*, ed. Reva Basch, 13-30. Brookfield, Vt.: Gower Publishing.

Arthur D. Little, Inc. 1981. *Electronic Document Delivery: The ARTEMIS Concept for Document Digitalization and Teletransmission*. Oxford: Learned Information.

Association of American Universities. 1979. *A National Strategy for Managing Scientific and Technical Information*. Washington, D.C.: Association of American Universities.

Association for Research Libraries. 1998. SPARC publisher partnership programs. Available from <http://www.arl.org/sparc>.

Astle, D. L. 1989. The scholarly journal: Whence or whither? *Journal of Academic Librarianship* 15: 151-156.

Auerbach Corp. 1965. *DOD User Needs Study, Phase I, Final Technical Report*: Vol. 2. 1151-TR-3. Philadelphia. Available from NTIS AD61 6501; AD 616502.

Badger, R., and M. Wallace. 1993. Electronic journals: The Red Sage approach. *Newsletter on Serials Pricing Issues* 91(2).

Bailey, Charles W., Jr. 1992. The coalition for networked information's acquisition-on-demand model: An exploration and critique. *Serials Review* 18(1/2): 78-81.

—. 1992. Network-based electronic serials. *Information Technology and Libraries* 11(1): 29-35.

—. 1998. *Scholarly Electronic Publishing Bibliography*. 22d ed. Houston: University of Houston Libraries.

Baker, N. R., J. Siegmann, and A. H. Rubenstein. 1967. The effects of perceived needs and means on the generation of ideas for industrial research and development projects. IEEE *Transactions on Engineering Management* 14.

Bamford, Harold E., Jr., and W. Savin. 1978. Electronic information exchange: The National Science Foundation's developing role. *Bulletin of the American Society for Information Science* 4(5): 12-13.

Barinova, Z. B., et al. 1979. Investigation of scientific journals as communication channels: Appraising the contribution of individual countries to the world scientific information flow. In *The Scientific Journal,* ed. A. J. Meadows, London: Aslib.

Barlow, John Perry. 1994. The economy of ideas: A framework for patents and copyrights in the digital age (Everything you know about intellectual property is wrong). *Wired* 2(3): 84-129.

Barnett, Michael P. 1965. *Computer Typesetting: Experiments and Prospects.* Cambridge: The MIT Press.

Barschall, H. H. 1992. Electronic version of printed journals. *Serials Review* 18(1/2): 49-51.

Baruch, J. J., and N. A. Bhagat. 1975. The IEEE Annals: An experiment in selective dissemination. *IEEE Transactions and Professional Communication* 18(3): 196-308.

Basch, Reva. 1995. *Electronic Information Delivery: Ensuring Quality and Value.* Brookfield, Vt.: Gower Publishing.

Basova, I. M., and I. F. Kuznetsova. 1979. The depositing of scientific papers. In *The Scientific Journal,* ed. A. J. Meadows, 256-68. London: Aslib.

Bayer, Alan E., and Gerald Jahoda. 1979. Background characteristics of industrial and academic users and nonusers of online bibliographic search services. *Online Review* 3(1): 95-105.

Beardsley, Charles W. 1972. Keeping on top of your field. IEEE *Spectrum* (December): 68-71.

Bennett, Scott. 1993. Copyright and innovation in electronic publishing: A commentary. *The Journal of Academic Librarianship* 19(2): 87-91.

—. 1994. The copyright challenge: Strengthening the public interest in the digital age. *Library Journal* 119(19): 34-37.

Berg, S. V. 1973. An economic analysis of the demand for scientific journals. *Journal of the American Society for Information Science* 23(1): 23-29.

Berghel, Hal, and Lawrence O'Gorman. 1996. Protecting ownership rights through digital watermarking. *Computer* 29(7): 101-03.

Bernard, Jessie, Charles W. Shilling, and Joe W. Tyson. 1963. Information communication among bioscientists. *Biological Sciences Communications Project.* Washington, D.C.: George Washington University; Part 1, 1963; Part 2, 1964.

Berge, Z.L., and M.P. Collins. 1996. IPCT Journal Readership Survey. *Journal of the American Society for Information Science* 47(9): 701-10.

Bernal, J.D. 1948. *Report on the Royal Society Scientific Information Conference.* London: Royal Society.

—. 1979. Provisional scheme for central distribution of scientific publications. In *The Scientific Journal,* ed. A. J. Meadows, 273-78. London: Aslib.

Beutler, Earl. 1995. Assuring data integrity and quality: A database producer's perspective. In *Electronic Information Delivery : Ensuring Quality and Value,* ed. Reva Basch, 59-87. Brookfield, Vt.: Gower Publishing.

Bever, Arley T. 1969. The duality of quick and archival communication. *Journal of Chemical Documentation* 9(3): 3-6.

Bichteler, Julie, and Ward Dederick. 1989. Information-seeking behavior of geoscientists. *Special Libraries* 80(3): 169-78.

Bickner, Robert E. 1983. Concepts of economic costs. In *Key Papers in the Economics of Information,* eds. Donald W. King, Nancy K. Roderer, and Harold A. Olsen, 107-46. New York: Knowledge Industry Publications.

Bishop, Ann Peterson. 1994. The role of computer networks in aerospace engineering. *Library Trends* 42(4): 694-729.

—. 1995. Scholarly journals on the Net: A reader's assessment. *Library Trends* 43(4): 544-70.

—. 1999. Document structure and digital libraries: How researchers mobilize information in journal articles. *Information Processing and Management* 35: 255-79.

Bishop, Ann Peterson, and Susan Leigh Star. 1996. Social informatics of digital library use and infrastructure. In *Annual Review of Information Science and Technology,* ed. Martha E. Williams, vol. 31, 301-401. Medford, N.J.: Information Today, Inc.

Blecic, Deborah D. 1999. Measurements of journal use: An analysis of the correlations between three methods. *Bulletin of the Medical Library Association* 87(1): 2026.

Borghuis, Marthyn, et al. 1999. *1996 TULIP Final Report.* New York: Elsevier Science.

Borgman, Christine L. 1989. All users of information retrieval systems are not created equal: An exploration into individual differences. *Information Processing & Management* 25(3): 237-51.

—. 1999. Books, bytes, and behavior: Rethinking scholarly communication for a global information infrastructure. In Is there a future for information research? ed. Tony Cawkel. *Information Services and Use* 19(2).

———. 2000. *From Gutenberg to the Global Information Infrastructure: Access to Information in the Networked Word.* Cambridge: The MIT Press.

Bosseau, Don. 1992. Confronting the influence of technology. *Journal of Academic Librarianship* 18: 302-03.

Bottoms, John W., and Linda W. Helgerson. 1988. Data conversion: The first step toward publishing on CD-ROM. In *The CD-ROM Handbook,* ed. Chris Sherman, 269-308. New York: Intertext Publications.

Bourne, Charles P., and Trudi Bellardo Hahn. 2000. *A History of the Early Online Industry and Technology.* Washington, D.C.: American Society for Information Science.

Bowden, Mary Ellen, Trudi Bellardo Hahn, and Robert V. Williams, eds. 1999. *Proceedings of the 1998 Conference on the History and Heritage of Science Information Systems.* Medford, N.J.: Information Today, Inc.

Bowen, D. H. M. 1979. Costs in selecting manuscripts. *Scholarly Publishing* 43-46.

Boyce, P. B., and H. Dalterio. 1996. Electronic publishing of scientific journals. *Physics Today* (January): 42-47.

Boyer, E.L. 1990. *Scholarship Reconsidered: Priorities of the Professoriate.* Princeton, N.J.: Carnegie Foundation for the Advancement of Teaching.

Brandao, C. 1996. Rewiring the ivory tower (Putting scholarly journals online). *Canadian Business Technology* Special Issue: 61-64M.

Branscomb, Anne Wells. 1986. *Accommodation of Intellectual Property Law to the Introduction of New Technologies.* Washington, D.C.: Office of Technology Assessment.

—. 1986. Law and culture in the information society. *Information Society* 4(4): 279-311.

—. 1988. Who owns creativity? Property rights in the information age. *Technology Review* 9(4): 38-46.

—. 1994. *Who Owns Information? From Privacy to Public Access.* New York: Basic Books, A Division of Harper Collins Publishers.

—. 1995. Public and private domains of information: Defining the legal boundaries. *Bulletin of the American Society for Information Science* 21(2): 14-18.

Braunstein, Yale M. 1985. Information as a factor of production: Substitutability and productivity. *Information Society* 3(3): 261-73.

Brichford, Maynard, and William Maher. 1995. Archival issues in networked electronic publications. *Library Trends* 43(4): 701-12.

Brinberg, Herbert R. 1989. Information economics: Valuing information. *Information Management Review* 4(3): 59-63.

Broadbent, Margaret. 1979. Standardization in production of journals: A black and white case? In *The Scientific Journal,* ed. A. J. Meadows, 71-72. London: Aslib.

Broadbent, Marianne, and Hans Lofgren. 1991. *Priorities, Performance, and Benefits: An Exploratory Study of Library and Information Units.* Melbourne, Australia: CIRCUIT and ACLIS.

Brock, William Hudson. 1992. *The Fontana History of Chemistry.* London: Fontana Press.

Brogan, M. 1979. Costs in copy editing. *Scholarly Publishing* 47-53.

Brown, Cecelia M. 1999. Information seeking behavior of scientists in the electronic information age: Astronomers, chemists, mathematicians, and physicists. *Journal of the American Society for Information Science* 50(10): 929-43.

Brown, David J., comp. 1996. *Electronic Publishing and Libraries: Planning for the Impact and Growth to 2003.* London; New Jersey: Bowker Saur.

Brown, Elizabeth W., and Andrea L. Duda. 1996. Electronic publishing programs in science and technology. Part 1: The journals. *Issues in Science and Technology Librarianship* (13). Available from <http://www.library.ucsb.edu/istl/96-fall/brown-duda.html>.

—. 1996. Electronic publishing programs: Issues to consider. *Issues in Science and Technology Librarianship* (13): Available from <http://www.library.ucsb.edu/istl/96-fall/brown-duda2.html>.

Brown, W. S., J. R. Pierce, and J. F. Traub. 1967. The future of scientific journals. *Science* 158: 1153-159.

Browning, John. 1993. Libraries without walls for books without pages. *Wired* 1(1): 62-110.

Brownrigg, Edwin. 1990. Developing the information superhighway. In *Library Perspectives on NREN: The National Research and Education Network,* ed. Carol A. Parkhurst, 55-63. Chicago: Library and Information Technology Association.

Bruwelheide, Janis H. 1995. *The copyright primer for librarians and educators* 2d ed. Chicago: American Library Association.

Buckland, Lawrence F. 1966. Problems of machine recording of textual information during scientific publication. In *Computer Applications in Scientific Publications: Transcript of Proceedings of the Information Systems Colloquium.* Washington, D.C.: National Science Foundation.

Buckland, Michael K. 1992. Emanuel Goldberg, electronic document retrieval, and Vannevar Bush's message. *Journal of the American Society for Information Science* 43(4): 284-94.

———. 1997. What is a document? *Journal of the American Society for Information Science* 48(9): 804-09.

Budd, John. 1988. Publication in library and information science: The state of the literature. *Library Journal* 113(14): 125-31.

Budd, John M., and Lynn Silipigni Connaway. 1997. University faculty and networked information: Results of a survey. *Journal of the American Society for Information Science* 48(9): 843-52.

Busch, Joseph A. 1994. Thinking ambigiously: Organizing source materials for historical research. In *Challenges in Indexing Electronic Text and Images,* eds. Raya Fidel, Trudi Bellardo Hahn, Edie M. Rasmussen, and Philip J. Smith, 23-55. Medford, N.J.: Learned Information, Inc.

Bush, Vannevar. 1945. As we may think. *Atlantic Monthly* 176(1): 101-08.

Butler, Brett. 1992. Electronic editions of serials: The virtual library model. *Serials Review* 102-06.

Butler, Declan. 1999. The writing is on the web for science journals in print. *Nature* 397: 195-200.

Butler, H. Julene. 1995. Where does scholarly electronic publishing get you? *Journal of Scholarly Publishing* 26(4): 174-86.

Butler, Meredith A., and Bruce R. Kingma, eds. 1996. *The Economics of Information in the Networked Enviroment.* Washington, D.C. Association for Research Libraries.

Buxton, A. B., and Arthur Jack Meadows. 1978. Categorization of the information in experimental papers and their author abstracts. *Journal of Research Communication Studies* 1(2): 161-82.

Campanario, Juan Miguel. 1996. The competition for journal space among referees and other authors and its influence on journals' impact factors. *Journal of the American Society for Information Science* 47(3): 184-92.

———. 1998a. Peer review for journals as it stands today-Part 1.*Science Communication* 19 (3): 181-211.

—. 1998b. Peer review for journals as it stands today-Part 2. *Science Communication* 19 (4): 277-306.

Campbell, Jerry D. 1995. Intellectual property in a networked world: Balancing fair use and commercial interests. *Library Acquisitions: Practice and Theory.* 19(2): 179-84.

Campbell, David T. H., and Jane Edmisten. 1964. *Characteristics of Professional Scientific Journals.* Washington, D.C.: Herner and Company. Available from NTIS: PB 166 088.

Carrigan, Dennis. 1993. From interlibrary lending to document delivery: The British Library Document Supply Centre. *The Journal of Academic Librarianship* 19(4): 220-24.

—. 1996. Commercial journal publishers and university libraries: Retrospect and prospect. *Journal of Scholarly Publishing* 27(4): 208-21.

Carter, Launor, Gordon Contley, John T. Rowell, Louise Schultz, Herbert R. Seiden, Everett Wallace, Richard Watson, and Ronald E. Wyllys. 1967. *National Document-Handling Systems for Science and Technology.* New York: Wiley.

Case, Donald. 1985. The personal computer: Missing links to the electronic journal. *Journal of the American Society for Information Science* 35(5): 309-13.

Cawkel, Tony, ed. 1999. Is there a future for information research? A Cranfield conference in honour of Jack Meadows. *Information Services and Use* 19(2).

Chakrabarti, Alok K., and Albert H. Rubenstein. 1976. Interorganization transfer of technology: A study of adoption of NASA innovations. IEEE *Transactions on Engineering Management* BM-23(1): 20-34.

Chakrabarti, Alok K., Stephen Feinman, and William Fuentevilla. 1983. Characteristics of sources, channels, and contents for scientific and technical information systems in industrial R&D. *IEEE Transactions on Engineering Management* EM-30(2).

Charles River Associates. 1978. *Development of a Model of the Demand for Scientific and Technical Information Services.* Cambridge, Mass.: Charles River Associates.

Chen, C. C. 1972. The use patterns of physics journals in a large academic library. *Journal of the American Society for Information Science* 23(4): 254-70.

Chen, Hsinchun, ed. 2000. Special Topic Issue: Digital Libraries: Part 1. *Journal of the American Society for the Information Science* 51(3).

—. 2000. Special Topic Issue: Digital Libraries: Part 2. *Journal of the American Society for the Information Science* 51(70).

Choo, Chun Wei, and Ethel Auster. 1993. Environmental scanning: Acquisition and use of information by managers. In *Annual Review of Information Science and Technology,* ed. Martha E. Williams, vol. 28, 279-314. Medford, N.J.: Learned Information, Inc.

Chressanthis, George A., and June D. Chressanthis. 1994. The determinants of library subscription prices of the top-ranked economics journals: An econometric analysis. *The Journal of Economic Education* 25(4): 367-82.

—. 1994. A general econometric model of the determinants of library subscription prices of scholarly journals: The role of exchange rate risk and other factors. *The Library Quarterly* 64(3): 270-93.

Chrzastowski, Tina E., and Brian M. Olesko.1997. Chemistry journal use and cost results of a longitudinal study. *LRTS* 41(2): 101-11.

Chu, H. 1994. E-mail in scientific communication. In *Fifteenth National Online Meeting*, -86. Medford, N. J.: Learned Information.

Chuang, J. S. I., and M. A. Sirbu. 1997. Network delivery of information goods: Optimal pricing of articles and subscriptions. In *Internet Publishing and Beyond: The Economics of Digital Information and Intellectual Property*, eds. S. D. Hurley, Brian Kahin, and Hal R. Varian. Cambridge: The MIT Press.

Cisler, Steve. 1992. Convergent electronic cultures. *Serials Review* 18(1/2): 55-57.

Clarke-Kraut, Karen Rebecca. 1993. *A Spreadsheet-Based Decision Model for the Choice of Indexing and Abstracting Data Delivery Option for Academic Libraries.* Ph.D. diss., University of Hawaii at Manoa.

Cleverdon, Cyril W., Jack Mills, and E. Michael Keen. 1966. *Factors determining the performance of indexing systems.* London: Aslib Cranfield Research Project.

Coffman, S., and P. Wiedensohler. 1993. *Fiscal Directory of Fee-based Research and Document Supply Services.* 4th ed. Chicago: American Library Association.

Collier, Harry. 1998. *The Electronic Publishing Maze: Strategies in the Electronic Publishing Industry.* Tetbury, Gloucestershire, England: Infonortics.

Cooper, Michael D. 1973. The economics of information. In *Annual Review of Information Science and Technology*, ed. Carlos A. Cuadra, vol. 8, 5-40. Washington, D.C.: American Society for Information Science.

Council on Library Resources. 1978. *A National Periodicals Center: Technical Development Plan.* Washington, D.C.: Council on Library Resources.

Council of Library Resources/American Association of Publishers. 1995. *Libraries and Publishers in the Scholarly Information Process.* Washington, D.C.: Council on Library and Information Resources.

Crane, Diana. 1969. Social structure in a group of scientists: A test of the invisible college'. *American Sociological Review* 34(3). Reprinted in *Key papers in information science,* ed. Belver C. Griffith, 10-27. White Plains, N.Y.: Knowledge Industry Publications, 1980.

—. 1971. Information needs and uses. In *Annual Review of Information Science and Technology*, ed. Carlos A. Cuadra, vol. 6, 3-39. Chicago: Encyclopedia Brittanica.

Crawford, Susan. 1971. Informal communication among scientists in sleep research. *Journal of American Society for Information Science* 22(5). Reprinted in *Key Papers in Information Science*, ed. Belver C. Griffith, 28-37. White Plains, N.Y.: Knowledge Industry Publications, 1980.

—.1978. Information needs and uses. In *Annual Review of Information Science and Technolog*, ed. Martha E Williams, vol. 13, 61-81. White Plains, N.Y.: Knowledge Industry Publications, Inc.

Crawford, Susan Y., Julie M. Hurd, and Ann C. Weller. 1996. *From Print to Electronic: The Transformation of Scientific Communication*. Medford, N.J.: Information Today, Inc.

Crews, Kenneth D., ed. 1999. Perspectives on copyright and fair-use guidelines for education and libraries. *Journal of the American Society for Information Science* 50(14).

Cronin, Blaise, and Elisabeth Davenport. 1993. Social intelligence. In *Annual Review of Information Science and Technology*, ed. Martha E. Williams, vol. 28, 3-44. Medford, N.J.: Learned Information.

Cronin, Blaise, and Kara Overfelt. 1995. E-Journals and tenure. *Journal of the American Society for Information Science* 46(9): 700-03.

Crossing the Border from Print to Online to . . .   1990. *NFAIS Newsletter* 32(1): 1-4.

Cummings, Anthony M. 1986. *The Economics of Research Libraries*. Washington, D.C.: Council on Research Libraries.

Cummings, Anthony M., Marcia L Witte, William G. Bowen, Laura O. Lazarus, and Richard H. Ekman. 1992. *University Libraries and Scholarly Communication: A Study Prepared for the Andrew W. Mellon Foundation*. The Association of Research Libraries for the Andrew W. Mellon Foundation.

Cunningham, Ann Marie, and Wendy Wicks, eds. 1993. *Three Views of the Internet*. NFAIS Report Series. Philadelphia: National Federation of Abstracting and Information Services.

Dannelly, Gay N. 1995. Resource sharing in the electronic era: Potentials and paradoxes. *Library Trends* 43(4): 663-78.

Daval, Nicola, and Patricia Brennan. 1994. *ARL statistics 1992-93: A Compilation of Statistics from the One Hundred and Nineteen Members of the Association of Research Libraries*. Washington, D.C.: Association of Research Libraries.

Daval, N., and A. Lichtenstein. 1987. ARL library data table totals. In *ARL Statistics 1985-86: A Compilation of Statistics from the One Hundred and Eighteen Members of the Association of Research Libraries*, comps., N. Daval and A. Lichtenstein, 27. Washington, D.C.: Association of Research Libraries.

Davenport, Elisabeth, and Blaise Cronin. 1990. Hypertext and the conduct of science. *The Journal of Documentation* 46(3): 175-92.

Davis, Richard M. 1975. *Technical Writing: Its Place in Engineering Curricula - a Survey of the Experience and Opinions of Prominent Engineers*. Wright-Patterson Air Force Base, Ohio: NTS ADA015906

Davis, R. A., and C. A. Bailey. 1964. *Bibliography of Use Studies*. Philadelphia: Graduate School of Library Science, Drexel Institute of Technology.

Day, Colin. 1995. Pricing electronic products. In *Filling the Pipeline and Paying the Piper: Proceedings of the 4th Symposium*, ed. Ann Okerson, 51-6. Washington, D.C.: Association of Research Libraries.

Day, R. A. 1973. Economics of printing. In *Economics of Scientific Publications*. Washington, D.C.: Council of Biological Editors.

DeGennaro, Richard. 1977. Escalating journal prices: Time to fight back. *American Libraries* 69-74.

DeLoughry, Thomas J., 1989. Scholarly journals in electronic form seen as means to speed pace of publication and promote dialogue. *The Chronicle of Higher Education* 35(28): A11, A16.

—. 1995. Copyright in cyberspace. *The Chronicle of Higher Education* 42(September 15): A22, A24.

Denning, Peter J. 1996. The ACM electronic publishing plan and interim copyright policies. *The Serials Librarian* 28(1/2): 57-62.

Denning, Peter J., and Bernard Rous. 1994. The ACM electronic publishing plan. ACM, Inc.

Dervin, Brenda, and Michael Nilan. 1986. Information needs and uses. In *Annual Review of Information Science and Technology*, ed. Martha E. Williams, vol. 21, 3-33. White Plains, N.Y.: Knowledge Industry Publications, Inc.

Doebler, Paul D. 1970. Publication and distribution of information. In *Annual Review of Information Science and Technology*, eds. Carlos A. Cuadra and Ann W. Luke, vol. 5, 223-57. Chicago: Encyclopedia Britannica.

Dosa, Marta, Mona Farid, and Pal Vasarhelyi. 1988. *From Informal Gatekeeper to Information Counselor: Emergence of a New Professional Role.* Syracuse: School of Information Studies, Syracuse University; 1988. 87p.

Drabenstott, Karen M. 1994. *Analytical Review of the Library of the Future.* Washington, D.C.: Council on Library Resources.

Drake, Miriam A., 1990. What became of the paperless library? *NFAIS Newsletter* 32(1): 4-5.

—. 1992. Buying articles in the future. *Serials Review* 18(1/2): 75-77.

Dubinskaya,S. A. 1967. Investigation of information service needs of chemical specialists. *Nauchno-Tekhnicheskaya Informatsiya* 2(n4): 3-6.

Duggan, Mary Kay. 1991. Copyright of electronic information: issues and questions. *Online* 15(3): 20-26.

Economic Consulting Services, Inc. 1989. A study of trends in average prices and costs of certain serials over time. In *Report of the ARL Serials Prices Project*, 1-43. Washington, D.C.: Association of Research Libraries.

Edwards, Paul N. 1999. Personal communication.

Elias, Arthur W. 1992. *The NFAIS Yearbook of the Information Industry 1992.* Medford, N.J.: Learned Information, Inc.

—. 1993. *The NFAIS Yearbook of the Information Industry 1993.* Medford, N.J.: Learned Information, Inc.

Elias, Arthur W., and Betty Unruh. 1990. *Economies of database production.* NFAIS Report Series, vol. 1. Philadelphia: National Federation of Abstracting and Information Services.

Elliott, Carolyn S. 1994. NREN update, 1993: Washington policy. *The Reference Librarian* (41/42): 237-59.

Elsdon-Dew, R. 1955. The library from the point of view of the research worker. *South African Libraries* 23: 51-54.

Englebart, Douglas C. 1970. Coordinated information service for a discipline — Or mission-oriented community. In *Time sharing: Past, Present, and Future: Second Annual Computer Communications Conference.* Association of Computing Machinery.

Ensor, Pat, and Thomas Wilson, eds. 1990-. *The Public-Access Computer Systems Review (The PACS Review).* Houston: University of Houston Libraries. Founded by Charles W. Bailey who was editor-in-chief through 1996.

Entlich, Richard, Lorrin Garson, Michael Lesk, Lorraine Normore, Jan Olsen, and Stuart Weibel. 1997. Making a digital library: The contents of the CORE project. *ACM Transactions on Information Systems* 15(2): 103-23.

—. 1996. Testing a digital library: User response to the CORE project. *Library Hi Tech* 14(4): 99-118.

Ernst and Young and LLP Magazine Publishers of America. 1997. *Magazine publishers and the business of online publishing.*

Esler, Sandra L., and Michael L. Nelson. 1998. Evolution of scientific and technical information distribution. *Journal of American Society for Information Science* 49(1).

Ettlie, John E. 1976. The timing and sources of information for the adoption and implementation of production innovations. IEEE *Transactions on Engineering Management* 23(1): 62-68.

Feldman, Susan. n.d. *Computational science. Digital Library Project Final Report: Recommendations.* Ithaca, N.Y.: Datasearch.

Final Report, President's Task Force on the Value of the Information Professional. 1987. Washington, D.C.: Special Libraries Association.

Finnigan, Georgia. 1994. Conversation with Williams, J.

—. 1994. Conversation with Dean, N.

—. 1994. Conversation with Fishel, M.

—. 1994. Conversation with Rugge, S.

—. 1995. The rise of value-added document delivery services. In *Document Delivery in an Electronic Age,* ed. Dick Kaser. Philadelphia: National Federation of Abstracting and Indexing Services.

Fisher, Janet. 1994. Chicago journal of theoretical computer science. *Newsletter on Serials Pricing Issues* 104, paper no. 104.3.

—. 1994. 2020: A publisher's view into the crystal ball. *The Serials Librarian* 24(3/4): 69-72.

—. 1995. The true costs of an electronic journal. *Serials Review* 21(1): 88-90.

Flanagin, A., R. M. Glass, and G. D Lundberg. 1992. Electronic journals and duplicate publication: Is a byte a word? *The Journal of the American Medical Association* 267(17): 2374.

Fletcher, Lloyd Alan. 1996. The new economics of online. *SEARCHER: The Magazine for Database Professionals* 4(5): 30-44.

Florentine, Harry. 1979. Subscription fulfillment. In *The Scientific Journal*, ed. A. J. Meadows, 56-58. London: Aslib.

Flowers, B.H. 1965. Survey of information needs of physicists and chemists. *Journal of Documentation* 21(2): 83-112.

Fox, Edward A. ed. 1999. The digital libraries initiative: Update and discussion. *Bulletin of the American Society of Information Science* 26(1).

Fox, Edward A., Robert M. Akscyn, Richard K. Furuta, and John J. Leggett, eds. 1995. Digital Libraries. *Communications of the ACM* 38(4).

Fox, Edward A., and Lois F. Lunin, eds. 1993. Perspectives on digital libraries. *Journal of American Society for Information Science* 44(8).

Franks, John. 1993. The impact of electronic publication on scholarly journals. *Notices of the American Mathematical Society* 40(9): 1200-202.

Frazier, Kenneth. 1995. Protecting copyright and preserving fair use in the electronic future. *The Chronicle of Higher Education* 41(June 30): A40.

Friend, Frederick. 2000. Keeping your head in a revolution. *Journal of Electronic Publishing* 5(3). Available from <http://www.press.umich.edu/jep/05-03/friend.html>.

Frost, Penelope A., and Richard Whitley. 1971. Communication patterns in a research laboratory. *R&D Management* 1: 71-79.

Fry, B. M., and H. S. White. 1976. *Publishers and Libraries: A Study of Scholarly and Research Journals*. Lexington, Mass.: Lexington Books.

Fuller, Steve. 1995a. Cyberplatonism: An inadequate constitution for the republic of science. *The Information Society* 11: 293-303.

—.1995b. Cybermaterialism, or why there is no free lunch in cyberspace. *The Information Society* 11(4): 325-32.

Fuseler, Elizabeth A. 1994. Providing access to journals—just in time or just in case? *College & Research Libraries News* no. 3 (March): 130-132, 148.

Gaines, Brian R. 1993. An agenda for digital journals: The socio-technical infrastructure of knowledge dissemination. *Journal of Organizational Computing* 3(2): 135-93.

Gannett, Elwood K. 1973. Primary publication systems and services. In *Annual Review of Information Science and Technolog,* eds. Carlos A. Cuadra and Ann W. Luke, vol. 8, 243-75. Washington, D.C.: American Society for Information Science.

Garcia, D. Linda. 1990. Information exchange: The impact of scholarly communication. *EDUCOM Review* 25(3): 28-32.

Garcia, J. J. E. 1994. Can there be texts without audiences? The identity and function of audiences. *Review of Metaphysics* 47(4): 711-35.

Gardner, William. 1990. The electronic archive: Scientific publishing for the 1990s. *Psychological Science* 1(6): 333-41.

Garrett, John R., and M. Stuart Lynn. 1994. Storerights, access rights, and copyright law: The base of the iceberg. *Serials Review* 20(4): 15-6.

Garrison, F. H. 1934. The medical and scientific periodicals of the seventeenth and eighteenth centuries. *Bulletin of the History of Medicine, Johns Hopkins University* 2(5): 285-341.

Garson, Lorrin R. 1996. Can e-journals save us? — A publisher's view. In *The Economics of Information in The Networked Environment*, eds. M.A. Butler and B. R. Kingma, 115-21. Washington, D.C.: Association of Research Libraries.

Garvey, William D., ed. 1979. *Communication: The Essence of Science.* Oxford: Pergamon Press.

Garvey, William D., and Bertita E. Compton. 1967. The flood and how to survive it. *The Johns Hopkins Magazine* 3.

Garvey, William D., and S. D. Gottfreddson. 1975. Scientific communication as an interactive social process: *U.S./U.S.S.R. Symposium held at Yale University.* Washington, D.C., National Science Foundation.

Garvey, William D., and Belver C. Griffith. 1963. *The American Psychological Association's Project on Scientific Information Exchange in Psychology.* Report No. 9. Washington, D.C.: American Psychological Association.

—.1971. Scientific communication: Its role in the conduct of research and creation of knowledge. *American Psychologist* 26(4): 14. Reprinted in *Key Papers in Information Science*, ed. Belver C. Griffith, 38-51. White Plains, N.Y.: Knowledge Industry Publications, 1980.

—. 1972. Communication and information processing within scientfic disciplines: Emperical findings for pyschology. *Information Storage and Retrieval* 5: 123-36.

Garvey, William D., Nan Lin, and Carnot E. Nelson. 1970. Communication in the physical and social sciences. *Science* 170(3963): 1166-73.

—.1979. Research studies in patterns of scientific communication: III. Information-exchange processes associated with the production of journal articles. In *The Scientific Journal*, ed. A. J. Meadows, 73-87. London: Aslib.

Garvey, William D., Nan Lin, and Kazuo Tomita. 1972. Research studies in patterns of scientific communication. III Information exchange processes associated with the production of journal articles. *Information Storage and Retrieval* 8: 207-21

Garvey, William D., Kazuo Tomita, and Patricia Woolf. 1974. The dynamic scientific-information user. In *Information Storage and Retrieval*, vol. 10, 115-31. Oxford; Elmsford, N.Y.: Pergamon Press.

Gasaway, Laura N. 1994. Copyright in the electronic era. *The Serials Librarian* 24(3/4): 153-62.

—. 1994. Serials 2020. *The Serials Librarian* 24(3/4): 63-67.

—. 1995. Scholarly publication and copyright in networked electronic publishing. *Library Trends* 43(4): 679-700.

Gasaway, Laura N., and James E. Rush. 1992-93. Protecting intellectual property. *Bulletin of the American Society for Information Science* 19(2): 11-15.

Gates, Y. 1983. User needs and technology options for electronic document delivery. *Aslib Proceedings* 35(4): 195-203.

Gerstberger, Peter G. and Thomas J. Allen. 1968. Criteria used by research and development engineers in the selection of an information source. *Journal of Applied Psychology* 52(4): 272-79.

—. 1971. *The Preservation and Transfer of Technology in Research and Development Organizations*. Ph.D. diss., Sloan School of Management, Massachusetts Institute of Technology, Cambridge.

Gerstenfeld, Arthur., and Paul Berger. 1980. An analysis of utilization differences for scientific and technical information. *Management Science* 26(2): 165-79.

Gerstl, J.E., and S.P. Hutton. 1966. *Engineers: The Anatomy of a Profession*. London; New York: Tavistock Publications.

Getz, Malcolm. 1991. Document Delivery. *Bottom Line* 5(4): 40-44.

—. 1992. Electronic publishing: An economic view. *Serials Review* 18(1/2): 25-31.

—. 1997. Evaluating digital strategies for storing and retrieving scholarly information. *Journal of Library Administration* 24: 81-98.

—. 1999a. Electronic publishing in academia: An economic perspective. *The Serials Librarian* 36(1/2): 263-300.

—. 1999b. Academic publishing: Networks and prices. In *ACRL Ninth National Conference*, 13-27. Detroit, Mich.

Gillespie, Robert G. 1994. Legislation and the NII. *Educom Review* 22-25.

Ginsparg, Paul. 1994. First steps towards electronic research communication. *Computers in Physics* 8(4): 390-96.

—. 1996. Winners and losers in the global research village. Available from <http://xxx. lanl.gov/blurb/pg96unesco.html>.

Givler, Peter, 1999. Scholarships waits to be reinvented. In Scholarly publishing in an electronic age: 8 views of the future. *Chronicle of Higher Education* 45 (June 25): B7.

Glaser, Edward, and Samuel H. Taylor. 1973. Factors influencing the success of applied research. *American Psychologist* 28(2). Reprinted in *Key Papers in Information Science*, ed. Belver C. Griffith, 96-102. White Plains, N.Y.: Knowledge Industry Publications, 1980.

Glueck, William F., and Lawrence R. Jauch. 1975. Sources of research ideas among productive scholars. *Journal of Higher Education* 46(1): 103-14.

GOGSIP Study Group, John Hopkins University. 1971. *Some Preliminary Results from a Survey of Graduate Students in Psychology*. Washington, D.C.: American Psychological Association.

Goodwin, H.B. 1959. Some thoughts on improved technical services. *Special Libraries* 50(9): 443-46

Goodyear, Marilu, and Jane Dodd. 1994. From the library of record to the library as gateway: An analysis of three electronic table-of-contents services. *Library Acquisitions: Practice and Theory* 18: 253-64.

Götze, Dietrich. 1995. Electronic journals—Market and technology. *Publishing Research Quarterly* 11(1): 3-20.

Gould, Constance C., and Karla Pearce. 1991 *Information Needs in the Sciences: An Assessment.* PRIMA (Program for Research Information Management). Mountain View, Calif.: Research Libraries Group, Inc.

Grajek, Susan. 1998. Annual University of Yale Medical Library survey. Available from <http://its.med.yale.edu/about_itsmed/research/index.html>.

Grant, Joan. 1964. *Information for Industry — A Study in Communications.* Pretoria, Republic of South Africa: Council for Scientific and Industrial Research.

Gray, Carolyn M. 1993. Building electronic bridges between scholars and information: New roles for librarians. In *Clinic on Library Applications of Data Processing*, 19-33. Urbana-Champaign: Graduate School of Library and Information Science, University of Illinois at Urbana-Champaign.

Green, Lois, and Susan T. Hill. 1974. *Survey of Authors, Reviewers, and Subscribers to Journals in the Life Sciences.* Editorial Processing Centers: A study to determine economic and technical feasibility. Westat, Inc. Report. Washington, D.C.: National Science Foundation. Available from dwking@umich.edu.

Green, Paul E., and Yoram Wind. 1975. New ways to measure consumers' judgments. *Harvard Business Review* 107-18.

Griffith, Belver C., and Nicholas Mullins. 1972. Coherent social groups in scientific change. *Science* 177(September 15). Reprinted in *Key Papers in Information Science,* ed. Belver C. Griffith, 52-57. White Plains, N.Y.: Knowledge Industry Publications, 1980.

Griffiths, José-Marie. 1982. The value of information and related systems, products, and services. In *Annual Review of Information Science and Technology,* ed. Martha E. Williams, vol. 17, 269-84. White Plains, N.Y.: Knowledge Industry Publications.

—.1994. Measures of economics of information and information economics. In *Changing Information Technologies: Research Challenges in the Economics of Information. The Third Information Research Conference,* eds. M. Feeney and M. Grieves, 95-122. London: Bowker Saur.

—. 1998. Why the Web is not a library. In *The Mirage of Continuity: Reconfiguring Academic Information Resources for the Twenty-first Century,* eds. Brian L. Hawkins and Patricia Battin, 229-46. Washington, D.C.: Council on Library and Information Resources and the Association of American Universities.

Griffiths, José-Marie, Bonnie C. Carroll, Donald W. King, Martha E. Williams, and Christine M. Sheetz. 1991. *Description of scientific and technical information in the United States: Current status and trends.* Knoxville: School of Information Sciences, University of Tennessee.

Griffiths, José-Marie, and Donald W. King. 1982. Alternative technologies and systems for distribution of separates. In *Proceedings of the Sixth International Online Information Meeting,* 83-89. Medford, N.J.: Learned Information.

—.1986. A study of library staffing. King Research Report. Long Beach: California State University, dwking@umich.edu.

—. 1991. *A Manual on the Evaluation of Information Centers and Services: NATO, AGARD.* New York: American Institute of Aeronautics and Astronautics.

—. 1993. *Special Libraries: Increasing the Information Edge,* Washington, D.C.: Special Libraries Association.

Grogan, D.J. 1982. *Science and Technology: An Introduction to the Literature.* 4th ed. London: Bingley.

Grossner, Kerry. 1991. Human networks in organizational information processing. In *Annual Review of Information Science and Technology,* ed. Martha E. Williams, vol. 26, 349-402. Medford, N.J.: Learned Information.

Grotenhuis, Albert J. te, and Selma J. Heijnekamp. 1995. The user pays: Cost billing in a company library. *Special Libraries* 86(2): 110-16.

Grycz, Czeslaw Jan. 1992. Economic models for networked information. *Serials Review* 18(1/2): 11-8.

Guédon, Jean-Claude. 1995. Research libraries and electronic scholarly journals: Challenges or opportunities? *The Serials Librarian* 26(3/4): 1-20.

—. 1996. The seminar, the encyclopedia, and the eco-museum as possible future forms of electronic publishing. In *Scholarly Publishing: The Electronic Frontier,* eds. Robin P. Peek and Gregory B. Newby, 71-101. Cambridge: The MIT Press.

Gupta, R.C. 1988. Skill development to assess information needs and seeking behavior. *Lucknow Librarian* 20(2): 52-8.

Gurnsey, J., ed. 1982. *Electronic publishing trends in the United States and Europe. Vol. III. Electronic Document Delivery,* ed. Oxford: Learned Information.

Gushee, David E. 1968. Reading behavior of chemists. *Journal of Chemical Documentation* 8(4): 191-94.

Guthrie, K.M. 1999. JSTOR: The development of a cost-driven, value-based pricing model. In *Technology and scholarly communication,* eds. R. Ekman and R.E. Quant, 133-144. University of California Press.

Hagstrom, Warren O. 1970. Factors related to the use of different modes of publishing research in four scientific fields. In *Communication Among Scientists and Engineers,* eds. Carnot E. Nelson and Donald K. Pollack, 85-124. Lexington, Mass.: D.C. Heath.

Halbert, Michael H., and Russell L. Ackoff. 1959. An operations research study of the dissemination of scientific information. In *International Conference on Scientific Information,* 87-120. Washington, D.C.: National Academy of Sciences, National Research Council.

Hall, Angela M., P. Clague, and T. M. Aitchison. 1972. *The Effect of the Use of an SDI Service on the Information-Gathering Habits of Scientists and Technologists.* London: The Institution of Electrical Engineers.

Hallgren, M. M., and A. K. McAdams. 1997. The economic efficiency of Internet public goods. In *Internet Economics,* eds. L. W. McKnight and J. P. Bailey, 455-78. Cambridge: The MIT Press.

Hallmark, Julie. 1994. Scientists' access and retrieval of references cited in their recent journal articles. *College & Research Libraries* 55(3): 199-209.

Halvorson, T. R. 1995. Selected aspects of legal liabilities of independent information professionals. In *ElectronicInformation Delivery: Ensuring Quality and Value,* ed. Reva Basch, 171-87. Brookfield, Vt.: Gower Publishing.

Hammer, Donald P. 1967. National information issues and trends. In *Annual Review of Information Science and Technology,* ed. Carlos A. Cuadra, vol. 2, 385-417. New York: Interscience Publishers.

Harnad, Stevan. 1990. Scholarly skywriting and the prepublication continuum of scientific inquiry. *Pscyhological Science* 1: 342-44.

—. 1991. Post-Gutenberg galaxy: The fourth revolution in the means of production of knowledge. *The Public-Access Computer Systems Review* 2(1): 39-53.

—. 1992. Interactive publication: Extending the american physical Society's discipline-specific model for electronic publishing. *Serials Review* 18(1/2): 58-61.

—. 1995. Sorting the esoterica from the exoterica: There's plenty of room in cyberspace. A response to Fuller. *The Information Society* 11(4): 305-24. Available from http://cogsci.soton.ac.uk/~harnad/THES/harful.html>.

—. 1996. Implementing peer review on the Net: Scientific quality control in scholarly electronic journals. In *Scholarly Publishing: The Electronic Frontier,* eds. Robin P. Peek and Gregory B. Newby, 103-18. Cambridge: The MIT Press.

—.1998. On-line Journals and Financial Fire-walls. *Nature* 395: 127-128

Harnad, Stevan, and M. Hemus. 1997. All-or-none: No stable hybrid or half-way solutions for launching the learned periodical literature into the PostGutenberg Galaxy. In *The Impact of Electronic Publishing on the Academic Community,* ed. I. Butterworth, London: Portland Press: 18-27.

Harrison, Teresa M., and Timothy D. Stephen. 1995. The electronic journal as the heart of an online scholarly community. *Library Trends* 43(4): 592-608.

Harrison, Teresa M., Timothy D. Stephen, and James Winter. 1991. Online journals: Disciplinary designs for electronic scholarship. *The Public-Access Computer Systems Review* 2(1): 25-38.

Harter, Stephen P. 1996. The impact of electronic journals on scholarly communication: A citation analysis. *The Public-Access Computer Systems Review* 7(5): 5-34.

—. 1998. Scholarly communication and electronic journals: An impact study. *Journal of the American Society for Information Science* 49: 507-16.

Harter, Stephen P., and Hak Joon Kim. 1996. Accessing electronic journals and other e-publications: An empirical study. *College & Research Libraries* 57(5): 440-456.

Hauptman, R., and S. Motin. 1994. The internet, cybernetics, and virtual morality. *Online* 18(2): 8-9.

Hawkins, Brian L. 1998. The unsustainability of the traditional library and the threat to higher education. In *The Mirage of Continuity: Reconfiguring Academic Resources for the 21st Century,* eds. Brian L. Hawkins and Patricia Battin, 129-53. Washington, D.C.: Council on Library and Information Resources and the Association of American Universities.

Hawkins, Brian L., and Patricia Battin, eds. 1998. *The Mirage of Continuity: Reconfiguring Academic Information Resources for the 21st Century.* Washington, D.C.: Council on Library and Information Resources and the Association of American Universities.

Hawkins, Donald T. 1992. Forces shaping the electronic publishing industry of the 1990s. *Electronic Networking* 2: 38-60.

Hayes, Brian. 1996. The economic quandary of the network publisher. In *Scholarly Publishing: The Electronic Frontier,* eds. Robin P. Peek and Gregory B. Newby, 121-32. Cambridge: The MIT Press.

Hayes, J.R. 1995 The Internet's first victim? *Forbes* (December) 200-01.

Hayes, Robert M., and T. Erickson. 1982. Added value as a function of purchasing information services. *Information Society* 1(4): 307-38.

Hazell, J.C., and J.N. Potter. 1968. Information practices of agricultural scientists. *Australian Library Journal* 17(5): 147-59.

Hazen, Dan C. 1992. Is money the issue? Research resources and our collections crisis. *Journal of Academic Librarianship* vol.? 13-15.

Heller, Stephen. 1997. *Proceedings of the 1997 Chemical Information Conference* 17-26. Tetbury: Infornortics.

Henderson, Albert. 1998/99. Should authors pay publishers? The desperation of the new paradigm. *Publishing Research Quarterly* (Winter): 3-8.

—. 1999. Information science and information policy: The use of constant dollars and other indicators to manage research investments. *Journal of the American Society for Information Science* 50(4): 366-79.

Henderson, Madeline B. 1999. A retrospective review of early information retrieval systems. In *The proceedings of the 1998 Conference on the History and Heritage of Science-Information Systems,* eds. Mary Ellen Bowden, Trudi Bellardo Hahn and Robert V. Williams. Medford, N.J.: Information Today, Inc.

Henderson, Tona. 1994. MOOving towards a virtual reference service. *The Reference Librarian* 41/42: 173-84.

Herner, Saul. 1959. The information-gathering habits of american medical scientists. In *Proceedings of the International Conference on Scientific Information,* vol. 1; 1958 November 16-21; Washington, D.C. Washington, D.C.: National Academy of Sciences, National Research Council; 1959. 277-85.

Herner, Saul, and Mary Herner. 1967. Information needs and uses. In *Annual Review of Information Science and Technology*, ed. Carlos A. Cuadra, vol. 2, 1-34. New York: John Wiley & Sons, Interscience Publishers.

Hernon, Peter, and Charles R. McClure. 1993. Electronic U.S. government information: Policy issues and directions. In *Annual Review of Information Science and Technology*, ed. Martha E. Williams, vol. 28 , 45-110. Medford, N.J.: Learned Information.

Herschman, Arthur. 1970. The primary journal: Past, present, and future. *Journal of Chemical Documentation* 10(1): 37-42.

Hewins, Elizabeth T. 1990. Information Needs and Use Studies. In: Williams, Martha E., ed. *Annual Review of Information Science and Technology* vol. 25, 145-72. Amsterdam; New York: Elsevier Science Publishers.

Hickey, Thomas B. 1995. Present and future capabilities of the online journal. *Library Trends* 43(4): 528-43.

Hills, J. A. 1972. *A review of the literature on primary communications in science and technology*. London: Aslib.

Hills, Philip, ed. 1980. *The Future of the Printed Word: The Impact and the Implications of the New Communications Technology*. London: Francis Pinter.

—. 1983. The scholarly communication process. In *Annual Review of Information Science and Technology*, ed. Martha E.Williams, vol.18, 99-125. White Plains, N.Y.: Knowledge Industry Publications, Inc.

Hilz, Starr Roxanne, and Murray Turoff. 1978. The Networks Nation. Human Communication via Computer. Reading, Mass: Addison-wesley Publishing Company, Inc.

Hinrichs, J.R. 1964. Communications Activity of Industrial Personnel. *Personnel Psychology* 17: 193-204.

Hitchcock, Steve, Leslie Carr, and Wendy Hall. 1996. A survey of STM online journals 1990-1995: The calm before the storm. In *Directory of Electronic Journals, Newsletters and Academic Discussion Lists* ,6th ed., ed. Dru Mogge, 7-32. Washington, D.C.: Association of Research Libraries.

Hoban, Charles F. 1967. *Survey of Professional Journals in Field of Public Communication, Including New Media of Education*. Philadelphia: University of Philadelphia.

Hoffert, Barbara. 1994. The encyclopedia wars. *Library Journal* 119(14): 142-45.

Holder, Steve. 1988. The new Gutenbergs. In *The CD-ROM Handbook*, ed. Chris Sherman, 51-76. New York: Intertext Publications.

Holland, Maurita P., Thomas E. Pinelli, Rebecca O. Barclay, and John M. Kennedy. 1991. *Engineers as Information Processors: A Survey of U.S. Aerospace Engineering Faculty and Students* Paper 20. Available from NTIS: 92N28155. Reprinted from *European Journal of Engineering Education*. 16(4): 317-36.

Holland, Maurita Peterson, and Christina Kelleher Powell. 1995. A longitudinal survey of the information seeking and use habits of some engineers. *College & Research Libraries* 56: 7-15.

Holmes, Aldyth. 1997. Electronic publishing in science: Reality check. *Canadian Journal of Communication* 22(3/4) (special issue): 105-16.

Horowitz, Irving Louis, and Mary E. Curtis. 1982. The impact of technology on scholarly publishing. *Scholarly Publishing* 13(3): 211-28.

—. 1994. Politics and publishing in a democratic society: Technical breakthroughs and research agendas. *Publishing Research Quarterly* 10(3): 22-30.

Houghton, Bernard. 1975. *Scientific Periodicals: Their Historical Development, Characteristics and Control.* Hamden, Conn.: Linnet Books & Clive Bingley.

Hudnut, Sophie K. 1995. Standardizing online information: An impossibility? In *Electronic Information Delivery: Ensuring Quality and Value*, ed. Reva Basch, 31-45. Brookfield, Vt.: Gower Publishing.

Hunter, Karen. 1990. A publisher's perspective. *Library Acquisitions: Practice and Theory* 14: 5-13.

—. 1993. An electronic field of dreams: Journal publishing and the Internet. *In Three Views of the Internet*, eds. Ann Marie Cunningham and Wendy Wicks, 33-52. Philadelphia: National Federation of Indexing and Abstracting Services.

Huth, Edward J. 1989. The Underused Medical Literature. *Annuals of Internal Medicine* 110(2): 99-100.

Institute of Physics. 1976. *Author/subscribers survey: Summary of results.* Bristol, England: The Institute of Physics.

Jackson, Mary E. 1997. Measuring the performance of interlibrary loan and document delivery services. *ARL: A Bimonthly Newsletter of Research Library Issues and Actions* 195: 1-3.

Jacob, M. E. L. 1993. New technology, new tools, new librarians: Shaping the future. In *Designing Information: New Roles for Librarians*, 204-11. Urbana-Champaign. Graduate School of Library and Information Science, University of Illinois at Urbana-Champaign.

Jacobson, Robert L. 1995. Publishers and the net. *Chronicle of Higher Education* 41(41): A17-A18.

—. 1995. Research universities consider plan to distribute scholarly work online. *The Chronicle of Higher Education* 42 (November 3): A32.

Jacso, Peter. 1995. Testing the quality of CD-ROM databases. In *Electronic Information Delivery: Ensuring Quality and Value,* ed. Reva Basch, 141-68. Brookfield, Vt.: Gower Publishing.

John, Nancy R. 1996. Putting content on the Internet: The library's role as creator of electronic information. *First Monday* 1(2). Available from <http://www.firstmonday.dk/issues/issue2/content/index.html>.

Johnson, Richard M. 1974. Trade-off analysis of consumer values. *Journal of Marketing Research* 11: 121-27.

Johnston, Ron, and Michael Gibbon. 1975. Characteristics of information usage in technological invention. IEEE *Transactions on Engineering Management.* EM-22(1): 27-34.

Jones, Paul E., Vincent E. Giuliano, and Robert M. Curtice. 1967a. Selected collection statistics and data analyses. *Papers on automatic language processing.* Arthur D. Little. Available from NTIS: AD649 037.

—. 1967b. Linear models for associative retrieval. *Papers on automatic language processing.* Arthur D. Little. Available from NTIS: AD649 038.

—.1967c. Development of string indexing techniques. *Papers on automatic language processing.* Arthur D. Little. Available from NTIS: AD649 039.

Jonscher, Charles. 1983. Information resources and economic productivity. *Information Economics and Policy* 1(1): 13-35.

Judson, H. F. 1994. Structural transformations of the sciences and the end of peer review. *The Journal of the American Medical Association* 272(2): 92-4.

Jul, Erik. 1992. Of barriers and breakthroughs. *Computers in Libraries* 12(3): 20-2.

—. 1992. Present at the beginning. *Computers in Libraries* 12(4): 44-6.

Kahin, Brian. 1994. A cooperative framework for enhancing research communication in science and technology. *Serials Review* 20(4): 17-20.

—. 1994. The copyright law: How it works and new issues in electronic settings. *The Serials Librarian* 24(3/4): 163-72.

Kahn, Robert. 1992. National information infrastructure components. *Serials Review* 13(1/2): 85-7.

Kantor, Paul B. and Tefko Saracevic. 1999. *Valuing Special Libraries and Information Services.* Alexander Project Laboratory, Rutgers University Report. Washington, D.C.: Special Libraries Association.

Kaplan, Jeremiah. 1993. For books, another brave new world. *Scholarly Publishing* 24(3): 157-60.

Kaser, Dick., ed. 1995 *Document delivery in an electronic age: A collection of views and viewpoints*. New Technologies and New Relationships. Philadelphia, PA: National Federation of Abstracting and Information Services.

Katz, Ralph and Michael Tushman. 1979. Communications patterns, project performances, and task characteristics: An emperical evaluation and integration in an R & D setting. *Organizational Behavior and Human Performance* 23(2): 139-62.

Katz, Richard N. 1992. Academic information management at the crossroads: Time again to review the economics. *Serials Review* 18(1/2): 41-4.

Katzen, May. 1977. *The Visual Impact of Scholarly Journal Articles: Report of a Feasibility Study to Isolate the Factors Which May Govern the Impact of Research Articles on Readers and to Outline a Methodology for Their Determination.* Leicester, UK: University of Leicester Primary Communications Research Centre.

Keenan, Stella. 1996. Target 2000. Electronicpublishing: A subvensive proposal, on even more subversive proposal, and a counter argument. *Online & CDROM Review* 20(2): 93-94.

Keenan, Stella, and Margaret Slater. 1967. *Results of a Survey on Current Awareness Methods Used by Physicists.* London; New York: Institute of Electrical Engineers; American Institute of Physics.

Keister, Lucinda H. 1994. User types and queries: Impact on image access systems. In *Challenges in Indexing Electronic Text and Images*, eds. Raya Fidel, Trudi Bellardo Hahn, Edie M. Rasmussen, and Philip J. Smith, Medford, N.J.: Learned Information.

Kendall, M. G. 1979. The bibliography of operational research. In *Aslib Reader*, 2d ed, eds. Peter Taylor, A. J. Meadows, and Ruth Riner, 151-6. London: Aslib.

Kent, A. J. 1980. Scientific and technical publishing in the 1980s. In *The Future of the Printed Word: The Impact and the Implications of the New Communications Technology*, ed. Philip Hills, 163-69. London: Frances Pinter.

Kent, A., K. L. Montgomery, J. Cohen, J. G. Williams, S. Bulick, R. Flynn, W. N. Sabar, and J. R. Kern. 1978. *A cost-benefit model of some critical library operations in terms of use of materials.* Pittsburgh: University of Pittsburgh Press.

Kessler, M. M. 1967. Some very general design considerations. In *TIP system report*, Appendix H. Cambridge: Massachusetts Institute of Technology.

Ketcham, Lee, and Kathleen Born. 1995. Serials vs. the dollar dilemma: Currency swings and rising costs play havoc with prices. *Library Journal* 120(7): 43-49.

Ketcham-Van Orsdel, Lee and Kathleen Born. 1998. E-Journals come of age: 38th Annual Peridical Prize Survey. *Library Journal* 123(7) 40–45.

Keyes, Alison M. 1995. The value of the special library: Review and analysis. *Special Libraries* 16: 172-81.

Kiernan, Vincent. 1997. University libraries debate the value of package deals on electronic journals. *The Chronicle of Higher Education* 44(3): A31-A33.

—. 1999a. Why do some electronic-only journals struggle, while others flourish? *Chronicle of Higher Education* 45(37): A25-A27.

—. 1999b. NIH Proceeds with On-Line Archive for Papers in the Life Sciences. Available from <http://chronicle.com/infotech>.

Killion, Vicki. 1994. Information resources for nursing research: The Sigma Theta Tau International Electronic Library and Online Journal. *Medical Reference Services Quarterly* 13(3): 1-17.

King, David. 1987. The contribution of hospital library information services to clinical care: A study in eight hospitals. *Bulletin of the Medical Library Association* 75(4): 291-301.

King, Donald W., ed. 1970. *Innovations in Communications* Springfield, Vir.: NTIS

—. 1977a. Some potential pitfalls in the economics of information products and services. *Bulletin of the American Society for Information Science* 3(5): 39,40.

—. 1977b. Systemic and economic interdependence in journal publication. *IEEE Transactions on Professional Communication* PC-20, no. 2.

—. 1979. Total cost of communicating scientific and technical information. In *The Scientific Journal*, ed. A. J. Meadows, 29-49. London: Aslib.

—. 1980. Electronic alternatives to paper-based publishing in science and technology. In *The Future of the Printed Word: The Impact and the Implications of the New Communications Technology*, ed. Philip Hills, 99-110. London: Frances Pinter.

—. 1981. Roadblocks to future ideal information transfer. In *Telecommunications and Libraries: A Primer for Librarians and Information Managers*. White Plains, N.Y.: Knowledge Industry Publications, Inc.

—. 1982. Marketing secondary information products and services. *Journal of the American Society for Information Science* 33(3): 168-74.

—. 1987. Testimony. *Report of the Registrar of Copyrights on the effects of 17 U.S.C. 108.* Washington, D.C.

—. 1998. Some economic aspects of the Internet. *Journal of the American Society for Information Science* 49: 990-1002.

—. 1998. Some economic aspects of publishing scholarly jounrals on the Web. *NEWS-DIC: Newsletter of the European Association of Information Services* 138: 11-15.

King, Donald W., and Edward D. Bryant. 1971. *The Evaluation of Information Services and Products.* Washington, D.C.: Information Resources Press.

King, Donald W. with Jane Casto, and Heather Jones. 1994. *Communication by Engineers: A Literature Review of Engineers' Information Needs, Seeking Processes and Use.* Washington, D.C.: Council on Library Resources.

King, Donald W., Patricia M. Dowd-Reisin, R. Boyd Ladd, Dennis D. McDonald, Vernon E. Palmour, and Nancy K. Roderer. 1977. *Library Photocopying in the United States.* Washington, D.C.: U.S. Government Printing Office.

King, Donald W. and Jose'-Marie Griffiths. 1984. *UMI Article Clearinghouse Market Analysis.* King Research Report. Ann Arbor, Mich.: UMI (now Bell & Howell), dwking@umich.edu.

—. 1987. *Survey of Library Networks and Cooperative Library Organizations*: 1985-86. Washington, D.C.: U.S. Government Printing Office. cs 87-349c.

—. 1989. *Library Systems in New York State.* King Research Report. Albany: New York State Library, Division of Library Development, dwking@umich.edu.

—. 1990. *A Study of Interlibrary Loan and Reference Referral Services in the State of Arizona.* King Research Report. Phoenix: Arizona Department of Library, Archives, and Public Records, dwking@umich.edu.

—. 1991. *Massachusetts Libraries: An Alliance for the Future. 1. Executive Summary. 2. Final Report.* King Research Report. Boston: Massachusetts Board of Library Commissioners, dwking@umich.edu.

—. 1995. Economic issues concerning electronic publishing and distribution of scholarly articles. *Library Trends* 43(4): 713-40.

King, Donald W., José-Marie Griffiths, Ellen A. Sweet, and Robert R. V. Wiederkehr. 1984. *The Value of Libraries as an Intermediary Information Servi*ce. King Research Report. Office of Science and Technology Information and Washington, D.C.: U.S. Department of Energy, dwking@umich.edu.

King, Donald W., F. W. Lancaster, Dennis D. McDonald, Nancy K. Roderer, and Barbara L. Wood. 1976a. *Statistical Indicators of Scientific and Technical Communications (1960-1980): Vol. I. A Summary Report.* Washington, D.C. GPO 083-000-00295-3.

—. 1976b. *Statistical Indicators of Scientific and Technical Communications (1960-1980): Vol. II. A Research Report.*

King, Donald W., Dennis D. McDonald, and Candace H. Olsen. 1978. *A Survey of Readers, Subscribers, and Authors of the Journal of the National Cancer Institute*. Washington, D.C.: National Cancer Institute. Available from King Research, Inc., dwking@umich.edu.

King, Donald W., Dennis D. McDonald, and Nancy K. Roderer. 1981. *Scientific Journals in the United States: Their Production, Use, and Economics*. Stroudsburg, Penn.: Hutchinson Ross Publishing Company, dwking@umich.edu.

King, Donald W., Dennis D. McDonald, Nancy K. Roderer, Colleen G. Schell, Charles G. Schueller, and Barbara L. Wood. 1977. *Statistical Indicators of Scientific and Technical Information Communication (1960-1980)*. Washington, D.C.: U.S. Government Printing Office. Available from NTIS, PB 278-279.

King, Donald W., and Hugh V. O'Neill, eds. 1969. *Time-sharing Innovation for Operations Research and Decision Making*. Washington, D.C.: Washington Operations Research Council.

King, Donald W., and Vernon E. Palmour. 1974. User Behavior. In *Changing Patterns in Information Retrieval*, ed. Carol Fenichel, 7-33, Philadelphia: ASIS.

King, Donald W., and Nancy K. Roderer. 1978. *Systems Analysis of Scientific and Technical Communication in the United States: The Electronic Alternative to communication through paper-based journals*. Washington, D.C.: King Research. Available from NTIS PB 281-847.

—. 1981. The AIP journal system: Relationship of price, page charges, demand, cost, and income. In *AIP Function Planning*, Appendix B. New York: American Institute of Physics.

—. 1982. Communication in physics: The use of journals. *Physics Today* 35(10): 43, 45.

King, Donald W., Nancy K. Roderer, and Harold A. Olsen, eds. 1983. *Key Papers in the Economics of Information*. White Plains, N.Y.: Knowledge Industry Publications.

King, Donald W. and Carol Tenopir. 1998a. Electronic journal publishing: Economics of production, distribution, and use. In *Information networking bridge to the third millennium: Proceedings of the Pan American Congress on Health Sciences Information, Costa Rica, March 1998*.

—. 1998b. Economic cost models of scientific scholarly journals. In *Economics, Real Costs and Benefits of Electronic Publishing in Science—A Technical Study: Proceedings of the UCSU Press Workshop, Keble College, Oxford, UK March 31 to April 2, 1998*, eds. Dennis Shaw and David Price. Available from <http://www.bodley.ox.ac.uk/icsu/ kingppr.htm>.

—. 1999a. Electronic journal pricing: The dilemma, The opportunity. *NFAIS Newletter* 41(6): 85-90

—. 1999b. Evolving journal costs: Implications for publishers, libraries, and readers. *Learned Publishing (Journal of the Association of Learned & Professional Society Publishers, UK)* 12(4): 221-58.

—. 2000a. Scholarly journal & digital database pricing: Threat or opportunity? In *Proceedings of the Economics and Usage of Digital Library Collections Conference.* March 23-24, Ann Arbor, Mich. Available from <http://www.si.umich.edu/PBAK-2000/proceedings. htm>.

—. 2000b. Using and readings scholarly literature. *In Annual Review of Information Science and Technology,* ed. Martha E. Williams, vol. 34. Medford, N.J.: Information Today, Inc. In press.

King Research, Inc. 1977. *Library Photocopying in the United States: With Implications for the Development of a Copyright Royalty Payment Mechanism.* Washington, D.C.: U. S. Government Printing Office.

King, Timothy B. 1991. The impact of electronic and networking technologies on the delivery of scholarly information. *The Serials Librarian* 21(2/3): 5-13.

Kingma, B. R. 1995. *Economics of access versus ownership: The costs and benefits of access to scholarly articles via interlibrary loan and journal subscription.* Washington, D.C.: Council on Library Resources.

Kingma, Bruce. 1999. ACM: The economics of digital access: The early Canadiana online project. Available from <http://www.canadiana.org>.

Klemperer, Katharina. 1993. Delivering a variety of information in a networked environment. In *Designing Information: New Roles for Librarians,* 178-86. Urbana-Champaign, IL: Graduate School of Library and Information Science, University of Illinois at Urbana-Champaign. Paper presented at the 1992 Clinic on Library Applications of Data Processing, April 5-7, 1992.

Kling, Rob, and Roberta Lamb. 1996. Analyzing alternate visions of electronic publishing and digital libraries. In *Scholarly Publishing: The Electronic Frontier,* eds. Robin P. Peek and Gregory B. Newby, 17-54. Cambridge: The MIT Press.

Kling, Rob, and Geoffrey McKim. 1999. Scholarly communication and the continuum of electronic publishing. *Journal of the American Society for Information Science* 50(10): 890-906.

Kochen, M., and R. Tagliacozzo. 1974. Matching authors and readers of scientific papers. *Information Storage and Retrieval* 10: 197-210.

Koenig, Michael E. D. 1990. Information services and downstream productivity. In *Annual Review of Information Science and Technology,* ed. Martha E. Williams, vol. 25, 55-86. Amsterdam; New York: Elsevier Science Publications.

—. 1991. The information environment and the productivity of research. In *The Moin-treux 1991 International Chemical Information Conference*, 133-43. Annecy, France.

—. 1992. The importance of information services for productivity: Under-recognized and under-invested. *Special Libraries* 83(4): 199-210.

Koenig, Michael E. D., and Daniel J. Gans. 1975. The productivity of research effort in the U.S. pharmaceutical industry. *Research Policy* 4(4): 331-49.

Kost, Robert. 1992. Technology Giveth. *Serials Review* 18(1/2): 67-70.

Kovacs, Diane K., Kara L. Robinson, and Jeanne Dixon. 1995. Scholarly e-conferences on the academic networks: How library and information science professionals use them. *Journal of the American Society for Information Science* 46(4): 244-53.

Kovacs, Michael J., and Diane K. Kovacs. 1991. The state of scholarly electronic confer-encing. *Electronic Networking* 1(2): 29-36.

Krikeles, James. 1983. Information-seeking behavior: Patterns and concepts. *Drexel Library Quarterly* 19(2): 5-20.

Krockel, H. 1991. Advanced materials data systems for engineering. In *Scientific and Technical Data in a New Era*, ed. P. S. Cloeser. New York: Hemisphere.

Kronick, David A. 1976. *A History of Scientific and Technical Periodicals: The Origins and Development of the Scientific and Technological Press, 1665-1790*. 2d ed. Metuchen, N.J.: Scarecrow Press.

Kuhn, Thomas S. 1962. *The Structure of Scientific Revolutions*. Chicago: University of Chicago Press.

Kuney, Joseph H. 1965. Computers and scientific periodicals. In *Automation and Elec-tronics Publishing*, eds. Lowell H. Hattery and George P. Bash, 27-37. Washington, D.C.: Sparton Books.

—. 1966. Computer typesetting as input to information systems. In *International Com-puter Typesetting Conference*.

—. 1968. Publication and distribution of information. In *Annual Review of Information Science and Technology*, ed. Carlos A. Cuadra, vol. 3, 31-59. Chicago: Encyclopedia Bri-tannica.

Kurosman, Kathleen. 1994. Document delivery: A comparison of commercial docu-ment suppliers and interlibrary loan services. *College & Research Libraries* 55: 129-39.

Kutz, Myer. 1992. Distributing the costs of scholarly journals: Should readers con-tribute? *Serials Review* 18(1/2): 73-77.

Kvalnes, Florence H. 1999. The history of managing technical information at DuPont. In *The Proceedings of the 1998 Conference on the History and Heritage of Science Information Systems*. eds. Mary Ellen Bowden, Trudi Bellardo Hahn, and Robert V. Williams. Medford, N.J.: Information Today, Inc.

Kyrillidou, Martha, Kaylyn E. Hipps, and Kendon Stubbs, comp. 1995. *ARL statistics, 1993-94: A compilation of statistics from the one hundred and nineteen members of the Association of Research Libraries*. Washington, D.C.: Association of Research Libraries.

Ladendorf, Janice M. 1970. Information flow in science, technology and commerce: A review of the concepts of the sixties. *Special Libraries* 61(5): 215-22.

—. 1973. Information flow in science, technology and commerce: A review of the concepts of the sixties. In *Reader in Science Information*, eds. John Sherrod and Alfred Hodina, 70-75. New York: Microcard Edition Books.

Lago, Jane. 1993. A decade of electronic editing. *Scholarly Publishing* 24(1): 101-12.

Lambert, Jill. 1985. *Scientific and Technical Journals*. London: Clive Bingley.

Lancaster, F. W. 1978. *Toward Paperless Information Systems*. New York: Academic Press.

—. 1985. The paperless society revisited. *American Libraries* 16(8): 553-55.

—. 1989. Electronic publishing. *Library Trends* 37(3): 316-25.

—. 1995a. Attitudes in academia toward feasibility and desirability of networked scholarly publishing. *Library Trends* 43(4): 741-52.

—. 1995b. The evolution of electronic publishing. *Library Trends* 43(4): 518-27. Available from Mag Coll 79K3280 InfoTrac.

Lancaster, F.W., ed 1995. Networked scholarly publishing. *Library Trends* 43(4): 515-770

Lancaster, F. W., L. Drasgow, and E. Marks. 1980. *The Impact of a Paperless Society on the Research Library of the Future: A Report to the National Science Foundation*. Urbana, IL: University of Illinois, Graduate School of Information Science. Available from NTIS: PB80-204548.

Lancaster, F. W., Constance J. Gillespie. 1970. Design and evaluation of information Systems. In *Annual Review of Information Science and Technology*, ed. Carlos A.Cuadra, vol. 5, 33-70. Chicago: Encyclopaedia Brittanica.

Lancaster, F. W., and Donald W. King. 1998. A cost-benefit analysis of the library services at the Vienna International Center. Library Research Center, GSLIS, *University of Illinois Report*. Vienna: International Atomic Energy Agency.

Landau, Herbert B. 1969. Document Dissemination. In *Annual Review of Information Science and Technology,* ed. Carlos A. Cuadra, vol. 4, 229-70. Chicago: Encyclopedia Brittanica.

Landau, Robert M., ed. 1971. *Proceedings of the ASIS Workshop on Computer Composition.* Washington, D.C.: American Society for Information Science.

Langschied, Linda. 1992. Electronic journal forum: Column 1. *Serials Review* 18(1/2): 131-36.

—. 1994. Electronic journal forum: VPIEJ-L: An online discussion group for electronic journal publishing concerns. *Serials Review* 20(1): 89-80.

LaPorte, Ronald E., Eric Marler, Shunichi Akazawa, Francois Sauer, Carlos Gamboa, Chris Shenton, Caryle Glosser, Anthony Villasenor, and Malcolm Maclure. 1995. The death of biomedical journals. *British Medical Journal* 310: 1387-90.

Lawrence, Barbara. 1995. Application of TQM to the continuous improvement of database production. In *Electronic Information Delivery: Ensuring Quality and Value,* ed. Reva Basch, 69-87. Brookfield, Vt.: Gower Publishing.

Laws, Kenneth I. 1992. Net Journalism. *Serials Review* 18(1-2): 82-84.

Lazinger, S. S., J. Bar-Ilan, and B. C. Peritz. 1997. Internet use by faculty members in various disciplines. *Journal of the American Society for Information Science* 48: 508-18.

Lederberg, J. 1993. Communication as the root of scientific progress. *Current Contents* 1: 5-11.

Lee, Alfred T. 1996. *Reading electronic text.* Cupertino, Calif.: Beta Research.

Lehman, Bruce A. 1995. *Intellectual property and the national information infrastructure: The report of the Working Group on Intellectual Property Rights.* Washington, D.C.

Lenares, Deborah. 1999. Faculty use of electronic journals at research institutions. In Racing toward tomorrow. *Proceedings of the Ninth National Conference of the Association of College and Research Libraries,* ed. Hugh A. Thompson, 329-334. Chicago: Association of College and Research Libraries.

Lenzini, R. T., and W. Shaw. 1992. UnCover and UnCover 2: An article citation database and service featuring document delivery. *Interlending and Document Supply* 20(1): 12-15.

Lerner, Rita 1984. The professional society in a changing world. *Library Quarterly* 54(1): 36-47.

Lerner, Rita, Ted Metaxas, John T. Scott, Peter D. Adams, and Peggy Judd. 1983. Primary publication systems and scientific text processing. In *Annual Review of Information Science and Technology,* ed. Martha E. Williams, vol. 18, 127-149. White Plains, N.Y.: Knowledge Industries, Inc.

Lesk, Michael. 1992. Pricing electronic information. *Serials Review* 18(1)-2: 38-40.

—.1997. *Practical Digital Libraries: Books, Bytes, and Bucks.* The Morgan Kaufmann Series in Multimedia Information and Systems, ed. Edward Fox. San Francisco: Morgan Kaufmann Publishers.

Levine, Arthur, ed. 1990. *Global Copyright Issues in the Secondary Information Industry.* NFAIS Report Series, 4. Philadelphia: National Federation of Abstracting and Information Services.

Lewis, David W. 1988. Inventing the electronic university. *College & Research Libraries* 49(4): 291-304.

Libbey, Miles A., and Gerald Zaltman. 1967. *The Role and Distribution of Written and Information Communication in Theoretical High Energy Physics.* New York: American Institute of Physics.

Lichtenberg, James. 1995. Of steeds and stalking horses: Academics meet publishers on the field of copyright. *Educom Review* 30(3): 40-43.

Licklider, Joseph C. R. 1966. A crux in scientific and technical communication. *American Psychologist* 21: 1044-51.

—. 1967. Graphic input: A survey of techniques. In *Computer Graphics — Utility/Production/Art,* ed. Fred Gruenberger. Washington, D.C.: Thompson.

Licklider, Joseph C. R., and Robert Taylor. 1968. The computer as a communication device. *Science and Technology* (April 16).

Liebscher, P., Eileen Abels, and D. W. Denman. 1997. Factors that influence the use of electronic networks by science and engineering faculty at small institutions. Part II. Preliminary use indicators. *Journal of the American Society for Information Science* 48: 498-507.

Lin, Nan, and William Garvey. 1971. The formal communication structure in science. In *American Sociological Association Annual Meeting* Washington, D.C.: American Sociological Association.

—.1972. Information needs and uses. In *Annual Review of Information Science and Technology,* eds. Carlos A. Cuadra and Ann W. Luke, vol. 7, 5-37. Chicago: Encyclopedia Britannica.

Lin, Nan, William D. Garvey, and Carnot E. Nelson. 1970. A study of the communication structure of science. In *Communication Among Scientists and Engineers,* eds. Carnot E. Nelson and Donald K. Pollack, 23-60. Lexington, Mass.: D.C. Heath.

Lin, Nan, and Carnot E. Nelson. 1969. Bibliographic reference patterns in core sociological journals. 1965-1966. *The American Sociologist* 4(1): 47-50.

Line, Maurice B. 1971. The information uses and needs of social scientists: An overview of INFROSS. *Aslib Proceedings* 23(8): 412-34.

Lipetz, Ben-Ami. 1970. Information needs and uses. In *Annual Review of Information Science and Technology*, ed. Carlos A. Cuadra, vol. 5, 3-32. Chicago: Encyclopaedia Brittanica.

Liston, D. M., Donald W. King, Gail L. Kutner, and Ronald G. Havelock. 1985. Analysis of technology assistance available to small high-technology firms. King Research Report to Small Business Administration, dwking@umich.edu.

Little, S. B. 1989. The research and development process and its relationship to the evolution of scientific and technical literature: A model for teaching research. *The Technical Writing Teacher* 16: 68-76.

Login, Elisabeth, and Marvin Pollard, eds. 1997. Special topic issue: Structural information/standards for document architectures. *Journal of the American Society for Information Science* 48(7).

Lohmann, Victor L. 1969. How to identify the special reading needs of library users. *AHIL Quarterly* IX(2): 40-46.

Longuet-Higgins, H.C. 1970. The language of science. *Times Literary Supplement* (UK). May 7; 3558: 505-506.

Lorimer, Rowland, John H.V. Gilbert, and Ruth J. Patrick, eds. 1997. Scholarly communication in the millennium. *Canadian Journal of Communication* 22(3/4), special issue.

Lu, Kathleen. 1994. Technological challenges to artists' rights in the age of multimedia: The future role of moral rights. *Reference Services Review* 22(1): 9-19.

Lubans, John, Jr. 1987. Scholars and serials. *American Libraries* 18(3): 180-182.

Lucier, Richard E. 1993. Embedding the library into scientific and scholarly communication through knowledge management. In *Designing Information: New Roles for Librarians*, 5-18. Urbana-Champaign: Graduate School of Library and Information Science, University of Illinois at Urbana-Champaign.

Ludwig, Walter. 1997. An evaluation for scholarly societies and non-profit associations: Self publish or go commercial - Critical issues for boards and managers. *Canadian Journal of Communication* 22(3/4), special issue: 117-25.

Lufkin, J. M., ed. 1973. Special Issue: Record of the Conference of the Future of Scientific and Technical Journals. *IEEE Transactions on Professional Communication* (September).

—. 1975. Special Issue: Record of the 1975 IEEE Conference on Scientific Journals. *IEEE Transactions on Professional Communication* September, PC-18. No. 3.

Lufkin, J. M., and E. H. Miller. 1966. The reading habits of engineers: A preliminary study. *IEEE Transactions on Education* E-9(4): 179-82.

Luhn, Hans P. 1958. A business intelligence system. *IBM Journal of Research and Development* 2(4): 314-19.

Lundeen, Gerald, Carol Tenopir, and Paul Wermager. 1994. Information needs of rural health care practitioners in Hawaii. *Bulletin of the Medical Library Association* 82: 197-205.

Lunin, Lois F. 1994. Analyzing art objects for an image database. In *Challenges in Indexing Electronic Text and Images*, eds. Raya Fidel, Trudi Bellardo Hahn, Edie M. Rasmussen, and Philip J. Smith, 57-72. Medford, N.J.: Learned Information.

Lustig, H. 1996. The finances of electronic publishing. *APS News* 5(10): 2.

Lyman, Peter. 1992. Can the network reduce the cost of scholarly information? *Serials Review* 18(1/2): 98-99, 112.

Lynch, Clifford A. 1992. Reaction, response, and realization: From the crisis in scholarly communication to the age of networked information. *Serials Review* 18(1/2): 107-12.

—.1996. Integrity issues in electronic publishing. In *Scholarly publishing: The electronic frontier*, eds. Robin P. Peek and Gregory B. Newby, 133-45. Cambridge: The MIT Press.

———. 1998. The evolving Internet: Application and network service infrastructure. In Perspectives on Internet issues, eds. C. Tenopir and L.F. Lunin. *Journal of the American Society for Information Science* 49(11): 961-72.

MacEwan, Bonnie, and Mira Geffner. 1996. The Committee on Institutional Cooperation Electronic Journals Collection (CIC-EJC): A new model for library management of scholarly journals published on the Internet. *Public-Access Computer Systems Review* 7(4): 5-15.

Machlup, Fritz. 1962. *The Production and Distribution of Knowledge in the United States.* Princeton: Princeton University Press.

—. 1979. Uses, value, and benefits of knowledge. In *Knowledge: Creation, Diffusion, and Utilization.* Beverly Hills: Sage Publications.

Machlup, Fritz, and Kenneth W. Leeson. 1978. *Information through the printed word: The Dissemination of Scholarly, Scientific, and Intellectual Knowledge. Vol. 2, Journals.* New York: Praeger.

—. 1980. *Information through the Printed Word: The Dissemination of Scholarly, Scientific, and Intellectual Knowledge. Vol.4: Books, Journals, and Bibliographic services.* New York: Praeger.

MacKie-Mason, J. K., L. Murphy, and J. Murphy. 1997. Responsive pricing in the Internet. In *Internet Economics*, eds. L. W. McKnight and J. P. Bailey, 279-303. Cambridge: The MIT Press.

MacKie-Mason, J. K., S. Shenker, and H. R. Varian. 1996. Service architecture and content provision. The network provider as an editor. *Telecommunications Policy* 20(3): 203-17.

MacKie-Mason, J. K., and Hal R. Varian. 1995. Some FAQs about usage-based pricing. *Computer Networks and ISDN Systems* 28: 257-65.

—. 1997. Economic FAQs about the Internet. In *Internet Economics*, ed. L. W. McKnight and J. P. Bailey, 27-62. Cambridge: The MIT Press.

—. 1997. Economic FAQs about the Internet. *Journal of Economic Perspectives* 8(3): 6.

MacKie-Mason, Jeffrey K., and A. L. L. Jankovich. 1997. Peak: Pricing electronic access to knowledge. *Library Acquisitions, Practice and Theory* 21(3): 281-95.

MacLennan, Birdie. 1999. Presenation and access issues for electronic journals in a medium-sized academic institution. *Journal of Electronic Publishing*. Available from <http://www.press.umich.edu/jep/>.

Mailloux, Elizabeth N. 1989. Engineering information systems. In *Annual Review of Information Science and Technology*, ed. Martha E. Williams, vol. 24. 239-66. Amsterdam; New York: Elsevier Science Publishers.

Maizell, R. B. 1958. The most creative chemists read more. *Industrial and Engineering Chemistry* 50: 64a-5a.

Malakoff, David. 1998. New journals launched to fight rising prices. *Sciences* 282: 853-54.

Manheim, Frank T. 1979. The scientific referee. In *The Scientific Journal*, ed. A. J. Meadows, 99-103. London: Aslib.

Manoff, Marlene, Eileen Dorschner, Marilyn Geller, Keith Morgan, and Carter Snowden. 1992. Report of the Electronic Journals Task Force, MIT Libraries. *Serials Review* 18(1/2): 113-29.

Marks, Kenneth E., Steven P. Nielsen, H. Craig Petersen, and Peter E. Wagner. 1991. Longitudinal study of scientific journal prices in a research library. *College & Research Libraries* 52 (March): 125-138.

Marks, Robert H. 1995. The economic challenges of publishing electronic journals. *Serials Review: Economics of Electronic Publishing* 21(1): 85-88.

—. 1998. Personal communication.

Marshall, G. 1988. The economics of journal publishing: A case study. In *Serials Information from Publisher to User: Practice, Programs, and Progress*, eds. L.A. Chatterton and M.E. Clack. New York: The Haworth Press.

Marshall, Joanne G. 1993. *The impact of the special library on corporate decision making*. Washington, D.C.: Special Libraries Association.

Martin, Miles W., and Russell L. Ackoff. 1963. The dissemination and use of recorded scientific information. *Management Science* 9: 322-36.

Martyn, John. 1979. Proliferation and fragmentation of journals. In *The Scientific Journal*, ed. A. J. Meadows, 68-70. London: Aslib.

Matarazzo, James M., and Laurence Prusak. 1990. *Valuing corporate libraries*. Washington, D.C.: Special Libraries Association.

Marquis, Donald G., and Thomas J. Allen. 1966. Communications patterns in applied technology. *American Psychologist* 21(11): 1052-060.

Marquis, D. G., and D. M. Straight. 1966. Organizational factors in project performance. In *Research Program Effectiveness, Proceedings. Conference on Research Program Effectiveness*, ed. M.C. Yovits, 441-58. Washington, D.C. New York: Gordon & Breach.

Martin, Miles W. 1962. *IEEE Transactions in engineering management* 9: 66+.

Martyn, John. 1974. Information needs and uses. In *Annual Review of Information Science and Technology*, ed. Carlos A. Cuadra, vol. 9, 3-23. Washington, D.C.: American Society for Information Science.

McCabe, Mark J. 1998. *The Impact of Publisher Mergers on Journal Prices: A Preliminary Report*. Washington, D.C. Association of Research Libraries. Available from <http://www.arl.org/newsltr/200/mccabe.html>.

—. 1999. Personal communication.

McCarthy, Paul. 1994. Serial killers: Academic libraries respond to soaring costs. *Library Journal* 19(11): 41-44.

McClung, Patricia A., ed. 1995. *RLG Digital Image Access Project Symposium*. Mountain View, Calif.: Research Libraries Group.

McClure, C. R. n.d. *Electronic Networks, the Research Process, and Scholarly Communications*. Syracuse, N.Y.: School of Information Management, Syracuse University.

McClure, C. R., J. C. Bertot, and J. C. Beachboard. 1995. Internet costs and cost models for public libraries. In *Final Report to the National Commission on Libraries and Information Service*. Washington, D.C.: U.S. Government Printing Office.

McDonald, Dennis D. 1979. Interactions Between Scientists and the Journal Publishing Process. King Research Report to the National Science Foundation, dwking@ umich.edu.

McDonald, Dennis D., and Colleen G. Bush. 1982. Libraries, Publishers and Photocopying: Final report of surveys conducted for the U.S. Copyright Office. King Research Report. Washington, D.C.; U.S. Copyright Office. Available from ERIC ED 226-732.

McEldowney, Philip F. 1995. Scholarly electronic journals, trends, and academic attitudes: A research proposal. Master's project, Department of Library and Information Studies, University of North Carolina at Greensboro. Available from <http://www.people.virgnia.edu/~pm9k/libsci/95/ejs95.html>.

McFarland, Patricia A. 1990. Electronic delivery for paper pushers? *NFAIS Newsletter* 32(1): 1-2.

McKie, Douglas. 1979. The scientific periodical from 1665 to 1798. In *The Scientific Journal*, ed. A. J. Meadows, 7-17. London: Aslib.

McKiernan, Gerry. 2000. Morning becomes electric: Post-modern scholarly information access, organization, and navigation. Available from <http://www.public.iastate.edu./~CYBERSTACKS/Morning.htm>.

McKnight, Cliff. 1993. Electronic journals—past, present ... and future? *Aslib Proceedings* 45(1): 1-30.

McKnight, L. W., and J. P. Bailey. 1997. An introduction to Internet economics. In *Internet Economics*, eds. L. W. McKnight and J. P. Bailey, 3-24 Cambridge: The MIT Press.

McMillan, Gail. 1993. Electronic journals: Access through libraries. In *The Virtual Library*, 111-29, Westport, Conn.: Meckler.

—. 1995. Scholarly Communications Project: Publishers and libraries. In *Filling the Pipeline and Paying the Piper: Proceedings of the Fourth Symposium*, ed. Ann Okerson. Washington, D.C.: Association of Research Libraries.

Meadows, A. J. 1974. *Communication in Science*. London: Butterworths.

—. 1979. The problem of refereeing. In *The Scientific Journal*, ed. A. J. Meadows, 104-11. London: Aslib.

—. 1994. *Innovation in information: Twenty Years of the British Library Research and Development Department*. London: Bowker Saur.

—. 1998. *Communicating Research*. New York: Academic Press.

—. 1999. Personal communication.

Meadows, A. J., and P. Buckle. 1993. Changing communication activities in the british scientific community. *Journal of Documentation* 48(3): 276-290.

Meadows, A. J., and J. G. Conner. 1969. *An Investigation of Information Retrieval in Astronomy and Space Science.* Leicester, UK: Astronomy Department, Leicester University.

Meadows, Jack, David Pullinger, and Peter Such. 1995a. Publishing and costing an electronic journal. In *Project Elvyn: An Experiment in Electronic Journal Delivery*, eds. Fytton Rowland, Cliff McKnight, and Jack Meadows. London: Bowker Saur.

—. 1995b. The cost of implementing on electronic journal. *Journal Scholarly Publishing* (July): 167+.

Meadows, Jack, and Alan Singleton. 1995. Introduction. In *Project Elvyn: An Experiment in Electronic Journal Delivery*, eds. Fytton Rowland, Cliff McKnight, and Jack Meadows, 1-14. London: Bowker Saur.

Menzel, Herbert. 1962. Planned and unplanned scientific communication. In *Sociology of Science*, eds. B. Barber and Walter Hirsch. New York: Macmillan Free Press.

—. 1966. Information needs and uses in science and technology. In *Annual Review of Information Science and Technology*, ed. Carlos A. Cuadra, vol. 1, 41-69. New York: John Wiley & Sons.

—. 1970. *Formal and Information Satisfaction of the Information Requirements of Chemists.* New York: Columbia University, Bureau of Applied Social Research.

Menzel, Herbert, L. Lieberman, and J. Dulchin. 1960. *Review of Studies in the Flow of Information Among Scientists.* New York: Columbia University Press.

Mercer, Linda S. 2000. Measuring the use and value of electronic journals and books. In *Issues in Science and Technology Librarianship* (Winter). Available from <http://www.library.ucsb.edu/istl/00-winter/article1.html>.

Merton, R.K. 1968. Social Theory and Social Structure. New York: Free Press.

Metoyer-Duran, Cheryl. 1993. Information gatekeepers. In *Annual Review of Information Science and Technology*, ed. Martha E. Williams, vol. 28, 111-50. Medford, N.J.: Learned Information.

Mick, Colin K., Georg N. Lindsey, Daniel Callahan, and Frederick Spielberg. 1979. *Towards Usable User Studies: Assessing the Information Behavior of Scientists and Engineers*, December 1979. Washington, D.C.: National Science Foundation, Division of Information Science and Technology. Available from NSF/IST: 78-10531F; NTIS: PB80-177165.

Miller, David C. 1987. Special Report: Publishers, libraries and CD-ROM: Implications of digital optical printing. DCM Associates. Report distributed to the registrants of the

Optical Publishing and Libraries: Cheers or Tears? Preconference Institute to the 1987 ALA Annual Conference, June 24-26, 1987, San Francisco.

Miller, George. 1983. Foreword. In *The Study of Information*, eds. Fritz Machlup and Una Mansfield. New York: John Wiley and Sons.

—.1968. Psychology and information. *American Documentation* 19(3): 286-89.

Mintz, Anne. 1995. Quality issues in information retrieval: A publisher perspective. In *Electronic Information Delivery: Ensuring Quality and Value,* ed. Reva Basch, 47-58. Brookfield, Vt.: Gower Publishing.

Molyneux, Robert E. 1989. ACRL library data table: Summary data. In *ACRL University Library Statistics 1987-88,* 26. Chicago: American Library Association, Association of College and Research Libraries.

Mondschein, Lawrence G. 1990. Selective dissemination of information (SDI) use and productivity in the corporate research environment. *Special Libraries* 81(4): 265-79.

Mooney, Carolyn J. 1991. In 2 years, a million refereed articles, 300,000 books, chapters, monographs. *Chronicle of Higher Education* (May 22): A17.

Moore, J. A. 1972. An inquiry on new forms of primary publications. *Journal of Chemical Documentation* 12: 75-78.

Moravcsik, Michael J. 1965. Private and public communications in physics. *Physics Today* 18: 23-6.

—. 1966. Physics information exchange — A communications experiment. *Physics Today* 19: 62+.

Morgan, Bruce. 1997. Is the journal as we know it an article of faith? An open letter to the faculty. *The Public-Access Computer Systems Review* 8(2): 1.

Mountbatten, Earl. 1966. Controlling the information explosion. *Radio and Electronic Engineer* 31: 195-208.

Murray, Herbert, Jr. 1966. *Methods for Satisfying the Needs of the Scientist and Engineer for Scientific and Technical Information.* Redstone Arsenal.

Myers, Judy E., Thomas C. Wilson, and John H. Lienhard. 1993. Surfing the sea of stories: Riding the information revolution. *Internet Librarian* 13(6): 30A-7A.

Narin, Francis, Mark Carpenter, and Nancy C. Berlt. 1979. Interrelationships of scientific journals. In *The Scientific Journal,* ed. A. J. Meadows, 163-71. London: Aslib.

National Commission on Libraries and Information Science. 1977. *Effective Access to the Periodical Literature: A National Program.* Washington, D.C.: National Commission on Libraries and Information Science.

National Research Council. Committee on Issues in the Transborder Flow of Scientific Data. 1997. *Bits of power: Issues in global access to scientific data.* Chair R. S. Berry and Study Director P. F. Uhlir. Washington, D.C.: National Academy Press.

National Research Council (NRC) Canada. 1993. *NRC-CNRC: A History of CISTI: Canada Institute for Scientific and Technical Information.* NRCC No. 38022:53. Ottawa: National Research Council Canada.

National Science Foundation. 1964. *Characteristics of Scientific Journals, 1949-1959.* Washington, D.C.: U. S. Government Printing Office.

Nelke, Margareta. 1998. *Knowledge Management in Swedish Corporations: The Value of Information and Information Services.* Stockholm: Swedish Society for Technical Documentation.

Nelson, Carnot E., and Donald K. Pollack, eds. 1970. *Communication Among Scientists and Engineers.* Lexington, Mass.: D.C. Heath.

Neuman, Michael, and Paul Mangiafico. 1994. Providing and accessing information via the Internet: The Georgetown Catalog of Projects in Electronic Text. *The Reference Librarian* (41/42): 319-32.

New Jour: Electronic Journals & News Sources. Muncie, Ind.: Ball State University Libraries. Available from <http://www.bsu.edu/library/ejournal/newjour.html>.

Noam, E. M. 1995. Electronics and the dim future of the university. *Science* 270: 247-49.

Noll, R., and W. E. Steinmueller. 1992. An economic analysis of scientific journal prices: Preliminary results. *Serials Review* 18(1/2): 32-37.

Norman, Sandy. 1995. Database quality and liability: The UK campaign. In *Electronic Information Delivery: Ensuring Quality and Value,* ed. Reva Basch, 189-202. Brookfield, Vt.: Gower Publishing.

Novikov, Yu A. 1979. Optimizing the structure of scientific publications. In *The Scientific Journal,* ed. A. J. Meadows, 248-25. London: Aslib.

Odlyzko, Andrew M. 1996a. On the road to electronic publishing. *Euromath Bulletin* 2.

O'Donnell, Michael J. 1995. Electronic journals: Scholarly invariants in a changing medium. *Journal of Scholarly Publishing* 26(3): 183-99.

—. 1996b. Tragic loss or good riddance? The impending demise of traditional scholarly journals. In *Scholarly Publishing: The Electronic Frontier,* eds. Robin P. Peek and Gregory B. Newby, 91-101. Cambridge: The MIT Press.

—. 1997. The economics of electronic journals. *First Monday* 2(8). Available from <http://www.firstmonday.dk/issues/issue2_8/odlyzko/index.html>.

—. 1998. Competition and cooperation: Libraries and publishers in the transition to electronic scholarly journals. *Journal of Electronic Publishing* 4(4). Available from <http://www.press.umich.edu/jep/>.

—. 1999. Personal communication.

Okerson, Ann. 1988. Accessing electronic journals: A survey of Canadian and American libraries. *Serials Librarian* 15(3): 73-83.

—. 1989a. Married to the library. *Library Acquisitions: Practice and Theory* 13(2): 155-60.

—. 1989b. Of making many books there is no end: Report on serial prices. *Report of the ARL Serials Prices Project.* Washington, D.C.: Association of Research Libraries.

—. 1990. Report on the ARL Serials Project. *Serials Librarian* 17(3): 111-19.

—. 1991a. Back to academia? The case for American universities to publish their own research. *Logos* 2(2): 106-12.

—. 1991b. The electronic journal: What, whence, and when? *The Public-Access Computer Systems Review* 2(1): 5-24.

—. 1991c. With feathers: Effects of copyright and ownership on scholarly publishing. *College & Research Libraries* 52(5): 425-38.

—. 1992a. The missing model: A "circle of gifts." *Serials Review* 18(1/2): 92-96.

—. 1992b. Publishing through the network: The 1990s debutante. *Scholarly Publishing* 23(3): 170-77.

—. 1992c. The old order changes: A plan for action. *Journal of Library Administration* 16(3): 3-23.

—. 1992d. ARL annual statistics 1990-91: Remembrance of things past, present... and future? *Publishers Weekly* 34(27): 22-23.

—. 1992e. Electronic journals: Current issues. *Quarterly Bulletin of the International Association of Agricultural Librarians and Documentalists* 37(1/2): 46-54.

—. 1994. Oh Lord, won't you buy me a Mercedes Benz? Or, there is a there there. *Surfaces* IV.102, Folio 1.

—. 1996. Whose work is it anyway? Perspectives on the stakeholders and the stakes in the current copyright scene. *The Serials Librarian* 28(1/2): 69-87.

—. 1999. LibLicense: Licensing digital information: A resource for librarians. Yale University. Available from <www.library.yale.edu/~llicense/index.shtml>.

Okerson, Ann, and James J. O'Donnell, eds. 1995. *Scholarly Journals at the Crossroads: A Subversive Proposal for Electronic Publishing. An Internet Discussion about Scientific and Scholarly Journals and their Future.* Washington, D.C.: Association of Research Libraries.

—. *New Jour: Electronic Journals and Newsletters.* University of California at San Diego Libraires. Avaliable from <http://gort.ucsd.edu/newjour/>.

Okerson, Ann, D. L. Rodgers, and B. MacLennan. Come into my parlor, said the spider: World Wide Web and the Mosaic interface. *Serials Librarian* (25): 27-32.

Okerson, Ann, and Kendon Stubbs. 1991. The library "Doomsday Machine." (Sharp price increase for scholarly journals). *Publishers Weekly* 238(8): 36-38.

Olsen, J. 1993. *Electronic Journal Literature: Implications for Scholars.* Westport, Conn.: Mecklermedia.

Online journals: The way ahead for OCLC. 1993. *Information World Review*: 5-6.

Operations Research Group. A Case Institute of Technology. 1960. *An Operations Research Study of the Dissemination and Use of Recorded Scientific Information.* Cleveland, Ohio: Case Institute of Technology.

Oram, A. 1997. The end of Internet socialism? In *Internet Economics,* eds.Lee W. McKnight and Joseph B. Bailey. Cambridge: The MIT Press.

Ordover, J. A., and W. J. Baumol. 1975. *Public Good Properties in Reality: The Case of Scientific Journals.* New York: New York University.

Orenstein, Ruth, ed. 1996. *Fulltext Sources Online.* Vol. 8. Needham Heights, Mass.: BiblioData.

Orr, Richard H. 1970. The scientist as an information processor: A conceptual model illustrated with data on variables related to library utilization. In *Communication Among Scientists and Engineers,* eds. Carnot E. Nelson and Donald K. Pollack, 143-89. Lexington, Mass.: D.C. Heath.

O'Shea, Robert and Owen Hansen. 1998. The hidden costs of electronic publishing. In *Economics, Real Costs, and Benefits of Electronics Publishing in Science—A Technical Report.* eds. Dennis Shaw and David Price. Proceedings of ICSU Press Workshop. Available from <http://www.bodley.ox.ac.uk/icsu/proceedings.htm>.

Otlet, P. 1934. *Traité de Documentation.* Brussels: Editiones mundaneum.

—. 1935. *Monde, Essai D'universalisme! Connaissances du Monde, Sentiments du Monde, Action Organisée et Plan du Monde.* Brussels: D. Van Keerberghen.

Page, Gillian, Robert Campbell, and Jack Meadows. 1987. *Journal Publishing: Principles and Practice.* London: Butterworths.

—. 1997. *Journal Publishing*. Cambridge: Cambridge University Press.

Paisley, William J. 1968. Information needs and uses. In *Annual Review of Information Science and Technology*, ed. Carlos A. Cuadra, vol. 3, 1-30. Chicago: Encyclopedia Brittanica.

—. 1971. *Clustering Scientific Articles to Form "Minijournals" — I. Preliminary Considerations*. Stanford: Stanford University, Department of Communications.

—. 1965. *The Flow of (Behavioral) Science Information: A Review of the Research Literature*. Stanford: Stanford University, Institute for Communication Research.

Palmour, V. E., M. C. Bellassai, and L. M. Gray. 1974. *Access to Periodical Resources: A National Plan*. Washington, D.C.: Association of Research Libraries.

Parker, E. B., D. A. Lingwood, and W. J. Paisley. 1968. *Communication and Research Productivity in an Interdisciplinary Behavioral Science Research Area*. Stanford: Stanford University Press.

Passman, Sydney. 1969. *Scientific and Technological Communication*. Exeter, Great Britain: Pergamon Press.

Pasternack, Simon. 1966. Criticism of the proposed physics information exchange. *Physics Today* 19: 63+.

Pederson, Wayne, and David Gregory. 1994. Interlibrary loan and commercial document supply: Finding the right fit. *The Journal of Academic Librarianship* 20: 263-72.

Peek, Robin P. 1994. Where is publishing going? A perspective on change. *Journal of the American Society for Information Science* 45(10): 730-36.

—. 1996. Scholarly publishing: Facing the new frontiers. In *Scholarly publishing: The Electronic Frontier*, eds. Robin P. Peek and Gregory B. Newby, 3-15. Cambridge: The MIT Press.

Peek, Robin P., ed. 1994. Perspectives on Electronic Publishing. *Journal of the American Society for Information Science* 45(10).

Peek, Robin P., and Gregory B. Newby, eds. 1996. *Scholarly Publishing: The Electronic Frontier*. Cambridge: The MIT Press.

Peek, Robin P., and Jeffery Pomerantz. 1998. Electronic scholarly journal publishing. *Annual Review of Information Science and Technology*, ed. Martha E Williams, vol. 33, 321-56. Medford, N.J.: Information Today, Inc.

Peters, John. 1995. The hundred years war started today: An exploration of electronic peer review. *Internet Research: Electronic Networking Applications and Policy* 5(4): 3-9.

Penniman, W. David. 1994. Tomorrow's library. *Computer Methods and Programs in Biomedicine* 44: 149-153.

Peters, Paul Evan. 1992. Making the market for networked information: An introduction to a proposed program for licensing electronic uses. *Serials Review* 18(1/2): 19-24.

Petersen, H. Craig. 1989. Variations in journal prices: A statistical analysis. *Serials Librarian* 17: 1-9.

Pigou, A. C. 1920. *The Economics of Welfare*. London: Macmillan.

Pinelli, Thomas E. 1991. The Relationship Between the Use of U.S. Government *Technical Reports by U.S. Aerospace Engineers and Scientists and Selected Institutional and Sociometric Variables*. *Report 6*. Washington, D.C.: National Aeronautics and Space Administration. Available from NASA: TM-102774; NTIS: 91N18898

Pinelli, Thomas E., Rebecca O. Barclay, Maurita Peterson Holland, Michael L. Keene, and John M. Kennedy. 1991. Technological innovation and technical communications: Their place in aerospace engineering curricula. A survey of European, Japanese and U.S. aerospace engineers and scientists. *European Journal of Engineering Education* 16(4): 337-51.

Pinelli, Thomas E., Myron Glassman, Walter E. Oliu, and Rebecca O. Barclay. 1989. *Technical Communication in Aeronautics: Results of Phase 1 Pilot Study*. Washington, DC: National Aeronautics and Space Administration. NASA TM-101534.

Piternick, Anne B. 1989. Attempts to find alternatives to the scientific journal: A brief review. *The Journal of Academic Librarianship* 15(5): 260-66.

—. 1989. Serials and new technology: The state of the "electronic journal." *Canadian Library Journal* 46(2): 93-7.

Porter, Michael E., and Victor E. Millar. 1985. How information gives you competitive advantage. *Harvard Business Review* 63: 149-60.

Potter, William. 1986. Readers in search of authors: The changing face of the middleman. *Wilson Library Bulletin* 60: 20-23.

Price, Derek J. de Solla. 1963. *Little Science, Big Science*. New York: Columbia University Press.

—. 1975. *Science Since Babylon*. Enlarged ed. New Haven: Yale University Press.

—. 1979. Networks of scientific papers: The pattern of bibliographic references indicates the nature of the scientific research front. In *The Scientific Journal*, ed. A. J. Meadows, 157-62. London: Aslib.

Price, D. S. and S. Gursey. 1974. *Transcience and Continuance in Scientific Authorship*. *Studies in Scientometrics*. New Haven: Yale University Press.

Prusak, Laurence, and James M. Matarazzo. 1992. *Information Management and Japanese Success*. Washington, D.C.: Special Libraries Association.

Pullinger, David. 1999. Academics and the new information environment: The impact of local factors on use of electronic journals. *Journal of Information Science* 25(2): 164-172.

Qin, Jian. 1995. Issues in scientific communication and the potential for information marketing in China. *Bulletin of the American Society for Information Science* 21(5): 7-8.

Quinn, Frank. 1995. Roadkill on the electronic highway? The threat to the mathematical literature. *Notices of the American Mathematical Society*.

Quinn, Frank, and Gail McMillan. 1995. Library copublication of electronic journals. *Serials Review* 21(1): 80-83.

Raitt, David Iain. 1984. *The Communication and Information-Seeking and Use Habits of Scientists and Engineers in International Organizations Based in Europe National Aerospace Research Establishments*. Ph.D. diss. Loughborough , U.K.: Loughborough University of Technology; 1984.

Rawlins, Gregory J. E. 1992. The new publishing: Technology's impact on the publishing industry over the next decade. *The Public-Access Computer Systems Review* 3(8): 5-63.

—. 1993. Publishing over the next decade. *Journal of the American Society for Information Science* 44(8): 474-79.

Rayward, W. Boyd. 1999. H. G. Wells' idea of a world brain: A critical reassessment. *Journal of the American Society for Information Science* 50(7): 557-73.

Reich, Vicky. 1992. Discipline-specific literature bases: A view of the APS model. *Serials Review* 18(1-2): 52-54, 65+.

Reichel, M. 1989. Ethics and library instruction: Is there a connection? *RQ* 28(4): 477-80.

Repo, Aatto J. 1987. Economics of information. In *Annual Review of Information Science and Technology*, ed. Martha E. Williams, vol. 22, 3-35. Amsterdam; New York: Elsevier Science Publishers.

Report of the AAU Task Force. 1994. *A National Strategy for Managing Scientific and Technical Information*. Available from <http://arl.cni.org/aau/STITOC.html>.

Report of the ARL Serials Prices Project. 1989. Washington, D.C.: Association of Research Libraries.

Reynolds, Linda. 1979. Legibility studies: Their relevance to present-day documentation methods. *Journal of Documentation* 35(4): 307-40.

Richardson, Robert J. 1981. End-user online searching in a high-technology engineering environment. *Online* 5(4): 44-57.

Rickards, Janice, Peter Linn, and Diana Best. Information needs and resoruces of engineering firms: Survery of Brisbane and the Gold Coast of Queensland. *Australasian College Libraries* 7(2): 63-72.

Rider, F. 1944. *The Scholar and the Future of the Research Library*. New York: Hadham Press.

Risher, Carol A., and Laura N. Gasaway. 1994. The great copyright debate. *Library Journal* 119(15): 34-37.

Ritchie, E., and A. Hindle. 1976. *Communication Networks in R & D: A Contribution to Methodology and Some Results in a Particular Laboratory*. Lancaster: Department of Operational Research, University of Lancaster.

Robert Ubell Associates. 1996. *Cost Centers and Measures in the Networked Information Value Chain*. Washington, D.C.: Center for Networked Information.

Robertson, S.E. 1997. Overview of the Okapi projects. *Journal of Documentation* 53(1): 3-7.

Roche, M., ed. 1993. *ARL/RLG Interlibrary Loan Cost: A Joint Effort by the Association of Research Libraries and Research Libraries Group: 63*. Washington, D.C.: Association of Research Libraries.

Roderer, Nancy K. 1994. LITA's Role in the NII. *LITA Newsletter* 16(1): 1, 18.

——. 1998. Collection development in the era of digital libraries. Paper presented at the CRICS IV Conference, 25-27 March, at San Jose, Costa Rica.

Roderer, Nancy K., and C. G. Schell. 1977b. *Statistical Indicators of Scientific and Technical Communication Worldwide*. Washington, D.C.: U. S. Government Printing Office. Available from NTIS: PB 283-439.

Rodgers, David L. 1994. Scholarly journals in 2020. *The Serials Librarian* 24(3/4): 73-76.

Rogers, Michael. 1993. OCLC to produce first online nursing journal. *Library Journal* 118(10): 40.

Rogers, Sharon J., and Charlene S. Hurt. 1990. How scholarly communication should work in the 21st century. *College & Research Libraries* 51(1): 5-8.

Roistacher, R. C. 1978. The virtual journal. *Computer Networks and ISDN Systems* 2(1): 18-24.

Rosenberg, Victor. 1994. Will new information technology destroy copyright? *The Electronic Library* 12(5): 285-87.

Rosenbloom, Richard S., and Francis W. Wolek. 1967. *Technology, Information & Organization: Information Transfer in Industrial R & D*. Boston: Harvard University.

—. 1970. *Technology and Information Transfer: A Survey of Practice in Industrial Organizations*. Boston: Harvard University.

Rothwell, Roy. 1980. Patterns of information flow during the innovation process. In *Key Papers in Information Science*, ed. Belver C. Griffith, 103-12. White Plains, N.Y.: Knowledge Industry Publications.

Rous, Bernard. 1999. ACM: A case study. *Journal of Electronic Publishing*. Available from <http://www.press.umich.edu/jep/04-04/rous.html>.

Rowland, Fytton (J.F.B.). 1982. Economic position of some British primary scientific journals. *Journal of Documentation* 38(2): 94-106.

—. 1995a. Recent and current electronic journal projects. In *Project Elvyn: An Experiment in Electronic Journal Delivery*, eds. Fytton Rowland, Cliff McKnight, and Jack Meadows, 15-36. London: Bowker Saur.

—. 1995b. Electronic journals: Neither free nor easy. *The Information Society* 11(4): 273-74.

—. 1996. Electronic journals: Delivery, use, and access. *IFLA Journal* 22(3): 226-28.

—. 1998. Policy issues in electronic publishing. In *Information Policy in the Electronic Age*, ed. M. Grieves, 133-163. London: Bowker-Saur.

Rowland, Fytton, Cliff McKnight, and Jack Meadows, eds. 1995. *Project Elvyn: An Experiment in Electronic Journal Delivery*. London: Bowker Saur.

Rusbridge, Chris. 1995. New relationships in scholarly publishing. In *Managing the Intellectual Record*, eds. Lorcan Dempsey, Derek Law, and Ian Mowat, 79-89. *Networking and the Future of Libraries*, London: Library Association Publishing.

Sabine, Gordon A., and Patricia L. Sabine. 1986. How people use books and journals. *Library Quarterly* 56(4): 399-408.

Salton, Gerald. 1968. *Automatic Text Processing*. Reading, Mass.: Addison-Wesley.

—. 1971. *The SMART Retrieval System: Experiments in Automatic Document Processing*. Englewood Cliffs, N.J.: Prentice Hall.

Samuel, A. L. 1964. The banishment of paperwork. *New Scientist* 21(380): 529-30.

Samuelson, Pamela. 1991. Digital media and the law. *Communications of the ACM* 34(10): 3-28.

—. 1992. Copyright law and electronic compilations of data. *Communications of the ACM* 35(2): 27-32.

—. 1995. Copyright's fair use doctrine and digital data. *Publishing Research Quarterly* 11(1): 27-39.

—. 1996. Intellectual property rights and the global information economy. *Communications of the ACM* 39(1): 23-28.

—. 1996. The copyright grab. *Wired* 4(1): 134-91.

SantaVicca, Edmund F. 1994. The Internet as a reference and research tool: A model for educators. *The Reference Librarian* (41/42): 225-36.

Saracevic, Tefko, and Paul B. Kantor. 1997. Studying the value of library and information sciences. Part I. Establishing a theoretical framework. Part II. Methodology and taxonomy. *Journal of the American Society for Information Science* 48: 527-63.

Schackel, B. 1983. The BLEND System: Programme for the study of some "electronic journals." *Journal of the American Society for Information Science* 34(1): 22-30.

Schaffner, Ann C. 1994. The future of scientific journals: Lessons from the past. *Information Technology and Libraries* 13: 239-47.

Schauder, Don. 1994. Electronic publishing of professional articles: Attitudes of academics and implications for the scholarly communication industry. *Journal of the American Society for Information Science* 45(2): 73-100.

Scholarly Communication: The Report of the National Enquiry. 1979. Baltimore: Johns Hopkins University Press.

Schwartz, Candy. 1998. Web search engines. In Perspectives on Internet issues, eds. Carol Tenopir and Lois F. Lunin. *Journal of the American Society for Information Science* 49(11): 973-82.

Schwartz, Charles A. 1994. Scholarly communication as a loosely coupled system: Reassessing prospects for structural reform. *College & Research Libraries* 55(2): 101-17.

—. 1994. The Strength of weak ties in electronic development of the scholarly communication system. *College & Research Libraries* 55(6): 529-40.

Scott, John. 1998. The perils of oversimplification: What are the real costs of online journals? In *ICSU Press Workshop on Economics, Real Costs, and Benefits of Electronic Publishing in Science—A Technical Study*, eds. Dennis Shaw and David Price. Available from <http://www.bodley.ox.ac.uk/icsu/proceedings.htm>.

Scoville, L. 1995. *Librarians and Publishers in the Scholarly Information Process: Transition in the Electronic Age.* New York: Association of American Publishers, Inc.

Seiler, L. H., and J. Raben. 1981. The electronic journal. *Society* 18(6): 76-83.

Senders, J. W. 1977. An online scientific journal. *The Information Scientist* 11(1): 3-9.

Senders, John. 1979. An on-line scientific journal. In *The Scientific Journal,* ed. A. J. Meadows, 289-95. London: Aslib.

Senders, J. W., C. M. B. Anderson, and C. P. Hecht. 1975. *Scientific Publications Systems: An Analysis of Past, Present, and Future Methods of Scientific Communication.* Toronto: University of Toronto.

Shamp, S. A. 1992. Prospects for electronic publication in communication: A survey of potential users. *Communication Quarterly* 40(3): 297-304.

Shapin, Steven. 1994. *A Social History of Truth: Civility and Science in Seventeenth-century England. Science and Its Conceptual Foundations.* Chicago: University of Chicago Press.

Shapin, Steven, and Simon Schaffer. 1985. *Leviathan and the Air Pump: Hobbes, Boyle, and the Experimental Life.* Princeton: Princeton University Press.

Shapiro, Carl and Hal R. Varian. 1998. *Information Rules: A Strategic Guide to the Network Economy.* Boston: Harvard Business School Press.

Shaw, Debora. 1991. The human-computer interface for information retrieval. In *Annual Review of Information Science and Technology,* ed. Martha E. Williams, vol. 26, 155-95. Medford, N.J.: Learned Information.

Shaw, Dennis and David Price, eds. 1998. *Economics, Real Costs and Benefits of Electronic Publishing in Science—A Technical Study: Proceedings of the UCSU Press Workshop, Keble College, Oxford, UK March 31 to April 2, 1998.* Available from <http://www.bodley.ox.ac.uk/icsu/proceedings.htm>.

Shaw, R. R. 1956. *Pilot Study on the Use of Scientific Literature by Scientists.* Washington, D.C.: National Science Foundation.

Shenker, S., D. Clark, D. Estrin, and S. Herzog. 1996. Pricing in computer networks: Reshaping the research agenda. In *The Internet and Telecommunications Policy,* eds. G. W. Brock and G. L. Rosston, 19. Mahwah, N.J.: Erlbaum.

Shephard, David A. 1979. Some effects of delay in publication of information in medical journals, and implications for the future. In *The Scientific Journal,* ed. A. J. Meadows, 89-93. London: Aslib.

Sherlock, Ellen Lyons. 1993. Final report on electronic publishing. *Canadian Mathematical Society Publications Committee.*

Sherman, Chris. 1988. *The CD ROM - Handbook.* New York: McGraw-Hill.

Shilling, C. W., and Jessie Bernard. 1964. Informal communication among bio-scientists. In *Biological Sciences Communication Project Report.* Washington, D.C.: George Washington University.

Shoham, Snunith. 1998. Scholarly communication: A study of Israeli academic research. *Journal of Librarianship and Information Science* 30(2): 118-121.

Shotwell, Thomas K. 1971. Information flow in an industrial research laboratory: A case study. *IEEE Transactions on Engineering Management* EM-18(1): 26-33.

Shuchman, Hedvah L. 1981. *Information Transfer in Engineering*. Glastonbury, Conn.: The Futures Group.

Siess, Judith A. 1982. Information needs and information-gathering behavior of research engineers. In *Proceedings of the Eleventh ASIS Mid-year Meeting Held in Silver Spring, MD*, 13-60. Washington, D.C.: American Society for Information Science.

Silverman, Robert J. 1996. The impact of electronic publishing on the academic community. In *Scholarly Publishing: The Electronic Frontier*, ed. Robin P. Peek and Gregory B. Newby, 55-69. Cambridge: The MIT Press.

Simpson, Annette. 1988. Academic journal usage. *British Journal of Academic Librarianship* 3: 25-36.

Singleton, Alan. 1979. Journal ranking and selection: A review in physics. In *The Scientific Journal*, ed. A. J. Meadows, 186-217. London: Aslib.

Singleton, Alan, and D. J. Pullinger. 1984. Ways of viewing costs of journals: Cost evaluation of the BLEND experiment. *Electronic Publishing Review* 4(1): 59-71.

Sirbu, M. A. 1995. Creating an open market for information. *The Journal of Academic Librarianship* (Managing technology issue): 467-71.

Smith, Clagett G. 1966. *Organizational Factors in Scientific Performance in an Industrial Research Laboratory*. Madison: Center for Advanced Study in Organization Science, University of Wisconsin.

Sparck Jones, Karen, and M. Kay. 1973. *Linguistics and Information Science*. New York: Academic Press.

Speier, Cheri, Jonathan Palmer, Daniel Wren, and Susan Hahn. 1999. Faculty perceptions of electronic journals as scholarly communication: A question of prestige and legitimacy. *Journal of the American Society for Information Science* 50(6): 537-43.

Spigai, Fran. 1991. Information pricing. In *Annual Review of Information Science and Technology*, ed. Martha E. Williams, vol. 26, 39-73. Medford, N.J.: Learned Information.

Spilhaus, A. F., Jr. 1998. Values, limits and progress. In *ICSU Press Workshop on Economics, Real Costs, and Benefits of Electronic Publishing in Science — A Technical Study*, eds. Dennis Shaw and David Price. Available from <http://www.bodley.ox.ac.uk/icsu/proceedings.htm>.

Spilhaus, A. F., Jr., and Judy C. Holoviak. 1972. Geoscience publications. In *Toward the Development of a Geological Information System*. Geological Information Society Sixth Annual Meeting held in Washington, D.C. Washington, DC.: Geological Information Society.

Spretnak, Charles M. 1982. A survey of the frequency and importance of technical communication in an engineering career. *Technical Writing Teacher* 9: 133-36.

Spring, Michael B. 1991. *Electronic Printing and Publishing: The Document Processing Revolution*. New York: Marcel Dekker.

—. 1991. Information technology standards. In *Annual Review of Information Science and Technology*, ed. Martha E. Williams, vol. 26, 79-111. Medford, N.J.: Learned Information.

Staiger, David L. 1971. Unit publications. In *National Federation of Science Abstracting and Indexing Services*, Annual Meeting, 91-96. Philadelphia: National Federation of Abstracting and Indexing Services.

Starr, Susan S. 1994. Evaluating physical science reference sources on the Internet. *The Reference Librarian* (41/42): 261-73.

Stebelman, Scott. 1994. Analysis of retrieval performance in four cross-disciplinary databases: Article1st, Faxon Finder, UnCover, and a locally mounted database. *College & Research Libraries* 55: 562-67.

Stern, B.T. 1982. ADONIS. *Proceedings of the 6th Online Information Meeting*. Medford, N.J.: Learned Information.

—. 1992. The new ADONIS. *Serials* 5(3): 37-43.

Stewart, Linda. 1996. User acceptance of electronic journals: Interviews with chemists at Cornell University. *College & Research Libraries* 57(4): 339-49.

Stix, G. 1994. The speed of write. *Scientific American* 271(6): 106-11.

Stodolsky, David S. 1995. Consensus journals: Invitational journals based upon peer review. *The Information Society* 11(4): 247-60.

Stoller, Michael A., Robert Christopherson, and Michael A. Miranda. 1996. The economics of professional journal pricing. *College & Research Libraries* 57: 9-21.

Stoller, Michael E. 1992. Electronic journals in the humanities: A survey and critique. *Library Trends* 40(4): 647-66.

Storey, Tom. 1994. The Internet and OCLC: Broadening access to the world's information. *The Reference Librarian* (41/42): 375-85.

Subramanyam, K. 1981. *Scientific and Technical Information Sources*. New York: Marcel Dekker.

SuperJournal Project Staff. 1999. Summary of SuperJournal findings: Readers (draft). Available from <http://www.superjournal.ac.uk/sj/findread.htm>.

Sutton, J.R. 1976. Information requirements of engineering designers. AGARD Tip Meetings. *The Problem of Optimizations of User Benefit in Scientific and Technical Information Transfer*. Copenhagen AGARD CP-179. 12.1-12.8.

Taylor, P. 1996. Internet users: Likely to reach 500m by 2000. *Financial Times* London edition (May 13): 4.

Taylor, R. S. 1986. *Value-added Processes in Information Systems*. Norwood, N.J.: Ablex Publishing.

Taylor, Robert L. 1975. The Technological Gatekeeper. *R&D Management*. 5(3): 239-42.

Tenopir, Carol. 1988. Searching full-text databases. *Library Journal* 113(8): 60-61.

—. 1994. Electronic publishing. *Library Journal* 119(6): 40-42.

—. 1995a. Authors and readers: The keys to success or failure for electronic publishing. *Library Trends* 43(4): 571-91.

—. 1995b. Priorities of quality. In *Electronic Information Delivery: Ensuring Quality and Value*, ed. Reva Basch, 119-39. Brookfield, Vt.: Gower Publishing.

—.1997. Complexities of electronic journals. *Library Journal* 122(2): 37-38.

Tenopir, Carol, and Donald W. King. 1996. Setting the record straight on journal publishing: Myth vs. reality. *Library Journal* 121(5): 32-35.

—. 1996. Electronic publishing: A study of functions and participants. In *Proceedings of the Seventeenth National Online Meeting*, ed. Martha E. Williams, 375-84. Medford, N.J.: Information Today.

—. 1997a. Managing scientific journals in a digital era. *Information Outlook* 1: 14-17.

—. 1997b. Trends in scientific scholarly journal publishing in the United States. *Journal of Scholarly Publishing* 28(3): 135-70.

—. 1998a. Designing the future of electronic journals with lessons learned from the past: Economic and use patterns of scientific journals. In *Proceedings of the Socioeconomic Dimensions of Electronic Publishing Workshop, Santa Barbara, CA, April 23-25, 1998*, sponsored by the National Science Foundation and IEEE Foundation in cooperation with the 1998 IEEE International Conference on Advances in Digital Libraries (ADL19988) 11-17.

—. 1998b. Designing the future of electronic journals with lessons learned from the past: Economic and use patterns of scientific journals. *Journal of Electronic Publishing*. Available from <http://www.press.umich.edu/jep/04-02/king.html>.

Tenopir, Carol, and Lois F. Lunin, eds.1998. Perspectives on Internet Issues. *Journal of the American Society for Information Society* 49(11).

Tenopir, Carol, and Jung Soon Ro. 1990. *Full-text databases*. Westport, Conn.: Greenwood Publishing Group.

Terleckyj, Nestor E. 1984. A growth model of the U.S. communication industry, 1948-1980. In *Communication and Information Economics: New Perspectives*. eds. Meheroo Jusawalla and Helene Ebenfield, 119-45. New York: North-Holland.

Terrant, Seldon W., and Lorrin R. Garson. 1977. Evaluation of a dual concept journal. *Journal of Chemical Information and Computer Science* 17(2): 61-67.

—. 1979. Evaluation of a dual journal concept. In *The Scientific Journal*, ed. A. J. Meadows, 279-88. London: Aslib.

The Seybold Report on Internet Publishing. 1996-1999. Media, Penn.: Seybold Publications.

Treloar, Andrew. 1996. Electronic scholarly publishing and the World Wide Web. *Journal of Scholarly Publishing* 27(3): 135-50.

—.1998. Libraries' new role in electronic scholarly publishing. *Communications of the ACM* 41(4): 88-89.

Trivette, Don. 1990. Electronic encyclopedias merge text, high-res visuals, and sound (three CD-ROM based electronic encyclopedias). *PC Magazine* 9(16): 537-39.

Tsay, Ming-Yueh. 1998. The relationship between journal use in a medical library and citation use. *Bulletin of the Medical Library Association* 86(1): 31-39.

Turner, Judith, ed. 2000. PubMed Central: A good idea. Journal of Electronic Publishing 5(3). Available from <http://www.press.umich.edu/jep/05-03/turner0503.html>.

Turoff, Murray, and Julian Scher. 1975. Computerized conferencing and its impact on engineering management. *Joint Engineering Management Conference*: 59-70.

—. 1978. The EIES experience: Electronic Information Exchange System. *Bulletin of the American Society for Information Science* 4(5): 9-10.

Turoff, Murray, and Starr Roxanne Hiltz. 1982. The electronic journal: A progress report. *Journal of the American Society for Information Science* 33(4): 195-202.

Ulrich's International Periodicals Directory. New York: Bowker Saur.

University of Houston Index. Houston: University of Houston Press.

Unruh, Betty, and Wendy Schipper, eds. 1991. *Information Distribution Issues for the 90s*. Philadelphia: The National Federation of Abstracting and Information Services.

Unsworth, John. 1996. Electronic scholarship; or, scholarly publishing and the public. *Journal of Scholarly Publishing* 28(1): 3-12.

U.S. Department of Commerce, Bureau of the Census. 1989. *Computer Use in the United States.* Washington, D.C.: U.S. Government Printing Office.

Utterback, J. M. 1969. *The Process of Technical Innovation in Industrial Firms.* Ph.D. diss. Cambridge: Sloan School of Management, Massachusetts Institute of Technology.

Van Brakel, Pieter A. 1995. Electronic journals: Publishing via Internet's World Wide Web. *The Electronic Library* 13(4): 389-96.

Van Cott, Harold P. 1970. National information system for psychology: A proposed system for a pressing problem. *American Psychologist* 25(5): i-xx.

Van House, Nancy A. 1990. *Library Resources and Research Productivity in Science and Engineering.* A report to the National Science Foundation from the Council on Library Resources. Washington, D.C.: Council on Library Resources.

VandenBos, Gary R. 1998. Electronic costs of an all-electronic journal. In *Economics, Real Costs and Benefits of Electronic Publishing in Science—A Technical Study: Proceedings of the UCSU Press Workshop, Keble College, Oxford, UK March 31 to April 2, 1998,* eds. Dennis Shaw and David Price. Available from <http://www.bodley.ox.ac.uk/icsu/vanden-bosppr.htm>.

Varian, Hal R. 1995. The information economy. How much will two bits be worth in the digital marketplace? *Scientific American* September: 200-01.

—. 1996a. Differential pricing and efficiency. *First Monday* 1(2). Available from <http://www.firstmonday.dk/issues/issue2/different/>.

—. 1996b. Economic issues facing the Internet. Available from <http://www.sims.berkeley.edu/~hal/Papers/econ-issues-internet.html>.

—. 1996c. Pricing electronic journals. *D-Lib Magazine* (June). Available from <http://www.dlib.org/dlib/june96/06varian.html>.

—. 1998. The future of electronic journals. *Journal of Electronic Publishing* 4(1). Avaliable from <http://www.press.umich.edu/jep/>.

Voge, Susan. 1994. Searching electronic databases to locate tests and measures. *Reference Services Review*: 75-79.

Von Seggern, Marilyn, and Janet M. Jourdain. 1996. Technical communications in engineering and science: The practices within a government defense laboratory. *Special Libraries* 87(2): 98-119.

Voorbij, Henk J. 1999. Searching scientific information on the Internet: A Dutch academic user survey. *Journal of the American Society for Information Science* 50(7): 598-615.

Wade, Philip. 1963. Subscriptions to journals. *The Lancet* 27: 950.

Walker, G. L. 1966. Processing mathematical text for publication. In *Transcript of Proceedings, Information Systems Colloquium, Computer Applications in Scientific Publications.* Washington, D.C.: National Science Foundation.

Walker, Mark. 1998. As online journals advance, new challenges emerge. *The Seybold Report on Internet Publishing* 3(1): 3.

Walker, Thomas J. 1996. Electronic reprints: Segueing into electronic publication of biological journals. *BioScience* 45: 171.

—. 1998a. The future of scientific journals: free access or pay per view? *American Entomologist* 44(3). Available from <http://csssrvr.entnem.ufl.edu/~walker/fewww/aecom3.html>.

—. 1998b. Free Internet access to traditional journals. *American Scientist* 86(5): 463-71. Available from <http://www.amsci.org/amsci/articles/98articles/walker.html>.

Wang, Peiling, and Marilyn D. White. 1999. A cognitive model of document use during a research project. Study II. Decisions at the reading and citing stages. *Journal of the American Society for Information Science* 50(2): 98-114.

Weibel, Stuart L. 1995. The World Wide Web and emerging Internet resource discovery standards for scholarly literature. *Library Trends* 43(4): 627-44.

Wei-He, Peter and Trudi E. Jacobsen. 1996. What are they doing with the Internet? A study of user information seeking behaviors. *Internet Reference Services Quarterly* 1(1): 31-51.

Weil, Ben H. 1977. *Benefits from Researcher Use of the Published Literature at the Exxon Research Center.* Washington, D.C.: National Information Conference and Exposition.

—. 1980. Benefits from research use of the published literature at the Exxon research center. In *Special Librarianship: A New Reader,* ed. Eugene B. Jackson, 586-594. Metuchen, N.J.: Scarecrow Press.

Wells, H. G. 1938. *World Brain.* London: Methuen.

Werbach, K. 1997. *Digital Tornado: The Internet and Telecommunications Policy.* Springfield, Va.: National Technical Information Service. PB 97 161 905.

Werler, Ruth W. 1975. Hospital journal title use study. *Special Libraries* 66(11): 532-37.

White, B. 1970. *Planners and Information.* London: Library Association.

White, Herbert S., and Bernard M. Fry. 1979. Economic interaction between special libraries and publishers of scholarly and research journals. In *The Scientific Journal,* ed. A. J. Meadows, 50-5. London: Aslib.

Wilder, Stanley J. 1998. Comparing value and estimated revenue of scitech journals. *ARL: A Bimonthly Newsletter of Research Library Issues and Actions*: 13-16.

Wilkinson, Sophie. 1998. Electronic publishing takes journals into a new realm. *Chemical and Engineering News* 76:10-18. Available from <http://pubs.acs.org/hotartcl/cenear/980518/elec.html>.

—. 1999. Behind the scenes at journals. *Chemical Engineering News*. September 13: 25-31.

Willenbrock, F. Karl. 1996. Spectral lines: Importance of secondary publications. *IEEE Spectrum* 3: 39.

Williams, G. R. 1975. Library subscription decisions. *IEEE Transactions on Professional Communication* 18(3): 207-09.

Williams, L. A. 1993. How chemists use the literature. *Learned Publishing* 6(2): 7-14.

Williams, Martha E. 1986. Transparent Information Systems Through Gateways, Front Ends, Intermediaries, and Interfaces. *Journal of the American Society for Information Science* 37(4): 204-14.

—. 1989. *Information Market Indicators Reports*. Monticello, Ill.: Information Market Indicators.

—.1990. Highlights of the online database industry and the quality of information and data. In *National Online Meeting Proceedings*, ed. M. E. Williams, 1-4 Medford, N.J.: Learned Information.

—. 1991. The state of databases today. In *Computer-Readable Databases: A Directory and Data Sourcebook*, eds. Kathleen Maraccio, Julie Adams, and Kathleen J. Edgar. Detroit: Gale Research.

—. 1994. The Internet: Implications for the information industry and database providers. *Online and CDROM Review* 18(3): 149-56.

Willis, Katherine, Ken Alexander, William A. Gosling, Gregory R. Peters, Jr., Robert Schwarzwalder, and Beth Forrest Warner. 1994. TULIP- The University Licensing Program: Experience at the University of Michigan. *Serials Review* Fall: 39-47.

Wills, Matthew, and Gordon Wills. 1996. The ins and the outs of electronic publishing. *Internet Research: Electronic Networking Applications and Policy* 6(1): 10-21.

Wilson, David L. 1991. Testing time for electronic journals. *The Chronicle of Higher Education* 38 (September 11): A22-A24.

—. 1994. The appeal of hypertext. *The Chronicle of Higher Education* 41(5): A25, A27, A30.

Wilson, L. 1940. *The Academic Man: A Study in the Sociology of a Profession.* New York: Oxford University Press.

Wilson, J.M., A. F. MacDougal, and H. M. Woodward. 1986. Economic consequences of libraries acquiring electronic journal articles. *British Journal of Academic Librarianship* 1(3): 228-35.

Winkler, Karen J. 1997. Academic presses look to the Internet to save scholarly monograph. *The Chronicle of Higher Education* 43(3): A18-A21.

Winner, L. 1996. Who will we be in cyberspace? *Information Society* 12(1): 63-72.

Wissoker, Ken. 1997. Scholarly monographs are flourishing, not dying. *The Chronicle of Higher Education* 43(3): B4-B5.

Wolek, Francis W. 1970. The complexity of messages in science and engineering: An influence on patterns of communication. In *Communication Among Scientists and Engineers*, eds. Carnot E. Nelson and Donald K.Pollard, 233-65. Lexington, Mass.: Heath Lexington Books.

Wolek, Francis, and Belver C. Griffith. Policy and informal communications in applied science and technology. In *Key Papers in Information Science*, ed. Belver C. Griffith, 113-22. White Plains, N.Y.: Knowledge Industry Publications.

Wood, Barbara L. 1977. *Review of Scientific and Technical Numeric Data Base Activities.* Washington, D.C. Available from PB 278-254.

Wood, M. Sandra, ed. 1985. *Cost Analysis, Cost Recovery, Marketing, and Fee-based Services: A Guide for the Health Sciences Librarian.* New York: The Haworth Press.

Woodward, A. M. 1976a. The applicability of Editorial Processing Centres to U.K. publishing. *Aslib Proceedings* 28(8): 266-70.

—. 1976b. *Editorial Processing Centres: Scope in the United Kingdom.* London: British Library Research and Development Department.

Woodward, Hazel M., and Cliff McKnight. 1995. Electronic journals: Issues of access and bibliographical control. *Serials Review* 21: 71-78.

Woodward, Hazel M., Fytton Rowland, Cliff McKnight, Jack Meadows, and C. Pritchett. 1997. Electronic journals: Myths and realities. *Library Management* 18: 155-62.

Wooster, Harold. 1979. The future of scientific publishing or, what will scientists be doing for brownie points? In *The Scientific Journal*, ed. A. J. Meadows, 63-70. London: Aslib.

Wootton, Christopher B. 1977. *Trends in Size, Growth and Cost of the Literature Science 1955.* Report No. 5323 HC. London. The British Library Research & Development Department.

Wouters, Paul. 1999. The creation of the Science Citation Index. In *Proceedings of the 1998 Conference on the History and Heritage of Science Information Systems,* eds. Mary Ellen Bowden, Trudi Bellardo Hahn, and Robert V. Williams, 127-36. Medford, N.J.: Information Today, Inc.

Wuest, F. J. 1965. *Studies in the methodology of measuring information requirements and use patterns*: Report No. 1. Bethlehem, Penn.: Center for the Information Sciences, Lehigh University.

Wulf, W. A. 1993. The collaborative opportunity. *Science* 261: 854-56.

Wyly, Brendan J. 1998. Competition in scholarly publishing? What published profits reveal. *ARL: A Bimonthly Newsletter of Research Library Issues and Actions*: 6-13.

Yavarkovsky, Jerome. 1990. A university-based electronic publishing network. *EDUCOM Review* 25(3): 14-20.

Yokote, G. and R. A. Utterback. 1974. Time lapses in information dissemination: Research lab to physician's office. *Bulletin of the Medical Library Association* 62: 251-57.

Young, Peter R. 1992. National Corporation for Scholarly Publishing: Presentation and description of the model. *Serials Review* 18(1/2): 100-01.

Zuckerman, Harriet, and Robert K. Merton. 1979. Patterns of evaluation in science: Institutionalization, structure, and functions of the referee system. In *The Scientific Journal*, ed. A. J. Meadows, 112-46. London: Aslib.

Author Index

A

Abels, Eileen, 366, 367, 403, 437
Ackoff, Russell L. (R. L.), 71, 127, 129, 403, 423, 441
A. C. Nielsen Media Research, 366
Adams, Julie, 461
Adams, Peter D., 436
Aitchison, J., 69, 75, 165, 403, 423
Akazawa, Shunichi, 436
Akscyn, Robert M., 418
Albritton, Everett C., 403
Alexander, Adrian, 404
Alexander, Julie S., 404
Alexander, Ken, 461
Allen, Bryce, 404
Allen, Thomas J., 65, 128, 129, 134, 135, 165, 172, 173, 404, 405, 420, 441
Almquist, E., 405
Altbach, Philip G., 405
American Association of Publishers, 413
American Chemical Society, 405
American Mathematical Society, 405
American Psychological Association, 65, 165, 170, 405

Amiran, Eyal, 134, 136, 137, 151, 152, 346, 348, 405
Amy, S., 77, 405
Anania, L., 359, 405
Anderla, J. Georges, 66, 67, 87, 405, 406
Anderson, C. M. B., 72, 454
Anderson, G., 148, 325, 346, 348, 406
Andrien, Maurice P. Jr., 172, 405
Anthony, L. J., 406
Ardito, Stephanie C., 406
Arms, William Y., 326, 406
Armstrong, C. J., 406
Arnold, Kenneth, 406
Arnold, Stephen E., 406
Arthur D. Little, Inc., 77, 406
Association of American Universities, 92, 99, 406
Association of Research Libraries, 406
Astle, D. L., 162, 406
Auerbach Corp., 406
Auster, Ethel, 412

B

Badger, R., 80, 406
Bailey, C. A., 415

Bailey, Charles W., Jr., 151, 326, 406, 407, 416
Bailey, Joseph P. (J. P.), 355, 405, 423, 446, 442, 447
Baker, N. R., 407
Bamford, Harold E., Jr., 74, 407
Barber, B., 443
Barclay, Rebecca O., 129, 130, 132, 142, 160, 200, 426, 449
Bar-Ilan, J., 367, 436
Barinova, Z. B., 407
Barlow, John Perry, 407
Barnett, Michael P., 64, 407
Barschall, H. H., 407
Baruch, Jordon (J. J.), 162, 407
Basch, Reva, 406, 407, 408, 423, 427,428, 444, 445, 457
Bash, George P., 434
Basova, I. M., 407
Battin, Patricia, 422, 424, 425
Baumol, William J. (W. J.), 287, 447
Bayer, Alan E., 407
Beachboard, J. C., 350, 358, 441
Beardsley, Charles W., 407
Bellardo Hahn, Trudi, 63, 409, 411, 425, 429, 435, 439, 463
Bellassai, M. C., 74, 448
Bennett, Scott, 407
Berg, S. V., 287, 407
Berge, Z. L., 408
Berger, Paul, 128, 420
Berghel, Hal, 408
Berlt, Nancy C., 444
Bernal, J. D., 408
Bernard, C. W., 454
Bernard, Jessie, 172, 408, 454
Berry, R. Stephen (R. S.), 445
Bertot, J. C., 358, 441
Berul, Lawrence M., 73
Best, Diana, 451
Beutler, Earl, 408
Bever, Arley T., 408
Bhagat, Nazir (N. A.), 162, 407
Bichteler, Julie, 408
Bickner, Robert E., 110, 408
Bishop, Ann Peterson, 366, 408
Blecic, Deborah D., 408
Borghuis, Marthyn, 408

Borgman, Christine L., 95, 409
Born, Kathleen, 279, 280, 429, 430
Bosseau, Don, 409
Bottoms, John W., 409
Bourne, Charles P., 63, 409
Bowden, Mary Ellen, 409, 425, 435, 463
Bowen, D. H. M., 256, 257, 409
Bowen, William G., 32, 414
Boyce, P. B., 372, 409
Boyer, E. L., 19, 409
Brandao, C., 372, 409
Branscomb, Anne Wells, 409
Braunstein, Yale, 206, 410
Brennan, Patricia, 414
Brett, 358
Brinberg, Herbert R., 410
Brinckman, Hans, 408
Brichford, Maynard, 410
Broadbent, Margaret, 410
Broadbent, Marianne, 210, 410
Brock, William Hudson, 57, 410
Brogan, M., 256, 410
Brown, Cecelia M., 169, 388, 389, 410
Brown, David J., 32, 80, 87, 282, 393, 410
Brown, Elizabeth W., 410
Brown, W. S., 68, 410
Browning, John, 410
Brownrigg, Edwin, 79, 410
Bruwelheide, Janis H., 410
Bryant, Edward C., 110, 161, 431
Buckland, Lawrence F., 64, 411
Buckland, Michael K., 61, 411
Buckle, P., 443
Budd, John, 411
Budd, John M., 388, 411
Bulick, S., 216, 297, 429
Busch, Joseph A., 411
Bush, Colleen G., 191, 442
Bush, Vannevar, 21, 61, 411
Butler, Brett, 411
Butler, Declan, 411
Butler, Julene H., 411
Butler, Meredith A., 411, 419
Buxton, A. B., 411

C

Callahan, Daniel, 129, 443
Campanario, Juan Miguel (J. M.), 139, 411, 412
Campell, David T. H., 279, 280, 412
Campbell, Jerry D., 28, 412
Campbell, Robert, 6, 37, 253, 256, 260, 302, 303, 304, 310, 313, 315, 447, 448
Cargill, Jennifer, 404
Carpender, Mark, 444
Carrigan, Dennis (D.), 192, 317, 412
Carr, Leslie, 121, 344, 346, 426
Carroll, Bonnie C., 78, 85, 93, 136, 168, 422
Carter, Launor, 412
Case, Donald, 386, 412
Casto, Jane, 66, 431
Cawkell, Tony, 409, 412
Chakrabarti, Alok K., 412
Charles River Associates, 174, 412
Chaski, C., 138, 151, 405
Chatterton, L. A., 441
Chen, Ching-Chih (C-C), 216, 297, 412
Chen, Hsinchun, 412
Choo, Chun Wei, 412
Chressanthis, George A., 287, 413
Chressanthis, June D., 287, 413
Christopherson, Robert, 287, 456
Chrzastowski, Tina E., 413
Chu, H., 367, 413
Chuang, J. S. I., 287, 393, 413
Cisler, Steve, 413
Clack, M. E., 441
Clague, P., 75, 165, 423
Clark, D., 359, 454
Clarke-Kraut, Karen Rebecca, 413
Cleverdon, Cyril W., 75, 413
Coffman, S., 193, 413
Cohen, J., 216, 297, 429
Cohen, Stephen I., 405
Collier, Harry, 65, 358, 362, 376, 392, 413
Collins, M. P., 408
Compton, Bertita E., 67, 419
Connaway, Lynn Silipigni, 388, 411
Contley, Gordon, 412
Cooper, Michael D., 413
Council on Library Resources, 74, 310, 413
Cowan, T. A., 71, 403

Crane, Diana, 413, 414
Crawford, Susan Y., 3, 61, 88, 362, 414
Crews, Kenneth D., 414
Cronin, Blaise, 414, 415
Cuadra, Carlos A., 404, 413, 414, 415, 418, 423, 426, 434, 435, 437, 438, 443, 448
Cummings, Anthony M., 32, 414
Cunningham, Ann Marie, 414, 427
Curtis, Mary E., 326, 427
Curtice, Robert M., 63, 428

D

Dalterio, H., 409
Dannelly, Gay N., 414
Daval, Nicola (N.), 192, 193, 414, 415
Davenport, Elisabeth, 414
David, Carl W., 131
Davis, P., 71, 403
Davis, R. A., 415
Davis, Richard M., 129, 130, 131, 415
Day, Colin, 415
Day, R. A., 256, 415
Dean, N., 417
Dederick, Ward, 408
DeGennaro, Richard, 284, 415
DeLoughry, Thomas J., 152, 415
Denman, D. W., 366, 367, 437
Denning, Peter J., 415
Dervin, Brenda, 415
Dixon, Jeanne, 434
Dodd, Jane, 421
Doebler, Paul D., 63, 415
Dorschner, Eileen, 440
Dosa, Marta, 416
Dowd-Reisen, Patricia M., 431
Drabenstott, Karen M., 81, 416
Drake, Miriam A., 416
Drasgow, L., 71, 72, 435
Dubinskaya, S. A., 416
Duda, Andrea, 410
Duggan, Mary K., 416
Dulchn, J., 127, 129, 181, 443

E

East, H., 406
Ebenfield, Helene, 458

Economic Consulting Services, Inc., 283, 284, 416
Edgar, Kathleen J., 461
Edmisten, Jane, 279, 280, 412
Edwards, Paul N., 20, 416
Ekman, R., 423
Ekman, Richard H., 32, 414
Elias, Arthur W., 416
Elliott, Carolyn S., 416
Elsdon-Dew, R., 416
Elton, M. C. J., 71, 403
Emery, J. C., 71, 403
Englebart, Douglas C., 62, 416
Ensor, Pat, 416
Entlich, Richard, 417
Erickson, T., 206, 425
Ernst and Young, 362, 417
Esler, Sandra L., 417
Estrin, D., 359, 454
Ettlie, John E., 417

F
Farid, Mona, 416
Feeney, M., 422
Feinman, Stephen, 412
Feldman, Susan, 417
Fidel, Raya, 411, 429, 439
Finnigan, Georgia, 192, 417
Fischer, Albert, 408
Fishel, M., 417
Fisher, Janet H., 81, 256, 417
Flanagin, A. R., 137, 417
Fletcher, Lloyd Alan, 417
Florentine, Harry, 418
Flowers, B. H., 418
Flynn, R., 216, 297, 429
Fox, Edward A., 418
Franks, John, 418
Frazier, Kenneth, 418
Friend, Frederick, 418
Frost, Penelope A., 418
Fry, Bernard M. (B. M.), 70, 199, 255, 310, 315, 418, 460
Fuentevilla, William, 412
Fuller, Steve, 418
Furuta, Richard K., 418

Fuseler, Elizabeth (Beth) Avery (A.), 418

G
Gaines, Brian R., 418
Gamboa, Carlos, 436
Gannett, Elwood K., 63, 418
Gans, Daniel J., 206, 434
Garcia, D. Linda, 418
Garcia, J. J. E., 148, 149, 419
Gardner, William, 419
Garrett, John R., 419
Garrison, F. H., 57, 419
Garson, Lorrin R., 69, 417, 419, 458
Garvey, William D., 2, 60, 66, 67, 68, 88, 89, 153, 154, 161, 162, 419, 420, 437
Gasaway, Laura N., 420, 451
Gates, Y., 77, 420
Geffner, Mira, 439
Geller, Marilyn, 440
Gerstberger, Peter G., 128, 173, 405, 420
Gerstenfeld, Arthur, 128, 405
Gerstl, J. E., 420
Getz, Malcolm, 344, 345, 401, 402, 420
Gibbon, Michael, 428
Gilbert, John H. V., 438
Gillespie, Constance J., 435
Gillespie, Robert G., 420
Ginsparg, Paul, 81
Giuliano, Vincent E., 63, 428
Givler, Peter, 381, 384, 421
Glaser, Edward, 421
Glass, R. M., 137, 417
Glassman, Myron, 129, 130, 132, 142, 160, 200, 449
Glosser, Caryle, 436
Glueck, William F., 421
GOGSIP Study Group, John Hopkins University, 421
Goodwin, H. B., 99, 421
Goodyear, Marilu, 404, 421
Gosling, William A., 461
Gottfreddson, S. D., 68, 419
Götze, Dietrich, 421
Gould, Constance C., 421
Grajek, Susan, 421
Grant, Joan, 421

Graves, Diana, 404
Gray, Carolyn M., 421
Gray, L. M., 74, 448
Green, Lois, 145, 155, 421
Green, Paul E., 224, 422
Gregory, David, 448
Grieves, M., 422, 452
Griffith, Belver C., 66, 88, 89, 161, 162, 404,
    414, 419, 421, 422, 452, 462
Griffiths, José-Marie (J-M), 78, 80, 85, 87,
    93, 104, 112, 116, 126, 128, 136, 163,
    164, 167, 168, 170, 179, 180, 181, 188,
    195, 196, 202, 203, 205, 209, 210, 212,
    216, 224, 228, 289, 291, 295, 296, 364,
    382, 383, 422, 431
Grogan, D. J., 422
Grossner, Kerry, 422
Grotenhuis, Alert J. te, 422
Grueberger, Fred, 437
Grycz, Czeslaw Jan, 423
Guédon, Jean-Claude, 423
Gupta, R. C., 423
Gurnsey, J., 77, 423
Gursey, S., 142, 449
Gushee, David E., 423
Guthrie, K. M., 383, 423

H
Hagstrom, Warren O., 69, 423
Hahn, Susan, 390, 455
Halbert, Michael H., 127, 129, 423
Hall, Angela M., 75, 165, 423
Hall, Wendy, 121, 344, 346, 426
Hallgren, M. M., 356, 423
Hallmark, Julie, 423
Halvorson, T. R., 423
Hambrecht, 355
Hammer, Donald P., 66, 424
Hansen, Owen, 374, 445
Harnad, Stevan, 24, 81, 148, 167, 372, 424
Harrison, Teresa M., 424
Harter, Stephen P., 390, 424
Hattery, Lowell H., 434
Hauptman, R., 150, 424
Havelock, Ronald G., 196, 202, 438
Hawkins, Brian L., 32, 422, 424, 425

Hawkins, Donald T., 327, 425
Hayes, Brian, 425
Hayes, J. R., 425
Hayes, Robert M., 206, 425
Hazell, J. C., 425
Hazen, Dan C., 425
Hecht, C. P., 72, 454
Heijnekamp, Selma J., 422
Helgerson, Linda W., 409
Heller, Stephen, 376, 425
Hemus, M., 424
Henderson, Albert (A.), 27, 32, 212, 282,
    425
Henderson, Madeline B., 62, 425
Henderson, Tona, 425
Herner, Mary, 66, 426
Herner, Saul, 66, 425, 426
Hernon, Peter, 426
Herschman, Arthur, 70, 426
Herzog, S., 359, 454
Hewins, Elizabeth T., 426
Hickey, Thomas B., 426
Hills, J. A., 69, 426
Hills, Philip, 426, 429, 430
Hill, Susan T., 145, 155, 421
Hiltz, Starr Roxanne, 23, 72, 74, 147, 426,
    458
Hindle, A., 451
Hinrichs, J. R., 426
Hipps, Kaylyn E., 435
Hirsch, Walter, 443
Hitchcock, Steve, 121, 344, 346, 426
Hoban, Charles F., 426
Hodina, Alfred, 435
Hoffert, Barbara, 426
Holder, Steve, 426
Holland, Maurita Peterson (P.), 426, 427,
    449
Holmes, Aldyth, 256, 258, 260, 263, 264,
    371, 375,427
Holoviak, Judy C., 70, 456
Horowitz, Irving Louis, 326, 427
Houghton, Bernard, 56, 57, 427
Hudnut, Sophie K., 427
Hunter, Karen, 408, 427
Hurd, Julie M., 3, 61, 88, 362, 414

Hurley, S. D., 413
Hurt, Charlene S., 138, 451
Huth, Edward J., 427
Hutton, S. P., 420

I
Intelquest, 366
Institute of Physics, 75, 155, 174, 312, 313, 427

J
Jackson, Eugene B., 460
Jackson, Mary E., 186, 191, 224, 227, 228, 295, 427
Jacob, M. E. L., 427
Jacobsen, Trudi E., 460
Jacobson, Robert L., 427, 428
Jacso, Peter, 428
Jahoda, Gerald, 407
Jankovich, A. L. L., 393, 440
Jauch, Lawerence R., 421
John, Nancy R., 428
Johnson, Richard M., 224, 428
Johnston, Ron, 428
Jones, Heather, 66, 431
Jones, Paul E., 63, 428
Jonscher, Charles, 206, 428
Jourdain, Janet M., 144, 459
Judd, Peggy, 436
Judson, H. F., 137, 148, 167, 326, 428
Jul, Erik, 428
Jusawalla, Meheroo, 428, 458

K
Kahin, Brian, 413, 428
Kahn, Robert, 428
Kantor, Paul B., 210, 403, 428, 453
Kaplan, Jeremiah, 134, 326, 429
Kaser, Dick, 192, 417, 429
Katz, Ralph, 128, 429
Katz, Richard N., 429
Katzen, May, 429
Kay, M., 75, 455
Keen, E. Michael, 75, 413
Keenan, Stella, 429
Keene, Michael L., 449
Keister, Lucinda H., 429

Kendall, M. G., 429
Kennedy, John M., 429, 449
Kent, A., 216, 297, 429
Kent, A. J., 429
Kern, J. R., 216, 297, 429
Kessler, M. M., 60, 429
Ketcham, Lee, 429
Ketcham-Van Orsdel, Lee, 279, 280, 430
Keyes, Alison M., 210, 430
Kiernan, Vincent 6, 386, 393, 430
Killion, Vicki, 430
Kim, Hak Joon, 424
King, David, 212, 430
King, Donald W., 7, 59, 60, 66, 67, 68, 69, 71, 72, 73, 74, 78, 80, 82, 83, 85, 87, 91, 92, 93, 99, 104, 110, 112, 116, 118, 120, 126, 128, 136, 139, 142, 144, 156, 161, 162, 163, 164, 165, 167, 168, 170, 179, 180, 181, 184, 186, 187, 188, 193, 194, 195, 196, 202, 203, 205, 209, 216, 224, 228, 236, 237, 240, 241, 252, 253, 255, 256, 258, 260, 261, 267, 268, 270, 271, 275, 276, 277, 279, 280, 282, 289, 291, 295, 296, 310, 311, 312, 313, 314, 324, 327, 351, 382, 386, 388, 398, 400, 409, 422, 430, 431, 432, 433, 435, 438, 457
Kingma, Bruce R. (B.R.), 181, 186, 215, 216, 227, 228, 295, 296, 297, 298, 318, 411, 419, 433
King Research, Inc., 74, 191, 433
King, Timothy B., 433
Klemperer, Katharina, 433
Kling, Rob, 390, 433
Kochen, Manfred (M.), 152, 433
Koenig, Michael E. D., 206, 210, 211, 433, 434
Kost, Robert, 434
Kovacs, Diana K., 434
Kovacs, Michael J., 434
Krikeles, James, 434
Krockel, H., 87, 434
Kronick, David A., 56, 434
Kuhn, Thomas S., 57, 434
Kuney, Joseph H., 64, 264, 434
Kurosman, Kathleen, 434
Kutner, Gail L., 196, 202, 438
Kutz, Myer, 434

Kuznetsova, I. F., 407
Kvalnes, Florence H., 63, 435
Kyrillidou, Martha, 435

L
Ladd, R. Boyd, 431
Ladendorf, Janice M., 435
Lago, J., 256, 435
Lambert, Jill, 75, 374, 377, 435
Lamb, Roberta, 433
Lancaster, F. W., 72, 76, 88, 91, 112, 143, 160,
    327, 388, 431, 435
Landau, Herbert B., 436
Landau, Robert M., 64, 69, 436
Langschied, Linda, 436
LaPorte, Ronald E., 436
Lawrence, Barbara, 436
Laws, Kenneth I., 436
Lazarus, Laura O., 32, 414
Lazinger, S. S., 367, 436
Lederberg, J., 148, 167, 436
Lee, Alfred T., 377, 436
Leeson, Kenneth W., 70, 73, 255, 258, 260,
    262, 263, 271, 272, 310, 311, 439
Leggett, John J., 418
Lehman, Bruce A., 436
Lenares, Deborah, 388, 390, 436
Lenzini, R. T., 81, 436
Lerner, Rita, 256, 258, 260, 310, 311, 436
Lesk, Michael, 22, 61, 64, 65, 78, 80, 329,
    417, 437
Levine, Arthur, 437
Lewis, David W., 437
Libbey, Miles A., 437
Lichtenberg, James, 437
Lichtenstein, A., 192, 415
Licklider, Joseph C. R. (J. C. R.), 62, 64, 65,
    66, 437
Liebscher, P., 366, 367, 437
Lieberman, L., 127, 129, 181, 443
Lienhard, John H., 444
Lindsey, Georg N., 129, 443
Lingwood, D. A., 172, 448
Lin, Nan, 60, 68, 88, 89, 153, 154, 419, 437
Line, Maurice B., 438
Linn, Peter, 451

Lipetz, Ben-Ami, 438
Liston, David M., 196, 202, 438
Little, S. B., 87, 438
LLP Magazine Publishers of America, 417
Lofgren, Hans, 210, 410
Login, Elisabeth, 438
Lohmann, Victor L., 438
Lonquet-Higgins, H. C., 438
Loo, Eleonore van der, 408
Lorimer, Rowland, 438
Lu, Kathleen, 438
Lubans, John Jr., 146, 438
Lucier, Richard E., 92, 438
Ludwig, Walter, 256, 263, 438
Lufkin, J. M., 128, 173, 438, 439
Luhn, Hans Peter (P.), 439
Luke, Ann W., 415, 418, 437
Lundberg, G. D., 137, 417
Lundeen, Gerald, 439
Lunin, Lois F., 403, 418, 439, 458
Lustig, H., 375, 439
Lyman, Peter, 439
Lynch, Clifford A., 439
Lynn, M. Stuart, 419

M
Macdougal, A. F., 462
MacEwan, Bonnie, 439
Machlup, Fritz, 61, 70, 73, 170, 255, 258,
    260, 262, 263, 271, 272, 309, 310, 439,
    444
MacKie-Mason, Jeffrey K., 352, 358, 359,
    393, 440
Maclure, Malcolm, 436
MacLennan, Birdie (B.), 388, 440, 447
Maher, William, 410
Mailloux, Elizabeth N., 440
Maizell, R. B., 172, 440
Malakoff, David, 440
Mangiafico, Paul, 445
Manheim, Frank T., 440
Manoff, Marlene, 440
Mansfield, Una, 444
Maraccio, Kathleen, 461
Marks, E., 72, 435
Marks, Kenneth E., 279, 280, 283, 440

Marks, Robert H. (R. H.), 253, 256, 257, 258, 263, 265, 440
Marler, Eric, 436
Marquis, Donald G. (D. G.), 441
Marshall, G., 256, 260, 263, 310, 441
Marshall, Joanne G., 211, 212, 441
Martin, Miles W., 127, 181, 441
Martyn, John, 441
Matarazzo, James M., 210, 211, 441, 450
McAdams, A. K., 356, 423
McCabe, Mark J., 282, 307, 317, 318, 319, 441
McCarthy, Paul, 300, 441
McClung, Patricia A., 441
McClure, Charles R., 358, 426, 441
McDonald, Dennis D., 7, 59, 67, 72, 74, 87, 91, 92, 118, 120, 139, 142, 153, 155, 156, 162, 163, 164, 165, 174, 175, 179, 180, 181, 191, 194, 255, 257, 258, 260, 279, 280, 282, 310, 312, 313, 324, 327, 382, 386, 431, 432, 442
McEldowney, Philip, 121, 343, 442
McFarland, Patricia A., 442
McKie, Douglas, 442
McKiernan, Gerry, 442
McKim, Geoffrey, 390, 433
McKnight, Cliff, 75, 442, 443, 452, 462
McKnight, Lee W. (L. W.), 355, 405, 423, 440, 442, 447
McMillan, Gail, 442, 450
Meadows, Jack (A. J., Arthur Jack), 6, 19, 37, 56, 57, 66, 75, 160, 253, 256, 260, 263, 302, 303, 304, 310, 313, 315, 407, 408, 410, 411, 418, 419, 429, 430, 441, 442, 443, 444, 445, 447, 448, 452, 454, 455, 458, 460, 462, 463
Meditz, M. L., 71, 403
Menzel, Herbert, 65, 66, 127, 129, 170, 181, 443
Mercer, Linda, 443
Merton, Robert K. (R. K.), 443, 463
Metaxas, Ted, 436
Metoyer-Duran, Cheryl, 443
Mick, Colin K., 443
Millar, Victor A., 449

Miller, David C., 443
Miller, E. H., 128, 173, 439
Miller, George, 61, 444
Mills, Jack, 75, 413
Mintz, Anne, 444
Miranda, Michael A., 287, 456
Mogge, Dru, 426
Molyneux, Robert E., 192, 444
Mondschein, Lawrence G., 444
Montgomery, K. L., 216, 297, 429
Mooney, Carolyn J., 141, 144, 444
Moore, J. A., 162, 444
Morgan, Bruce, 444
Mors, Rob ter, 408
Moravesik, Michael J., 81, 444
Morgan, Keith, 440
Mostert, Paul, 408
Motin, S., 150, 424
Mountbatten, Earl, 67, 444
Mullins, Nicholas, 422
Murphy, J., 358, 440
Murphy, K. L., 358, 440
Murray, Herbert Jr., 67, 444
Myers, Judy E., 444

N
Narin, Francis, 444
National Commission on Libraries and Information Science, 74, 44
National Research Council,(Canada), 192
National Research Council (US), 360, 362, 396, 445
National Science Foundation, 445
Nelke, Margareta, 210, 445
Nelson, Carnot E., 68, 88, 89, 154, 419, 423, 437, 445, 447, 462
Nelson, Michael L., 417
Neuman, Michael, 445
Network Wizards, 364
Newby, Gregory B., 423, 424, 425, 439, 445, 447, 455
Nielsen, Steven P., 279, 280, 283, 440
Nilan, Michael, 415
Noam, E. M., 445
Noll, R., 275, 287, 445

Norman, Sandy, 445
Normore, Lorraine, 417
Novikov, Yu A., 445

O
Odlyzko, Andrew, 3, 24, 81, 241, 259, 271,
    281, 318, 326, 342, 371, 374, 382, 445,
    446
O'Donnell, James J., 375, 445, 447
O'Donnell, Michael J. (Mike J.), 138, 445
O'Gorman, Lawrence, 408
Okerson, Ann, 167, 279, 280, 284, 325, 326,
    375, 398, 415, 442, 446, 447
Oleska, Brian M., 413
Oliu, Walter E., 129, 130, 132, 142, 160, 200,
    449
Olsen, Candace H., 165, 432
Olsen, Harold A., 408, 432
Olsen, Jan (J.), 166, 167, 168, 346, 348, 417,
    447
O'Neill, Hugh V., 69, 432
Operations Research Group, Case
    Institute of Technology, 127, 129, 165,
    172, 188, 447
Oram, A., 360, 447
Ordover, J. A., 287, 447
Orenstein, Ruth, 447
Orr, Elaine, 134, 136, 151, 152, 346, 405
Orr, Richard H., 172, 200, 447
O'Shea, Robert, 374, 447
Otlet, P., 61, 447
Overfelt, Kara, 414

P
Page, Gillian, 6, 37, 253, 256, 260, 263, 302,
    303, 304, 310, 313, 315, 447, 448
Paisley, William J. (W. J.), 65, 69, 172, 448
Palmer, Jonathan, 390, 455
Palmour, Vernon (V. E.), 74, 431, 432, 448
Parker, Edward (E. B.), 65, 172, 448
Parkhurst, Carol A., 410
Passman, Sidney, 448
Pasternack, Simon, 448
Patrick, Ruth J., 438
Pearce, Karla, 421
Pederson, Wayne, 448

Peek, Robin P., 423, 424, 425, 439, 445, 448,
    455
Penniman, W. David, 449
Peritz, B. C., 367, 436
Peters, Gregory R., 461
Peters, John, 448
Peters, Paul Evan, 449
Petersen, H. Craig, 279, 280, 283, 287, 440,
    449
Pierce, J. R., 68, 410
Pigou, A. C., 394, 449
Pinelli, Thomas E., 129, 130, 132, 142, 160,
    200, 426, 449
Piternick, Anne B., 449
Pollack, Donald K., 423, 437, 445, 447, 462
Pollard, Marvin, 438
Pomerantz, Jefferey, 448
Porter, Michael E., 449
Potter, J. N., 425
Potter, William, 323, 449
Powell, Christina Kelleher, 427
President's Task Force, 210
Price, David, 432, 447, 453, 454, 455, 459
Price, Derek J. DeSolla (D.S.), 18, 56, 57, 58,
    67, 142, 146, 148, 168, 449
Pritchett, C., 462
Prusak, Laurence, 210, 211, 441, 450
Pullinger, David (D. J.), 443, 450, 455

Q
Quant, R. E., 423
Quist, 355
Qin, Jian, 450
Quinn, Frank, 450

R
Raben, J., 136, 152, 167, 453
Raitt, David Iain, 450
Rasmussen, Edie M., 411, 429, 439
Rawlins, Gregory J. E., 150, 348, 450
Rayward, W. Boyd, 61, 450
Reich, Vicky, 450
Reichel, M., 193, 450
Repo, Aatto J., 210, 450
Reynolds, Linda, 450
Richardson, Robert J., 451

Rickards, Janice, 451
Rider, F., 21, 61, 451
Riner, Ruth, 429
Risher, Carol A., 451
Ritchie, E., 451
Robertson, S. E., 75, 451
Robert Ubell Associates, 253, 451
Robinson, Kara L., 434
Roche, M., 193, 451
Roderer, Nancy K., 7, 59, 61, 67, 71, 72, 74,
    76, 82, 87, 91, 118, 120, 139, 142, 156,
    162, 163, 164, 165, 179, 180, 181, 194,
    195, 201, 255, 257, 258, 260, 268, 276,
    279, 280, 282, 310, 311, 312, 313, 324,
    327, 382, 386, 408, 431, 432, 451
Rodgers, David L. (D. L.), 447, 451
Rogers, Michael, 451
Rogers, Sharon J., 138, 451
Roistacher, R. C., 138, 451
Ro, Jung Soon, 65, 458
Rosenberg, Victor, 451
Rosenbloom, Richard S., 65, 132, 133, 452
Rothwell, Roy, 452
Rous, Bernard, 386, 415, 452
Rowell, John T., 412
Rowland, Fytton (J. F. B.), 75, 77, 80, 314,
    443, 452, 462
Royal Society, 315
Rubenstein, Albert H. (A. H.), 407, 412
Rugge, S., 417
Rusbridge, Chris, 452
Rush, James E., 420

S
Sabar, W. N., 216, 297, 429
Sabine, Gordon A., 452
Sabine, Patricia L., 452
Sachs, W. M., 71, 403
Salton, Gerard, 63, 452
Samuel, A. L., 22, 452
Samuelson, Pamela, 452, 453
SantaVicca, Edmund F., 453
Saracevic, Tefko, 210, 403, 428, 453
Sauer, Francois, 436
Saunders, Laverna, 406
Savin, W., 74, 407

Schackel, B., 76, 453
Schaffer, Simon, 21, 454
Schaffner, Ann C., 453
Schauder, Don, 143, 146, 147, 149, 152, 161,
    324, 325, 378, 453
Schell, Colleen G. (Bush), 71, 432, 451
Scher, Julian, 129, 458
Schipper, Wendy, 458
Scholarly Communication: The Report of
    the National Enquiry, 71, 453
Schueller, C. G., 71, 432
Schultz, Louise, 412
Schwartz, C., 364, 453
Schwartz, Charles A., 453
Schwartzwalder, Robert, 461
Scott, John T., 265, 436, 453
Scoville, L., 253, 263, 316, 453
Seiden, Herbert R., 412
Seiler, R. H., 136, 152, 167, 453
Senders, John W. (J. W.), 72, 77, 453, 454
Shamp, S. A., 147, 454
Shapin, Steven, 21, 454
Shapiro, Carl, 454
Shaw, Debora, 454
Shaw, Dennis, 432, 447, 453, 454, 455, 459
Shaw, R. R., 132, 454
Shaw, W., 81, 436
Sheetz, Christine M., 78, 85, 93, 136, 168,
    422
Shenker, S., 359, 440, 454
Shenton, Chris, 436
Shephard, David A., 454
Sherlock, Ellen Lyons, 454
Sherman, Chris, 426, 454
Sherrod, John, 435
Shilling, Charles W. (C. W.), 172, 408, 454
Shoham, Snunith, 455
Shotwell, Thomas K., 455
Shuchman, Hedvah L., 455
Siegmann, J., 407
Siess, Judith A., 201, 455
Silverman, Robert J., 455
Simpson, Annette, 455
Singleton, Alan, 57, 75, 443, 455
Sirbu, M. A., 287, 374, 393, 396, 397, 413,
    455

Slater, Margaret (M. J.), 406, 429
Smith, Clagette G., 455
Smith, Philip J., 411, 429, 439
Snowden, Carter, 440
Soloman, R. J., 359, 405
Sparck Jones, Karen (K.), 75, 455
Speier, Cheri, 390, 455
Spielberg, Frederick, 129, 443
Spigai, Fran, 455
Spilhaus, A. F. Jr., 70, 95, 455, 456
Spretnak, Charles M., 130, 456
Spring, Michael B., 456
Staiger, David L., 69, 456
Star, Susan Leigh, 408
Starr, Susan S., 456
Stebelman, Scott, 456
Steinmueller, W. E., 275, 287, 445
Stephen, Timothy D., 424
Stern, Barrie (B. T.), 80, 456
Stewart, Linda, 456
Stix, G., 24, 81, 347, 348, 362, 456
Stodolsky, David S., 456
Stoller, Michael A., 287, 456
Stoller, Michael E., 456
Storey, Tom, 456
Straight, D. M., 441
Stubbs, Kendon, 435, 447
Subramanyam, K., 88, 456
Such, Peter, 443
Sutton, J. R., 457
Sweet, Ellen A., 209, 431

T
Tagliacozzo, R., 152, 433
Taylor, Peter (P.), 366, 429, 457
Taylor, Robert, 65, 437
Taylor, Robert L., 457
Taylor, Robert S., 100, 457
Taylor, Samuel H., 421
Tenopir, Carol, 59, 65, 67, 83, 96, 118, 144,
    146, 151, 163, 164, 180, 181, 184, 186,
    187, 188, 195, 236, 237, 240, 241, 252,
    257, 261, 267, 268, 270, 271, 275, 277,
    279, 280, 314, 432, 433, 439, 457, 458
Terleckyj, Nestor E., 206, 458
Terrant, Seldon W., 69, 458

Thompson, Hugh A., 436
Tomita, Kazuo, 153, 419, 420
Traub, J. F., 68, 410
Treloar, Andrew, 458
Trivette, Don, 458
Tsay, Ming-Yueh, 458
Turner, Judith, 458
Turoff, Murray, 23, 72, 73, 74, 129, 147, 426,
    458,
Tushman, Michael, 128, 429
Tyson, Joe W., 408

U
Uhlir, Paul, 445
Unruh, Betty, 416, 458
Unsworth, John, 134, 136, 151, 152, 348,
    405, 459
US Department of Commerce, Census
    Bureau, 458
Utterback, J. M., 459
Utterback, R. A., 88, 463

V
Van Brakel, Pieter A., 459
Van Cott, Harold P., 69, 459
VandenBos, Gary R., 372, 373, 459
Van House, Nancy A., 206, 459
Varian, Hal R., 326, 352, 356, 357, 359, 365,
    383, 393, 394, 395, 413, 440, 454, 459
Vasarhelyi, Pal, 416
Villasenor, Anthony, 436
Voge, Susan, 459
Von Seggern, Marilyn, 144, 459
Voorbij, Henk J., 390, 459

W
Wade, Philip, 317, 460
Wagner, Peter E., 279, 280, 283, 440
Walker, G. L., 64, 460
Walker, Mark, 460
Walker, Thomas J., 81, 383, 385, 386, 460
Wallace, Everett, 412
Wallace, M., 80, 406
Wang, Peiling, 460
Warner, Beth Forrest, 461
Watson, Richard, 412

Wei-He, Peter, 367, 460
Weibel, Stuart L., 417, 460
Weil, Ben H., 165, 460
Weller, Ann C., 3, 61, 88, 362, 414
Wells, H. G., 61, 460
Werbach, K., 355, 364, 366, 460
Werler, Ruth W., 460
Wermager, Paul, 439
White, B., 181, 460
White, Herbert S. (H. S.), 70, 119, 255, 310, 315, 418, 460
White, Marilyn, 460
Whitley, Richard, 418
Wicks, Wendy, 414, 427
Wiedensohler, P., 193, 413
Wiederkehr, Robert R. V., 209, 431
Wilder, Stanley J., 182, 216, 379, 461
Wilkinson, Sophie, 461
Willenbrock, F. Karl, 66, 461
Williams, G. R., 161, 178, 461
Williams, J., 417
Williams, J. G., 216, 297, 429
Williams, L. A., 461
Williams, Martha E. (M. E.), 78, 79, 85, 93, 121, 136, 168, 323, 363, 408, 412, 414, 415, 422, 433, 436, 440, 443, 448, 450, 454, 456, 457, 461
Williams, Robert V., 409, 425, 426, 435, 463
Willis, Katherine, 461
Wills, Gordon, 461
Wills, Matthew, 461
Wilson, David L., 461

Wilson, J. M., 462
Wilson, L., 146, 462
Wilson, Thomas C., 416, 444
Wind, Yoram, 224, 422
Winkler, Karen J., 462
Winner, Langdon, 462
Wissoker, Ken, 462
Witte, Marcia L., 32, 414
Wolek, Francis W., 65, 132, 133, 452, 462
Wood, Barbara (B. L.), 71, 91, 431, 432, 462
Wood, M. Sandra, 462
Woodward, A. M., 75, 462
Woodward, Hazel M. (H.M.), 82, 462
Woolf, Patricia, 420
Wooster, Harold, 462
Wootton, Christopher B., 279, 280, 462
Wouters, Paul, 63, 463
Wren, Daniel, 390, 455, 463
Wuest, F. J., 463
Wulf, W. A., 148, 463
Wyllys, Ronald E., 412
Wyly, Brendan J., 316, 318, 320, 463

X,Y,Z
Yankee Group, 366
Yates, John G., 73
Yavarkovsky, Jerome, 436
Yokote, G., 88, 463
Young, Peter R., 463
Zaltman, Gerald, 437
Zijlstra, Jaco, 408
Zuckerman, Harriet, 463

Subject Index

A

Academic Press, 80
Ackoff, Russell L., 65, 71
ACM Digital Library, 386-388
ADONIS, 24, 76, 80
ADRS (Automated Document Request
    Service), 77
ADSL (Asymmetric Digital Subscriber
    Line), 368
Air Products & Chemicals, Inc., 112
Alabama Power Company, 112
Allen, Thomas J., 65, 66
America Online (AOL), 331, 336, 339,
    353, 357
American Association for the
    Advancement of Science (AAAS),
    81, 325
American Can Company, 73
American Chemical Society (ACS), 23, 52,
    64, 69, 81, 256, 257, 265, 345, 375,
    388
American Council of Learned Societies,
    146
American Geological Institute (AGI), 64

American Institute of Physics (AIP), 23, 63,
    64, 74, 81, 256, 265, 309-311, 345,
    375
American Library Association (ALA), 335
American Mathematical Society (AMS), 64,
    342, 372, 388
American Physical Society, 390
American Psychological Association (APA),
    63, 69, 81, 161, 170, 372
AMS e-math system, 388
*Annual Review of Information Science and
    Technology*, 210
APOLLO (Article Procurement with
    Online Local Ordering), 77
ARTEMIS, 24, 77
Arthur D. Little, Inc., 77
article copies, databases, 191-196
    electronic access to articles, 341-342,
        377-379, 380-381, 389
    interlibrary loan/document delivery, 7,
        191-193, 389
        See also library services,
    photocopying, 194-196
    preprints and reprints, 7, 194
    separates, 7, 193-195, 387-388

Advanced Research Projects Agency
    (ARPA), 70
ASCII, 329, 331
Aslib, 62, 75
Aspen Systems Corporation, 73, 80
Association of American Publishers (AAP),
    80, 309–310
Association of American Universities
    (AAU), 284
Association of American University
    Presses, 310
Association of Research Libraries (ARL),
    120, 191, 279–280, 283, 295, 325,
    387–388
attributes. *See* journal systems
AT&T Bell Laboratories, xviii, 80, 112, 115,
    169, 238
authorship/authors
    activities involved, 145
    articles
        amount of articles written, 27
        cost per article and reading, 27–28,
            145
        proportion who write, 27, 141
        rejection rate. *See* publishing,
            scholarly journals; publishing lag
            or speed
        time spent writing, 135, 145–146
        trends in authorship. *See* trends
    description of authors, 142–143
    goals, incentives, motives. *See* goals,
        motives, incentives of
    writing, 127, 129, 130–132
    See also journal systems—participants
automated searching of bibliographic
        databases
    amount of searching/proportion of
        readings, 178–179, 182, 185–186,
        190–191
    capabilities of database, 329, 330–331,
        363
    cost/price of, 207, 363, 382, 400
    importance of, 30, 31, 45, 51, 52, 63–64,
        79, 363–364, 365–366

B
Bailar, John C. III, 112, 162
Bailey, Charles W. Sr., 369
Bamford, Harold E. Jr., 70, 73
Baxter Healthcare, 112
Berul, Lawrence M., 73
Bhagat, Nazir, 71
BioMedNet, 344
BIOSIS, 63
Blackwell Publishers; Blackwell-Scientific,
    80 336, 345
BLEND (Birmingham Loughborough
    Electronic Network
    Development), 24, 76
BLAISE (British Library Information
    Services), 77
Boardwatch Directories of Internet Providers,
    355
Booher, Edwin, 71
Bookstein, Abraham, 138
Boston Public Library, 202
Braunstein, Yale, xix
Bristol-Myers Squib, 112, 382
British Library, 76
British Library (Lending Division), 74,
    76–77, 192
British Library Research & Development
    Department (BLRDD), 24, 62,
    75–77
Brownson, Helen L., 70
BT Tymnet, 332
Buck Consultants, 360
Buckland, Lawrence E., 64
Bush, Vannevar, 61

C
Carrigan, Dennis, 317
CARL UnCover, 74, 81, 389
Case Institute of Technology
    (Case–Western) 65, 127–128
CD-ROM
    journal medium, 2, 24, 39, 50, 80, 85, 94,
        97, 181, 328–329, 338–342, 346
    pricing, 45–46, 370, 372, 392, 394, 401
    other, 79, 100, 178, 207, 331–334, 336,
        349

CERN, 20, 79
Center for Research Libraries (CRL), 74
Chadwyck-Healy, 92
Charles River Associates, 174
Chemical Abstracts Service, 63–64
CIC (Committee on Institutional
        Cooperation), 369, 371
CISTI, 192
citation analysis, xix, 71
Clark, D., 360
Colgate Palmolive Company, 112
Commission of European Communities
        (CEC), 77
Communications Decency Act of 1995
        (US), 365
computerized photocomposition, 64, 69,
        70
communication
    alternatives, 69–70
    channels, 2, 60, 65, 69, 88, 128, 133, 135,
        324
    cycle, 87
    distribution means, 2, 324, 333–337
    history of. See history of
        communication
    media, 2, 328–333
    modes, 2, 324
    paths/links, 324
    redundancy in, 2–4
    time spent in, 126–130
CompuServe, 331
Consumers Union, 365
copyright law, ix, 100, 150, 294–295, 339,
        392
Copyright Clearance Center (CCC), 339,
        340, 398
Copyright Office (US), 112, 191
cost comparisons (tradeoffs) between
        services with breakeven point in
        reading, 10, 32, 184–186, 229–231,
        282, 292–298, 371–381
costs. See
    article copies, separates, databases
    authorship/authors
    automated searching/bibliographic
        databases
    electronic publishing/journals
        Internet, economics of

communication infrastructure
    information infrastructure
    library services
    publishing, scholarly journal
    reading
    scientists
costs, defined
    average, 247–249
    fixed, 247–248, 356
    incremental, 247, 248
    total, 247–248
    variable, 247-248, 356
creators. See journal systems—
        participants
Cuadra, Carlos A., 121
Current Contents, 178

D
DARPA, 78
databases
    article text. See electronic article text
        databases
    bibliographic. See automated searching
        of bibliographic databases
David, Carl W., 131
Department of Defense (DOD), 62, 65
Department of Justice (DOJ), 112
Department of Labor (DOL), 112
Department of Transportation (DOT), 112
DDN/MILNET, 79
DIALOG, 74, 121, 331, 336, 341, 363
digital libraries, 61, 63, 81, 364, 386–388
Directory of Electronic Journals, Newsletters
        and Academic Discussion Lists, 120,
        343, 369
diskettes/floppy disks, 328, 332
Docline, 192
document delivery. See journal systems—
        participants; article copies,
        separates, databases; library
        services
Dongarra and Grosse netlib system, 342,
        388
DRINET, 79
DuPont Company, 62, 112

E

Eastman Chemicals Company, 112
Eastman Kodak Company, 112
EasyNet, 336, 279–281, 336
Economic Consulting Services, Inc.,
    283–284
economic interdependencies. *See* journal
    systems
economies of scale, 259
editorial processing centers (EPCs), 22, 73,
    75, 80
EIES (Electronic Information Exchange
    System), 73, 76, 147
electronic article text databases, 6, 10–11,
    23, 39, 72, 74
electronic delivery. *See* electronic
    publishing/journals; article
    copies, separates, databases
electronic distribution. *See* electronic
    publishing/journals; article
    copies, separates, databases
electronic format. *See* electronic
    publishing/journals
electronic publishing/journals, 80
    granularity, 337–339
    interactivity, 333–334
    delivery, 331–333, 341–346
    format, 328–331, 333, 342
    circulation, 386
    costs, 40–41, 369–381
    effects of, 347–349
    innovations (value-added
        processes/features), 12, 40, 68–70,
        71–73, 75–77, 88–90, 337–339, 376,
        381–382, 383–384, 392–393
    number of journals, 341–346
    pricing, 41, 43–46, 100, 392–402
    site licenses, 39, 41, 43, 45–46, 48, 57,
        398–400
    stages, 21–25, 326–328, 382–383
    types 371–376
    use of, 342, 388–390
Elsevier ScienceDirect, 345
Elsevier Science Publishers, 80, 345
ELVYN, 24, 76
Encyclopædia Britannica, 318, 340

Engineering Information (EI), 63, 81
Engineering Information Village, 336
ESNET, 79
exchange rates, international, 282, 284–285
extranets, 358

F

fax delivery, 333
Faxon, 281, 287
Federal Bureau of Investigation Academy,
    112
financing journals
    operations, 37, 304–309, 311, 313,
        373–374
    re-capitalization/research and
        development, 37
    sources of revenue, 309–313
    starting new journal, 6, 36–37, 302–304,
        373–374
Florida Entomological Society, 383
forecasts
    electronic publishing, 10–12, 38–41,
        43–44, 386
    growth of the literature/journals, 58–59,
        67, 71
    number of scientists, 19
Forrester, Jay, 71
Fry, Bernard M. (B. M.), 119
FTP (File Transfer Protocol), 332
Fulltext Sources Online, 120–121, 341, 369
functions. *See* journal systems
funders of scientists and libraries, 52–54,
        97. *See also* journal systems—
        participants

G

Gale Directory of Databases, 120–121, 341,
    369
Gale Group, 335–336, 338
Garvey, William D., 65, 88, 161
gatekeepers, 65–66
gateways, subscription agents,
        information brokers, library
        networks, and consortia, 335–337,
        343–344. *See also* journal
        systems—participants

Getz, Malcolm, 401–402
GIF, 330
Ginsparg, Paul, xvii, 6, 24, 143, 195, 362, 382, 388
goals, incentives, motives of
    authors and readers, 134, 147–155, 312
    libraries, 49–51
    organizations served by libraries, 206, 208
    publishers, 325–326
    readers, 164–168, 173–175, 312, 390
government agencies—See individual agency name
Griffith, Belver C., 65, 88
Group Lens, 365–366
Gursey, S., 143

H
Hambrecht and Quist, 355
Harnad, Stevan, 138, 347
Harvard University, 65
Hebrew University, 367
Hellman, Eric, 259
Henderson, Ronald L., 64
HERMES, 77
HighWire Press, 345, 388
Hilz, Starr Roxanne, 72
history of
    communication, 17–56
    electronic publishing, 5–6, 21–25, 61–82
    scholarly journals, 56–61
    science, 17–18
Houghton, Bernard, 57
HTML, 38, 247, 330
Hubble Space Telescope, 352
human genome research, 352
H.W. Wilson Company, 340

I
IBM, 63
IEE, 62
IEEE, 64, 81
incentives. See goals, incentives, motives of
Indiana University, 119

information
    information content, defined, 85, 351
    information form, defined, 85
    life cycle, 88–92, 324
information brokers, 192
information explosion, 9, 66–67
information seeking patterns, 30, 174, 177–183, 288–289
Information Today, Inc., 121
innovations. See electronic publications/journals—innovations (value-added processes/features)
Institute for Scientific Information (ISI), 63, 71, 119–120, 317
Institute of Physics, 76, 155, 345, 390
interlibrary loan (borrowing). See articles copies, separates, databases; library services
International Atomic Energy Agency, 112
International Committee of Medical Journal Editors, 137
Internet, economics of, 334, 351–368
    communication infrastructure, 351–353, 355–360
    information infrastructure, 351–353, 360–368
intranets, 358
ISDN, 368
ISI/OATS (Original Article Tear Sheets)

J
John Wiley & Sons, 80, 316, 318
Johns Hopkins University, 65, 80, 112, 187, 195
Johns Hopkins University Press, 80, 344–345, 388
Johnson & Johnson (Orthopedics, Vistakon), 112
journal prices/pricing of. See publishing, scholarly journals; electronic publishing/journals
journals, history. See history of scholarly journals

journals, number of. *See* publishing,
    scholarly journals; electronic
    publishing/journals
journal names
  electronic
    Canadian Journal of Communications,
        372
    *Chicago Journal of Theoretical
        Computer Science*, 81, 138
    Complexity International, 346
    Computer Human Factors Journal, 76
    Economist, 392
    Electronic Journal of Combinatorics,
        348, 371
    *Electronic Journal of Differential
        Equations*, 346
    *Electronic Research Announcements of
        the American Mathematical Society*,
        346
    Florida Entomologist, 386, 401
    Harvard Business Review, 336
    Journal of Electronic Publishing, 81
    *MARS Internet Journal of Nitride
        Semi-Conductor Research*, 259
    Mental Workload, 147
    *Online Journal of Current Clinical
        Trials*, 81
    Postmodern Culture, 136, 348
    Psycoloquy, 81, 138, 348
    Wall Street Journal, 392
  print
    American Libraries, 281
    American Mechanics Magazine, 57
    Astrophysical Journal, 153, 154, 174
    Behavioral and Brain Sciences, 138
    Cancer Research, 153, 154
    Chronicle of Higher Education, 6
    Forbes, 317
    Harvard Business Review, 224
    Journal des Scavans, 56
    Journal of Applied Technology, 69
    Journal of Marketing Research, 224
    Journal of Organic Chemistry, 162
    *Journal of the American Society for
        Information Science*, 304
    Journal of the Franklin Institute, 57
    *Journal of the National Cancer
        Institute*, xiii, 112, 162, 163

    Library Journal, 279, 280
    Library Trends, xviii
    Nature, 303, 401
    Philosophical Transactions, 56
    SAE Transactions, 69
    Science, xviii, 112, 161
    Science Indicators, 71
    Scientific American, 347–348
    Transactions, 57, 59
journals, scholarly. *See* electronic publish-
    ing/journals; publishing, scholarly
journals, type of. *See* publishing, scholarly
    journals; electronic
    publishing/journals
journal systems,
    attributes, 99–100
    economic interdependencies, 83,
        103–104, 311–313
    functions/processes, 83, 92–95, 351–352
    participants 83, 95–98, 323–324
        authors 96, 130–132, 134–136,
            141–157, 324, 335
        copyright granting/royalty
            collection agencies, 97
        costs, 4, 28–29, 33, 391
        creators, 96
        document delivery services, 52–54,
            97
        funders, 97
        gateway organizations, 97, 324, 336
        information brokers, 97, 337
        libraries 97, 335
        library
            networks/consortia/cooperatives,
                202, 337
        primary publishers, 96, 324, 335
        readers 97, 132–136
        reviewers/referees, 136–139
        searchers, 324
        second-party distributors, 97, 335
        secondary publishers, 97, 324
        subscription agents, 97, 336
        teritary publishers, 324
        third-party distributors, 335
    roles, 26–27, 95, 325–326, 364
journal use. *See* readership; publishing,
    scholarly journals; electronic
    publishing/journals.

JPEG, 330
JSTOR, 92, 342, 345, 383

K

King, Donald W., 73, 112, 128, 131,
King Research, Inc., xvii, xix, 6, 71–72, 105,
    112–113, 119, 162, 200, 259
Kingma, Bruce R., 216, 297, 345
Knight-Ridder, 336
Kronick, David A., 57

L

LAN (Local Area Network), 353, 358
Lancaster, F. W., xvii, 161, 162, 327, 328–329
LANDSAT, 352
Leeson, Kenneth. W., 259
LEXIS-NEXIS, 121, 331, 336, 341, 363
library goals, incentives, motives. *See*
    goals, incentives, motives of
library services
    cost of library services
        per reading, 29
            electronic access to separate
                copies of articles, 380–381
            electronic subscriptions,
                379–381
            interlibrary borrowing/
                document delivery, 207,
                230, 282, 295–297,
            journal collections, current
                periodicals, stacks, 207,
                216–218, 282, 291,
                295–296
            photocopying, 196, 207,
                295–296, 379
            purchase for department or
                personal use, 207, 223
            routed journals, 207, 221–222,
                282
        per scientist, 282
    cost/savings, 389–381, 399
    unit costs, 204–205, 207
    usefulness and value of library services,
        29, 188, 218–220, 222–223
    usefulness indicators, 205–208
    use of library services, 29, 187, 215–217,
        220–221, 223–229, 279, 296–297

value indicators, 208–212
    See also journal systems—participants
Licklider, Joseph C. R. (J. C. R.), 65
Lifecycle. *See* information—life cycle
LINC (Loughborough Information
    Network Community), 76
Linda Hall Library, 74
Lindsay Ross, 374, 332
Listservs, 332
lognormal distribution of,
    library journal use, 101, 216, 297
    scientific communities, 101
Los Alamos National Laboratory (LANL)
    Preprint Archive, 6, 7, 24, 81, 195,
        342, 362, 382, 388–389
Lotka's Law, 143
Loughborough University (HUSAT
    Research Group), 76

M

Machlup, Fritz, 61, 259
magnetic tape, 328
Marshall, Joanne G., 212
Martin, Sperling, 73
Maxwell, Robert, 317
McDonald, Dennis D., 154
MCI, 353
Meade, J. N., 64
Meadows, Jack (A. J.), 57, 106–111
measures
    framework, 106–111
    description of measures, publishing,
        library services 107–110, 126,
        203–204, 354
MEDLARS/MEDLINE, 331
methods/research/studies—definitions
    assessments of value, 208, 209, 212
    conjoint measurement, 224–227
    cost finding, 33, 117–119
        library services, 204–205, 209, 221,
            380, 382
        publishing, 251–252, 255–256, 257,
            265
        scientist activities, 171, 377, 380
    Delphi, 72
    experiments, 68–70, 73, 74
    journal tracking, 71, 114, 119–120, 278,
        315

Markov chain, 156–157
multiple regression, 172, 286, 287, 317
price-demand, 276, 299
surveys
    critical incidents, 65, 115, 116
    institutions, 70–71, 112–113
    scientists, 65, 66, 88, 111–117, 144,
        161–162, 168, 188, 209, 378
    systems analysis, 71–72
MIT (Massachusetts Institute of
        Technology), 60, 65, 71, 216
MIT Press, 345
monopoly of journals, 317–319
monopsony of libraries, 288
Moore's Law, 356
Mosaic (web browser), 79
motives. *See* goals, incentives, motives of
MUSE (Johns Hopkins University), 80,
        344, 345, 388

N
National Aeronautics and Space
        Administration (NASA), 62
National Center for Supercomputing
        Applications (NCSA), 79
National Endowment for the Humanitites
        (NEH), 71
National Institutes of Health, xviii, 69, 112,
        115, 164, 169, 216, 382
National Library of Medicine (NLM), 22,
        62, 64, 363
National Oceanic and Atmospheric
        Administration (NOAA), 112
National Periodicals Center, 23, 72, 74
National Physical Laboratory, 76
National Research Council (NRC), (US),
        xvii, 66, 362
National Rural Electric Cooperatives
        Association, 112
National Science Board, 27
National Science Foundation (NSF),
        xvii–xviii, 6–7, 18, 21–22, 24, 57,
        61–63, 65, 67, 70, 73–75, 78, 85,
        111–112, 117–120, 145, 163, 174,
        236, 255, 259–260, 355, 356
National Technical Information Service
        (NTIS), 400

Netcom, 353
New Jersey Institute of Technology, 73
New York Public Library, 202
New York Reference and Research Library
        Resources Systems, 202
New York University, xix
NewJour, 369
Newsgroups, 332
Next Generation Internet (NGI), 356
NSFNET, 79, 356

O
Oak Ridge National Laboratory (ORNL),
        xviii, 112, 170
Oberlin Group, 224
OCLC (Online Computer Library Center),
        74, 81, 192, 325, 344–345
OCR/scanning, 73, 80, 330, 364
Odlyzko, Andrew, 359, 374, 382, 388
O'Donnell, Michael J., 138
Olsen, Jan., 167
OVID, 341

P
page charges/fees, 155, 309–313
Parker, Edward, B., 65
participants. *See* journal systems
Patent and Trade Office (US), 62
Pergamon Press, 80, 317
photocopies. *See* article copies, separates,
        databases; library services
PICS (platform for Internet selection), 365
PIRA, 77
Plenum Publishing, 316
postal rates, 256, 262, 263
preprints. *See* article copies, separates,
        databases
Price, Derek J. DeSolla, 66, 143
Price's Law, 143
price/pricing of journals,
    current versus constant dollars, 277
    factors affecting increases, 32–36,
        281–288
    government information, 396
    price-demand relationship, 274–276,
        281–300, 319, 361, 376–377

price per title versus price per
    subscription, 274
strategies/policies, 11, 42–48, 51, 100,
    239, 341, 361, 392–400
    See also CD-ROM
Procter & Gamble, 112
Project Quartet, 76
ProQuest Direct (Bell & Howell), 81, 341
PSI, 353
primary publishers. *See* journal systems—
    participants
privacy, 365–366
Pronko, Eugene, 70
publisher goals, incentives, motives.
        See goals, incentives, motives of
publishers
    commercial, 37–38, 60, 236–242,
        269–271, 274–277, 303, 397–308,
        313–320
    educational/university presses, 236–242,
        269–271, 274–275, 277, 314
    other type, 236–238, 241–242, 269–271,
        274–275, 277, 314
    society, 236–238, 241–242, 269–271, 274,
        277, 314
publishing lag or speed, 9, 153, 156–157,
    257, 312
publishing, scholarly journals
    activities, 96, 238, 244, 253–255
    by field of science, 236–237, 240–241,
        278
    circulation
        individual/personal, 243
        institutional/library, 243, 275
        personal subscriptions per scientist,
            171, 181, 243, 277, 289
        per title, average, median,
            distribution, 10, 28, 100, 241–242,
            269, 274–275
    costs of
        article processing, 34, 238, 255–259,
            305–307
        by circulation, 35, 36, 259, 265–266,
            282
        by number of articles, 35, 259,
            267–268

by time, 267–268
distribution, 238, 262–263, 305–307
fixed versus variable, 34, 35,
    247–249, 252, 266
non-article processing, 328,
    259–260, 305–307
reproduction, 238, 260–262, 305–307
sources of, 255–256
support, 239, 263–264, 305–307
total/unit, 239, 241–242, 264, 308
validation, 265
economic characteristics, 244–246
financing. *See* financing
flaws, 8–10, 21–22, 31, 66–68
number of titles, 28, 57, 60, 236
price/pricing, journal—by type of
    subscriber
    individual/personal, 239, 241, 274,
        278
    institutional/library, 239, 241, 274,
        275, 276, 278–281
    size, 28, 236–237, 259, 261, 262,
        266–267
value, 4, 246
See also electronic publishing/journals

R
Ramsey Pricing, 396
reader goals—incentives, motives. *See*
        goals, incentives, motives of
readers. *See* journal systems—participants
readership—patterns
    general
        amount of reading, 132–133
        sources of materials read, 132–134
        time spent reading, 126–130
    readings per journal, 183–186, 288–289,
        292–293, 297–299
        library journals read—number,
            distribution/frequency of
            readings
            per journal, 182, 186–188, 297–299
                per scientist, 182
        purpose of, 25, 218
        reading—defined, 25, 160
        reading on a screen, 51, 370,
            378–379

readings
  by university versus other
    scientists, 9, 163–164
  per article, 10, 28, 67, 133, 160,
    162, 163
  per journal, 9–10, 160, 163, 174,
    182
  per scientist, 19, 25, 133, 160, 163,
    288, 389
  time spent
    per reading, 30, 135, 162, 165–166
    per scientist, 26, 30, 135, 160,
      164–165, 171
  usefulness of information read, 25,
    160, 168–170, 218
  use of library journal collections,
    187–188
  value of information read, 26, 160,
    169–173, 219–220, 222–224, 229
scholarly journals/articles
  age of articles read, 30–31, 188–191
  cost per reading, 30, 171, 184, 289,
    290, 291, 295–297
  journals read—number,
    distribution/frequency of
Red Sage, 24, 80, 388
Reed Elsevier, 316–317
Reed International, 331
refereeing (peer review)
  cost per manuscript, 139
  importance of, 136, 137, 155, 175
  rejection rates, 145, 257
  time spent per manuscript, 139
Reitman, David, 317–318
reprints. *See* article copies, separates,
    databases
resources, costs. *See* journal systems
reviewers/referees. *See* journal systems—
    participants
Rider, F., 61
Robbe-Grillet, Alain, 149
Rockwell International, 112
Rocky Flats Nuclear Center, 112
roles. *See* journal systems
Rosenbloom, Richard S., 65
Royal Society, 21, 56, 62, 66, 75–76

S
SCATT (Scientific Communication and
    Technology Transfer) system, 71
Schauder, Don, 324
Scholarly Electronic Bibliography, 369
Schwartz, Stephan,
science, 19–21
Science Citation Index, 52, 279–280
scientists
  cost savings due to electronic journals,
    276–278
  costs to scientists, 207–209, 276–278,
    289–291
    of reading. *See* readership,
      scholarly journal, cost per
      reading
    goals, incentives, motives. *See*
      goals, incentives, motives
  number of, 18–19, 27, 144, 267
  time of, 4–5, 126–130, 150
SCONUL, 76
search, analyst. *See* journal systems—
    participants; library services
Seybold, J. W., 64
SGML, 38, 80, 247, 330
SIAM Journals Online, 388
Silver Platter, 336
site licenses. *See* price/pricing, journal;
    strategies, policies
Society of Automotive Engineers (SAE), 69
SPARC (Scholarly Publishing and
    Academic Resources Coalition),
    49, 320, 325–326
Special Libraries Association (SLA), xviii,
    211
SPIES (Stanford Public Information
    Retrieval System), 389
SPIN (American Institute of Physics), 74
Springer Link, 345
Springer-Verlag, 80, 345
Springer-Verlag Online Journals, 388
Sprint, 353
SprintNet, 332
stakeholders. *See* journal systems—
    participants

Standard & Poor's (S&P) 500 companies, 316
standards, codes, publishing markup, 24, 73
  ASCII (American Standard Code for information Interchange), 329, 331
  Electronic Manuscript Standards, 80
  GIF, 330
  HTML (hypertext markup language), 38, 247, 330
  JPEG, 330
  SGML (standard generalized markup language), 38, 80, 247, 330
  TeX, 330
  XML, 38
Stanford University, 65
Steven I. Goldspiel Memorial Research Grant, xviii, 211
STN International, 341
Super JANET, 76
systematic interdependencies, 83, 102–103, 311–313
systemic interdependencies. *See* journal systems
systems analysis, 71–72 *See also* publishing, scholarly journals; electronic publishing/journals

T
Tagliacozzo, R., 152
Taylor and Francis, 345
TCP/IP, 353
Telecommunications Act of 1995, 356
Telnet, 331
TeX, 330
third-party distributors. *See* journal systems—participants
trends
  article copies (separates), 6–7, 193–195
  authorship, authors, 27–28, 144
  funding, 52–54
  interlibrary loan/document delivery, 7, 29, 193
  circulation/subscriptions, 28, 32, 181, 243–244, 268, 281, 314, 386
  number of articles, 144
  number of journals, 26, 28, 57–60, 66–67, 82, 242, 267
  size of journals, 9, 28, 242, 268
  costs, 29, 33–34, 267–268, 377
  libraries, 29, 32–33, 45–51, 282, 387
  perceptions/expectations/hype concerning electronic publishing/journals, 5, 6–7, 22–24, 38, 77, 381–383
  prices, 28, 32. 214, 243–244, 276–281
  publishers, 28 44–48
  reading, 28, 30, 163–164, 179–181, 214
  science, 1
  scientists and science, 5, 9, 18–19, 27–28, 30, 51–52, 127, 135, 144
TULIP (The University Licensing Program), 24, 80, 325, 344
Turoff, Murray, 72, 73

U
UDP (user-defined protocols), 353
UKCIS, 62
Ulrich's International Periodicals Directory, 119–120, 242–243, 315
UMI (Bell & Howell), 112, 330–331, 335, 338
UMI Article Clearinghouse, 74 (*see also* ProQuest Direct)
University College London, 75
University Corporation for Advanced Internet Development, 356
University of New York, Albany, 367
University of California at Berkeley, 130
University of California at San Diego, 369
University of California at San Francisco (libraries), 80
University of Chicago, 369
University of Chicago Press, 345
University of Houston, 369
University of Illinois, 112, 182, 379
University of Michigan, School of Information, 23
University of Michigan Press, 82
University of Oklahoma, 389–390
University of Pittsburgh, 215, 216

University of Tennessee, xviii, 105, 112,
     131, 159, 163, 187, 195, 200, 224,
     367, 378
University of Tennessee, School of
     Information Sciences, xvii, 105
University of Toronto, 71
UUNet, 353

V
value-added processes. *See* electronic
     publishing/journals—
     innovations, (value-added
     processes/features)
VandenBos, Gary R., 374
VandenBos' Law, 374
Varian, Hal R., 360, 384, 394–396
Volpe National Transportation Systems
     Center, 112

W
Waverly, Inc., 318
West Group, 363
Westat, Inc., 73
Westlaw, 336, 341
Wolters Kluwer, 316, 318, 345

X, Y, Z
XML, 38
Yale University Medical Center, 201, 388
Ziff-Davis, 338